PROGRAMMING IN VISUAL C# 2008

PROGRAMMING IN
VISUAL C# 2008

Julia Case Bradley

Anita C. Millspaugh

 **Higher Education**

Boston   Burr Ridge, IL   Dubuque, IA   New York   San Francisco   St. Louis
Bangkok   Bogotá   Caracas   Kuala Lumpur   Lisbon   London   Madrid   Mexico City
Milan   Montreal   New Delhi   Santiago   Seoul   Singapore   Sydney   Taipei   Toronto

Higher Education

PROGRAMMING IN VISUAL C# 2008

Published by McGraw-Hill, a business unit of The McGraw-Hill Companies, Inc., 1221 Avenue of the Americas, New York, NY, 10020. Copyright © 2010 by The McGraw-Hill Companies, Inc. All rights reserved. Previous editions © 2004 and 2008. No part of this publication may be reproduced or distributed in any form or by any means, or stored in a database or retrieval system, without the prior written consent of The McGraw-Hill Companies, Inc., including, but not limited to, in any network or other electronic storage or transmission, or broadcast for distance learning.

Some ancillaries, including electronic and print components, may not be available to customers outside the United States.

This book is printed on acid-free paper.

2 3 4 5 6 7 8 9 0 QPD/QPD 0 9

ISBN 978-0-07-351721-6
MHID 0-07-351721-6

Vice president/Editor in chief: *Elizabeth Haefele*
Vice president/Director of marketing: *John E. Biernat*
Senior sponsoring editor: *Scott Davidson*
Developmental editor II: *Alaina Grayson*
Marketing manager: *Tiffany Wendt*
Lead media producer: *Damian Moshak*
Director, Editing/Design/Production: *Jess Ann Kosic*
Project manager: *Marlena Pechan*
Senior production supervisor: *Janean A. Utley*
Senior designer: *Srdjan Savanovic*
Media developmental editor: *William Mulford*
Media project manager: *Mark A. S. Dierker*
Cover design: *Jessica Lazar*
Typeface: *11/13 Bodoni*
Compositor: *Aptara, Inc.*
Printer: *Quebecor World Dubuque Inc.*

Library of Congress Cataloging-in-Publication Data

Bradley, Julia Case.
    Programming in Visual C# 2008 / Julia Case Bradley, Anita C. Millspaugh.
    p. cm.
    Includes index.
    ISBN-13: 978-0-07-351721-6 (alk. paper)
    ISBN-10: 0-07-351721-6 (alk. paper)
    1. C# (Computer program language) 2. Microsoft Visual C#. 3. Visual programming
    languages (Computer science) I. Millspaugh, A. C. (Anita C.) II. Title.

QA76.73.C154B7324 2010
006.6'63—dc22

                                                2008031694

The Internet addresses listed in the text were accurate at the time of publication. The inclusion of a Web site does not indicate an endorsement by the authors or McGraw-Hill, and McGraw-Hill does not guarantee the accuracy of the information presented at these sites.

PREFACE

Visual C# (C Sharp) is a relatively new language introduced by Microsoft along with Visual Studio. Its goal was to provide the ease of working with Visual Basic with the flexibility and power of the Java and C++ languages. The syntax of C# is similar to Java and C++ but the ease of creating a graphical user interface and an event-driven application rivals Visual Basic.

C# is fully object-oriented, compatible with many other languages using the .NET Framework. This book incorporates the object-oriented concepts throughout, as well as the syntax and terminology of the language.

C# is designed to allow the programmer to develop applications that run under Windows and/or in a Web browser without the complexity generally associated with programming. With very little effort, the programmer can design a screen that holds standard elements such as buttons, check boxes, radio buttons, text boxes, and list boxes. Each of these objects operates as expected, producing a "standard" Windows or Web user interface.

About This Text

This textbook is intended for use in an introductory programming course, which assumes no prior knowledge of computer programming. The later chapters are also appropriate for professional programmers who are learning a new language to upgrade their skills.

This text assumes that the student is familiar with the Windows operating environment and can use an Internet browser application.

Approach

This text incorporates the basic concepts of programming, problem solving, and programming logic, as well as the design techniques of an object-oriented event-driven language.

Chapter topics are presented in a sequence that allows the programmer to learn how to deal with a visual interface while acquiring important programming skills such as creating projects with objects, decisions, loops, and data management.

A high priority is given to writing applications that are easy for the user to understand and use. Students are presented with interface design guidelines throughout the text.

This text follows essentially the same sequence as the Bradley/Millspaugh *Visual Basic* text. Object-oriented programming (OOP) is introduced in Chapter 1 and is used consistently in every chapter of the book.

The code for all in-chapter projects is available to instructors.

TEXT FEATURES

Object-Oriented Concepts

are presented throughout the text to offer students an introduction to object-oriented design before learning to create their own classes.

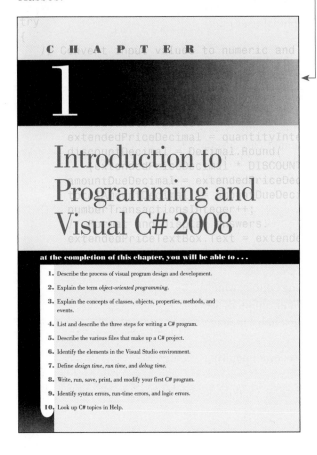

Interface Design Guidelines

are presented to offer students a better understanding of meeting user needs and employing industry standards.

Good Programming Habits

1. Always test the tab order on your forms. Fix it if necessary by changing the TabIndex properties of the controls.
2. Provide visual separation for input fields and output fields and always make it clear to the user which are which.
3. Make sure that your forms can be navigated and entered from the keyboard. Always set a default button (AcceptButton property) for every form.
4. To make a label maintain its size regardless of the value of the Text property, set AutoSize to *false*.
5. To make the text in a text box right justified or centered, set the TextAlign property.
6. You can use the Checked property of a check box to set other properties that must be *true* or *false*.

Tips

in the margins help students avoid potential trouble spots in their programs and encourage them to develop good programming habits.

Use two ampersands when you want to make an ampersand appear in the Text property: &Health && Welfare for "<u>H</u>ealth & Welfare". ■

Feedback Questions

give the students time to reflect on the current topic and to evaluate their understanding of the details.

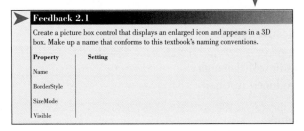

Hands-On Programming Examples

guide students through the process of planning, writing, and executing C# programs.

Your Hands-On Programming Example

In this project, Look Sharp Fitness Center needs to expand the clothing sale project done previously in this chapter. In addition to calculating individual sales and discounts, management wants to know the total amount of sales and the number of transactions.

Add exception handling to the program so that missing or nonnumeric data will not cause a run-time error.

Help the user by adding ToolTips wherever you think they will be useful.

Programming Exercises

test students' understanding of the programming skills covered in that chapter.

at the completion of this chapter, you will be able to . . .

1. Use database terminology correctly.

2. Create Windows and Web projects that display database data.

3. Display data in a DataGridView control.

4. Bind data to text boxes and labels.

5. Allow the user to select from a combo box or list box and display the corresponding record in data-bound controls.

6. Query an object using LINQ.

Case Studies

provide continuing-theme exercises that may be used throughout the course, providing many opportunities to expand on previous projects.

Learning Objectives

tell students what will be covered in the chapter and what they will be able to do after completing the chapter.

Online Learning Center

Visit the Visual C# 2008 Web site at www.mhhe.com/C#2008/ for instructor and student resoures.

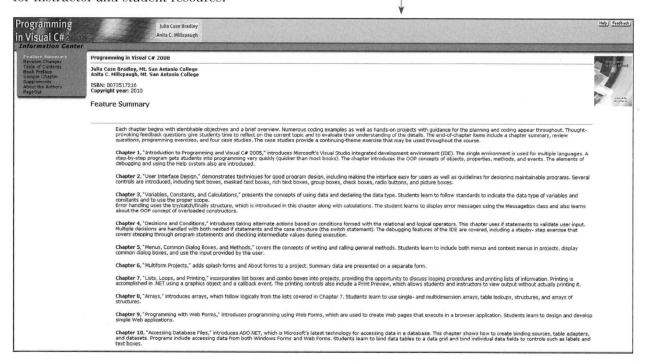

Changes in This Edition

This revision of the text is based on the Professional Edition of Visual Studio (VS) 2008. The 2008 version of VS includes Language-Integrated Queries (LINQ) for a more consistent means of querying a variety of data sources. The Windows Presentation Foundation (WPF) brings new dimensions to interface design. AJAX also has been added to provide faster postbacks for Web pages.

Microsoft has made many enhancements to the integrated development environment (IDE). The Editor now has a much richer IntelliSense. New tool windows for creating, managing, and applying styles in Web applications are now included in Chapter 9.

A new PrintForm component makes printing a form extremely easy and convenient for a classroom environment. The PrintForm component is part of a Microsoft download called the *Visual Basic Power Packs*, which can be added to the IDE for use with a C# program. PrintForm is covered in Chapter 2 for output to either the printer or a Print Preview window. Standard printing is still covered in Chapter 7.

LINQ is covered in Chapter 10 ("Database Applications") and again in the XML section of Chapter 14.

Chapter 11 ("Data Files") includes a simplified method for writing small amounts of data without performing an open operation.

Drag-and-drop for images is now covered in the graphics chapter (Chapter 13). Students learn the development techniques for this familiar operation.

Chapter 14 includes XML data files and an introduction to programming with WPF.

The text narrative, step-by-step exercises, screen captures, and appendixes have all been updated to Visual Studio 2008. The screen captures are all based on Windows Vista.

Features of This Text

Each chapter begins with identifiable objectives and a brief overview. Numerous coding examples as well as hands-on projects with guidance for the planning and coding appear throughout. Thought-provoking feedback questions give students time to reflect on the current topic and to evaluate their understanding of the details. The end-of-chapter items include a chapter summary, review questions, programming exercises, and four case studies. The case studies provide a continuing-theme exercise that may be used throughout the course.

> *Chapter 1, "Introduction to Programming and Visual C# 2008,"* introduces Microsoft's Visual Studio integrated development environment (IDE). The single environment is used for multiple languages. A step-by-step program gets students into programming very quickly (quicker than most books). The chapter introduces the OOP concepts of objects, properties, methods, and events. The elements of debugging and using the Help system also are introduced.

> *Chapter 2, "User Interface Design,"* demonstrates techniques for good program design, including making the interface easy for users as well as guidelines for designing maintainable programs. Several controls are introduced, including text boxes, masked text boxes, rich text boxes, group boxes, check boxes, radio buttons, and picture boxes. A new section covers the controls in the Power Pack including PrintForm and the Shape and Line controls.

Chapter 3, *"Variables, Constants, and Calculations,"* presents the concepts of using data and declaring the data type. Students learn to follow standards to indicate the data type of variables and constants and to use the proper scope.

Error handling uses the `try/catch/finally` structure, which is introduced in this chapter along with calculations. The student learns to display error messages using the MessageBox class and also learns about the OOP concept of overloaded constructors.

Chapter 4, *"Decisions and Conditions,"* introduces taking alternate actions based on expressions formed with the relational and logical operators. This chapter uses `if` statements to validate user input. Multiple decisions are handled with both nested `if` statements and the case structure (the `switch` statement).

The debugging features of the IDE are covered, including a step-by-step exercise that covers stepping through program statements and checking intermediate values during execution.

Chapter 5, *"Menus, Common Dialog Boxes, and Methods,"* covers the concepts of writing and calling general methods. Students learn to include both menus and context menus in projects, display common dialog boxes, and use the input provided by the user.

Chapter 6, *"Multiform Projects,"* adds splash forms and About forms to a project. Summary data are presented on a separate form.

Chapter 7, *"Lists, Loops, and Printing,"* incorporates list boxes and combo boxes into projects, providing the opportunity to discuss looping procedures and printing lists of information. Printing is accomplished in .NET using a graphics object and a callback event. The printing controls also include a Print Preview, which allows students and instructors to view output without actually printing it.

Chapter 8, *"Arrays,"* introduces arrays, which follow logically from the lists covered in Chapter 7. Students learn to use single- and multidimension arrays, table lookups, structures, and arrays of structures.

Chapter 9, *"Web Applications,"* introduces programming using Web Forms, which are used to create Web pages that execute in a browser application. Students learn to design and develop simple Web applications. CSS styles and AJAX provide the ability to create improved, more efficient Web sites.

Chapter 10, *"Database Applications,"* introduces ADO.NET, which is Microsoft's technology for accessing data in a database. This chapter shows how to create binding sources, table adapters, and datasets. Programs include accessing data from both Windows Forms and Web Forms. Students learn to bind data tables to a data grid and bind individual data fields to controls such as labels and text boxes. LINQ is used to query an array and a database.

Chapter 11, *"Data Files,"* presents the techniques for data file handling. Students learn to save and read small amounts of data using streams. The StreamWriter and StreamReader objects are used to store and reload the contents of a combo box.

Chapter 12, *"OOP: Creating Object-Oriented Programs,"* explains more of the theory of object-oriented programming. Although we have been using OOP concepts since Chapter 1, in this chapter students learn the terminology and application of OOP. Inheritance is covered for visual objects (forms) and for extending existing classes. The samples are kept simple enough for an introductory class.

Chapter 13, "Graphics, Animation, Sound, and Drag-and-Drop," covers the classes and methods of GDI+. The chapter covers graphics objects, pens, and brushes for drawing shapes and lines. Animation is accomplished using the Timer control and the SetBounds method for moving controls. Students learn to play sounds using the SoundPlayer class. Video files are played using Windows Media Player. Drag-and-drop events are used to transfer images and the contents of a text box to a list box.

Chapter 14, "Additional Topics in C#," introduces some advanced programming topics. This final chapter covers validating user input using Error Providers and the Validating event of controls. Students learn to create applications using multiple document interfaces (MDI), create toolbars and status bars using ToolStrip and StatusStrip controls, and add Web content to a Windows Form using the WebBrowser control. The code-snippet feature is introduced. Reading and writing XML text files are covered. The chapter also covers LINQ to XML.

An introduction to Windows Presentation Framework (WPF) includes using WPF Interoperability with a standard Windows Form and creating a WPF Form project.

The appendixes offer important additional material. Appendix A holds the answers to all Feedback questions. Appendix B covers methods for dates, math, and string handling. In the OOP programming style, actions are accomplished with methods of the Math class and String class. Appendix C gives tips and shortcuts for mastering the Visual Studio environment, and Appendix D discusses security issues for both Windows and Web programming.

Thank You

Many people have worked very hard to design and produce this text. We would like to thank our editors, Scott Davidson and Alaina Grayson. Our thanks also to the many people who produced this text, including Marlena Pechan and Betsy Blumenthal.

We greatly appreciate Robert Price and Peter van der Goes for their thorough technical reviews, constructive criticism, and many valuable suggestions. Thank you to Theresa Berry for her work on the exercise solutions. And, most importantly, we are grateful to Dennis and Richard for their support and understanding through the long days and busy phone lines.

The Authors

We have had fun writing about C#. We hope that this feeling is evident as you read this book and that you will enjoy learning or teaching this outstanding programming language.

Julia Case Bradley
Anita C. Millspaugh

TO THE STUDENT

The best way to learn to program in Visual C# is to do it. If you enter and run the sample projects, you will be on your way to writing applications. Reading the examples without trying to run them is like trying to learn a foreign language or mathematics by just reading about it. Enter the projects, look up your questions in the extensive MSDN Help files, and make those projects *run*.

Installing Visual C#

For the programs in this text, you need to install the .NET Framework v 3.5, Visual C# 2008, and the MSDN (Microsoft Developers Network) library, which contains all of Help and many instructive articles.

You can download the Express Edition of Visual C# and Visual Web Developer from msdn.microsoft.com/express. Using these two products, you can complete most of the exercises in this text.

Format Used for Visual C# Statements

Visual C# statements, methods, and functions are shown in `this font`. Any values that you must supply are in *italics*.

As you work your way through this textbook, note that you may see a subset of the available options for a C# statement or method. Generally, the options that are included reflect those covered in the chapter. If you want to see the complete format for any statement or all versions of a method, refer to Help.

J.C.B.
A.C.M.

About the Authors

Julia Bradley is a professor emeritus of Computer Information Systems at Mt. San Antonio College. She developed and taught computer programming courses for 25 years and then took early retirement from teaching in order to write full time. Most recently she has taught courses in introductory and advanced Visual Basic, Access programming, and Microsoft Office. She began writing BASIC textbooks in 1984 using MS-BASIC (GW-BASIC) and has authored or co-authored texts in Macintosh Basic, QuickBasic, QBasic, Visual Basic, C#, Java, the Internet, and desktop publishing.

Anita Millspaugh teaches programming courses in Visual Basic, C#, and Java at Mt. San Antonio College and has served as chair of the department for eight years. She received her MBA from California State Polytechnic University, with a bachelor's degree in Computer Information Systems. She has taught faculty at the National Computer Educator's Institute and also has led Great Teacher's Conferences for Mt. SAC and for California Vocational Faculty.

BRIEF CONTENTS

CONTENTS

12 OOP: Creating Object-Oriented Programs 481

13 Graphics, Animation, Sound, and Drag-and-Drop 535

1

Introduction to Programming and Visual C# 2008

1. Describe the process of visual program design and development.

2. Explain the term *object-oriented programming*.

3. Explain the concepts of classes, objects, properties, methods, and events.

4. List and describe the three steps for writing a C# program.

5. Describe the various files that make up a C# project.

6. Identify the elements in the Visual Studio environment.

7. Define *design time*, *run time*, and *debug time*.

8. Write, run, save, print, and modify your first C# program.

9. Identify syntax errors, run-time errors, and logic errors.

10. Look up C# topics in Help.

Writing Windows Applications with Visual C#

Using this text, you will learn to write computer programs that run in the Microsoft Windows environment. Your projects will look and act like standard Windows programs. You will use the tools in C# (C sharp) and Windows Forms to create windows with familiar elements such as labels, text boxes, buttons, radio buttons, check boxes, list boxes, menus, and scroll bars. Figure 1.1 shows some sample Windows user interfaces.

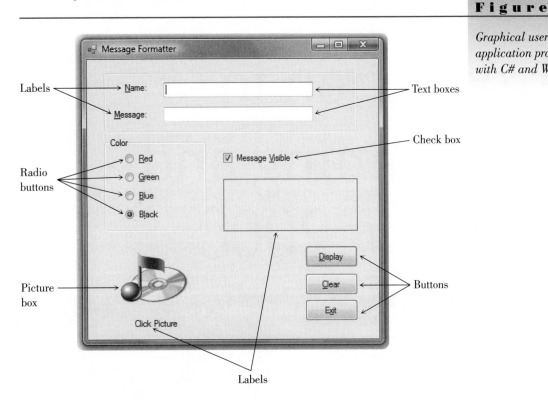

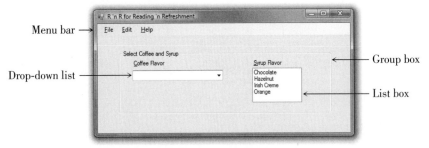

Beginning in Chapter 9 you will create programs using Web Forms and Visual Web Developer. You can run Web applications in a browser such as Internet Explorer or Mozilla FireFox, on the Internet, or on a company intranet. Figure 1.2 shows a Web Forms application.

You also will become acquainted with Microsoft's new screen design technology, Windows Presentation Foundation (WPF), which is covered in Chapter 14. WPF uses its own designer and design elements, which are different from those used for Windows forms.

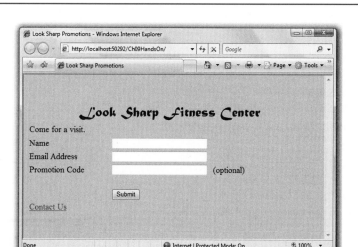

Figure 1.2

*A Web Forms application
running in a browser.*

The Windows Graphical User Interface

Microsoft Windows uses a **graphical user interface**, or **GUI** (pronounced "gooey"). The Windows GUI defines how the various elements look and function. As a C# programmer, you have available a **toolbox** of these elements. You will create new windows, called *forms*. Then you will use the toolbox to add the various elements, called *controls*. The projects that you will write follow a programming technique called *object-oriented programming (OOP)*.

Programming Languages—Procedural, Event Driven, and Object Oriented

There are literally hundreds of programming languages. Each was developed to solve a particular type of problem. Most traditional languages, such as BASIC, C, COBOL, FORTRAN, PL/1, and Pascal, are considered *procedural* languages. That is, the program specifies the exact sequence of all operations. Program logic determines the next instruction to execute in response to conditions and user requests.

The newer programming languages such as C#, Java, and Visual Basic (VB) use a different approach: *object-oriented programming (OOP)*.

In the OOP model, programs are no longer procedural. They do not follow a sequential logic. You, as the programmer, do not take control and determine the sequence of execution. Instead, the user can press keys and click various buttons and boxes in a window. Each user action can cause an event to occur, which triggers a method (a set of programming statements) that you have written. For example, the user clicks on a button labeled Calculate. The clicking causes the button's Click event to occur, and the program automatically jumps to a method you have written to do the calculation.

The Object Model

In C# you will work with objects, which have properties, methods, and events. Each object is based on a class.

Objects

Think of an **object** as a thing, or a noun. Examples of objects are forms and controls. *Forms* are the windows and dialog boxes you place on the screen; *controls* are the components you place inside a form, such as text boxes, buttons, and list boxes.

Properties

Properties tell something about or control the behavior of an object such as its name, color, size, or location. You can think of properties as adjectives that describe objects.

When you refer to a property, you first name the object, add a period, and then name the property. For example, refer to the Text property of a form called SalesForm as SalesForm.Text (pronounced "sales form dot text").

The term *members* is used to refer to both properties and methods. ∎

Methods

Actions associated with objects are called *methods*. **Methods** are the verbs of object-oriented programming. Some typical methods are `Close`, `Show`, and `Clear`. Each of the predefined objects has a set of methods that you can use. You will learn to write additional methods to perform actions in your programs.

You refer to methods as Object.Method ("object dot method"). For example, a `Show` method can apply to different objects: `BillingForm.Show` shows the form object called BillingForm; `exitButton.Show` shows the button object called exitButton.

Events

You can write methods that execute when a particular event occurs. An **event** occurs when the user takes an action such as clicking a button, pressing a key, scrolling, or closing a window. Events also can be triggered by actions of other objects, such as repainting a form or a timer reaching a preset point.

Classes

A **class** is a template or blueprint used to create a new object. Classes contain the definition of all available properties, methods, and events.

Each time that you create a new object, it must be based on a class. For example, you may decide to place three buttons on your form. Each button is based on the Button class and is considered one object, called an *instance* of the class. Each button (or instance) has its own set of properties, methods, and events. One button may be labeled "OK", one "Cancel", and one "Exit". When the user clicks the *OK* button, that button's Click event occurs; if the user clicks on the *Exit* button, that button's Click event occurs. And, of course, you have written different program instructions for each of the button's Click events.

An Analogy

If the concepts of classes, objects, properties, methods, and events are still a little unclear, maybe an analogy will help. Consider an Automobile class. When we say *automobile,* we are not referring to a particular auto, but we know that an automobile has a make and model, a color, an engine, and a number of doors. These elements are the *properties* of the Automobile class.

Each individual auto is an object, or an instance of the Automobile class. Each Automobile object has its own settings for the available properties. For example, each Automobile object has a Color property, such as myAuto.Color = Blue and yourAuto.Color = Red.

The methods, or actions, of the Automobile class might be `Start`, `SpeedUp`, `SlowDown`, and `Stop`. To refer to the methods of a specific object of the class, use `myAuto.Start` and `yourAuto.Stop`.

The events of an Automobile class could be Arrive or Crash. In a C# program, you write event-handling methods that specify the actions you want to take when a particular event occurs for an object. For example, you might write a method to handle the yourAuto.Crash event.

Note: Chapter 12 presents object-oriented programming in greater depth.

Microsoft's Visual Studio

The latest version of Microsoft's Visual Studio, called Visual Studio 2008, includes C#, Visual C++, Visual Basic, and the .NET 3.5 Framework.

The .NET Framework

The programming languages in Visual Studio run in the .NET Framework. The Framework provides for easier development of Web-based and Windows-based applications, allows objects from different languages to operate together, and standardizes how the languages refer to data and objects. Several third-party vendors have produced versions of other programming languages to run in the .NET Framework, including .NET versions of APL by Dyalog, FORTRAN by Lahey Computer Systems, COBOL by Fujitsu Software Corporation, Pascal by the Queensland University of Technology (free), PERL by ActiveState, RPG by ASNA, and Java, known as IKVM.NET.

The .NET languages all compile to (are translated to) a common machine language, called Microsoft Intermediate Language (MSIL). The MSIL code, called *managed code,* runs in the Common Language Runtime (CLR), which is part of the .NET Framework.

C#

Microsoft C# is a part of Visual Studio. You also can purchase C# by itself (without the other languages but *with* the .NET Framework). C# is available in an **Express Edition**, a **Standard Edition,** a **Professional Edition**, and four specialized versions of **Team System** Editions for large enterprise application development. You can find a matrix showing the features of each edition in Help. Anyone planning to do professional application development that includes the advanced features of database management should use the Professional Edition or the Team System Database version. The full Professional Edition is available to educational institutions through the Microsoft Academic Alliance program and is the best possible deal. When a campus department purchases the Academic Alliance, the school can install Visual Studio on all classroom and lab computers and provide the software to all students and faculty at no additional charge. For more information, have your instructor visit: http://msdn.microsoft.com/en-us/academic/default.aspx

Microsoft provides an Express Edition of each of the programming languages, which you can download for free (www.microsoft.com/express/download/). You can use Visual C# Express for Windows development and Visual Web Developer Express for the Web applications in Chapters 9 and 10.

This text is based on the Professional Edition of Visual Studio 2008, the current version. You cannot run the projects in this text in any earlier version of C#.

Writing C# Programs

When you write a C# application, you follow a three-step process for planning the project and then repeat the three-step process for creating the project. The three steps involve setting up the user interface, defining the properties, and then creating the code.

The Three-Step Process

Planning

1. *Design the user interface.* When you plan the **user interface**, you draw a sketch of the screens the user will see when running your project. On your sketch, show the forms and all the controls that you plan to use. Indicate the names that you plan to give the form and each of the objects on the form. Refer to Figure 1.1 for examples of user interfaces.

   Before you proceed with any more steps, consult with your user and make sure that you both agree on the look and feel of the project.

2. *Plan the properties.* For each object, write down the properties that you plan to set or change during the design of the form.

3. *Plan the C# code.* In this step you plan the classes and methods that will execute when your project runs. You will determine which events require action to be taken and then make a step-by-step plan for those actions.

   Later, when you actually write the C# **code**, you must follow the language syntax rules. But during the planning stage, you will write out the actions using **pseudocode**, which is an English expression or comment that describes the action. For example, you must plan for the event that occurs when the user clicks on the *Exit* button. The pseudocode for the event could be *End the project* or *Quit*.

Programming

After you have completed the planning steps and have approval from your user, you are ready to begin the actual construction of the project. Use the same three-step process that you used for planning.

1. *Define the user interface.* When you define the user interface, you create the forms and controls that you designed in the planning stage.

   Think of this step as defining the objects you will use in your application.

2. *Set the properties*. When you set the properties of the objects, you give each object a name and define such attributes as the contents of a label, the size of the text, and the words that appear on top of a button and in the form's title bar.

   You might think of this step as describing each object.

3. *Write the code*. You will use C# programming statements (called *C# code*) to carry out the actions needed by your program. You will be surprised and pleased by how few statements you need to create a powerful Windows program.

   You can think of this third step as defining the actions of your program.

C# Application Files

A C# application, called a ***solution***, can consist of one or more projects. Since all of the solutions in this text have only one project, you can think of one solution = one project. Each project can contain one or more form files. In Chapters 1 through 5, all projects have only one form, so you can think of one project = one form. Starting in Chapter 6, your projects will contain multiple forms and additional files. As an example, the HelloWorld application that you will create later in this chapter creates the following files:

File Name	File Icon	Description
HelloWorld.sln		The **solution file**. A text file that holds information about the solution and the projects it contains. This is the primary file for the solution—the one that you open to work on or run your project. Note the "9" on the icon, which refers to Visual Studio version 9.
HelloWorld.suo		Solution user options file. Stores information about the state of the integrated development environment (IDE) so that all customizations can be restored each time you open the solution.
HelloForm.cs		A .cs (C#) file that holds the code methods that you write. This is a text file that you can open in any editor. *Warning*: You should not modify this file unless you are using the editor in the Visual Studio environment.
HelloForm.Designer.cs		A .cs (C#) file created by the Form Designer that holds the definition of the form and its controls. You should not modify this file directly, but instead make changes in the Designer and allow it to update the file.
HelloForm.resx		A resource file for the form. This text file defines all resources used by the form, including strings of text, numbers, and any graphics.

File Name	File Icon	Description
HelloWorld.csproj		The **project file** that describes the project and lists the files that are included in the project.
HelloWorld.csproj.user		The project user options file. This text file holds IDE option settings so that the next time you open the project, all customizations will be restored.
Program.cs		A .cs (C#) file that contains automatically generated code that runs first when you execute your application.

Note: You can display file extensions. In Windows Vista, open the Explorer and select *Organize / Folders and Search Options*, click on the *View* tab and deselect the check box for *Hide extensions for known file types*. In Windows XP, in the My Computer *Tools* menu, select *Folder Options* and the *View* tab. Deselect the check box for *Hide extensions for known file types*. If you do not display the extensions, you can identify the file types by their icons.

After you run your project, you will find several more files created by the system. The only file that you open directly is the .sln, or solution file.

The Visual Studio Environment

The **Visual Studio environment** is where you create and test your projects. A development environment such as Visual Studio is called an ***integrated development environment* (IDE)**. The IDE consists of various tools, including a form designer, which allows you to visually create a form; an editor, for entering and modifying program code; a compiler, for translating the C# statements into the intermediate machine code; a debugger, to help locate and correct program errors; an object browser, to view the available classes, objects, properties, methods, and events; and a Help facility.

In versions of Visual Studio prior to .NET, each language had its own IDE. For example, to create a Visual Basic project you would use the Visual Basic IDE, and to create a C++ project you would use the C++ IDE. But in Visual Studio, you use the one IDE to create projects in any of the supported languages.

Default Environment Settings

The full version of Visual Studio 2008 provides an option that allows the programmer to select the default profile for the IDE. The first time you open Visual Studio, you are presented with the *Choose Default Environment Settings* dialog box (Figure 1.3), where you can choose *Visual C# Development Settings*. This text uses the Visual C# settings.

Figure 1.3

Note: If you plan to develop in more than one language, such as VB and C#, you can save each group of settings and switch back and forth between the two. Select *Tools / Import and Export Settings* and choose to *Reset all settings*.

The IDE Initial Screen

When you open the Visual Studio IDE, you generally see an empty environment with a Start Page (Figure 1.4). However, it's easy to customize the environment, so you may see a different view. In the step-by-step exercise later in this chapter, you will learn to reset the IDE layout to its default view.

The contents of the Start Page vary, depending on whether you are connected to the Internet. Microsoft has included links that can be updated, so you may find new and interesting information on the Start Page each time you open it. To display or hide the Start Page, select *View / Other Windows / Start Page*.

You can open an existing project or begin a new project using the Start Page or the *File* menu. The examples in this text use the menus.

The New Project Dialog

You will create your first C# projects by selecting *File / New Project*, which opens the *New Project* dialog (Figure 1.5). In the *New Project* dialog, you may need to expand the node for *Other Languages*, depending on your installation. Under *Visual C#*, select *Windows*, and in the *Templates* pane, select *Windows Forms Application*. You also give the project a name in this dialog. Deselect the check box for *Create directory for solution*, which creates an extra level of folders for our single-project solutions.

Figure 1.4

The Visual Studio IDE with the Start Page open, as it first appears in Windows Vista, without an open project. You can close the Start Page by clicking on its Close button.

Close button for
Start Page

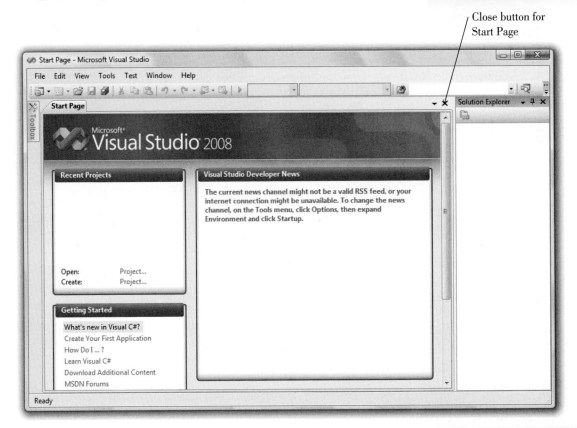

Figure 1.5

Begin a new C# Windows project using the Windows Forms Application template.

Select the Windows Forms
Application template

Enter the project name

Select Visual C# Windows

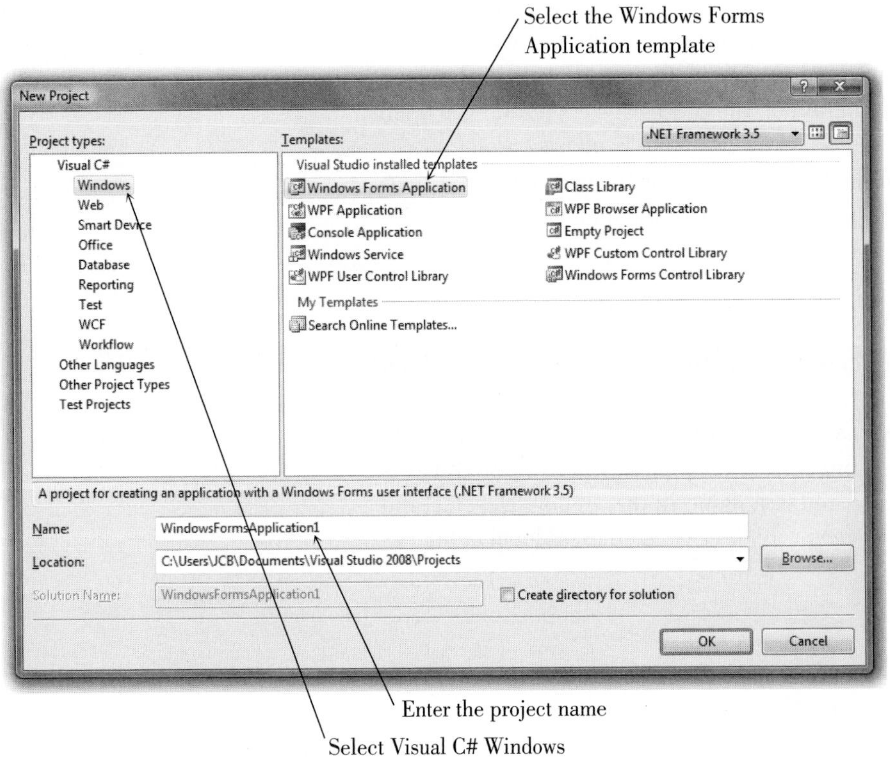

The IDE Main Window

Figure 1.6 shows the Visual Studio environment's main window and its various child windows. Note that each window can be moved, resized, opened, closed, and customized. Some windows have tabs that allow you to display different contents. Your screen may not look exactly like Figure 1.6; in all likelihood, you will want to customize the placement of the various windows. The Designer and Editor windows are generally displayed in tabs in the center of the screen (the Document window), and the various tool windows are docked along the edges and bottom of the IDE, but the locations and the docking behavior are all customizable.

The IDE main window holds the Visual Studio menu bar and the toolbars. You can display or hide the various windows from the *View* menu.

Figure 1.6

The Visual Studio environment. Each window can be moved, resized, closed, or customized.

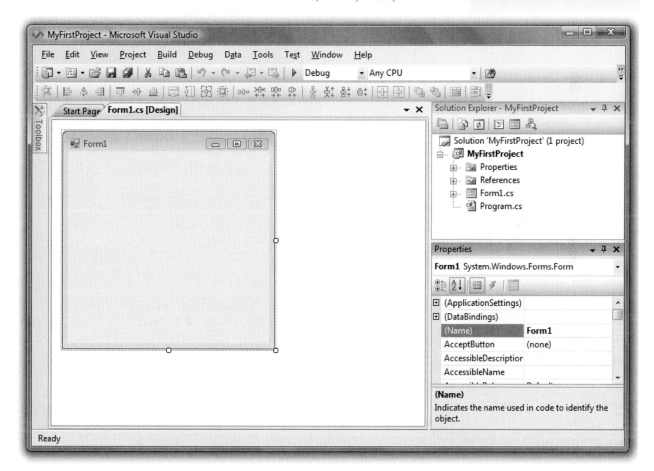

The Toolbars

You can use the buttons on the **toolbars** as shortcuts for frequently used operations. Each button represents a command that also can be selected from a menu. Figure 1.7*a* shows the toolbar buttons on the Standard toolbar for the Professional Edition, which displays in the main window of the IDE; Figure 1.7*b* shows the Layout toolbar, which is useful for designing forms in the Form Designer; and Figure 1.7*c* shows the Text Editor toolbar, which contains buttons to use in the Editor window. Select *View / Toolbars* to display or hide these and other toolbars.

Figure 1.7

The Visual Studio toolbars contain buttons that are shortcuts for menu commands. You can display or hide each of the toolbars: a. the Standard toolbar; b. the Layout toolbar; and c. the Text Editor toolbar.

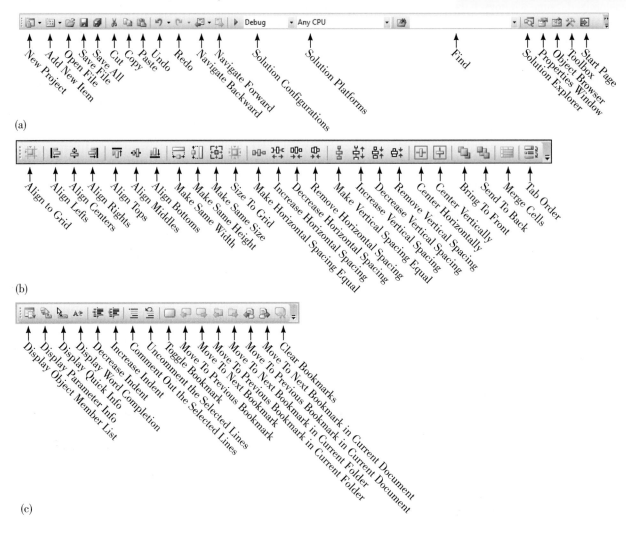

(a)

(b)

(c)

The Document Window

The largest window in the center of the screen is the **Document window**. Notice the tabs across the top of the window, which allow you to switch between open documents. The items that display in the Document window include the Form Designer, the Code Editor, the Project Designer, the Database Designer, and the Object Browser.

    You can switch from one tab to another, or close any of the documents using its Close button.

Use Ctrl + Tab to switch to another open document in the Document window. ■

The Form Designer

The **Form Designer** is where you design a form that makes up your user interface. In Figure 1.6, the Form Designer for Form1 is currently displaying. You can drag the form's sizing handles or selection border to change the size of the form.

When you begin a new C# Windows application, a new form is added to the project with the default name Form1. In the step-by-step exercise later in the chapter, you will learn to change the form's name.

The Solution Explorer Window

The **Solution Explorer window** holds the filenames for the files included in your project and a list of the classes it references. The Solution Explorer window and the environment's title bar hold the name of your solution (.sln) file, which is WindowsFormsApplication1 by default unless you give it a new value in the *New Project* dialog box. In Figure 1.6, the name of the solution is MyFirstProject.

The Properties Window

You use the **Properties window** to set the properties for the objects in your project. See "Set Properties" later in this chapter for instructions on changing properties.

The Toolbox

The toolbox holds the tools you use to place controls on a form. You may have more or different tools in your toolbox, depending on the edition of C# you are using (Express, Standard, Professional, or Team System). Figure 1.8 shows the toolbox.

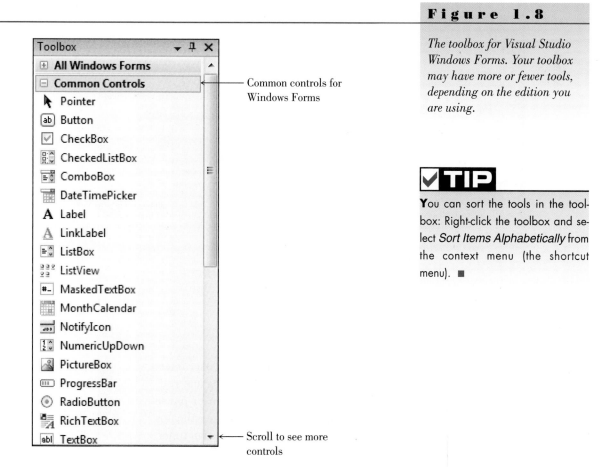

Common controls for Windows Forms

Scroll to see more controls

☑TIP

You can sort the properties in the window either alphabetically or by categories. Use the buttons on the Properties window. ∎

Figure 1.8

The toolbox for Visual Studio Windows Forms. Your toolbox may have more or fewer tools, depending on the edition you are using.

☑TIP

You can sort the tools in the toolbox: Right-click the toolbox and select *Sort Items Alphabetically* from the context menu (the shortcut menu). ∎

Help

Visual Studio has an extensive **Help** feature, which includes the Microsoft Developer Network library (MSDN). You can find reference materials for C#, C++, VB, and Visual Studio; several books; technical articles; and the Microsoft Knowledge Base, a database of frequently asked questions and their answers.

Help includes the entire reference manual, as well as many coding examples. See the topic "Visual Studio Help" later in this chapter for help on Help.

When you make a selection from the *Help* menu, the requested item appears in a new window that floats on top of the IDE window (Figure 1.9), so you can keep both open at the same time. It's a good idea to set the *Filtered By* entry to *Visual C#*.

Figure 1.9

Help displays in a new window, independent of the Visual Studio IDE window.

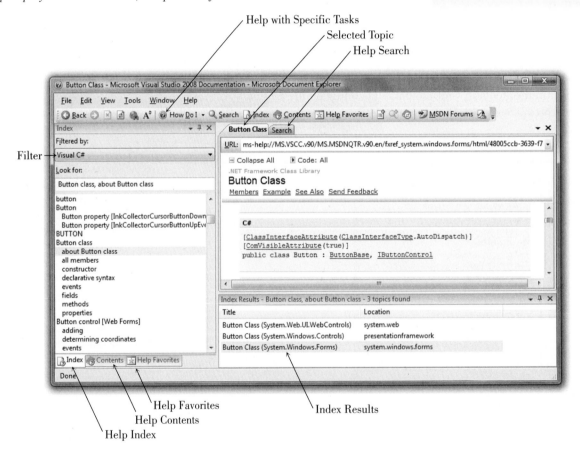

Design Time, Run Time, and Debug Time

Visual Studio has three distinct modes. While you are designing the user interface and writing code, you are in **design time**. When you are testing and running your project, you are in **run time**. If you get a run-time error or pause program execution, you are in **debug time**. The IDE window title bar indicates (Running) or (Debugging) to indicate that a project is no longer in design time.

Writing Your First C# Project

For your first C# project, you will create a form with three controls (see Figure 1.10). This simple project will *display* the message "Hello World" in a label when the user clicks the *Display* button and will terminate when the user clicks the *Exit* button.

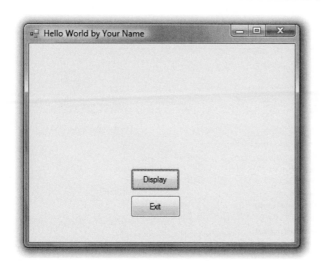

Figure 1.10

*The Hello World form. The "Hello World" message will appear in a label when the user clicks on the **Display** button. The label does not appear until the button is pressed.*

Set Up Your Workspace

Before you can begin a project, you must open the Visual Studio IDE. You also may need to customize your workspace.

Run Visual Studio

These instructions assume that Visual Studio 2008 is installed in the default location. If you are running in a classroom or lab, the program may be installed in an alternate location, such as directly on the desktop.

STEP 1: Click the Windows *Start* button and move the mouse pointer to *All Programs*.

STEP 2: Locate *Microsoft Visual Studio 2008*.

STEP 3: If a submenu appears, select *Microsoft Visual Studio 2008* or *Microsoft Visual C# 2008 Express*.

   Visual Studio will start and display the Start Page (refer to Figure 1.4). If you are using Visual Studio Professional and this is the first time that VS has been opened for this user, you will need to select *Visual C# Development Settings* from the *Choose Default Environment Settings* dialog box (refer to Figure 1.3).

   Note: The VS IDE can be customized to not show the Start Page when it opens.

Start a New Project

STEP 1: Select *File / New / Project*; the *New Project* dialog box opens (refer to Figure 1.5). Make sure that *Visual C#* and *Windows* are selected for

Project types and *Windows Forms Application* is selected for the template. If you are using Visual C# Express, the dialog box differs slightly and you don't have to choose the language, but you can still choose a Windows Forms Application.

STEP 2: Enter "HelloWorld" (without the quotes) for the name of the new project (Figure 1.11) and click the *OK* button. The new project opens (Figure 1.12). At this point, your project is stored in a temporary directory. You can specify a new location for the project later when you save it.

Enter the name for the new project.

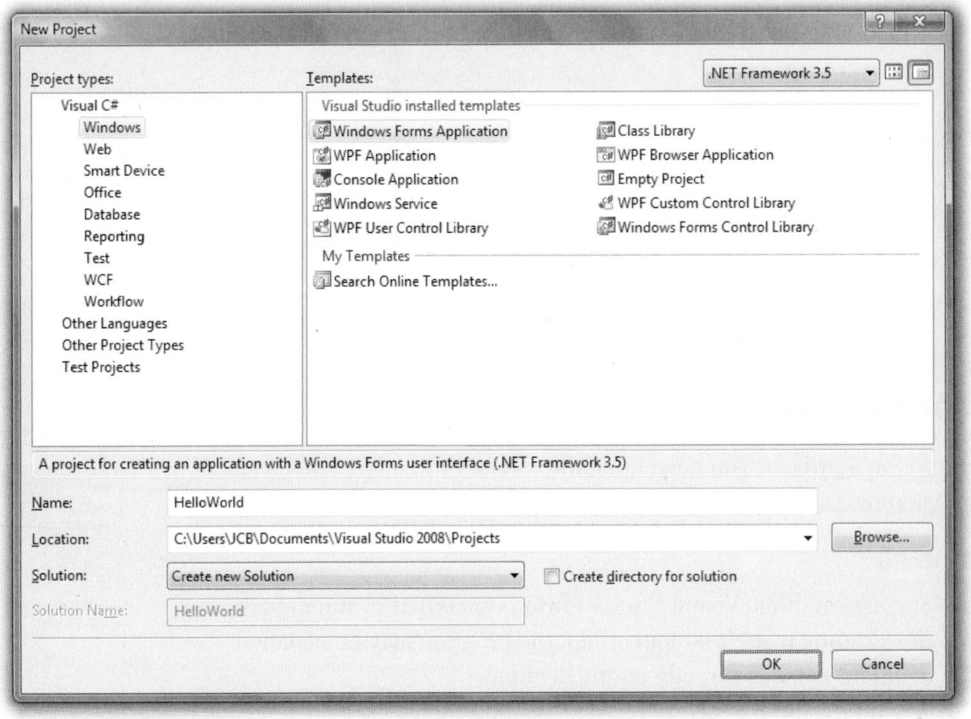

Set Up Your Environment

In this section, you will customize the environment. For more information on customizing windows, floating and docking windows, and altering the location and contents of the various windows, see Appendix C.

STEP 1: Reset the IDE's default layout by choosing *Window / Reset Window Layout* and responding *Yes*. The IDE should now match Figure 1.12.

STEP 2: Point to the icon for the toolbox at the left of the IDE window. The Toolbox window pops open. Notice the pushpin icon at the top of the window (Figure 1.13); clicking this icon pins the window open rather than allowing it to Auto Hide.

STEP 3: Click the Auto Hide pushpin icon for the Toolbox window; the toolbox will remain open.

Figure 1.12

The Visual Studio IDE with the new HelloWorld C# project. Your screen may look significantly different from the figure since the environment can be customized.

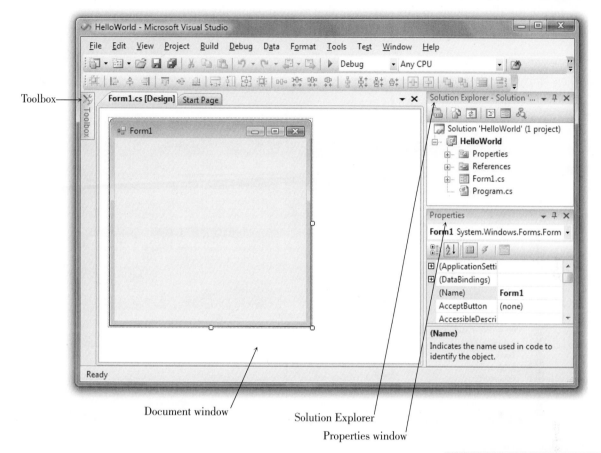

Toolbox

Document window   Solution Explorer

                                   Properties window

Figure 1.13

The Toolbox window.

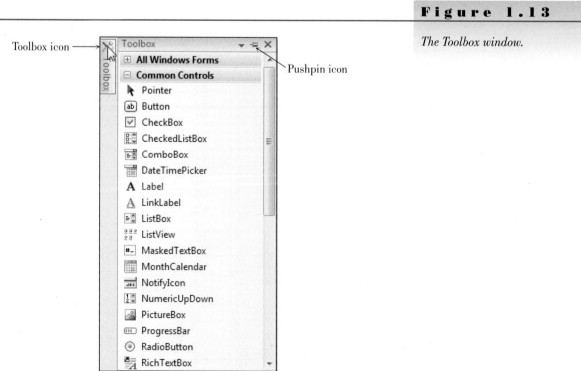

Toolbox icon

Pushpin icon

STEP 4: Optional: Select *Tools / Options*. In the *Options* dialog box, select *Startup* under *Environment*, drop down the *At startup* list and select *Show empty environment* (Figure 1.14), and click *OK*. This selection causes the Start Page to not appear and will make your environment match the illustrations in this text. Note that you can show the Start Page at any time by selecting *View / Other Windows / Start Page*.

Figure 1.14

*Select **Show empty environment** for the environment's **Startup** option in the **Options** dialog box.*

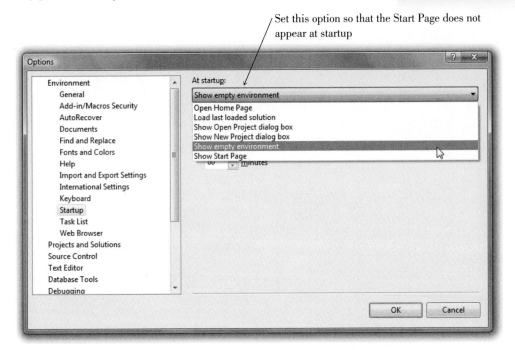

Plan the Project

The first step in planning is to design the user interface. Figure 1.15 shows a sketch of the form that includes a label and two buttons. You will refer to the sketch as you create the project.

Figure 1.15

A sketch of the Hello World form for planning.

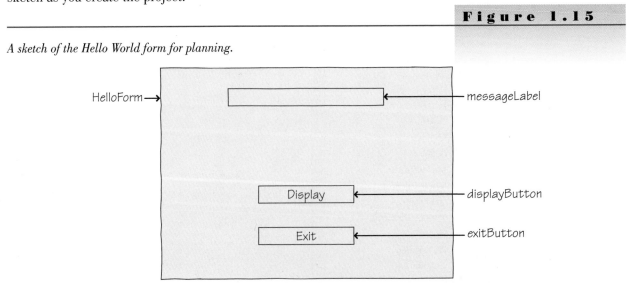

The next two steps, planning the properties and the code, have already been done for this first sample project. You will be given the values in the steps that follow.

Define the User Interface

Set Up the Form

Notice that the new form in the Document window has all the standard Windows features, such as a title bar, maximize and minimize buttons, and a Close button.

STEP 1: Resize the form in the Document window: Drag the handle in the lower-right corner down and to the right (Figure 1.16).

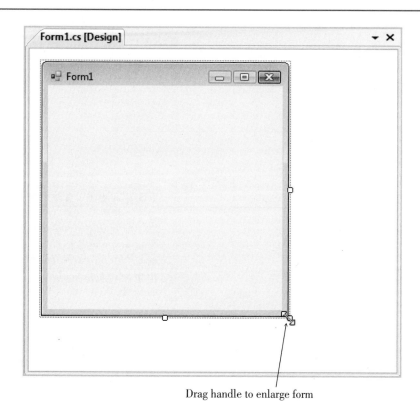

Drag handle to enlarge form

Figure 1.16

Make the form larger by dragging its lower-right handle diagonally. The handles disappear as you drag the corner of the form.

Place Controls on the Form

You are going to place three controls on the form: a **label** and two **buttons**.

STEP 1: Point to the Label tool in the toolbox and double-click; a Label control appears on the form. Drag the label to the desired location (Figure 1.17). Later you will adjust the label's size.

As long as the label is selected, you can press the Delete key to delete it, or drag it to a new location.

You can tell that a label is selected; it has a dotted border, as shown in Figure 1.17, when the AutoSize property is *true* (the default) or sizing handles if you set the AutoSize property to *false*.

STEP 2: Draw a button on the form: Click on the Button tool in the toolbox, position the crosshair pointer for one corner of the button, and drag to the diagonally opposite corner (Figure 1.18). When you release the mouse button, the new button should appear selected and have

Figure 1.17

The newly created label appears outlined, indicating that it is selected. Notice that the contents of the label are set to the control's name (label1) by default.

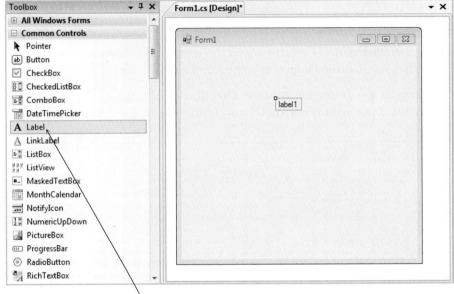

Double-click the Label tool

Figure 1.18

Select the Button tool and drag diagonally to create a new Button control. The blue snap lines help to align controls.

Snap line

Draw the Button control using the crosshair pointer

resizing handles. The blue lines that appear are called **snap lines**, which can help you align your controls.

While a control is selected, you can delete it or move it. If it has resizing handles, you also can resize it. Refer to Table 1.1 for instructions for selecting, deleting, moving, and resizing controls. Click outside of a control to deselect it.

Selecting, Deleting, Moving, and Resizing Controls on a Form.   Table   1.1

Select a control	Click on the control.
Delete a control	Select the control and then press the Delete key on the keyboard.
Move a control	Select the control, point inside the control (not on a handle), press the mouse button, and drag it to a new location.
Resize a control	Make sure the control is selected and has resizing handles; then either point to one of the handles, press the mouse button, and drag the handle; or drag the form's bottom border to change the height or the side border to change the width. Note that the default format for labels does not allow resizing.

STEP 3: While the first button is still selected, point to the Button tool in the toolbox and double-click. A new button of the default size will appear on top of the last-drawn control (Figure 1.19).

Figure 1.19

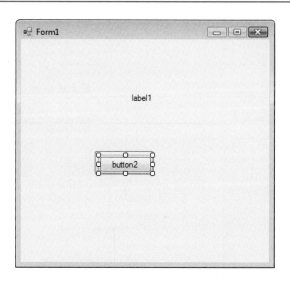

Place a new button on the form by double-clicking the Button tool in the toolbox. The new button appears on top of the previously selected control.

STEP 4: Keep the new button selected, point anywhere inside the button (not on a handle), and drag the button below your first button (Figure 1.20).

STEP 5: Select each control and move and resize the controls as necessary. Make the two buttons the same size and line them up. Use the snap lines to help with the size and alignment. Note that you can move but not resize the label.

At this point you have designed the user interface and are ready to set the properties.

Set Properties

Set the Name and Text Properties for the Label

STEP 1: Click on the label you placed on the form; a dotted outline appears around the control. If the Properties window is not displaying, select *View / Properties Window* or press the F4 key. Click on the title bar of the Properties window to make it the active window (Figure 1.21).

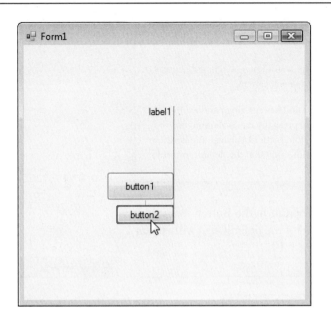

Drag the new button (button2) below button1.

If no control is selected when you double-click a tool, the new control is added to the upper-left corner of the form. ■

The currently selected control is shown in the Properties window.

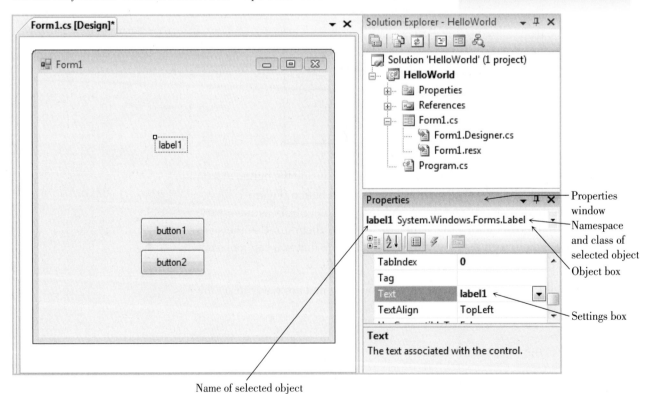

Notice that the Object box at the top of the Properties window is showing *label1* (the name of the object) and *System.Windows.Forms.Label* as the class of the object. The actual class is Label; System.Windows.Forms is called the **namespace**, or the hierarchy used to locate the class.

STEP 2: In the Properties window, click on the Alphabetical button to make sure the properties are sorted in alphabetic order. Then select the Name property, which appears near the top of the list. Click on *(Name)* and notice that the Settings box shows *label1*, the default name of the label (Figure 1.22).

If the Properties window is not visible, you can choose *View / Properties Window* or press the F4 key to show it. ■

Figure 1.22

The Properties window. Click on the Name property to change the value in the Settings box.

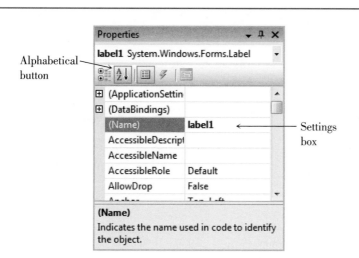

STEP 3: Type "messageLabel" (without the quotation marks). See Figure 1.23. As a shortcut, you may wish to delete the "1" from the end of "label1", press the Home key to get to the beginning of the word, and then type "message". Change the "l" for label to uppercase.

After you change the name of the control and press Enter or Tab, you can see the new name in the Object box's drop-down list.

Figure 1.23

Type "messageLabel" into the Settings box for the Name property.

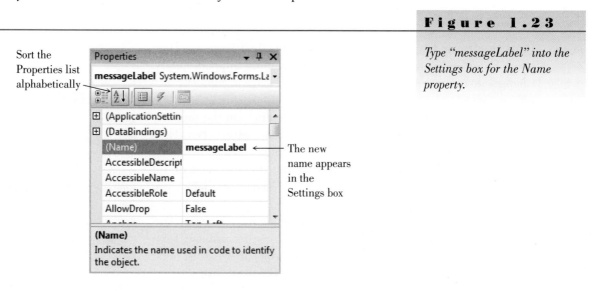

STEP 4: Select the AutoSize property and change the value to False. You can easily change a property from True to False in several ways: (1) Click in the word "True" and type only the letter "f", and the value changes automatically; (2) Double-click on either the property name (Auto-Size) or the property value (True), and the value toggles each time you double-click; or (3) Click on either the property name or the property value, and a drop-down arrow appears at the right end of the Settings box. Drop down the list and make your selection from the possible values (True or False, in this case).

STEP 5: Click on the Text property to select it. (Scroll the Properties list if necessary.)

The **Text property** of a control determines what will be displayed on the form. Because nothing should display when the program begins, you must delete the value of the Text property (as described in the next two steps).

STEP 6: Double-click on *label1* in the Settings box; the entry should appear selected (highlighted). See Figure 1.24.

F i g u r e   1 . 2 4

Double-click in the Settings box to select the entry.

Name of control

Value in Settings box is selected

Text
The text associated with the control.

STEP 7: Press the Delete key to delete the value of the Text property. Then press Enter and notice that the label on the form appears empty. Changes do not appear until you press Enter or move to another property or control.

As an alternate technique, you can double-click on the property name, which automatically selects the entry in the Settings box. Then you can press the Delete key or just begin typing to change the entry.

All you see is a very small selection border (Figure 1.25), and if you click anywhere else on the form, which deselects the label, you cannot see it at all.

If you need to select the label after deselecting it, you can click in the approximate spot on the form or use the Properties window: Drop down the Object list at the top of the window; you can see a list of all controls on the form and can make a selection (Figure 1.26).

☑TIP

Don't confuse the Name property with the Text property. You will use the Name property to refer to the control in your C# code. The Text property determines what the user will see on the form. C# sets both of these properties to the same value by default and it is easy to confuse them. ■

Figure 1.25

Delete the value for the Text property from the Settings box; the label on the form also appears empty.

Label is empty and selected

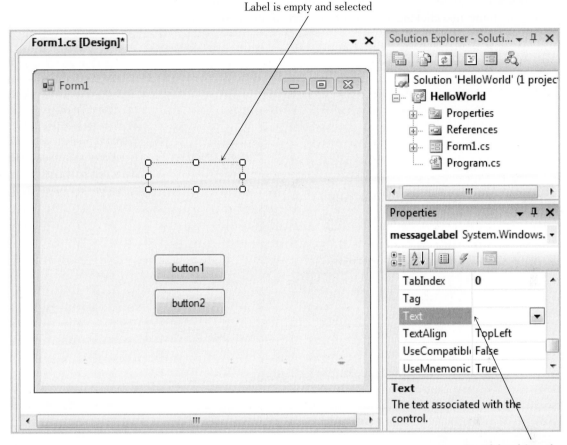

Text deleted from the
Settings box

Figure 1.26

*Drop down the Object box in
the Properties window to select
any control on the form.*

Lock the Controls

STEP 1: Point anywhere on the form and click the right mouse button to
display a **context menu**. On the context menu, select *Lock Controls*
(Figure 1.27). Locking prevents you from accidentally moving the

controls. When your controls are locked, a selected control has a small lock icon in the upper-left corner instead of resizing handles (Figure 1.28).

Note: You can unlock the controls at any time if you wish to redesign the form. Just click again on *Lock Controls* on the context menu to deselect it.

Figure 1.27

*After the controls are placed into the desired location, lock them in place by selecting **Lock Controls** from the context menu. Remember that context menus differ depending on the current operation and system setup.*

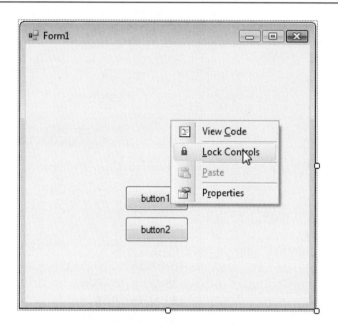

Figure 1.28

After you lock the controls on a form, a selected control has a lock icon instead of resizing handles.

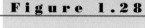

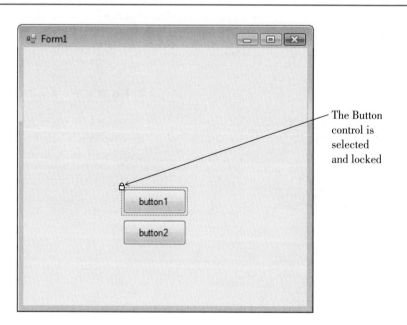

The Button control is selected and locked

Set the Name and Text Properties for the First Button

STEP 1: Click on the first button (button1) to select it and then look at the Properties window. The Object box should show the name (*button1*) and class (*System.Windows.Forms.Button*) of the button (Figure 1.29).

Figure 1.29

Change the properties of the first button.

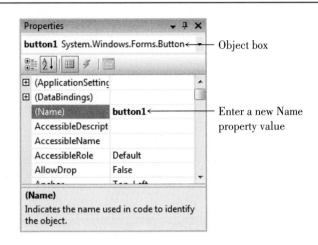

Problem? If you should double-click and code appears in the Document window, simply click on the *Form1.cs [Design]* tab at the top of the window.

STEP 2: Change the Name property of the button to "displayButton" (without the quotation marks).

Although the project would work fine without this step, we prefer to give this button a meaningful name, rather than use button1, its default name. The guidelines for naming controls appear later in this chapter in the section "Naming Rules and Conventions for Objects."

STEP 3: Change the Text property to "Display" (without the quotation marks). This step changes the words that appear on top of the button.

Set the Name and Text Properties for the Second Button

STEP 1: Select button2 and change its Name property to "exitButton."

STEP 2: Change the Text property to "Exit."

Change Properties of the Form

STEP 1: Click anywhere on the form, except on a control. The Properties window Object box should now show the form as the selected object (*Form1* as the object's name and *System.Windows.Forms.Form* as its class).

STEP 2: Change the Text property to "Hello World by Your Name" (again, no quotation marks and use your own name).

The Text property of a form determines the text that appears in the title bar. Your screen should now look like Figure 1.30.

STEP 3: In the Properties window, click on the StartPosition property and notice the arrow on the property setting, indicating a drop-down list. Drop down the list and select *CenterScreen*. This will make your form appear in the center of the screen when the program runs.

STEP 4: In the Solution Explorer, right-click on Form1.cs and choose *Rename* from the context menu. Change the file name to "HelloForm.cs", making sure to retain the .cs extension. Press Enter when finished and click *Yes* on the confirmation dialog box. This changes the name of the file that saves to disk (Figure 1.31) as well as the name of the class.

TIP

Always set the Name property of controls before writing code. Although the program will still work if you reverse the order, the method names won't match the control names, which can cause confusion. ∎

The form's Text property appears in the title bar

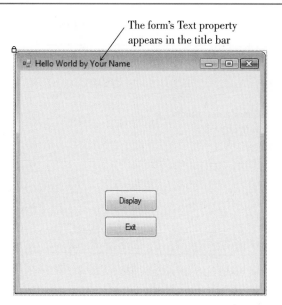

Figure 1.31

The Properties window shows the file's properties with the new name for the file. You can change the filename in the Properties window or the Solution Explorer.

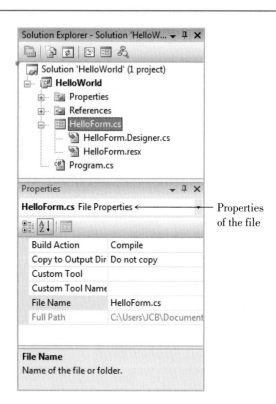

Properties of the file

STEP 5: Click on the form in the Document window, anywhere except on a control. The name of the file appears on the tab at the top of the Designer window and the Properties window shows properties for the form's class, not the file. The C# designer changed the name of the form's class to match the name of the file (Figure 1.32).

The Properties window for the form. The form's class name now matches the name of the form's file.

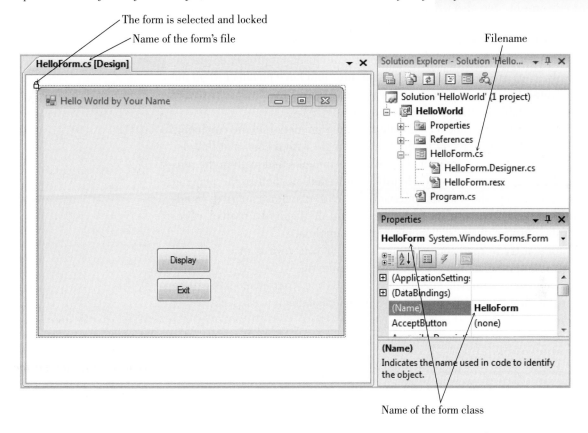

The form is selected and locked

Name of the form's file

Filename

Name of the form class

Write Code

C# Events

While your project is running, the user can do many things, such as move the mouse around; click either button; move, resize, or close your form's window; or jump to another application. Each action by the user causes an event to occur in your C# project. Some events (like clicking on a button) you care about, and some events (like moving the mouse and resizing the window) you do not care about. If you write code for a particular event, then C# will respond to the event and automatically execute your method. *C# ignores events for which no methods are written.*

C# Event Handlers

You write code in C# in methods. For now, each method will begin with the words `private void` and the code will be enclosed in opening and closing braces { }.

C# automatically names your **event-handling methods** (also called *event handlers*). The name consists of the object name, an underscore (_), and the name of the event. For example, the Click event for your button called display-Button will be displayButton_Click. For the sample project you are writing, you will have a displayButton_Click method and an exitButton_Click method.

> **TIP**
>
> If you change the form's filename before changing the form's class name, the IDE automatically changes the form's class name to match the filename. It does not make the change if you have changed the form's class name yourself. ∎

C# Code Statements

This first project requires two C# statements: the **comment** and the **assignment statement**. You also will execute a method of an object.

The Comment Statement

Comment statements, sometimes called *remarks*, are used for project documentation only. They are not considered "executable" and have no effect when the program runs. The purpose of comments is to make the project more readable and understandable by the people who read it.

Good programming practices dictate that programmers include comments to clarify their projects. Every method should begin with a comment that describes its purpose. Every project should have comments that explain the purpose of the program and provide identifying information such as the name of the programmer and the date the program was written and/or modified. In addition, it is a good idea to place comments within the logic of a project, especially if the purpose of any statements might be unclear.

When you try to read someone else's code or your own after a period of time, you will appreciate the generous use of comments.

C# comments begin with slashes. Most of the time, your comments will be on a separate line. You also can add slashes and a comment to the right end of a line of code.

The Comment Statement—Examples

```
// This project was written by Jonathon Edwards.
// Exit the project.
messageLabel.Text = "Hello World"; // Assign the message to the Text property.
```

Multiline Comments You also can create multiline comments by placing /* at the beginning and */ at the end. The enclosing symbols can be on lines by themselves or on existing lines. As you type additional lines between the beginning and ending symbols, the editor adds an asterisk at the start of each line, indicating that it is a comment line. However, you do not need the * at the beginning of each line. When you want to turn multiple lines of code into comments, just add the opening /* and ending */.

```
/*
 *    Project:      Ch01HandsOn
 *    Programmer:   Bradley/Millspaugh
 *    Date:         June 2009
 *    Description:  This project displays a Hello World message
 *                     using labels and buttons.
 * */

/*Project:    Ch01HandsOn
Programmer:   Bradley/Millspaugh
Date:         June 2009
Description:  This project displays a Hello World message
                 using labels and buttons. */
```

Ending a Statement

Most C# statements must be terminated by a semicolon (;). Comments and a few other statements (which you will learn about later) do not end with a semi-colon. A C# statement may extend over multiple lines; the semicolon indicates that the statement is complete.

The Assignment Statement

The assignment statement assigns a value to a property or variable (you learn about variables in Chapter 3). Assignment statements operate from right to left; that is, the value that appears on the right side of the equal sign is assigned to the property named on the left of the equal sign. It is often helpful to read the equal sign as "is replaced by." For example, the following assignment statement would read "messageLabel.Text is replaced by Hello World."

```
messageLabel.Text = "Hello World";
```

The Assignment Statement—General Form

General Form

```
Object.Property = value;
```

The value named on the right side of the equal sign is assigned to (or placed into) the property named on the left.

The Assignment Statement—Examples

Examples

```
titleLabel.Text = "A Snazzy Program";
addressLabel.Text = "1234 South North Street";
messageLabel.AutoSize = true;
numberInteger = 12;
```

Notice that when the value to assign is some actual text (called a *literal*), it is enclosed in quotation marks. This convention allows you to type any combination of alpha and numeric characters. If the value is numeric, do not enclose it in quotation marks. And do not place quotation marks around the terms *true* and *false*, which C# recognizes as special key terms.

Ending a Program by Executing a Method

To execute a method of an object, you write:

```
Object.Method();
```

Notice that methods always have parentheses. Although this might seem like a bother, it's helpful to distinguish between properties and methods: Methods always have parentheses; properties don't.

Examples

```
helloButton.Hide();
messageLabel.Show();
```

To execute a method of the current form, you use the **this** keyword for the object. And the method that closes the form and terminates the project execution is `Close`.

```
this.Close();
```

In most cases, you will include `this.Close()` in the event-handling method for an *Exit* button or an *Exit* menu choice.

Note: Remember, the keyword `this` refers to the current object. You can omit `this` since a method without an object reference defaults to the current object.

Code the Event-Handling Methods for Hello World

Code the Click Event Handler for the Display Button

STEP 1: Double-click the *Display* button. The Visual Studio editor opens with the header line of your method already in place, with the insertion point indented inside the opening and closing braces (Figure 1.33).

Figure 1.33

The Editor window, showing the first line of the displayButton_Click event handler with the insertion point between the opening and closing braces.

Insertion point

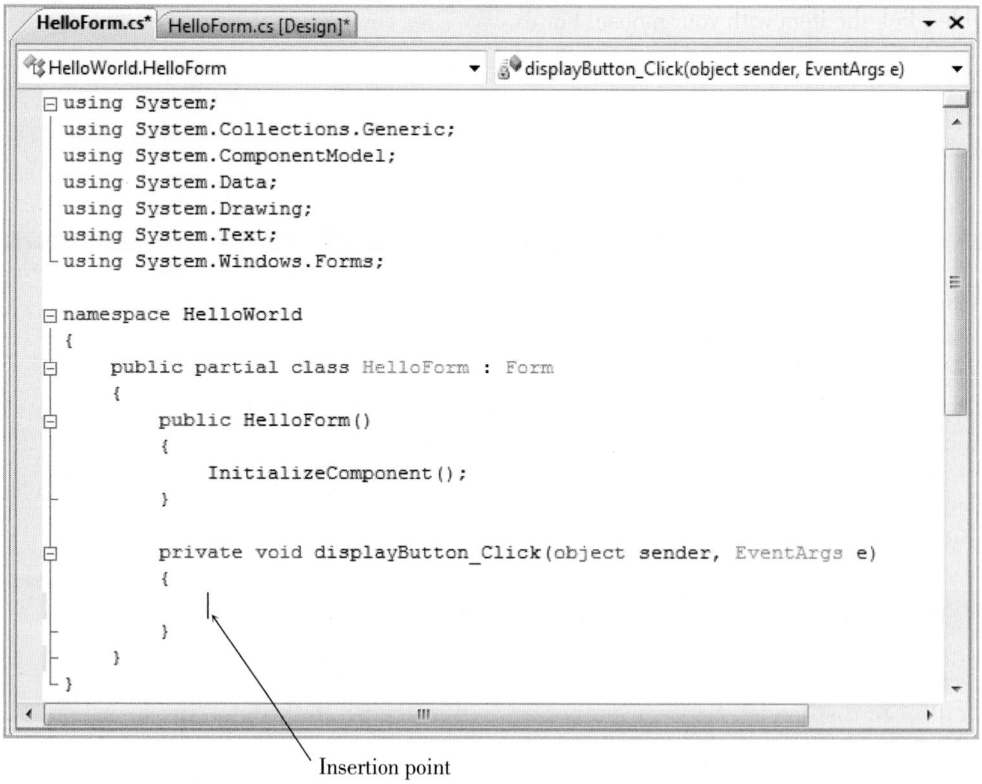

STEP 2: Type this comment statement:

```
// Display the Hello World message.
```

Notice that the editor automatically displays comments in green (unless you or someone else has changed the color with an Environment option).

Follow good coding conventions and indent all lines between the opening and closing braces. The smart editor attempts to help you follow this convention. Also, always leave a blank line after the comments at the top of a method.

STEP 3: Press Enter twice and then type this assignment statement:

```
messageLabel.Text = "Hello World";
```

Note: When you type the names of objects and properties, allow IntelliSense to help you. When you type the first character of a name, such as the "m" of "messageLabel", IntelliSense pops up a list of possible object names from your program (Figure 1.34). When several items match the first letter, you can type additional characters until you get a match, or use your keyboard down arrow or the mouse to highlight the correct item. To accept the correct item when it is highlighted, press the punctuation character that should follow the item, such as the period, spacebar, equal sign, semicolon, Tab key, or Enter key, or double-click the item with your mouse. For example, accept "messageLabel" by pressing the period and accept "Text" by pressing the spacebar, since those are the characters that follow the selected items.

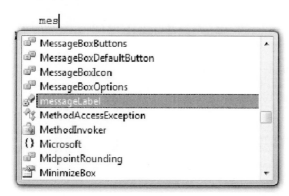

```
private void displayButton_Click(object sender, EventArgs e)
{
    // Display the Hello World message.

    mes|
```

Figure   1.34

IntelliSense pops up to help you. Select the correct item from the list and press the period, spacebar, semicolon, Tab key, or Enter key to accept the text.

☑ **TIP**

Accept an entry from the IntelliSense popup list by typing the punctuation that follows the entry, by pressing the spacebar, the Tab key, or the Enter key. You also can scroll the list and select with your mouse. ■

The assignment statement

```
messageLabel.Text = "Hello World";
```

assigns the literal "Hello World" to the Text property of the control called messageLabel. Compare your screen to Figure 1.35.

STEP 4: Return to the Form Designer (refer to Figure 1.32) by clicking on the *HelloForm.cs [Design]* tab on the Document window (refer to Figure 1.35).

Editor tab   Form Designer tab

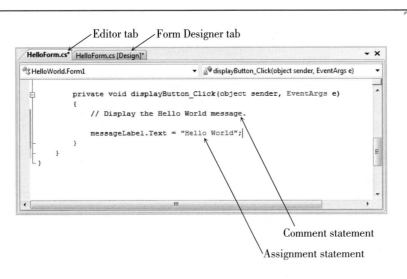

Comment statement

Assignment statement

Figure 1.35

Type the comment and assignment statement for the displayButton_Click event handler.

✓TIP

Allow the Editor and IntelliSense to help you. If the IntelliSense list does not pop up, likely you misspelled the name of the control. ■

Code the Click Event Handler for the Exit Button

STEP 1: Double-click the *Exit* button to open the editor for the exitButton_Click event handler.

STEP 2: Type this comment:

```
// Exit the project.
```

STEP 3: Press Enter twice and type this C# statement:

```
this.Close();
```

STEP 4: Make sure your code looks like the code shown in Figure 1.36.

Figure 1.36

Type the code for the exitButton_Click event handler. Notice that an asterisk appears on the tab at the top of the window, indicating that there are unsaved changes in the file.

Asterisk indicates unsaved changes

```
private void displayButton_Click(object sender, EventArgs e)
{
    // Display the Hello World message.

    messageLabel.Text = "Hello World";
}

private void exitButton_Click(object sender, EventArgs e)
{
    // Exit the project.

    this.Close();
}
```

Run the Project

After you have finished writing the code, you are ready to run the project. Use one of these three techniques:

1. Open the *Debug* menu and choose *Start Debugging*.
2. Press the *Start Debugging* button on the toolbar.
3. Press F5, the shortcut key for the *Start Debugging* command.

Start the Project Running

STEP 1: Choose one of the three methods previously listed to start your project running.

Problems? See "Finding and Fixing Errors" later in this chapter. You must correct any errors and restart the program.

If all went well, the form appears and the Visual Studio title bar now indicates that you are in run time (Figure 1.37).

TIP

If your form disappears during run time, click its button on the Windows task bar. ∎

Figure 1.37

The form of the running application.

IDE title bar indicates that the program is in run time

Running program, Editor tab is locked

Running program, Form Designer tab locked

Form for the running application

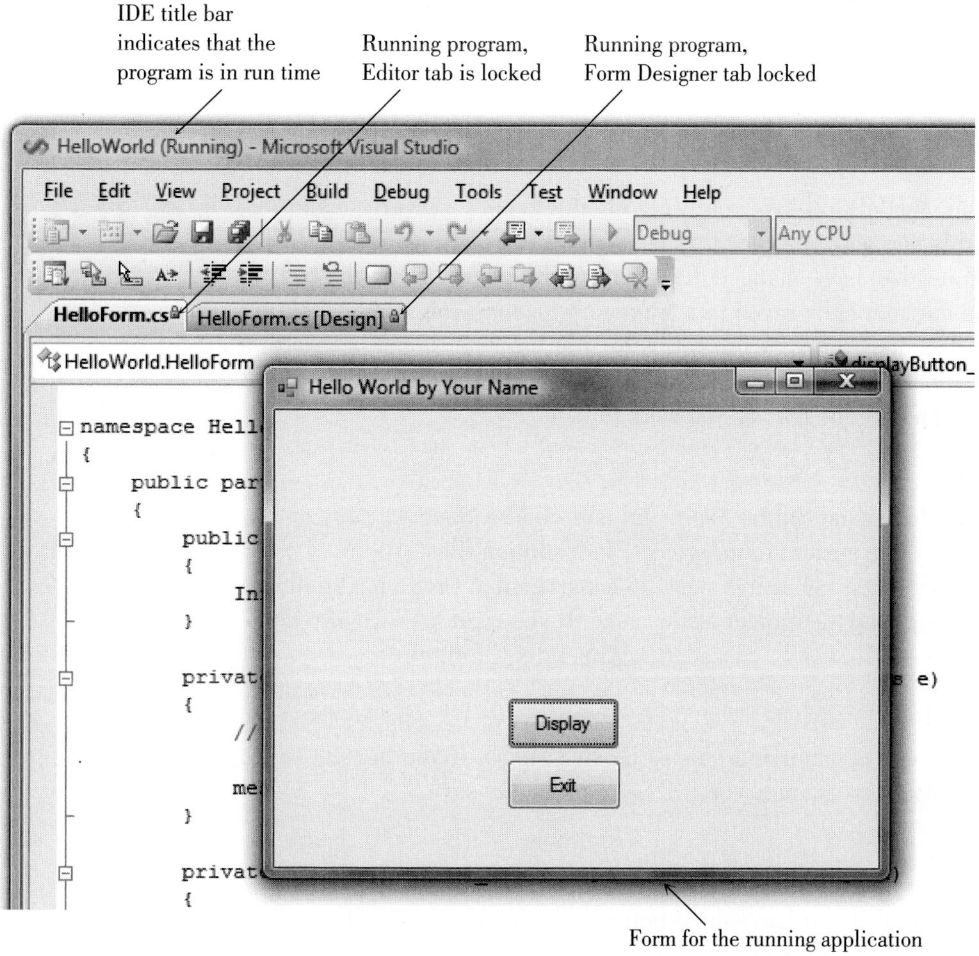

Click the Display Button

STEP 1: Click the *Display* button. Your "Hello World" message appears in the label (Figure 1.38).

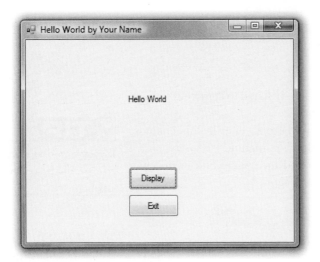

Figure 1.38

Click the Display button and "Hello World" appears in the label.

Click the Exit Button

STEP 1: Click the *Exit* button. Your project terminates, and you return to design time.

Save Your Work

Of course, you must always save your work often. Except for a very small project such as this one, you will usually save your work as you go along. Unless you (or someone else) have changed the setting in the IDE's *Options* dialog box, your files are automatically saved in a temporary location each time you build (compile) or execute (run) your project. After you have performed a save to a different location, files are automatically resaved each time you compile or run. You also can save the files as you work.

TIP

Click the *Save All* toolbar button to quickly save all of your work. ■

Save the Files

STEP 1: Open the Visual Studio *File* menu and choose *Save All*. This option will save the current form, project, and solution files.

    Note: When saving a project, do not attempt to save a modified version by giving the project a new name. If you want to move or rename the project, it must be closed. See Appendix C for help.

Close the Project

STEP 1: Open the *File* menu and choose *Close Solution*. If you haven't saved since your last change, you will be prompted to save.

Open the Project

Now is the time to test your save operation by opening the project from disk. You can choose one of three ways to open a saved project:

- Select *Open Project* from the Visual Studio *File* menu and browse to find your .sln file, which has a small "9" as part of the file's icon.

- Choose the project from the *File / Recent Projects* menu item.

- Choose the project from Recent Projects (if available) on the Start Page (*View / Other Windows / Start Page*).

Open the Project File

STEP 1: Open your project by choosing one of the previously listed techniques. Remember that the file to open is the .sln file.

    If you do not see your form on the screen, check the Solution Explorer window—it should say *HelloWorld* for the project. Select the icon for your form: HelloForm.cs. You can double-click the icon or single-click and click on the *View Designer* button at the top of the Solution Explorer (Figure 1.39); your form will appear in the Designer window. Notice that you also can click on the *View Code* button to display your form's code in the Editor window.

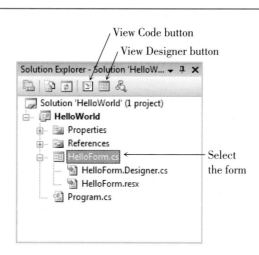

View Code button
View Designer button
Select the form

Figure 1.39

*To display the form layout, select the form name and click on the **View Designer** button, or double-click on the form name. Click on the **View Code** button to display the code in the editor.*

Modify the Project

Now it's time to make some changes to the project. We'll change the size of the "Hello World" message, display the message in two different languages, and display the programmer name (that's you) on the form.

Change the Size and Alignment of the Message

STEP 1: Right-click the form to display the context menu. If your controls are currently locked, select *Lock Controls* to unlock the controls so that you can make changes.

STEP 2: Drop down the Object list at the top of the Properties window and select messageLabel, which will make the label appear selected.

STEP 3: Scroll to the Font property in the Properties window. The Font property is actually a Font object that has a number of properties. To see the Font properties, click on the small plus sign on the left (Figure 1.40); the Font properties will appear showing the current values (Figure 1.41).

    You can change any of the Font properties in the Properties window, such as setting the Font's Size, Bold, or Italic properties. You also can display the *Font* dialog box and make changes there.

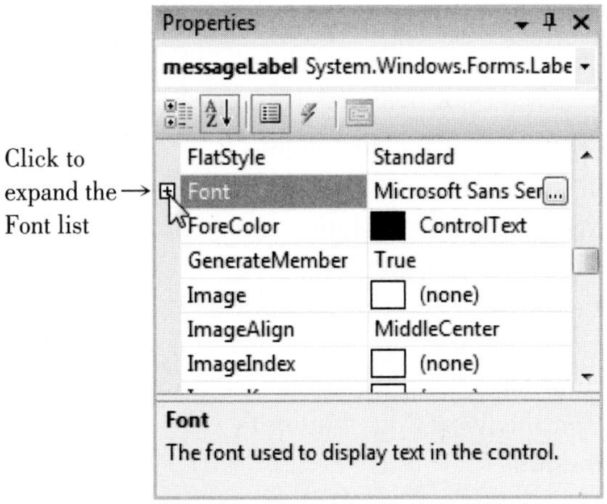

Figure 1.40

Click on the Font's plus sign to view the properties of the Font object.

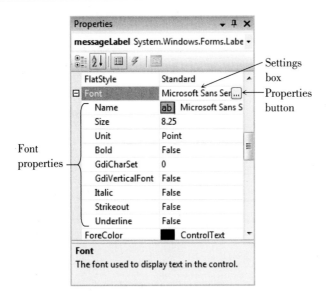

Click to expand the → Font list

Figure 1.41

You can change the individual properties of the Font object.

STEP 4: Click the Properties button for the font (the button with the ellipsis on top) to display the *Font* dialog box (Figure 1.42). Select 12 point if it is available. (If it isn't available, choose another number larger than the current setting.) Click *OK* to close the *Font* dialog box.

STEP 5: Select the TextAlign property. The Properties button that appears with the down-pointing arrow indicates a drop-down list of choices. Drop down the list (Figure 1.43) and choose the center box; the alignment property changes to *MiddleCenter*.

Add a New Label for Your Name

STEP 1: Click on the Label tool in the toolbox and create a new label along the bottom edge of your form (Figure 1.44). (You can resize the form if necessary.)

STEP 2: Change the label's Text property to "by Your Name." (Use your name and omit the quotation marks.)

> *Note*: You do not need to rename this label because it will never be referred to in the code.

☑ **TIP**

When you change a property from its default value, the property name appears bolded; you can scan down the property list and easily identify the properties that are changed from their default value. ■

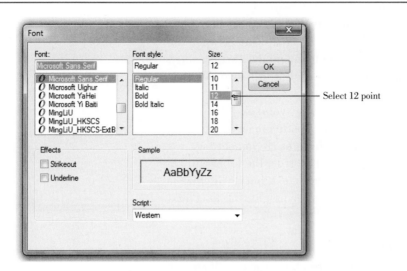

Figure 1.42

Choose 12 point on the Font dialog box.

Select 12 point

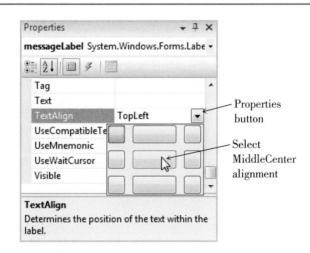

Figure 1.43

Select the center box for the TextAlign property.

Properties button

Select MiddleCenter alignment

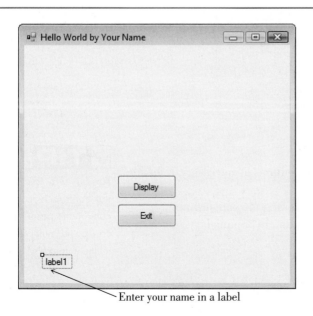

Enter your name in a label

Figure 1.44

Add a new label for your name at the bottom of the form.

TIP

You can change the Font property of the form, which sets the default Font for all objects on the form. ■

The Label's AutoSize Property   Earlier you changed the AutoSize property of messageLabel to False, a step that allows you to set the size of the label yourself. When AutoSize is set to True (the default), the label resizes automatically to accommodate the Text property, which can be an advantage when the text or font size may change. However, if you plan to delete the Text property, as you did for messageLabel, the label resizes to such a tiny size that it is difficult to see.

Any time that you want to set the size of a label yourself, change the AutoSize property to False. This setting also allows you to create taller labels that allow a long Text property to wrap to multiple lines. If you set the Text property to a very long value when AutoSize is set to True, the label will resize only to the edge of the form and cut off any excess text, but if AutoSize is set to False and the label has been resized to a taller height, the long Text property will wrap.

Change the Text of the Display Button

Because we plan to display the message in one of two languages, we'll change the text on the *Display* button to "English" and move the buttons to allow for another button.

STEP 1:   Select the *Display* button and change its Text property to "English."
STEP 2:   Move the *English* button and the *Exit* button to the right and leave room for a *Spanish* button (Figure 1.45).

F i g u r e   1 . 4 5

Move the English and Exit buttons and add a Spanish button.

Add a Spanish Button

STEP 1:   Add a new button. Move and resize the buttons as necessary, referring to Figure 1.45.
STEP 2:   Change the Name property of the new button to spanishButton.
STEP 3:   Change the Text property of the new button to "Spanish."

☑ TIP

An easy way to create multiple similar controls is to copy an existing control and paste it on the form. You can paste multiple times to create multiple controls. ■

Add an Event Handler for the Spanish Button

STEP 1: Double-click on the *Spanish* button to open the editor for spanishButton_Click.

STEP 2: Add a comment:

```
// Display the Hello World message in Spanish.
```

STEP 3: Press Enter twice and type the following line of C# code.

```
messageLabel.Text = "Hola Mundo";
```

STEP 4: Return to design view.

Lock the Controls

STEP 1: When you are satisfied with the placement of the controls on the form, display the context menu and select *Lock Controls* again.

Save and Run the Project

STEP 1: Save your project again. You can use the *File / Save All* menu command or the *Save All* toolbar button.

STEP 2: Run your project again. Try clicking on the *English* button and the *Spanish* button.

Problems? See "Finding and Fixing Errors" later in this chapter.

STEP 3: Click the *Exit* button to end program execution.

Add Comments

Good documentation guidelines require some more comments in the project. Always begin each method with comments that tell the purpose of the method. In addition, each project file needs identifying comments at the top.

STEP 1: Display the code in the editor and click in front of the first line (using System;). Make sure that you have an insertion point; if the entire first line is selected, press the left arrow to set the insertion point.

STEP 2: Press Enter to create a blank line.

Warning: If you accidentally deleted the first line, click *Undo* (or press Ctrl + Z) and try again.

STEP 3: Move the insertion point up to the blank line and type the following comments, one per line (Figure 1.46):

Press Ctrl + Home to quickly move the insertion point to the top of the file. ■

```
/*
 * Project:      Hello World
 * Programmer:   Your Name (Use your own name here.)
 * Date:         (Fill in today's date.)
 * Description:  This project will display a "Hello World"
 *               message in two different languages.
 */
```

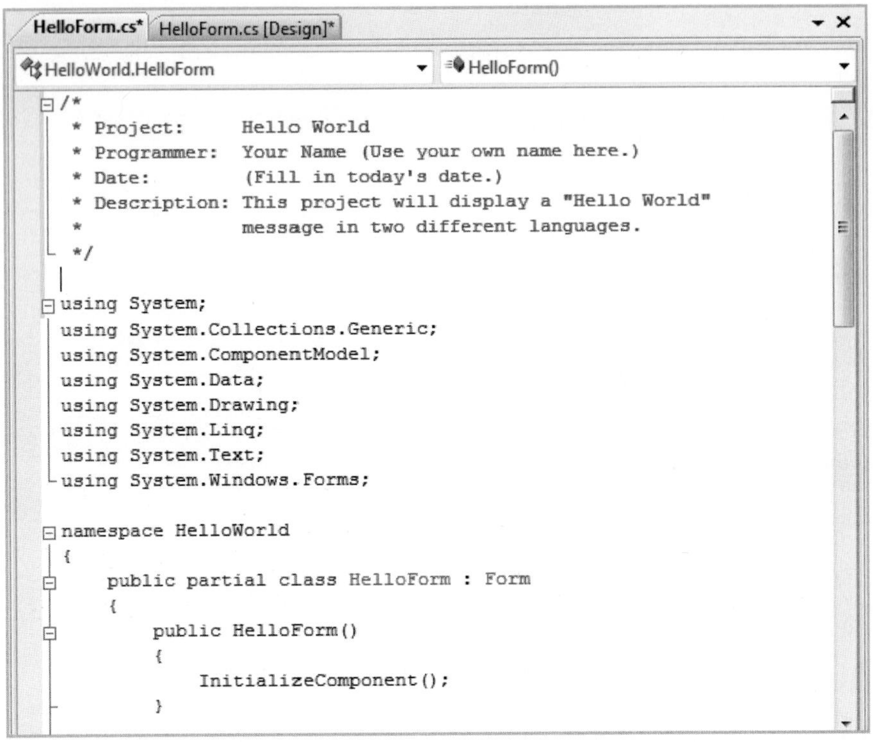

Figure 1.46

Enter the comments at the top of the form file.

```
HelloForm.cs*  HelloForm.cs [Design]*                          ▾ ✕
🔧 HelloWorld.HelloForm              ▾    ≡◆ HelloForm()              ▾
⊟ /*
    * Project:      Hello World
    * Programmer:   Your Name (Use your own name here.)
    * Date:         (Fill in today's date.)
    * Description: This project will display a "Hello World"
    *              message in two different languages.
    */

⊟ using System;
  using System.Collections.Generic;
  using System.ComponentModel;
  using System.Data;
  using System.Drawing;
  using System.Linq;
  using System.Text;
  using System.Windows.Forms;

⊟ namespace HelloWorld
  {
⊟     public partial class HelloForm : Form
      {
⊟         public HelloForm()
          {
              InitializeComponent();
          }
```

Finish Up

STEP 1: Run the project again. Test each language button multiple times; then click the *Exit* button.

Print the Code

Select the Printing Options

STEP 1: Make sure that the Editor window is open and showing your form's code. The *File / Print* command is disabled unless the code is displaying and its window selected.

STEP 2: Open the *File* menu and choose *Print*. Click *OK*.

View Event Handlers

You also can get to the event-handling methods for a control using the Properties window in design mode. With a button control selected, click on the *Events* button (lightning bolt) in the Properties window; all of the events for that control display (Figure 1.47). If you've already written code for the Click event, the method name appears bold in the Properties window. When you double-click on the event, the editor takes you to the method in the code window.

To write an event-handling method for any of the available events of a control, double-click the event name. You will be transferred to the Code Editor window with the insertion point inside the template for the new event handler. You also can click in any event name in the Properties window and then drop down a list of all previously written methods and select a method to assign as the event handler.

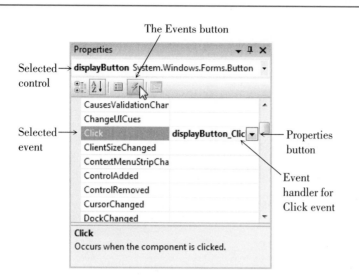

The Events button

Selected control

Selected event

Properties button

Event handler for Click event

Figure 1.47

Click on the Events button to see the available events for a selected control. Any event handlers that are already written appear in bold. Double-click an event to jump to the Editor window inside the event handler for that method, or drop down the list to select a method to assign as the handler for the event.

A Sample Printout

This output is produced when you print the form's code. An explanation of some of the features of the code follows the listing.

```
C:\Users\. . .\Ch01HelloWorld\HelloForm.cs            1
/*
 * Project:       Hello World
 * Programmer:    Your Name (Use your own name here.)
 * Date:          (Fill in today's date.)
 * Description:   This project will display a "Hello World"
 *                message in two different languages.
 */

using System;
using System.Collections.Generic;
using System.ComponentModel;
using System.Data;
using System.Drawing;
using System.Linq;
using System.Text;
using System.Windows.Forms;

namespace HelloWorld
{
    public partial class HelloForm : Form
    {
        public HelloForm()
        {
            InitializeComponent();
        }

        private void displayButton_Click(object sender, EventArgs e)
        {
            // Display the Hello World message.
```

```csharp
        messageLabel.Text = "Hello World";
    }

    private void exitButton_Click(object sender, EventArgs e)
    {
        // Exit the project.

        this.Close();
    }

    private void spanishButton_Click(object sender, EventArgs e)
    {
        // Display the Hello World message in Spanish.

        messageLabel.Text = "Hola Mundo";
    }
  }
}
```

Automatically Generated Code

In the preceding code listing, you see many statements that you wrote, plus some more that appeared "automatically." Although a programmer *could* begin a C# program by using a simple text editor and write all of the necessary statements to make the program run, using the development tools of the Visual Studio IDE is much quicker and more efficient. The IDE adds a group of statements by default and sets up the files for the project to accommodate the majority of applications. Later, when your programs include database tables, you will have to write additional using statements.

The Using Statements

The using statements appear at the top of the file after the comments that you wrote. Using statements provide references to standard groups of classes from the language library. For example, the statement using System.Windows. Forms; allows your program to refer to all of the Windows controls that appear in the toolbox. Without the using statement, each time that you wanted to refer to a Label control, for example, you would have to specify the complete reference: System.Windows.Forms.Label.messageLabel. Instead, in the program with the using statement, you can just refer to messageLabel.

The Namespace Statement

As mentioned earlier, a namespace provides a way to refer to programming components by location or organization. In the Label example in the preceding section, "Label" is the class and "System.Windows.Forms" is the namespace, or library grouping where "Label" is found. You can think of a namespace as similar to a telephone area code: In any one area code, a single phone number can appear only once, but that same phone number can appear in any number of other area codes.

Using the .NET Framework, every program component is required to have a namespace. The VS IDE automatically adds a namespace statement to your program. The default namespace is the name of your solution, but you can use a different name if you wish. Many companies use the namespace to organize applications such as the company name and functional organization, `LookSharpFitnessCenter.Payroll`, for example.

In Visual Studio, one solution can contain multiple projects. All of the solutions in this text contain only one project, so you can think of a solution and a project as being equal.

The Class Statement

In object-oriented programming, code is organized into classes. A new class can be based on (inherit from) another class, which gives the new class all of the properties and methods of the original class (the base class).

When you create a new form, you declare a new class (HelloForm in the earlier example). The new class inherits from the Form base class, which makes your new form behave like a standard form, with a title bar, maximize and minimize buttons, and resizable borders, among other behaviors.

A class may be split into multiple files. VS uses this feature, to place most of the code automatically generated by the Form Designer in a separate file that is part of the form's class.

The automatically generated statement

```
public partial class HelloForm : Form
```

means that this is a new class called HelloForm that inherits from the Form class. The new class is a partial class, so another file can exist that also contains statements that are part of the HelloForm class. You will learn more about classes and files in later chapters.

Finding and Fixing Errors

You already may have seen some errors as you entered the first sample project. Programming errors come in three varieties: syntax errors, run-time errors, and logic errors.

Syntax Errors

When you break C#'s rules for punctuation, format, or spelling, you generate a **syntax error**. Fortunately, the smart editor finds most syntax errors and even corrects many of them for you. The syntax errors that the editor cannot identify are found and reported by the compiler as it attempts to convert the code into intermediate machine language. A compiler-reported syntax error may be referred to as a *compile error*.

The editor identifies syntax errors as you move off the offending line. A red squiggly line appears under the part of the line that the editor cannot interpret. You can view the error message by pausing the mouse pointer over the error, which pops up a box that describes the error (Figure 1.48). You also can display an Error List window, which appears at the bottom of the Editor window and shows all error messages along with the line number of the statement that caused the error. You can display line numbers on the source code (Figure 1.49) with *Tools / Options / Text Editor / C# / General / Display / Line Numbers*.

Figure 1.48

The editor identifies a syntax error with a squiggly red line; you can point to an error to pop up the error message.

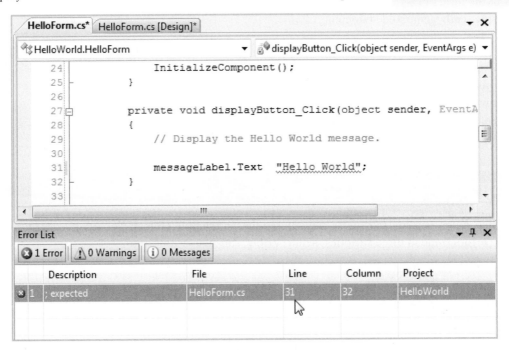

Figure 1.49

You can display the Error List window and line numbers in the source code to help locate the error lines.

The quickest way to jump to an error line is to point to a message in the Error List window and double-click. The line in error will display in the Editor window with the error highlighted (Figure 1.50).

If a syntax error is found by the compiler, you will see the dialog box shown in Figure 1.51. Click *No* and return to the editor, correct your errors, and run the program again.

Run-Time Errors

If your project halts during execution, it is called a **run-time error** or an **exception**. C# displays a dialog box and highlights the statement causing the problem.

Statements that cannot execute correctly cause run-time errors. The statements are correctly formed C# statements that pass the syntax checking; however, the statements fail to execute due to some serious issue. You can cause

Figure 1.50

Quickly jump to the line in error by double-clicking on the error message in the Error List window.

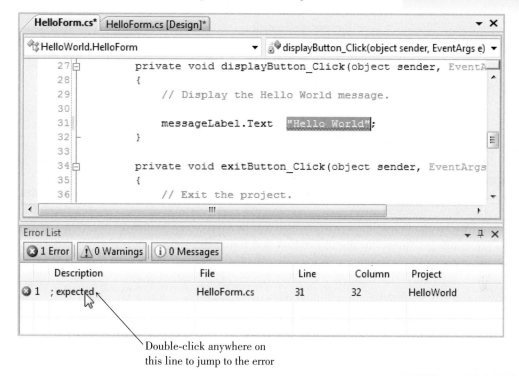

Double-click anywhere on
this line to jump to the error

Figure 1.51

When the compiler identifies syntax errors, it cannot continue. Click No to return to the editor and correct the error.

run-time errors by attempting to do impossible arithmetic operations, such as calculate with nonnumeric data, divide by zero, or find the square root of a negative number.

In Chapter 3 you will learn to catch exceptions so that the program does not come to a halt when an error occurs.

Logic Errors

When your program contains **logic errors**, the program runs but produces incorrect results. Perhaps the results of a calculation are incorrect or the wrong text appears or the text is okay but appears in the wrong location.

Beginning programmers often overlook their logic errors. If the project runs, it must be right—right? All too often, that statement is not correct. You may need to use a calculator to check the output. Check all aspects of the project output: computations, text, and spacing.

For example, the Hello World project in this chapter has event-handling methods for displaying "Hello World" in English and in Spanish. If the contents of the two methods were switched, the program would work, but the results would be incorrect.

The following code does not give the proper instructions to display the message in Spanish:

```
private void spanishButton_Click(object sender, EventArgs e)
{
    // Display the Hello World message in Spanish.

    messageLabel.Text = "Hello World";
}
```

Project Debugging

If you talk to any computer programmer, you will learn that programs don't have errors—programs get "bugs" in them. Finding and fixing these bugs is called **debugging**.

For syntax errors and run-time errors, your job is easier. C# displays the Editor window with the offending line highlighted. However, you must identify and locate logic errors yourself.

C# also includes a very popular feature: edit-and-continue. If you are able to identify the run-time error and fix it, you can continue project execution from that location by clicking on the *Start Debugging* button, pressing F5, or choosing *Debug / Continue*. You also can correct the error and restart from the beginning.

The Visual Studio IDE has some very helpful tools to aid in debugging your projects. The debugging tools are covered in Chapter 4.

TIP

If you get the message "There were build errors. Continue?" always say *No*. If you say *Yes*, the last cleanly compiled version runs rather than the current version. ■

A Clean Compile

When you start executing your program, the first step is called *compiling*, which means that the C# statements are converted to Microsoft Intermediate Language (MSIL). Your goal is to have no errors during the compile process: a **clean compile**. Figure 1.52 shows the Error List window for a clean compile: 0 Errors; 0 Warnings; 0 Messages.

Figure 1.52

Zero errors, warnings, and messages mean that you have a clean compile.

Modifying an Event Handler

When you double-click a Button control to begin writing an event-handling method for the Click event, several things happen. As an example, say that you have a button on your form called *button1*. If you double-click button1, the Editor window opens with a template for the new method:

```
private void button1_Click(object sender, EventArgs e)
{

}
```

The insertion point appears between the opening and closing braces, where you can begin typing your new method. But behind the scenes, VS also adds a line to the (hidden) *FormName*.Designer.cs file that assigns this new method to the Click event of the button.

As long as you keep the name of the button unchanged and don't delete the method, all is well. But if you want to rename the button, or perhaps delete the method (maybe you accidentally double-clicked a label or the form and have a method that you really don't want or need), then you will need to take additional steps.

Deleting an Event Handler

Assume that you have double-clicked the form called Form1 and now have an extra event handler that you do not want. If you simply delete the event handler, your program generates an error message due to the extra code that appears in the Form's designer.cs file. When you double-click on the form, the extra Form Load event handler looks like this:

```
private void Form1_Load(object sender, EventArgs e)
{

}
```

If you delete these lines of code and try to run the program, you receive an error message that "'WindowsApplication1.Form1' does not contain a definition for 'Form1_Load'." If you double-click on the error message, it takes you to a line in the Form1.Designer.cs file. You can delete the line of code that it takes you to, which, in this example, is

```
this.Load += new System.EventHandler(this.Form1_Load);
```

The preferable way to remove the statement that assigns the event handler is to use the Properties window in the designer. First, make sure to select the form or control that has the unwanted event handler assigned; then click on the *Events* button in the Properties window (Figure 1.53). You will see the event-handling method's name for the name of the event. You can select and delete the name of the method, which removes the assignment statement from the Designer.cs file, and you will not generate an error message when you delete the code lines.

Renaming a Control

You can receive an error if you rename a control after you write the code for its event. For this example, assume that you add a button that is originally called *button1*. You write the code for the button1_Click event handler and then decide to change the button's name to exitButton. (This scenario occurs quite often, especially with beginning programmers.)

Figure 1.53

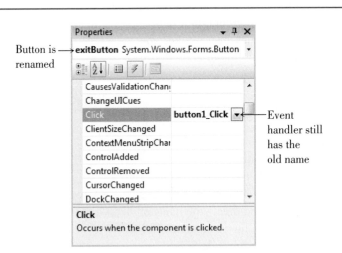

If you simply change the Name property of button1 to exitButton in the Form Designer, your program will still run without an error message. But you may be surprised to see that the event handler is still named button1_Click. If you check the events in the Properties window, you will see why (Figure 1.54): Although the control was renamed, the event handler was not. And if you type a new name into the Properties window (exitButton_Click, for example), a new (empty) method template will appear in your code. The code that you wrote in the button1_Click method is still there and the new exitButton_Click method is empty. One solution is to just cut-and-paste the code from the old method to the new one. You can safely delete the empty button1_Click method since it no longer is assigned as the event handler.

Another way to change the name of an event handler is to use refactoring, which allows you to make changes to an existing object. After you change the name of the control using the designer, switch to the Editor window and right-click on the name of the event-handling method (button1_Click in this example). From the context menu, select *Refactor / Rename*. The *Rename* dialog box shows the current name of the method (Figure 1.55). Enter the new name, making sure to include the "_Click." When you click *OK*, you see a *Preview Changes-Rename* dialog box with the proposed changes highlighted (Figure 1.56). Click *Apply* and all references to the old name are changed to the new one, which corrects the line in the Designer.cs file that assigns the event handler.

Figure 1.55

*Change the name of the event-handling method using **Refactor / Rename**, which changes the name of the method and the assignment of the event handler in the form's Designer.cs file.*

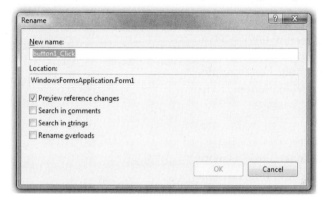
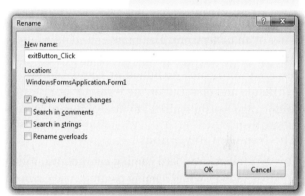

Figure 1.56

*The **Preview Changes-Rename** dialog box shows the changes that you are about to make. Click **Apply** to complete the Rename operation.*

Naming Rules and Conventions for Objects

Using good consistent names for objects can make a project easier to read and understand, as well as easier to debug. You *must* follow the C# rules for naming objects, methods, and variables. In addition, conscientious programmers also follow certain naming conventions.

Most professional programming shops have a set of standards that their programmers must use. Those standards may differ from the ones you find in this book, but the most important point is this: *Good programmers follow standards. You should have a set of standards and always follow them.*

The Naming Rules

When you select a name for an object, C# requires the name to begin with a letter or an underscore. The name can contain letters, digits, and underscores. An object name cannot include a space or punctuation mark and cannot be a reserved word, such as button or Close, but can contain one. For example, exitButton and closeButton are legal. C# is case sensitive, so exitbutton, Exit-Button, and exitButton refer to three different objects.

The Naming Conventions

This text follows standard naming conventions, which help make projects more understandable. When naming controls, use **camel casing**, which means that you begin the name with a lowercase character and capitalize each additional word in the name. Make up a meaningful name and append the full name of the control's class. Do not use abbreviations unless it is a commonly used term that everyone will understand. All names must be meaningful and indicate the purpose of the object.

Examples
messageLabel
exitButton
discountRateLabel

Do not keep the default names assigned by C#, such as button1 and label3. Also, do not name your objects with numbers. The exception to this rule is for labels that never change during program execution. These labels usually hold items such as titles, instructions, and labels for other controls. Leaving these labels with their default names is perfectly acceptable and is practiced in this text.

For forms and other classes, capitalize the first letter of the name and all other words within the name. You will find this style of capitalization referred to as **pascal casing** in the MSDN Help files. Always append the word *Form* to the end of a form name.

Examples
HelloForm
MainForm
AboutForm

Refer to Table 1.2 for sample object names.

Recommended Naming Conventions for C# Objects.

Object Class	Example
Form	DataEntryForm
Button	exitButton
Label	totalLabel
TextBox	paymentAmountTextBox
RadioButton	boldRadioButton
CheckBox	printSummaryCheckBox
PictureBox	landscapePictureBox
ComboBox	bookListComboBox
ListBox	ingredientsListBox
SoundPlayer	introPageSoundPlayer

Visual Studio Help

Visual Studio has an extensive Help facility, which contains much more information than you will ever use. You can look up any C# statement, class, property, method, or programming concept. Many coding examples are available, and you can copy and paste the examples into your own project, modifying them if you wish.

The VS Help facility includes all of the Microsoft Developer Network library (MSDN), which contains several books, technical articles, and the Microsoft Knowledge Base, a database of frequently asked questions and their answers. MSDN includes reference materials for the VS IDE, the .NET Framework, C#, Visual Basic, and C++. You will want to filter the information to display only the Visual C# and related information.

Installing and Running MSDN

You can run MSDN from a hard drive, or online. Of course, if you plan to access MSDN online, you must have a live Internet connection as you work.

Depending on how you install C#, you are given the option to refer first to online, first to local, or only to local. You can change this setting later in the *Options* dialog box (Figure 1.57). Select *Tools / Options* and expand the *Environment* node and the *Help* node. Click on *Online*. You can choose the options to *Try online first, then local*; *Try local first, then online*; or *Try local only, not online*. Notice also that you can select sites to include in Help topics.

The extensive Help is a two-edged sword: You have available a wealth of materials, but it may take some time to find the topic you want.

Figure 1.57

In the Options dialog box, you can specify the preferred source for Help content and choose the Help providers.

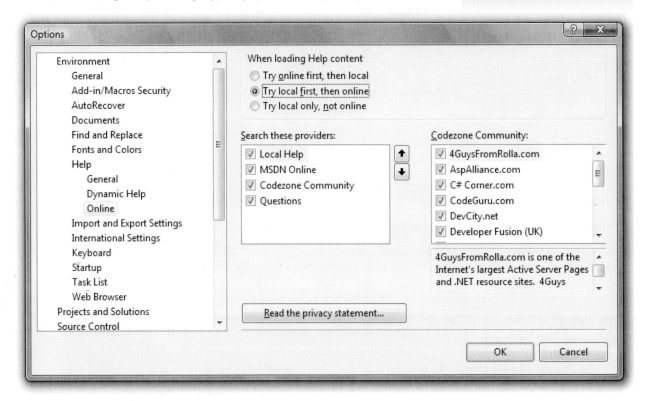

Viewing Help Topics

The Help system in Visual Studio 2008 allows you to view the Help topics in a separate window from the VS IDE, so you can have both windows open at the same time. When you choose *How Do I, Search, Contents, Index,* or *Help Favorites* from the *Help* menu, a new window opens on top of the IDE window (Figure 1.58). You can switch from one window to the other, or resize the windows to view both on the screen if your screen is large enough.

You can choose to filter the Help topics so that you don't have to view topics for all of the languages when you search for a particular topic. In the Index or Contents window, drop down the *Filtered by* list and choose *Visual C# Express Edition* for the Express Edition or *Visual C#* for the Professional Edition (Figure 1.59).

In the Search window, you can choose additional filter options, such as the technology and topic type. Drop down a list and select any desired options (Figure 1.60).

In the Help Index window, you see main topics and subtopics (indented beneath the main topics). All main topics and some subtopics have multiple entries available. When you choose a topic that has more than one possible entry, the *Index Results* pane opens up below the main Document window (refer to Figure 1.58). Click on the entry for which you are searching and the corresponding page appears in the Document window. For most controls, such as the Label control that appears in Figure 1.58, you will find references for mobile controls, Web controls, and Windows Forms. For now, always choose Windows Forms. Chapters 1 to 8 deal with Windows Forms exclusively; Web Forms are introduced in Chapter 9.

Figure 1.58

The Help window. The Help topic and Search appear in tabbed windows in the main Document window; Index, Contents, and Help Favorites appear in tabbed windows docked at the left of the main window.

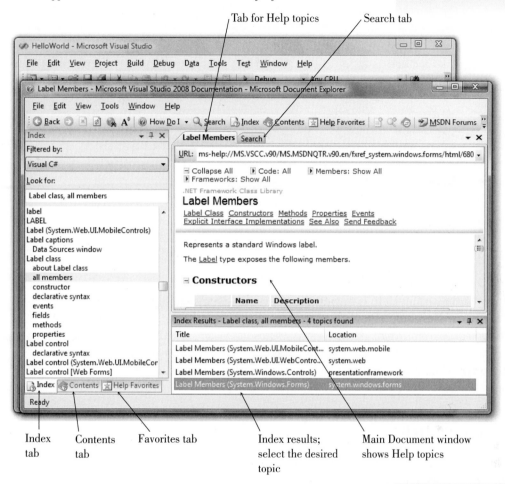

Tab for Help topics

Search tab

Index tab

Contents tab

Favorites tab

Index results; select the desired topic

Main Document window shows Help topics

Figure 1.59

Filter the Help topics so that only the C# topics appear.

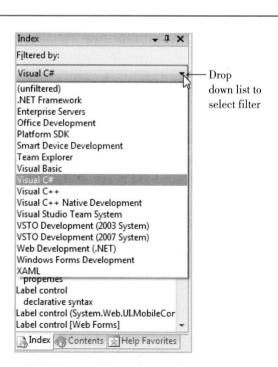

Drop down list to select filter

Figure 1.60

*Drop down the **Content Type** list to make selections for the Search window.*

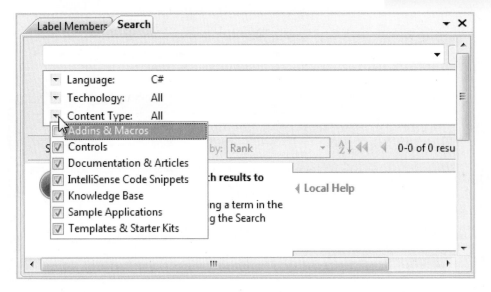

A good way to start using Help is to view the topics that demonstrate how to look up topics in Help. On the Help *Contents* tab, select *Help on Help (Microsoft Document Explorer Help)*. Then choose *Microsoft Document Explorer Overview* and *What's New in Document Explorer*. Make sure to visit *Managing Help Topics and Windows*, which has subtopics describing how to copy topics and print topics.

Context-Sensitive Help

A quick way to view Help on any topic is to use **context-sensitive Help**. Select a C# object, such as a form or a control, or place the insertion point in a word in the editor and press F1. The Help window pops up with the corresponding Help topic displayed, if possible, saving you a search. You can display context-sensitive Help about the environment by clicking in an area of the screen and pressing Shift + F1.

Managing Windows

At times you may have more windows and tabs open than you want. You can hide or close any window, or switch to a different window.

- To close a window that is a part of a tabbed window, click the window's *Close* button. Only the top window will close.

- To switch to another window that is part of a tabbed window, click on its tab.

For additional help with the environment, see Appendix C, "Tips and Shortcuts for Mastering the Visual Studio Environment."

> ### Feedback 1.1

Note: Answers for Feedback questions appear in Appendix A.

1. Display the Help Index, filter by *Visual C#* (or *Visual C# Express Edition*), and type "button control." In the Index list, notice multiple entries for button controls. Depending on the edition of C#, you may see entries for HTML, Web Forms, and Windows Forms. Click on the main topic, *Button control [Windows Forms]*: and click on the entry for *about Button control*. The topics included for the Professional Edition are more extensive than those for the Express Edition. In the Express Edition, only one page matches the selection and it appears in the main Document window. In the Professional Edition, several topics appear in the *Index Results* list. Click on a title in the *Index Results* to display the corresponding page in the Document window. Notice that additional links appear in the text in the Document window. You can click on a link to view another topic.

2. Display the Editor window of your Hello World project. Click on the `Close` method to place the insertion point. Press the F1 key to view context-sensitive Help.

3. Select each of the options from the VS IDE's *Help* menu to see how they respond.

Your Hands-On Programming Example

Write a program for the Look Sharp Fitness Center to display the current promotions. Include a label for the current special and buttons for each of the following departments: Clothing, Equipment and Accessories, Juice Bar, Membership, and Personal Training.

The user interface should also have an *Exit* button and a label with the programmer's name. Use appropriate names for all controls. Make sure to change the Text property of the form.

Planning the Project

Sketch a form (Figure 1.61), which your users sign off as meeting their needs.

Figure 1.61

A planning sketch of the form for the hands-on programming example.

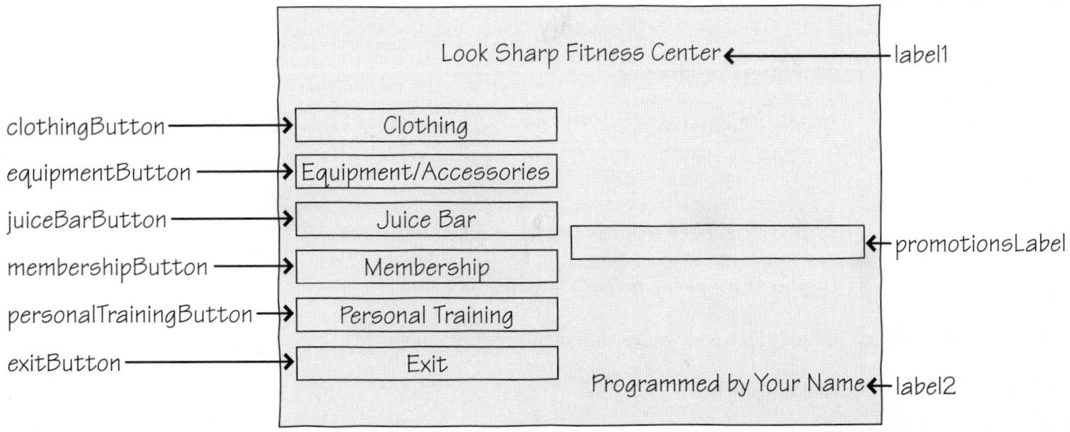

Note: Although this step may seem unnecessary, having your users sign off is standard programming practice and documents that your users have been involved and have approved the design.

Plan the Objects and Properties

Plan the property settings for the form and for each control.

Object	Property	Setting	
PromotionForm	Name	PromotionForm	
	Text	Current Promotions	
	StartPosition	CenterScreen	
label1	Text	Look Sharp Fitness Center	Hint: Do not change the name of this label.
	Font	18 pt.	
label2	Text	Programmed by Your Name	
promotionsLabel	Name	promotionsLabel	
	AutoSize	True	
	Text	(blank)	
	TextAlign	MiddleLeft	
	Font	12 pt.	
clothingButton	Name	clothingButton	
	Text	Clothing	
equipmentButton	Name	equipmentButton	
	Text	Equipment/Accessories	
juiceBarButton	Name	juiceBarButton	
	Text	Juice Bar	
membershipButton	Name	membershipButton	
	Text	Membership	
personalTrainingButton	Name	personalTrainingButton	
	Text	Personal Training	
exitButton	Name	exitButton	
	Text	Exit	

Plan the Event Methods You will need event-handling methods for each button.

Method	Actions—Pseudocode
clothingButton_Click	Display "Take an extra 30% off the clearance items." in the label.
equipmentButton_Click	Display "Yoga mats—25% off."
juiceBarButton_Click	Display "Try a free serving of our new WheatBerry Shake."
membershipButton_Click	Display "First month personal training included."
personalTrainingButton_Click	Display "3 free sessions with membership renewal."
exitButton_Click	End the project.

Write the Project Follow the sketch in Figure 1.61 to create the form. Figure 1.62 shows the completed form.

- Set the properties of each object, as you have planned.

- Working from the pseudocode, write each event-handling method.

- When you complete the code, thoroughly test the project.

Figure 1.62

The form for the hands-on programming example.

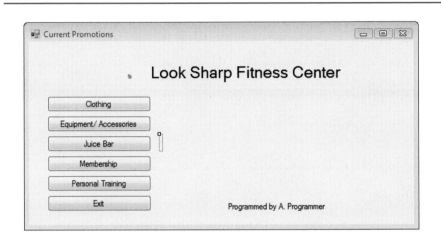

The Project Coding Solution

```
/*
 * Project:      Ch01HandsOn
 * Programmer:   Bradley/Millspaugh
 * Date:         June 2009
 * Description:  This project displays current sales for
 *               each department.
 */

using System;
using System.Collections.Generic;
using System.ComponentModel;
using System.Data;
using System.Drawing;
using System.Linq;
using System.Text;
using System.Windows.Forms;

namespace Ch01HandsOn
{
    public partial class PromotionsForm : Form
    {
        public Form1()
        {
            InitializeComponent();
        }
```

```csharp
        private void exitButton_Click(object sender, EventArgs e)
        {
            // End the project.

            this.Close();
        }

        private void clothingButton_Click(object sender, EventArgs e)
        {
            // Display current promotion.

            promotionsLabel.Text = "Take an extra 30% off the clearance items.";
        }

        private void equipmentLabel_Click(object sender, EventArgs e)
        {
            // Display current promotion.

            promotionsLabel.Text = "Yoga mats--25% off.";
        }

        private void juiceBarButton_Click(object sender, EventArgs e)
        {
            // Display current promotion.

            promotionsLabel.Text = "Try a free serving of our new WheatBerry Shake.";
        }

        private void membershipButton_Click(object sender, EventArgs e)
        {
            // Display current promotion.

            promotionsLabel.Text = "First month personal training included.";
        }

        private void personalTrainingButton_Click(object sender, EventArgs e)
        {
            // Display current promotion.

            promotionsLabel.Text = "3 free sessions with membership renewal.";
        }
    }
}
```

Summary

1. Visual C# is an object-oriented language primarily used to write application programs that run in Windows or on the Internet using a graphical user interface (GUI).
2. In the OOP object model, classes are used to create objects that have properties, methods, and events.
3. The current release of C# is called Visual C# 2008 and is one part of Visual Studio. C# is available individually in an Express Edition or in Visual Studio Professional Edition and Team System versions.

4. The .NET Framework provides an environment for the objects from many languages to interoperate. Each language compiles to Microsoft Intermediate Language (MSIL) and runs in the Common Language Runtime (CLR).

5. To plan a project, first sketch the user interface and then list the objects and properties needed. Then plan the necessary event-handling methods.

6. The three steps to creating a C# project are (1) define the user interface, (2) set the properties, and (3) write the code.

7. A C# application is called a *solution*. Each solution may contain multiple projects, and each project may contain multiple forms and additional files. The solution file has an extension of .sln, a project file has an extension of .csproj, and form files and additional C# files have an extension of .cs. In addition, the Visual Studio environment and the C# compiler both create several more files.

8. The Visual Studio integrated development environment (IDE) consists of several tools, including a form designer, an editor, a compiler, a debugger, an object browser, and a Help facility.

9. Visual Studio has three modes: design time, run time, and debug time.

10. You can customize the Visual Studio IDE and reset all customizations back to their default state.

11. You create the user interface for an application by adding controls from the toolbox to a form. You can move, resize, and delete the controls.

12. The Name property of a control is used to refer to the control in code. The Text property holds the words that the user sees on the screen.

13. C# code is written in methods. Method bodies begin and end with braces { }.

14. Project comments are used for documentation. Good programming practice requires comments in every method and at the top of a file.

15. Most C# statements must be terminated by a semicolon. A statement may appear on multiple lines; the semicolon determines the end of the statement. Comments and some other statements do not end with semicolons.

16. Assignment statements assign a value to a property or a variable. Assignment statements work from right to left, assigning the value on the right side of the equal sign to the property or variable named on the left side of the equal sign.

17. The `this.Close()` method terminates program execution.

18. Each event to which you want to respond requires an event-handling method, also called an *event handler*.

19. You can print out the C# code for documentation.

20. Three types of errors can occur in a C# project: syntax errors, which violate the syntax rules of the C# language; run-time errors, which contain a statement that cannot execute properly; and logic errors, which produce erroneous results.

21. Finding and fixing program errors is called *debugging*.

22. You must have a clean compile before you run the program.

23. Following good naming conventions can help make a project easier to debug.

24. C# Help has very complete descriptions of all project elements and their uses. You can use the *How Do I*, *Contents*, *Index*, *Search*, *Help Favorites*, or context-sensitive Help.

Key Terms

assignment statement   *30*
button   *19*
camel casing   *52*
class   *4*
clean compile   *48*
code   *6*
comment   *30*
context menu   *25*
context-sensitive Help   *56*
control   *3*
debug time   *14*
debugging   *48*
design time   *14*
Document window   *12*
event   *4*
event handler   *29*
event-handling method   *29*
exception   *46*
Express Edition   *5*
form   *3*
Form Designer   *12*
graphical user interface (GUI)   *3*
Help   *14*
integrated development
   environment (IDE)   *8*
label   *19*
logic error   *47*

method   *4*
namespace   *23*
object   *4*
object-oriented
   programming (OOP)   *3*
pascal casing   *52*
Professional Edition   *5*
project file   *8*
Properties window   *13*
property   *4*
pseudocode   *6*
resizing handle   *20*
run time   *14*
run-time error   *46*
snap lines   *20*
solution   *6*
Solution Explorer window   *13*
solution file   *7*
Standard Edition   *5*
syntax error   *45*
Team System   *5*
Text property   *24*
`this`   *32*
toolbar   *11*
toolbox   *3*
user interface   *6*
Visual Studio environment   *8*

Review Questions

1. What are objects and properties? How are they related to each other?
2. What are the three steps for planning and creating C# projects? Describe what happens in each step.
3. What is the purpose of these C# file types: .sln, .suo, and .cs?
4. When is C# in design time? run time? debug time?
5. What is the purpose of the Name property of a control?
6. Which property determines what appears on the form for a Label control?
7. What is the purpose of the Text property of a button? the Text property of a form?
8. What does displayButton_Click mean? To what does displayButton refer? To what does Click refer?
9. What is a C# event? Give some examples of events.
10. What property must be set to center text in a label? What should be the value of the property?
11. Describe the two types of comments in a C# program and tell where each is generally used.

12. What is meant by the term *debugging*?
13. What is a syntax error, when does it occur, and what might cause it?
14. What is a run-time error, when does it occur, and what might cause it?
15. What is a logic error, when does it occur, and what might cause it?
16. Tell the class of control and the likely purpose of each of these object names:

>   addressLabel
>   exitButton
>   nameTextBox

17. What does context-sensitive Help mean? How can you use it to see the Help page for a button?

Programming Exercises

1.1 For your first C# exercise, you must first complete the Hello World project. Then add buttons and event-handling methods to display the "Hello World" message in two more languages. You may substitute any other languages for those shown. Feel free to modify the user interface to suit yourself (or your instructor).

Make sure to use meaningful names for your new buttons, following the naming conventions in Table 1.2. Include comments at the top of every method and at the top of the file.

>   "Hello World" in French: Bonjour tout le monde
>   "Hello World" in Italian: Ciao Mondo

1.2 Create a project that displays the hours for each department on campus. Include buttons for Student Learning, Financial Aid, Counseling, and the Bookstore. Each button should display the hours for that department in a label. The interface should have one label for the hours, one label for the programmer name, buttons for each department, and an *Exit* button.

Make sure to use meaningful names for your new buttons, following the naming conventions in Table 1.2. Include comments at the top of every method and at the top of the file.

1.3 Write a project that displays four sayings, such as "The early bird gets the worm" or "A penny saved is a penny earned." (You will want to keep the sayings short, as each must be entered on one line. However, when the saying displays on your form, you can set the label's properties to allow long lines to wrap within the label.)

Make a button for each saying with a descriptive Text property for each, as well as a button to exit the project.

Include a label that holds your name at the bottom of the form. Also, make sure to change the form's title bar to something meaningful.

If your sayings are too long to display on one line, set the label's Auto-Size property to False and resize the height of the label to hold multiple lines. You may change the Font properties of the label to the font and size of your choice.

Make sure the buttons are large enough to hold their entire Text properties.

Follow good naming conventions for object names; include comments at the top of every method and at the top of the file.

1.4 Write a project to display company contact information. Include buttons and labels for the contact person, department, and phone. When the user clicks on one of the buttons, display the contact information in the corresponding label. Include a button to exit.

Include a label that holds your name at the bottom of the form and change the title bar of the form to something meaningful.

You may change the Font properties of the labels to the font and size of your choice.

Follow good naming conventions for object names; include comments at the top of every method and at the top of the file.

1.5 Create a project to display the daily specials for "your" diner. Make up a name for your diner and display it in a label at the top of the form. Add a label to display the appropriate special depending on the button that is pressed. The buttons should be

- Soup of the Day

- Chef's Special

- Daily Fish

  Also include an *Exit* button.

Sample Data: Dorothy's Diner is offering Tortilla Soup, a California Cobb Salad, and Hazelnut-Coated Mahi Mahi.

Case Studies

Custom Supplies Mail Order

If you don't have the time to look for all those hard-to-find items, tell us what you're looking for. We'll send you a catalog from the appropriate company or order for you.

We can place an order and ship it to you. We also help with shopping for gifts; your order can be gift wrapped and sent anywhere you wish.

The company title will be shortened to CS Mail Order. Include this name on the title bar of the first form of each project that you create for this case study.

Your first job is to create a project that will display the name and telephone number for the contact person for the customer relations, marketing, order processing, and shipping departments.

Include a button for each department. When the user clicks on the button for a department, display the

name and telephone number for the contact person in two labels. Also include identifying labels with Text "Department Contact" and "Telephone Number."

Be sure to include a button for *Exit*.

Include a label at the bottom of the form that holds your name and give the form a meaningful title bar.

Test Data

Department	Department Contact	Telephone Number
Customer Relations	Tricia Mills	500-1111
Marketing	Michelle Rigner	500-2222
Order Processing	Kenna DeVoss	500-3333
Shipping	Eric Andrews	500-4444

Christopher's Car Center

Christopher's Car Center will meet all of your automobile needs. The center has facilities with everything for your vehicles including sales and leasing for new and used cars and RVs, auto service and repair, detail shop, car wash, and auto parts.

Your first job is to create a project that will display current notices.

Include four buttons labeled "Auto Sales," "Service Center," "Detail Shop," and "Employment Opportunities." One label will be used to display the information when the buttons are clicked. Be sure to include a button for *Exit*.

Include your name in a label at the bottom of the form.

Test Data

Button	Label Text
Auto Sales	Family wagon, immaculate condition $12,995
Service Center	Lube, oil, filter $25.99
Detail Shop	Complete detail $79.95 for most cars
Employment Opportunities	Sales position, contact Mr. Mann 551-2134 x475

Xtreme Cinema

This neighborhood store is an independently owned video rental business. The owners would like to allow their customers to use the computer to look up the aisle number for movies by category.

Create a form with a button for each category. When the user clicks on a button, display the corresponding aisle number in a label. Include a button to exit.

Include a label that holds your name at the bottom of the form and change the title bar of the form to Xtreme Cinema.

You may change the font properties of the labels to the font and size of your choice. Include additional categories, if you wish.

Follow good programming conventions for object names; include comments at the top of every method and at the top of the file.

Test Data

Button	Location
Comedy	Aisle 1
Drama	Aisle 2
Action	Aisle 3
Sci-Fi	Aisle 4
Horror	Aisle 5
New Releases	Back Wall

Cool Boards

This chain of stores features a full line of clothing and equipment for snowboard and skateboard enthusiasts. Management wants a computer application to allow their employees to display the address and hours for each of their branches.

Create a form with a button for each store branch. When the user clicks on a button, display the correct address and hours.

Include a label that holds your name at the bottom of the form and change the title bar of the form to Cool Boards.

You may change the font properties of the labels to the font and size of your choice.

Follow good programming conventions for object names; include comments at the top of every method and at the top of the file.

Store Branches: The three branches are Downtown, Mall, and Suburbs. Make up hours and locations for each.

2

User Interface Design

at the completion of this chapter, you will be able to . . .

1. Use text boxes, masked text boxes, rich text boxes, group boxes, check boxes, radio buttons, and picture boxes effectively.

2. Set the BorderStyle property to make controls appear flat or three-dimensional.

3. Select multiple controls and move them, align them, and set common properties.

4. Make your projects easy for the user to understand and operate by defining access keys, setting an *Accept* and a *Cancel* button, controlling the tab sequence, resetting the focus during program execution, and causing ToolTips to appear.

5. Clear the contents of text boxes and labels.

6. Make a control visible or invisible at run time by setting its Visible property.

7. Disable and enable controls at design time and run time.

8. Change text color during program execution.

9. Concatenate (join) strings of text.

10. Download the Line and Shape controls, add them to the toolbox, and use the controls on your forms.

Introducing More Controls

In Chapter 1 you learned to use labels and buttons. In this chapter you will learn to use several more control types: text boxes, group boxes, check boxes, radio buttons, and picture boxes. Figure 2.1 shows the toolbox with the tools for these controls labeled. Figure 2.2 shows some of these controls on a form.

Each class of controls has its own set of properties. To see a complete list of the properties for any class of control, you can (1) place a control on a form and examine the properties list or (2) click on a tool or a control and press F1 for context-sensitive Help. Visual Studio will display the Help page for that control, and you can view a list of the properties and an explanation of their use.

Figure 2.1

The toolbox showing the controls that are covered in this chapter.

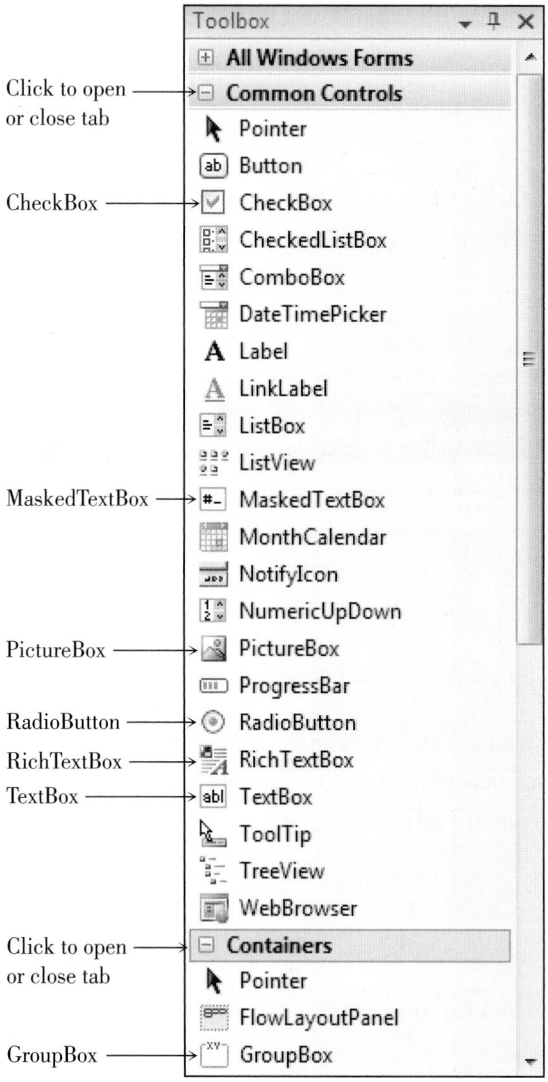

Text Boxes

Use a **text box** control when you want the user to type some input. The form in Figure 2.2 has two text boxes. The user can move from one box to the next, make

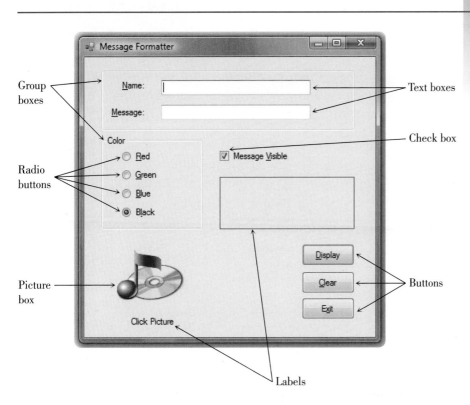

corrections, cut and paste if desired, and click the *Display* button when finished. In your program code, you can use the **Text property** of each text box.

Example

```
nameLabel.Text = nameTextBox.Text;
```

In this example, whatever the user enters into the text box is assigned to the Text property of nameLabel. If you want to display some text in a text box during program execution, assign a literal to the Text property:

```
messageTextBox.Text = "Watson, come here.";
```

You can set the **TextAlign property** of text boxes to change the alignment of text within the box. In the Properties window, set the property to Left, Right, or Center. In code, you can set the property using these values:

HorizontalAlignment.Left
HorizontalAlignment.Right
HorizontalAlignment.Center

```
messageTextBox.TextAlign = HorizontalAlignment.Left;
```

Example Names for Text Boxes

```
titleTextBox
companyNameTextBox
```

Figure 2.3

Select a format for the input mask in the Input Mask *dialog box, which supplies the Mask property of the MaskedTextBox control.*

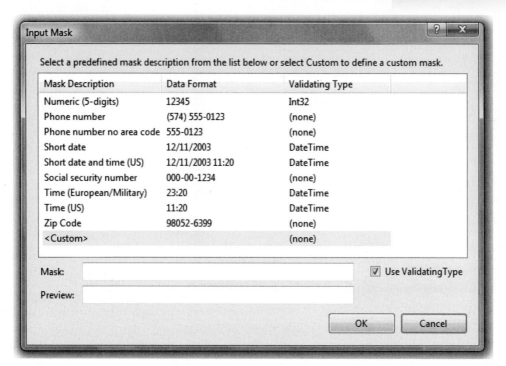

Masked Text Boxes

A specialized form of the TextBox control is the **MaskedTextBox**. You can specify the format (the Mask property) of the data required of the user. For example, you can select a mask for a ZIP code, a date, a phone number, or a social security number. Figure 2.3 shows the *Input Mask* dialog box, where you can select the mask and even try it out. At run time, the user cannot enter characters that do not conform to the mask. For example, the phone number and social security number masks do not allow input other than numeric digits.

Example Names for Masked Text Boxes

```
dateMaskedTextBox
phoneMaskedTextBox
```

Note: For a date or time mask, the user can enter only numeric digits but may possibly enter an invalid value; for example, a month or hour greater than 12. The mask will accept any numeric digits, which could possibly cause your program to generate a run-time error. You will learn to check the input values in Chapter 4.

Rich Text Boxes

Another variety of text box is the **RichTextBox** control, which offers several formatting features (Figure 2.4). In a regular text box, all of the text is formatted

Figure 2.4

*Using a RichTextBox control
you can apply font styles to
selected text, show formatted
URLs, and display text from
a formatted .rtf file.*

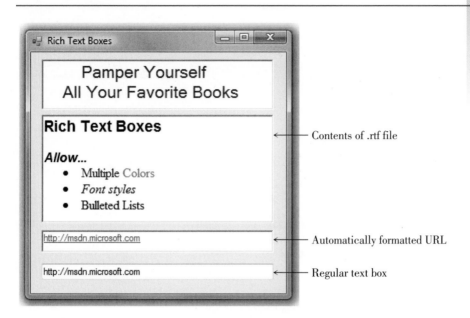

Contents of .rtf file

Automatically formatted URL

Regular text box

the same, but in a rich text box, the user can apply character and paragraph formatting to selected text, much like using a word processor.

One common use for a rich text box is for displaying URL addresses. In a regular text box, the address appears in the default font color, but the rich text box displays it as a link when the DetectUrl property is set to *true*. Note that it is not an active link, but it does have the formatting to show the URL as an address.

You also can load formatted text into a rich text box from a file stored in rich text format (rtf). Use the `LoadFile` method of the rich text box. In Figure 2.4, the file "Rich Text Boxes.rtf" is stored in the bin\debug folder, but you could include the complete path to load a file from another location.

```
sampleRichTextBox.LoadFile("Rich Text Boxes.rtf");
```

Displaying Text on Multiple Lines

Both the regular text box and the rich text box have properties that allow you to display text on multiple lines. The **WordWrap property** determines whether the contents should wrap to a second line if they do not fit on a single line. The property is set to *true* by default. Both controls also have a **Multiline property**, which is set to *false* by default on a text box and *true* by default on a rich text box. Both WordWrap and Multiline must be set to *true* for text to wrap to a second line.

For a regular text box, you must set Multiline to *true* and then adjust the height to accommodate multiple lines. If Multiline is *false* (the default), a text box does not have resizing handles for vertical resizing. Be aware that a text box will not automatically resize to display multiple lines even though Multiline is *true*; you must make the height tall enough to display the lines.

Figure 2.5

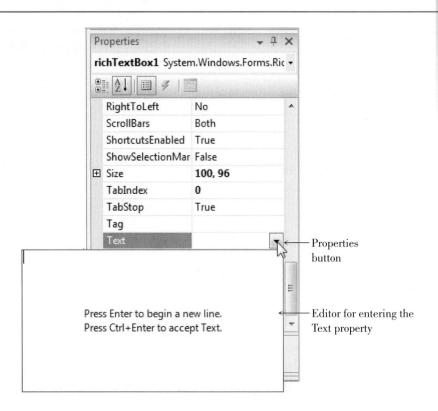

You can set the Text property of a multiline text box (or rich text box) to a very long value; the value will wrap to fit in the width of the box. You also can enter multiple lines and choose the location of the line breaks; the techniques differ depending on whether you set the Text property at design time or in code. At design time, click on the Text property in the Properties window and click on the Properties button (the down arrow); a small editing window pops up with instructions to press Enter at the end of each line and Ctrl + Enter to accept the text (Figure 2.5). In code, you can use a **NewLine character** (`Environment.NewLine`) in the text string where you want the line to break. Joining strings of text is called *concatenation* and is covered in the section "Concatenating Text" later in this chapter.

```
titleRichTextBox.Text = "    Pamper Yourself" +
    Environment.NewLine + "All Your Favorite Books";
```

Group Boxes

Group boxes are used as **containers** for other controls. Usually, groups of radio buttons or check boxes are placed in group boxes. Using group boxes to group controls can make your forms easier to understand by separating the controls into logical groups. You can find the **GroupBox** control in the *Containers* tab of the toolbox.

Set a group box's Text property to the words you want to appear on the top edge of the box.

Example Names for Group Boxes

```
colorGroupBox
styleGroupBox
```

You only need to change the name of a group box if you plan to refer to it in code. One reason to use it in code is to set the Enabled property of the group box to *false*, which disables all of the controls inside the box.

Check Boxes

Check boxes allow the user to select (or deselect) an option. In any group of check boxes, any number can be selected. The **Checked property** of a check box is set to *false* if unchecked or *true* if checked.

You can write an event handler for the CheckedChanged event, which executes when the user clicks in the box. In Chapter 4, when you learn about `if` statements, you can take one action when the box is checked and another action when it is unchecked.

Use the Text property of a check box for the text you want to appear next to the box.

Example Names for Check Boxes

```
boldCheckBox
italicCheckBox
```

Radio Buttons

Use **radio buttons** when only one button of a group may be selected. Any radio buttons that you place directly on the form (not in a group box) function as a group. A group of radio buttons inside a group box function together. The best method is to first create a group box and then create each radio button inside the group box.

When you need separate lists of radio buttons for different purposes, you must include each list in a separate group box. You can find an example program later in this chapter that demonstrates using two groups of radio buttons, one for setting the background color of the form and a second set for selecting the color of the text on the form. See "Using Radio Buttons for Selecting Colors."

The Checked property of a radio button is set to *true* if selected or to *false* if unselected. You can write an event handler to execute when the user selects a radio button using the control's CheckedChanged event. In Chapter 4 you will learn to determine in your code whether or not a button is selected.

Set a radio button's Text property to the text you want to appear next to the button.

Example Names for Radio Buttons

```
yellowRadioButton
blueRadioButton
```

Picture Boxes

A **PictureBox control** can hold an image. You can set a picture box's **Image property** to a graphic file with an extension of .bmp, .gif, .jpg, .jpeg, .png, .ico, .emf, or .wmf. You first add your images to the project's resources; then you can assign the resource to the Image property of a PictureBox control.

Place a PictureBox control on a form and then select its Image property in the Properties window. Click on the Properties button (Figure 2.6) to display a **Select Resource dialog box,** where you can select images that you have already added or add new images (Figure 2.7).

Figure 2.6

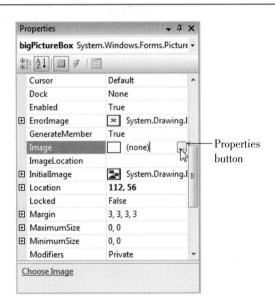

Properties button

Click on the Image property for a PictureBox control, and a Properties button appears. Click on the Properties button to view the Select Resource dialog box.

Figure 2.7

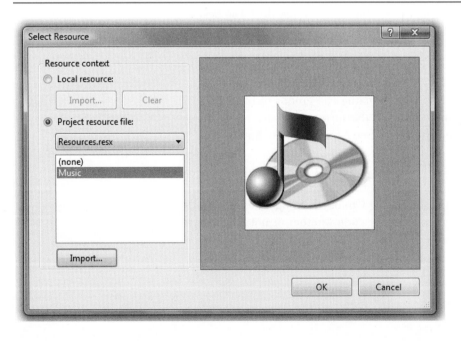

The Select Resource dialog box. Make your selection here for the graphic file you want to appear in the PictureBox control; click Import to add an image to the list.

Drop down
File-type list

Click on the *Import* button of the *Select Resource* dialog box to add images. An *Open* dialog box appears (Figure 2.8), where you can navigate to your image files. A preview of the image appears in the preview box.

Note: To add files with an .ico extension, drop down the *File Type* list and select *All Files* in the *Open* dialog box.

You can use any graphic file (with the proper format) that you have available. You will find many graphic files in the StudentData\Images folder from the textbook Web site: www.mhhe.com/csharp2008.

PictureBox controls have several useful properties that you can set at design time or run time. For example, set the **SizeMode property** to *StretchImage* to make the graphic resize to fill the control. You can set the **Visible property** to *false* to make the picture box disappear.

For example, to make a picture box invisible at run time, use this code statement:

```
logoPictureBox.Visible = false;
```

Assigning an Image to a Picture Box

To assign a graphic from the Resources folder at run time, you refer to the project name (ChangePictures in the following example), the Resources folder in the project's properties, and the name of the graphic resource:

```
samplePictureBox.Image = ChangePictures.Properties.Resources.Water_Lilies;
```

Clearing a Picture Box

Sometimes you may wish to keep the picture box visible but remove the picture. To accomplish this, set the Image property to `null`, which means empty.

```
samplePictureBox.Image = null;
```

Adding and Removing Resources

In Figure 2.7 you saw the easiest way to add a new graphic to the Resources folder, which you perform as you set the Image property of a PictureBox control. You also can add, remove, and rename resources using the Visual Studio **Project Designer**. From the *Project* menu, select *ProjectName Properties* (which always shows the name of the selected project). The Project Designer opens in the main Document window; click on the *Resources* tab to display the project resources (Figure 2.9). You can use the buttons at the top of the window to add and remove images, or right-click an existing resource to rename or remove it.

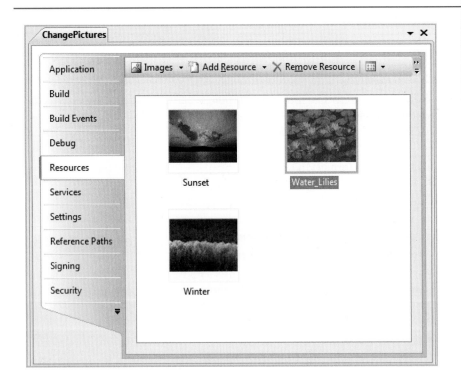

Figure 2.9

Click on the Resources tab of the Project Designer to work with project resources. You can add, remove, and rename resources on this page.

Using Smart Tags

You can use smart tags to set the most common properties of many controls. When you add a PictureBox or a TextBox to a form, for example, you see a small arrow in the upper-right corner of the control. Click on the arrow to open

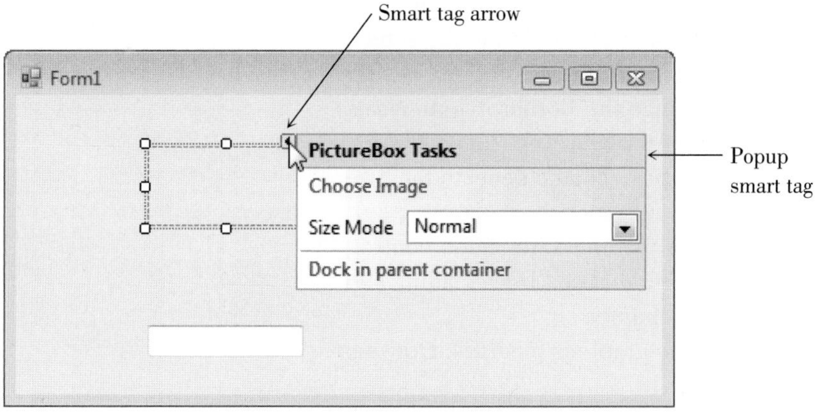

Figure 2.10

Smart tag arrow

PictureBox Tasks

Popup smart tag

Point to the smart tag arrow to open the smart tag for a control. For this PictureBox control, you can set the Image, SizeMode, and Dock properties in the smart tag.

the smart tag for that control (Figure 2.10). The smart tag shows a few properties that you can set from there, which is just a shortcut for making the changes from the Properties window.

Using Images for Forms and Controls

You can use an image as the background of a form or a control. For a form, set the BackgroundImage property to a graphic resource; also set the form's BackgroundImageLayout property to *Tile*, *Center*, *Stretch*, or *Zoom*.

Controls such as buttons, check boxes, and radio buttons have an Image property that you can set to a graphic from the project's resources.

Setting a Border and Style

Most controls can appear to be three-dimensional or flat. Labels, text boxes, and picture boxes all have a **BorderStyle property** with choices of *None*, *FixedSingle*, or *Fixed3D*. Text boxes default to *Fixed3D*; labels and picture boxes default to *None*. Of course, you can change the property to the style of your choice.

Feedback 2.1

Create a picture box control that displays an enlarged icon and appears in a 3D box. Make up a name that conforms to this textbook's naming conventions.

Property	Setting
Name	
BorderStyle	
SizeMode	
Visible	

Drawing a Line

You can draw a line on a form by using the Label control. You may want to include lines when creating a logo or you may simply want to divide the screen by drawing a line. To create the look of a line, set the AutoSize property of your label to *false*, set the Text property to blank, change the BorderStyle to *None*, and change the Backcolor to the color you want for the line. You can control the size of the line with the Width and Height properties, located beneath the Size property.

Another way to draw a line on a form is to use the LineShape control, which you can download and install into Visual Studio. See "Downloading and Using the Line and Shape Controls" later in this chapter.

You also can draw a line on the form using the graphics methods. Drawing graphics is covered in Chapter 13.

Working with Multiple Controls

You can select more than one control at a time, which means that you can move the controls as a group, set similar properties for the group, and align the controls.

Selecting Multiple Controls

There are several methods of selecting multiple controls. If the controls are near each other, the easiest technique is to use the mouse to drag a selection box around the controls. Point to a spot that you want to be one corner of a box surrounding the controls, press the mouse button, and drag to the opposite corner (Figure 2.11). When you release the mouse button, the controls will all be selected (Figure 2.12). Note that selected labels and check boxes with AutoSize set to *true* do not have resizing handles; other selected controls do have resizing handles.

You also can select multiple controls, one at a time. Click on one control to select it, hold down the Ctrl key or the Shift key, and click on the next control. You can keep the Ctrl or Shift key down and continue clicking on controls you wish to select. Ctrl–click (or Shift–click) on a control a second time to deselect it without changing the rest of the group.

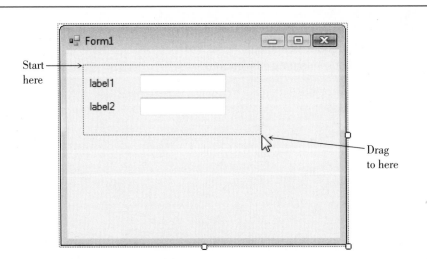

Figure 2.11

Use the pointer to drag a selection box around the controls you wish to select.

Figure 2.12

When multiple controls are selected, each has resizing handles (if resizable).

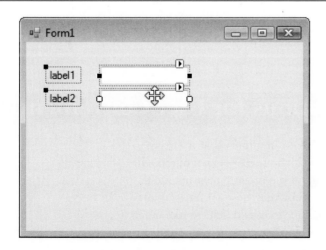

Selection handles

Resizing handles

When you want to select most of the controls on the form, use a combination of the two methods. Drag a selection box around all of the controls to select them and then Ctrl–click on the ones you want to deselect. You also can select all of the controls using the *Select All* option on the *Edit* menu or its keyboard shortcut: Ctrl + A.

Deselecting a Group of Controls

When you are finished working with a group of controls, it's easy to deselect them. Just click anywhere on the form (not on a control) or select another previously unselected control.

☑TIP

Make sure to read Appendix C for tips and shortcuts for working with controls. ■

Moving Controls as a Group

After selecting multiple controls, you can move them as a group. To do this, point inside one of the selected controls, press the mouse button, and drag the entire group to a new location (Figure 2.13).

Figure 2.13

Drag a group of selected controls to move the entire group to a new location.

Setting Properties for Multiple Controls

You can set some common properties for groups of controls. After selecting the group, look at the Properties window. Any properties that appear in the window are shared by all of the controls and can be changed all at once. For example, you may want to set the BorderStyle property for a group of controls to three-dimensional or change the font used for a group of labels. Some properties appear empty; even though those properties are common to all the selected controls, they do not share a common value. You can enter a new value that will apply to all selected controls.

TIP

Setting the font for the form changes the default font for all controls on the form. ■

Aligning Controls

After you select a group of controls, it is easy to resize and align them using the buttons on the Layout toolbar (Figure 2.14) or the corresponding items on the *Format* menu. Select your group of controls and choose any of the resizing buttons. These can make the controls equal in width, height, or both. Then select another button to align the tops, bottoms, or centers of the controls. You also can move the entire group to a new location.

Note: The alignment options align the group of controls to the control that is active (indicated by white sizing handles). Referring to Figure 2.13, the lower text box is the active control. To make another selected control the active control, simply click on it.

To set the spacing between controls, use the buttons for horizontal and/or vertical spacing. These buttons enable you to create equal spacing between controls or to increase or decrease the space between controls.

Note: If the Layout toolbar is not displaying, select *View / Toolbars / Layout*.

Figure 2.14

Resize and align multiple controls using the Layout toolbar.

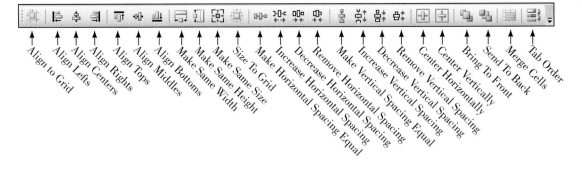

Designing Your Applications for User Convenience

One of the goals of good programming is to create programs that are easy to use. Your user interface should be clear and consistent. One school of thought says that if users misuse a program, it's the fault of the programmer, not the users. Because most of your users will already know how to operate Windows programs, you should strive to make your programs look and behave like other Windows programs. Some of the ways to accomplish this are to make the controls operate in the standard way, define keyboard access keys, set an Accept button, and make the Tab key work correctly. You also can define ToolTips, which are those small labels that pop up when the user pauses the mouse pointer over a control.

Designing the User Interface

The design of the screen should be easy to understand and "comfortable" for the user. The best way that we can accomplish these goals is to follow industry standards for the color, size, and placement of controls. Once users become accustomed to a screen design, they will expect (and feel more familiar with) applications that follow the same design criteria.

You should design your applications to match other Windows applications. Microsoft has done extensive program testing with users of different ages, genders, nationalities, and disabilities. We should take advantage of this research and follow their guidelines. Take some time to examine the screens and dialog boxes in Microsoft Office as well as those in Visual Studio.

One recommendation about interface design concerns color. You have probably noticed that Windows applications are predominantly gray. A reason for this choice is that many people are color blind. Also, research shows that gray is easiest for the majority of users. Although you may personally prefer brighter colors, you will stick with gray, or the system palette the user chooses, if you want your applications to look professional.

Note: By default the BackColor property of forms and controls is set to *Control*, which is a color included in the operating system's palette. If the user changes the system theme or color, your forms and controls will conform to their settings.

Colors can indicate to the user what is expected. Use a white background for text boxes to indicate that the user should input information. Use a gray background for labels, which the user cannot change. Labels that will display a message should have a border around them; labels that provide text on the screen should have no border (the default).

Group your controls on the form to aid the user. A good practice is to create group boxes to hold related items, especially those controls that require user input. This visual aid helps the user understand the information that is being presented or requested.

Use a sans serif font on your forms, such as the default MS Sans Serif, and do not make them boldface. Limit large font sizes to a few items, such as the company name.

Defining Keyboard Access Keys

Many people prefer to use the keyboard, rather than a mouse, for most operations. Windows is set up so that most functions can be done with either the keyboard or a mouse. You can make your projects respond to the keyboard by defining **access keys**, also called *hot keys*. For example, in Figure 2.15 you can select the *OK* button with Alt + o and the *Exit* button with Alt + x.

You can set access keys for buttons, radio buttons, and check boxes when you define their Text properties. Type an ampersand (&) in front of the character you want for the access key; Visual Studio underlines the character. You

Figure 2.15

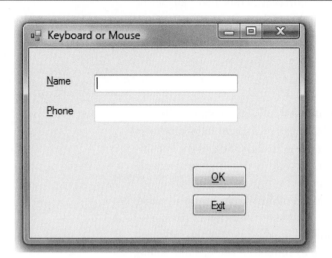

also can set an access key for a label; see "Setting the Tab Order for Controls" later in this chapter.

For examples of access keys on buttons, type the following for the button's Text property:

&OK for O̲K
E&xit for Ex̲it

When you define access keys, you need to watch for several pitfalls. First, try to use the Windows standard keys whenever possible. For example, use the x̲ of Exit and the S̲ of Save. Second, make sure you don't give two controls the same access key. It confuses the user and doesn't work correctly. Only the next control (from the currently active control) in the tab sequence is activated when the user presses the access key.

Note: To view the access keys on controls or menus in Windows 2000, Windows XP, or Windows Vista, you may have to press the Alt key, depending on your system settings. You can set Windows Vista to always show underlined shortcuts in the Control Panel's *Ease of Access Center*. Select *Change how your keyboard works* and check the box for *Underline keyboard shortcuts and access keys* in the *Make the keyboard easier to use* dialog .

TIP

Use two ampersands when you want to make an ampersand appear in the Text property: &Health && Welfare for "H̲ealth & Welfare". ∎

Setting the Accept and Cancel Buttons

Are you a keyboard user? If so, do you mind having to pick up the mouse and click a button after typing text into a text box? Once a person's fingers are on the keyboard, most people prefer to press the Enter key, rather than to click the mouse. If one of the buttons on the form is the Accept button, pressing Enter is the same as clicking the button.

You can make one of your buttons the Accept button by setting the **AcceptButton property** of the form to the button name. The Accept button is visually indicated to the user by a thicker border (in default color scheme, it's black) around the button. When the user presses the Enter key, that button is automatically selected.

You also can select a Cancel button. The Cancel button is the button that is selected when the user presses the Esc key. You can make a button the

Cancel button by setting the form's **CancelButton property**. An example of a good time to set the CancelButton property is on a form with *OK* and *Cancel* buttons. You may want to set the form's AcceptButton to okButton and the CancelButton property to cancelButton.

Setting the Tab Order for Controls

In Windows programs, one control on the form always has the **focus**. You can see the focus change as you tab from control to control. For many controls, such as buttons, the focus appears as a thick border. Other controls indicate the focus by a dotted line or a shaded background. For text boxes, the insertion point (also called the *cursor*) appears inside the box.

Some controls can receive the focus; others cannot. For example, text boxes and buttons can receive the focus, but labels and picture boxes cannot.

The Tab Order

Two properties determine whether the focus stops on a control and the order in which the focus moves. Controls that are capable of receiving focus have a **TabStop property**, which you can set to *true* or *false*. If you do not want the focus to stop on a control when the user presses the Tab key, set the TabStop property to *false*.

The **TabIndex property** determines the order the focus moves as the Tab key is pressed. As you create controls on your form, Visual Studio assigns the TabIndex property in sequence. Most of the time that order is correct, but if you want to tab in some other sequence or if you add controls later, you will need to modify the TabIndex properties of your controls.

When your program begins running, the focus is on the control with the lowest TabIndex (usually 0). Since you generally want the insertion point to appear in the first control on the form, its TabIndex should be set to 0. The next control should be set to 1; the next to 2; and so forth.

You may be puzzled by the properties of labels, which have a TabIndex property but not a TabStop. A label cannot receive focus, but it has a location in the tab sequence. This fact allows you to create keyboard access keys for text boxes. When the user types an access key that is in a label, such as Alt + N, the focus jumps to the first TabIndex following the label (the text box). See Figure 2.16.

Figure 2.16

To use a keyboard access key for a text box, the TabIndex of the label must precede the TabIndex of the text box.

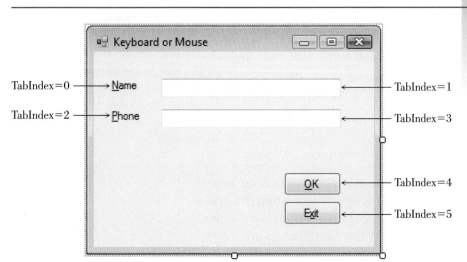

TabIndex=0 →Name   TabIndex=1
TabIndex=2 →Phone   TabIndex=3
OK — TabIndex=4
Exit — TabIndex=5

By default, buttons, text boxes, and radio buttons have their TabStop property set to *true*. Be aware that the behavior of radio buttons in the tab sequence is different from other controls: The Tab key takes you only to one radio button in a group (the selected button), even though all buttons in the group have their TabStop and TabIndex properties set. If you are using the keyboard to select radio buttons, you must tab to the group and then use your Up and Down arrow keys to select the correct button.

Setting the Tab Order

To set the tab order for controls, you can set each control's TabIndex property in the Properties window. Or you can use Visual Studio's great feature that helps you set TabIndexes automatically. To use this feature, make sure that the Design window is active and select *View / Tab Order* or click the *Tab Order* button on the Layout toolbar. (The *Tab Order* item does not appear on the menu and is not available on the Layout toolbar unless the Design window is active.) Small numbers appear in the upper-left corner of each control; these are the current TabIndex properties of the controls. Click first in the control that you want to be TabIndex zero, then click on the control for TabIndex one, and then click on the next control until you have set the TabIndex for all controls (Figure 2.17).

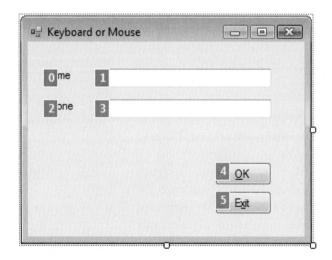

Figure 2.17

Click on each control, in sequence, to set the TabIndex property of the controls automatically.

When you have finished setting the TabIndex for all controls, the white numbered boxes change to blue. Select *View / Tab Order* again to hide the sequence numbers or press the Esc key. If you make a mistake and want to change the tab order, turn the option off and on again, and start over with TabIndex zero again, or you can keep clicking on the control until the number wraps around to the desired value.

Setting the Form's Location on the Screen

When your project runs, the form appears in the upper-left corner of the screen by default. You can set the form's screen position by setting the **StartPosition property** of the form. Figure 2.18 shows your choices for the property setting. To center your form on the user's screen, set the StartPosition property to *CenterScreen*.

Figure 2.18

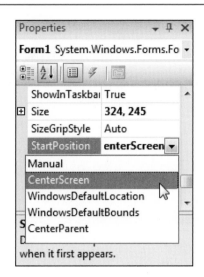

*Set the StartPosition property
of the form to CenterScreen to
make the form appear in the
center of the user's screen when
the program runs.*

Creating ToolTips

If you are a Windows user, you probably appreciate and rely on **ToolTips**, those small labels that pop up when you pause your mouse pointer over a toolbar button or control. You can easily add ToolTips to your projects by adding a **ToolTip component** to a form. After you add the component to your form, each of the form's controls has a new property: **ToolTip on toolTip1**, assuming that you keep the default name, toolTip1, for the control.

To define ToolTips, select the ToolTip tool from the toolbox (Figure 2.19) and click anywhere on the form or double-click the ToolTip tool in the toolbox. The new control appears in the component tray that opens at the bottom of the Form Designer (Figure 2.20). The **component tray** holds controls that do not have a visual representation at run time. You will see more controls that use the component tray later in this text.

Figure 2.19

*Add a ToolTip component to
your form; each of the form's
controls will have a new
property to hold the text of
the ToolTip.*

ToolTip

After you add the ToolTip component, examine the properties list for other controls on the form, such as buttons, text boxes, labels, radio buttons, check boxes, and even the form itself. Each has a new ToolTip on toolTip1 property.

Try this example: Add a button to any form and add a ToolTip component. Change the button's Text property to Exit and set its ToolTip on toolTip1 property to *Close and Exit the program*. Now run the project, point to the *Exit* button, and pause; the ToolTip will appear (Figure 2.21).

You also can add multiline ToolTips. In the ToolTip on ToolTip1 property, click the drop-down arrow. This drops down a white editing box in which you enter the text of the ToolTip. Type the first line and press Enter to create a

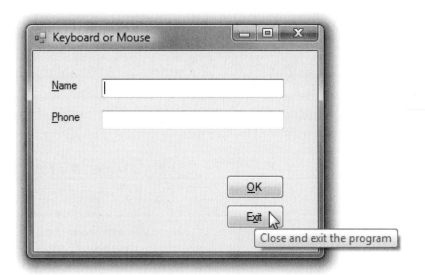

Figure 2.21

Use the ToolTip on toolTip1 property to define a ToolTip.

second line; press Ctrl + Enter to accept the text (or click somewhere outside the Property window).

You can modify the appearance of a ToolTip by setting properties of the ToolTip component. Select the ToolTip component in the component tray and try changing the BackColor and ForeColor properties. You also can set the IsBalloon property to *true* for a different appearance and include an icon in the ToolTips by selecting an icon for the ToolTipIcon property (Figure 2.22). Once you set properties for a ToolTip component, they apply to all ToolTips displayed with that component. If you want to create a variety of appearances, the best

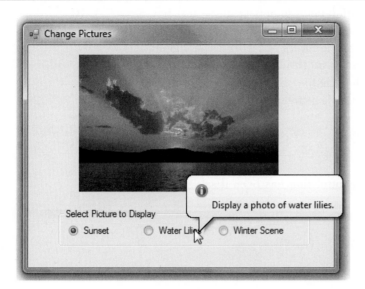

approach is to create multiple ToolTip components, giving each a unique name. For example, you might create three ToolTip components, in which case you would have properties for ToolTip on toolTip1, ToolTip on toolTip2, and ToolTip on toolTip3 for the form and each control.

Coding for the Controls

You already know how to set initial properties for controls at design time. You also may want to set some properties in code, as your project executes. You can clear out the contents of text boxes and labels; reset the focus (the active control); change the color of text, or change the text in a ToolTip.

Clearing Text Boxes and Labels

You can clear out the contents of a text box or label by setting the property to an **empty string**. Use `""` (no space between the two quotation marks). This empty string is also called a *null string* or *zero-length string*. You also can clear out a text box using the `Clear` method or setting the Text property to `string.Empty`. Note that the `Clear` method works for text boxes but not for labels.

Examples

```
// Clear the contents of text boxes and labels.
nameTextBox.Text = "";
messageLabel.Text = "";
dataTextBox.Clear();
messageLabel.Text = string.Empty;
```

Resetting the Focus

As your program runs, you want the insertion point to appear in the text box where the user is expected to type. The focus should therefore begin in the first text box. But what about later? If you clear the form's text boxes, you should reset the focus to the first text box. The **Focus method** handles this situation. Remember, the convention is Object.Method, so the statement to set the insertion point in the text box called nameTextBox is as follows:

```
// Make the insertion point appear in this text box.
nameTextBox.Focus();
```

Note: You cannot set the focus to a control that has been disabled. See "Disabling Controls" later in the text.

Setting the Checked Property of Radio Buttons and Check Boxes

Of course, the purpose of radio buttons and check boxes is to allow the user to make selections. However, at times you need to select or deselect a control in code. You can select or deselect radio buttons and check boxes at design time (to set initial status) or at run time (to respond to an event).

To make a radio button or check box appear selected initially, set its Checked property to *true* in the Properties window. In code, assign *true* to its Checked property:

```
// Make button selected.
redRadioButton.Checked = true;

// Make box checked.
displayCheckBox.Checked = true;

// Make box unchecked.
displayCheckBox.Checked = false;
```

At times, you need to reset the selected radio button at run time, usually for a second request. You only need to set the Checked property to *true* for one button of the group; the rest of the buttons in the group will set to *false* automatically. Recall that only one radio button of a group can be selected at one time.

Setting Visibility at Run Time

You can set the visibility of a control at run time.

```
// Make label invisible.
messageLabel.Visible = false;
```

You may want the visibility of a control to depend on the selection a user makes in a check box or radio button. This statement makes the visibility match the check box: When the check box is checked (Checked = *true*), the label is visible (Visible = *true*).

```
// Make the visibility of the label match the setting in the check box.
messageLabel.Visible = displayCheckBox.Checked;
```

Disabling Controls

The **Enabled property** of a control determines whether the control is available or "grayed out." The Enabled property for controls is set to *true* by default, but you can change the value at either design time or run time. You might want to disable a button or other control initially and enable it in code, depending on an action of the user. If you disable a button control (Enabled = *false*) at design time, you can use the following code to enable the button at run time.

```
displayButton.Enabled = true;
```

When you have a choice to disable or hide a control, it's usually best to disable it. Having a control disabled is more understandable to a user than having it disappear.

To disable radio buttons, consider disabling the group box holding the buttons, rather than the buttons themselves. Disabling the group box grays all of the controls in the group box.

```
departmentGroupBox.Enabled = false;
```

Note: Even though the control has the TabStop property set to *true* and the TabIndex is in the proper order, you cannot tab to a control that has been disabled.

Setting Properties Based on User Actions

Often you need to change the Enabled or Visible property of a control based on an action of the user. For example, you may have controls that are disabled or invisible until the user signs in. In the following example, when the user logs in and clicks the *Sign In* button, a rich text box becomes visible and the radio buttons are enabled:

```
private void signInButton_Click(object sender, EventArgs e)
{
    // Set visibility and enable controls.

    welcomeRichTextBox.Visible = true;
    clothingRadioButton.Enabled = true;
    equipmentRadioButton.Enabled = true;
    juiceBarRadioButton.Enabled = true;
    membershipRadioButton.Enabled = true;
    personalTrainingRadioButton.Enabled = true;
}
```

Feedback 2.2

1. Write the statements to clear the text box called companyTextBox and reset the insertion point into the box.
2. Write the statements to clear the label called customerLabel and place the insertion point into a text box called orderTextBox.
3. What will be the effect of each of these C# statements?
   (a) `printCheckBox.Checked = true;`
   (b) `colorRadioButton.Checked = true;`
   (c) `drawingPictureBox.Visible = false;`
   (d) `locationLabel.BorderStyle = BorderStyle.Fixed3D;`
   (e) `cityLabel.Text = cityTextBox.Text;`
   (f) `redRadioButton.Enabled = true;`

Changing the Color of Text

You can change the color of text by changing the **ForeColor property** of a control. Actually, most controls have a ForeColor and a BackColor property. The ForeColor property changes the color of the text; the BackColor property determines the color around the text.

The Color Constants

C# provides an easy way to specify a large number of colors. These **color constants** are in the Color class. If you type the keyword `Color` and a period in the editor, you can see a full list of colors. Some of the colors are listed below.

```
Color.AliceBlue
Color.AntiqueWhite
Color.Bisque
Color.BlanchedAlmond
Color.Blue
```

Examples

```
nameTextBox.ForeColor = Color.Red;
messageLabel.ForeColor = Color.White;
```

Using Radio Buttons for Selecting Colors

Here is a small example (Figure 2.23) that demonstrates using two groups of radio buttons to change the color of the form (the form's BackColor property) and the color of the text (the form's ForeColor property). The radio buttons in each group box operate together, independently from those in the other group box.

Figure 2.23

The radio buttons in each group box function independently from the other group. Each button changes a property of the form: BackColor to change the background of the form itself or ForeColor to change the color of the text on the form.

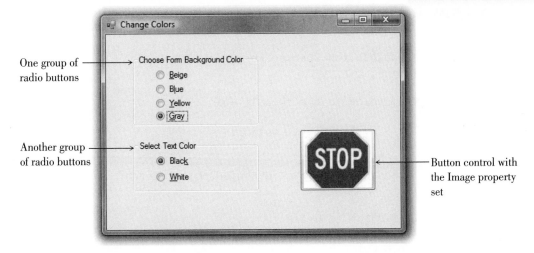

```
/* Project:      Ch02RadioButtons
 * Programmer:   Bradley/Millspaugh
 * Date:         Jan 2009
 * Description: This project demonstrates changing a form's background
 *              and foreground colors using two groups of radio buttons.
 */
using System;
using System.Collections.Generic;
using System.ComponentModel;
using System.Data;
using System.Drawing;
using System.Text;
using System.Windows.Forms;

namespace Ch02RadioButtons
{
    public partial class ColorsForm : Form
    {
        public ColorsForm()
        {
            InitializeComponent();
        }

        private void beigeRadioButton_CheckedChanged(object sender,
            EventArgs e)
        {
            // Set the form color to beige.

            this.BackColor = Color.Beige;
        }

        private void blueRadioButton_CheckedChanged(object sender,
            EventArgs e)
        {
            // Set the form color to light blue.

            this.BackColor = Color.LightBlue;
        }
```

```csharp
        private void yellowRadioButton_CheckedChanged(object sender,
            EventArgs e)
        {
            // Set the form color to yellow.

            this.BackColor = Color.LightGoldenrodYellow;
        }

        private void grayRadioButton_CheckedChanged(object sender,
            EventArgs e)
        {
            // Set the form color to the default color.

            this.BackColor = SystemColors.Control;
        }

        private void blackRadioButton_CheckedChanged(object sender,
            EventArgs e)
        {
            // Set the Text color to black.

            this.ForeColor = Color.Black;
        }

        private void whiteRadioButton_CheckedChanged(object sender,
            EventArgs e)
        {
            // Set the Text color to white.

            this.ForeColor = Color.White;
        }

        private void exitButton_Click(object sender, EventArgs e)
        {
            // End the project.

            this.Close();
        }
    }
}
```

Concatenating Text

At times you need to join strings of text. For example, you may want to join a literal and a property. You can "tack" one string of characters to the end of another in the process called **concatenation**. Use a plus sign (+) between the two strings.

Examples

```csharp
messageLabel.Text = "Your name is: " + nameTextBox.Text;
nameAndAddressLabel.Text = nameTextBox.Text + " " + addressTextBox.Text;
```

You also can concatenate a NewLine character (Environment.NewLine) into a long line to set up multiple lines:

```csharp
welcomeRichTextBox.Text = "Welcome Member #" + memberIDMaskedTextBox.Text
    + Environment.NewLine + nameTextBox.Text;
```

Downloading and Using the Line and Shape Controls

You can add graphic shapes to your forms using a set of controls that Microsoft makes available in a PowerPack, which is a separate and free download. After you download the PowerPack, you run the installation file, which installs the controls into Visual Studio. Once installed, you can add the controls to the Visual Studio toolbox. Note that although the set of controls is called Visual Basic PowerPacks, the controls work just fine in C# and are a great new addition for creating Windows Forms applications.

Download and Install the Controls

The first step is to download from Microsoft's site, msdn2.microsoft.com/en-us/vbasic/bb735936.aspx, and follow the links to download.

It's best to download the file VisualBasicPowerPacks3Setup.exe to your hard drive (save it somewhere easy to find, such as the Desktop). After the download is complete, make sure that Visual Studio is not running and double-click the setup filename to run the setup.

If you are using the Professional Edition or above and Visual Studio is closed, the new tools are automatically added to a new section of the toolbox. You can find the new section, called Visual Basic Power Packs 3.0, at the bottom of the toolbox (Figure 2.24).

For the Express Edition, or the Professional Edition if the IDE was open when you ran setup, you must manually add the controls to the toolbox. Open Visual Studio or Visual C# Express and start a new project so that you can see the Form Designer and the toolbox. Right-click in the toolbox and select *Add Tab*. Type "Visual Basic Power Packs 3.0" as the Tab name, then right-click on the

F i g u r e   2 . 2 4

The Line, Shape, and PrintForm controls in the toolbox, with some sample controls on the form.

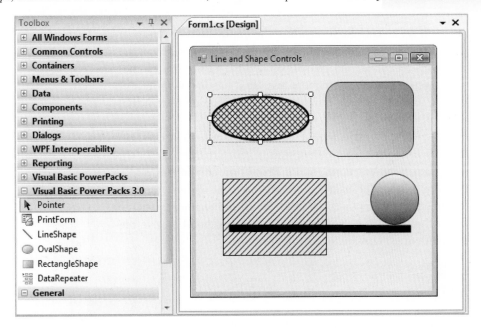

new tab, and select *Choose Items* from the context menu. The *Choose Toolbox Items* dialog box appears with the list of all available tools. You can save some time by typing "Power" in the *Filter* box, which will limit the list to the PowerPack controls. Then select *LineShape*, *OvalShape*, *RectangleShape*, and *PrintForm*. If you have multiple versions of the controls listed, choose the highest version number (9.0.0.0 as of this writing). Then click *OK* to return to the toolbox. The new tools should appear in the Visual Basic PowerPacks 3.0 tab of the toolbox.

Note: The controls appear in the section of the toolbox that is active when you select *Choose Toolbox Items*.

Place the Controls on a Form

To place a control on the form, click on the tool in the toolbox and use the mouse pointer to draw the shape that you want on the form. Alternately, you can double-click one of the tools to create a default size control that you can move and resize as desired.

The Line and Shape controls have many properties that you can set, as well as events, such as Click and DoubleClick, for which you can write event handlers.

Properties of a Line include BorderStyle (*Solid*, *Dot*, *Dash*, and a few more), BorderWidth (the width of the line, in pixels), BorderColor, and the locations for the two endpoints of the line (X1, X2, X3, X4). Of course, you can move and resize the line visually, but it sometimes is more precise to set the pixel location exactly.

The properties of the Shape controls are more interesting. You can set transparency with the BackStyle property and the border with BorderColor, BorderStyle, and BorderWidth. Set the interior of the shape using FillColor, FillGradientColor, FillGradientStyle, and FillStyle. You can make a rectangle have rounded corners by setting the CornerRadius, which defaults to zero for square corners.

Printing a Form

Would you like to print an image of a form while the application is running? You can use the new PrintForm component that you added to the toolbox in the preceding section (refer to Figure 2.24). When you add the PrintForm component to your form, it appears in the component tray, as it has no visual representation on the form. Note that this is similar to the ToolTip component that you used earlier in this chapter.

You can choose to send the printer output to the printer or to the Print Preview window, which saves paper while you are testing your program.

To add printing to a Windows Form, add a PrintForm component and a *Print* button to the form so that the user can select the print option. You can leave the default name of the component as printForm1 and change the name of the button to printButton. In the printButton_Click event handler, use the PrintForm's `Print` method to send the form to the printer:

```
// Print the form on the printer.
printForm1.Print();
```

To send the output to the Print Preview window, set the PrintForm's PrintAction property before executing the `Print` method. Allow IntelliSense to help you select the PrintAction property.

```
// Print to the Print Preview window.
printForm1.PrintAction = System.Drawing.Printing.PrintAction.PrintToPreview;
printForm1.Print();
```

Your Hands-On Programming Example

Create a login for members to view specials for Look Sharp Fitness Center. The member name is entered in a text box and the member ID in a masked text box that allows five numeric digits. Include three buttons, one for Sign In, one for Print, and one for Exit. Set the AcceptButton to the *Sign In* button and use the *Exit* button for the CancelButton. Include keyboard shortcuts as needed.

Use a group box of radio buttons for each of the departments; the buttons should be disabled when the program begins.

A check box allows the user to choose whether an image should display for the selected department. You will need an image to display for each department. You can use any images that you have available, find them on the Web, or use images from the StudentData\Images folder.

Place a line below the company name.

When the user clicks on the *Sign In* button, the data entry boxes and labels should disappear, the promotions box should appear, and the radio buttons should be enabled. The special for the selected department displays in a rich text box concatenated to the member name.

Add a ToolTip to the member ID text box that says, "Your 5 digit member number."

Allow the user to print the form to the Print Preview window.

Planning the Project

Sketch a form (Figure 2.25), which your users sign off as meeting their needs.

Figure 2.25

A planning sketch of the form for the hands-on programming example.

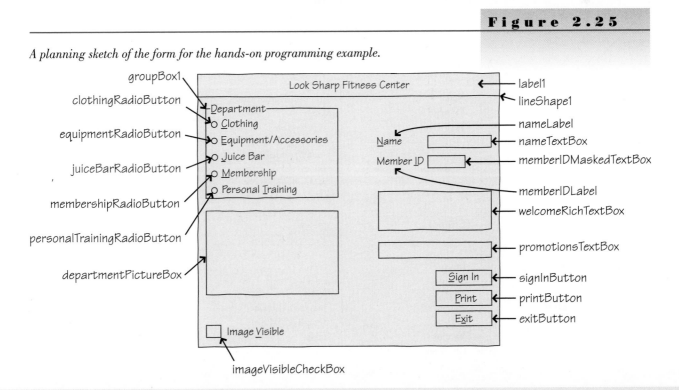

Plan the Objects and Properties

Plan the property settings for the form and for each control.

Object	Property	Setting	
PromotionForm	Name	PromotionForm	
	Text	blank	
	AcceptButton	signInButton	
	CancelButton	exitButton	
	StartPosition	CenterScreen	
label1	Text	Look Sharp Fitness Center	Hint: Do not change the name of labels not referenced in code.
	ForeColor	Select a shade of blue	
	Font.Size	14 Point	
lineShape1	BorderColor	Select a shade of blue	
	BorderWidth	5	
nameLabel	Text	&Name	
nameTextBox	Name	nameTextBox	
	Text	(blank)	
memberIDLabel	Text	Member &ID	
memberIDMaskedTextBox	Name	memberIDMaskedTextBox	
	Mask	00000	
	Text	(blank)	
	ToolTip on toolTip1	Your 5 digit member number.	
groupBox1	Text	Department	
clothingRadioButton	Name	clothingRadioButton	
	Enabled	false	
	Text	&Clothing	
equipmentRadioButton	Name	equipmentRadioButton	
	Enabled	false	
	Text	&Equipment/Accessories	
juiceBarRadioButton	Name	juiceBarRadioButton	
	Enabled	false	
	Text	&Juice Bar	
membershipRadioButton	Name	membershipRadioButton	
	Enabled	false	
	Text	&Membership	
personalTrainingRadioButton	Name	personalTrainingRadioButton	
	Enabled	false	
	Text	Personal &Training	
departmentPictureBox	Image	(none)	
	Visible	false	
imageVisibleCheckBox	Name	imageVisibleCheckBox	
	Text	Image &Visible	
	Visible	false	
	Checked	false	

welcomeRichTextBox	Text	welcomeRichTextBox
	Multiline	true
	Visible	false
promotionsTextBox	Name	promotionsTextBox
	BorderStyle	FixedSingle
	TabStop	false
	Visible	false
signInButton	Name	signInButton
	Text	&Sign In
printButton	Name	printButton
	Text	&Print
exitButton	Name	exitButton
	Text	E&xit

Plan the Event-Handling Methods You will need event handlers for each button, radio button, and check box.

Method	Actions—Pseudocode
signInButton_Click	Display a welcome in the welcomeRichTextBox concatenating the member name and number. Set the sign-in controls Visible = false. Set the promotions and welcome Visible = true. Display the image and the image visible check box. Enable the radio buttons.
printButton_Click	Set the PrintAction to PrintToPreview. Print the form.
exitButton_Click	End the project.
clothingRadioButton_CheckedChanged	Set the image and promotion for the clothing department.
equipmentRadioButton_CheckedChanged	Set the image and promotion for the equipment department.
juiceBarRadioButton_CheckedChanged	Set the image and promotion for the juice bar.
membershipRadioButton_CheckedChanged	Set the image and promotion for the membership department.
personalTrainingRadioButton_CheckedChanged	Set the image and promotion for the personal training department.
imageVisibleCheckBox_CheckedChanged	Make picture box visibility match that of check box.

Write the Project Follow the sketch in Figure 2.25 to create the form. Figure 2.26 shows the completed form.

- Set the properties of each object, as you have planned. Make sure to set the tab order of the controls.

- Working from the pseudocode, write each event-handling method.

- When you complete the code, thoroughly test the project. Make sure to select every department, with the image check box both selected and not selected.

Figure 2.26

The form for the hands-on programming example.

The Project Coding Solution

```
/*
 * Project:        Ch02HandsOn
 * Programmer:     Bradley/Millspaugh
 * Date:           Jan 2009
 * Description:    Allow the user to sign in and display
 *                 current sales promotions.
 */

using System;
using System.Collections.Generic;
using System.ComponentModel;
using System.Data;
using System.Drawing;
using System.Text;
using System.Windows.Forms;

namespace Ch02HandsOn
{
    public partial class PromotionForm : Form
    {
        public PromotionForm()
        {
            InitializeComponent();
        }

        private void signInButton_Click(object sender, EventArgs e)
        {
            // Display the specials, set the visibility of the controls.

            welcomeRichTextBox.Text = "Welcome Member #"
                        + memberIDMaskedTextBox.Text
                        + Environment.NewLine + nameTextBox.Text;
```

```
        // Set visibility properties.
        memberIDLabel.Visible = false;
        memberIDMaskedTextBox.Visible = false;
        nameLabel.Visible = false;
        nameTextBox.Visible = false;
        welcomeRichTextBox.Visible = true;
        promotionsTextBox.Visible = true;
        imageVisibleCheckBox.Visible = true;
        departmentPictureBox.Visible = true;

        // Enable the radio buttons.
        departmentGroupBox.Enabled = true;
    }

    private void printButton_Click(object sender, EventArgs e)
    {
        // Print the form as a print preview.

        printForm1.PrintAction =
            System.Drawing.Printing.PrintAction.PrintToPreview;
        printForm1.Print();
    }

    private void exitButton_Click(object sender, EventArgs e)
    {
        // End the project.

        this.Close();
    }

    private void clothingRadioButton_CheckedChanged(object sender,
        EventArgs e)
    {
        // Display the clothing image and show the special.

        departmentPictureBox.Image =
            Ch02HandsOn.Properties.Resources.GymClothing;
        promotionsTextBox.Text = "30% off clearance items.";
    }

    private void equipmentRadioButton_CheckedChanged(object sender,
        EventArgs e)
    {
        // Display the equipment image and show the special.

        departmentPictureBox.Image =
            Ch02HandsOn.Properties.Resources.GymEquipment2;
        promotionsTextBox.Text = "25% off all equipment.";
    }

    private void juiceBarRadioButton_CheckedChanged(object sender,
        EventArgs e)
    {
        // Display the juice bar image and show the special.

        departmentPictureBox.Image =
            Ch02HandsOn.Properties.Resources.JuiceBar2;
        promotionsTextBox.Text = "Free serving of WheatBerry Shake.";
    }
```

```csharp
private void membershipRadioButton_CheckedChanged(object sender,
    EventArgs e)
{
    // Display the membership image and show the special.

    departmentPictureBox.Image =
        Ch02HandsOn.Properties.Resources.Fitness1;
    promotionsTextBox.Text = "Free Personal Trainer for 1st month.";
}

private void personalTrainingRadioButton_CheckedChanged(object sender,
    EventArgs e)
{
    // Display the personal training image and show the special.

    departmentPictureBox.Image =
        Ch02HandsOn.Properties.Resources.PersonalTrainer;
    promotionsTextBox.Text = "3 free sessions with membership renewal.";
}

private void imageVisibleCheckBox_CheckedChanged(object sender,
    EventArgs e)
{
    // Set the visibility of the department image.

    departmentPictureBox.Visible = imageVisibleCheckBox.Checked;
}
}
}
```

Good Programming Habits

1. Always test the tab order on your forms. Fix it if necessary by changing the TabIndex properties of the controls.
2. Provide visual separation for input fields and output fields and always make it clear to the user which are which.
3. Make sure that your forms can be navigated and entered from the keyboard. Always set a default button (AcceptButton property) for every form.
4. To make a label maintain its size regardless of the value of the Text property, set AutoSize to *false*.
5. To make the text in a text box right justified or centered, set the TextAlign property.
6. You can use the Checked property of a check box to set other properties that must be *true* or *false*.

Summary

1. Text boxes are used primarily for user input. The Text property holds the value input by the user. You also can assign a literal to the Text property during design time or run time.
2. A MaskedTextBox has a Mask property that allows you to specify the data type and format of the input data.

3. A RichTextBox is a specialized text box that allows additional formatting to the text.

4. Both text boxes and rich text boxes have Multiline and WordWrap properties that can allow a long Text property to wrap to multiple lines. The text will wrap to the width of the control, which must be tall enough to display multiple lines. A NewLine character can be included in the text to specify the location to split the line.

5. Group boxes are used as containers for other controls and to group like items on a form.

6. Check boxes and radio buttons allow the user to make choices. In a group of radio buttons, only one can be selected; but in a group of check boxes, any number of the boxes may be selected.

7. The current state of check boxes and radio buttons is stored in the Checked property; the CheckedChanged event occurs when the user clicks on one of the controls.

8. Picture box controls hold a graphic, which is assigned to the Image property. Set the SizeMode property to *StretchImage* to make the image resize to fit the control.

9. The *Resources* tab of the Project Designer can be used to add, remove, and rename images in the project Resources folder.

10. The BorderStyle property of many controls can be set to *None*, *FixedSingle*, or *Fixed3D*, to determine whether the control appears flat or three-dimensional.

11. Forms and controls can display images from the project's resources. Use the form's BackgroundImage property and a control's Image property.

12. To create a line on a form, you can use a Label control or use the new LineShape control included in the Power Packs.

13. You can select multiple controls and treat them as a group, including setting common properties at once, moving them, or aligning them.

14. Make your programs easier to use by following Windows standard guidelines for colors, control size and placement, access keys, Accept and Cancel buttons, and tab order.

15. Define keyboard access keys by including an ampersand (&) in the Text property of buttons, radio buttons, check boxes, and labels. Use a double ampersand (&&) when you want an ampersand to actually display.

16. Set the AcceptButton property of the form to the desired button so that the user can press Enter to select the button. If you set the form's CancelButton property to a button, that button will be selected when the user presses the Esc key.

17. The focus moves from control to control as the user presses the Tab key. The sequence for tabbing is determined by the TabIndex properties of the controls. The Tab key stops only on controls that have their TabStop property set to *true* and are enabled.

18. Set the form's location on the screen by setting the StartPosition property.

19. Add a ToolTip control to a form and then set the ToolTip on toolTip1 property of a control to make a ToolTip appear when the user pauses the mouse pointer over the control. You can set properties of the ToolTip component to modify the background, foreground, shape, and an icon for the ToolTips.

20. Clear the Text property of a text box or a label by setting it to an empty string. Text boxes also can be cleared using the `Clear` method.

21. To make a control have the focus, which makes it the active control, use the `Focus` method. Using the `Focus` method of a text box makes the insertion point appear in the text box. You cannot set the focus to a disabled control.

22. You can set the Checked property of a radio button or check box at run time and also set the Visible property of controls in code.
23. Controls can be disabled by setting the Enabled property to *false*.
24. Change the color of text in a control by changing its ForeColor property.
25. You can use the color constants to change colors during run time.
26. Joining two strings of text is called *concatenation* and is accomplished by placing a plus sign between the two elements.
27. You can download and use PowerPack controls for LineShape, OvalShape, RectangleShape, and a PrintForm component.

Key Terms

Review Questions

1. You can display program output in a text box or a label. When should you use a text box? When is a label appropriate?
2. What would be the advantage of using a masked text box rather than a text box?
3. When would it be appropriate to use a rich text box instead of a text box?
4. What properties of a TextBox and RichTextBox must be set to allow a long Text property to wrap to multiple lines?
5. How does the behavior of radio buttons differ from the behavior of check boxes?
6. If you want two groups of radio buttons on a form, how can you make the groups operate independently?
7. Explain how to make a graphic appear in a picture box control.
8. Describe how to select several labels and set them all to 12-point font size at once.

9. What is the purpose of keyboard access keys? How can you define them in your project? How do they operate at run time?

10. Explain the purpose of the AcceptButton and CancelButton properties of the form. Give an example of a good use for each.

11. What is the focus? How can you control which object has the focus?

12. Assume you are testing your project and don't like the initial position of the insertion point. Explain how to make the insertion point appear in a different text box when the program begins.

13. During program execution, you want to return the insertion point to a text box called addressTextBox. What statement will you use to make that happen?

14. What is a ToolTip? How can you make a ToolTip appear?

15. What statements will clear the current contents of a text box and a label?

16. What is concatenation and when would it be useful?

Programming Exercises

Graphics Files: The StudentData folder, which is available on the text Web site (www.mhhe.com/csharp2008), holds many graphic files. You also can use any graphics that you have available or find on the Web.

2.1 Create a project for the Pamper Your Soles Shoe Sales catalog. Allow the user to select either women's or men's shoes. Have a group box for each, which contains radio buttons for shoe styles. The styles for women are dress shoes, running shoes, boots, and sandals. Men's styles are dress shoes, work boots, western boots, tennis shoes, and sandals. (*Hint*: When the user selects the radio button for women's shoes, make the group box of women's styles visible; the radio button for men's shoes displays the men's styles.)

Download two appropriate pictures from the Web for each style and give a name to the style. Display the name of the style in a text box below the image for the shoes along with the category. For example, the Cinderella-style heels should display the concatenated style: "Women's Dress Shoe Cinderella".

Include an *Exit* button that is set as both the Cancel and Accept buttons of the form. A *Clear* button should set the user interface to display only a logo and the options for Men's or Women's shoes. A *Print* button should send the form to the Print Preview window. Use keyboard access keys and include ToolTips.

2.2 Write a project to display the flags of four different countries, depending on the setting of the radio buttons. In addition, display the name of the country in the large label under the flag picture box. The user also can choose to display or hide the form's title, the country name, and the name of the programmer. Use check boxes for the display/hide choices.

Include keyboard access keys for all radio buttons, check boxes, and buttons. Make the *Exit* button the Cancel button. Include a *Print* button and ToolTips.

You can choose the countries and flags. (The StudentData\Images\ MicrosoftIcons folder holds flag icons for four countries, which you can use if you wish.)

Hints: When a project begins running, the focus goes to the control with the lowest TabIndex. Because that control likely is a radio button, one button will appear selected. You must either display the first flag to match the radio button or make the focus begin in a different control. You might consider beginning the focus on a button.

Set the Visible property of a control to the Checked property of the corresponding check box. That way when the check box is selected, the control becomes visible.

Because all three selectable controls will be visible when the project begins, set the Checked property of the three check boxes to *true* at design time.

2.3   Write a project to display a weather report for a Sporting Goods Store. The user will input his or her name in a text box and can choose one of the radio buttons for the weather—rain, snow, cloudy, and sunny. Display an image and a message. The message should give the weather report in words and include the person's name (taken from the text box at the top of the form). For example, if the user chooses the *Sunny* button, you might display "It looks like a good day for golf, John" (assuming that the user entered *John* in the text box).

Include keyboard access keys for the buttons and radio buttons. Make the *Exit* button the Cancel button and include a *Print* button and ToolTips.

Note: The StudentData\Images\MicrosoftIcons folder has icon files that you can use, if you wish. Available are Cloud.ico, Rain.ico, Snow.ico, and Sun.ico.

2.4   BratPack BackPacks needs an application to display products. The categories are school bags, sling backpacks, daypacks, weekend hiking backpacks, and cycling backpacks. When the user selects a category, display an image of the appropriate style. Include a *Print* button, a *Clear* button, and an *Exit* button.

2.5   Create a project that allows the user to input name and address information and then display the lines of output for a mailing label in a rich text box.

Use text boxes for entry of the first name, last name, street address, city, and state, and a masked text box for the ZIP code. Give meaningful names to the text boxes and set the initial Text properties to blank. Add appropriate labels to each text box to tell the user which data will be entered into each box and also provide ToolTips.

Use buttons for *Display Label Info*, *Clear*, *Print*, and *Exit*. Make the *Display* button the Accept button and the *Clear* button the Cancel button.

When the user clicks on the *Display Label Info* button, display the following in a rich text box:

Line 1—The first name and last name concatenated together, with a space between the two.
Line 2—The street address.
Line 3—The city, state, and ZIP code concatenated together. (Make sure to concatenate a comma and a space between the city and state, using "," and two spaces between the state and ZIP code.)

Case Studies

Custom Supplies Mail Order

Design and code a project that displays shipping information.

Use an appropriate image in a picture box in the upper-left corner of the form.

Use text boxes with identifying labels for Catalog Code, Page Number, and Part Number.

Use two groups of radio buttons on the form; enclose each group in a group box. The first group box should have a Text property of Shipping and contain radio buttons for Express and Ground. Make the second group box have a Text property of Payment Type and include radio buttons for Charge, COD, and Money Order.

Use a check box for New Customer.

Create a group box for Order Summary. The group box will contain a rich text box to display the catalog information and labels for the other details. Have a new customer label that is visible when the box is checked. Display the shipping method and payment type in labels when a radio button is selected.

Add buttons for *Display Catalog Information*, *Clear*, *Print*, and *Exit*. Make the *Display Catalog Information* button the Accept button and the *Clear* button the Cancel button.

The *Display Catalog Information* button should display the Catalog Code, page number, and part number in a text box.

Add ToolTips as appropriate.

Christopher's Car Center

Modify the project from the Chapter 1 Car Center case study, replacing the buttons with images in picture boxes. (See "Copy and Move Projects" in Appendix C for help in making a copy of the Chapter 1 project to use for this project.) Above each picture box, place a label that indicates which department or command the graphic represents. A click on a picture box will produce the appropriate information in the special notices label.

Add an image in a picture box that clears the special notices label. Include a ToolTip for each picture box to help the user understand the purpose of the graphic.

Add radio buttons that will allow the user to view the special notices label in different colors.

Include a check box labeled Hours. When the check box is selected, a new label will display the message "Open 24 Hours—7 days a week". Include a *Print* button that displays the form in the Print Preview window.

Department/Command	Suggested Image for Picture box (Available in Images\MicrosoftIcons)
Auto Sales	Cars.ico
Service Center	Wrench.ico
Detail Shop	Water.ico
Employment Opportunities	Mail12.ico
Exit	Msgbox01.ico

Xtreme Cinema

Design and code a project that displays the location of videos using radio buttons. Use a radio button for each of the movie categories and a label to display the aisle number. A check box will allow the user to display or hide a message for members. When the check box is selected, a message stating "All Members Receive a 10% Discount" will appear.

Include buttons (with keyboard access keys) for *Clear*, *Print*, and *Exit*. The *Clear* button should be set as the Accept button and the *Exit* as the Cancel button.

Place a label on the form in a 24-point font that reads *Xtreme Cinema*. Use a line to separate the label from the rest of the user interface. Include an image in a picture box.

Radio Button	Location
Comedy	Aisle 1
Drama	Aisle 2
Action	Aisle 3
Sci-Fi	Aisle 4
Horror	Aisle 5
New Releases	Back wall

Cool Boards

Create a project to display an advertising screen for Cool Boards. Include the company name, programmer name, a slogan (use "The very best in boards" or make up your own slogan), and a graphic image for a logo. You may use the graphic Skateboard.gif from StudentData\Images or use one of your own.

Allow the user to select the color for the slogan text using radio buttons. Additionally, the user may choose to display or hide the company name, the slogan, and the logo. Use check boxes for the display options so that the user can select each option independently.

Include keyboard access keys for the radio buttons and the buttons. Make the *Exit* button the Cancel button; the *Print* button should display the form in the Print Preview window. Create ToolTips for the company name ("Our company name"), the slogan ("Our slogan"), and the logo ("Our logo").

When the project begins execution, the slogan text should be red and the Red radio button selected. When the user selects a new color, change the color of the slogan text to match.

Each of the check boxes must appear selected initially, since the company name, slogan, logo, and programmer name display when the form appears. Each time the user selects or deselects a check box, make the corresponding item display or hide.

Make the form appear in the center of the screen.

3

Variables, Constants, and Calculations

at the completion of this chapter, you will be able to . . .

1. Distinguish between variables, constants, and controls.

2. Differentiate among the various data types.

3. Apply naming conventions incorporating standards and indicating the data type.

4. Declare variables and constants.

5. Select the appropriate scope for a variable.

6. Convert text input to numeric values.

7. Perform calculations using variables and constants.

8. Convert between numeric data types using implicit and explicit conversions.

9. Round decimal values using the decimal.Round method.

10. Format values for output using the ToString method.

11. Use try/catch blocks for error handling.

12. Display message boxes with error messages.

13. Accumulate sums and generate counts.

In this chapter you will learn to do calculations. You will start with text values input by the user, convert them to numeric values, and perform calculations on them. You also learn to format the results of your calculations and display them for the user.

Although the calculations themselves are quite simple (addition, subtraction, multiplication, and division), there are some important issues to discuss first. You must learn about variables and constants, the various types of data used by Visual C#, and how and where to declare variables and constants. Variables are declared differently, depending on where you want to use them and how long you need to retain their values.

The code below is a small preview to show the calculation of the product of two text boxes. The first group of statements declares the variables and their data types. The second group of statements converts the text box contents to numeric and places the values into the variables. The last line performs the multiplication and places the result into a variable. The following sections of this chapter describe how to set up your code for calculations.

```
// Declare the variables.
int quantityInteger;
decimal priceDecimal, extendedPriceDecimal;

// Convert input text to numeric and assign values to variables.
quantityInteger = int.Parse(quantityTextBox.Text);
priceDecimal = decimal.Parse(priceTextBox.Text);

// Calculate the product.
extendedPriceDecimal = quantityInteger * priceDecimal;
```

Data—Variables and Constants

So far, all data you have used in your projects have been properties of objects. You have worked with the Text property of text boxes and labels. Now you will work with values that are not properties. C# allows you to set up locations in memory and give each location a name. You can visualize each memory location as a scratch pad; the contents of the scratch pad can change as the need arises. In this example, the memory location is called *maximumInteger*.

```
maximumInteger = 100;
```

maximumInteger
100

After executing this statement, the value of maximumInteger is 100. You can change the value of maximumInteger, use it in calculations, or display it in a control.

In the preceding example, the memory location called maximumInteger is a **variable**. Memory locations that hold data that can be changed during project execution are called *variables*; locations that hold data that cannot change during execution are called **constants**. For example, the customer's name will vary as the information for each individual is processed. However, the name of the company and the sales tax rate will remain the same (at least for that day).

When you declare a variable or a **named constant**, C# reserves an area of memory and assigns it a name, called an **identifier**. You specify identifier names according to the rules of C# as well as some recommended naming conventions.

The **declaration** statements establish your project's variables and constants, give them names, and specify the type of data they will hold. The statements are not considered executable; that is, they are not executed in the flow of instructions during program execution. An exception to this rule occurs when you initialize a variable on the same line as the declaration.

Here are some sample declaration statements:

```
// Declare a string variable.
string nameString;

// Declare integer variables.
int counterInteger;
int maxInteger = 100;

// Declare a named constant.
const decimal DISCOUNT_RATE_Decimal = .15M;
```

The next few sections describe the data types, the rules for naming variables and constants, and the format of the declarations.

Data Types

The **data type** of a variable or constant indicates what type of information will be stored in the allocated memory space: perhaps a name, a dollar amount, a date, or a total. You can think of the data types in C# as classes, and the variables as objects of the class. Table 3.1 shows the data types.

same in all .NET languages

**The C# Data Types, .NET Common Language Runtime (CLR)
Data Types, the Kind of Data Each Type Holds, and the
Amount of Memory Allocated for Each.**

Table 3.1

C# Data Type	.NET Common Language Runtime (CLR) Data Type	Use for	Storage size in bytes
bool	Boolean	*true* or *false* values	2
byte	Byte	0 to 255, binary data	1
char	Char	Single Unicode character	2
DateTime	DateTime	1/1/0001 00:00:00 through 12/31/9999 23:59:59	8
decimal	Decimal	Decimal fractions, such as dollars and cents, with a precision of 28 digits	16
float	Single	Single-precision floating-point numbers with six digits of accuracy	4
double	Double	Double-precision floating-point numbers with 14 digits of accuracy	8
short	Int16	Small integer in the range −32,768 to +32,767	2
int	Int32	Whole numbers in the range −2,147,483,648 to +2,147,483,647	4
long	Int64	Larger whole numbers	8
string	String	Alphanumeric data: letters, digits, and other characters	varies
object	Object	Any type of data	4

Note: Generally you will use the C# data types, but for some conversion methods, you must use the corresponding CLR data type.

Note that C# has unsigned integral fields—uint, ushort, and ulong—and a signed byte data type: sbyte.

The most common types of variables and constants we will use are string, int, and decimal. When deciding which data type to use, follow this guideline: If the data will be used in a calculation, then it must be numeric (usually int or decimal); if it is not used in a calculation, it will be string. Use decimal as the data type for any decimal fractions in business applications; float and double data types are generally used in scientific applications.

Consider the following examples:

Contents	Data type	Reason
Social security number	string	Not used in a calculation.
Pay rate	decimal	Used in a calculation; contains a decimal point.
Hours worked	decimal	Used in a calculation; may contain a decimal point. (Decimal can be used for any decimal fraction, not just dollars.)
Phone number	string	Not used in a calculation.
Quantity	int	Used in calculations; contains a whole number.

Naming Rules

A programmer has to name (identify) the variables and named constants that will be used in a project. C# requires identifiers for variables and named constants to follow these rules: names may consist of letters, digits, and underscores; they must begin with a letter or underscore; they cannot contain any spaces or periods; and they may not be reserved words. (Reserved words, also called *keywords*, are words to which C# has assigned some meaning, such as *print*, *name*, and *value*.)

Identifiers in C# are case sensitive. Therefore, the names sumInteger, SumInteger, suminteger, and SUMINTEGER all refer to different variables.

Naming Conventions

When naming variables and constants, you *must* follow the rules of C#. In addition, you *should* follow some naming conventions. Conventions are the guidelines that separate good names from bad (or not so good) names. The meaning and use of all identifiers should always be clear.

Just as we established conventions for naming objects in Chapter 1, in this chapter we adopt conventions for naming variables and constants. The following conventions are widely used in the programming industry:

1. *Identifiers must be meaningful.* Choose a name that clearly indicates its purpose. Do not abbreviate unless the meaning is obvious and do not use very short identifiers, such as *X* or *Y*.
2. *Include the class (data type) of the variable.*

3. *Begin with a lowercase letter and then capitalize each successive word of the name.* Always use mixed case for variables; uppercase for constants.

Sample Identifiers

Field of data	Possible identifier
Social security number	socialSecurityNumberString
Pay rate	payRateDecimal
Hours worked	hoursWorkedDecimal
Phone number	phoneNumberString
Quantity	quantityInteger
Tax rate (constant)	TAX_RATE_Decimal
Quota (constant)	QUOTA_Integer
Population	populationLong

Feedback 3.1

Indicate whether each of the following identifiers conforms to the rules of C# and to the naming conventions. If the identifier is invalid, give the reason. Remember, the answers to Feedback questions are found in Appendix A.

1. omitted
2. #SoldInteger
3. Number Sold Integer
4. Number.Sold.Integer
5. amount$Decimal
6. class
7. subString
8. Text
9. maximum
10. minimumRate
11. maximumCheckDecimal
12. companyNameString

Constants: Named and Intrinsic

Constants provide a way to use words to describe a value that doesn't change. In Chapter 2 you used the Visual Studio constants Color.Blue, Color.Red, Color.Yellow, and so on. Those constants are built into the environment and called *intrinsic constants*; you don't need to define them anywhere. The constants that you define for yourself are called *named constants*.

Named Constants

You declare named constants using the keyword const. You give the constant a name, a data type, and a value. Once a value is declared as a constant, its value cannot be changed during the execution of the project. The data type that you declare and the data type of the value must match. For example, if you declare an integer constant, you must give it an integer value.

You will find two important advantages to using named constants rather than the actual values in code. The code is easier to read; for example, seeing the identifier MAXIMUM_PAY_Decimal is more meaningful than seeing a number such as 1000. In addition, if you need to change the value at a later time, you need to change the constant declaration only once; you do not have to change every reference to it throughout the code.

const Statement—General Form

```
const Datatype Identifier = Value;
```

Naming conventions for constants require that you include the data type in the name. Use all uppercase for the name with individual words separated by underscores.

This example sets the company name, address, and the sales tax rate as constants:

const Statement—Examples

```
const string COMPANY_NAME_String = "R 'n R -- for Reading 'n Refreshment";
const string COMPANY_ADDRESS_String = "101 S. Main Street";
const decimal SALES_TAX_RATE_Decimal = .08m;
```

Assigning Values to Constants

The values you assign to constants must follow certain rules. You have already seen that a text (string) value must be enclosed in quotation marks; numeric values are not enclosed. However, you must be aware of some additional rules.

Numeric constants may contain only the digits (0–9), a decimal point, and a sign (+ or −) at the left side. You cannot include a comma, dollar sign, any other special characters, or a sign at the right side. You can declare the data type of numeric constants by appending a type-declaration character. If you do not append a type-declaration character to a numeric constant, any whole number is assumed to be integer and any fractional value is assumed to be double. The type-declaration characters are

decimal	M or m
double	D or d
long	L or l
short	S or s
float	F or f

String literals (also called string constants) may contain letters, digits, and special characters such as $#@%&*. You will have a problem when you want to include quotation marks inside a string literal since quotation marks enclose the literal. The solution is to precede the quotation mark with a backslash (\), which specifies that the character following should be rendered as is.

Example

```
"He said, \"I like it.\" " produces this string: He said, "I like it."
```

You can use two backslashes when you need to include a backslash in a string literal. The first backslash specifies that you want the following character rendered as it appears.

Example

```
string filePathString = "C:\\PersonalDocuments\\PersonalLetter";
```

Although you can use numeric digits inside a string literal, remember that these numbers are text and cannot be used for calculations.

The string values are referred to as **string literals** because they contain exactly (literally) whatever is inside the quotation marks. (Remember that the backslash is a special escape character, so, after the assignment above, `filePathString` contains `"C:\PersonalDocuments\PersonalLetter"`.) Another technique for including a backslash character in a string literal is to place an at sign (@) in front of the string literal, which tells the compiler to use the characters exactly as typed. The following example places the same string into `filePathString` as the above example:

```
string filePathString = @"C:\PersonalDocuments\PersonalLetter";
```

The following table lists example constants.

Data type	Constant value example
int	5 125 2170 2000 −100 12345678
float	101.25f −5.0f
decimal	850.50m −100m
double	52875.8 52875.8d −52875.8d
long	1342579871 −8250758L

string literals	`"Visual C#"`
	`"ABC Incorporated"`
	`"1415 J Street"`
	`"102"`
	`"She said \"Hello.\""`

Intrinsic Constants

Intrinsic constants are system-defined constants. Many sets of intrinsic constants are declared in system class libraries and are available for use in your C# programs. For example, the color constants that you used in Chapter 2 are intrinsic constants.

You must specify the class name or group name as well as the constant name when you use intrinsic constants. For example, Color.Red is the constant "Red" in the class "Color." Later in this chapter, you will learn to use constants from the MessageBox class for displaying message boxes to the user.

Declaring Variables

You declare a variable by specifying the data type followed by an identifier. You also can assign an initial value to the variable. Later in this chapter, you will learn to declare variables using the `public` or `private` statement.

Declaration Statements—General Form

> **General Form**
>
> ```
> datatype identifier;
> datatype identifier = LiteralOfCorrectType;
> public | private datatype identifier;
> ```

Declaration Statement—Examples

> **Examples**
>
> ```
> string customerNameString;
> string customerNameString = "None";
> private int totalSoldInteger;
> int totalSoldInteger = 0;
> float temperatureFloat;
> float temperatureFloat = 32f;
> decimal priceDecimal;
> private decimal priceDecimal = 99.95m;
> ```

You also can declare several variables in one statement; the data type named at the beginning of the statement applies to all of the variables. Separate the variable names with commas and place a semicolon at the end of the statement. Here are some sample declarations:

```
string nameString, addressString, phoneString;
decimal priceDecimal, totalDecimal;
int countInteger = 0, totalInteger = 0;
```

> **☑TIP**
>
> **R**ename a variable or control using refactoring. Right-click on the name and choose *Refactor / Rename* from the context menu. Enter a new name and the identifier will be changed everywhere it occurs. ■

Initializing Numeric Variables

Numeric variables must be assigned a value before they can be used. In other words, the variable must appear on the left side of an equal sign (an assignment) before it can be used on the right side of an equal sign. You can initialize a variable when you declare it:

```
int quantityInteger = 0;
```

Or you can declare it without an initial value and assign the value later:

```
int quantityInteger;
quantityInteger = int.Parse(quantityTextBox.Text);
```

The preceding example also could be declared and initialized with this statement:

```
int quantityInteger = int.Parse(quantityTextBox.Text);
```

If you refer to a variable without first assigning it a value, the compiler will generate an error message.

```
int quantityInteger;
totalInteger = quantityInteger; // Generates a compiler error.
```

Note: Later in this chapter, you will learn about class-level variables, which do not require initialization because C# initializes them automatically. See "Scope and Lifetime of Variables."

Entering Declaration Statements

The IntelliSense feature helps you enter declaration statements. After you type the first letter, a list pops up (Figure 3.1). This list shows the possible entries for data type to complete the statement. The easiest way to complete the statement is to begin typing the correct entry; the list automatically scrolls to the correct section (Figure 3.2). When the correct entry is highlighted, press Enter, Tab, or the spacebar to select the entry, or double-click if you prefer using the mouse.

Figure 3.1

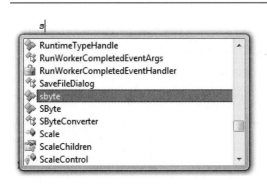

As soon as you begin typing on a line, IntelliSense pops up. You can make a selection from the list with your mouse or the keyboard.

Figure 3.2

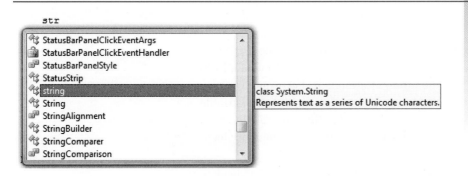

Type the first few characters of the data type and the IntelliSense list quickly scrolls to the correct section. When the correct word is highlighted, press Enter, Tab, or the spacebar to select the entry.

Note: Some people find the IntelliSense feature annoying rather than helpful. You can turn off the feature by selecting *Tools / Options*. In the *Options* dialog box, choose *Text Editor / C# / General*; deselect *Auto list members* and

Parameter information. If you are using the C# Express Edition, you must select *Show all settings* in the *Options* dialog box to make the selections.

Feedback 3.2

Write a declaration for the following situations; make up appropriate variable identifiers.

1. You need variables for payroll processing to store the following:
   (a) Number of hours, which can hold a decimal value.
   (b) Employee's name.
   (c) Department number (not used in calculations).
2. You need variables for inventory control to store the following:
   (a) Integer quantity.
   (b) Description of the item.
   (c) Part number.
   (d) Cost.
   (e) Selling price.

Scope and Lifetime of Variables

A variable may exist and be visible for all classes in a project, a single class, a single form (which is a class), a single method in a class, or inside a single block in a method. The visibility of a variable is referred to as its **scope**. Visibility really means "this variable can be used or 'seen' in this location." The scope is said to be namespace, class level, local, or block. A **namespace variable** may be used in all methods of the namespace, which is generally the entire project. **Class-level variables** are accessible in all methods of a form or other class. A **local variable** may be used only within the method in which it is declared, and a **block variable** is used only within a block of code inside a method. A block is defined as the code enclosed in curly braces.

You declare the scope of a variable by choosing where to declare it.

Note: Some programming languages and some programmers refer to namespace variables as *global variables*.

Variable Lifetime

When you create a variable, you must be aware of its **lifetime**. The *lifetime* of a variable is the period of time that the variable exists. The lifetime of a local or block variable is normally one execution of a method. For example, each time you execute a method, the local declarations are executed. Each variable is created as a "fresh" new one, with the initial value that you assign for it. When the method finishes, its variables disappear; that is, their memory locations are released.

The lifetime of a class-level variable is the entire time the class is loaded, generally the lifetime of the entire project. If you want to maintain the value of a variable for multiple executions of a method, for example, to calculate a running total, you must use a class-level variable (or a variable declared as static, which is discussed in Chapter 12).

Local Declarations

Any variable that you declare inside a method is local in scope, which means that it is known only to that method. The keywords public and private are not used on local variables. A declaration may appear anywhere inside the method as long as it appears prior to the first use of the variable in a statement. However, good programming practices dictate that all declarations appear at the top of the method, prior to all other code statements (after the comments).

```
// Class-level declarations.
private const decimal DISCOUNT_RATE_Decimal = 0.15m;

private void calculateButton_Click(object sender, EventArgs e)
{
  // Calculate the price and discount.
  int quantityInteger;
  decimal priceDecimal, extendedPriceDecimal, discountDecimal,
    discountedPriceDecimal;

  // Convert input values to numeric variables.
  quantityInteger = int.Parse(quantityTextBox.Text);
  priceDecimal = decimal.Parse(priceTextBox.Text);

  // Calculate values.
  extendedPriceDecimal = quantityInteger * priceDecimal;
  discountDecimal = decimal.Round((extendedPriceDecimal * DISCOUNT_RATE_Decimal), 2);
  discountedPriceDecimal = extendedPriceDecimal - discountDecimal;
```

Notice the private const statement in the preceding example. Although you can declare named constants to be local, block level, class level, or namespace in scope, just as you can variables, good programming practices dictate that constants should be declared at the class level. This technique places all constant declarations at the top of the code and makes them easy to find in case you need to make changes.

Class-Level Declarations

At times you need to be able to use a variable or constant in more than one method of a form. When you declare a variable or constant as class level, you can use it anywhere in that form's class. When you write class-level declarations, you can use the public or private keywords or just use the data type. In Chapter 12 you will learn how and why to choose public or private, but good programming practices dictate that you use the private keyword unless you need a variable to be public.

Place the declarations for class-level variables and constants after the opening brace for the class, outside of any method. *If you wish to accumulate a sum or count items for multiple executions of a method, you should declare the variable at the class level.*

Figure 3.3

The variables you declare inside a method are local. Variables that you declare outside a method are class level.

```
namespace MyProjectNamespace
{
        public partial class MyProjectForm : ...
        {
                declare classVariables
                declare namedConstants

                private calculateButton_Click(...)
                {
                        declare localVariables
                        ...
                }

                private summaryButton_Click(...)
                {
                        declare localVariables
                        ...
                }

                private clearButton_Click(...)
                {
                        declare localVariables
                        {
                                declare blockLevelVariables
                        }
                }
        }
}
```

Figure 3.3 illustrates the locations for coding local variables and class-level variables.

Coding Class-Level Declarations

To enter class-level declarations, place the insertion point on a new line after the class declaration and its opening curly brace (Figure 3.4). Declare the variables and constants after the class declaration but before your first method.

Figure 3.4

Code class-level declarations at the top of a class.

```
namespace Ch03Discounts
{
    public partial class DiscountForm : Form
    {
        private int quantitySumInteger, saleCountInteger;
        private decimal discountSumDecimal;
        private const decimal MAXIMUM_DISCOUNT_Decimal = 100.0m;

        public DiscountForm()
        {
            InitializeComponent();
        }
    }
}
```

Class variables and constants

It isn't necessary to initialize class-level variables, as it is with local variables because C# automatically initializes numeric variables to zero and string variables to an empty string. However, most programmers prefer to initialize all variables themselves.

Block-Level and Namespace-Level Declarations

You won't use block-level or namespace-level declarations in this chapter. Block-level variables and constants have a scope of a block of code, i.e. the code contained within a pair of curly braces ({}). These statements are covered later in this text.

Namespace-level variables and constants can sometimes be useful when a project has multiple forms and/or classes, but good programming practices exclude the use of namespace-level variables.

Feedback 3.3

Write the declarations for each of the following situations and indicate where each statement will appear.

1. The total of the payroll that will be needed in a Calculate event-handling method and in a Summary event-handling method.
2. The sales tax rate that cannot be changed during execution of the program but will be used by multiple methods.
3. The number of participants that are being counted in the Calculate event-handling method but not displayed until the Summary event-handling method.

Calculations

In programming, you can perform calculations with variables, with constants, and with the properties of certain objects. The properties you will use, such as the Text property of a text box or a label, are usually strings of text characters. These character strings, such as "Howdy" or "12345", cannot be used directly in calculations unless you first convert them to the correct data type.

Converting Strings to a Numeric Data Type

You can use a Parse method to convert the Text property of a control to its numeric form before you use the value in a calculation. The class that you use depends on the data type of the variable to which you are assigning the value. For example, to convert text to an integer, use the int.Parse method; to convert to a decimal value, use decimal.Parse. Pass the text string that you want to convert as an **argument** of the Parse method.

```
// Convert input values to numeric variables.
quantityInteger = int.Parse(quantityTextBox.Text);
priceDecimal = decimal.Parse(priceTextBox.Text);

// Calculate the extended price.
extendedPriceDecimal = quantityInteger * priceDecimal;
```

In the preceding example, the String value from the quantityTextBox.Text property is converted into an int data type and the string from priceTextBox.Text is converted into a decimal data type.

Using the Parse Methods

As you know, objects have methods that perform actions, such as the Focus method for a text box. The data types that you use to declare variables are classes, which have properties and methods. Each of the numeric data type classes has a Parse method, which you will use to convert text strings into the correct numeric value for that type. The decimal class has a Parse method that converts the value inside the parentheses to a decimal value while the int class has a Parse method to convert the value to an integer.

The Parse Methods—General Form

General Form

```
// Convert to int.
int.Parse(StringToConvert);

// Convert to decimal.
decimal.Parse(StringToConvert);
```

The expression you wish to convert can be the property of a control, a string variable, or a string constant. The Parse method returns (produces) a value that can be used as a part of a statement, such as the assignment statements in the following examples.

The Parse Methods—Examples

Examples

```
quantityInteger = int.Parse(quantityTextBox.Text);
priceDecimal = decimal.Parse(priceTextBox.Text);
wholeNumberInteger = int.Parse(digitString);
```

The Parse methods examine the value stored in the argument and attempt to convert it to a number in a process called *parsing*, which means to pick apart, character by character, and convert to another format.

When a Parse method encounters a value that it cannot parse to a number, such as a blank or nonnumeric character, an error occurs. You will learn how to avoid those errors later in this chapter in the section titled "Handling Exceptions."

You will use the int.Parse and decimal.Parse methods for most of your programs. But in case you need to convert to long, float, or double, C# also has a Parse method for each of those data type classes.

Converting to String

When you assign a value to a variable, you must take care to assign like types. For example, you assign an integer value to an int variable and a decimal value to a decimal variable. Any value that you assign to a string variable or the Text property of a control must be string. You can convert any of the numeric data types to a string value using the ToString method. Later in this chapter, you will learn to format numbers for output using parameters of the ToString method.

Note: The rule about assigning only like types has some exceptions. See "Implicit Conversions" later in this chapter.

Examples

```
resultTextBox.Text = resultDecimal.ToString();
countTextBox.Text = countInteger.ToString();
idString = idInteger.ToString();
```

Arithmetic Operations

The arithmetic operations you can perform in C# include addition, subtraction, multiplication, division, and modulus.

Operator	Operation
+	Addition
−	Subtraction
*	Multiplication
/	Division
%	Modulus—remainder of division

The first four operations are self-explanatory, but you may not be familiar with modulus.

Modulus

The % operator returns the remainder of a division operation. For example, if totalMinutesInteger = 150, then

```
minutesInteger = totalMinutesInteger % 60;
```

returns 30 for minutesInteger (150 divided by 60 equals 2 with a remainder of 30).

Division

The division operator (/) can be used to divide fractional values or integers. The operation depends on the data types of the operands. If at least one of the operands is fractional, the result will be fractional. However, if you divide one integer value by another, C# will truncate (drop) any fractional result and produce an integer result. For example, if minutesInteger = 150, then

```
hoursInteger = minutesInteger / 60;
```

returns 2 for hoursInteger. But

```
hoursFloat = minutesInteger / 60.0f;
```

returns 2.5 for hoursFloat. Note that if you omit the "f" on the divisor, C# performs integer division and returns 2.0 for hoursFloat.

Exponentiation

C# does not have an operator for exponentiation; instead, it uses the `Pow` method of the Math class. You can refer to Appendix B for the Math methods. Additionally, Chapter 5 has an example that uses the `Pow` method in the section titled "Writing a Method with Multiple Arguments."

Order of Operations

The order in which operations are performed determines the result. Consider the expression 3 + 4 * 2. What is the result? If the addition is done first, the result is 14. However, if the multiplication is done first, the result is 11.

The hierarchy of operations, or **order of precedence**, in arithmetic expressions from highest to lowest is

1. Any operation inside parentheses.
2. Multiplication and division.
3. Modulus.
4. Addition and subtraction

In the previous example, the multiplication is performed before the addition, yielding a result of 11. To change the order of evaluation, use parentheses. The expression

(3 + 4) * 2

will yield 14 as the result. One set of parentheses may be used inside another set. In that case, the parentheses are said to be *nested*. The following is an example of nested parentheses:

```
((score1Integer + score2Integer + score3Integer) / 3.0f) * 1.2f
```

Extra parentheses can always be used for clarity. The expressions

```
2 * costDecimal * rateDecimal and (2 * costDecimal) * rateDecimal
```

are equivalent, but the second is easier to understand.

Multiple operations at the same level (such as multiplication and division) are performed from left to right. The example 8 / 4 * 2 yields 4 as its result, not 1. The first operation is 8 / 4, and 2 * 2 is the second.

Evaluation of an expression occurs in this order:

1. All operations within parentheses. Multiple operations within the parentheses are performed according to the rules of precedence.
2. All multiplication and division. Multiple operations are performed from left to right.
3. Modulus operations. Multiple operations are performed from left to right.
4. All addition and subtraction are performed from left to right.

Although the precedence of operations in C# is the same as in algebra, take note of one important difference: There are no implied operations in C#.

Use extra parentheses to make the precedence clearer. The operation will be easier to understand and the parentheses have no negative effect on execution. ■

The following expressions would be valid in mathematics, but they are not valid in C#:

Mathematical notation	Equivalent C# function
2A	2 * A
3(X + Y)	3 * (X + Y)
(X + Y)(X – Y)	(X + Y) * (X – Y)

Feedback 3.4

What will be the result of the following calculations using the order of precedence?

Assume that xInteger = 2, yInteger = 4, zInteger = 3

```
1. xInteger + yInteger / 2
2. 8 / yInteger / xInteger
3. xInteger * (xInteger + 1)
4. xInteger * xInteger + 1
5. yInteger * xInteger + zInteger * 2
6. yInteger * (xInteger + zInteger) * 2
7. (yInteger * xInteger) + zInteger * 2
8. ((yInteger * xInteger) + zInteger) * 2
```

Using Calculations in Code

You perform calculations in assignment statements. Recall that whatever appears on the right side of an = (assignment operator) is assigned to the item on the left. The left side may be the property of a control or a variable. It cannot be a constant.

Examples

```
averageDecimal = sumDecimal / countInteger;
amountDueLabel.Text = (priceDecimal – (priceDecimal *
  discountRateDecimal)).ToString();
commissionTextBox.Text = (salesTotalDecimal * commissionRateDecimal).ToString();
```

In the preceding examples, the results of the calculations were assigned to a variable, the Text property of a label, and the Text property of a text box. In most cases, you will assign calculation results to variables or to the Text properties of text boxes or labels. When you assign the result of a calculation to a Text property, place parentheses around the entire calculation and convert the result of the calculation to a string.

Assignment Operators

In addition to the equal sign (=) as an **assignment operator**, C# has several operators that can perform a calculation and assign the result as one operation. The combined assignment operators are +=, – =, *=, /=, %=, and += (string). Each of these combined assignment operators is a shortcut for the standard method; you can use the standard (longer) form or the shortcut. The shortcuts allow you to type a variable name only once instead of having to type it on both sides of the equal sign.

For example, to add salesDecimal to totalSalesDecimal, the long version is

```
// Accumulate a total.
totalSalesDecimal = totalSalesDecimal + salesDecimal;
```

Instead you can use the shortcut assignment operator:

```
// Accumulate a total.
totalSalesDecimal += salesDecimal;
```

The two statements have the same effect.

To subtract 1 from a variable, the long version is

```
// Subtract 1 from a variable.
countDownInteger = countDownInteger - 1;
```

and the shortcut, using the − = operator:

```
// Subtract 1 from a variable.
countDownInteger -= 1;
```

The assignment operators that you will use most often are += and − =. The following are examples of other assignment operators:

```
// Multiply resultInteger by 2 and assign the result to resultInteger.
resultInteger *= 2;

// Divide sumDecimal by countInteger and assign the result to sumDecimal.
sumDecimal /= countInteger;

// Concatenate smallString to the end of bigString.
bigString += smallString;
// If bigString = "Large" and smallString = "Tiny" then
// bigString will equal "LargeTiny" after the assignment.
```

Increment and Decrement Operators

C# also has operators that allow you to add 1 or subtract 1 from a number. The **increment operator** (++) adds 1 to a variable:

```
countInteger++;
```

The **decrement operator** (−−) subtracts 1 from the variable:

```
countDownInteger--;
```

You can place the increment or decrement operator before the variable, called a ***prefix notation***. If you prefix the operator, the order of calculation changes, which can modify the result if there are multiple operations:

```
resultInteger = 100 - ++countInteger;
```

means "add 1 to countInteger before subtracting it from 100."

Placing the operator after the variable is called a ***postfix notation***. When you use postfix notation, the increment (or decrement) is performed after other operations:

```
resultInteger = 100 - countInteger++;
```

subtracts countInteger from 100 before incrementing countInteger.

Feedback 3.5

1. Write three statements to add 1 to countInteger, using (*a*) the standard, long version; (*b*) the assignment operator; and (*c*) the increment operator.
2. Write two statements to add 5 to countInteger, using (*a*) the standard, long version and (*b*) the assignment operator.
3. Write two statements to subtract withdrawalDecimal from balanceDecimal, using (*a*) the standard, long version and (*b*) the assignment operator.
4. Write two statements to multiply priceDecimal by countInteger and place the result into priceDecimal. Use (*a*) the standard, long version and (*b*) the assignment operator.

Converting between Numeric Data Types

In C# you can convert data from one numeric data type to another. Some conversions can be performed implicitly (automatically) and some you must specify explicitly. And some cannot be converted if the value would be lost in the conversion.

Implicit Conversions

If you are converting a value from a narrower data type to a wider type, where there is no danger of losing any precision, the conversion can be performed by an **implicit conversion**. For example, the statement

```
bigNumberDouble = smallNumberInteger;
```

does not generate any error message, assuming that both variables are properly declared. The value of smallNumberInteger is successfully converted and stored in bigNumberDouble. However, to convert in the opposite direction could cause problems and cannot be done implicitly.

The following list shows selected data type conversions that can be performed implicitly in C#:

From	To
byte	short, int, long, float, double, or decimal
short	int, long, float, double, or decimal
int	long, float, double, or decimal
long	float, double, or decimal
float	double

Notice that no implicit conversions exist to convert from decimal data type to another type and you cannot convert implicitly from floating point (float or double) to decimal. Double does not convert implicitly to any other type.

Explicit Conversions

If you want to convert between data types that do not have implicit conversions, you must use an **explicit conversion**, also called *casting*. But beware: If you perform a cast that causes significant digits to be lost, an exception is generated. (Exceptions are covered later in this chapter in the section titled "Handling Exceptions.")

To cast, you specify the destination data type in parentheses before the data value to convert.

Examples

```
numberDecimal = (decimal) numberFloat; // Cast from float to decimal.
valueInt = (int) valueDouble;      // Cast from double to int.
amountFloat = (float) amountDouble; // Cast from double to float.
```

You also can use methods of the Convert class to convert between data types. The Convert class has methods that begin with "To" for each of the data types: `ToDecimal`, `ToSingle`, and `ToDouble`. However, you must specify the integer data types using their .NET class names.

For the C# data type	Use the method for the .NET CLR data type
short	`ToInt16`
int	`ToInt32`
long	`ToInt64`

The following are examples of explicit conversions using the Convert class. For each, assume that the variables are already declared following the textbook naming standards.

```
numberDecimal = Convert.ToDecimal(numberSingle);
valueInteger = Convert.ToInt32(valueDouble);
```

You should perform a conversion from a wider data type to a narrower one only when you know that the value will fit without losing significant digits. Fractional values are rounded to fit into integer data types, and a float or double value converted to decimal is rounded to fit in 28 digits.

Performing Calculations with Unlike Data Types

When you perform calculations with unlike data types, C# performs the calculation using the wider data type. For example, `countInteger / numberDecimal` produces a decimal result. If you want to convert the result to a different data type, you must perform a cast: `(int) countInteger / numberDecimal` or (float) countInteger / numberDecimal. Note, however, that C# does not convert to a different data type until it is necessary. The expression countInteger / 2 * amountDecimal is evaluated as integer division for countInteger / 2, producing an integer intermediate result; then the multiplication is performed on the integer and decimal value (amountDecimal), producing a decimal result.

Rounding Numbers

At times you may want to round decimal fractions. You can use the decimal. Round method to round decimal values to the desired number of decimal positions.

The Round Method—General Form

```
decimal.Round(DecimalValue, IntegerNumberOfDecimalPositions);
```

The decimal.Round method returns a decimal result, rounded to the specified number of decimal positions, which can be an integer in the range 0–28.

The Round Method—Examples

```
// Round to two decimal positions.
resultDecimal = decimal.Round(amountDecimal, 2);
// Round to zero decimal positions.
wholeDollarsDecimal = decimal.Round(dollarsAndCentsDecimal, 0);
// Round the result of a calculation.
discountDecimal = decimal.Round(extendedPriceDecimal * DISCOUNT_RATE_Decimal, 2);
```

The decimal.Round method and the Convert methods round using a technique called "rounding toward even." If the digit to the right of the final digit is exactly 5, the number is rounded so that the final digit is even.

Examples

Decimal value to round	Number of decimal positions	Result
1.455	2	1.46
1.445	2	1.44
1.5	0	2
2.5	0	2

In addition to the `decimal.Round` method, you can use the `Round` method of the Math class to round either decimal or double values. See Appendix B for the methods of the Math class.

Formatting Data for Display

When you want to display numeric data in the Text property of a label or text box, you must first convert the value to string. You also can **format** the data for display, which controls the way the output looks. For example, 12 is just a number, but $12.00 conveys more meaning for dollar amounts. Using the `ToString` method and formatting codes, you can choose to display a dollar sign, a percent sign, and commas. You also can specify the number of digits to appear to the right of the decimal point. C# rounds the value to return the requested number of decimal positions.

If you use the `ToString` method with an empty argument, the method returns an unformatted string. This is perfectly acceptable when displaying integer values. For example, the following statement converts numberInteger to a string and displays it in displayTextBox.Text.

```
displayTextBox.Text = numberInteger.ToString();
```

Using Format Specifier Codes

You can use the **format specifier codes** to format the display of output. These predefined codes can format a numeric value to have commas and dollar signs, if you wish.

Note: The default format of each of the formatting codes is based on the computer's regional setting. The formats presented here are for the default English (United States) values.

```
// Display as currency.
extendedPriceTextBox.Text = (quantityInteger * priceDecimal).ToString("C");
```

The `"C"` code specifies *currency*. By default, the string will be formatted with a dollar sign, commas separating each group of three digits, and two digits to the right of the decimal point.

```
// Display as numeric.
discountTextBox.Text = discountDecimal.ToString("N");
```

The `"N"` code stands for *number*. By default, the string will be formatted with commas separating each group of three digits, with two digits to the right of the decimal point.

You can specify the number of decimal positions by placing a numeric digit following the code. For example, `"C0"` displays as currency with zero digits to the right of the decimal point. The value is rounded to the specified number of decimal positions.

Format specifier codes	Name	Description
C or c	Currency	Formats with a dollar sign, commas, and two decimal places. Negative values are enclosed in parentheses.
F or f	Fixed-point	Formats as a string of numeric digits, no commas, two decimal places, and a minus sign at the left for negative values.
N or n	Number	Formats with commas, two decimal places, and a minus sign at the left for negative values.
D or d	Digits	Use only for *integer* data types. Formats with a left minus sign for negative values. Usually used to force a specified number of digits to display.
P or p	Percent	Multiplies the value by 100, adds a space and a percent sign, and rounds to two decimal places; negative values have a minus sign at the left.

Examples

Variable	Value	Format specifier code	Output
totalDecimal	1125.6744	"C"	$1,125.67
totalDecimal	1125.6744	"N"	1,125.67
totalDecimal	1125.6744	"N0"	1,126
balanceDecimal	1125.6744	"N3"	1,125.674
balanceDecimal	1125.6744	"F0"	1126
pinInteger	123	"D6"	000123
rateDecimal	0.075	"P"	7.50 %
rateDecimal	0.075	"P3"	7.500 %
rateDecimal	0.075	"P0"	8 %
valueInteger	–10	"C"	($10.00)
valueInteger	–10	"N"	–10.00
valueInteger	–10	"D3"	–010

Note that the formatted value returned by the `ToString` method is no longer purely numeric and cannot be used in further calculations. For example, consider the following lines of code:

```
amountDecimal += chargesDecimal;
amountTextBox.Text = amountDecimal.ToString("C");
```

Assume that amountDecimal holds 1050 after the calculation, and amount-TextBox.Text displays $1,050.00. If you want to do any further calculations with this amount, such as adding it to a total, you must use amountDecimal, not amountTextBox.Text. The variable amountDecimal holds a numeric value; amountTextBox.Text holds a string of (nonnumeric) characters.

You also can format DateTime values using format codes and the `ToString` method. Unlike the numeric format codes, the date codes are case sensitive. The strings returned are based on the computer's regional settings and can be changed. The following are default values for U.S. English in Windows Vista.

Date specifier code	Name	Description	Example of default setting
d	short date	mm/dd/yyyy	6/15/2009
D	long date	Day, Month dd, yyyy	Monday, June 15, 2009
t	short time	hh:mm AM|PM	4:55 PM
T	long time	hh:mm:ss AM|PM	4:55:45 PM
f	full date/time (short time)	Day, Month dd, yyyy hh:mm AM|PM	Monday, June 15, 2009 4:55 PM
F	full date/time (long time)	Day, Month dd, yyyy hh:mm:ss AM|PM	Monday, June 15, 2009 4:55:45 PM
g	general (short time)	mm/dd/yyyy hh:mm AM|PM	6/15/2009 11:00 AM
G	general (long time)	mm/dd/yyyy hh:mm:ss AM|PM	6/15/2009 11:00:15 AM
M or m	month	Month dd	June 15
R or r	GMT pattern	Day, dd Mmm yyyy hh:mm:ss GMT	Mon, 15 Jun 2009 11:00:15 GMT

Note that you also can use methods of the DateTime structure for formatting dates: `ToLongDateString`, `ToShortDateString`, `ToLongTimeString`, `ToShortTimeString`. See Appendix B or MSDN for additional information.

Choosing the Controls for Program Output

Some programmers prefer to display program output in labels; others prefer text boxes. Both approaches have advantages, but whichever approach you use, you should clearly differentiate between (editable) input areas and (uneditable) output areas.

Users generally get clues about input and output fields from their color. By Windows convention, input text boxes have a white background; output text has a gray background. The default background color of text boxes (BackColor property) is set to white; the default BackColor of labels is gray.

However, you can change the BackColor property and the BorderStyle property of both text boxes and labels so that the two controls look very similar. You might wonder why a person would want to do that, but there are some very good reasons.

Using text boxes for output can provide some advantages: The controls do not disappear when the Text property is cleared, and the borders and sizes of the output boxes can match those of the input boxes, making the form more visually uniform. Also, the user can select the text and copy it to another program using the Windows clipboard.

If you choose to display output in labels (the traditional approach), set the AutoSize property to *false* so that the label does not disappear when the Text property is blank. You also generally set the BorderStyle property of the labels to Fixed3D or FixedSingle so that the outline of the label appears.

To use a text box for output, set its ReadOnly property to *true* (to prevent the user from attempting to edit the text) and set its TabStop property to *false*, so that the focus will not stop on that control when the user tabs from one control to the next. Notice that when you set ReadOnly to *true*, the BackColor property automatically changes to Control, which is the system default for labels.

The example programs in this chapter use text boxes, rather than labels, for output.

TIP

To change the ForeColor property of a ReadOnly text box in code, set the control's BackColor property as well. You can set BackColor to SystemColors.Control, which is the default for a ReadOnly text box, and the ForeColor change will show up. ■

Feedback 3.6

Give the line of code that assigns the formatted output and explain how the output will display for the specified value.

1. A calculated variable called averagePayDecimal has a value of 123.456 and should display in a text box called averagePayTextBox.
2. The variable quantityInteger, which contains 176123, must be displayed in the text box called quantityTextBox.
3. The total amount collected in a fund drive is being accumulated in a variable called totalCollectedDecimal. What statement will display the variable in a text box called totalTextBox with commas and two decimal positions but no dollar signs?

A Calculation Programming Example

Look Sharp Fitness Center needs to calculate prices and discounts for clothing sold. The company is currently having a big sale, offering a 30 percent discount on all clearance clothing items. In this project, you will calculate the amount due for items sold, determine the 30 percent discount, and deduct the discount, giving the new amount due—the discounted amount. Use text boxes with the ReadOnly property set to *true* for the output fields.

Planning the Project

Sketch a form (Figure 3.5) that meets the needs of your users.

Figure 3.5

A planning sketch of the form for the calculation programming example.

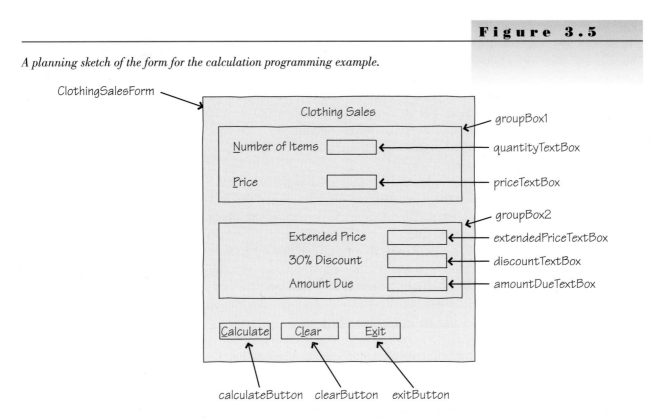

Plan the Objects and Properties

Plan the property settings for the form and each of the controls.

Object	Property	Setting
ClothingSalesForm	Name Text AcceptButton CancelButton	ClothingSalesForm Look Sharp Fitness Center calculateButton clearButton
label1	Text	Clothing Sales
groupBox1	Text	(blank)
label2	Text	&Number of Items
quantityTextBox	Name	quantityTextBox
label3	Text	&Price
priceTextBox	Name	priceTextBox
groupBox2	Text	(blank)
label4	Text	Extended Price
extendedPriceTextBox	Name TextAlign ReadOnly TabStop	extendedPriceTextBox Right True False

label5	Text	30% Discount
discountTextBox	Name TextAlign ReadOnly TabStop	discountTextBox Right True False
label6	Text	Amount Due
amountDueTextBox	Name TextAlign ReadOnly TabStop	amountDueTextBox Right True False
calculateButton	Name Text	calculateButton &Calculate
clearButton	Name Text	clearButton C&lear
exitButton	Name Text	exitButton E&xit

Plan the Event Handlers

Since you have three buttons, you need to plan the actions for three event-handling methods.

Event handlers	Actions—Pseudocode
calculateButton_Click	Declare the variables. Convert the input Quantity and Price to numeric. Calculate Extended Price = Quantity * Price. Calculate and round: Discount = Extended Price * Discount Rate. Calculate Discounted Price = Extended Price − Discount. Format and display the output in text boxes.
clearButton_Click	Clear each text box. Set the focus in the first text box.
exitButton_Click	Exit the project.

Write the Project

Follow the sketch in Figure 3.5 to create the form. Figure 3.6 shows the completed form.

1. Set the properties of each object, as you have planned.
2. Write the code. Working from the pseudocode, write each event method.
3. When you complete the code, use a variety of test data to thoroughly test the project.

Figure 3.6

The form for the calculation programming example.

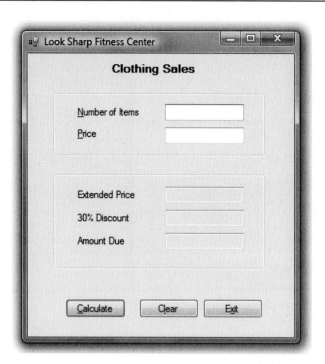

Note: If the user enters nonnumeric data or leaves a numeric field blank, the program will cancel with a run-time error. In the "Handling Exceptions" section that follows this program, you will learn to handle the errors.

The Project Coding Solution

```
/*Project:     Ch03ClothingSales
 *Date:        June 2009
 *Programmer:  Bradley/Millspaugh
 *Description: This project inputs sales information for clothing.
 *             It calculates the extended price and discount for
 *                 a sale.
 *             Uses variables, constants, and calculations.
 *             Note that no error trapping is included in this version
 *                 of the program.
 */
using System;
using System.Collections.Generic;
using System.ComponentModel;
using System.Data;
using System.Drawing;
using System.Text;
using System.Windows.Forms;

namespace Ch03ClothingSales
{
    public partial class ClothingSalesForm : Form
    {
        // Declare the constant.
        private const decimal DISCOUNT_RATE_Decimal = 0.3m;
```

```csharp
public ClothingSalesForm()
{
    InitializeComponent();
}

private void calculateButton_Click(object sender, EventArgs e)
{
    // Calculate the discount and amount due.

    // Declare the variables.
    int quantityInteger;
    decimal priceDecimal, extendedPriceDecimal, discountDecimal,
        amountDueDecimal;

    // Convert input values to numeric and assign to variables.
    quantityInteger = int.Parse(quantityTextBox.Text);
    priceDecimal = decimal.Parse(priceTextBox.Text);

    // Calculate values.
    extendedPriceDecimal = quantityInteger * priceDecimal;
    discountDecimal = Decimal.Round(
        (extendedPriceDecimal * DISCOUNT_RATE_Decimal), 2);
    amountDueDecimal = extendedPriceDecimal - discountDecimal;

    // Format and display answers.
    extendedPriceTextBox.Text = extendedPriceDecimal.ToString("C");
    discountTextBox.Text = discountDecimal.ToString("N");
    amountDueTextBox.Text = amountDueDecimal.ToString("C");
}

private void clearButton_Click(object sender, EventArgs e)
{
    // Clear the text boxes.

    quantityTextBox.Clear();
    priceTextBox.Clear();
    discountTextBox.Clear();
    extendedPriceTextBox.Clear();
    amountDueTextBox.Clear();
    quantityTextBox.Focus();
}

private void exitButton_Click(object sender, EventArgs e)
{
    // End the program.

    this.Close();
}
    }
}
```

Handling Exceptions

When you allow users to input numbers and use those numbers in calculations, lots of things can go wrong. The Parse methods, int.Parse and decimal.Parse, fail if the user enters nonnumeric data or leaves the text box blank. Or your user may enter a number that results in an attempt to divide by zero. Each of those situations causes an **exception** to occur, or, as programmers like to say, *throws an exception*.

You can easily "catch" program exceptions by using structured exception handling. You catch the exceptions before they can cause a run-time error and handle the situation, if possible, within the program. Catching exceptions as they happen and writing code to take care of the problems is called *exception handling*. The exception handling in Visual Studio .NET is standardized for all of the languages that use the Common Language Runtime.

try/catch Blocks

To trap or catch exceptions, enclose any statement(s) that might cause an error in a **try/catch block**. If an exception occurs while the statements in the `try` block are executing, program control transfers to the `catch` block; if a `finally` statement is included, the code in that section executes last, whether or not an exception occurred.

The try Block—General Form

```
try
{
    // Statements that may cause error.
}
catch [(ExceptionType [VariableName])]
{
    // Statements for action when exception occurs.
}
[finally
{
    // Statements that always execute before exit of try block.
}]
```

Note: The code shown in square brackets is optional.

The try Block—Example

```
try
{
    quantityInteger = int.Parse(quantityTextBox.Text);
    quantityTextBox.Text = quantityInteger.ToString();
}
catch
{
    messageLabel.Text = "Error in input data.";
}
```

The `catch` as it appears in the preceding example will catch any exception. You also can specify the type of exception that you want to catch, and even write several `catch` statements, each to catch a different type of exception. For example, you might want to display one message for bad input data and a different message for a calculation problem.

To specify a particular type of exception to catch, use one of the predefined exception classes, which are all based on, or derived from, the SystemException class. Table 3.2 shows some of the common exception classes.

To catch bad input data that cannot be converted to numeric, write this catch statement:

```
catch (FormatException)
{
    messageLabel.Text = "Error in input data.";
}
```

The Exception Class

Each exception is an instance of the Exception class. The properties of this class allow you to determine the code location of the error, the type of error, and the cause. The Message property contains a text message about the error and the Source property contains the name of the object causing the error. The StackTrace property can identify the location in the code where the error occurred.

Common Exception Classes Table 3.2

Exception	Caused by
FormatException	Failure of a numeric conversion, such as `int.Parse` or `decimal.Parse`. Usually blank or nonnumeric data.
InvalidCastException	Failure of a casting operation. May be caused by loss of significant digits or an illegal conversion.
ArithmeticException	A calculation error, such as division by zero or overflow of a variable.
System.IO.EndofStream Exception	Failure of an input or output operation such as reading from a file.
OutOfMemoryException	Not enough memory to create an object.
Exception	Generic.

You can include the text message associated with the type of exception by specifying the Message property of the Exception object, as declared by the variable you named on the catch statement. Be aware that the messages for exceptions are usually somewhat terse and not oriented to users, but they can sometimes be helpful.

```
catch (FormatException theException)
{
    messageLabel.Text = "Error in input data: " + theException.Message;
}
```

Handling Multiple Exceptions

If you want to trap for more than one type of exception, you can include multiple catch blocks (handlers). When an exception occurs, the catch statements are checked in sequence. The first one with a matching exception type is used.

```
catch (FormatException theException)
{
    // Statements for nonnumeric data.
}
catch (ArithmeticException theException)
{
    // Statements for calculation problem.
}
catch (Exception theException)
{
    // Statements for any other exception.
}
```

The last `catch` will handle any exceptions that do not match either of the first two exception types. Note that it is acceptable to use the same variable name for multiple `catch` statements; each `catch` represents a separate code block, so the variable's scope is only that block. You can omit the variable name for the exception if you don't need to refer to the properties of the exception object in the `catch` block.

Later in this chapter, in the "Testing Multiple Fields" section, you will see how to nest one `try`/`catch` block inside another one.

Compiler Warnings

Some of the preceding statements will generate warnings from the compiler. If you declare a variable for the exception on the `catch` statement but do not use the variable, the compiler sends the message: "The variable 'theException' is declared but never used." You can choose to ignore the message; warnings do not stop program execution. Or you can choose to eliminate the variable or use the value of the variable within the catch block.

Displaying Messages in Message Boxes

You may want to display a message when the user has entered invalid data or neglected to enter a required data value. You can display a message to the user in a message box, which is a special type of window. You can specify the message, an optional icon, title bar text, and button(s) for the message box (Figure 3.7).

You use the **Show method** of the **MessageBox** object to display a message box. The MessageBox object is a predefined instance of the MessageBox class that you can use any time you need to display a message.

Figure 3.7

Two sample message boxes created with the MessageBox class.

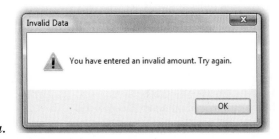

a.

b.

The MessageBox Object—General Form

There is more than one way to call the Show method of the MessageBox class. Each of the following statements is a valid call; you can choose the format you want to use. It's very important that the arguments you supply exactly match one of the formats. For example, you cannot reverse, transpose, or leave out any of the arguments. When there are multiple ways to call a method, the method is said to be *overloaded*. See the section "Using Overloaded Methods" later in this chapter.

General Form

```
MessageBox.Show(TextMessage);
MessageBox.Show(TextMessage, TitlebarText);
MessageBox.Show(TextMessage, TitlebarText, MessageBoxButtons);
MessageBox.Show(TextMessage, TitlebarText, MessageBoxButtons, MessageBoxIcon);
```

The TextMessage is the message you want to appear in the message box. The TitlebarText appears on the title bar of the MessageBox window. The MessageBoxButtons argument specifies the buttons to display. And the MessageBoxIcon determines the icon to display.

The MessageBox Statement—Examples

Examples

```
MessageBox.Show("Enter numeric data.");

MessageBox.Show("Try again.", "Data Entry Error");

MessageBox.Show("This is a message.", "This is a title bar", MessageBoxButtons.OK);

try
{
    quantityInteger = int.Parse(quantityTextBox.Text);
    outputTextBox.Text = quantityInteger.ToString();
}
catch (FormatException)
{
    MessageBox.Show("Nonnumeric Data.", "Error",
      MessageBoxButtons.OK, MessageBoxIcon.Exclamation);
}
```

The TextMessage String

The message string you display may be a string literal enclosed in quotes or a string variable. You also may want to concatenate several items, for example, combining a literal with a value from a variable. If the message you specify is too long for one line, it will wrap to the next line.

The Titlebar Text

The string that you specify for TitlebarText will appear in the title bar of the message box. If you choose the first form of the Show method, without the TitlebarText, the title bar will appear empty.

MessageBoxButtons

When you show a message box, you can specify the button(s) to display. In Chapter 4, after you learn to make selections using the `if` statement, you will display more than one button and take alternate actions based on which button the user clicks. You specify the buttons using the MessageBoxButtons constants from the MessageBox class. The choices are OK, OKCancel, RetryCancel, YesNo, YesNoCancel, and AbortRetryIgnore. The default for the `Show` method is OK, so unless you specify otherwise, you will get only the OK button in your message box.

MessageBoxIcon

The easy way to select the icon to display is to type MessageBoxIcon and a period into the editor; the IntelliSense list pops up with the complete list. The actual appearance of the icons varies from one operating system to another. You can see a description of the icons in Help under the "MessageBoxIcon Enumeration" topic.

Constants for MessageBoxIcon

Asterisk
Error
Exclamation
Hand
Information
None
Question
Stop
Warning

Using Overloaded Methods

As you saw earlier, you can call the `Show` method with several different argument lists. This feature, called ***overloading***, allows the `Show` method to act differently for different arguments. Each argument list is called a ***signature***, so you can say that the `Show` method has several signatures.

When you call the `Show` method, the arguments that you supply must exactly match one of the signatures provided by the method. You must supply the correct number of arguments of the correct data type and in the correct sequence.

Fortunately the Visual Studio smart editor helps you enter the arguments; you don't have to memorize or look up the argument lists. Type "MessageBox. Show(" and IntelliSense pops up with one signature for the `Show` method (Figure 3.8). Notice in the figure that there are 21 possible forms of the argument list, or 21 signatures for the `Show` method. (We only show 4 of the 21 signatures in the previous example, to simplify the concept.)

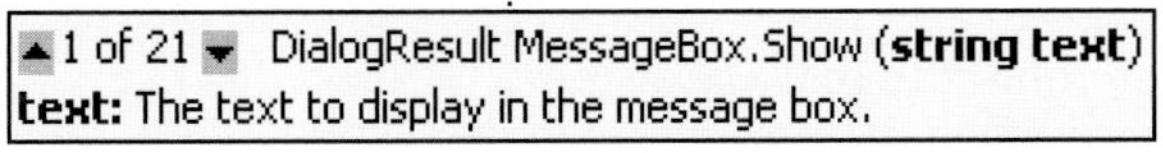

Figure 3.8

```
▲ 1 of 21 ▼  DialogResult MessageBox.Show (string text)
text: The text to display in the message box.
```

Figure 3.8

IntelliSense pops up the first of 21 signatures for the Show *method. Use the Up and Down arrows to see the other possible argument lists.*

To select the signature that you want to use, use the Up and Down arrows at the left end of the IntelliSense popup. For example, to select the signature that needs only the text of the message and the title bar caption, select the third format (Figure 3.9). The argument that you are expected to enter is shown in bold, and a description of that argument appears in the last line of the popup. After you type the text of the message and a comma, the second argument appears in bold and the description changes to tell you about that argument (Figure 3.10).

You can use the keyboard Up and Down arrow keys rather than the mouse to view and select the signature. The on-screen arrows jump around from one signature to the next, making mouse selection difficult. ■

Figure 3.9

```
▲ 3 of 21 ▼  DialogResult MessageBox.Show (string text, string caption)
text: The text to display in the message box.
```

Select the third signature to see the argument list. The currently selected argument is shown in bold and the description of the argument appears in the last line of the popup.

Figure 3.10

Type the first argument and a comma, and IntelliSense bolds the second argument and displays a description of the needed data.

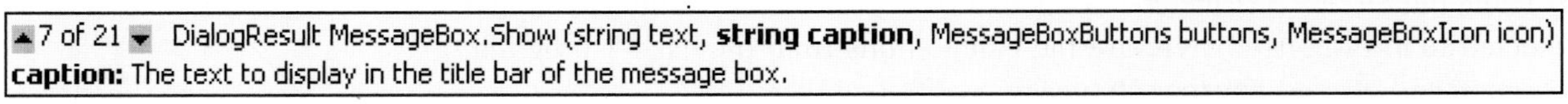

```
▲ 7 of 21 ▼  DialogResult MessageBox.Show (string text, string caption, MessageBoxButtons buttons, MessageBoxIcon icon)
caption: The text to display in the title bar of the message box.
```

Testing Multiple Fields

When you have more than one input field, each field presents an opportunity for an exception. If you would like your exception messages to indicate the field that caused the error, you can nest one try/catch block inside another one.

Nested try/catch Blocks

One try/catch block that is completely contained inside another one is called a **nested try/catch block**. You can nest another try/catch block within the try block or the catch block.

```
try     // Outer try block for the first field.
{
    // Convert first field to numeric.
    try // Inner try block for the second field.
    {
        // Convert second field to numeric.

        // Perform the calculations for the fields that passed conversion.
    }
    catch (FormatException secondException)
    {
        // Handle any exceptions for the second field.

        // Display a message and reset the focus for the second field.

    } // End of inner try block for the second field.
}
catch (FormatException firstException)
{
    // Handle exceptions for the first field.

    // Display a message and reset the focus for the first field.
}
catch (Exception anyOtherException)
{
    // Handle any generic exceptions.

    // Display a message.
}
```

You can nest the try/catch blocks as deeply as you need. *Make sure to place the calculations within the most deeply nested try*; you do not want to perform the calculations unless all of the input values are converted without an exception.

By testing each Parse method individually, you can be specific about which field caused the error and set the focus back to the field in error. Also, by using the SelectAll method of the text box, you can make the text appear selected to aid the user. Here are the calculations from the earlier program, rewritten with nested try/catch blocks.

```
private void calculateButton_Click(object sender, EventArgs e)
{
    // Declare the variables.
    int quantityInteger;
    decimal priceDecimal, extendedPriceDecimal, discountDecimal,
        amountDueDecimal;

    try
    {
        // Convert input values to numeric and assign to variables.
        quantityInteger = int.Parse(quantityTextBox.Text);
        try
        {
            priceDecimal = decimal.Parse(priceTextBox.Text);
```

```
        // Calculate values.
        extendedPriceDecimal = quantityInteger * priceDecimal;
        discountDecimal = Decimal.Round(
            (extendedPriceDecimal * DISCOUNT_RATE_Decimal), 2);
        amountDueDecimal = extendedPriceDecimal - discountDecimal;

        // Format and display answers.
        extendedPriceTextBox.Text = extendedPriceDecimal.ToString("C");
        discountTextBox.Text = discountDecimal.ToString("N");
        amountDueTextBox.Text = amountDueDecimal.ToString("C");
    }
    catch
    {
        // Invalid price.
        MessageBox.Show("Invalid price.","Data Error");
        priceTextBox.Focus();
        priceTextBox.SelectAll();
    }
}
catch
{
    // Invalid quantity.
    MessageBox.Show("Invalid quantity.", "Data Error");
    quantityTextBox.Focus();
    quantityTextBox.SelectAll();
}
}
```

Counting and Accumulating Sums

Programs often need to calculate the sum of numbers. For example, in the previous programming exercise each sale is displayed individually. If you want to accumulate totals of the sales amounts, of the discounts, or of the number of books sold, you need some new variables and new techniques.

As you know, the variables you declare inside a method are local to that method. They are re-created each time the method is called; that is, their lifetime is one time through the method. Each time the method is entered, you have a new fresh variable. If you want a variable to retain its value for multiple calls, in order to accumulate totals, you must declare the variable as class level. (Another approach, using static variables, is discussed in Chapter 12.)

Summing Numbers

The technique for summing the sales amounts for multiple sales is to declare a class-level variable for the total. Then, in the calculateButton_Click event handler for each sale, add the current amount to the total:

```
totalAmountDecimal += amountDecimal;
```

This assignment statement adds the current value for amountDecimal into the sum held in totalAmountDecimal.

Counting

If you want to count something, such as the number of sales in the previous example, you need another class-level variable. Declare a counter variable as integer:

```
int saleCountInteger;
```

Then, in the calculateButton_Click event method, add 1 to the counter variable:

```
saleCountInteger ++;
```

This statement adds 1 to the current contents of saleCountInteger. The statement will execute one time for each time the calculateButton_Click event method executes. Therefore, saleCountInteger will always hold a running count of the number of sales.

Calculating an Average

To calculate an average, divide the sum of the items by the count of the items. In the Look Sharp Fitness Center example, we can calculate the average clothing sale by dividing the sum of the total sales by the number of sales transactions:

```
averageSaleDecimal = totalAmountDecimal / saleCountInteger;
```

Your Hands-On Programming Example

In this project, Look Sharp Fitness Center needs to expand the clothing sale project done previously in this chapter. In addition to calculating individual sales and discounts, management wants to know the total amount of sales and the number of transactions.

Add exception handling to the program so that missing or nonnumeric data will not cause a run-time error.

Help the user by adding ToolTips wherever you think they will be useful.

Planning the Project

Sketch a form (Figure 3.11) that your users sign off as meeting their needs.

Plan the Objects and Properties   Plan the property settings for the form and each control. These objects and properties are the same as for the previous example, with the addition of the summary information beginning with groupBox3.

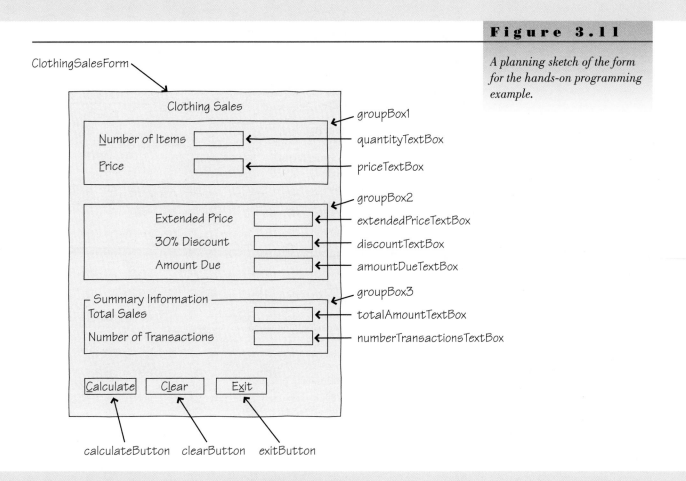

ClothingSalesForm

Clothing Sales

groupBox1

Number of Items — quantityTextBox

Price — priceTextBox

groupBox2

Extended Price — extendedPriceTextBox

30% Discount — discountTextBox

Amount Due — amountDueTextBox

groupBox3

Summary Information
Total Sales — totalAmountTextBox

Number of Transactions — numberTransactionsTextBox

Calculate   Clear   Exit

calculateButton   clearButton   exitButton

Note: The ToolTips have not been added to the planning forms. Make up and add your own.

Object	Property	Setting
ClothingSalesForm	Name	ClothingSalesForm
	Text	Look Sharp Fitness Center
	AcceptButton	calculateButton
	CancelButton	clearButton
label1	Text	Clothing Sales
groupBox1	Text	(blank)
label2	Text	&Number of Items
quantityTextBox	Name	quantityTextBox
label3	Text	&Price
priceTextBox	Name	priceTextBox
groupBox2	Text	(blank)
label4	Text	Extended Price

Object	Property	Setting
extendedPriceTextBox	Name	extendedPriceTextBox
	TextAlign	Right
	ReadOnly	True
	TabStop	False
label5	Text	30% Discount
discountTextBox	Name	discountTextBox
	TextAlign	Right
	ReadOnly	True
	TabStop	False
label6	Text	Amount Due
amountDueTextBox	Name	amountDueTextBox
	TextAlign	Right
	ReadOnly	True
	TabStop	False
groupBox3	Text	Summary Information
label7	Text	Total Sales
totalAmountTextBox	Name	totalAmountTextBox
	TextAlign	Right
	ReadOnly	True
	TabStop	False
label8	Text	Number of Transactions
numberTransactionsTextBox	Name	numberTransactionsTextBox
	TextAlign	Right
	ReadOnly	True
	TabStop	False
calculateButton	Name	calculateButton
	Text	&Calculate
clearButton	Name	clearButton
	Text	C&lear
exitButton	Name	exitButton
	Text	E&xit

Plan the Event-Handling Methods The planning that you did for the previous example will save you time now. The only method that requires more steps is the calculateButton_Click event handler.

Event Handler	Actions—Pseudocode

calculateButton_Click	Declare the variables.
	try
	      Convert the input Quantity to numeric.
	      try
	            Convert the input Price to numeric.
	            Calculate Extended Price = Quantity * Price.
	            Calculate Discount = Extended Price * Discount Rate.
	            Calculate Discounted Price = Extended Price − Discount.

Calculate the summary values:
    Add Amount Due to Total Amount.
    Add 1 to Sale Count.
Format and display sale output.
Format and display summary values.
catch any Quantity exception
    Display error message and reset the focus to Quantity.
catch any Price exception
    Display error message and reset the focus to Price.

clearButton_Click	Clear each text box except Summary fields. Set the focus in the first text box.
exitButton_Click	Exit the project.

Write the Project Following the sketch in Figure 3.11, create the form. Figure 3.12 shows the completed form.

- Set the properties of each of the objects, as you have planned.

- Write the code. Working from the pseudocode, write each event-handling method.

- When you complete the code, use a variety of test data to thoroughly test the project. Test with nonnumeric data and blank entries.

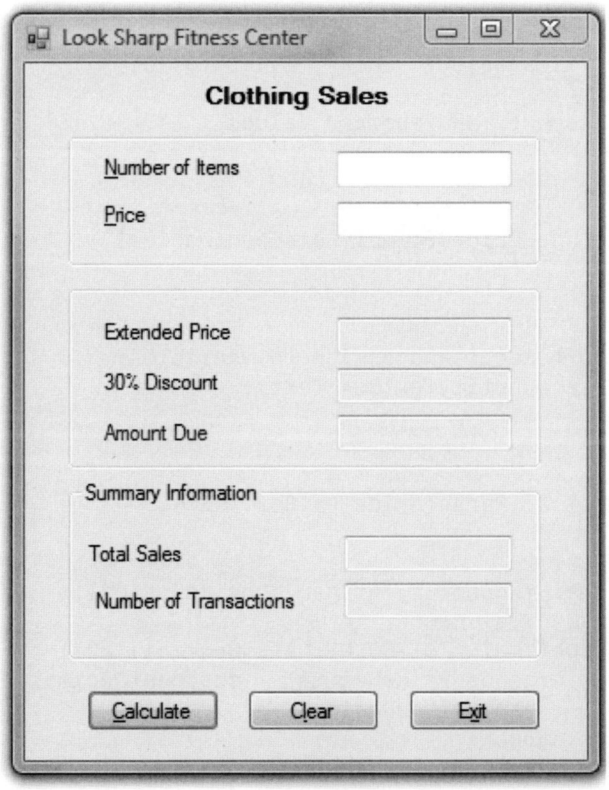

Figure 3.12

The form for the hands-on programming example.

The Project Coding Solution

```csharp
/*Project:      Ch03HandsOn
 *Date:         June 2009
 *Programmer:   Bradley/Millspaugh
 *Description:  This project inputs sales information for clothing.
 *                 It calculates the extended price and discount for
 *                    a sale.
 *                 Uses variables, constants, and calculations.
 *                 Includes error trapping and summary calculations.
 */
using System;
using System.Collections.Generic;
using System.ComponentModel;
using System.Data;
using System.Drawing;
using System.Text;
using System.Windows.Forms;

namespace Ch03ClothingSales
{
    public partial class ClothingSalesForm : Form
    {
        // Declare the constant and summary variables.
        private const decimal DISCOUNT_RATE_Decimal = 0.3m;
        private decimal totalAmountDecimal;
        private int numberTransactionsInteger;

        public ClothingSalesForm()
        {
            InitializeComponent();
        }

        private void calculateButton_Click(object sender, EventArgs e)
        {
            // Calculate the sale, discount, and summary values.

            // Declare the variables.
            int quantityInteger;
            decimal priceDecimal, extendedPriceDecimal, discountDecimal,
                amountDueDecimal;
        try
        {
            // Convert input values to numeric and assign to variables.
            quantityInteger = int.Parse(quantityTextBox.Text);

                try
                {
                    priceDecimal = decimal.Parse(priceTextBox.Text);

                    // Calculate values.
                    extendedPriceDecimal = quantityInteger * priceDecimal;
                    discountDecimal = Decimal.Round(
                        (extendedPriceDecimal * DISCOUNT_RATE_Decimal), 2);
                    amountDueDecimal = extendedPriceDecimal - discountDecimal;
                    totalAmountDecimal += amountDueDecimal;
                    numberTransactionsInteger++;
```

```
                    // Format and display answers.
                    extendedPriceTextBox.Text = extendedPriceDecimal.ToString("C");
                    discountTextBox.Text = discountDecimal.ToString("N");
                    amountDueTextBox.Text = amountDueDecimal.ToString("C");

                    // Format and display summary information.
                    totalAmountTextBox.Text = totalAmountDecimal.ToString("C");
                    numberTransactionsTextBox.Text =
                        numberTransactionsInteger.ToString();
                }
                catch
                {
                    // Invalid price.
                    MessageBox.Show("Invalid price.", "Data Error");
                    priceTextBox.Focus();
                    priceTextBox.SelectAll();
                }
            }
            catch
            {

                // Invalid quantity.
                MessageBox.Show("Invalid quantity.", "Data Error");
                quantityTextBox.Focus();
                quantityTextBox.SelectAll();
            }
        }

        private void clearButton_Click(object sender, EventArgs e)
        {
            // Clear the text boxes.

            quantityTextBox.Clear();
            priceTextBox.Clear();
            discountTextBox.Clear();
            extendedPriceTextBox.Clear();
            amountDueTextBox.Clear();
            quantityTextBox.Focus();
        }

        private void exitButton_Click(object sender, EventArgs e)
        {
            // End the program.

            this.Close();
        }
    }
}
```

Summary

1. Variables are temporary memory locations that have a name (called an *identifier*), a data type, and a scope. A constant also has a name, data type, and scope, but it also must have a value assigned to it. The value stored in a variable can be changed during the execution of the project; the values stored in constants cannot change.

2. The data type determines what type of values may be assigned to a variable or constant. The most common data types are string, int, decimal, single, and bool.

3. Identifiers for variables and constants must follow the C# naming rules and should follow good naming standards, called *conventions*. An identifier should be meaningful and have the data type appended at the end. Variable names should begin with a lowercase character and be mixed upper- and lowercase while constants are all uppercase.

4. Identifiers should include the data type of the variable or constant.

5. Intrinsic constants, such as Color.Red and Color.Blue, are predefined and built into the .NET Framework. Named constants are programmer-defined constants and are declared using the `const` statement. The location of the `const` statement determines the scope of the constant.

6. The location of the declaration statement determines the scope of the variable. Use the data type without the `private` or `public` keyword to declare local variables inside a method; declare class-level variables at the top of the class, outside of any method; you can use the `private` keyword to declare class-level variables.

7. The scope of a variable may be namespace, class level, local, or block level. Block level and local variables are available only within the method in which they are declared; class-level variables are accessible in all methods within a class; namespace variables are available in all methods of all classes in a namespace, which is usually the entire project.

8. The lifetime of local and block-level variables is one execution of the method in which they are declared. The lifetime of class-level variables is the length of time that the class is loaded.

9. Use the `Parse` methods to convert text values to numeric before performing any calculations.

10. Calculations may be performed using the values of numeric variables, constants, and the properties of controls. The result of a calculation may be assigned to a numeric variable or to the property of a control.

11. A calculation operation with more than one operator follows the order of precedence in determining the result of the calculation. Parentheses alter the order of operations.

12. To explicitly convert between numeric data types, use casting or the Convert class. Some conversions can be performed implicitly.

13. The `decimal.Round` method rounds a decimal value to the specified number of decimal positions.

14. The `ToString` method can be used to specify the appearance of values for display. By using formatting codes, you can specify dollar signs, commas, percent signs, and the number of decimal digits to display. The method rounds values to fit the format.

15. `try`/`catch`/`finally` statements provide a method for checking for user errors such as blank or nonnumeric data or an entry that might result in a calculation error.

16. A run-time error is called an *exception*; catching and taking care of exceptions is called *exception handling*.

17. You can trap for different types of errors by specifying the exception type on the `catch` statement, and you can have multiple `catch` statements to catch more than one type of exception. Each exception is an instance of the Exception class; you can refer to the properties of the Exception object for further information.

18. A message box is a window for displaying information to the user.

19. The Show method of the MessageBox class is overloaded, which means that the method may be called with different argument lists, called *signatures*.

20. You can calculate a sum by adding each transaction to a class-level variable. In a similar fashion, you can calculate a count by adding to a class-level variable.

Key Terms

argument *119*

assignment operator *123*

block variable *116*

casting *126*

class-level variable *116*

constant *108*

data type *109*

declaration *109*

decrement operator *124*

exception *136*

explicit conversion *126*

format *128*

format specifier codes *128*

identifier *108*

implicit conversion *125*

increment operator *124*

intrinsic constant *113*

lifetime *116*

local variable *116*

MessageBox *138*

named constant *108*

namespace variable *116*

nested try/catch
   block *141*

order of precedence *122*

overloading *140*

postfix notation *125*

prefix notation *124*

scope *116*

Show method *138*

signature *140*

string literal *113*

try/catch block *136*

variable *108*

Review Questions

1. Name and give the purpose of five data types available in C#.

2. What does *declaring a variable* mean?

3. What effect does the location of a declaration statement have on the variable it declares?

4. Explain the difference between a constant and a variable.

5. What is the purpose of the int.Parse method? The decimal.Parse method?

6. Explain the order of precedence of operators for calculations.

7. What statement(s) can be used to declare a variable?

8. Explain how to make an interest rate stored in rateDecimal display in rateTextBox as a percentage with three decimal digits.

9. What are implicit conversions? explicit conversions? When would each be used?

10. When should you use try/catch blocks? Why?

11. What is a message box and when should you use one?

12. Explain why the MessageBox.Show method has multiple signatures.

13. Why must you use class-level variables if you want to accumulate a running total of transactions?

Programming Exercises

3.1 In retail sales, management needs to know the average inventory figure and the turnover of merchandise. Create a project that allows the user to enter the beginning inventory, the ending inventory, and the cost of goods sold.

Form: Include labeled text boxes for the beginning inventory, the ending inventory, and the cost of goods sold. After calculating the answers, display the average inventory and the turnover formatted in text boxes.

Include buttons for *Calculate*, *Clear*, *Print*, and *Exit*. The formulas for the calculations are

$$\text{Average inventory} = \frac{\text{Beginning inventory} + \text{Ending inventory}}{2}$$

$$\text{Turnover} = \frac{\text{Cost of goods sold}}{\text{Average inventory}}$$

Note: The average inventory is expressed in dollars; the turnover is the number of times the inventory turns over.

Code: Include methods for the click event of each button. Display the results in text boxes. Format the average inventory as currency and the turnover as a number with one digit to the right of the decimal. Make sure to catch any bad input data and display a message to the user.

Test Data

Beginning	Ending	Cost of goods sold	Average inventory	Turnover
58500	47000	40000	$52,750.00	.8
75300	13600	51540	44,450.00	1.2
3000	19600	4800	11,300.00	.4

3.2 A local recording studio rents its facilities for $200 per hour. Management charges only for the number of minutes used. Create a project in which the input is the name of the group and the number of minutes it used the studio. Your program calculates the appropriate charges, accumulates the total charges for all groups, and computes the average charge and the number of groups that used the studio.

Form: Use labeled text boxes for the name of the group and the number of minutes used. The charges for the current group should be displayed formatted in a text box. Create a group box for the summary information. Inside the group box, display the total charges for all groups, the number of groups, and the average charge per group. Format all output appropriately. Include buttons for *Calculate*, *Clear*, *Print*, and *Exit*.

Code: Use a constant for the rental rate per hour; divide that by 60 to get the rental rate per minute. Do not allow bad input data to cancel the program.

Test Data

Group	Minutes
Pooches	95
Hounds	5
Mutts	480

Check Figures

Total charges for group	Total number of groups	Average charge	Total charges for all groups
$316.67	1	$316.67	$316.67
$16.67	2	$166.67	$333.33
$1,600.00	3	$644.44	$1,933.33

3.3   Create a project that determines the future value of an investment at a given interest rate for a given number of years. The formula for the calculation is

Future value = Investment amount * (1 + Interest rate) ^ Years

Form: Use labeled text boxes for the amount of investment, the interest rate (as a decimal fraction), and the number of years the investment will be held. Display the future value in a text box formatted as currency.

Include buttons for *Calculate*, *Clear*, *Print*, and *Exit*. Format all dollar amounts. Display a message to the user for nonnumeric or missing input data.

Test Data

Amount	Rate	Years
2000.00	.15	5
1234.56	.075	3

| Check Figures

Hint: You must use the Math.Pow method for exponentiation (the ^ in the formula). The Math.Pow method operates only on double data types, so you must cast values of any other data type to double. You can refer to Appendix B for the Math methods. Additionally, Chapter 5 has an example that uses the Pow method in the section titled "Writing a Method with Multiple Arguments."

3.4   Write a project that calculates the shipping charge for a package if the shipping rate is $0.12 per ounce.

Form: Use labeled text boxes for the package-identification code (a six-digit code) and the weight of the package—one box for pounds and another one for ounces. Use a text box to display the shipping charge.

Include buttons for *Calculate*, *Clear*, *Print*, and *Exit*.

Code: Include event-handling methods for each button. Use a constant for the shipping rate, calculate the shipping charge, and display it formatted in a text box. Display a message to the user for any bad input data.

Calculation hint: There are 16 ounces in a pound.

ID	Weight	Shipping Charge
L5496P	0 lb. 5 oz.	$0.60
J1955K	2 lb. 0 oz.	$3.84
Z0000Z	1 lb. 1 oz.	$2.04

3.5   Create a project for the local car rental agency that calculates rental charges. The agency charges $15 per day plus $0.12 per mile.

Form: Use text boxes for the customer name, address, city, state, Zip code, beginning odometer reading, ending odometer reading, and the number of days the car was used. Use text boxes to display the miles driven and the total charge. Format the output appropriately.

Include buttons for *Calculate*, *Clear*, *Print*, and *Exit*.

Code: Include an event-handling method for each button. For the calculation, subtract the beginning odometer reading from the ending odometer reading to get the number of miles traveled. Use a constant for the $15 per day charge and the $0.12 mileage rate. Display a message to the user for any bad input data.

3.6   Create a project that will input an employee's sales and calculate the gross pay, deductions, and net pay. Each employee will receive a base pay of $900 plus a sales commission of 6 percent of sales.

After calculating the net pay, calculate the budget amount for each category based on the percentages given.

Pay

Base pay	$900; use a named constant
Commission	6% of sales
Gross pay	Sum of base pay and commission
Deductions	18% of gross pay
Net pay	Gross pay minus deductions

Budget

Housing	30% of net pay
Food and clothing	15% of net pay
Entertainment	50% of net pay
Miscellaneous	5% of net pay

Form: Use text boxes to input the employee's name and the dollar amount of the sales. Use text boxes to display the results of the calculations.

Provide buttons for *Calculate*, *Clear*, *Print*, and *Exit*. Display a message to the user for any bad input data.

Case Studies

Custom Supplies Mail Order

The company has instituted a bonus program to give its employees an incentive to sell more. For every dollar the store makes in a four-week period, the employees receive 2 percent of sales. The amount of bonus each employee receives is based on the percentage of hours he or she worked during the bonus period (a total of 160 hours).

The screen will allow the user to enter the employee's name, the total hours worked, and the amount of the store's total sales. The amount of sales needs to be entered only for the first employee. (*Hint*: Don't clear it.)

The *Calculate* button will determine the bonus earned by this employee, and the *Clear* button will clear only the name, hours-worked, and bonus amount fields. A *Print* button allows the user to print the form. Do not allow missing or bad input data to cancel the program; instead display a message to the user.

Christopher's Car Center

Salespeople for used cars are compensated using a commission system. The commission is based on the costs incurred for the vehicle.

Commission = Commission rate *
(Sales price − Cost value)

The form will allow the user to enter the salesperson's name, the selling price of the vehicle, and the cost value of the vehicle. Use a constant of 20 percent for the commission rate.

The *Calculate* button will determine the commission earned by the salesperson; the *Clear* button will clear the text boxes. A *Print* button allows the user to print the form. Do not allow bad input data to cancel the program; instead, display a message to the user.

Xtreme Cinema

Design and code a project to calculate the amount due and provide a summary of rentals. All movies rent for $4.50 and all customers receive a 10 percent discount.

The form should contain input for the member number and the number of movies rented. Inside a group box, display the rental amount, the 10 percent discount, and the amount due. Inside a second group box, display the number of customers served and the total rental income (after discount).

Include buttons for *Calculate*, *Clear*, *Print*, and *Exit*. The *Clear* button clears the information for the current rental but does not clear the summary information. Do not allow bad input data to cancel the program; instead, display a message to the user.

Cool Boards

Cool Boards rents snowboards during the snow season. A person can rent a snowboard without boots or with boots. Create a project that will calculate and display the information for each customer's rentals. In addition, calculate the summary information for each day's rentals.

For each rental, input the person's name, the driver's license or ID number, the number of snowboards, and the number of snowboards with boots. Snowboards without boots rent for $20; snowboards with boots rent for $30.

Calculate and display the charges for snowboards and snowboards with boots, and the rental total. In addition, maintain summary totals. Use constants for the snowboard rental rate and the snowboard with boots rental rate.

Create a summary frame with boxes to indicate the day's totals for the number of snowboards and snowboards with boots rented, total charges, and average charge per customer.

Include buttons for *Calculate Order*, *Clear*, *Clear All*, *Print*, and *Exit*. The *Clear All* button should clear the summary totals to begin a new day's summary. *Hint*: You must set each of the summary variables to zero as well as clear the summary boxes.

Make your buttons easy to use for keyboard entry. Make the *Calculate* button the Accept button and the *Clear* button the Cancel button.

Do not allow bad input data to cancel the program; instead, display a message to the user.

4

Decisions and Conditions

1. Use if statements to control the flow of logic.

2. Understand and use nested if statements.

3. Read and create action diagrams that illustrate the logic in a selection process.

4. Evaluate Boolean expressions using the relational or comparison operators.

5. Combine expressions using logical operators && (and), || (or), and ! (not).

6. Test the Checked property of radio buttons and check boxes.

7. Perform validation on numeric fields using if statements.

8. Use a switch structure for multiple decisions.

9. Use one event handler to respond to the events for multiple controls.

10. Call an event handler from other methods.

11. Create message boxes with multiple buttons and choose alternate actions based on the user response.

12. Debug projects using breakpoints, stepping program execution, and displaying intermediate results.

In this chapter, you will learn to write applications that can take one action or another, based on a condition. For example, you may need to keep track of sales separately for different classes of employees, different sections of the country, or different departments. You also will learn alternate techniques for checking the validity of input data and how to display multiple buttons in a message box and take different actions depending on the user response.

if Statements

A powerful capability of the computer is its ability to make decisions and to take alternate courses of action based on the outcome.

A decision made by the computer is formed as a question: Is a given condition true or false? If it is true, do one thing; if it is false, do something else.

if *the sun is shining*	(condition)
go to the beach	(action to take if condition is true)
else	
go to class	(action to take if condition is false)
(See Figure 4.1.)	

or

if *you don't succeed*	(condition)
try, try again	(action)
(See Figure 4.2.)	

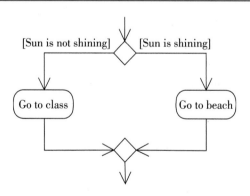

Figure 4.1

The logic of an if/else *statement in Unified Modeling Language (UML) activity diagram form.*

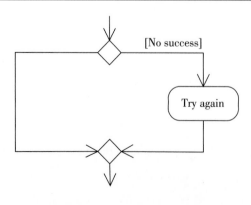

Figure 4.2

The logic of an if *statement without an* else *action in UML activity diagram form.*

Notice in the second example that no action is specified if the condition is not true.

In an **if statement,** when the condition is *true,* only the statement following the if is executed. When the condition is *false,* only the statement following the else clause, if present, is executed. You can use a block (braces) to include multiple statements in the if or else portion of the statement. Although not required, it is considered good programming practice to always use braces, even when you have only one statement for the if or else.

if Statement—General Form

```
if (condition)
{
    // Statement(s)
}
[else
{
    // Statements(s)
}]
```

Only the first statement following an if or an else is considered a part of the statement unless you create a block of statements using braces. Notice that the if and else statements do not have semicolons. If you accidentally place a semicolon after the if or else, that terminates the statement and any statement(s) following will execute unconditionally.

The statements under the if and else clauses are indented for readability and clarity.

if Statement—Examples

When the number of units in unitsDecimal is less than 32, select the radio button for Freshman; otherwise, make sure the radio button is deselected (see Figure 4.3). Remember that when a radio button is selected, the Checked property has a Boolean value of *true.*

```
unitsDecimal = decimal.Parse(unitsTextBox.Text);
if (unitsDecimal < 32m)
{
    freshmanRadioButton.Checked = true;
}
else
{
    freshmanRadioButton.Checked = false;
}
```

When you type an if statement and press Enter, the editor places the insertion point on a blank line, indented from the if. If you have multiple statements on either the if or the else, you must place those statements in braces; otherwise, only the first statement belongs to the if. The editor properly places the

Figure 4.3

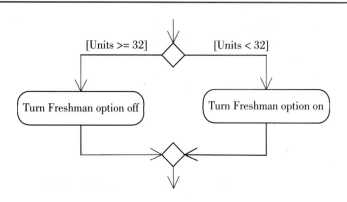

braces directly under the if or else when you type the brace at the position of the insertion point on the blank line.

Charting if Statements

A Unified Modeling Language (UML) activity diagram is a useful tool for showing the logic of an if statement. It has been said that one picture is worth a thousand words. Many programmers find that a diagram helps them organize their thoughts and design projects more quickly.

The UML specification includes several types of diagrams. The activity diagram is a visual planning tool for decisions and actions for an entire application or a single method. The diamond-shape symbol (called a *decision symbol*) represents a condition. The branches from the decision symbol indicate which path to take for different results of the decision (Figure 4.4).

Figure 4.4

The UML activity diagram symbols used for program decisions and activities.

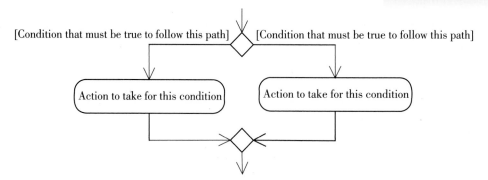

Boolean Expressions

The test in an if statement is a **Boolean expression**, which evaluates as *true* or *false*. To form Boolean expressions, also referred to as **conditions**, you use **relational operators** (Table 4.1), also called **comparison operators**. The comparison is evaluated and the result is either *true* or *false*.

Boolean expressions can be formed with numeric variables and constants, string variables and constants, object properties, and arithmetic expressions.

The Relational Operators

Table 4.1

Symbol	Relation tested	Examples
>	greater than	`decimal.Parse(amountTextBox.Text) > limitDecimal` `correctInteger > 75`
<	less than	`int.Parse(salesTextBox.Text) < 10000` `saleDecimal < limitDecimal`
==	equal to	`passwordTextBox.Text == "101"` `nameTextBox.Text == nameString`
!=	not equal to	`freshmanRadioButton.Checked != true` `nameTextBox.Text != ""`
>=	greater than or equal to	`int.Parse(quantityTextBox.Text) >= 500`
<=	less than or equal to	`countInteger <= maximumInteger`

However, it is important to note that comparisons must be made on like types; that is, strings can be compared only to other strings, and numeric values can be compared only to other numeric values, whether a variable, constant, property, or arithmetic expression.

Comparing Numeric Variables and Constants

When numeric values are involved in a test, an algebraic comparison is made; that is, the sign of the number is taken into account. Therefore, negative 20 is less than 10, and negative 2 is less than negative 1.

In a comparison, the double equal sign is used to test for equality. An equal sign (=) means replacement in an assignment statement. For example, the Boolean expression in the statement

TIP

If you accidentally use an = (assignment) instead of an == (equal to) operator in a comparison, the compiler generates an error. ■

```
if (decimal.Parse(priceTextBox.Text) == maximumDecimal)
```

means "Is the current numeric value stored in priceTextBox.Text equal to the value stored in maximumDecimal?"

Sample Comparisons

alphaInteger	bravoInteger	charlieInteger
5	4	–5

Boolean expression	Evaluates
`alphaInteger == bravoInteger`	*false*
`charlieInteger < 0`	*true*
`bravoInteger > alphaInteger`	*false*
`charlieInteger <= bravoInteger`	*true*
`alphaInteger >= 5`	*true*
`alphaInteger != charlieInteger`	*true*

Comparing Character Data

You can use the relational operators to compare character data stored in the char data type. As you recall, char variables hold only a single character. The determination of which character is less than another is based on the code used to store characters internally in the computer. C# stores characters using the 16-bit Unicode, which is designed to hold characters in any language, such as Japanese and Chinese. However, the Latin alphabet, numerals, and punctuation have the same values in Unicode as they do in the **ANSI code,** which is the most common coding method used for microcomputers. ANSI has an established order (called the *collating sequence*) for all letters, numbers, and special characters. Note in Table 4.2 that the uppercase letters are lower than the lowercase letters, and all numeric digits are less than all letters. Some special symbols are lower than the numbers and some are higher, and the blank space is lower than the rest of the characters shown.

You can compare a char variable to a literal, another char variable, an escape sequence, or the code number. You can enclose char literals in single or double quotes, which then compares to the value of the literal. Without the quote, you are comparing to the code number (from the code chart).

TIP

Although the editor helps you indent properly as you enter an if statement, when you modify code, the indentation can get messed up. Take the time to fix any indentation errors—you will save yourself debugging time and the indentation helps to visualize the intended logic. You can use *Edit / Advanced / Format Document* or *Format Selection* to reformat automatically. ■

```
(sexChar == 'F')    // Compare to the uppercase letter 'F'.
(codeChar != '\0')  // Compare to a null character (character 0).
(codeChar == '9')   // Compare to the digit 9.
(codeChar == 9)     // Compare to the ANSI code 9 (the Tab character).
```

Selected ANSI Codes   T a b l e   4 . 2

Code	Value	Code	Value	Code	Value
0	Null	38	&	60	<
8	Backspace	39	'	61	=
9	Tab	40	(	62	>
10	Linefeed	41	)	63	?
12	Formfeed	42	*	64	@
13	Carriage return	43	+	65–90	A–Z
27	Escape	44	,	91	[
32	Space	45	-	92	\
33	!	46	.	93	]
34	"	47	/	94	^
35	#	48–57	0–9	95	_
36	$	58	:	96	`
37	%	59	;	97–122	a–z

Examples

```
char upperCaseChar = 'C';
char lowerCaseChar = 'c';
```

The expression (`lowerCaseChar > upperCaseChar`) is *true* because the ANSI code for `'C'` is 67, while the code for `'c'` is 99.

```
char questionMarkChar = '?';
char exclamationChar = '!';
```

The expression (`questionMarkChar < exclamationChar`) is *false* because the ANSI code for `'?'` is 63 while the ANSI code for `'!'` is 33.

Comparing Strings

You can use the equal to (`==`) and not equal to (`!=`) relational operators for comparing strings. The comparison begins with the leftmost character and proceeds one character at a time from left to right. As soon as a character in one string is not equal to the corresponding character in the second string, the comparison is terminated and the Boolean expression returns *false*.

Example

```
string name1String = "Joan";
string name2String = "John";
```

The expression

```
if (name1String == name2String)
```

evaluates to *false*. The a in Joan is lower ranking than the h in John. However, when you need to compare for *less than* or *greater than*, such as arranging strings alphabetically, you cannot use the relational operators, but you *can* use the `CompareTo` method.

The CompareTo Method

Use the `CompareTo` method to determine *less than* or *greater than*. The `CompareTo` method returns an integer with one of three possible values.

```
aString.CompareTo(bString)
```

If the two strings are equal, the method returns zero; when aString is greater than bString, a positive number returns. A negative number is returned when bString is greater than aString. To use this method effectively, you can set up a condition using the return value and a relational operator.

```
if (aString.CompareTo(bString) == 0) // Are the strings equal?
if (aString.CompareTo(bString) != 0) // Are the strings different?
if (aString.CompareTo(bString) > 0)  // Is aString greater than bString?
```

Example

```
string word1String = "Hope";
string word2String = "Hopeless";
// Compare the strings.
if (word1String.CompareTo(word2String) < 0)
    // Display a message -- What will it be?
```

Will the result of the preceding comparison test be *true* or *false*? Before reading any further, stop and figure it out.

Ready? When one string is shorter than the other, the comparison proceeds as if the shorter string is padded with blanks to the right of the string, and the blank space is compared to a character in the longer string. So in the `CompareTo` method, `"Hope"` is less than `"Hopeless"`, the method returns a negative number, and the condition is *true*.

Example

```
string car1String = "300ZX";
string car2String = "Porsche";
```

The expression

```
if (car1String.CompareTo(car2String) > 0)
```

evaluates *false*. When the number 3 is compared to the letter P, the 3 is lower—all numbers are lower than all letters. The `CompareTo` method returns a negative number and the comparison is *false*.

Feedback 4.1

count1Integer	count2Integer	count3Integer	word1TextBox.Text	word2TextBox.Text
5	5	−5	"Bit"	"bit"

Determine which Boolean expressions will evaluate *true* and which ones will evaluate *false*.

1. `count1Integer >= count2Integer`
2. `count3Integer < 0`
3. `count3Integer < count2Integer`
4. `count1Integer != count2Integer`
5. `count1Integer + 2 > count2Integer + 2`
6. `word1TextBox.Text == word2TextBox.Text`
7. `word1TextBox.Text != ""`
8. `word1TextBox.Text == "bit"`
9. `"2" != "Two"`
10. `'$' <= '?'`
11. `word1TextBox.Text.CompareTo(word2TextBox.Text) > 0`

Testing for True or False

You can use shortcuts when testing for *true* or *false*. C# evaluates the expression in an `if` statement. If the condition is a Boolean variable or property, it holds the values *true* or *false*.

Example

```
if (blueRadioButton.Checked == true)
```

is equivalent to

```
if (blueRadioButton.Checked)
```

Comparing Uppercase and Lowercase Characters

When comparing strings, the case of the characters is important. An uppercase *Y* is not equal to a lowercase *y*. Because the user may type a name or word in uppercase, in lowercase, or as a combination of cases, we must check user input for all possibilities. The best way is to use the **ToUpper** and **ToLower** **methods** of the string class, which return the uppercase or lowercase equivalent of a string, respectively.

The ToUpper and ToLower Methods—General Form

```
TextString.ToUpper()
TextString.ToLower()
```

The ToUpper and ToLower Methods—Examples

nameTextBox.Text Value	nameTextBox.Text.ToUpper()	nameTextBox.Text.ToLower()
Richard	RICHARD	richard
PROGRAMMING	PROGRAMMING	programming
Robert Jones	ROBERT JONES	robert jones
hello	HELLO	hello

An example of a Boolean expression using the `ToUpper` method follows.

```
if (nameTextBox.Text.ToUpper() == "PROGRAMMING")
{
    // Do something.
}
```

Note that when you convert nameTextBox.Text to uppercase, you must compare it to an uppercase literal ("PROGRAMMING") if you want it to evaluate as *true*.

Compound Boolean Expressions

You can use **compound Boolean expressions** to test more than one condition. Create compound expressions by joining conditions with **logical operators**, which compare each expression and return a boolean result. The logical operators are || (or), && (and), and ! (not).

Logical operator	Meaning	Example	Explanation
|| (or)	If one expression or both expressions are *true*, the entire expression is *true*.	`int.Parse(numberLabel.Text) == 1 ||` `  int.Parse(numberLabel.Text) == 2`	Evaluates *true* when numberLabel.Text is either "1" or "2".
&& (and)	Both expressions must be *true* for the entire expression to be *true*.	`int.Parse(numberTextBox.Text) > 0 &&` `  int.Parse(numberTextBox.Text) < 10`	Evaluates *true* when numberTextBox.Text is "1", "2", "3", "4", "5", "6", "7", "8", or "9".
! (not)	Reverses the Boolean expression so that a *true* expression will evaluate *false* and vice versa.	`! foundBool`	Evaluates *true* when the Boolean value is *false*.

Compound Boolean Expression Examples

```
if (maleRadioButton.Checked && int.Parse(ageTextBox.Text) < 21)
{
    minorMaleCountInteger++;
}
if (juniorRadioButton.Checked || seniorRadioButton.Checked)
{
    upperClassmanInteger++;
}
```

The first example requires that both the radio button test and the age test be *true* for the count to be incremented. In the second example, only one of the conditions must be true.

One caution when using compound Boolean expressions: Each side of the logical operator must be a complete expression. For example,

```
countInteger > 10 || < 0
```

is incorrect. Instead, it must be

```
countInteger > 10 || countInteger < 0
```

Combining Logical Operators

You can create compound Boolean expressions that combine multiple && and ||
conditions. When you have both an && and an ||, the && is evaluated before
the ||. However, you can change the order of evaluation by using parentheses;
any expression inside parentheses will be evaluated first.

For example, will the following condition evaluate *true* or *false*? Try it with
various values for saleDecimal, discountRadioButton, and stateTextBox.Text.

```
if (saleDecimal > 1000.0m || discountRadioButton.Checked &&
    stateTextBox.Text.ToUpper() != "CA" )
{
    // Code here to calculate the discount.
}
```

saleDecimal	discountRadioButton.Checked	stateTextBox.Text.ToUpper	Evaluates
1500.0	*false*	CA	*true*
1000.0	*true*	OH	*true*
1000.0	*true*	CA	*false*
1500.0	*true*	NY	*true*
1000.0	*false*	CA	*false*

Short-Circuit Operations

When evaluating a compound Boolean expression, sometimes the second ex-
pression is never evaluated. If a compound expression has an || and the first
expression evaluates *true*, there is no reason to evaluate the second expression.
For example, if you have the condition

```
totalInteger < 0 || totalInteger > 10
```

and totalInteger = −1 (negative 1), as soon as the first expression is tested, the
entire expression is deemed *true* and the comparison stops, called **short
circuiting** the operation. Likewise, if you have a compound expression with an
&& and the first expression evaluates *false*, there is no reason to evaluate the
second expression.

```
countInteger >= 0 && countInteger <= 10
```

If countInteger = −1, the first expression is evaluated *false* and the comparison
stops.

Most of the time you don't care whether it evaluates both expressions or not. But sometimes the result may not be what you expected. For example, consider the condition

```
amountInteger > 0 && balanceDecimal++ < limitDecimal
```

When amountInteger is less than or equal to 0, the first condition is *false* and there is no need to evaluate the second expression. This may have some surprising results: if you were performing an increment in the second expression, the increment may never occur.

If you need to have both comparisons made, you can avoid short circuiting by using a single comparison operator, rather than the double operator.

And—Short circuit	And—Regular (forces comparison to occur)	Or—Short circuit	Or—Regular (forces comparison to occur)
&&	&	||	|

The following condition forces the second condition to be tested, even when the first condition is *false*, and so guarantees that the increment operator is processed.

```
amountInteger > 0 & balanceDecimal++ < limitDecimal
```

Nested if Statements

In many situations, another `if` statement is one of the statements to be executed when a condition tests *true* or *false*. An `if` statement that contains additional `if` statements is said to be a **nested if** statement. The following example shows a nested `if` statement in which the second `if` occurs in the *true* result of the first `if` (Figure 4.5).

```
if (tempInteger > 32)
{
    if (tempInteger > 80)
    {
        commentLabel.Text =  "Hot";
    }
    else
    {
        commentLabel.Text = "Moderate";
    }
}
else
{
    commentLabel.Text = "Freezing";
{
```

To nest `if` statements in the `else` portion, you may use either of the following approaches; however, your code is simpler if you use the second method (using `else if`).

Figure 4.5

Diagramming a nested if *statement.*

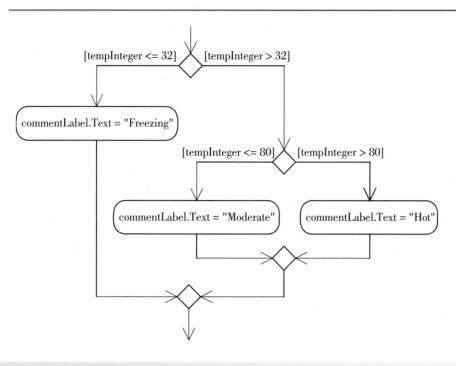

```
if (tempInteger <= 32)
{
    commentLabel.Text = "Freezing";
}
else
{
    if (tempInteger > 80)
    {
        commentLabel.Text = "Hot";
    }
    else
    {
        commentLabel.Text = "Moderate";
    }
}
```

This code has the same logic but uses an else if:

```
if (tempInteger <= 32)
{
    commentLabel.Text = "Freezing";
}
else if (tempInteger > 80)
{
    commentLabel.Text = "Hot";
}
else
{
    commentLabel.Text = "Moderate";
}
```

You can nest ifs in both the *true* block and the else block. In fact, you may continue to nest ifs within ifs (Figure 4.6). However, projects become very difficult to follow (and may not perform as intended) when `if`s become too deeply nested.

Figure 4.6

A diagram of a nested `if` statement with `if`s nested on both sides of the original `if`.

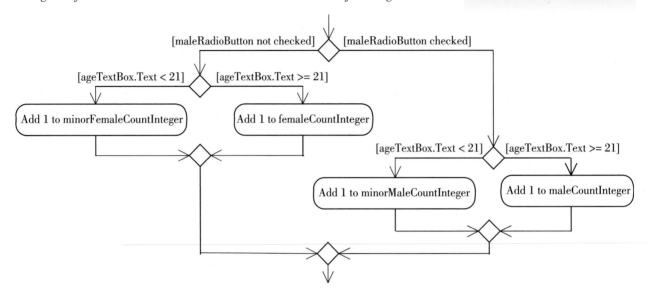

```
if (maleRadioButton.Checked)
{
    if (int.Parse(ageTextBox.Text) < 21)
    {
        minorMaleCountInteger++;
    }
    else
    {
        maleCountInteger++;
    }
}
else
{
    if (int.Parse(ageTextBox.Text) < 21)
    {
        minorFemaleCountInteger++;
    }
    else
    {
        femaleCountInteger++;
    }
}
```

Coding an else if

When you need to write another `if` in the `else` portion of the original `if` statement, you can choose the spacing. You can place the second (nested) `if` on a line by itself or on the same line as the `else`. You can choose to write the preceding nested `if` statement this way:

```
if (maleRadioButton.Checked)
{
    if (int.Parse(ageTextBox.Text) < 21)
    {
        minorMaleCountInteger++;
    }
    else
    {
        maleCountInteger++;
    }
}
else if (int.Parse(ageTextBox.Text) < 21)
{
    minorFemaleCountInteger++;
}
else
{
    femaleCountInteger++;
}
```

Notice that the indentation changes when you write else if on one line, and the logic of the entire nested if may not be quite as clear. Most programmers code else if on one line when they must test multiple conditions.

```
if (twelveOunceRadioButton.Checked)
{
    itemPriceDecimal = 3m;
}
else if (sixteenOunceRadioButton.Checked)
{
    itemPriceDecimal = 3.5m;
}
else if (twentyOunceRadioButton.Checked)
{
    itemPriceDecimal = 4m;
else
{
    MessageBox.Show("Select the desired size", "Required Entry");
}
```

Feedback 4.2

Assume that frogsInteger = 10, toadsInteger = 5, and polliwogsInteger = 6. What will be displayed for each of the following statements?

```
1. if (frogsInteger > polliwogsInteger)
   {
       frogsRadioButton.Checked = true;
   }
   else
   {
       polliwogsRadioButton.Checked = true;
   }
```

2.
```csharp
if (frogsInteger > toadsInteger + polliwogsInteger)
{
    resultLabel.Text = "It's the frogs";
}
else
{
    resultLabel.Text = "It's the toads and the polliwogs";
}
```

3.
```csharp
if (polliwogsInteger > toadsInteger && frogsInteger != 0
    || toadsInteger == 0)
{
    resultLabel.Text = "It's true";
}
else
{
    resultLabel.Text = "It's false";
}
```

4. Write the statements necessary to compare the numeric values stored in applesTextBox.Text and orangesTextBox.Text. Display in mostTextBox.Text which has more, the apples or the oranges, or a tie.

5. Write the statements that will test the current value of balanceDecimal. When balanceDecimal is greater than zero, the check box for Funds Available, called fundsCheckBox, should be selected, balanceDecimal is set back to zero, and countInteger is incremented by one. When balanceDecimal is zero or less, fundsCheckBox should not be selected (do not change the value of balanceDecimal or increment the counter).

Using if Statements with Radio Buttons and Check Boxes

In Chapter 2 you used the CheckedChanged event for radio buttons and check boxes to carry out the desired action. Now that you can use if statements, you should not take action in the CheckedChanged event handlers for these controls. Instead, use if statements to determine which options are selected.

To conform to good programming practice and make your programs consistent with standard Windows applications, place your code in the Click event handler of buttons, such as an *OK* button or an *Apply* button. For example, refer to the Visual Studio *Options* dialog box (Figure 4.7); no action will occur when you click on a radio button or check box. Instead, when you click on the *OK* button, VS checks to see which options are selected.

In an application such as the radio button project in Chapter 2 (refer to Figure 2.23), you could modify the code for the button to include code similar to the following:

Figure 4.7

*The Visual Studio **Options** dialog box. When the user clicks **OK**, the program checks the state of all radio buttons and check boxes.*

```
if (beigeRadioButton.Checked)
{
    this.BackColor = Color.Beige;
}
else if (blueRadioButton.Checked)
{
    this.BackColor = Color.Blue;
}
else if (yellowRadioButton.Checked)
{
    this.BackColor = Color.Yellow;
}
else if (grayRadioButton.Checked)
{
    this.BackColor = Color.Gray;
}
```

Additional Examples

```
if (fastShipCheckBox.Checked)
  totalDecimal += fastShipRateDecimal;

if (giftWrapCheckBox.Checked)
  totalDecimal += wrapAmountDecimal;
```

A "Simple Sample"

Test your understanding of the use of the `if` statement by coding some short examples.

Test the Value of a Check Box

Create a small project that contains a check box, a label, and a button. Name the button testButton, the check box testCheckBox, and the label message-Label. In the Click event handler for testButton, check the value of the check box. If the check box is currently checked, display "Check box is checked" in messageLabel.

```csharp
private void testButton_Click(object sender, EventArgs e)
{
    // Test the value of the check box.
    if (testCheckBox.Checked)
    {
        messageLabel.Text = "Check box is checked.";
    }
}
```

Test your project. When it works, add an `else` to the code that displays "Check box is not checked".

Test the State of Radio Buttons

Remove the check box from the previous project and replace it with two radio buttons, named freshmanRadioButton and sophomoreRadioButton and labeled "< 30 units" and ">= 30 units". Now change the `if` statement to display "Freshman" or "Sophomore" in the label.

```csharp
if (freshmanRadioButton.Checked)
{
    messageLabel.Text = "Freshman";
}
else
{
    messageLabel.Text = "Sophomore";
}
```

Can you modify the sample to work for Freshman, Sophomore, Junior, and Senior? In the sections that follow, you will see code for testing multiple radio buttons and check boxes.

Checking the State of a Radio Button Group

Nested `if` statements work very well for determining which button of a radio button group is selected. Recall that in any group of radio buttons, only one button can be selected. Assume that your form has a group of radio buttons for Freshman, Sophomore, Junior, and Senior. In a calculation method, you want to add 1 to one of four counter variables, depending on which radio button is selected:

```csharp
if (freshmanRadioButton.Checked)
{
    freshmanCountInteger++;
}
else if (sophomoreRadioButton.Checked)
{
    sophomoreCountInteger++;
}
```

```
else if (juniorRadioButton.Checked)
{
    juniorCountInteger++;
}
else if (seniorRadioButton.Checked)
{
    seniorCountInteger++;
}
```

Note that, in most situations, the final test is unnecessary. You should be able to just code an `else` and add to seniorRadioButton if the first three expressions are *false*. You might prefer to code the expression to make the statement more clear, or if no radio button is set initially, or if the program sets all radio buttons to false.

Clearing and Testing Radio Buttons

You can clear all radio buttons in a group by setting the Checked property of each to *false*. However, this leads to a lot of programming if you have a long list of radio buttons. *Remember*: When you set one button to *true*, all of the others are automatically set to *false*. You can use this fact to easily clear a set of radio buttons. Add an extra button to the group and set its Visible property to *false*. When you want to clear the visible buttons, set the Checked property of the invisible radio button to *true*.

```
noColorRadioButton.Checked = true;
```

If you are using this technique, you should set the initial value of the invisible radio button to Checked = *true* in the Form Designer.

Testing whether the User Has Selected an Option When you use an invisible radio button, you can verify in code that the user has made a selection by testing the Checked property of the button:

```
if (noColorRadioButton.Checked)
{
    MessageBox.Show("Please select a color.", "Required Entry");
}
else
{
    // A selection was made; take any appropriate action.
}
```

Checking the State of Multiple Check Boxes

Although nested `if` statements work very well for groups of radio buttons, the same is not true for a series of check boxes. Recall that if you have a series of check boxes, any number of the boxes may be selected. In this situation, assume that you have check boxes for Discount, Taxable, and Delivery. You will need separate `if` statements for each condition.

```
if (discountCheckBox.Checked)
{
    // Calculate the discount.
}
if (taxableCheckBox.Checked)
{
    // Calculate the tax.
}
if (deliveryCheckBox.Checked)
{
    // Calculate the delivery charges.
}
```

Enhancing Message Boxes

In Chapter 3 you learned to display a message box to the user. Now it's time to add such features as controlling the format of the message, displaying multiple buttons, checking which button the user clicks, and performing alternate actions depending on the user's selection.

Displaying the Message String

The message string you display in a message box may be a string literal enclosed in quotes or a string variable. You also may want to concatenate several items, for example, combining a literal with a value from a variable. It's usually a good idea to create a variable for the message and format the message before calling the Show method; if nothing else, it makes your code easier to read and follow.

Combining Values into a Message String

You can concatenate a literal such as "Total Sales: " with the value from a variable. You may need to include an extra space inside the literal to make sure that the value is separated from the literal.

```
string messageString = "Total Sales: " + totalDecimalSales.ToString("C");
MessageBox.Show(messageString, "Sales Summary", MessageBoxButtons.OK);
```

Creating Multiple Lines of Output

If your message is too long for one line, the message wraps to a second line. But if you would like to control the line length and position of the split, you can insert a **NewLine (\n) character** into the string message. You can concatenate this constant into a message string to set up multiple lines.

In this example, a second line is added to the MessageBox from the previous example.

```
string formattedTotalString = totalSalesDecimal.ToString("N");
string formattedAvgString = averageSaleDecimal.ToString("N");
string messageString = "Total Sales: " + formattedTotalString + "\n"
  + "Average Sale: " + formattedAvgString;
MessageBox.Show(messageString, "Sales Summary", MessageBoxButtons.OK);
```

✓TIP

Specify only the message for a "quick and dirty" message box for debugging purposes. It will display an *OK* button and an empty title bar: MessageBox.Show("I'm here.");. ■

You can combine multiple NewLine constants to achieve double spacing and create multiple message lines (Figure 4.8).

Figure 4.8

A message box with multiple lines of output, created by concatenating two NewLine characters at the end of each line.

```
// Concatenate the text for the message.
string summaryString = "Drinks Sold: " + drinksInteger.ToString() + "\n\n" +
                       "Number of Orders: " + ordersInteger.ToString() + "\n\n" +
                       "Total Sales: " + totalSalesDecimal.ToString("C");

// Display the message box.
MessageBox.Show(summaryString, "Juice Bar Sales Summary", MessageBoxButtons.OK,
  MessageBoxIcon.Information);
```

Using the Character Escape Sequences

You can use several other constants from the character escape sequence (\) list, in addition to the \n constant.

Escape sequence	Description
\'	Includes a single quote in a character literal.
\"	Includes a double quote in a string literal.
\\	Includes a backslash in a string literal.
\n	New line.
\r	Carriage return.
\b	Backspace character.
\f	Formfeed character (not useful in Microsoft Windows).
\t	Horizontal tab.

Displaying Multiple Buttons

You can choose the buttons to display in the message box using the Message-BoxButtons constants (Figure 4.9). Figure 4.10 shows a MessageBox with two buttons using the `MessageBoxButtons.YesNo` constant. The `Show` method

```
MessageBoxButtons.AbortRetryIgnore
MessageBoxButtons.OK
MessageBoxButtons.OKCancel
MessageBoxButtons.RetryCancel
MessageBoxButtons.YesNo
MessageBoxButtons.YesNoCancel
```

Figure 4.10

Display Yes and No buttons on a message box using `MessageBoxButtons. YesNo.`

Clear Order

? Clear the current order figures?

Yes   No

returns a **DialogResult object** that you can check to see which button the user clicked.

Determining the Return Type of a Method

How do you know that the Show method returns an object of the DialogResult class? An easy way is to point to the Show keyword and pause; the popup displays the type of the return value (Figure 4.11).

Figure 4.11

Pause the mouse pointer over the Show keyword and IntelliSense pops up with an argument list and the method's return type.

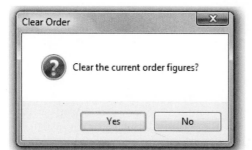

```
MessageBox.Show(messageString, "Coffee Sales Summary")
```
Public Shared Function Show(text As String, caption As String) As System.Windows.Forms.DialogResult
Displays a message box with specified text and caption.

Declaring an Object Variable for the Method Return

To capture the information about the outcome of the Show method, you must declare a variable that can hold an instance of the DialogResult type.

```
DialogResult whichButtonDialogResult;
```

Then you assign the return value of the Show method to the new variable.

```
string messageString = "Clear the current order figures?";
whichButtonDialogResult = MessageBox.Show(messageString, "Clear Order",
  MessageBoxButtons.YesNo, MessageBoxIcon.Question);
```

The next step is to check the value of the return, comparing to the DialogResult constants, such as Yes, No, OK, Retry, Abort, and Cancel.

```
if (whichButtonDialogResult == DialogResult.Yes)
{
    // Code to clear the order.
}
```

Specifying a Default Button and Options

Two additional signatures for the MessageBox.Show method are as follows:

General Form

```
MessageBox.Show(TextMessage, TitlebarText, MessageBoxButtons, MessageBoxIcons,
    MessageBoxDefaultButton);
MessageBox.Show(TextMessage, TitlebarText, MessageBoxButtons, MessageBoxIcons,
    MessageBoxDefaultButton, MessageBoxOptions);
```

When you display multiple buttons, you may want one of the buttons to be the default (the Accept button). For example, to make the second button (the *No* button) the default, use this statement:

```
string messageString = "Clear the current order figures?";
whichButtonDialogResult = MessageBox.Show(messageString, "Clear Order",
    MessageBoxButtons.YesNo, MessageBoxIcon.Question,
    MessageBoxDefaultButton.Button2);
```

You can right-align the text in the message box by setting the MessageBox-Options argument:

```
string messageString = "Clear the current order figures?";
whichButtonDialogResult = MessageBox.Show(messageString, "Clear Order",
    MessageBoxButtons.YesNo, MessageBoxIcon.Question,
    MessageBoxDefaultButton.Button2, MessageBoxOptions.RightAlign);
```

Input Validation

Careful programmers check the values entered into text boxes before beginning the calculations. Validation is a form of self-protection; it is better to reject bad data than to spend hours (and sometimes days) trying to find an error, only to discover that the problem was caused by a "user error." Finding and correcting the error early can often keep the program from producing erroneous results or halting with a run-time error.

Checking to verify that appropriate values have been provided as input is called **validation**. The validation may include making sure that the input is numeric, checking for specific values, checking a range of values, or making sure that required items are entered.

In Chapter 3 you learned to use try/catch blocks to trap for nonnumeric values. This chapter presents some additional validation techniques using if statements.

Note: Chapter 14 covers some advanced validation techniques using the Validating event and error providers.

Checking for a Range of Values

Data validation may include checking the reasonableness of a value. Assume you are using a text box to input the number of hours worked in a day. Even with overtime, the company does not allow more than 10 work hours in a single day. You could check the input for reasonableness with this code:

```
if (int.Parse(hoursTextBox.Text) > 10)
{
    MessageBox.Show("Too many hours.", "Invalid Data", MessageBoxButtons.OK);
}
```

Checking for a Required Field

Sometimes you need to be certain that a value has been entered into a text box before proceeding. You can compare a text box value to an empty string literal.

```
if (nameTextBox.Text != "")
{
    // Good data -- Perform some action.
}
else
{
    MessageBox.Show("Required entry.", "Invalid Data", MessageBoxButtons.OK);
}
```

Many programmers prefer to reverse the test in an if statement, so that invalid entries are caught in the *true* portion of the test. This practice can be easier to read and understand. The preceding validation could be written as follows, which does not require the use of *not* (!).

```
if (nameTextBox.Text == "")
{
    MessageBox.Show("Required entry.", "Invalid Data", MessageBoxButtons.OK);
}
else
{
    // Good data -- Perform some action.
}
```

By checking separately for blank or nonnumeric data, you can display a better message to the user. Make sure to check for blanks first, since a blank field will throw an exception with a parsing method. For example, if you reverse the order of the if and try blocks in the following example, blanks in quantityTextBox will always trigger the nonnumeric message in the catch block.

```
if (quantityTextBox.Text != "") // Not blank.
{
    try
        quantityDecimal = decimal.Parse(quantityTextBox.Text);
    catch              // Nonnumeric data.
    {
        messageString = "Nonnumeric data entered for quantity.";
        MessageBox.Show(messageString, "Data Entry Error");
    }
}
else                   // Missing data.
{
    messageString = "The quantity is required.";
    MessageBox.Show(messageString, "Data entry error");
}
```

Performing Multiple Validations

When you need to validate several input fields, how many message boxes do you want to display for the user? Assume that the user has neglected to fill five text boxes or make a required selection and clicked on *Calculate*. You can avoid displaying multiple message boxes in a row by using a nested if statement. This way you check the second value only if the first one passes, and you can exit the processing if a problem is found with a single field.

```
if (nameTextBox.Text != "")
{
    try
    {
        unitsDecimal = decimal.Parse(unitsTextBox.Text);
        if (freshmanRadioButton.Checked || sophomoreRadioButton.Checked
           || juniorRadioButton.Checked || seniorRadioButton.Checked)
        {
            // Data valid -- Do calculations or processing here.
        }
        else
        {
            MessageBox.Show("Please select a grade level.",
               "Data Entry Error", MessageBoxButtons.OK);
        }
    }
    catch(FormatException)
    {
        MessageBox.Show("Enter number of units.", "Data Entry Error",
          MessageBoxButtons.OK);
        unitsTextBox.Focus();
    }
}
```

```
else
{
    MessageBox.Show ("Please enter a name", "Data Entry Error",
        MessageBoxButtons.OK);
    nameTextBox.Focus();
}
```

The switch Statement

Earlier you used the if statement for testing conditions and making
decisions. Whenever you want to test a single variable for multiple values,
the **switch statement** provides a flexible and powerful solution. Any
decisions that you can code with a switch statement also can be coded
with nested if statements, but usually the switch statement is simpler and
more clear.

The switch Statement—General Form

General Form

```
switch (expression)
{
    case testValue1:
        [statement(s);
        break;]
    [case testValue2:
        statement(s);
        break;]
    .
    .
    .
    [default:]
        statement(s);
        break;]
}
```

The expression in a switch statement is usually a variable or property that you
wish to test. The test values are the values that you want to match; they may be
numeric or string constants or variables, and must match the data type of the
expression you are testing.

There is no limit to the number of case blocks that you can include, and no
limit to the number of statements that can follow a case statement. After all of
the statements for a case statement, you must place a break statement. The
break causes the switch to terminate.

The switch Statement—Examples

```
switch (listIndexInteger)
{
    case 0:
        // Code to handle selection of zero.
        break;
    case 1:
        // Code to handle selection of one.
        break;
    default:
        // Code to handle no selection made or no match.
        break;
}
switch (scoreInteger/10)
{
    case 10:
    case 9:
        messageLabel1.Text = "Excellent Score";
        messageLabel2.Text = "Give yourself a pat on the back.";
        break;
    case 8:
        messageLabel1.Text = "Very Good";
        messageLabel2.Text = "You should be proud.";
        break;
    case 7:
        messageLabel1.Text = "Satisfactory Score";
        messageLabel2.Text = "You should have a nice warm feeling.";
        break;
    default:
        messageLabel1.Text = "Your score shows room for improvement.";
        messageLabel2.Text = "";
        break;
}
```

Notice in the second example above that case 10: has no code. In this case, the code beneath Case 9: executes for both 10 and 9.

When you want to test for a string value, you must include quotation marks around the literals.

Example

```
switch (teamNameTextBox.Text)
{
    case "Tigers":
        // Code for Tigers.
        break;
    case "Leopards":
        // Code for Leopards.
        break;
    case "Cougars":
    case "Panthers":
        // Code for Cougars and Panthers.
        break;
    default:
        // Code for any nonmatch.
        break;
}
```

Note that, in the previous example, the capitalization must also match exactly. A better solution would be

```
switch (teamNameTextBox.Text.ToUpper())
{
    case "TIGERS":
        // Code for Tigers.
        break;
    case "LEOPARDS":
        // Code for Leopards.
        break;
    case "COUGARS":
    case "PANTHERS":
        // Code for Cougars and Panthers.
        break;
    default:
        // Code for any nonmatch.
        break;
}
```

Although the `default` clause is optional, generally you will want to include it in `switch` statements. The statements you code beneath `default` execute only if none of the other `case` expressions is matched. This clause provides checking for any invalid or unforeseen values of the expression being tested. If the `default` clause is omitted and none of the `case` conditions is *true*, the program continues execution at the statement following the closing brace for the `switch` block.

The final `break` statement in the last `case` or `default` statement seems unnecessary, but the compiler generates an error message if you leave it out.

If more than one `case` value is matched by the expression, only the statements in the *first* matched `case` clause execute.

▶ Feedback 4.3

1. Convert the following `if` statement to a `switch` statement:

```
if (codeString == "A")
{
    outputLabel.Text = "Excellent";
}
else if (codeString == "B")
{
    outputLabel.Text = "Good";
}
else if (codeString == "C" || codeString == "D")
{
    outputLabel.Text = "Satisfactory";
}
else
{
    outputLabel.Text = "Not Satisfactory";
}
```

2. Rewrite the switch statement from question 1 to handle upper- or lowercase values for codeString.

3. Write the switch statement to convert this if statement to a switch statement:

```csharp
if (countInteger == 0)
{
    MessageBox.Show("Invalid value");
}
else
{
    averageDecimal = sumDecimal / countInteger;
    MessageBox.Show("The average is: " + averageDecimal.ToString());
}
```

Sharing an Event Handler

A very handy feature of C# is the ability to share an event-handling method for the events of multiple controls. For example, assume that you have a group of four radio buttons to allow the user to choose a color (Figure 4.12). Each of the radio buttons must have its own name and will ordinarily have its own event-handling method. You can code the event-handling method for one of the radio buttons and then connect the other radio buttons to the same method.

To share an event-handling method, first double-click on one of the radio buttons; the editor creates the event handler for that button. Then select another radio button and click on the *Events* button in the Properties window. You will see a list of the available events for the selected control (Figure 4.13).

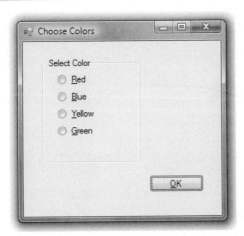

Properties button
Events button

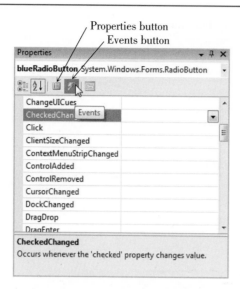

TIP

When you share an event handler, rename the method to more clearly reflect its purpose, such as radio-Buttons_CheckedChanged instead of blueRadioButton_Checked-Changed. Right-click on the method name in the Code Editor and select Refactor / Rename from the context menu to rename the method everywhere it occurs. ■

You can set the handler for the CheckedChanged event for a control to an existing method by selecting the method from the drop-down list (Figure 4.14).

After you have selected a single event-handling method for multiple controls, this method will execute when the user selects *any* of the radio buttons.

A good, professional technique is to set up a class-level variable to hold the selection that the user makes. Then, in the *OK* button's event-handling method, you can take action based on which of the buttons was selected.

The key to using the shared event handler is the sender argument that is passed to the CheckedChanged method. The sender is defined as a generic

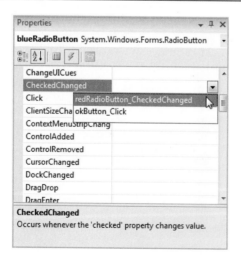

F i g u r e   4 . 1 4

Select the redRadioButton_ CheckedChanged *method to handle the CheckedChanged event for blueRadioButton.*

object. To use its Name property, you must cast sender to a RadioButton type. Then you can use its Name property in a `switch` statement to determine which radio button the user selected.

```
// Declare class-level variable.
Color selectedColor;
```

You can declare a class-level variable as a Color data type, assign the chosen color in the shared event handler, and then apply the color in the *OK* button's click event handler. In this example, we used *Refactor / Rename* to rename the shared event handler from redRadioButton_CheckedChanged to radioButtons_CheckedChanged, to make the name more generic.

```csharp
public partial class ChangeColorForm : Form
{
    // Declare class-level variable.
    Color selectedColor;

    public ChangeColorForm()
    {
        InitializeComponent();
    }

    private void radioButtons_CheckedChanged(object sender, EventArgs e)
    {
        // Set the selected color to match the radio button.
        // Handles all four radio buttons.

        // Cast the sender argument to a RadioButton data type.
        RadioButton selectedRadioButton = (RadioButton)sender;
        switch (selectedRadioButton.Name)
        {
            case "redRadioButton":
                selectedColor = Color.Red;
                break;
            case "blueRadioButton":
                selectedColor = Color.Blue;
                break;
            case "yellowRadioButton":
                selectedColor = Color.Yellow;
                break;
            case "greenRadioButton":
                selectedColor = Color.Green;
                break;
        }
    }

    private void okButton_Click(object sender, EventArgs e)
    {
        // Change the color based on the selected radio button.

        this.BackColor = selectedColor;
    }
}
```

Calling Event Handlers

If you wish to perform a set of instructions in more than one location, you should never duplicate the code. Write the instructions once, in an event-handling method, and "call" the method from another method. When you **call** a method, the entire method is executed and then execution returns to the statement following the call.

The Call Statement—General Form

```
MethodName();
```

You must include the parentheses; if the method that you are calling requires arguments, then place the arguments within the parentheses; otherwise, leave them empty. Note that all method calls in this chapter *do* require arguments. Chapter 5 covers more options including writing additional methods, with and without arguments.

The Call Statement—Example

```
clearButton_Click(sender, e);
```

Notice the arguments for the call statement. You are passing the same two arguments that were passed to the calling method. If you examine any of the editor-generated event-handling method headers, you can see that every event handler requires these two arguments, which can be used to track the object that generated the event.

```
private void newOrderButton_Click(object sender, System.EventArgs e)
{
    // . . .
    // Call the clearButton_Click event-handling method.
    clearButton_Click(sender, e);
}
```

In the programming example that follows, you will accumulate individual items for one customer. When that customer's order is complete, you need to clear the entire order and begin an order for the next customer. Refer to the form in Figure 4.15; notice the two buttons: *Clear for Next Item* and *New Order*. The button for next item clears the text boxes on the screen. The button for a new order must clear the screen text boxes and clear the subtotal fields. Rather than repeat the instructions to clear the individual screen text boxes, we can call the event handler for clearButton_Click from the newOrderButton_Click method.

Figure 4.15

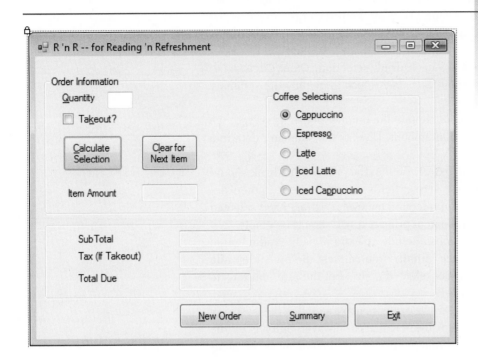

A form with buttons that perform overlapping functions. The New Order button must include the same tasks as Clear for Next Item.

```csharp
private void newOrderButton_Click(object sender, System.EventArgs e)
{
    // Clear the current order and add to totals.

    DialogResult      responseDialogResult;
    string            messageString;

    // Confirm clear of current order.
    messageString = "Clear the current order figures?";
    responseDialogResult = MessageBox.Show(messageString, "Clear Order",
        MessageBoxButtons.YesNo, MessageBoxIcon.Question,
        MessageBoxDefaultButton.Button2);

    if (responseDialogResult == DialogResult.Yes)  // User said Yes.
    {
        clearButton_Click(sender, e); // Clear the current order fields.
        // Continue with statements to clear the subtotals.
    }
}
```

In the newOrderButton_Click handler, all the instructions in clearButton_Click are executed. Then execution returns to the next statement following the call.

Your Hands-On Programming Example

Create a project for the juice bar at Look Sharp Fitness Center. The application must calculate the amount due for individual orders and maintain accumulated totals for a summary. Have option buttons for the size (12, 16, and 20 ounce) and options for the drink selections. Two juices are available and three smoothie flavors. Have a check box for the three extra additive choices.

The prices for the drinks are 3.00, 3.50, and 4.00, depending on size. Each additive is an additional 50 cents. Display the price of the drink as the options are selected. Only add it to the order when the *Add to Order* button is selected.

The buttons are *Add to Order* for each drink selection, *Order Complete* to display the amount due for the order, *Summary Report* to display the summary information, and *Exit*.

The summary information should contain the number of drinks served, the number of orders, and the total dollar amount. Display the summary data in a message box.

When the user clicks the *Add to Order* button, the price of the drink should be added to the order totals and the screen fields should be reset to their default values, which are as follows: No selection for size or extras, *Fruit* selected for Juices and *1* for quantity, and the item price text box should be empty.

For the Size group of radio buttons, include an extra invisible radio button with its Checked property set to *true* initially. You can test the invisible radio button to make sure that the user has selected a size. Set the radio buttons to *true* when you need to clear the others.

When the user clicks the *Order Complete* button, make sure that the last drink order was added into the total. You will know that an unsaved order is on the screen if the *Item Price* text box has a value (it is cleared when the order is calculated). If the user wants to add the last drink order into the total, call the event handler for the *Add to Order* button, rather than write the code a second time.

Planning the Project

Sketch a form (Figure 4.16), which your users sign as meeting their needs.

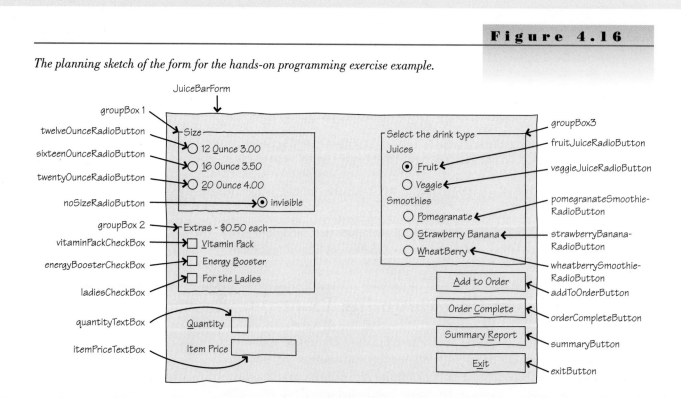

Figure 4.16

The planning sketch of the form for the hands-on programming exercise example.

Plan the Objects and Properties. Plan the property settings for the form and each of the controls.

Object	Property	Setting
JuiceBarForm	Name	JuiceBarForm
	Text	Juice Bar Orders
	AcceptButton	addToOrderButton
	CancelButton	exitButton
groupBox1	Text	Size
twelveOunceRadioButton	Name	twelveOunceRadioButton
	Text	12 &Ounce
sixteenOunceRadioButton	Name	sixteenOunceRadioButton
	Text	&16 Ounce
twentyOunceRadioButton	Name	twentyOunceRadioButton
	Text	&20 Ounce
noSizeRadioButton	Name	noSizeRadioButton
	Checked	true
	Visible	false
groupBox2	Text	Extras - $0.50 each
vitaminPackCheckBox	Name	vitaminPackCheckBox
	Text	&Vitamin Pack
energyBoosterCheckBox	Name	energyBoosterCheckBox
	Text	Energy &Booster
ladiesCheckBox	Name	ladiesCheckBox
	Text	For the &Ladies
groupBox3	Text	Select the drink type
label1	Text	Juices
fruitJuiceRadioButton	Name	fruitJuiceRadioButton
	Text	&Fruit
	Checked	true
veggieJuiceRadioButton	Name	veggieJuiceRadioButton
	Text	Ve&ggie
label2	Text	Smoothies
pomegranateSmoothieRadioButton	Name	pomegranateSmoothieRadioButton
	Text	&Pomegranate
strawberryBananaRadioButton	Name	strawberryBananaRadioButton
	Text	&Strawberry Banana
wheatberrySmoothieRadioButton	Name	wheatberrySmoothieRadioButton
	Text	&WheatBerry
label3	Text	&Quantity

Object	Property	Setting
quantityTextBox	Name Text	quantityTextBox (blank)
label4	Text	Item Price
itemPriceTextBox	Name Text ReadOnly TabStop	itemPriceTextBox (blank) true false
addToOrderButton	Name Text	addToOrderButton &Add to Order
orderCompleteButton	Name Text Enabled	orderCompleteButton Order &Complete false
summaryButton	Name Text Enabled	summaryButton Summary &Report false
exitButton	Name Text	exitButton E&xit

Plan the Event Handlers. You need to plan the actions for five event handlers for the buttons.

Object	Method	Action
addToOrderButton	Click	Check if size is selected. Validate for blank or nonnumeric amount. Multiply price by quantity. Add to the number of drinks. Enable the Order Complete button. Reset controls to default values

orderCompleteButton	Click	If last item not cleared from screen
		  Ask user whether to add it.
		  If yes
		    Call addToOrderButton_Click.
		Display the price of the order.
		Add to the number of orders and totalSales.
		Enable the Summary and Order Complete buttons.
		Clear the order amount

summaryButton	Click	Display the summary totals in a message box.
exitButton	Click	Terminate the project.
Size radio buttons	CheckedChanged	Clear the Extras variable. Find price of selected size.

Write the Project Follow the sketch in Figure 4.16 to create the form. Figure 4.17 shows the completed form.

- Set the properties of each object as you have planned.
- Write the code. Working from the pseudocode, write each event-handling method.
- When you complete the code, use a variety of data to thoroughly test the project.

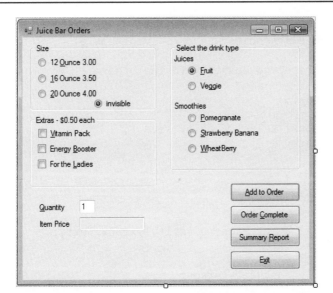

Figure 4.17

The form for the hands-on programming exercise.

The Project Coding Solution

```
/*
 *  Program Name:      Ch04HandsOn
 *  Programmer:        Bradley/Millspaugh
 *  Date:              June 2009
 *
 *  Description:       This project calculates the amount due
 *                     based on the customer selection
 *                     and accumulates summary data for the day.
 *
 *
 */

using System;
using System.Collections.Generic;
using System.ComponentModel;
using System.Data;
using System.Drawing;
using System.Text;
using System.Windows.Forms;
```

```csharp
namespace Ch04HandsOn
{
    public partial class JuiceBarForm : Form
    {
        // Declare class variables.
        private decimal itemPriceDecimal,
                        totalOrderDecimal,
                        totalSalesDecimal;
        private int    drinksInteger,
                       ordersInteger;

        public JuiceBarForm()
        {
            InitializeComponent();
        }
        private void addToOrderButton_Click(object sender, EventArgs e)
        {
            // Add the current item price and quantity to the order.

            if (noSizeRadioButton.Checked)
            {
                MessageBox.Show("You must select a drink size.",
                  "Missing required entry");
            }
            else
            {
                try
                {
                    int quantityInteger = int.Parse(quantityTextBox.Text);
                    if (quantityInteger != 0)
                    {
                        drinksInteger += quantityInteger;
                        totalOrderDecimal += itemPriceDecimal * quantityInteger;
                        orderCompleteButton.Enabled = true;

                        // Reset defaults for next item.
                        noSizeRadioButton.Checked = true;
                        fruitJuiceRadioButton.Checked = true;
                        vitaminPackCheckBox.Checked = false;
                        energyBoosterCheckBox.Checked = false;
                        ladiesCheckBox.Checked = false;
                        itemPriceTextBox.Clear();
                        quantityTextBox.Text = "1";
                    }
                    else
                    {
                        MessageBox.Show("Please enter a quantity.",
                          "Missing Required Entry");
                    }
                }
                catch (FormatException)
                {
                    MessageBox.Show("Invalid quantity.", "Data Entry Error");
                    quantityTextBox.Focus();
                    quantityTextBox.SelectAll();
                }
            }
        }
    }
```

```csharp
private void orderCompleteButton_Click(object sender, EventArgs e)
{
    // Order is complete, add to summary and clear order.
    // Check if the last item was added to the total.
    if (itemPriceTextBox.Text != "")
    {
        DialogResult responseDialogResult;
        string messageString = "Current Item not recorded. Add to order?";
        responseDialogResult = MessageBox.Show(messageString,
            "Verify Last Drink Purchase",
            MessageBoxButtons.YesNo,
            MessageBoxIcon.Question);
        if (responseDialogResult == DialogResult.Yes)
        {
            addToOrderButton_Click(sender, e);
        }
    }

    // Display amount due.
    string dueString = "Amount Due " + totalOrderDecimal.ToString("C");
    MessageBox.Show(dueString, "Order Complete");

    // Add to summary totals.
    ordersInteger++;
    totalSalesDecimal += totalOrderDecimal;

    // Reset buttons and total for new order.
    summaryButton.Enabled = true;
    orderCompleteButton.Enabled = false;
    totalOrderDecimal = 0m;
}

private void summaryButton_Click(object sender, EventArgs e)
{
    // Display the summary information in a message box.

    string summaryString = "Drinks Sold:        "
            + drinksInteger.ToString()
            + "\n\n" + "Number of Orders: "
            + ordersInteger.ToString()
            + "\n\n" + "Total Sales:        "
            + totalSalesDecimal.ToString("C");
    MessageBox.Show(summaryString, "Juice Bar Sales Summary",
        MessageBoxButtons.OK,
        MessageBoxIcon.Information);
}

private void exitButton_Click(object sender, EventArgs e)
{
    // End the application.

    this.Close();
}

private void twelveOunceRadioButton_CheckedChanged(object sender,
    EventArgs e)
{
    // Calculate and display the price for the selected item.
    // Handles all check boxes and radio buttons.
    int extrasInteger = 0;
```

```
            if (twelveOunceRadioButton.Checked)
            {
                itemPriceDecimal = 3m;
            }
            else if (sixteenOunceRadioButton.Checked)
            {
                itemPriceDecimal = 3.5m;
            }
            else if (twentyOunceRadioButton.Checked)
            {
                itemPriceDecimal = 4m;
            }
            extrasInteger = 0;
            if (vitaminPackCheckBox.Checked)
            {
                extrasInteger++;
            }
            if (energyBoosterCheckBox.Checked)
            {
                extrasInteger++;
            }
            if (ladiesCheckBox.Checked)
            {
                extrasInteger++;
            }
            itemPriceDecimal += extrasInteger * .5m; // 50 cents for each extra.
            itemPriceTextBox.Text = itemPriceDecimal.ToString("C");
        }
    }
}
```

Debugging C# Projects

One of the advantages of programming in the Visual Studio environment is the availability of debugging tools. You can use these tools to help find and eliminate logic and run-time errors. The debugging tools also can help you to follow the logic of existing projects to better understand how they work.

Sometimes it's helpful to know the result of a Boolean expression, the value of a variable or property, or the sequence of execution of your program. You can follow program logic in Debug mode by single-stepping through code; you also can get information about execution without breaking the program run, using the WriteLine method of the Console class.

In the following sections, you will learn to use many of the debugging tools on the Debug toolbar (Figure 4.18) and the *Debug* menu (Figure 4.19). Note that the Debug toolbar appears automatically when you choose the *Start* command; you also can make the toolbar display full-time by right-clicking on any toolbar and choosing *Debug* from the popup menu.

Figure 4.18

The Debug toolbar with its tools for debugging programs.

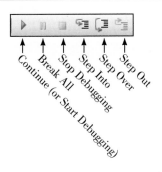

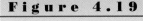

Figure 4.19

The debugging options on the Debug menu.

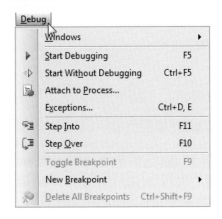

Writing to the Output Window

You can place a **Console.WriteLine method** in your code. In the argument, you can specify a message to write or an object that you want tracked.

The Console.WriteLine Method—General Form

```
Console.WriteLine(TextString);
Console.WriteLine(Object);
```

The `Console.WriteLine` method is overloaded, so that you can pass it a string argument or the name of an object.

The Console.WriteLine Method—Examples

```
Console.WriteLine("calculateButton method entered.");
Console.WriteLine(quantityTextBox);
Console.WriteLine("quantityInteger = " + quantityInteger);
```

When the `Console.WriteLine` method executes, its output appears in the Output window. Figure 4.20 shows the output of the three example statements above. Notice the second line of output, for quantityTextBox—the class of the object displays along with its current contents.

Note: If the Output window is not displaying, select *View/ Other Windows / Output*.

Figure 4.20

The Output window shows the output of the `Console.WriteLine` *method.*

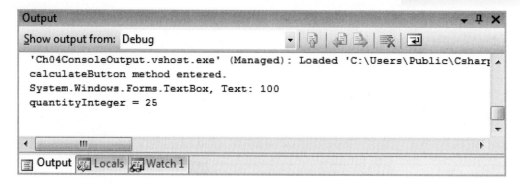

You may find it useful to place `WriteLine` methods in `if` statements so that you can see which branch the logic followed.

```csharp
if (intCount > 10)
{
    Console.WriteLine("Count is greater than 10.");
    // Other processing.
}
else
{
    Console.WriteLine("Count is not greater than 10.");
    // Other processing.
}
```

An advantage of using `WriteLine`, rather than the other debugging techniques that follow, is that you do not have to break program execution.

Pausing Execution with the Break All Button

You can click on the *Break All* button to pause execution. This step places the project into Debugging mode at the current line. However, generally you will prefer to break in the middle of a method. To choose the location of the break, you can force a break with a breakpoint.

Forcing a Break

During the debugging process, often you want to stop at a particular location in code and watch what happens (which branch of an `if`/`else`; which methods were executed; the value of a variable just before or just after a calculation). You can force the project to break by inserting a **breakpoint** in code.

To set a breakpoint, place the mouse pointer in the gray margin indicator area at the left edge of the Editor window on a line of executable code and click; the line will be highlighted in red and a large red dot will display in the margin indicator (Figure 4.21).

After setting a breakpoint, start execution. When the project reaches the breakpoint, it will halt, display the line, and go into debug mode.

You can remove a breakpoint by clicking again in the gray margin area, or clear all breakpoints from the *Debug* menu.

Place the insertion point in the line you want as a breakpoint and press F9. Press F9 again to toggle the breakpoint off. ■

Figure 4.21

A program statement with a breakpoint set appears highlighted and a dot appears in the gray margin indicator area.

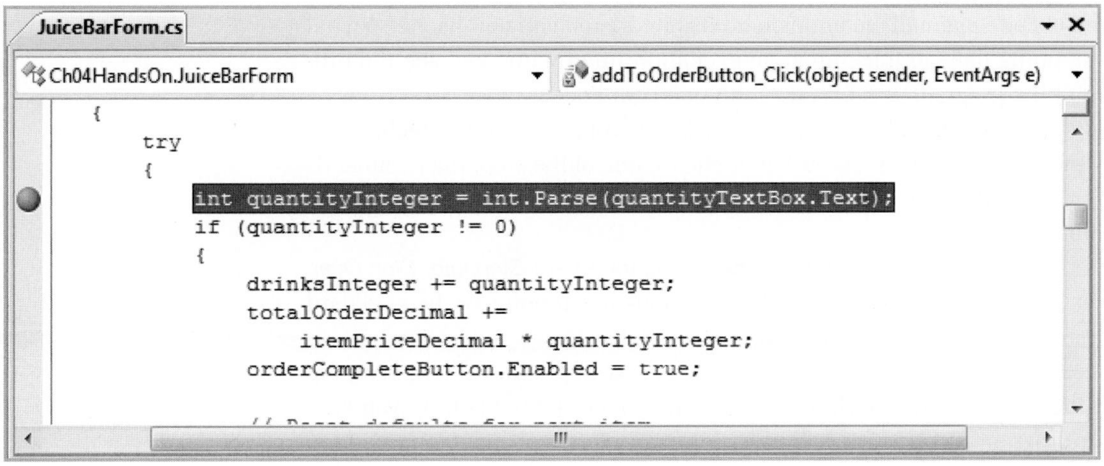

Checking the Current Values of Expressions

You can quickly check the current value of an expression such as a variable, a control, a Boolean expression, or an arithmetic expression. During debug mode, display the Editor window and point to the name of the expression that you want to view; a small label, called a *DataTip*, pops up and displays the current contents of the expression.

The steps for viewing the contents of a variable during run time are

1. Break the execution using a breakpoint.
2. If the code does not appear in the Editor, click on the editor's tab in the Document window.
3. Point to the variable or expression in the current procedure that you wish to view.

The current contents of the expression will pop up in a label (Figure 4.22), when the expression is in scope.

Figure 4.22

Point to a variable name in code and its current value displays in a DataTip.

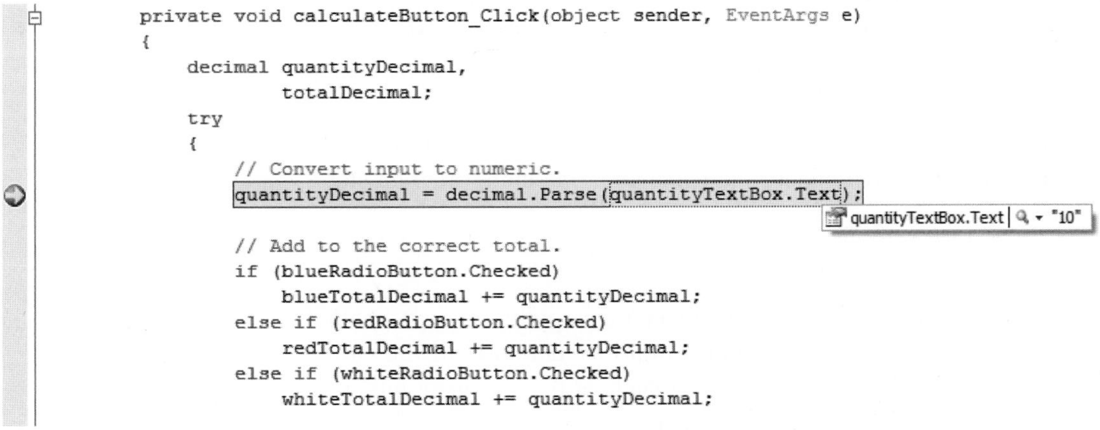

Stepping through Code

The best way to debug a project is to thoroughly understand what the project is doing every step of the way. Previously, this task was performed by following each line of code manually to understand its effect. You can now use the Visual Studio stepping tools to trace program execution line by line and see the progression of the program as it executes through your code.

You step through code at debug time. You can use one of the techniques already mentioned to break execution or choose one of the stepping commands at design time; the program will begin running and immediately transfer to debug time.

The three stepping commands on the *Debug* menu are *Step Into*, *Step Over*, and *Step Out*. You also can use the toolbar buttons for stepping or the keyboard shortcuts shown on the menu (refer to Figure 4.19).

These commands force the project to execute a single line at a time and to display the Editor window with the current statement highlighted. As you execute the program, by clicking a button, for example, the Click event occurs. Execution transfers to the event-handling method, the Editor window for that method appears on the screen, and you can follow line-by-line execution.

Step Into

Most likely you will use the **Step Into** command more than the other two stepping commands. When you choose *Step Into* (from the menu, the toolbar button, or F11), the next line of code executes and the program pauses again in debug time. If the line of code is a call to another method, the first line of code of the called method displays.

To continue stepping through your program execution, continue choosing the *Step Into* command. When a method is completed, your form will display again, awaiting an event. You can click on one of the form's buttons to continue stepping through code in an event-handling method. If you want to continue execution without stepping, choose the *Continue* command (from the menu, the toolbar button, or F5). *Note*: The keyboard shortcuts may differ, depending on the keyboard mapping selected in the *Options* dialog box. The shortcuts shown here are for C# development settings; if you are using general development settings, perhaps in a shared environment with other language development, the keyboard shortcuts may differ.

Step Over

The **Step Over** command also executes one line of code at a time. The difference between *Step Over* and *Step Into* occurs when your code has calls to other methods. *Step Over* displays only the lines of code in the current method being analyzed; it does not display lines of code in the called methods.

You can choose *Step Over* from the menu, from the toolbar button, or by pressing F10. Each time you choose the command, one more program statement executes.

Step Out

You use the third stepping command when you are stepping through a called method. The **Step Out** command continues rapid execution until the called method completes, and then returns to debug mode at the statement following the call, that is, the next line of the calling method.

Continuing Program Execution

When you have seen what you want to see, continue rapid execution by pressing F5 or choosing *Continue* from the Debug toolbar or the *Debug* menu. If you want to restart execution from the beginning, choose the *Restart* command.

Stopping Execution

Once you have located a problem in the program's code, usually you want to stop execution, correct the error, and run again. Stop execution by selecting *Stop Debugging* from the *Debug* menu or the toolbar button, or press the keyboard shortcut: Shift + F5.

Note: The keyboard shortcuts differ depending on the keyboard mapping scheme selected in *Tools / Options / Environment / Keyboard* with *Show All Settings* selected.

Edit and Continue

C# 2005 introduced a new feature: Edit and Continue. You can use this feature to save time when debugging programs. When your program goes into Debugging mode and you make minor modifications to the code in the Editor, you may be able to continue execution without stopping to recompile. Press F5 or choose *Debug / Continue*. If the changes to the code are too major to continue without recompiling, the debugger does not allow the changes. Stop program execution, make the changes, and recompile the program.

The Locals Window

Sometimes you may find that the **Locals window** displays just the information that you want (Figure 4.23). The Locals window displays all objects and variables that are within scope at debug time. That means that if you break execution in the calculateButton_Click event method, all variables local to that method display. You also can expand the `this` entry to see the state of the form's controls and the values of class-level variables. Display the Locals window from the toolbar button or the *Debug / Windows / Locals* menu item, which appears only when a program is running, either in run time or debug mode.

F i g u r e   4 . 2 3

The Locals window shows the values of the local variables that are within scope of the current statement.

Name	Value	Type
⊞ ⚷ this	{Ch04HandsOn.JuiceBarForm, Text: Juice Bar Orders}	Ch04HandsOn.JuiceBarForm
⊞ ⚷ sender	{Text = "&Add to Order"}	object {System.Windows.Forms.Button}
⊞ ⚷ e	{X = 55 Y = 16 Button = Left}	System.EventArgs {System.Windows.Form:
⚷ quantityInteger	10	int

🔲 Locals 🔲 Autos

The Autos Window

Another helpful debugging window is the **Autos window**. The Autos window "automatically" displays all variables and control contents that are referenced in the current statement and a few statements on either side of the current one (Figure 4.24). Note that the highlighted line in the Editor window is about to execute next; the "current" statement is the one just before the highlighted one.

F i g u r e   4 . 2 4

The Autos window automatically adjusts to show the variables and properties that appear in the previous few lines and the next few lines.

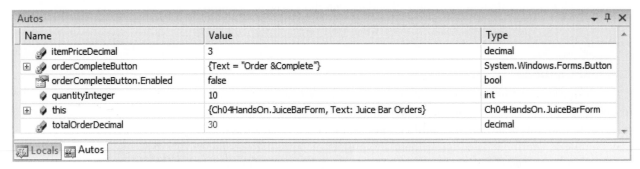

You can view the Autos window when your program stops at a breakpoint. Click on the Autos window tab if it appears, or open it using the *Debug / Windows / Autos* menu item. Again, you must be in either run time or debug mode to see the menu item.

Note: The Autos window is not available in the Express Edition.

✓ TIP

To use any of the debugging windows, you must be in debug mode. ■

Debugging Step-by-Step Tutorial

In this exercise, you will learn to set a breakpoint; pause program execution; single-step through program instructions; display the current values of properties, variables, and conditions; and debug a C# program.

Test the Project

STEP 1: Open the debugging project from the StudentData folder, which you downloaded from the text Web site (www.mhhe.com/C#2008). The project is found in the Ch04Debug folder.

STEP 2: Run the program.

STEP 3: Enter color Blue and quantity 100, and press Enter or click on the *Calculate* button.

STEP 4: Enter another color Blue and quantity 50, and press Enter. Are the totals correct?

STEP 5: Enter color Red and quantity 30, and press Enter.

STEP 6: Enter color Red and quantity 10, and press Enter. Are the totals correct?

STEP 7: Enter color White and quantity 50, and press Enter.

STEP 8: Enter color White and quantity 100, and press Enter. Are the totals correct?

STEP 9: Exit the project. You are going to locate and correct the errors in the red and white totals.

Break and Step Program Execution

STEP 1: Display the program code. Scroll to locate this line, which is the first calculation line in the calculateButton_Click event method:

```
quantityDecimal = decimal.Parse(quantityTextBox.Text);
```

STEP 2: Click in the gray margin indicator area to set a breakpoint on the selected line. Your screen should look like Figure 4.25.

Figure 4.25

A program statement with a breakpoint set appears highlighted, and a dot appears in the gray margin indicator area.

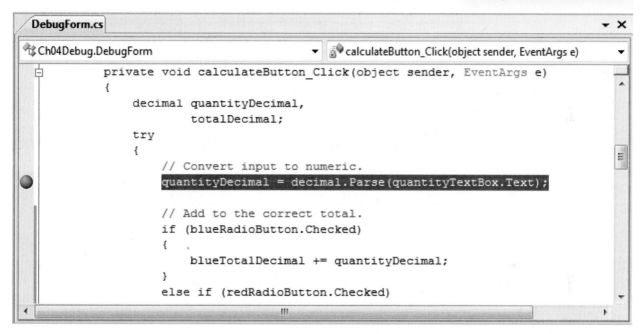

STEP 3: Run the project, enter Red and quantity 30, and press Enter. The project will transfer control to the calculateButton_Click method, stop when the breakpoint is reached, highlight the current line, and enter debug time (Figure 4.26). If the form is on top of the IDE window, click on the IDE or its taskbar button to make the VS IDE window appear on top. *Note*: The highlighted line has not yet executed.

STEP 4: Press the F11 key, which causes C# to execute the current program statement (the assignment statement). (F11 is the keyboard shortcut for *Debug / Step Into*.) The statement is executed, and the highlight moves to the next statement (the if statement).

STEP 5: Press F11 again; the condition (blueRadioButton.Checked) is tested and found to be *false*.

STEP 6: Continue pressing F11 a few more times and watch the order in which program statements execute.

You can change the current line of execution in debug mode by dragging the yellow current-line indicator arrow on the left side ■

Figure 4.26

When a breakpoint is reached during program execution, C# enters debug time, displays the Editor window, and highlights the breakpoint line.

```
DebugForm.cs                                                                    ▾ ✕
Ch04Debug.DebugForm              ▾   📄 calculateButton_Click(object sender, EventArgs e)    ▾
              {
                      // Convert input to numeric.
                      quantityDecimal = decimal.Parse(quantityTextBox.Text);

                      // Add to the correct total.
                      if (blueRadioButton.Checked)
                      {
                              blueTotalDecimal += quantityDecimal;
```

View the Contents of Properties, Variables, and Boolean Expressions

STEP 1: Scroll up if necessary and point to `quantityTextBox.Text` in the breakpoint line; the contents of the Text property pop up (Figure 4.27).

Figure 4.27

Point to a property reference in code and the current contents pop up.

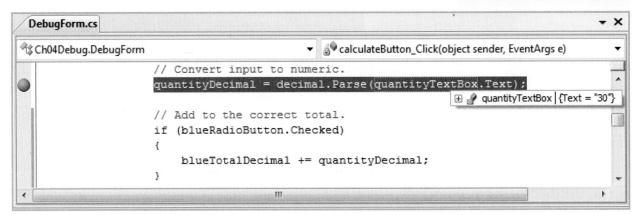

```
DebugForm.cs                                                                    ▾ ✕
Ch04Debug.DebugForm              ▾   📄 calculateButton_Click(object sender, EventArgs e)    ▾
                      // Convert input to numeric.
                      quantityDecimal = decimal.Parse(quantityTextBox.Text);
                                                    ⊞ 🔍 quantityTextBox │ {Text = "30"}
                      // Add to the correct total.
                      if (blueRadioButton.Checked)
                      {
                              blueTotalDecimal += quantityDecimal;
                      }
```

STEP 2: Point to `quantityDecimal` and view the contents of that variable. Notice that the Text property is enclosed in quotes and the numeric variable is not.

STEP 3: Point to `blueRadioButton.Checked` in the `if` statement; then point to `redRadioButton.Checked`. You can see the Boolean value for each of the radio buttons.

STEP 4: Point to `redTotalDecimal` to see the current value of that total variable. This value looks correct, since you just entered 30, which was added to the total.

Continue Program Execution

STEP 1: Press F5, the keyboard shortcut for the *Continue* command. The *Continue* command continues execution.

> If the current line is any line other than the closing brace } of the method, execution continues and your form reappears. If the current line is }, you may have to click on your project's Taskbar button to make the form reappear.

STEP 2: Enter color Red and quantity 10. When you press Enter, program execution will again break at the breakpoint.

STEP 3: The 10 you just entered should be added to the 30 previously entered for Red, producing 40 in the Red total.

STEP 4: Use the *Step Into* button on the Debug toolbar to step through execution. Keep pressing *Step Into* until the 10 is added to redTotalDecimal. Display the current contents of the total. Can you see what the problem is?

> *Hint*: redTotalDecimal has only the current amount, not the sum of the two amounts. The answer will appear a little later; try to find it yourself first.

> You will fix this error soon, after testing the White total.

Test the White Total

STEP 1: Press F5 to continue execution. If the form does not reappear, click the project's Taskbar button.

STEP 2: Enter color White and quantity 100, and press Enter.

> When execution halts at the breakpoint, press F5 to continue. This returns to rapid execution until the next breakpoint is reached.

> Enter color White and quantity 50, and press Enter.

> Press F11 several times when execution halts at the breakpoint until you execute the line that adds the quantity to the White total. Remember that the highlighted line has not yet executed; press *Step Into* one more time, if necessary, to execute the addition statement.

> Point to each variable name to see the current values (Figure 4.28). Can you see the problem?

TIP

You can execute several lines at once by right-clicking the line you would like to debug next and choosing *Run To Cursor.* ■

Figure 4.28

Point to the variable name in code and its current value displays as 2 decimal.

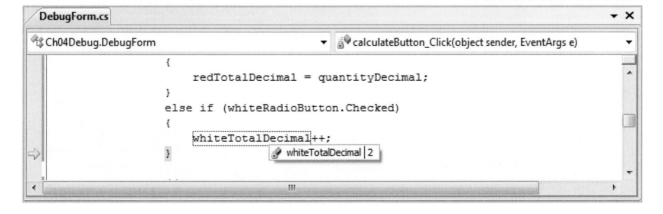

STEP 3: Display the Autos window by clicking on its tab. If the tab does not appear, select *Debug / Windows / Autos*. The Autos window displays the current value of all properties and variables referred to by a few statements before and after the current statement (Figure 4.29). *Note*: If you are using the Express Edition, you can substitute the Locals window for the Autos window.

Figure 4.29

The Autos window displays the current contents of variables and properties in the statements before and after the current statement.

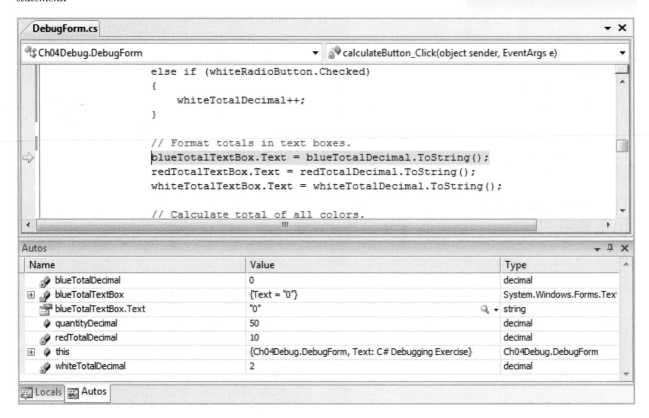

STEP 4: Identify all the errors. When you are ready to make the corrections, continue to the next step.

Correct the Red Total Error

STEP 1: Stop program execution by clicking on the *Stop Debugging* toolbar button (Figure 4.30).

Display keyboard shortcuts on ToolTips, as in Figure 4.30, by selecting *Tools / Customize / Show shortcut keys in ScreenTips.* ∎

Figure 4.30

Click on the Stop Debugging button on the Debug toolbar to halt program execution.

STEP 2: Locate this line:

```
redTotalDecimal = quantityDecimal;
```

This statement replaces the value of redTotalDecimal with quantityDecimal rather than adding to the total.

STEP 3: Change the line to read

```
redTotalDecimal += quantityDecimal;
```

Correct the White Total Error

STEP 1: Locate this line:

```
whiteTotalDecimal++;
```

Of course, this statement adds 1 to the White total, rather than adding the quantity.

STEP 2: Correct the line to read

```
whiteTotalDecimal += quantityDecimal;
```

Test the Corrections

STEP 1: Press F5 to start program execution. Enter color White and quantity 100; press Enter.

STEP 2: When the program stops at the breakpoint, press F5 to continue.

STEP 3: Enter White and 50, and press Enter.

STEP 4: At the breakpoint, clear the breakpoint by clicking on the red margin dot for the line.

STEP 5: Press F5 to continue and check the White total on the form. It should now be correct.

STEP 6: Enter values for Red twice and make sure the total is correct.

STEP 7: Test the totals for all three colors carefully and then click *Exit.*

Test the Exception Handling

STEP 1: Set a breakpoint again on the first calculation line in the calculateButton_Click event handler.

STEP 2: Run the program, this time entering nonnumeric characters for the amount. Click on *Calculate*; when the program stops at the breakpoint, press F11 repeatedly and watch program execution. The message box should appear.

STEP 3: Stop program execution.

Force a Run-Time Error

For this step, you will use a technique called *commenting out* code. Programmers often turn code lines to comments to test the code without those lines. Sometimes it works well to copy a section of code, comment out the original to keep it unchanged, and modify only the copy. You'll find it easy to uncomment the code later, after you finish testing.

In C# you can turn code lines into comments in several ways: You can add "//" to the beginning of a line, surround a group of lines with "/*" and "*/", or use the *Comment out the selected lines* toolbar button.

STEP 1: Select *Delete All Breakpoints* from the *Debug* menu if the menu item is available. The item is available only when there are breakpoints set in the program. Click *Yes* on the confirmation dialog.

STEP 2: At the left end of the line with the `try` statement, add two slashes, turning the line into a comment.

STEP 3: Scroll down and locate the exception-handling code. Highlight the lines beginning with `catch` and ending with the closing brace for the `catch` block (Figure 4.31).

Figure 4.31

Select the lines to convert to comments for debugging.

```
        }
        catch
        {
            MessageBox.Show("Enter numeric data.",
                "Data Error",
                MessageBoxButtons.OK,
                MessageBoxIcon.Information);
            quantityTextBox.Focus();
            quantityTextBox.SelectAll();
        }
    }
```

STEP 4: Click on the *Comment out the selected lines* button on the Text Editor toolbar (Figure 4.32). The editor adds double slashes to the start of each of the selected lines.

Figure 4.32

Comment out the selected lines.

Click the Comment out the selected lines toolbar button to temporarily make program lines into comments.

STEP 5: Run the project. This time click the *Calculate* button without entering a quantity.
A run-time error will occur (Figure 4.33).
Click *Stop Debugging* to cancel execution.

Figure 4.33

The missing data cause an exception and run-time error.

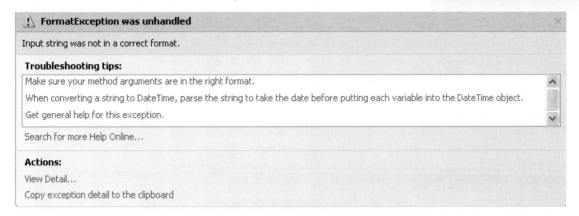

STEP 6: After you are finished testing the program, select the commented lines and click on the *Uncomment the selected lines* button (Figure 4.34).

Note: You can just click an insertion point in a line or select the entire line when you comment and uncomment lines.

Figure 4.34

Click the Uncomment the selected lines toolbar button after testing the program.

S u m m a r y

1. C# uses the `if/else` statement to make decisions. An `else` clause is optional and specifies the action to be taken if the expression evaluates *false*. If there are multiple statements for the `if` or `else`, the statements must be enclosed in braces.
2. UML activity diagrams can help visualize the logic of an `if/else` statement.
3. The Boolean expressions for an `if` statement are evaluated for *true* or *false*.
4. Boolean expressions can be composed of the relational operators, which compare items for equality, greater than, or less than. The comparison of numeric values is based on the quantity of the number, while character comparisons are based on the ANSI code table. Strings may use the equal and not equal operators or the string methods `Equals` and `CompareTo`.
5. The `ToUpper` and `ToLower` methods of the String class can convert a text value to upper- or lowercase.
6. The `&&`, `||`, `&`, and `|` logical operators may be used to combine multiple expressions. With the `&&` operator, both expressions must be true for the entire expression to evaluate *true*. For the `||` operator, if either or both expressions are true, the entire expression evaluates as *true*. When both `&&`

and || are used in a compound Boolean expression, the && expression is evaluated before the || expression. || and && short circuit the expression so that the second part of a compound expression may not be tested; use a single symbol (| or &) to not short circuit and thus force evaluation of all expressions.

7. A nested `if` statement contains an `if` statement within either the *true* or *false* actions of a previous `if` statement. An `else` clause always applies to the last unmatched `if` regardless of indentation.

8. The state of radio buttons and check boxes is better tested with `if` statements in the event handler for a button, rather than coding event handlers for the radio button or check box. Use individual `if` statements for check boxes and nested `if` statements for multiple radio buttons.

9. The `MessageBox.Show` method can display a multiline message if you concatenate a NewLine character (\n) to specify a line break.

10. You can choose to display multiple buttons in a message box. The `MessageBox.Show` method returns an object of the DialogResult class, which you can check using the DialogResult constants.

11. Data validation checks the reasonableness or appropriateness of the value in a variable or property.

12. The `switch` statement can test an expression for multiple values and substitute for nested `if` statements.

13. You can assign the event-handling method for a control in the Properties window. A single method can be assigned to multiple controls, so that the controls share the event handler.

14. You can use the `sender` argument in an event-handling method to determine which control caused the method to execute.

15. One method can call another method. To call an event-handling method, you must supply the `sender` and e arguments.

16. A variety of debugging tools are available in Visual Studio. These include writing to the Output window, breaking program execution, displaying the current contents of variables, and stepping through code.

Key Terms

Review Questions

1. What is the general format of the statement used to code decisions in an application?
2. What is a Boolean expression?
3. Explain the purpose of relational operators and logical operators.
4. How does a comparison performed on numeric data differ from a comparison performed on string data?
5. How does C# compare the Text property of a text box?
6. Why would it be useful to include the `ToUpper` method in a comparison?
7. Name the types of items that can be used in a comparison.
8. Explain a Boolean variable test for *true* and *false*. Give an example.
9. Give an example of a situation where nested `if`s would be appropriate.
10. Define the term *validation*. When is it appropriate to do validation?
11. Define the term *checking a range*.
12. When would it be appropriate to use a `switch` structure? Give an example.
13. Explain the difference between *Step Into* and *Step Over*.
14. What steps are necessary to view the current contents of a variable during program execution?

Programming Exercises

4.1 Lynette Rifle owns an image consulting shop. Her clients can select from the following services at the specified regular prices: Makeover $125, Hair Styling $60, Manicure $35, and Permanent Makeup $200. She has distributed discount coupons that advertise discounts of 10 percent and 20 percent off the regular price. Create a project that will allow the receptionist to select a discount rate of 10 percent, 20 percent, or none, and then select a service. Display the total price for the currently selected service and the total due for all services. A visit may include several services. Include buttons for *Calculate*, *Clear*, *Print*, and *Exit*.

4.2 Modify Programming Exercise 4.1 to allow for sales to additional patrons. Include buttons for *Next Patron* and *Summary*. When the receptionist clicks the *Summary* button, display in a summary message box the number of clients and the total dollar value for all services rendered. For *Next Patron*, confirm that the user wants to clear the totals for the current customer.

4.3 Create a project to compute your checking account balance.
Form: Include radio buttons to indicate the type of transaction: deposit, check, or service charge. A text box will allow the user to enter the amount of the transaction. Display the new balance in a ReadOnly text box or a label. Calculate the balance by adding deposits and subtracting service charges and checks. Include buttons for *Calculate*, *Clear*, *Print*, and *Exit*.

4.4   Add validation to Programming Exercise 4.3. Display a message box if the new balance would be a negative number. If there is not enough money to cover a check, do not deduct the check amount. Instead, display a message box with the message "Insufficient Funds" and deduct a service charge of $10.

4.5   Modify Programming Exercise 4.3 or 4.4 by adding a *Summary* button that displays the total number of deposits, the total dollar amount of deposits, the number of checks, and the dollar amount of the checks. Do not include checks that were returned for insufficient funds, but do include the service charges. Use a message box to display the summary information.

4.6   Piecework workers are paid by the piece. Workers who produce a greater quantity of output are often paid at a higher rate.

Form: Use text boxes to obtain the person's name and the number of pieces completed. Include a *Calculate* button to display the dollar amount earned. You will need a *Summary* button to display the total number of pieces, the total pay, and the average pay per person. A *Clear* button should clear the name and the number of pieces for the current employee and a *Clear All* button should clear the summary totals after confirming the operation with the user.

Include validation to check for missing data. If the user clicks on the *Calculate* button without first entering a name and the number of pieces, display a message box. Also, you need to make sure to not display a summary before any data are entered; you cannot calculate an average when no items have been calculated. You can check the number of employees in the Summary event handler or disable the *Summary* button until the first order has been calculated.

Pieces completed	Price paid per piece for all pieces
1–199	.50
200–399	.55
400–599	.60
600 or more	.65

4.7   Modify Programming Exercise 2.2 (the flag viewer) to treat radio buttons and check boxes in the proper way. Include a *Display* button and check the settings of the radio buttons and check boxes in the button's event handler, rather than making the changes in event handlers for each radio button and check box.

Note: For help in basing a new project on an existing project, see "Copy and Move a Windows Project" in Appendix C.

4.8   Create an application to calculate sales for Catherine's Catering. The program must determine the amount due for an event based on the number of guests, the menu selected, and the bar options. Additionally, the program maintains summary figures for multiple events.

Form: Use a text box to input the number of guests and radio buttons to allow a selection of Prime Rib, Chicken, or Pasta. Check boxes allow the user to select an Open Bar and/or Wine with Dinner. Include buttons for *Calculate*, *Clear*, *Summary*, and *Exit*. Display the amount due for the event in a label or ReadOnly text box.

Rates per Person

Prime Rib	25.95
Chicken	18.95
Pasta	12.95
Open Bar	25.00
Wine with Dinner	8.00

Summary: Display the number of events and the total dollar amount in a message box. Prompt the user to determine if he or she would like to clear the summary information. If the response is Yes, set the number of events and the total dollar amount to zero. Do not display the summary message box if there is no summary information. (Either disable the *Summary* button until a calculation has been made or test the total for a value.)

Case Studies

Custom Supplies Mail Order

Calculate the amount due for an order. For each order, the user should enter the following information into text boxes: customer name, address, city, state (two-letter abbreviation), and ZIP code. An order may consist of multiple items. For each item, the user will enter the product description, quantity, weight, and price into text boxes.

You will need buttons for *Add This Item*, *Update Summary*, *Clear*, and *Exit*.

For the *Add This Item* button, validate the quantity, weight, and price. Each must be present and numeric. For any bad data, display a message box. Calculate the charge for the current item and add the charge and weight into the appropriate totals, but do not display the summary until the user clicks the *Update Summary* button. Do not calculate shipping and handling on individual items; rather, calculate shipping and handling on the entire order.

When the user clicks *Add This Item* for a new order, the customer information should be disabled so that the state cannot be changed until the next customer.

When the *Update Summary* button is clicked, calculate the sales tax, shipping and handling, and the total amount due for the order. Sales tax is 8 percent of the total charge and is charged only for shipments to a California address. Do not charge sales tax on the shipping and handling charges. The shipping and handling should be calculated only for a complete order.

Optional: Disable the *Add This Item* button when the *Summary* button is pressed.

The *Clear* button clears the data and totals for the current customer.

The shipping and handling charges depend on the weight of the products. Calculate the shipping charge as $0.25 per pound and add that amount to the handling charge (taken from the following table).

Weight	Handling
Less than 10 pounds	$1.00
10 to 100 pounds	$3.00
Over 100 pounds	$5.00

Display the entire amount of the bill in controls titled *Dollar amount due*, *Sales tax*, *Shipping and handling*, and *Total amount due*.

Test data

Description	Quantity	Weight	Price
Planter	2	3	19.95
Mailbox	1	2	24.95
Planter Box	2	3	19.95

Test data output for taxable (if shipped to a California address)

Dollar Amount Due	$104.75
Sales Tax	8.38
Shipping and Handling	6.50
Total Amount Due	119.63

Test data output for nontaxable (if shipped outside of California)

Dollar Amount Due	$104.75
Sales Tax	0.00
Shipping and Handling	6.50
Total Amount Due	111.25

Christopher's Car Center

Create a project that determines the total amount due for the purchase of a vehicle. Include text boxes for the base price and the trade-in amount. Check boxes will indicate if the buyer wants additional accessories such as a stereo system, leather interior, and/or computer navigation. A group box for the exterior finish will contain radio buttons for Standard, Pearlized, or Customized detailing.

Have the trade-in amount default to zero; that is, if the user does not enter a trade-in amount, use zero in your calculation. Validate the values from the text boxes, displaying a message box if necessary.

To calculate, add the price of selected accessories and exterior finish to the base price and display the result in a control called *Subtotal*. Calculate the sales tax on the subtotal and display the result in a Sales Tax control. Calculate and display the total in a *Total* control. Then subtract any trade-in amount from the total and display the result in an *Amount Due* control.

Include buttons for *Calculate*, *Clear*, and *Exit*. The *Calculate* button must display the total amount due after trade-in.

Hint: Recall that you can make an ampersand appear in the Text property of a control by including two ampersands. See the tip on page 82 (Chapter 2).

Item	Price
Stereo System	425.76
Leather Interior	987.41
Computer Navigation	1,741.23
Standard	No additional charge
Pearlized	345.72
Customized Detailing	599.99
Tax Rate	8%

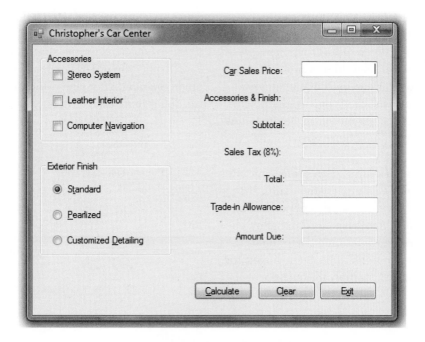

Xtreme Cinema

Design and code a project to calculate the amount due for rentals. Movies may be in Blu-Ray (BD) format or DVD format. BD rent for $5.00 each and DVDs rent for $4.50. New releases are $1 additional charge.

On the form include a text box to input the movie title and radio buttons to indicate whether the movie is in DVD or BD format. Use one check box to indicate whether the person is a member; members receive a 10 percent discount. Another check box indicates a new release.

Use buttons for *Calculate*, *Clear for Next Item*, *Order Complete*, *Summary*, and *Exit*. The *Calculate* button should display the item amount and add to the subtotal. The *Clear for Next Item* clears the check box for new releases, the movie title, and the radio buttons; the member check box cannot be changed until the current order is complete. Include validation to check for missing data. If the user clicks on the *Calculate* button without first entering the movie title and selecting the movie format, display a message box.

For the *Order Complete* button, first confirm the operation with the user and clear the controls on the form for a new customer.

The *Summary* button displays the number of customers and the sum of the rental amounts in a message box. Make sure to add to the customer count and rental sum for each customer order.

Cool Boards

Cool Boards does a big business in shirts, especially for groups and teams. They need a project that will calculate the price for individual orders, as well as a summary for all orders.

The store employee will enter the orders in an order form that has text boxes for customer name and order number. To specify the shirts, use a text box for the quantity, radio buttons to select the size (small, medium, large, extra large, and XXL), and check boxes to specify a monogram and/or a pocket. Display the shirt price for the current order and the order total in ReadOnly text boxes or labels.

Include buttons to add a shirt to an order, clear the current item, complete the order, and display the summary of all orders. Do not allow the summary to display if the current order is not complete. Also, disable the text boxes for customer name and order number after an order is started; enable them again when the user clicks on the button to begin a new order. Confirm the operation before clearing the current order.

When the user adds shirts to an order, validate the quantity, which must be greater than zero. If the entry does not pass the validation, do not perform any calculations but display a message box and allow the user to correct the value. Determine the price of the shirts from the radio buttons and check boxes for the monogram and pockets. Multiply the quantity by the price to determine the extended price, and add to the order total and summary total.

Use constants for the shirt prices.

Display the order summary in a message box. Include the number of shirts, the number of orders, and the dollar total of the orders.

Prices for the shirts

Small, medium, and large	$10
Extra large	11
XXL	12
Monogram	Add $2
Pocket	Add $1

5

Menus, Common Dialog Boxes, and Methods

1. Create menus and submenus for program control.

2. Display and use the Windows common dialog boxes.

3. Create context menus for controls and the form.

4. Write reusable code in methods and call the methods from other locations.

Menus

You have undoubtedly used menus quite extensively while working with the computer. **Menus** consist of a menu bar that contains menus, each of which drops down to display a list of menu items. You can use menu items in place of or in addition to buttons to execute a method.

Menu items are actually controls; they have properties and events. Each menu item has a Name property, a Text property, and a Click event, similar to a button. When the user selects a menu item, either with the mouse or the keyboard, the menu item's Click event-handling method executes.

It is easy to create menus for a Windows form using the Visual Studio environment's **Menu Designer**. Your menus will look and behave like standard Windows menus.

Defining Menus

To create menus for your application, you add a **MenuStrip component** to a form. The MenuStrip is a container to which you can add **ToolStripMenuItems**. You also can add ToolStripComboBoxes, ToolStripSeparators, and ToolStripTextBoxes, making the new menus considerably more powerful than those in C# Version 1.

The Visual Studio Menu Designer allows you to add menus and menu items to your forms. You must add a MenuStrip component from the toolbox (Figure 5.1), which appears in the component tray below the form. Once you have added the MenuStrip component, it is extremely easy to create the menu items for your menu. The words *Type Here* appear at the top of the form so that you can enter the text for your first menu (Figure 5.2). After you type the text for the first menu name and press Enter, the words *Type Here* appear both below the menu name and to the right of the menu name. You can choose next to enter menu items for the first menu, or to type the words for the second menu (Figure 5.3). Each time you type the text for a new menu, you are automatically adding a ToolStripMenuItem to the MenuStrip's Items collection.

Note: If you click elsewhere on the form, you deactivate the Menu Designer. You can click on the menu at the top of the form or on the MenuStrip component to activate the Menu Designer again.

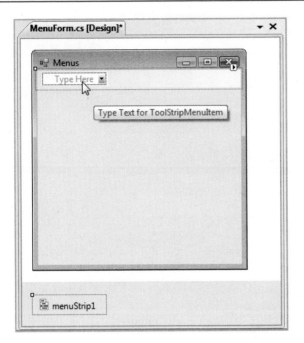

Figure 5.2

The MenuStrip component appears in the component tray below the form and the Menu Designer allows you to begin typing the text for the menu items.

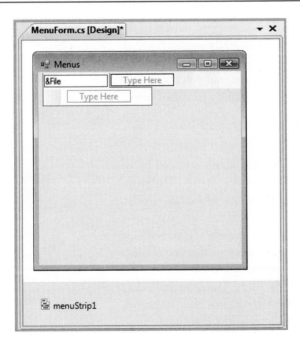

Figure 5.3

After typing the text for the first menu, you can add a second menu or add menu items below the menu name.

☑**TIP**

Do not use the same access key on a top-level menu as you use on a form control. However, access keys on menu items and submenus do not conflict with menu or control access keys. ∎

The Text Property

When you type the words for a menu or menu item, you are entering the Text property for an item. The Text property holds the words that you want to appear on the screen (just like the Text property of a button or label). To conform to Windows standards, your first menu's Text property should be File, with a keyboard access key. Use the ampersand (&) in the text to specify the key to use for keyboard access, as you learned to do in Chapter 2. For example, for <u>F</u>ile, the Text property should be &File.

You can enter and change the Text property for each of your menus and menu items using the Menu Designer. You also can change the Text property using the Properties window (Figure 5.4). Click on a menu or menu item to make its properties appear in the Properties window.

Modify the Text property of a menu item in the Properties window or the Menu Designer.

The Name Property

The Visual Studio Menu Designer is smart enough to give good names to the menu items. The File menu item that you add is automatically named *fileTool-StripMenuItem*. Since the new items are named so well, you won't have to change the Name property of any menu component. However, if you change the Text property of any menu item, the item is not automatically renamed; you'll have to rename it yourself in the Properties window.

The MenuStrip Items Collection

As you create new menus using the Menu Designer, each menu is added to the Items collection that belongs to the MenuStrip. You can display the ToolStrip-MenuItems in the collection, set other properties of the items, as well as reorder, add, and delete items, using the Items Collection Editor (Figure 5.5). To display the Items Collection Editor, first select the MenuStrip (be sure you've selected the MenuStrip and not one of the ToolStripMenuItems) and then use one of these three techniques: (1) in the Items property in the Properties window, click on the ellipsis button; (2) right-click on the MenuStrip in the Menu Designer and select *Edit Items* from the context menu; or (3) click on the MenuStrip's smart-tag arrow (at the right end of the strip) to display the smart tag and select *Edit Items*.

A Menu's DropDownItems Collection

The MenuStrip's Items collection holds the top-level menus; each of the menus has its own collection of the menu items that appear in that menu. The Tool-StripMenuItems that appear below a menu name belong to the menu's Drop-DownItems collection. Therefore, if the *File* menu contains menu items for *Print*, *Save*, and *Exit*, the menu's DropDownItems collection will contain three Tool-StripMenuItems. Notice the title bar in Figure 5.6, which shows the Drop-DownItems collection for the *File* menu (fileToolStripMenuItem).

Figure 5.5

Use the MenuStrip's Item Collection Editor to display and modify properties of the menus. You also can add new menus to the collection or modify the order of the menus.

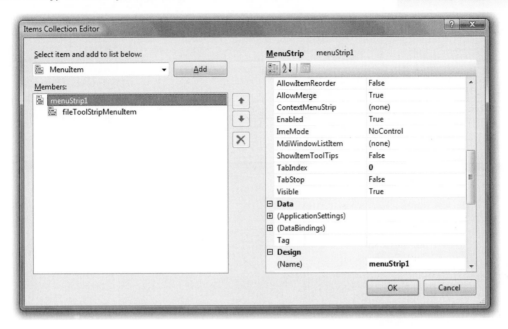

Figure 5.6

The Items Collection Editor for the DropDownItems collection, a property of the File menu's ToolStripMenuItem.

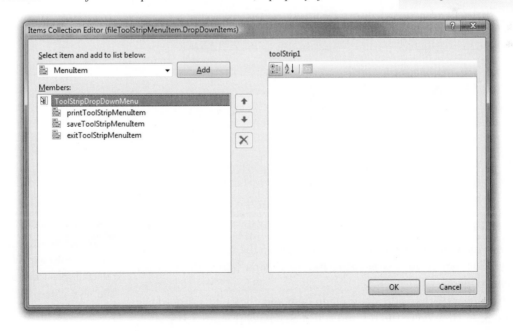

You can use the Items Collection Editor to rearrange or delete a menu item. You also can accomplish the same tasks using the Menu Designer; just drag a menu item to a new location or right-click a menu item and select *Delete*.

Submenus

The drop-down list of items below a menu name is called a *menu item*. When an item on the menu has another list of items that pops up, the new list is called a **submenu.** A filled triangle to the right of the item indicates that a menu item has a submenu (Figure 5.7). You create a submenu in the Menu Designer by moving to the right of a menu item and typing the next item's text (Figure 5.8).

Figure 5.7

A filled triangle on a menu item indicates that a submenu will appear.

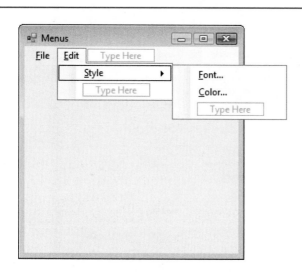

Figure 5.8

Create a submenu by typing to the right of the parent menu item.

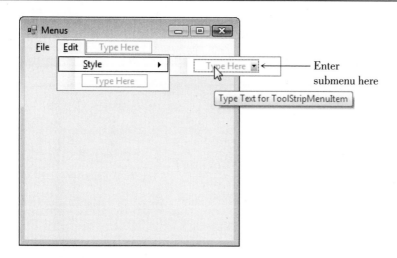

Separator Bars

When you have many items in a menu, you should group the items according to their purpose. You can create a **separator bar** in a menu, which draws a bar across the entire menu.

   To create a separator bar, add a new menu item and click on its drop-down arrow (Figure 5.9). Drop down the list and select *Separator* (Figure 5.10).

Other Features of ToolStrip Controls

You also can select ComboBox and TextBox for the type of menu item from the drop-down list. Using these features, you can create very powerful and professional menus and toolbars.

TIP

You can create a separator by typing a single hyphen where it says "Type Here" in the Menu Designer. ■

Figure 5.9

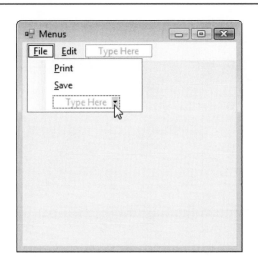

Figure 5.10

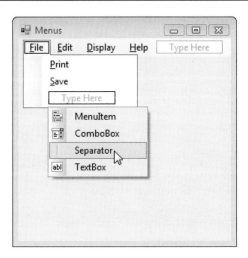

Another nice feature of the MenuStrip component is that you can now add a menu to other components on your form. For example, you could add a menu to a group box if it was appropriate.

Creating a Menu—Step-by-Step

You are going to create a project with one form and a menu bar that contains these menu items:

File	Help
Exit	*About*

Create the Menu Items

STEP 1: Begin a new Windows Forms project (or open an existing one to which you want to add a menu).

STEP 2: Add a MenuStrip component to the form. You can double-click or drag the tool to the form; the component will appear in the component tray at the bottom of the form (Figure 5.11).

When adding a MenuStrip to an existing form, the MenuStrip may overlap existing controls. To correct this, select all the controls on the form and drag them down. ■

Figure 5.11

Add a MenuStrip component to the form. It will appear in the component tray at the bottom of the form.

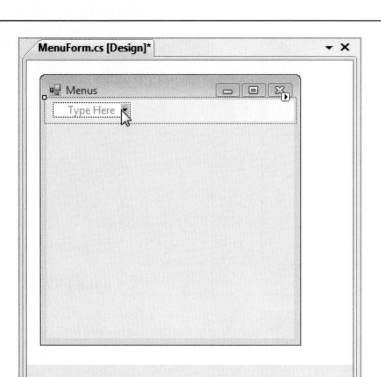

STEP 3: With the words "Type Here" selected, type "&File" over the words.

STEP 4: Move down to the "Type Here" words below the *File* menu and type "E&xit".

STEP 5: Move up and to the right and add the *Help* menu ("&Help").

STEP 6: Below the *Help* menu, add the *About* menu item ("&About").

Coding for Menu Items

After you create your form's menu bar, it appears on the form in design time. Double-click any menu item and the Editor window opens in the item's Click event handler where you can write the code. For example, in design time, open your form's *File* menu and double-click on *Exit*. The Editor window will open with the exitToolStripMenuItem_Click method displayed.

Note: The name of the ToolStripMenuItem is automatically named based on the text you entered into the Menu Designer.

Write the Code

STEP 1: Code the event-handling method for the *Exit* by pulling down the menu and double-clicking on the word *Exit*. Type a comment and a `this.Close();` statement.

STEP 2: Open the aboutToolStripMenuItem_Click event handler. Use a `MessageBox.Show` statement to display the About box. The message string should say "Programmer: " followed by your name (Figure 5.12).

STEP 3: Run the program and test your menu items.

Figure 5.12

Display a message box for an About box.

The Enabled Property

By default, all new menu items have their **Enabled property** set to *true*. An enabled menu item appears in black text and is available for selection, whereas the grayed out or **disabled** (Enabled = false) items are not available (Figure 5.13). You can set the Enabled property at design time or run time, in code.

```
instructionsToolStripMenuItem.Enabled = false;
```

Figure 5.13

Menu items can be disabled (grayed) or checked. A check mark usually indicates that the option is currently selected.

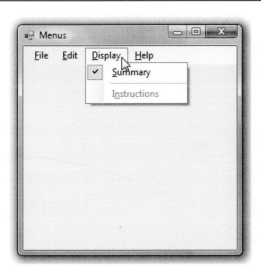

The Checked Property

A menu item may contain a check mark beside it (indicating that the item is checked). Usually a check mark next to a menu item indicates that the option is currently selected (refer to Figure 5.13). By default, the **Checked property** is set to *false*; you can change it at design time or in code.

```
summaryToolStripMenuItem.Checked = true;
```

Toggling Check Marks On and Off

If you create a menu item that can be turned on and off, you should include a check mark to indicate its current state. You can set the initial state of the Checked property in the Properties window (Figure 5.14).

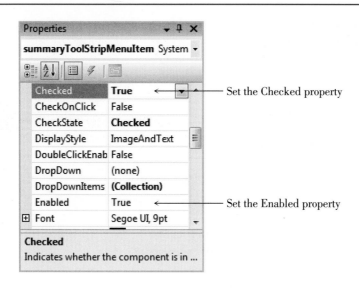

— Set the Checked property

— Set the Enabled property

To change a menu item's state in code, set its Checked property to *true* or *false*. For example, for a menu item that displays or hides a summary, called *summaryToolStripMenuItem*, a check mark indicates that the summary is currently selected. Choosing the menu item a second time should remove the check mark and hide the summary.

```csharp
private void summaryToolStripMenuItem_Click(object sender, EventArgs e)
{
    // Toggle the checkmark on the Summary menu item.

    if (summaryToolStripMenuItem.Checked)
    {
        // Uncheck the summary menu item.
        summaryToolStripMenuItem.Checked = false;
    }
    else
    {
        // Check the summary menu item.
        summaryToolStripMenuItem.Checked = true;
    }
}
```

Setting Keyboard Shortcuts

Many computer users prefer to use keyboard shortcuts for selecting menu items. For example, most applications from Microsoft use Ctrl + P for the *Print* menu item and Ctrl + S for *Save*. You can create keyboard shortcuts for your menu items and choose whether or not to display the shortcuts on the menu. (For example, you can exit most Windows applications using Alt + F4, but the keyboard shortcut rarely appears on any menu except the System menu.)

To set a keyboard shortcut for a menu item, first select the menu item in the designer. Then in the Properties window, select the ShortcutKeys property. Drop down the list to see the available choices and make your selection. You can use many combinations of function keys, the Alt key, the Shift key, and the Ctrl key. By default, the ShowShortcutKeys property is set to *true*; you can change it to *false* if you don't want the shortcut to show up on the menu.

☑TIP

You can toggle a Boolean value on and off using the Not operator (!): `summaryToolStripMenuItem.Checked != summaryToolStripMenuItem.Checked`. ∎

Standards for Windows Menus

When you write applications that run under Windows, your programs should follow the Windows standards. You should always include keyboard access keys; if you include keyboard shortcuts, such as Ctrl + key, stick with the standard keys, such as Ctrl + P for printing. Also, follow the Windows standards for placing the *File* menu on the left end of the menu bar and ending the menu with an *Exit* command. If you have a *Help* menu, it belongs at the right end of the menu bar.

Any menu item that will display a dialog box asking for more information from the user should have "…" appended to its Text property. Following Windows standards, the "…" indicates that a dialog box with further choices will appear if the user selects the menu item. You do not use the "…" for menu items that display dialog boxes that are informational only, such as an About box or a Summary form.

Plan your menus so that they look like other Windows programs. Your users will thank you.

Common Dialog Boxes

You can use a set of predefined standard dialog boxes in your projects for such tasks as specifying colors and fonts, printing, opening, and saving. Use the **common dialog** components in the *Dialogs* tab of the toolbox to display the dialog boxes that are provided as part of the Windows environment. The common dialog components provided with Visual Studio are ColorDialog, FolderBrowserDialog, FontDialog, OpenFileDialog, and SaveFileDialog (Figure 5.15).

To use a common dialog component, add the component to the form, placing it in the component tray. You can keep the default names for the components, such as colorDialog1 and fontDialog1, since you will have only one component of each type.

Figure 5.15

The common dialog tools in the toolbox.

Displaying a Windows Common Dialog Box

After you place a common dialog component on your form, you can display the dialog box at run time using the **ShowDialog** method.

ShowDialog Method—General Form

```
dialogObject.ShowDialog();
```

The dialogObject is the name of the common dialog component that you placed on the form. The name will be the default name, such as colorDialog1 or font-Dialog1.

ShowDialog Method—Examples

```
colorDialog1.ShowDialog();
fontDialog1.ShowDialog();
```

Place the code to show the dialog in the event handler for a menu item or button.

Modal versus Modeless Windows

You probably have noticed that when you display a Windows dialog box, it remains on top until you respond. But in many applications, you can display additional windows and switch back and forth between the windows. A dialog box is said to be **modal**, which means that it stays on top of the application and must be responded to. You use the ShowDialog method to display a dialog box, which is just a window displayed modally. In Chapter 6 you will learn to display additional windows that are **modeless**, which do not demand that you respond. You will use the Show method to display a modeless window.

Using the Information from the Dialog Box

Displaying the *Color* dialog box (Figure 5.16) doesn't make the color of anything change. You must take care of that in your program code. When the user clicks on *OK*, the selected color is stored in a property that you can access. You can assign the value to the properties of controls in your project.

Using the Color Dialog Box

The color selected by the user is stored in the Color property. You can assign this property to another object, such as a control.

```
titleLabel.BackColor = colorDialog1.Color;
```

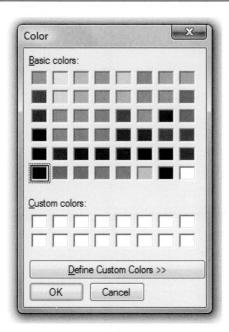

Because C# executes the statements in sequence, you would first display the dialog box with the `ShowDialog` method. (Execution then halts until the user responds to the dialog box.) Then you can use the Color property:

```
private void colorToolStripMenuItem_Click(object sender, EventArgs e)
{
    // Change the color of the total labels.

    colorDialog1.ShowDialog();
    totalLabel.ForeColor = colorDialog1.Color;
}
```

Note: You can change the ForeColor of a label that is disabled (Enabled = false), but you will not see the change until it is enabled. Likewise, you can change the ForeColor of a text box that is set to ReadOnly or disabled, but you will not notice the change until it is enabled or, for a ReadOnly text box, until you change the BackGround color or set ReadOnly to false (see the Tip on page 131).

Using the Font Dialog Box

When you display the *Font* common dialog box (Figure 5.17), the available fonts for the system display. After the user makes a selection, you can use the Font property of the dialog box object. You may want to assign the Font property to the Font property of other objects on your form.

```
private void fontToolStripMenuItem_Click(object sender, EventArgs e)
{
    // Change the font of the total label.

    fontDialog1.ShowDialog();
    totalLabel.Font = fontDialog1.Font;
}
```

Figure 5.17

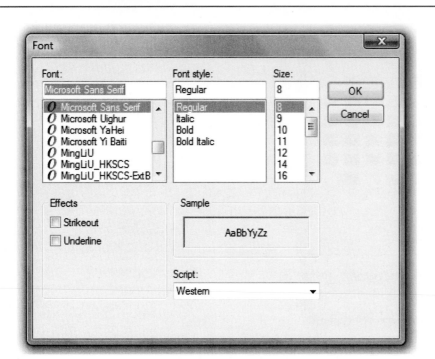

When the user clicks on the *Font* menu item, the *Font* dialog box appears on the screen. Execution halts until the user responds to the dialog box, by clicking either *OK* or *Cancel*.

Setting Initial Values

When a common dialog box for colors or fonts appears, what color or font do you want to display? It's best to assign initial values before showing the dialog box. Before executing the ShowDialog method, you should assign the existing values of the object's properties that will be altered. This step makes the current values selected when the dialog box appears. It also means that if the user selects the *Cancel* button, the property settings for the objects will remain unchanged.

```
// Change the color of the total label.
colorDialog1.Color = totalLabel.ForeColor;
colorDialog1.ShowDialog();
totalLabel.ForeColor = colorDialog1.Color;
```

or

```
// Change the font of the total label.
fontDialog1.Font = totalLabel.Font;
fontDialog1.ShowDialog();
totalLabel.Font = fontDialog1.Font;
```

Creating Context Menus

Since Windows 95, context menus have become a defacto standard Windows GUI feature. You should also add **context menus** to your applications. Context menus are the **shortcut menus** that pop up when you right-click. Generally, the items in a context menu are specific to the component to which you are pointing, listing the options available for that component or that situation.

Creating a context menu is similar to creating a menu. You add a **ContextMenuStrip component**, which appears in the component tray below the form. At the top of the form, in the Menu Designer, the words say *ContextMenuStrip* (Figure 5.18). A context menu does not have a top-level menu, only the menu items. Click on the words *Type Here* to type the text of your first menu item.

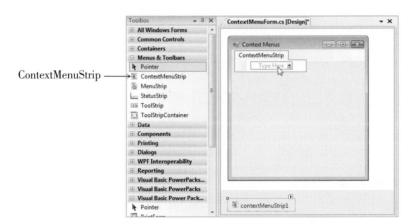

ContextMenuStrip

Figure 5.18

Add a ContextMenuStrip component to the component tray and create the context menu using the Menu Designer.

Your application can have more than one context menu. You assign the context menu to the form or control by setting its ContextMenuStrip property. For example, a form has a ContextMenuStrip property, a button has a ContextMenuStrip property, and all visible controls have ContextMenuStrip properties. You can assign the same ContextMenuStrip to the form and each of the controls, or a different context menu to each. If you have only one context menu, attach it to the form—it will pop up if the user right-clicks anywhere on the form, including on a control. However, some controls have an "automatic" context menu. For example, a text box has an automatic context menu that allows the user to cut, copy, and paste text. If you set the ContextMenuStrip property of a text box to your own context menu, your context menu will appear instead of the original (automatic) context menu.

Creating a Context Menu—Step-by-Step

You are going to create a context menu that contains these menu items:

Color...
Font...
Exit

Add the Context Menu Strip to a Form

STEP 1: Begin a new Windows project (or open an existing one to which you want to add a context menu). For a new project, change the form's file name to ContextMenuForm.

STEP 2:   Add a ContextMenuStrip component to the form; the component
          will appear in the component tray at the bottom of the form (refer to
          Figure 5.18).

STEP 3:   Click on the words *Type Here* below the words "ContextMenuStrip" in
          the Menu Designer.

STEP 4:   Type the text for the first menu item: "&Color…".

STEP 5:   Type the text for the second and third menu items: "&Font…" and
          "E&xit".

STEP 6:   Add a label named *messageLabel* to your form and set the Text prop-
          erty to "*Right-click for the Context Menu*".

STEP 7:   Set the form's ContextMenuStrip property to contextMenuStrip1. No-
          tice that the property box has a drop-down list. If you have more than
          one context menu defined, you can choose from the list.

STEP 8:   Add a ColorDialog component from the *Dialogs* tab of the toolbox.

STEP 9:   Add a FontDialog component from the toolbox.

In this example, right-clicking anywhere on the form allows you to change
the foreground color or the font of the form. As you know, if you haven't set
those properties for individual controls, the form's properties apply to all controls on the form.

STEP 10: Code the form as follows:

TIP

It's a good idea to set a ContextMenu property for all controls and for the form to allow users the option of using context menus. ∎

```
/* Program:        Ch05ContextMenus
 * Programmer:     Your Name
 * Date:           Today's date
 * Description:    Create and apply a context menu.
 */

using System;
using System.Collections.Generic;
using System.ComponentModel;
using System.Data;
using System.Drawing;
using System.Text;
using System.Windows.Forms;

namespace Ch05ContextMenus
{
    public partial class ContextMenuForm : Form
    {
        public ContextMenuForm()
        {
            InitializeComponent();
        }

        private void colorToolStripMenuItem_Click(object sender, EventArgs e)
        {
            // Change the form's ForeColor.
            // Applies to all conrols on the form that haven't had their
            // ForeColor explicitly modified.

            // Initialize the dialog box.
            colorDialog1.Color = this.ForeColor;
            // Display the dialog box.
            colorDialog1.ShowDialog();
            // Assign the new color.
            this.ForeColor = colorDialog1.Color;
        }
```

```
private void fontToolStripMenuItem_Click(object sender, EventArgs e)
{
    // Change the label's font.

    // Initialize the dialog box.
    fontDialog1.Font = messageLabel.Font;
    // Display the dialog box.
    fontDialog1.ShowDialog();
    // Assign the new font.
    messageLabel.Font = fontDialog1.Font;
}

private void exitToolStripMenuItem_Click(object sender, EventArgs e)
{
    // Exit the program.

    this.Close();
}
}
}
```

Test the Program

STEP 1: Experiment with right-clicking on the form and on the label. Test each of the options.

After you have the program working, experiment with adding more controls and more ContextMenuStrip components, and setting the ContextMenuStrip property of controls.

Sharing Methods

Most frequently, a context menu is added as an additional way to access a feature that is also available from another menu or a button. Recall from Chapter 4 that you can use a single method to handle multiple events by selecting the existing method in the Properties window (Figure 5.19).

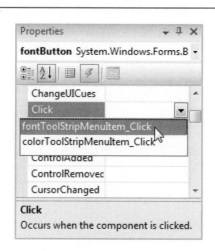

Figure 5.19

Select an existing method to handle an event to make a method handle the events of multiple objects.

Writing General Methods

Often you will encounter programming situations in which multiple methods perform the same operation. This condition can occur when the user can select either a button or a menu item to do the same thing. Rather than retyping the code, you should write reusable code in a **general method** and call it from both event handlers.

General methods are also useful in breaking down large sections of code into smaller units that perform a specific task. By breaking down your calculations into smaller tasks, you simplify any maintenance that needs to be done in a program in the future. For example, bowling statistics for a league may require calculations for handicap and series total. If the formula for calculating handicaps changes, wouldn't it be nice to have a method that calculates handicaps only instead of one that performs all the calculations?

Your method may return a value or not. You specify that the method returns a value by placing the return type of the method preceding the method name. You can return a value for any method that you create. Notice the event handlers:

```
private void fontToolStripMenuItem_Click(object sender, EventArgs e)
```

The keyword **void** indicates that the method does not return a value.

Creating a New Method

You can create a method in the Editor window by writing a method header and then enclosing the desired lines of code within a set of braces.

```
private void selectColor()
{
    // Display the color dialog box.

    colorDialog1.ShowDialog();
}
```

Note that C# has choices other than `private` for the access, such as `public`, `internal`, and `protected`. In Chapter 6 you will learn about the other types of methods; for now use `private` for all methods.

The coding for the new method is similar to the other methods we have been coding but is not yet attached to any event. Therefore, this code cannot be executed unless we specifically **call** the method from another method. To call a method, just give the method a name, which in this case is `selectColor`.

```
private void changeColorButton_Click(object sender, EventArgs e)
{
    // Change the color of the message.

    selectColor();
    messageLabel.ForeColor = colorDialog1.Color;
}
```

```
private void changeTitleButton_Click(object sender, EventArgs e)
{
    // Change the color of the title.

    selectColor();
    titleLabel.ForeColor = colorDialog1.Color;
}
```

Passing Arguments to Methods

At times you may need to use the value of a variable in one method and also in a second method that is called from the first. In this situation, you could declare the variable as class level, but that approach makes the variable visible to all other methods. To keep the scope of a variable as narrow as possible, consider declaring the variable as local and passing it to any called methods.

As an example, we will expand the capabilities of the previous selectColor method to display the original color when the dialog box appears. Because the selectColor method can be called from various locations, the original color must be passed to the method.

```
private void selectColor(Color incomingColor)
{
    // Display the color dialog box.

    colorDialog1.Color = incomingColor;
    colorDialog1.ShowDialog();
}

private void changeMessageButton_Click(object sender, EventArgs e)
{
    // Change the color of the message.

    Color originalColor = messageLabel.ForeColor;
    selectColor(originalColor);
    messageLabel.ForeColor = colorDialog1.Color;
}

private void changeTitleButton_Click(object sender, EventArgs e)
{
    // Change the color of the title.

    Color originalColor = titleLabel.ForeColor;
    selectColor(originalColor);
    titleLabel.ForeColor = colorDialog1.Color;
}
```

Notice that, in this example, the selectColor method now has a parameter inside the parentheses. This syntax specifies that, when called, an argument must be supplied.

When a method definition names a parameter, any call to that method must supply a value, called an *argument*. In addition, the data type of the parameter and the supplied argument must be the same. Notice that in the two calling methods (the changeMessageButton_Click and changeTitleButton_Click methods), the variable originalColor is declared as a Color data type.

Another important point is that the *names* of the parameter and the supplied argument do not have to be the same. The `selectColor` method will take whatever Color value it is passed and refer to it as incomingColor inside the method.

You may specify multiple parameters in the method header and supply multiple arguments in the call to the method. *The number of arguments, their sequence, and their data types must match the parameter list!* You will see some examples of multiple parameters in the sections that follow.

Writing Methods That Return Values

As a programmer, you may need to calculate a value that will be needed in several different methods or programs. You can write your own method that will calculate a value and return it to the place where the method is called. As an example, we will create a method called `commission`, which calculates and returns a salesperson's commission.

Since the method returns a value, you must specify a data type for the value.

A Method That Returns a Value—General Form

```
private DataType MethodName()
{

}
```

The method header includes a data type, which is the type of the value returned by the method.

A Method That Returns a Value—Example

```
private decimal commission()
{
    // Statements in method.
}
```

Remember that methods can have parameters. You supply arguments to a method that returns a value by placing a value or values inside the parentheses.

When you write a method, you declare the parameter(s) that the method needs. You give each parameter a data type and an identifier. The name that you give a parameter in the method header is the identifier that you will use inside the method to refer to the value passed as an argument.

Example

```
private decimal commission(decimal salesAmountDecimal)
```

In the method header, the parameter list you enter establishes the number of parameters, their type, and their sequence. When using multiple parameters, the sequence of the supplied arguments is critical, just as when you use predefined methods.

Returning the Result of a Method

A method can return one value, which must be the same data type as that named in the method header. The **return value** is passed back with a **return statement**. The keyword `return` is followed by a variable or expression that contains the value to return to the caller. Note that if the method header specifies `void` rather than a data type, you do not use the `return` keyword. Figure 5.20 shows a method header for a method that returns a value.

Figure 5.20

Include a data type on a method header for a method that returns a value.

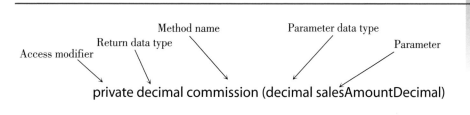

Writing a commission Method

The following `commission` method returns a commission amount of 15 percent for sales between $1,000 and $2,000. Sales over $2,000 earn 20 percent.

```
private decimal commission(decimal salesAmountDecimal)
{
    // Calculate the sales commission.

    if (salesAmountDecimal < 1000M)
    {
        return 0M;
    }
    else if (salesAmountDecimal <= 2000M)
    {
        return 0.15M * salesAmountDecimal;
    }
    else
    {
        return 0.2M * salesAmountDecimal;
    }
}
```

Calling the commission Method

In another method in the project, you can call your new `commission` method by using it in an expression.

```
private void calculateButton_Click(object sender, EventArgs e)
{
    // Calculate the commission.
    decimal salesDecimal;

    salesDecimal = decimal.Parse(salesTextBox.Text);
    commissionTextBox.Text = commission(salesDecimal).ToString("C");
}
```

Notice in the preceding example that the parameter named in the method call does not have the same name as the parameter named in the method definition. When the `commission` method is called, a copy of the value of salesDecimal is passed to the method and is assigned to the named parameter, in this case salesAmountDecimal. As the calculations are done (inside the method), for every reference to salesAmountDecimal, the value that was passed in, salesDecimal, is actually used.

You can combine the method calls, if you wish:

```
commissionTextBox.Text = commission(decimal.Parse(salesTextBox.Text)).ToString("C");
```

Converting selectColor to Return a Value

The selectColor method that we wrote earlier is a good candidate for a method that returns a value, since we need to return one value: the selected color.

```
private Color selectColor(Color incomingColor)
{
    // Display the color dialog box.

    colorDialog1.Color = incomingColor;
    colorDialog1.ShowDialog();
    return colorDialog1.Color;
}

private void changeMessageButton_Click(object sender, EventArgs e)
{
    // Change the color of the message.

    Color originalColor = messageLabel.ForeColor;
    messageLabel.ForeColor = selectColor(originalColor);
}

private void changeTitleButton_Click(object sender, EventArgs e)
{
    // Change the color of the title by calling selectColor differently.

    titleLabel.ForeColor = selectColor(titleLabel.ForeColor);
}
```

Methods with Multiple Parameters

A method can have multiple parameters. The sequence and data type of the arguments in the call must exactly match the parameters in the method header.

Writing a Method with Multiple Parameters

When you create a method with multiple parameters such as a payment method, you enclose the list of parameters within the parentheses. The following example indicates that three arguments are needed in the call: The first argument is the annual interest rate, the second is the time in years, and the third is the loan amount. All three argument values must have a data type of decimal, and the return value must be decimal.

Although the incoming parameters are decimal and the return value is decimal, inside the payment method the arguments must be converted to double. The reason for the conversion is that the `Math.Pow` method requires double data types. Look carefully at the following formula and notice how the identifiers in the parentheses are used.

```csharp
private decimal payment(decimal rateDecimal, decimal timeDecimal, decimal amountDecimal)
{
    // Calculate the payment using double values for the Pow function.
    double monthsDouble = (double)timeDecimal * 12D;
    double ratePerMonthDecimal = (double)rateDecimal / 12D;
    double amountDouble = (double)amountDecimal;

    double paymentDouble = (amountDouble * ratePerMonthDecimal)
        /(1 - (1 / Math.Pow((1 + ratePerMonthDecimal), monthsDouble)));
    // Cast the return value to a decimal value.
    return (decimal)paymentDouble;
}
```

Calling a Method with Multiple Parameters

To call this method from another method, use these statements:

```csharp
decimal rateDecimal = decimal.Parse(rateTextBox.Text);
decimal yearsDecimal = decimal.Parse(yearsTextBox.Text);
decimal principalDecimal = decimal.Parse(principalTextBox.Text);
decimal paymentDecimal = payment(rateDecimal, yearsDecimal, principalDecimal);
paymentLabel.Text = paymentDecimal.ToString("C");
```

You can format the result, as well as pass the value of the text boxes, by nesting methods:

```csharp
paymentLabel.Text = payment(decimal.Parse(rateTextBox.Text),
    decimal.Parse(yearsTextBox.Text),
    decimal.Parse(principalTextBox.Text)).ToString("C");
```

When you call the `payment` method, the smart editor shows you the parameters of your method (Figure 5.21), just as it does for built-in methods (assuming that you have already entered the method).

Figure 5.21

The Visual Studio IntelliSense feature pops up with the parameter list for your own newly written method.

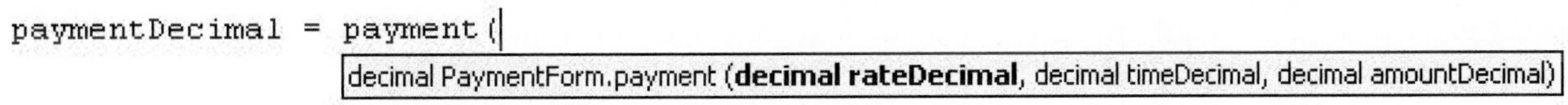

```
paymentDecimal = payment (|
            decimal PaymentForm.payment (decimal rateDecimal, decimal timeDecimal, decimal amountDecimal)
```

Reference and Output Parameters

Just as variables are either value types (holding the actual value) or reference types (holding a reference to the value), the arguments of methods also are either value parameters or reference parameters. In C#, by default, parameters are value parameters; that is, the variable named as a parameter of the method passes the value and does not refer back to the memory location of the original value in the calling method. A value parameter, also called an *In* parameter, acts like a local variable within the method. Any assignment that is made to the argument affects only the local value and does not affect the value in the calling method. When you do not specify a parameter type, the argument defaults to a value parameter.

In addition to value parameters, C# also has reference and output parameters. A reference parameter is declared by using the `ref` modifier. A reference parameter refers to the same location as the variable that was passed to the method; no new memory location is created. This means that the calling and called methods both have access to the same memory location. Note that OOP principles advise strongly against using reference parameters; only do so when you have a very strong reason.

Example Header for a Reference Parameter

```
private decimal commission(ref decimal salesDecimal)
```

Example Call for a Reference Parameter

```
commissionDecimal = commission(ref salesDecimal);
```

Note that both the method header and the call to the method must include the `ref` keyword.

The commission method receives the address of salesDecimal rather than the value. This would allow the `commission` method to alter the value of the salesDecimal variable. Don't do this unless it is needed; in this example, there is probably no reason for the `commission` method to change the value of salesDecimal.

An output parameter uses the `out` modifier in the method header. The primary purpose of output parameters is to allow a method to return more than one value. Both the method header and the call to the method must contain the `out` keyword, and the method must explicitly assign a value to each argument declared with the `out` keyword.

Example Header for an Output Parameter

```
private void commission(decimal salesAmountDecimal, out commissionOnDecimal,
    out commissionDecimal)
```

Example Call for an Output Parameter

```
commissionDecimal = commission(salesDecimal, out commissionCalulatedOnDecimal,
    out commissionAmountDecimal)
```

An output parameter is similar to a reference parameter in that the address is sent to the method rather than the value. The difference between a reference parameter and an output parameter is that the method *must* assign a value to any output parameter.

Breaking Calculations into Smaller Units

A project with many calculations can be easier to understand and write if you break the calculations into small units. Each unit should perform one program function or block of logic. In the following example that calculates bowling statistics, separate methods calculate the average, handicap, and series total, and find the high game.

```csharp
/* Project:        Ch05Bowling
 * Programmer:     Bradley/Millspaugh
 * Date:           June 2009
 * Description:    This project calculates bowling statistics using
 *                 multiple methods.
 */
using System;
using System.Collections.Generic;
using System.ComponentModel;
using System.Data;
using System.Drawing;
using System.Text;
using System.Windows.Forms;

namespace Ch05Bowling
{
    public partial class BowlingForm : Form
    {
        public BowlingForm()
        {
            InitializeComponent();
        }

        private void exitToolStripMenuItem_Click(object sender, EventArgs e)
        {
            // End the program.

            this.Close();
        }

        private void clearToolStripMenuItem_Click(object sender, EventArgs e)
        {
            // Clear the input area and individual bowler info.

            nameTextBox.Clear();
            nameTextBox.Focus();
            maleRadioButton.Checked = false;
            femaleRadioButton.Checked = false;
            score1TextBox.Clear();
            score2TextBox.Clear();
            score3TextBox.Clear();
            seriesTextBox.Text = "";
            averageTextBox.Text = "";
            highGameTextBox.Text = "";
            handicapTextBox.Text = "";
        }
        private void calculateToolStripMenuItem_Click(object sender, EventArgs e)
        {
            // Calculate individual and summary info.
            decimal averageDecimal, handicapDecimal;
            int seriesInteger, game1Integer, game2Integer, game3Integer;
            string highGameString;
```

```csharp
    try
    {
        game1Integer = int.Parse(score1TextBox.Text);
        game2Integer = int.Parse(score2TextBox.Text);
        game3Integer = int.Parse(score3TextBox.Text);

        // Perform all calculations.
        averageDecimal = findAverage(game1Integer, game2Integer,
            game3Integer);
        seriesInteger = findSeries(game1Integer, game2Integer,
            game3Integer);
        highGameString = findHighGame(game1Integer, game2Integer,
            game3Integer);
        handicapDecimal = findHandicap(averageDecimal);

        // Format the output.
        averageTextBox.Text = averageDecimal.ToString("N1");
        highGameTextBox.Text = highGameString;
        seriesTextBox.Text = seriesInteger.ToString() ;
        handicapTextBox.Text = handicapDecimal.ToString("N1");
    }
    catch
    {
        MessageBox.Show("Please Enter three scores.", "Missing Data",
            MessageBoxButtons.OK);
    }
}

private decimal findAverage(int score1Integer,int score2Integer,
    int score3Integer)
{
    // Return the average of three games.

    return (score1Integer + score2Integer + score3Integer) / 3M;
}

private decimal findHandicap(decimal averageDecimal)
{
    // Calculate the handicap.
    if (averageDecimal >= 200M)
        return 0;
    else
        return (200M – averageDecimal) * 0.8M;
}

private int findSeries(int game1Integer,int game2Integer,
    int game3Integer)
{
    // Calculate the series total.

    return game1Integer + game2Integer + game3Integer;
}

private string findHighGame(int game1Integer,int game2Integer,
    int game3Integer)
{
    // Find the highest game in the series.
```

```
            if (game1Integer > game2Integer && game1Integer > game3Integer)
                return "1";
            else if (game2Integer > game1Integer && game2Integer > game3Integer)
                return "2";
            else if (game3Integer > game1Integer && game3Integer > game2Integer)
                return "3";
            else
                return "Tie";
        }
    }
}
```

▶ **Feedback 5.1**

You need to write a method to calculate and return the average of three decimal values.

1. Write the header line of the method.
2. Write the calculation.
3. How is the calculated average passed back to the calling method?

Basing a New Project on an Existing Project

In this chapter, you will base a new project on an existing project but keep the previous project unchanged. To create a new project based on a previous one, you should copy the project folder. Then you can move it as necessary.

You can copy an entire Windows project folder from one location to another using the Windows Explorer. Make sure that the project is not open in Visual Studio and copy the entire folder.

- Make sure the project is not open (very important).

- Copy the folder to a new location using the Windows Explorer.

- Rename the new folder for the new project name, still using the Windows Explorer.

- Open the new project (the copy) in the Visual Studio IDE.

- In the IDE's Solution Explorer, rename the solution and the project. The best way to do this is to right-click on the name and choose the *Rename* command from the shortcut menu. To rename the solution, you must set the option to display the solution: *Tools / Options / Projects and Solutions / General / Always show solution.*

- Rename the forms, if desired.

- Open the Project Designer (*Project / ProjectName Properties*) and change the *Assembly name* and *Default namespace* entries to match your new project name.

Warning: Do not try to copy a project that is open using the *Save As* command, attempting to place a copy in a new location.

Your Hands-On Programming Example

Modify the hands-on programming example from Chapter 4 by adding menus and common dialog boxes. Write a general method to find the price of the extra additives and one for clearing for the next item. Allow the user to select the font of the title and the forecolor of the form. Use a `switch` statement for the size selection.

The *About* selection on the *Help* menu should display a message box with information about the programmer.

File	Edit	Help
Summary	Add to Order	About
Exit	Order Complete	
	————	
	Font...	
	Color...	

Planning the Project

Sketch a form (Figure 5.22), which your users sign as meeting their needs.

Figure 5.22

A sketch of the form for the hands-on programming example.

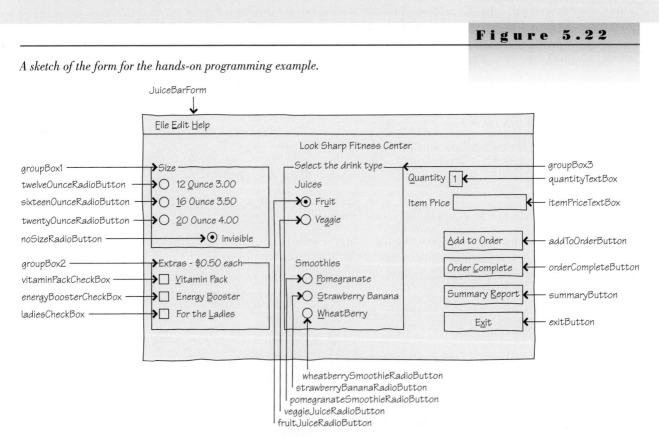

Plan the Objects and Properties Plan the property settings for the form and each of the controls.

Object	Property	Setting
JuiceBarForm	Name	JuiceBarForm
	Text	Juice Bar Orders
	AcceptButton	addToOrderButton
	CancelButton	exitButton
groupBox1	Text	Size
twelveOunceRadioButton	Name	twelveOunceRadioButton
	Text	12 &Ounce 3.00
sixteenOunceRadioButton	Name	sixteenOunceRadioButton
	Text	&16 Ounce 3.50
twentyOunceRadioButton	Name	twentyOunceRadioButton
	Text	&20 Ounce 4.00
noSizeRadioButton	Name	noSizeRadioButton
	Text	invisible
	Checked	true
	Visible	false
groupBox2	Text	Extras - $0.50 each
vitaminPackCheckBox	Name	vitaminPackCheckBox
	Text	&Vitamin Pack
energyBoosterCheckBox	Name	energyBoosterCheckBox
	Text	Energy &Booster
ladiesCheckBox	Name	ladiesCheckBox
	Text	For the &Ladies
groupBox3	Text	Select the drink type
label1	Text	Juices
fruitJuiceRadioButton	Name	fruitJuiceRadioButton
	Text	Fr&uit
	Checked	true
veggieJuiceRadioButton	Name	veggieJuiceRadioButton
	Text	Ve&ggie
label2	Text	Smoothies
pomegranateSmoothie-RadioButton	Name	pomegranateSmoothie-RadioButton
	Text	&Pomegranate
strawberryBananaRadioButton	Name	strawberryBananaRadioButton
	Text	&Strawberry Banana
wheatberrySmoothieRadioButton	Name	wheatberrySmoothieRadioButton
	Text	&WheatBerry
label3	Text	&Quantity

(Continued)

Object	Property	Setting
quantityTextBox	Name	quantityTextBox
	Text	(blank)
label4	Text	Item Price
itemPriceTextBox	Name	itemPriceTextBox
	Text	(blank)
	ReadOnly	true
	TabStop	false
addToOrderButton	Name	addToOrderButton
	Text	&Add to Order
orderCompleteButton	Name	orderCompleteButton
	Text	Order &Complete
	Enabled	false
summaryButton	Name	summaryButton
	Text	Summary &Report
	Enabled	false
exitButton	Name	exitButton
	Text	E&xit
fileToolStripMenuItem	Name	fileToolStripMenuItem
	Text	&File
summaryToolStripMenuItem	Name	summaryToolStripMenuItem
	Text	&Summary
exitToolStripMenuItem	Name	exitToolStripMenuItem
	Text	E&xit
editToolStripMenuItem	Name	editToolStripMenuItem
	Text	&Edit
addToOrderToolStripMenuItem	Name	addToOrderToolStripMenuItem
	Text	&Add to Order
orderCompleteToolStripMenuItem	Name	orderCompleteToolStripMenuItem
	Text	&Order Complete
fontToolStripMenuItem	Name	fontToolStripMenuItem
	Text	&Font…
colorToolStripMenuItem	Name	colorToolStripMenuItem
	Text	&Color…
helpToolStripMenuItem	Name	helpToolStripMenuItem
	Text	&Help
aboutToolStripMenuItem	Name	aboutToolStripMenuItem
	Text	&About
colorDialog1	Name	ColorDialog1
fontDialog1	Name	FontDialog1

Plan the Methods You need to plan the actions for the buttons and the actions of the menu items, as well as the general methods.

Object	Method	Action
addToOrderButton	Click	Check if size is selected. Validate for blank or nonnumeric amount. Add to number of drinks. Multiply price by quantity. Call clearForNextItem. Enable the Order Complete button.
orderCompleteButton	Click	If last item not cleared from screen Ask user whether to add it. If yes Call addToOrderButton_Click. Display the price of the order. Add to the number of orders and totalSales. Reset the controls for the next order. Clear the order amount
summaryButton	Click	Display the summary totals in a message box.
exitButton	Click	End the project.
Size radio buttons	CheckedChanged	Find the price of the selected size.
clearForNextItem	General method	Clear option buttons, check boxes, text boxes. Set quantity to default to 1.
findExtrasPrice	General method returns a decimal	Clear the extras variable. Find the price of extras.
Check boxes	CheckedChanged	Find the price of extras. Display the current drink price.
aboutToolStripMenuItem	Click	Display a message box showing programmer and version.
fontToolStripMenuItem	Click	Display the Font dialog box. Change the font of the title.
colorToolStripMenuItem	Click	Display the Color dialog box. Change the ForeColor of the form.

Write the Project Follow the sketch in Figure 5.22 to create the form. Figure 5.23 shows the completed form.

- Set the properties of each object according to your plan. If you are modifying the project from Chapter 4, add the menus and the common dialog controls.

- Write the code. Working from the pseudocode, write each event-handling method and general method.

- When you complete the code, use a variety of data to thoroughly test the project.

Figure 5.23

The form for the hands-on programming example.

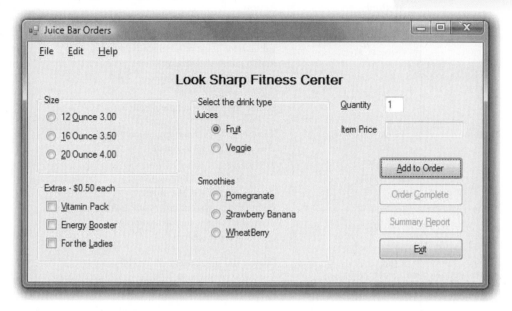

The Project Coding Solution

```
/*
 * Program Name:      Ch05HandsOn
 * Programmer:        Bradley/Millspaugh
 * Date:              June 2009
 *
 * Description:       This project calculates the amount due
 *                    based on the customer selection
 *                    and accumulates summary data for the day.
 *                    Includes menus, common dialog boxes, a
 *                    switch statement, and general methods.
 */

using System;
using System.Collections.Generic;
using System.ComponentModel;
using System.Data;
using System.Drawing;
using System.Text;
using System.Windows.Forms;

namespace Ch05HandsOn
{
    public partial class JuiceBarForm : Form
    {
        // Declare class variables.
        decimal itemSizeDecimal, totalOrderDecimal, totalSalesDecimal;
        decimal drinkDecimal;
        int drinksInteger, ordersInteger;
```

```csharp
public JuiceBarForm()
{
    InitializeComponent();
}

private void addToOrderButton_Click(object sender, EventArgs e)
{
    // Add the current item price and quantity to the order.

    if (noSizeRadioButton.Checked)
    {
        MessageBox.Show("You must select a drink and size.",
            "Missing required entry");
    }
    else
    {
        try
        {
            int quantityInteger = int.Parse(quantityTextBox.Text);
            if (quantityInteger > 0)
            {
                drinksInteger += quantityInteger;
                totalOrderDecimal += drinkDecimal * quantityInteger;
                clearForNextItem();
                orderCompleteButton.Enabled = true;
            }
            else
            {
                MessageBox.Show("Please enter a quantity",
                    "Missing Required Entry");
            }
        }
        catch (FormatException)
        {
            MessageBox.Show("Invalid Quantity", "Data Entry Error");
            quantityTextBox.Focus();
            quantityTextBox.SelectAll();
        }
    }
}

private void orderCompletebutton_Click(object sender, EventArgs e)
{
    // Order is complete, add to summary and clear order.

    // Check if the last item was added to the total.
    if (itemPriceTextBox.Text != "")
    {
        DialogResult responseDialogResult;
        string messageString = "Current item not recorded. Add to order?";
        responseDialogResult = MessageBox.Show(messageString,
            "Verify Last Drink Purchase", MessageBoxButtons.YesNo,
            MessageBoxIcon.Question);
        if (responseDialogResult == DialogResult.Yes)
        {
            addToOrderButton_Click(sender, e);
        }
    }
```

```csharp
            // Display amount due.
            string dueString = "Amount Due " + totalOrderDecimal.ToString("C");
            MessageBox.Show(dueString, "Order Complete");

            // Add to summary totals.
            ordersInteger++;
            totalSalesDecimal += totalOrderDecimal;

            // Reset all for new order.
            summaryButton.Enabled = true;
            summaryToolStripMenuItem.Enabled = true;
            orderCompleteButton.Enabled = false;
            orderCompleteToolStripMenuItem.Enabled = false;
            totalOrderDecimal = 0m;
        }

        private void summaryButton_Click(object sender, EventArgs e)
        {
            // Display the summary information in a message box.

            string summaryString = "Drinks Sold:      " + drinksInteger.ToString()
                + "\n\n" + "Number of Orders: " + ordersInteger.ToString()
                + "\n\n" + "Total Sales:      " + totalSalesDecimal.ToString("C");
            MessageBox.Show(summaryString, "Juice Bar Sales Summary",
                MessageBoxButtons.OK, MessageBoxIcon.Information);
        }

        private void exitButton_Click(object sender, EventArgs e)
        {
            // End the application.

            this.Close();
        }

        private void twelveOunceRadioButton_CheckedChanged(object sender, EventArgs e)
        {
            // Calculate and display the price for the selected item.
            // Handles all check boxes and radio buttons.

            // Cast the sender to a RadioButton type.
            RadioButton selectedSizeRadioButton = (RadioButton)sender;

            switch (selectedSizeRadioButton.Name)
            {
                case "twelveOunceRadioButton":
                    itemSizeDecimal = 3m;
                    break;
                case "sixteenOunceRadioButton":
                    itemSizeDecimal = 3.5m;
                    break;
                case "twentyOunceRadioButton":
                    itemSizeDecimal = 4m;
                    break;
            }
            drinkDecimal = itemSizeDecimal + findExtrasPrice();
            itemPriceTextBox.Text = drinkDecimal.ToString("C");
        }
```

```
private void clearForNextItem()
{
    // Clear radio buttons, check boxes, text boxes.

    noSizeRadioButton.Checked = true;
    fruitJuiceRadioButton.Checked = true;
    vitaminPackCheckBox.Checked = false;
    energyBoosterCheckBox.Checked = false;
    ladiesCheckBox.Checked = false;
    itemPriceTextBox.Clear();
    quantityTextBox.Text = "1";
}

private decimal findExtrasPrice()
{
    // Find price for additives.
    decimal extrasDecimal = 0m;

    if (vitaminPackCheckBox.Checked)
        extrasDecimal += .5m;
    if (energyBoosterCheckBox.Checked)
        extrasDecimal += .5m;
    if (ladiesCheckBox.Checked)
        extrasDecimal += .5m;

    return extrasDecimal;
}

private void vitaminPackCheckBox_CheckedChanged(object sender, EventArgs e)
{
    // Check price of additives and display current price.
    // Handles all three check boxes.

    drinkDecimal = itemSizeDecimal + findExtrasPrice();
    itemPriceTextBox.Text = drinkDecimal.ToString("C");
}

private void aboutToolStripMenuItem_Click(object sender, EventArgs e)
{
    // Display information in a message box.

    string aboutString = "Programmed by A. Programmer\nVersion 1.1";
    string captionString =
        "About Look Sharp Fitness Center Juice Bar Orders";
    MessageBox.Show(aboutString, captionString);
}

private void fontToolStripMenuItem_Click(object sender, EventArgs e)
{
    // Change the label's font.

    // Initialize the dialog box.
    fontDialog1.Font = titleLabel.Font;
    // Display the dialog box.
    fontDialog1.ShowDialog();
    // Assign the new font.
    titleLabel.Font = fontDialog1.Font;
}
```

```
private void colorToolStripMenuItem_Click(object sender, EventArgs e)
{
    // Change the form's ForeColor.
    // Applies to all controls on the form that haven't had their
    //    ForeColor explicitly modified.

    // Initialize the dialog box.
    colorDialog1.Color = this.ForeColor;
    // Display the dialog box.
    colorDialog1.ShowDialog();
    // Assign the new color.
    this.ForeColor = colorDialog1.Color;
}
}
}
```

Summary

1. The Visual Studio Menu Designer enables you to create menus by using MenuStrips, which contain ToolStripMenuItems that can have keyboard access keys assigned.
2. In the Menu Designer, you can set and modify the order and level of menu items.
3. You can modify menu items in the MenuStrip's Items Collection Editor.
4. A menu item can have a second list of choices, which is called a sub-menu.
5. Menu items can be disabled by setting the Enabled property = *false* and can be made to appear with a check mark by setting the Checked property = *true*.
6. Menus should follow Windows standards, use standard keyboard shortcuts, and include an ellipsis if further choices will be offered.
7. Each menu item has a Click event. The code to handle the actions for a menu item belongs in the item's Click event-handling method.
8. Common dialog boxes allow C# programs to display the predefined Windows dialog boxes for *Color*, *Font*, *Open File*, *Save File*, and *Folder browser*. These dialog boxes are part of the operating environment; therefore, it is an unnecessary duplication of effort to have each programmer create them again.
9. Context menus, or shortcut menus, are created using a ContextMenuStrip component and the Menu Designer. Context menus pop up when the user right-clicks.
10. The programmer can write reusable code in general methods. These methods may be called from any other procedure in the form class and may or may not return a value.
11. Methods that return a value must specify the data type of the return value and set the value to return using a `return` statement, which sends the value back to the location from which the method was called. If the return type is `void`, no value can be returned.

Key Terms

call *234*

Checked property *225*

common dialog *227*

context menu *231*

ContextMenuStrip component *231*

disabled *225*

Enabled property *225*

general method *234*

menu *218*

Menu Designer *218*

MenuStrip component *218*

modal *228*

modeless *228*

return statement *237*

return value *237*

separator bar *222*

shortcut menu *231*

ShowDialog method *228*

submenu *222*

ToolStripMenuItem *218*

void *234*

Review Questions

1. Explain the difference between a menu and a submenu.
2. How can the user know if a menu item contains a submenu?
3. What is a separator bar and how is it created?
4. Name at least three types of common dialog boxes.
5. What is a context menu? How would you attach a context menu to a control?
6. Why would you need methods that are not attached to an event?
7. Code the necessary statements to produce a color dialog box and use it to change the background color of a label.
8. Explain the difference between a method that returns a value and a method that doesn't return a value.
9. What is a return value? How can it be used?

Programming Exercises

5.1 Modify Programming Exercise 4.6 (piecework pay) to replace buttons with menus and add a method.

   This project will input the number of pieces and calculate the pay for multiple employees. It also must display a summary of the total number of pieces, the number of workers, the total pay, and the average pay for all employees.

Menu: The menu bar must have these items:

File	Edit	Help
Calculate Pay	Clear	About
Summary	Clear All	
Exit	————	
	Font...	
	Color...	

Piecework workers are paid by the piece. Workers who produce a greater quantity of output may be paid at a higher rate.

Use text boxes to obtain the name and the number of pieces completed. The *Calculate Pay* menu item calculates and displays the dollar amount earned. The *Summary* menu item displays the total number of pieces, the total number of workers, the total pay, and the average pay per person in a message box. The *Clear* menu choice clears the name and the number of pieces for the current employee and resets the focus.

The *Color* item should change the ForeColor of the objects on the form and *Font* items should change the font of the information displayed for the Amount Earned.

Use a message box to display the program name and your name for the *About* option on the *Help* menu.

Write a method to find the pay rate and return a value to the proper event-handling method.

Pieces completed	Price paid per piece for all pieces
1 to 199	.50
200 to 399	.55
400 to 599	.60
600 or more	.65

Optional Extra: Add a context menu to the Amount Earned label with the choices for font and color. Consider adding another context menu to the form for calculating and clearing.

Note: For help in basing a new project on an existing project, see "Basing a New Project on an Existing Project" in this chapter.

5.2   Redo the checking account programming exercises from Chapter 4 (4.3, 4.4, and 4.5) using menus and methods.

Menu:

File	Edit	Help
Transaction	Clear	About
Summary	————	
Print	Font...	
Exit	Color...	

Form: Use radio buttons to indicate the type of transaction—deposit, check, or service charge. Use a text box to allow the user to enter the amount of the transaction. Display the balance in a label or ReadOnly text box.

Include validation that displays a message box if the amount of the transaction is a negative number. If there is not enough money to cover a check, display a message box with the message "Insufficient Funds." Do not pay the check, but deduct a service charge of $10.

Write methods for processing deposits, checks, and service charges. The deposit method adds the deposit to the balance; the check method subtracts the transaction amount from the balance; the service charge method subtracts the transaction amount from the balance. Each of the methods must return the updated balance.

The *Summary* menu item displays the total number of deposits and the dollar amount of deposits, the number of checks, and the dollar amount of the checks in a message box.

The *Clear* menu item clears the radio buttons and the amount and resets the focus.

The *Color* menu item should change the form's ForeColor and the *Font* menu item should change the font of the information displayed for the balance.

Use a message box to display the program name and your name as the programmer for the *About* option on the *Help* menu.

Note: For help in basing a new project on an existing project, see "Basing a New Project on an Existing Project" in this chapter.

5.3   A salesperson earns a weekly base salary plus a commission when sales are at or above quota. Create a project that allows the user to input the weekly sales and the salesperson name, calculates the commission, and displays summary information.

Form: The form should have text boxes for the salesperson name and his or her weekly sales.

Menu:

File	Edit	Help
Pay	Clear	About
Summary	———	
Print	Font...	
Exit	Color...	

Use constants to establish the base pay, the quota, and the commission rate.

The *Pay* menu item calculates and displays the commission and the total pay for that person. However, if there is no commission, do not display the commission amount (do not display a zero-commission amount).

Write a method to calculate and return the commission. The method must compare sales to the quota. When the sales are equal to or greater than the quota, calculate the commission by multiplying sales by the commission rate.

Each salesperson receives the base pay plus the commission (if one has been earned). Format the dollar amounts to two decimal places; do not display a dollar sign.

The *Summary* menu item displays a message box that holds total sales, total commissions, and total pay for all salespersons. Display the numbers with two decimal places and dollar signs.

The *Clear* menu item clears the name, sales, commission, and pay for the current employee and then resets the focus.

The *Color* menu item should change the ForeColor of the objects on the form. The *Font* menu items should change the font of the information displayed for commission and total pay.

Use a message box to display the program name and your name as programmer for the *About* option on the *Help* menu.

Test Data: Quota = 1000; Commission rate = .15 (15%); and Base pay = $250.

Name	Sales
Sandy Smug	1,000.00
Sam Sadness	999.99
Joe Whiz	2,000.00

Totals should be

Sales	$3,999.99
Commissions	450.00
Pay	1,200.00

5.4   The local library has a summer reading program to encourage reading. The staff keeps a chart with readers' names and bonus points earned. Create a project using a menu and a method that determines and returns the bonus points.

Menu:

File	Edit	Help
Points	Clear	About
Summary	———	
Print	Font...	
Exit	Color...	

Form: Use text boxes to obtain the reader's name and the number of books read. Display the number of bonus points.

The *Points* menu item should call a method to calculate the points using this schedule: the first three books are worth 10 points each. The next three books are worth 15 points each. All books over six are worth 20 points each.

The *Summary* menu item displays the average number of books read for all readers that session.

The *Clear* menu item clears the name, the number of books read, and the bonus points and then resets the focus.

The *Color* menu item should change the color of the controls on the form; the *Font* menu item should change the font of the bonus points.

Use a message box to display the program name and your name as programmer for the *About* option on the *Help* menu.

Test Data: 7 books = 95 points.

5.5   Modify Programming Exercise 2.2 (the flag viewer) to use a menu instead of radio buttons, check boxes, and buttons. Include check marks next to the name of the currently selected country and next to the selected display options.

Use a message box to display the program name and your name as programmer for the *About* option on the *Help* menu.

Menu:

File	*Country*	*Display*	*Help*
Print	*United States*	*Title*	*About*
Exit	*Canada*	*Country Name*	
	Japan	*Programmer*	
	Mexico		

Note: For help in basing a new project on an existing project, see "Basing a New Project on an Existing Project" in this chapter.

Case Studies

Custom Supplies Mail Order

Modify the case study project from Chapter 4 to use menus and a method. Refer to Chapter 4 for project specifications.

Write a method to calculate and return the shipping and handling based on the weight for an entire order. (Do not calculate shipping and handling on individual items—wait until the order is complete.)

Apply the user's font changes to the Total Due; apply color changes to the form's ForeColor.

Use a message box to display the program name and your name as programmer for the *About* option on the *Help* menu.

Menu:

File	*Edit*	*Help*
Update Summary	*Add This Item*	*About*
Exit	*Clear*	
	———	
	Font. . .	
	Color. . .	

Note: For help in basing a new project on an existing project, see "Basing a New Project on an Existing Project" in this chapter.

Christopher's Car Center

Modify the case study project from Chapter 4 to use menus and a method. Refer to Chapter 4 for project specifications.

Write a method to calculate and return the sales tax.

Menu:

File	Edit	Help
Exit	Calculate	About
	Clear	
	————	
	Font. . .	
	Color. . .	

Apply the user's font changes to the Amount Due; apply the color changes to the form's ForeColor. Consider adding keyboard shortcuts to the menu commands.

Note: For help in basing a new project on an existing project, see "Basing a New Project on an Existing Project" in this chapter.

Xtreme Cinema

Modify the case study from Chapter 4 to use menus and a method. Refer to Chapter 4 for project specifications.

Write a method to calculate and return the rental fee based on the type of video.

The *Help* menu *About* option should display a message box with information about the program and the programmer. The *Color* option should change the background color of the form; the font changes can change the control of your choice.

Menu:

File	Edit	Help
Summary	Calculate	About
Exit	Clear for Next Item	
	Order Complete	
	————	
	Color. . .	
	Font. . .	

Optional extra: Set keyboard shortcuts for the menu commands.

Note: For help in basing a new project on an existing project, see "Basing a New Project on an Existing Project" in this chapter.

Cool Boards

Modify your case study project from Chapter 4 to add a menu and a method. Refer to Chapter 4 for the project specifications.

Write a method to calculate and return the price of shirts; display the *About* box in a message box.

Allow the user to change the font size and font color of the label that displays the company slogan.

Include keyboard shortcuts for the menu commands.

Menu:

File	Sale	Display	Help
Summary	Add to Order	Font. . .	About
————	Clear This Item	Color. . .	
Exit	Order Complete	————	
		Slogan	
		Logo	

The Slogan and Logo: Make up a slogan for the company, such as "We're Number One" or "The Best

in Boards." The logo should be a graphic; you can use an icon, any graphic you have available, or a graphic you create yourself with a draw or paint program.

The *Slogan* and *Logo* menu choices must toggle and display a check mark when selected. For example, when the slogan is displayed, the *Slogan* menu command is checked. If the user selects the *Slogan* command again, hide the slogan and uncheck the menu command. The *Slogan* and *Logo* commands operate independently; that is, the user may select either, both, or neither item.

When the project begins, the slogan and logo must both be displayed and their menu commands appear checked.

Note: For help in basing a new project on an existing project, see "Basing a New Project on an Existing Project" in this chapter.

6

Multiform Projects

1. Include multiple forms in an application.

2. Use a template to create an About box form.

3. Create a new instance of a form's class and show the new form.

4. Use the Show, ShowDialog, and Hide methods to display and hide forms.

5. Understand the various form events and select the best method for your code.

6. Declare variables with the correct scope and access level for multiform projects.

7. Create new properties of a form and pass data values from one form to another.

8. Create and display a splash screen.

9. Run your project outside of the IDE.

Using Multiple Forms

All the projects that you have created up to now have operated from a single form. It has probably occurred to you that the project could appear more professional if you could use different windows for different types of information. Consider the example in Chapter 5 in which summary information is displayed in a message box when the user presses the *Summary* button. You have very little control over the appearance of the message box. The summary information could be displayed in a much nicer format in a new window with identifying labels. Another window in C# is actually another form.

The first form a project displays is called the **startup form**. You can add more forms to the project and display them as needed. A project can have as many forms as you wish.

Creating New Forms

To add a new form to a project, select *Add Windows Form* from the *Project* menu. The *Add New Item* dialog box appears (Figure 6.1), in which you can select from many installed templates. You will learn about some of the other form types later in the chapter. For now, choose *Windows Forms* for *Category* and *Windows Form* for Template to add a regular new form.

Figure 6.1

Select Windows Forms *for* Category *and the* Windows Form *template to add a new form to a project. Your dialog box may have more or fewer item templates, depending on the version of Visual Studio you are using.*

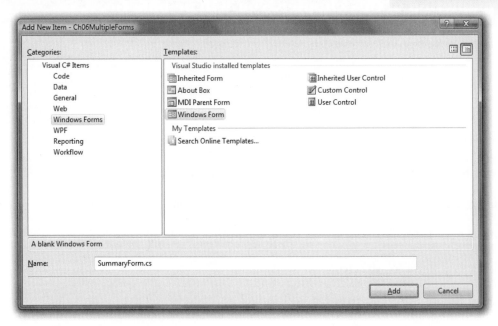

Adding a New Form to a Project

You can add a new form to a project following these steps:

STEP 1: Select *Add Windows Form* from the *Project* menu. *Note*: If the *Project* menu does not contain the *Add Windows Form* item, click in the main Document window to make it active and open the *Project* menu again.

STEP 2: In the *Categories* pane of the *Add New Item* dialog box, select *Windows Forms*. Then select the *Windows Form* from the *Templates* list.

STEP 3: Enter a name for the new form and click on *Add*.

The new form will display on the screen and be added to the Solution Explorer window (Figure 6.2).

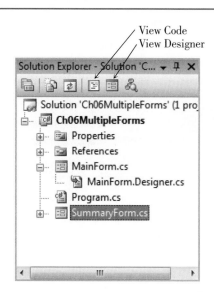

Figure 6.2

After adding a new form, the Solution Explorer shows the filename of the new form.

While in design time, you can switch between forms in several ways. In the Solution Explorer window, you can select a form name and click the *View Designer* button or the *View Code* button. Double-clicking a form name opens the form in the designer. But the easiest way to switch between forms is to use the tabs at the top of the Document window that appear after the form has been displayed (Figure 6.3). If there isn't room to display tabs for all open

Figure 6.3

Click on the tabs at the top of the Document window to switch among the Form Designer and Editor windows.

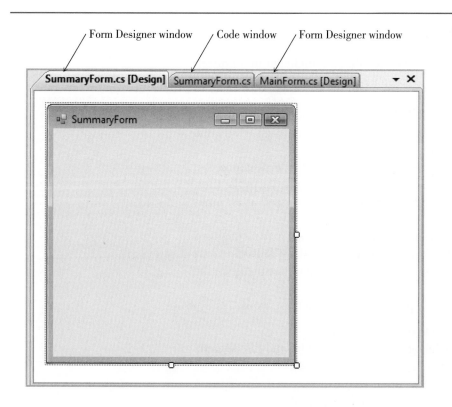

documents, you can click the *Active Files* button to drop down a list and make a selection (Figure 6.4).

Each form is a separate class and is stored in its own files. Later in this chapter, you will learn to display and hide each of the forms in a project.

Figure 6.4

You can drop down the list of available windows and select a form to view.

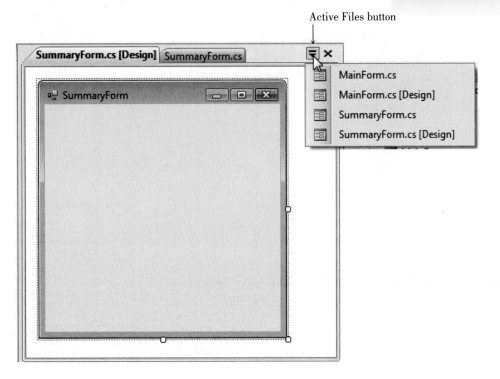

Active Files button

Adding and Removing Forms

The Solution Explorer window shows the files that are included in a project. You can add new files and remove files from a project.

Adding Existing Form Files to a Project

Forms may be used in more than one project. You might want to use a form that you created for one project in a new project.

Each form is saved as three separate files with the extensions .cs, designer.cs, and .resx. All of the information for the form resides in the files, which includes the code methods and the visual interface as well as all property settings for the controls.

To add an existing form to a project, use the *Add Existing Item* command on the *Project* menu and navigate to the form file to be added. You select only one filename: FormName.cs; all three files are automatically copied into the project folder.

You can add an existing form to a project by following these steps:

STEP 1: Select *Add Existing Item* from the *Project* menu.
STEP 2: In the *Add Existing Item* dialog box, locate the folder and file desired.
STEP 3: Click on *Add*.

Removing Forms from a Project

If you want to remove a file from a project, select its name in the Solution Explorer window. You can then either press the Delete key or right-click on the filename to display the context menu and choose *Delete*. You also can choose *Exclude From Project* to remove the form from the project but not delete the files.

Creating a New Instance of a Form

Each form in your project is a class, which you can use to create a new object. This is similar to the controls that you place on forms such as buttons, labels, and text boxes. You must create a new instance of a form before you can display it.

Note: See "Displaying an About Form" on page 266 for more explanation of creating a new instance.

```
private void summaryButton_Click(object sender, EventArgs e)
{
    // Show the summary form.

    // Declare a variable and instantiate the new object.
    SummaryForm aSummaryForm = new SummaryForm();
    // Show the new form object.
    aSummaryForm.ShowDialog();
}
```

> ☑ **TIP**
>
> **U**se the F7 key to switch to the *Form Code* tab and Shift + F7 for the *Form Designer Window* tab (depending on the keyboard settings). Use Ctrl + Tab to cycle through all open Document windows: while holding Ctrl, press Tab multiple times; when you reach the item you want, release the Ctrl key. ■

An About Box

One popular type of form in a project is an **About box**, such as the one you find in most Windows programs under *Help / About*. Usually an About box gives the name and version of the program as well as information about the programmer or company.

You can create your own About box by creating a new form and entering the information in labels. Of course, you may use any of the Windows controls on this new form, but About boxes typically hold labels and perhaps a picture box for a logo. Figure 6.5 shows a typical About box.

Figure 6.5

A typical About box that contains labels and a button.

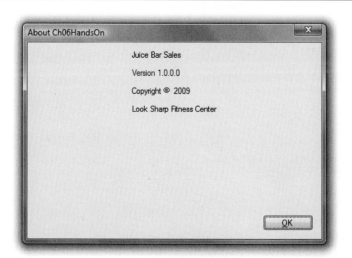

Using the About Box Template

You also can use Visual Studio's About Box template to create a new About box. Choose *Add Windows Form* from the *Project* menu, select *Windows Forms* for *Category*, and select *About Box* from the *Templates* list (Figure 6.6). A new form named AboutBox1 is added to your project (Figure 6.7) with controls you can modify. You can change the captions and image by setting the properties as you would on any other form. Once you create the form in your project, it is yours and may be modified as you please.

Select the About Box template to add a preformatted AboutBox form to a project.

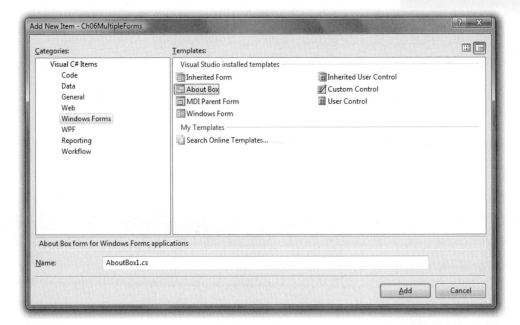

A new form created with the About Box template. You can customize the form by setting properties of the controls, adding controls, or removing controls.

Setting Assembly Information

Notice in Figure 6.7 that the About Box template form includes the product name, version, copyright, company name, and description. You can manually set the Text properties of the controls, but there's a better way that provides this information for the entire project. Open the Project Designer (Figure 6.8) from *Project / ProjectName Properties*. Click on the *Assembly Information* button and fill in the desired information in the *Assembly Information* dialog box (Figure 6.9).

Figure 6.8

Open the Project Designer and click on the **Assembly Information** *button to display the project's assembly information.*

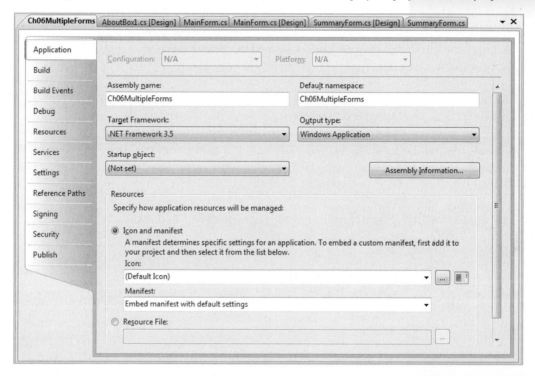

Figure 6.9

Enter or modify the project's information on the **Assembly Information** *dialog box.*

Once the information is entered into the *Assembly Information*, the code behind the AboutBox form retrieves and displays the information. Typically you find much of this same information on an application's splash screen. Splash screens are discussed later in this chapter in the section "A Splash Screen."

Feel free to customize the AboutBox form. You may change the picture, the fonts, or the fields to make it your own. If you want the *OK* button to close the form, you must code the okButton_Click event handler.

Displaying an About Form

In order to display the About Box template, you must create a new object of the form's class in code. You declare a new instance of the form by using the keyword new. Notice that the template you add to a project gets named the default name of *AboutBox1*. You can use that as a data type to create an aboutForm object.

```
// Create a new instance of the AboutBox1 form class.
AboutBox1 aboutForm = new AboutBox1();
```

Once you have created the form object, you can display it using a Show method or a ShowDialog method. These methods are discussed in more detail later in the chapter.

```
private void aboutToolStripMenuItem_Click(object sender, EventArgs e)
{
    // Display the about form.

    // Create a new instance of the AboutBox1 form class.
    AboutBox1 aboutForm = new AboutBox1();
    // Show the new aboutForm object.
    aboutForm.ShowDialog();
}
```

Using the Methods and Events of Forms

In code, you can use several methods to show, hide, and close forms.

Showing a Form

You generally display a new form in response to a user clicking a button or a menu item. In the event handler for the button or menu item, you can use either the Show or the ShowDialog method to display the new form.

Modal versus Modeless Forms

The **Show method** displays a form as **modeless**, which means that both forms are open and the user can navigate from one form to the other. When you use the **ShowDialog method**, the new form displays as **modal**; the user must respond to the form in some way, usually by clicking a button. No other program code can execute until the user responds to and hides or closes the modal form. However, if you display a modeless form, the user may switch to another form in the project without responding to the form.

Note: Even with a modal form, the user can switch to another application within Windows.

The Show Method—General Form

General Form

```
FormObjectName.Show();
```

The Show method displays a form object modelessly. The FormObjectName is the name of the form you wish to display. Note that you must first declare a form object in order to show it. Each time you use the new keyword you create a new object.

The Show Method—Example

```
SummaryForm aSummaryForm = new SummaryForm();
aSummaryForm.Show();
```

The ShowDialog Method—General Form

```
FormObjectName.ShowDialog();
```

Use the ShowDialog method when you want the user to notice, respond to, and close the form before proceeding with the application.

The ShowDialog Method—Example

```
SummaryForm aSummaryForm = new SummaryForm();
aSummaryForm.ShowDialog();
```

You generally place this code in a menu item or a button's click event handler:

```
private void summaryButton_Click(object sender, EventArgs e)
{
    // Show the summary form.

    // Create a new instance of the summary form.
    SummaryForm aSummaryForm = new SummaryForm();
    // Show the new form.
    aSummaryForm.ShowDialog();
}
```

Hiding or Closing a Form

You already know how to close the current form: this.Close();.
    You also can use the Close method to close any other form:

```
aSummaryForm.Close();
```

The Close method behaves differently for a modeless form (using the Show method) compared to a modal form (using the ShowDialog method). For a modeless form, Close destroys the form instance and removes it from memory; for a modal form, the form is only hidden. A second ShowDialog method of the same object displays the same form instance, which can have data left from the previous time the form was displayed. In contrast, a second Show method creates a new instance, so no leftover data can appear.

Note: Each time you use the new keyword, you create a new object. If you want to display the same form object several times, you must not use the new keyword each time.

You also can choose to use a form's **Hide method**, which sets the form's Visible property to *false* and keeps the form instance in memory.

The Hide Method—General Form

```
FormObjectName.Hide();
```

Hiding conceals a form but keeps it in memory, ready to be redisplayed. Use the Hide method rather than Close when the user is likely to display the form again. A good example might be a form with instructions or Help text, which the user may display multiple times.

The Hide Method—Example

```
aSummaryForm.Hide();
```

Responding to Form Events

The two primary events for which you may need to write code are the *Form-Name*.Load and *FormName*.Activated. The first time a form is shown in an application, both the Load and Activated events occur. The Load event occurs when the form is loaded into memory; the Activated event occurs after the Load event, just as control is passed to the form. Each subsequent time the form is shown, the Activated event occurs but the Load event does not. Therefore, if a form may be displayed multiple times, you may want to place initializing steps into the Activated event handler rather than into the Load. Also, if you wish to set the focus in a particular place on the new form, place the Focus method in the FormName_Activated method.

The Sequence of Form Events

Although you don't need to write event handlers for all of these form events, it's helpful to know the order in which they occur:

Load	Occurs before the form is displayed for the first time. Happens only once for any one form unless the form is closed rather than hidden.
Activated	Occurs each time the form is shown. This event handler is the correct location for initialization or SetFocus.
Paint	Occurs each time any portion of the form is redrawn, which happens each time a change is made or the form is moved or uncovered.

Deactivate	Occurs when the form is no longer the active form, such as when the user clicks on another window or the form is about to be hidden or closed.
FormClosing	Occurs as the form is about to close.
FormClosed	Occurs after the form is closed.

Notice that the **Form.Load event** occurs only once when the form is loaded into memory and the **Form.Activated event** occurs each time the form is shown. You will want to use the Form.Activated event to display data values that must be updated for current values, such as a summary form.

Writing Event Handlers for Selected Events

You are accustomed to double-clicking a control or form to open an event handler for its default event. If you double-click a form, the default event is *FormName*.Load. To open an event handler for the other events, you can select an event using the Properties window in the Form Designer. Click on the form to show its properties in the Properties window and click on the *Events* button to display the available events (Figure 6.10). The default event appears selected, but you can double-click any other event to create its event handler. You also can select a previously written method from the drop-down list for any event. When you want to switch the Properties window back to viewing properties, click on the *Properties* button.

Figure 6.10

Click on the Events button in the Properties window to see the list of possible events for which to write an event handler. Double-click on the event to create an empty event handler.

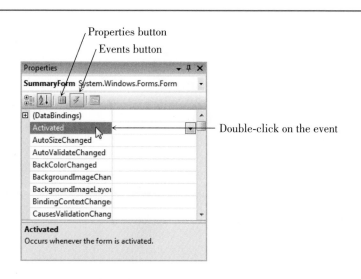

Properties button

Events button

Double-click on the event

Variables and Constants in Multiform Projects

When you have multiple forms in a project, the scope, access level, and lifetime of the variables and constants become a little more complicated. If you want class-level variables to be available in more than one form in a project, you must declare them as `public`. This approach presents a security problem and should be avoided.

In object-oriented programming, each object has properties that expose its values to other objects. For example, each Form object has many properties that you can view and some that you can change, such as the Name property and the Text property. Many other values are used internally by the Form class but are not available or visible to other code. Hiding internal values and exposing only certain values as properties is one of the key principles of object-oriented programming. (See Chapter 12 for a discussion of the theory and principles of object-oriented programming.)

When you want to pass variables from one form object to another, the correct approach is to set up properties of the form's class. For example, consider a total in a calculation form that you would like to display on a summary form. The variable for the total is private in the calculation form. You add a private variable in the summary form to hold the data and then use a property method to pass the value from one form to the other.

Creating Properties in a Class

To set up a new property of a form class, generally you need a private class-level variable to store the value and public property methods that allow other classes to view and/or set the property. The private class-level variable is available only to the methods and property blocks within the class.

When your program creates objects from your class, you will need to assign values to the properties. The class controls access to its properties through property methods.

Property Blocks

The way that your class allows its properties to be retrieved and set is with **accessor methods** in a **property block**. The block may contain a `get` accessor method to retrieve a property value and/or a `set` accessor method to assign a value to the property. The name that you use for the property block becomes the name of the property to the outside world. Create "friendly" property names, such as LastName or EmployeeNumber, that describe the property without using a data type or abbreviation.

The Property Block—General Form

General Form

```
// Class-level variable to hold the value internally.
Private DataType MemberVariable;

public DataType PropertyName
{
    get
    {
        return MemberVariable;
    }

    set
    {
        // Statements, such as validation.
        MemberVariable = value;
    }
}
```

The set statement uses the **value keyword** to refer to the incoming value for the property. You must specify the property block as public to allow external objects (objects created in other classes) to access them. The get accessor method is similar to a method declared with a return value: Somewhere inside the method, before the closing brace, you must assign a return value. The data type of the incoming value for a set must match the type of the return value of the corresponding get.

The Property Block—Example

```
private string lastNameString;

public string LastName
{
    get
    {
        return lastNameString;
    }

    set
    {
        lastNameString = value;
    }
}
```

Remember, the private class-level variable stores the value of the property. The get and set accessor methods in the property block retrieve the current value and/or assign a new value to the property.

Read-Only Properties

In some instances, you may wish to have a property that can be retrieved by an object but not changed. You can write a property block that contains only a get to create a read-only property.

```
// Private class-level variable to hold the property value.
private decimal payDecimal;

// Property block for read-only property.
public decimal Pay
{
    get
    {
        return payDecimal;
    }
}
```

Write-Only Properties

At times you may need to have a property that can be assigned by an object but not retrieved. You can create a property block that contains only a set to create a write-only property.

```
// Private class-level variable to hold the property value.
private decimal hoursDecimal;

// Property block for write-only property.
public decimal Hours
{
    set
    {
        hoursDecimal = value;
    }
}
```

Applying the Properties to Multiple Forms

Now let's apply this theory to display a total on a separate summary form. The hands-on projects in Chapters 4 and 5 calculate a decimal variable that holds the total sales. In those two projects, the total is displayed in a message box, but now it's time to create a new summary form to display a nicely formatted total.

The summary form must contain a private variable to hold the value for the total sales as well as a property set method to allow the value to be assigned. The name TotalSales is the "friendly" property name and totalSummarySalesDecimal is the private class-level variable to hold the value inside the class.

```
public partial class SummaryForm : Form
{
    private decimal totalSummarySalesDecimal;

    public decimal TotalSales
    {
        set
        {
            totalSummarySalesDecimal = value;
        }
    }
    // . . . More code for the rest of the Form class.
```

You already know how to display the summary form from another form, but first we need to pass the value from the private variable totalSalesDecimal in the main calculation form to the property of the summary form called Total-Sales, which will be stored internally in the SummaryForm as totalSummary-SalesDecimal. The following code appears on the main calculation form, which has a button or menu item to display the summary information. Notice that you assign the private variable totalSalesDecimal from the calculation form to the property TotalSales that is a property of the summary form.

```
// Event-handling method in the main calculation form.
private void summaryButton_Click(object sender, EventArgs e)
{
    // Display the summary form.
    SummaryForm aSummaryForm = new SummaryForm();

    aSummaryForm.TotalSales = totalSalesDecimal;
    aSummaryForm.ShowDialog();
}
```

Passing Summary Values among Forms

Occasionally, you may need to calculate in one form and display summary information in another form, but the summary form is not displayed from the calculation form. This situation can occur when a main form instantiates and displays both a data entry form, where the calculations are performed, and the summary form. The menu on the main form allows the user to display either the data entry form or the summary form as desired.

Earlier you learned to create a public property of a form, which is available to other objects in the project. But consider the example of a main form, a data entry form, and a summary form; each time the main form instantiates and displays the data entry form, a new fresh version of each property is created. If you want to maintain the value of a property for multiple instances of a class, you must declare the property as **static**. You can declare as static a total or a count that you wish to use in a summary calculation.

```
private static decimal totalDueDecimal;
```

Static variables retain their values for every object that is instantiated using the new keyword. Therefore, every call to the data entry form continues to increase the total.

You use the static keyword on both the private variable and the property method. When you use the static keyword in a property method, you are creating a public property that can be accessed from anywhere in the project without instantiating a specific object of the class. For more information about static properties, see "Instance Variables versus Static Variables" in Chapter 12.

In the following example, the data entry form, called OrderForm, accumulates the static variable totalDueDecimal. The OrderForm object exposes the total with a ReadOnly property called Total. The summary form can retrieve the current value of the property by referring to OrderForm.Total.

```
// OrderForm

private static decimal totalDueDecimal;

public static decimal Total
{
    get
    {
        return totalDueDecimal;
    }
}
```

By placing the static variable and property method in the data entry form, you can now access the total in the summary form.

```
// SummaryForm

private void SummaryForm_Activated(object sender, EventArgs e)
{
    // Display the total.

    totalTextBox.Text = OrderForm.Total.ToString("C");
}
```

Feedback 6.1

1. What is the purpose of a property method?
2. Write the statement to assign the private variable drinksSoldInteger to the DrinksSold property of aSummaryForm.
3. Write the property `set` method for DrinksSold.

A Splash Screen

Perhaps you have noticed the logo or window that often appears while a program is loading, such as the one in Figure 6.11. This initial form is called a **splash screen**. Professional applications use splash screens to tell the user that the program is loading and starting. It can make a large application appear to load and start faster, since something appears on the screen while the rest of the application loads.

Creating a Splash Screen

A splash screen is simply another form in a project. Typically you want to adjust some of the features such as eliminating the title bar and the close button. We will control the length of time that the splash screen appears using a Timer component.

After adding a form to the project, set the StartPosition to CenterScreen, leave the Text property blank, and set ControlBox to *false*. The control box eliminates the resize buttons and the close button. If you also leave the Text property blank, the title bar will disappear.

Property	Setting
StartPosition	CenterScreen
Text	(blank)
ControlBox	False
TopMost	True

On the form, add graphics and any information about your program that you wish to display. Many programs will use the same AssemblyInfo that displays on the AboutBox. In this example, we're going to just use text.

Controlling the Time a Splash Form Displays

In an application that must load data or has other time-consuming activities, the length of time the splash screen displays is governed by those activities. But in smaller applications, such as the ones you are writing, the splash form disappears before you have a chance to see it. So for these applications, we will control the display using a **Timer component**.

To use a timer on a splash screen form, you add a Timer component from the *Components* section of the toolbox. Then you can set properties of the timer to fire an event at a specified time interval and write code for the event in an event-handling method.

When you add a Timer component to a form, you must set two properties: Enabled and Interval. By default, the timer is not enabled, so you must set the Enabled property to *true*. Note that you can set the Enabled property either at design time or in code, but for a splash form, you will set it at design time. Set the timer's Interval property for the number of milliseconds the splash screen should display. For example, to make the form display for approximately five seconds, set the Interval to 5000.

Timer property	Setting
Enabled	True
Interval	Number of milliseconds to pass before firing an event.

When the specified interval passes, the timer's Tick event fires. This code for the timer closes the splash screen.

```
private void timer1_Tick(object sender, EventArgs e)
{
    // Close the splash form.

    this.Close();
}
```

Making the Splash Form Display First

C# programs actually begin execution in the file called Program.cs, which you can see in the Solution Explorer. Double-click on the filename to open the file and locate the Main method; you add code to the Main method to create the splash screen before the program begins execution.

```
static void Main()
{
    Application.EnableVisualStyles();
    Application.SetCompatibleTextRenderingDefault(false);
    SplashForm aSplashForm = new SplashForm();    ⎤ Add these statements to
    aSplashForm.ShowDialog();                     ⎦ display the splash form
    Application.Run(new MainForm());
}                                        └──────Name of the startup form
```

After the splash screen displays and the timer closes the splash screen, the application runs the startup form, MainForm in the preceding example.

Note: You can use either the `Show` or `ShowDialog` method to display the splash form. Using `ShowDialog`, the main form does not appear until the splash form closes; using `Show`, the main form appears behind the splash form.

Running Your Program Outside the IDE

Every time that you create and run an application, the executable file is placed in the project's bin\Debug folder. You can move that .exe file to another computer, place the file on the system desktop, or use it as a shortcut just like any other application on your system. If you copy the executable file to another system, you must make sure that the computer has the correct version of the Microsoft .NET Framework. Although Visual Studio 2008 includes an option to select a particular version of the .NET Framework, by default the programs target the .NET 3.5 Framework. It is possible to download the framework for free from the Microsoft Web site.

You also may want to change the icon for your program. The default icon is a standard window image. To change the icon to something more interesting, open the Project Designer (*Project / ProjectName Properties*). On the *Application* tab (Figure 6.12), click the *Browse* button next to *Icon* and browse to find another file with an .ico extension. When you select a new icon, the .ico file is copied into your project folder. Many icon files are in various folders in Windows, with a few in the StudentData folder. You must recompile (build) the project again after setting the icon.

F i g u r e   6 . 1 2

Select a different icon for your project in the Project Designer.

Your Hands-On Programming Example

Modify the hands-on project from Chapter 5 to include multiple forms. This version of the project requires four forms: JuiceBarForm, SummaryForm, SplashForm, and AboutBox.

Note: Follow the instructions in Chapter 5 "Basing a New Project on an Existing Project" or Appendix C "Copy and Move a Project" to begin this hands-on example.

JuiceBarForm: This is the JuiceBarForm form from Chapter 5, with a few modifications to display output on new forms rather than in message boxes.

SummaryForm: Create a form with the appropriate labels and text boxes for the summary information.

AboutBox form: Replace the message box for the *Help / About* menu item from Chapter 5 with a new form using the About Box template. Set the assembly information in the Project Designer.

SplashForm: Create a splash screen that displays the company name.

Planning the Project

Sketch the four forms (Figure 6.13), which the users approve and sign off as meeting their needs.

Figure 6.13

The planning sketches of the forms for the hands-on programming example. a. the main form (JuiceBarForm); b. the summary form (SummaryForm); c. the about form (AboutBox1); and d. the splash form (SplashForm).

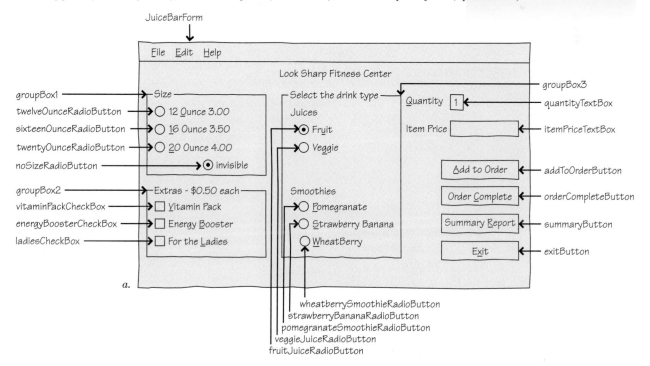

Figure 6.13

(concluded)

Juice Bar Sales Summary

Drinks Sold   [_____] ← drinksSoldTextBox

Number of Orders   [_____] ← numberOrdersTextBox

Total Sales   [_____] ← totalSalesTextBox

            [<u>O</u>K] ← okButton

b.

About Look Sharp Fitness Center Juice Bar Sales

Product Name

Version

Copyright

Company Name

[<u>O</u>K] ← okButton

c.

Look Sharp Fitness Center
Juice Bar Sales
Version 1.0

d.

Plan the Objects and Properties for the Main Form (JuiceBarForm) See the hands-on exercise for Chapter 5 for the objects and properties of JuiceBarForm, which are unchanged for this project. The only changes are to the methods that display the summary form and the About form.

Plan the Methods for the JuiceBarForm Most of the methods for JuiceBarForm are unchanged from the project in Chapter 5. You need two additional methods:

Object	Method	Actions
summaryButton	Click	Pass values to summary form properties. Display the summary form.
aboutToolStripMenuItem	Click	Display the About Box form.

Plan the Objects and Properties for the Summary Form

Object	Property	Setting
SummaryForm	Name	SummaryForm
	AcceptButton	okButton
	Title	Juice Bar Sales Summary
label1	Name	label1
	Text	Drinks Sold
drinksSoldTextBox	Name	drinksSoldTextBox
	ReadOnly	true
label2	Name	label2
	Text	Number Orders
numberOrdersTextBox	Name	numberOrdersTextBox
	ReadOnly	true
label3	Name	label3
	Text	Total Sales
totalSalesTextBox	Name	totalSalesTextBox
	ReadOnly	true
okButton	Name	okButton
	Text	&OK

Plan the Methods for the Summary Form

Object	Method	Actions
SummaryForm	Activated	Set the values of the labels from the form properties.
okButton	Click	Close this form.

Summary Form Properties Create new properties of the form:

Property	Data type	Access
TotalSales	decimal	write-only
NumberOrders	int	write-only
DrinksSold	int	write-only

Plan the Objects and Properties for the About Form Use the About Box template and consider changing the graphic.

Fill in the *Assembly Information* in the Project Designer so that the screen fields appear filled.

Plan the Method for the About Box

Object	Method	Actions
okButton	Click	Close this form.

Plan the Objects and Properties for the Splash Screen

Object	Property	Setting
SplashForm	Name	SplashForm
	Controlbox	False
	Text	(blank)
	StartupPosition	CenterScreen
	TopMost	True
timer1	Enabled	True
	Interval	2000
label1	Text	Look Sharp Fitness Center
	Font	Arial, 14 pt

Plan the Method for the Splash Screen

Object	Method	Actions
timer1	Tick	Close this form.

Plan the Code for Program.cs Add code to create and display the splash screen.

Write the Project

Follow the instructions in Chapter 5 "Basing a New Project on an Existing Project" or Appendix C "Copy and Move a Project" to base this project on Ch05HandsOn. If you have not written Ch05HandsOn, do so first before beginning this project.

Follow the sketches in Figure 6.13 to create the new forms. Use the About Box template. Figure 6.14 shows the completed forms.

- Set the properties of each of the objects according to your plan.

- Create new properties in the summary form.

- Write the additional code. Working from the pseudocode, write each method.

- When you complete the code, use a variety of data to thoroughly test the project.

Figure 6.14

The completed forms for the hands-on programming example. a. the main form (JuiceBarForm); b. the summary form (SummaryForm); c. the about form (AboutBox1); and d. the splash form (SplashForm).

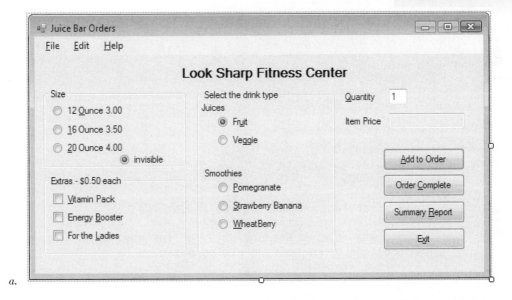

a.

b.

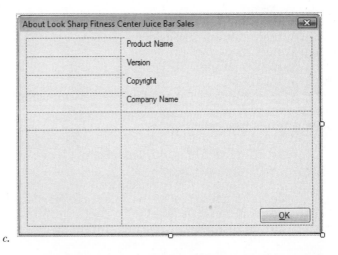

c.

Figure 6.14

(concluded)

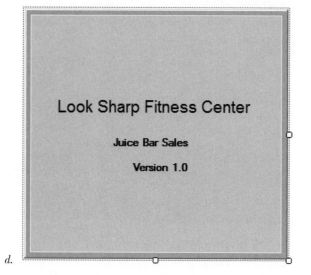

Look Sharp Fitness Center

Juice Bar Sales

Version 1.0

d.

The Project Coding Solution
JuiceBarForm

```
/*
 * Program Name:       Ch06HandsOn
 * Programmer:         Bradley/Millspaugh
 * Date:               June 2009
 *
 * Description:        This project calculates the amount due
 *                     based on the customer selection
 *                     and accumulates summary data for the day.
 *                     Includes menus, common dialog boxes, a
 *                     switch statement, and general methods.
 */

using System;
using System.Collections.Generic;
using System.ComponentModel;
using System.Data;
using System.Drawing;
using System.Text;
using System.Windows.Forms;

namespace Ch06HandsOn
{
    public partial class JuiceBarForm : Form
    {
        // Declare class variables.
        decimal itemSizeDecimal, totalOrderDecimal, totalSalesDecimal;
        decimal drinkDecimal;
        int drinksInteger, ordersInteger;

        public JuiceBarForm()
        {
```

```csharp
        InitializeComponent();
    }

    private void addToOrderButton_Click(object sender, EventArgs e)
    {
        // Add the current item price and quantity to the order.

        if (noSizeRadioButton.Checked)
        {
            MessageBox.Show("You must select a drink and size.",
                "Missing required entry");
        }
        else
        {
            try
            {
                int quantityInteger = int.Parse(quantityTextBox.Text);
                if (quantityInteger != 0)
                {
                    drinksInteger += quantityInteger;
                    totalOrderDecimal += drinkDecimal * quantityInteger;
                    clearForNextItem();
                    orderCompleteButton.Enabled = true;
                }
                else
                {
                    MessageBox.Show("Please enter a quantity",
                        "Missing Required Entry");
                }
            }
            catch (FormatException)
            {
                MessageBox.Show("Invalid Quantity", "Data Entry Error");
                quantityTextBox.Focus();
                quantityTextBox.SelectAll();
            }
        }
    }

    private void orderCompleteButton_Click(object sender, EventArgs e)
    {
        // Order is complete, add to summary and clear order.

        // Check if the last item was added to the total.
        if (itemPriceTextBox.Text != "")
        {
            DialogResult responseDialogResult;
            string messageString = "Current Item not recorded. Add to order?";
            responseDialogResult = MessageBox.Show(messageString,
                "Verify Last Drink Purchase", MessageBoxButtons.YesNo,
                MessageBoxIcon.Question);
            if (responseDialogResult == DialogResult.Yes)
            {
                addToOrderButton_Click(sender, e);
            }
        }
        // Display amount due.
        string dueString = "Amount Due " + totalOrderDecimal.ToString("C");
        MessageBox.Show(dueString, "Order Complete");
```

```
        // Add to summary totals.
        ordersInteger ++;
        totalSalesDecimal += totalOrderDecimal;

        // Reset all for new order.
        summaryButton.Enabled = true;
        summaryToolStripMenuItem.Enabled = true;
        orderCompleteButton.Enabled = false;
        orderCompleteToolStripMenuItem.Enabled = false;
        totalOrderDecimal = 0m;
    }

    private void summaryButton_Click(object sender, EventArgs e)
    {
        // Display the summary form.
        SummaryForm aSummaryForm = new SummaryForm();

        aSummaryForm.DrinksSold = drinksInteger;
        aSummaryForm.NumberOrders = ordersInteger;
        aSummaryForm.TotalSales = totalSalesDecimal;

        aSummaryForm.ShowDialog();
    }

    private void exitButton_Click(object sender, EventArgs e)
    {
        // End the application.

        this.Close();
    }

    private void clearForNextItem()
    {
        // Clear option buttons, check boxes, text boxes.

        noSizeRadioButton.Checked = true;
        fruitJuiceRadioButton.Checked = true;
        vitaminPackCheckBox.Checked = false;
        energyBoosterCheckBox.Checked = false;
        ladiesCheckBox.Checked = false;
        itemPriceTextBox.Clear();
        quantityTextBox.Text = "1";
    }

    private void twelveOunceRadioButton_CheckedChanged(object sender,
        EventArgs e)
    {
        // Calculate and display the price for the selected item.
        // Handles all check boxes and radio buttons.

        // Cast the sender to a RadioButton type.
        RadioButton selectedSizeRadioButton = (RadioButton)sender;

        switch (selectedSizeRadioButton.Name)
        {
            case "twelveOunceRadioButton":
                itemSizeDecimal = 3m;
                break;
            case "sixteenOunceRadioButton":
```

```
                itemSizeDecimal = 3.5m;
                break;
            case "twentyOunceRadioButton":
                itemSizeDecimal = 4m;
                break;
        }
        drinkDecimal = itemSizeDecimal + findExtrasPrice();
        itemPriceTextBox.Text = drinkDecimal.ToString("C");
    }

    private decimal findExtrasPrice()
    {
        // Find price for additives.
        decimal extrasDecimal = 0m;

        if (vitaminPackCheckBox.Checked)
            extrasDecimal += .5m;
        if (energyBoosterCheckBox.Checked)
            extrasDecimal += .5m;
        if (ladiesCheckBox.Checked)
            extrasDecimal += .5m;

        return extrasDecimal;
    }

    private void vitaminPackCheckBox_CheckedChanged(object sender, EventArgs e)
    {
        // Check price of additives and display current price.

        drinkDecimal = itemSizeDecimal + findExtrasPrice();
        itemPriceTextBox.Text = drinkDecimal.ToString("C");
    }

    private void aboutToolStripMenuItem_Click(object sender, EventArgs e)
    {
        // Display about form.
        AboutBox1 aboutForm = new AboutBox1();

        aboutForm.ShowDialog();
    }

    private void fontToolStripMenuItem_Click(object sender, EventArgs e)
    {
        // Change the label's font.

        // Initialize the dialog box.
        fontDialog1.Font = titleLabel.Font;
        // Display the dialog box.
        fontDialog1.ShowDialog();
        // Assign the new font.
        titleLabel.Font = fontDialog1.Font;
    }

    private void colorToolStripMenuItem_Click(object sender, EventArgs e)
    {
        // Change the form's ForeColor.
        // Applies to all controls on the form that haven't had their
        //    ForeColor explicitly modified.
```

```
            // Initialize the dialog box.
            colorDialog1.Color = this.ForeColor;
            // Display the dialog box.
            colorDialog1.ShowDialog();
            // Assign the new color.
            this.ForeColor = colorDialog1.Color;
        }
    }
}
```

SummaryForm

```
/*
 * Program Name:         Ch06HandsOn
 * Programmer:           Bradley/Millspaugh
 * Date:                 June 2009
 * Class:                SummaryForm
 *
 * Description:          Display the summary information.
 */

using System;
using System.Collections.Generic;
using System.ComponentModel;
using System.Data;
using System.Drawing;
using System.Text;
using System.Windows.Forms;

namespace Ch06HandsOn
{
    public partial class SummaryForm : Form
    {
        decimal totalSalesDecimal;
        int numberOrdersInteger, drinksSoldInteger;

        public decimal TotalSales
        {
            set
            {
                totalSalesDecimal = value;
            }
        }

        public int NumberOrders
        {
            set
            {
                numberOrdersInteger = value;
            }
        }

        public int DrinksSold
        {
            set
            {
                drinksSoldInteger = value;
            }
        }
```

```csharp
        public SummaryForm()
        {
            InitializeComponent();
        }

        private void okButton_Click(object sender, EventArgs e)
        {
            // Close the summary form.

            this.Close();
        }

        private void SummaryForm_Activated(object sender, EventArgs e)
        {
            // Get and display the summary data.

            drinksSoldTextBox.Text = drinksSoldInteger.ToString();
            numberOrdersTextBox.Text = numberOrdersInteger.ToString();
            totalSalesTextBox.Text = totalSalesDecimal.ToString("C");
        }
    }
}
```

AboutBox1

```csharp
private void okButton_Click(object sender, EventArgs e)
{
    // Close this form.

    this.Close();
}
```

SplashForm

```csharp
/*
 * Program Name:      Ch06HandsOn
 * Programmer:        Bradley/Millspaugh
 * Date:              June 2009
 * Class:             Splash Form
 *
 * Description:       Display the splash form at startup.
 */

using System;
using System.Collections.Generic;
using System.ComponentModel;
using System.Data;
using System.Drawing;
using System.Text;
using System.Windows.Forms;

namespace Ch06HandsOn
{
    public partial class SplashForm : Form
    {
        public SplashForm()
        {
            InitializeComponent();
        }
```

```
        private void timer1_Tick(object sender, EventArgs e)
        {
            // Close the splash form.

            this.Close();
        }
    }
}
```

Program.cs

```
/*
 * Program Name:        Ch06HandsOn
 * Programmer:          Bradley/Millspaugh
 * Date:                June 2009
 * Class:               Program
 *
 * Description:         Control program execution.
 */

using System;
using System.Collections.Generic;
using System.Windows.Forms;

namespace Ch06HandsOn
{
    static class Program
    {
        /// <summary>
        /// The main entry point for the application.
        /// </summary>
        [STAThread]
        static void Main()
        {
            Application.EnableVisualStyles();
            Application.SetCompatibleTextRenderingDefault(false);
            SplashForm aSplashForm = new SplashForm();
            aSplashForm.ShowDialog();
            Application.Run(new JuiceBarForm());
        }
    }
}
```

S u m m a r y

1. Projects may need more than one form—there is virtually no limit to the number of forms that can be used within a single project. The first form in the application (after the splash form) is called the *startup form*.
2. Forms used for one project can be added to another project. Forms also can be removed from a project.
3. To display a new form, you must declare and instantiate a form object.
4. An About box, which typically contains information about the version of an application and the programmer and copyrights, may be created by adding a new form. C# has an About Box template form that you can use to create an About box.

5. The About Box template automatically inserts information on the form from the project's assembly information; you can enter the information in the *Assembly Information* dialog box.

6. The Show (modeless) and ShowDialog (modal) methods are used to display a form on the screen.

7. A form displayed as modal requires a response from the user; it must be closed or unloaded before any execution continues. When a form is displayed as modeless, the user can switch to another form without closing the form.

8. The Form.Hide method hides the form but keeps it loaded in memory; the Form.Close method removes a modeless form from memory; the Form.Close method for a modal form actually hides the form rather than closing it.

9. The form's Load event occurs once for each loaded form; the form's Activated event can occur multiple times, each time the form is shown.

10. The form's FormClosing event occurs just before the form closes. You can write event handlers for any of the form's events.

11. Use property methods to transfer the values from the private variables in one form to the private variables in a second form.

12. To create a new property of a form, set up a private class-level variable to hold the value internally and write public accessor methods to allow the property to be set and retrieved. A property may be ReadOnly or WriteOnly if the property block contains only the appropriate get or set method.

13. To display a second form and pass a value to a property of the form, instantiate a new form object, assign a value to the form object's property, and show the form.

14. A splash screen is a form that appears as an application loads, before the main or startup form. A splash screen is created as a form without the title bar and the control buttons. Code to display the splash form belongs in the Main method of Program.cs.

15. Use a Timer component to control the length of time the form appears. Set the timer's Interval property to the number of milliseconds; the component's Tick event fires when the interval passes.

16. You can run a project outside the VS IDE by moving and running the .exe file. The target machine must have the correct version of the .NET Framework installed.

Key Terms

R e v i e w   Q u e s t i o n s

1. List some of the items generally found in an About box.
2. What is the purpose of a splash screen?
3. What is the term used for the first form to display in a project?
4. Explain how to include an existing form in a new project.
5. What is the *assembly information*? How can you change the information? How can you use the information?
6. Explain the difference between *modal* and *modeless*.
7. How does the `Show` method differ from the `ShowDialog` method?
8. Explain when the form's Load event and Activated event occur. In which event handler should you place code to initialize screen fields? Is the answer always the same?
9. How are variable values passed from one form to another?
10. How can you run a compiled C# program outside the Visual Studio IDE?

P r o g r a m m i n g   E x e r c i s e s

Note: For help in basing a new project on an existing project, see "Copy and Move a Project" in Appendix C.

6.1 Modify Programming Exercise 5.5 (the flag viewer) to include a splash screen and an About box.

6.2 Create a project that will produce a summary of the amounts due for Pat's Auto Repair Shop. Display a splash screen first; then display the Job Information form. If you wish, you can add a graphic to the form.

The Job Information Form Menu:

File	Edit	Help
Exit	Calculate	About
	Clear	

Job Information Form: The Job Information form must have text boxes for the user to enter the job number, customer name, amount charged for parts, and the hours of labor. Include labels and text boxes for Parts, Labor, Subtotal, Sales Tax, and Total.

The *Calculate* menu item finds the charges and displays them in labels. The tax rate and the hourly labor charge should be set up as named constants so that they can be easily modified if either changes. Current charges are $50 per hour for labor and 8 percent (.08) for the sales tax rate. Sales tax is charged only on parts, not on labor.

The *Clear* menu item clears the text boxes and resets the focus in the first text box.

The *Exit* menu item closes the Job Information form.

6.3 Modify Programming Exercise 6.2 so that summary information is maintained for the total dollar amount for parts, labor, sales tax, and total for all customers.

Add a *Summary* menu item under the *File* menu before the *Exit* item; include a separator bar between the two menu items. When the user selects the *Summary* menu item, display the summary information in a Summary form. The Summary form should have an *OK* button that closes the Summary form and returns the user to the Job Information form.

6.4   A battle is raging over the comparative taste of Prune Punch and Apple Ade. Each taste tester rates the two drinks on a scale of 1 to 10 (10 being best). The proof of the superiority of one over the other will be the average score for the two drinks.

Display a splash screen and then the New Tester form. You can add a graphic if you wish.

New Tester Form Menus:

File	Ratings	Help
Exit	Add Your Scores	About
	Summary	

The New Tester form allows the user to input test scores for each drink.

When the user clicks the *Add Your Scores* menu item, add the score for each type of drink to the drink's total, clear the text boxes, and reset the focus. If either score is blank when the menu item is selected, display a message in a message box and reset the focus to the box for the missing data.

Summary Menu Item: The *Summary* item displays a form that contains the current results of the taste test. It should display the winner, the total number of taste testers, and the average rating for each drink. The form contains an *OK* button that returns to the New Tester form. (The user will be able to display the summary at any time and as often as desired.)

About Box: The About box should display information about the program and the programmer. Include an *OK* button that returns the user to the New Tester form.

6.5   Modify Programming Exercise 5.1 (piecework pay) to add a Splash form, an About box, and a Summary form. Add a slogan and a logo that the user can hide or display from menu choices on the main form.

Splash Form: The Splash form must appear when the project begins execution. It should display the project name, programmer name, and at least one graphic.

About Box: The About box should have the program name, version number, and programmer name, as well as a graphic and an *OK* button. It must be displayed as modal.

Summary Form: The Summary form should display the summary information. Note that in Chapter 5 the summary information was displayed in a message box. You must remove the message box and display the summary information only on the Summary form. An *OK* button closes the form.

Slogan and Logo: Make up a slogan for the company, such as "We're Number One" or "We Do Chicken Right." For the logo, you can use an icon or any graphic you have available, or create one yourself with a draw or paint program.

The *Slogan* and *Logo* menu choices must toggle and display a check mark when selected. For example, when the slogan is displayed, the *Slogan* menu item is checked. If the user selects the *Slogan* command again, hide the slogan and uncheck the menu item. The *Slogan* and *Logo* commands operate independently; that is, the user may select either, both, or neither item.

When the project begins, the slogan and logo must both be displayed on the main form and their menu items appear checked.

Case Studies

Custom Supplies Mail Order

Modify the Custom Supplies Mail Order project from Chapter 5 to include a Splash screen, an About box, and a summary form.

Delete the summary information from the form from Chapter 5 and display the information on the summary form. Include an image on both the Splash form and the About box.

Christopher's Car Center

Create a project that uses four forms. Add the form from the Chapter 5 Christopher's Car Center case study and create a Main form, a Splash screen, and an About box.

Main Form: The Main form should display a large label with the words "Christopher's Car Center— Meeting all your vehicle's needs" and appropriate image(s). You must change the project's startup form to the new Main form. See page 275 for help in changing the startup form.

Main Form Menus:

File	Edit	Help
Input Sale	Color. . .	About
Exit	Font. . .	

The *Input Sale* item should display the form from Chapter 5.

The *Color* and *Font* items should allow the user to change the large label on the form.

Xtreme Cinema

Modify the Xtreme Cinema project from Chapter 5 to separate the project into multiple forms. Include a summary form, a Splash screen, and an About box.

Cool Boards

Modify the Cool Boards project from Chapter 5 to separate the project into multiple forms. Include a summary form, a Splash screen, and an About box.

7

Lists, Loops, and Printing

1. Create and use list boxes and combo boxes.

2. Differentiate among the available types of combo boxes.

3. Enter items into list boxes using the Items collection in the Properties window.

4. Add and remove items in a list at run time.

5. Determine which item in a list is selected.

6. Use the Items.Count property to determine the number of items in a list.

7. Display a selected item from a list.

8. Use do, while, and for loops to execute a series of statements.

9. Skip to the next iteration of a loop by using the continue statement.

10. Send information to the printer or the Print Preview window using the PrintDocument class.

Often you will want to offer the user a list of items from which to choose. You can use the Windows ListBox and ComboBox controls to display lists on a form. You may choose to add items to a list during design time, during run time, or perhaps a combination of both. Several styles of list boxes are available; the style you use is determined by design and space considerations as well as by whether you will allow users to add items to the list.

List Boxes and Combo Boxes

Both list boxes and combo boxes allow you to have a list of items from which the user can make a selection. Figure 7.1 shows the toolbox tools for creating the controls; Figure 7.2 shows several types of list boxes and combo boxes, including **simple list boxes**, **simple combo boxes**, **drop-down combo boxes**, and **drop-down lists**. The list boxes on the left of the form in Figure 7.2 are all created with the list box tool; the boxes on the right of the form are created with the combo box tool. Notice the three distinct styles of combo boxes.

ListBox controls and **ComboBox controls** have most of the same properties and operate in a similar fashion. One exception is that a combo box control has a DropDownStyle property, which determines whether or not the list box also has a text box for user entry and whether or not the list will drop down (refer to Figure 7.2).

Both list boxes and combo boxes have a great feature. If the box is too small to display all the items in the list at one time, C# automatically adds a scroll bar. You do not have to be concerned with the location of the scroll box in the scroll bar; the scrolling is handled automatically.

When you add a list control to a form, choose the style according to the space you have available and how you want the box to operate. Do you want the user to select from an existing list? If so, use a simple list box or a drop-down

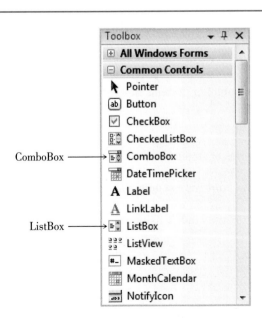

F i g u r e   7 . 1

Use the ListBox tool and ComboBox tool to create list boxes and combo boxes on your forms.

Figure 7.2

Various styles of list boxes and combo boxes.

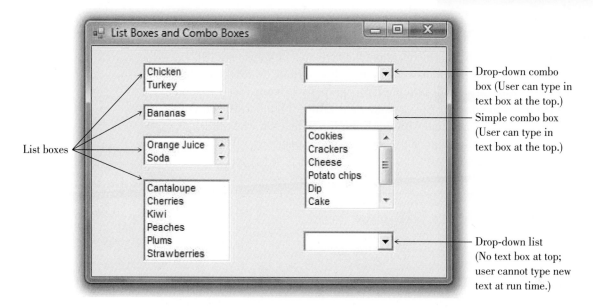

list (ComboBox DropDownStyle = DropDownList). Do you want the user to be able to type a new entry if necessary? In this case, use one of the two styles with an added text box: the drop-down combo box (DropDownStyle = Drop-Down) or the simple combo box (DropDownStyle = Simple).

At design time, the behavior of list boxes and combo boxes differs. For list boxes, C# displays the Name property in the control; for combo boxes, the Text property displays. Don't spend any time trying to make an empty list box appear empty during design time; the box will appear empty at run time. Combo boxes have a Text property, which you can set or remove at design time. List boxes also have a Text property, but you can access it only at run time.

The Items Collection

The list of items that displays in a list box or combo box is a **collection**. C# collections are objects that have properties and methods to allow you to add items, remove items, refer to individual elements, count the items, and clear the collection. In the sections that follow, you will learn to maintain and refer to the Items collection.

You can refer to the items in a collection by an index, which is zero based. For example, if a collection holds 10 items, the indexes to refer to the items range from 0 to 9. To refer to the first item in the Items collection, use Items[0].

Filling a List

You can use several methods to fill the Items collection of a list box and combo box. If you know the list contents at design time and the list never changes, you can define the Items collection in the Properties window. If you must add items to the list during program execution, you will use the `Items.Add` or `Items.Insert` method in a program method. In Chapter 11 you will learn to fill a list from a data file on disk, which allows the list contents to vary from one run to the next.

Using the Properties Window

The **Items property**, which is a collection, holds the list of items for a list box or combo box. To define the Items collection at design time, select the control and scroll the Properties window to the Items property (Figure 7.3). Click on the ellipsis button to open the String Collection Editor (Figure 7.4), and type your list items, ending each line with the Enter key. Click *OK* when finished. You can open the editor again to modify the list, if you wish.

Figure 7.3

Select the Items property of a list box to enter the list items.

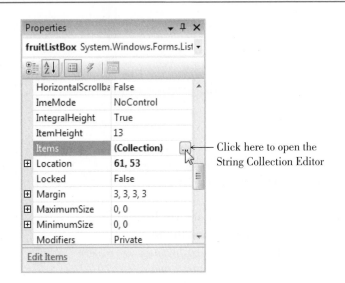

— Click here to open the String Collection Editor

Figure 7.4

In the String Collection Editor that opens, type each list item and press Enter to go to the next line.

Using the Items.Add Method

To add an item to a list at run time, use the **Items.Add method**. You can choose to add a variable, a constant, the contents of the text box at the top of a combo box, or the Text property of another control.

The Items.Add Method—General Form

```
Object.Items.Add(ItemValue);
```

ItemValue is the string value to add to the list. If the value is a string literal, enclose it in quotation marks.

The new item generally goes at the end of the list. However, you can alter the placement by setting the control's **Sorted property** to *true*. Then the new item will be placed alphabetically in the list.

The Items.Add Method—Examples

```
schoolsListBox.Items.Add("Harvard");
schoolsListBox.Items.Add("Stanford");
schoolsListBox.Items.Add(schoolsTextBox.Text);
majorsComboBox.Items.Add(majorsComboBox.Text);
majorsComboBox.Items.Add(majorString);
```

When the user types a new value in the text box portion of a combo box, that item is not automatically added to the list. If you want to add the newly entered text to the list, use the Items.Add method:

```
coffeeComboBox.Items.Add(coffeeComboBox.Text);
```

Similarly, you can add the contents of a text box to a list box.

```
schoolsListBox.Items.Add(schoolTextBox.Text);
```

Using the Items.Insert Method

You can choose the location for a new item added to the list. In the **Items. Insert method**, you specify the index position for the new item, which must be an existing position or the end of the list.

The Items.Insert Method—General Form

```
Object.Items.Insert(IndexPosition, ItemValue);
```

The index position is zero based. To insert a new item in the first position, use index position = 0.

The Items.Insert Method—Examples

```
schoolsListBox.Items.Insert(0, "Harvard");
majorsComboBox.Items.Insert(1, majorsComboBox.Text);
```

If you choose the index position of an item using the Insert method, do not set the list control's Sorted property to *true*. A sorted list is always sorted into alphabetic order, regardless of any other order that you request. Inserting an item beyond the end of the list throws an exception.

The SelectedIndex Property

When a project is running and the user selects (highlights) an item from the list, the index number of that item is stored in the **SelectedIndex property** of the list box. Recall that the index of the first item in the list is 0. If no list item is selected, the SelectedIndex property is set to negative 1 (–1).

You can use the SelectedIndex property to select an item in the list or deselect all items in code.

Examples

```
// Select the fourth item in list.
coffeeTypesListBox.SelectedIndex = 3;

// Deselect all items in list.
coffeeTypesListBox.SelectedIndex = -1;
```

The Items.Count Property

You can use the Count property of the Items collection to determine the number of items in the list. We will use the **Items.Count property** later in this chapter to process each element in the list. Items.Count is also handy when you need to display the count at some point in your project.

Remember: Items.Count is always one more than the highest possible SelectedIndex since the indexes begin with 0. For example, if there are five items in a list, Items.Count is 5 and the highest index is 4 (Figure 7.5).

Examples

```
totalItemsInteger = itemsListBox.Items.Count;
MessageBox.Show("The number of items in the list is " +
  itemsListBox.Items.Count.ToString());
```

F i g u r e   7 . 5

Items.SelectedIndex	Items.Count = 5
[0]	Harvard
[1]	Stanford
[2]	University of California
[3]	Miami University
[4]	University of New York

For a list of five items, the indexes range from 0 to 4.

Referencing the Items Collection

If you need to display one item from a list, you can refer to one element of the Items collection. The Items collection of a list box or combo box holds the text of all list elements. You specify which element you want by including an index. This technique can be useful if you need to display a list item in a label or on another form. Later in this chapter, we will use the Items property to send the contents of the list box to the printer.

TIP

Use square brackets to reference the index position of a list; use parentheses for method arguments: namesListBox.Items[index Integer]; and namesListBox. Items.Add("New Name"); ∎

Using the Items Collection—General Form

```
Object.Items[IndexPosition];
```

The index of the first list element is 0, so the highest index is Items.Count − 1. Notice that you use brackets, rather than parentheses.

You can retrieve the value of a list element or set an element to a different value.

Using the Items Collection—Examples

```
schoolsListBox.Items[2] = "University of California";
majorLabel.Text = majorsComboBox.Items[indexInteger].ToString();
selectedMajorLabel.Text = majorsComboBox.Items[majorsComboBox.SelectedIndex].ToString();
selectedMajorLabel.Text = majorsComboBox.Text;
```

To refer to the currently selected element of a list, you combine the Items property and the SelectedIndex property:

```
selectedFlavorString = flavorListBox.Items[flavorListBox.SelectedIndex].ToString();
```

You also can retrieve the selected list item by referring to the Text property of the control:

```
selectedMajorLabel.Text = majorsComboBox.Text;
```

Note that if you assign a value to a particular item, you replace the previous contents of that position. For example,

```
schoolsListBox.Items[0] = "My School";
```

places "My School" into the first position, replacing whatever was there already. It does not insert the item into the list or increase the value in Items.Count.

Removing an Item from a List

You can remove individual items from a list by specifying either the index of the item or the text of the item. Use the **Items.RemoveAt method** to remove an item by index and the **Items.Remove method** to remove by specifying the text.

The Items.RemoveAt Method—General Form

```
Object.Items.RemoveAt(IndexPosition);
```

The index is required; it specifies which element to remove. The index of the first list element is 0, and the index of the last element is Items.Count − 1. If you specify an invalid index, the system throws an IndexOutOfRange exception.

The Items.RemoveAt Method—Examples

```
// Remove the first name from the list.
namesListBox.Items.RemoveAt(0);
// Remove the item in position indexInteger.
schoolsComboBox.Items.RemoveAt(indexInteger);
// Remove the currently selected item.
coffeeComboBox.Items.RemoveAt(coffeeComboBox.SelectedIndex);
```

The Items.Remove Method—General Form

```
Object.Items.Remove(TextString);
```

The `Items.Remove` method looks for the specified string in the Items collection. If the string is found, it is removed; however, if it is not found, no exception is generated.

The Items.Remove Method—Examples

```
// Remove the specified item.
namesListBox.Items.Remove("My School");
// Remove the matching item.
schoolsComboBox.Items.Remove(schoolTextBox.Text);
// Remove the currently selected item.
coffeeComboBox.Items.Remove(coffeeComboBox.Text);
```

Clearing a List

In addition to removing individual items at run time, you also can clear all items from a list. Use the **Items.Clear method** to empty a combo box or list box.

The Items.Clear Method—General Form

```
Object.Items.Clear();
```

The Items.Clear Method—Examples

```
schoolsListBox.Items.Clear();
majorsComboBox.Items.Clear();
```

```
// Confirm clearing the majors list.
DialogResult responseDialogResult;

responseDialogResult = MessageBox.Show("Clear the majors list?",
    "Clear Majors List", MessageBoxButtons.YesNo, MessageBoxIcon.Question);

if (responseDialogResult == DialogResult.Yes)
{
    majorsComboBox.Items.Clear();
}
```

List Box and Combo Box Events

Later in the chapter, we will perform actions in event-handling methods for events of list boxes and combo boxes. Some useful events are the SelectedIndexChanged, TextChanged, Enter, and Leave.

Note: Although we haven't used these events up until this point, many other controls have similar events. For example, you can code event-handling methods for the TextChanged, Enter, and Leave events of text boxes.

The TextChanged Event

As the user types text into the text box portion of a combo box, the TextChanged event occurs. Each keystroke generates another TextChanged event. A list box does not have a TextChanged event because list boxes do not have associated text boxes.

The Enter Event

When a control receives the focus, an Enter event occurs. As the user tabs from control to control, an Enter event fires for each control. Later you will learn to make any existing text appear selected when the user tabs to a text box or the text portion of a combo box.

The Leave Event

You also can write code for the Leave event of a control. The Leave event fires when the control loses focus. Often Leave event handlers are used for validating input data. When the user tabs from one control to another, the Leave event is triggered before the Enter event of the next control.

> **✓ TIP**
>
> To write a method for an event that isn't the default event, you cannot just double-click the control. Instead, select the control, click on the *Events* button in the Properties window, and double-click on the event for which you want to write a handler; the Editor window will open with the method header written for you. ■

▶ Feedback 7.1

Describe the purpose of each of the following methods or properties for a list box or combo box control.

1. Sorted
2. SelectedIndex
3. Items

(*continued on next page*)

4. DropDownStyle
5. Items.Count
6. `Items.Add`
7. `Items.Insert`
8. `Items.Clear`
9. `Items.RemoveAt`
10. `Items.Remove`

The while and do/while Loops

Until now, there has been no way to repeat the same steps in a method without calling it a second time. The computer is capable of repeating a group of instructions many times without calling the method for each new set of data. The process of repeating a series of instructions is called *looping*. The group of repeated instructions is called a ***loop***. An **iteration** is a single execution of the statement(s) in the loop. In this section, you will learn about the `while` and `do/while` loops. Later in this chapter, you will learn about another type of loop—a `for` loop.

A **while** or **do/while loop** terminates based on a condition that you specify. Execution of the statements in the loop continues *while* a condition is *true*. Generally, you use `while` or `do/while` loops when you don't know ahead of time the exact number of iterations needed. (Later you will learn about `for` loops, which you use when you *do* know the exact number of iterations.)

The while and do/while Loop Statements—General Form

<table>
<tr><td>

```
    while (Condition)
    {
        // Statements in loop.
    }

or

    do
    {
        // Statements in loop.
    } while (Condition);
```

</td></tr>
</table>

The first form shown above, the `while` loop, tests for completion at the top of the loop. With this type of loop, also called a ***pretest*** or ***entry test***, the statements inside the loop may never be executed if the terminating condition is *true* the first time it is tested.

Example

```
totalInteger = 0;
while (totalInteger != 0)
{
    // Statements in loop (will never be done).
}
```

Because totalInteger is 0 the first time the condition is tested, the condition is *false* and the statements inside the loop will not execute. Control will pass to the statement following the end of the loop.

The do/while tests for completion at the bottom of the loop, which means that the statements inside the loop will *always* be executed at least once. This form of loop is sometimes called a ***posttest*** or ***exit test***. Changing the example to a posttest, you can see the difference.

```
totalInteger = 0;
do
{
    // Statements in loop (will be done only once).
} while (totalInteger != 0);
```

In this case, the statements inside the loop will be executed at least once. Assuming the value for totalInteger does not change inside the loop, the condition (totalInteger != 0) will be *false* the first time it is tested and control will pass to the first statement following the while statement. Figure 7.6 shows UML action diagrams of pretest and posttest loops, using both while and do/while.

UML action diagrams of loops: a. pretest (while) loop, and b. posttest (do/while) loop.

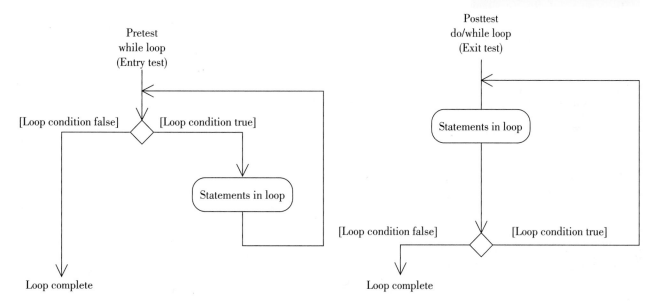

The while and do/while Loop Statements—Examples

```
while (itemInteger <= itemsListBox.Items.Count - 1)
{
    // Statements in loop.
}
do
{
    // Statements in loop.
} while (amountDecimal >= 10M && amountDecimal <= 20M);
```

The bool Data Type Revisited

In Chapter 2 you learned to use Boolean values to set and test for *true* or *false*. You will find Boolean variables very useful when setting and testing conditions for a loop.

An example of using a Boolean variable is when you want to search through a list for a specific value. The item may be found or not found, and you want to quit looking when a match is found.

Using a Boolean variable is usually a three-step process. First you must declare a variable and set its initial value. Then, when a particular situation occurs, you set the variable to *true*. A loop condition can then check for *true* (continue executing the loop as long as the condition is not *true*).

```
bool itemFoundBoolean = false;

while ( ! itemFoundBoolean)     // Loops when condition is false (not true).
{
    // Statement(s) in loop.
    // Must include a statement that sets itemFoundBoolean to true.
}
```

A Boolean variable is always in one of two states—*true* or *false*. Many programmers refer to Boolean variables as *switches* or *flags*. Switches have two states—on or off; flags are considered either up or down.

Using a while Loop with a List Box

This small example combines a Boolean variable with a `while` loop. Inside the loop, each element of the list is compared to newItemTextBox.Text for a match. The loop will terminate when a match is found or when all elements have been tested. Follow through the logic to see what happens when there is a match, when there isn't a match, when the match occurs on the first list element, and when the match occurs on the last list element.

```
private void findButton_Click(object sender, EventArgs e)
{
    // Look for a match between text box and list items.
    bool itemFoundBoolean = false;
    int itemInteger = 0;

    while (! itemFoundBoolean && itemInteger < itemsListBox.Items.Count)
    {
        if (newItemTextBox.Text == itemsListBox.Items[itemInteger].ToString())
        {
            itemFoundBoolean = true;
        }
        itemInteger++;
    }
    if (itemFoundBoolean)
    {
        MessageBox.Show("Item is in the list", "Item match",
            MessageBoxButtons.OK, MessageBoxIcon.Information);
    }
```

```
    else
    {
        MessageBox.Show("Item is not in the list", "No item match",
            MessageBoxButtons.OK, MessageBoxIcon.Information);
    }
}
```

Feedback 7.2

Explain the purpose of each line of the following code:

```
bool itemFoundBoolean = false;
int itemInteger = 0;

while (! itemFoundBoolean && itemInteger < itemsListBox.Items.Count)
{
    if (newItemTextBox.Text == itemsListBox.Items[itemInteger].ToString())
    {
        itemFoundBoolean = true;
    }
    itemInteger++;
}
```

for Loops

When you want to repeat the statements in a loop a specific number of times, the **for loop** is ideal. The for loop allows you to initialize values, test a condition, and perform actions.

```
int maximumInteger = schoolsListBox.Items.Count - 1;

for (int indexInteger = 0; indexInteger <= maximumInteger; indexInteger++)
{
    // The statements inside of the loop are indented.
    // and referred to as the body of the loop.
}
```

The for loop contains three parts: initialization, the condition, and the action to occur after each iteration. In the previous example, an integer variable called indexInteger, the **loop index**, is created and initialized to 0 (the initial value); the indexInteger variable is then compared to maximumInteger, which was assigned the value of schoolsListBox.Items.Count − 1. If the condition (indexInteger <= maximumInteger) is *true*, the statements in the loop are executed and then indexInteger is incremented by 1. Then control passes back to the for statement. Is the value of indexInteger less than or equal to maximumInteger? If so, the statements in the loop are executed again. When the test is made and the loop index *is* greater than the final value, control passes to the statement immediately following the loop's closing brace.

Use a semicolon to separate the three parts of the `for` statement. You can include more than one initialization action by separating each with commas. You also can write more than one action to execute at the end of each iteration of the loop.

The most common use of a `for` is to count the number of iterations when you know the number of times the loop must execute such as iterating through the items in a list box.

A counter-controlled loop generally has three elements (see Figure 7.7 for a UML action diagram of loop logic).

1. Initialize the counter.
2. Test the counter to determine when it is time to terminate the loop.
3. Increment the counter.

A `for` loop handles all three steps for you.

The for Loop—General Form

```
for (initialization [, additional initialization]; condition; action [, additional
action])
{
    // (Body of loop).
}
```

For the initialization, the loop index must be a properly initialized numeric variable. The condition should test the value of the loop index variable. The action is generally to add to or subtract from the loop index variable.

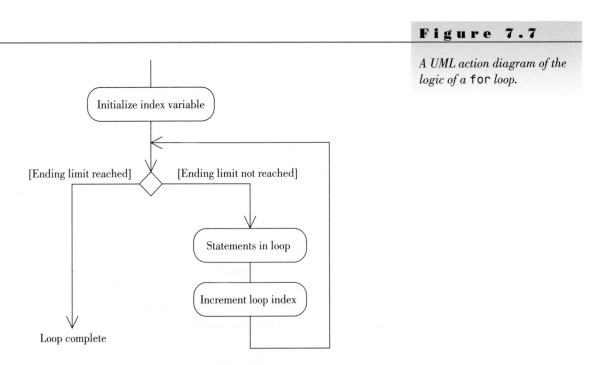

F i g u r e   7 . 7

A UML action diagram of the logic of a `for` loop.

The for Statement—Examples

```
for (int indexInteger = 2; indexInteger <= 100; indexInteger += 2)
for (countInteger = startInteger; countInteger < endInteger; countInteger +=
    incrementInteger)
for (int countInteger = 0; countInteger <= coffeeTypeComboBox.Items.Count - 1;
    countInteger++)
for (numberInteger = (numberCorrectInteger - 5); numberInteger < totalPossibleInteger;
    numberInteger++)
for (rateDecimal = 0.05M; rateDecimal < 0.25M; rateDecimal += 0.05M)
for (int countDownInteger = 10; countDownInteger > 0; countDownInteger--)
```

All statements between the pair of braces that follows the for statement are considered to be the body of the loop and will be executed the specified number of times.

The first for statement example will count from 2 to 100 by 2. The statements in the body of the loop will be executed 50 times—first with indexInteger = 2, next with indexInteger = 4, next with indexInteger = 6, and so forth.

When the comparison is done, the program checks the condition. If the *condition* is *true*, then it continues executing the loop; if the *condition* is *false*, then it exits the loop. When indexInteger = 100 in the preceding example, the body of the loop will execute one more time. Then, at the end of the loop, indexInteger will be incremented to 102, the test will be made, and control will pass to the statement following the closing brace.

Use a for loop when you know the number of iterations needed for the loop. Use a while or do/while when the loop should end based on a condition. ∎

Negative Increment or Counting Backward

You can decrement the counter variable, rather than increment it. In that case, you must write the condition to test for the lower bound. The loop will continue as long as the index variable is greater than the test value.

```
// Count down.
for (int countInteger = 10; countInteger > 0; countInteger--)
{
    // Statements in the body of the loop.
}
```

Conditions Satisfied before Entry

At times, the final value will be reached before entry into the loop. In that case, the statements in the body of the loop will not be executed at all.

```
// An unexecutable loop.
int finalInteger = 5;
for (int indexInteger = 6; indexInteger < finalInteger; indexInteger++)
{
    // The execution will never reach here.
}
```

Endless Loops

Changing the value of a loop index variable not only is considered a poor practice but also may lead to an endless loop. Your code could get into a loop that is impossible to exit. Consider the following example; when will the loop end?

```
// Poor Programming.
for (int indexInteger = 1; indexInteger < 10; indexInteger++)
{
    indexInteger = 1;
}
```

Exiting for Loops

In the previous example of an endless loop, you will have to break the program execution manually. You can click on your form's close box or use the VS IDE menu bar or toolbar to stop the program. If you can't see the menu bar or toolbar, you can usually move or resize your application's form to bring it into view. You may want to set a breakpoint and step program execution to see what is causing the problem.

Usually loops should proceed to normal completion. However, on occasion you may need to terminate a loop before the loop index reaches its final value. You can use the C# break statement for this situation. You have already seen the break statement as part of a switch statement. You also can use break to exit a for loop, a while loop, or a do/while loop. However, good programming practices dictate that you exit loops properly rather than use break.

Skipping to the Next Iteration of a Loop

At times you may be finished in the current iteration of a loop and want to skip to the next. The continue statement transfers control to the end of the loop and retests the loop exit condition. This effectively skips to the next iteration of the loop. Generally, the continue statement is part of an if statement.

Examples

```
// Continue a for loop.
for (int loopInteger = 0; loopInteger <= nameListBox.Items.Count - 1; loopInteger++)
{
    if (nameListBox.Items[loopInteger].ToString() == string.Empty)
    {
      continue;
    }
    // Code to do something with the name found.
    Console.WriteLine("Name = " + nameListBox.Items[loopInteger].ToString());
}

// Continue a while loop.
int indexInteger = -1;
while (indexInteger < nameListBox.Items.Count - 1)
{
```

```
      indexInteger++;
      if (nameListBox.Items[indexInteger].ToString() == string.Empty)
      {
        continue;
      }
      // Code to do something with the name found.
      Console.WriteLine("Name = " + nameListBox.Items[indexInteger].ToString());
}
```

Note: The two above examples do the same thing, but you'll notice that the `for` loop has two fewer lines of code. Because the number of iterations is known (`Items.Count`), the `for` statement is the preferred solution.

▶ ## Feedback 7.3

1. Identify the statements that are correctly formed and those that have errors. For those with errors, state what is wrong and how to correct it. You can assume that all variables are properly declared.
   (a) `for (indexDecimal = 3.5M, indexDecimal < 6.0M, indexDecimal += 0.5M)`
   (b) `for (indexInteger = beginInteger; incrementInteger < endInteger;`
       `     incrementInteger++)`
   (c) `for (4 = 1; 4 < 10; 4 += 2)`
   (d) `for (indexInteger = 100; indexInteger > 0; indexInteger -= 25)`
   (e) `for (indexInteger = 0; indexInteger < -10; indexInteger -= 1)`
2. How many times will the body of the loop be executed for each of these examples?
   (a) `for (countInteger = 1; countInteger < 3; countInteger++)`
   (b) `for (countInteger = 2; countInteger < 11; countInteger += 3)`
   (c) `for (countInteger = 10; countInteger > 0; countInteger--)`
   (d) `for (countDecimal = 3.0M; countDecimal < 6.0M; countDecimal += 0.5M)`

Making Entries Appear Selected

You can use several techniques to make the text in a text box or list appear selected.

Selecting the Entry in a Text Box

When the user tabs into a text box that already has an entry, how do you want the text to appear? Should the insertion point appear at either the left or right end of the text? Or should the entire entry appear selected? You also can apply this question to a text box that failed validation; shouldn't the entire entry be selected? The most user-friendly approach is to select the text, which you can do with the `SelectAll` method of the text box, which you saw in Chapter 3.

A good location to select the text is in the text box's Enter event handler, which occurs when the control receives the focus.

```csharp
private void newItemTextBox_Enter(object sender, System.EventArgs e)
{
    // Select any existing text.
    newItemTextBox.SelectAll();
}
```

Reminder: You can write the Enter event handler for a text box by double-clicking the Enter event in the *Events* list of the control's Properties window.

Sending Information to the Printer

So far, all program output has been on the screen. You can use the .NET Print-Document and PrintPreviewDialog components to produce output for the printer and also to preview the output on the screen. These components appear in the *Printing* tab of the toolbox.

C# was designed to run under Windows. The printing is done through the Windows environment, allowing you to take advantage of the fonts installed on any given system. The printing dialogs and page setup are the same ones that you have become familiar with using Microsoft products.

It is easy to create forms for interactive programs, but it is not as easy to print on the printer. Several companies sell utilities that do a nice job of designing and printing reports. The C# Professional Edition and Team System Edition include Crystal Reports for creating reports from database files.

The PrintDocument Component

You set up output for the printer using the methods and events of the **PrintDocument component**. When you add a PrintDocument component to a form, the component appears in the component tray below the form (Figure 7.8).

The PrintDocument Print Method

The **Print method** of the PrintDocument component sends the command to print the information according to the layout that you specify in the PrintPage event handler. The `Print` method belongs in the Click event handler for the *Print* button or menu item that the user selects to begin printing.

```csharp
private void printButton_Click(object sender, System.EventArgs e)
{
    // Print output on the printer.
    printDocument1.Print(); // Start the print process.
}
```

Setting Up the Print Output

The code that you write to set up the printed page belongs in the PrintDocument's **PrintPage event handler**. The PrintPage event is fired once for each page to be printed. This technique is referred to as a ***callback*** and is different from anything we have done so far. In a callback, the object notifies the program

Figure 7.8

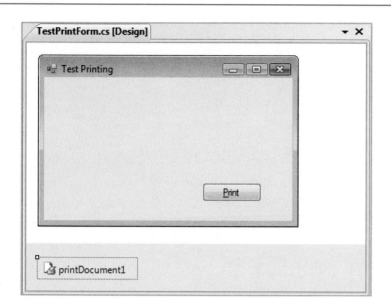

Add a PrintDocument
component to your application.
The component appears in the
form's component tray.

that it needs to do something or that a situation exists that the program needs to handle. The object notifies the program of the situation by firing an event.

When the user activates the PrintDocument Print method, usually from a menu option or a button click, the PrintPage event handler for the PrintDocument executes. The PrintPage event handler holds the code that describes exactly how pages should print. The PrintDocument object also fires events for BeginPrint and EndPrint, for which you can write code if you wish.

```
private void printDocument1_PrintPage(object sender,
    System.Drawing.Printing.PrintPageEventArgs e)
{
    // Set up actual output to print.
}
```

Notice the argument System.Drawing.Printing.PrintPageEventArgs e. We will use some of the properties and methods of the PrintPageEventArgs argument for such things as determining the page margins and sending a string of text to the page.

Getting Started with Printing—Step-by-Step

This simple project introduces you to printing by creating a document that sends your name to the printer. The sections that follow describe how to set up the printed page.

Create the Project

STEP 1: Create a project called Ch07Printing.

STEP 2: Add a button and a printDocument component to the form.

STEP 3: Name the button printButton and set the Text property to "&Print".

Set up the Print Document Component

STEP 1: Double-click on printDocument1 in the component tray. The Print-Page event handler appears.

STEP 2: Write the code. Note that the sections that follow explain the parameters for the *DrawString* method in detail. But as a quick overview, you are printing your name using Arial 36-point font in black, 100 pixels down from the top of the page (X) and 100 pixels to the right of the left edge of the page (Y).

```
// Information to print.
e.Graphics.DrawString("Your Name", new Font("Arial", 36),
    Brushes.Black, 100, 100);
```

Code the Print Button

STEP 1: Go to the Click event handler method for the printButton and add the code to call the `Print` method of the print document.

```
private void printButton_Click(object sender, EventArgs e)
{
    // Call the Print method of the print document component.

    printDocument1.Print();
}
```

Run the Program

STEP 1: Run the program and click on the *Print* button.
STEP 2: Change the font and location for the text. If you have a color printer, try changing the color for the brushes.
STEP 3: Run it again.

The Graphics Page

You set up a graphics page in memory and then the page is sent to the printer. The graphics page can contain strings of text as well as graphic elements.

You must specify the exact location on the graphics page for each element that you want to print. You can specify the upper-left corner of any element by giving its X and Y coordinates, or by using a Point structure or a Rectangle structure. We will stick with the X and Y coordinates in these examples (Figure 7.9).

F i g u r e   7 . 9

The X coordinate is the horizontal distance across a line from the left edge of the page; the Y coordinate is the vertical distance from the top of the page. The measurements are in pixels.

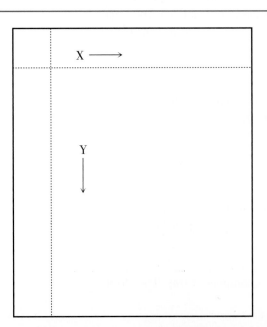

You can use multiple PrintDocument objects if you have more than one type of output or report. Each PrintDocument has its own PrintPage event. Code the graphics commands to precisely print the page in each document's PrintPage event handler.

Using the DrawString Method

You use the **DrawString method** to send a line of text to the graphics page. The DrawString method belongs to the Graphics object of the PrintPageEvent-Args argument. Refer back to the method header for the PrintPage event in "Setting Up the Print Output."

The DrawString Method—General Form

The DrawString method is overloaded, which means that there are several forms for calling the method. The form presented here is the least complicated and requires that page coordinates be given in X and Y format.

General Form

```
GraphicsObject.DrawString(StringToPrint, Font, Brush, Xcoordinate, Ycoordinate);
```

You supply the arguments of the DrawString method: what to print, what font and color to print it in, and where to print it. IntelliSense prompts you so there's no need to memorize the order of the arguments.

The DrawString Method—Examples

Examples

```
e.Graphics.DrawString(printLineString, printFont, Brushes.Black,
    horizontalPrintLocationFloat, verticalPrintLocationFloat);
e.Graphics.DrawString("My text string", myFont, Brushes.Black, 100.0, 100.0);
e.Graphics.DrawString(nameTextBox.Text, new Font("Arial", 10), Brushes.Red,
    leftMarginFloat, currentLineFloat);
```

Before you execute the DrawString method, you can set up the font that you want to use and the X and Y coordinates.

Setting the X and Y Coordinates

For each line that you want to print, you must specify the X and Y coordinates. It is helpful to set up some variables for setting these values, which should be declared as float data type.

```
float horizontalPrintLocationFloat;
float verticalPrintLocationFloat;
```

The PrintPageEventArgs argument has several useful properties (Figure 7.10), such as MarginBounds, PageBounds, and PageSettings. You can use these properties to determine the present settings. For example, you may want to set the X coordinate to the current left margin and the Y coordinate to the top margin.

```
horizontalPrintLocationFloat = e.MarginBounds.Left;
verticalPrintLocationFloat = e.MarginBounds.Top;
```

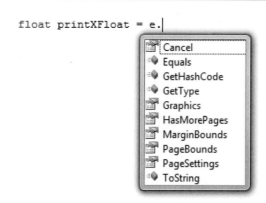

```
float printXFloat = e.|
```
| Cancel |
| Equals |
| GetHashCode |
| GetType |
| Graphics |
| HasMorePages |
| MarginBounds |
| PageBounds |
| PageSettings |
| ToString |

To send multiple lines to the print page, you must increment the Y coordinate, which forces the next line further down the page. You can add the height of a line to the previous Y coordinate to calculate the next line's Y coordinate. Find the height of a line in the current font using the font's **GetHeight method**.

```
// Declarations at the top of the method.
Font printFont = new Font("Arial", 12);
float lineHeightFloat = printFont.GetHeight;
horizontalPrintLocationFloat = e.MarginBounds.Left;
verticalPrintLocationFloat = e.MarginBounds.Top;

// Set up printline.
string printLineString = "Programmed by (Your Name)";
// Print a line.
e.Graphics.DrawString(printLineString, printFont, Brushes.Black,
    horizontalPrintLocationFloat, verticalPrintLocationFloat);
// Increment the Y position for the next line.
verticalPrintLocationFloat += lineHeightFloat;
```

Printing Summary

Although the steps for printing may sound confusing at first, you can follow these easy steps for nearly all printing tasks. Place the code for these actions in the PrintPage event handler for the PrintDocument component:

1. At the top of the event-handling method, define the font(s), line height, and X and Y coordinates.
2. Set up the line to print.
3. Print the line.
4. Increment the Y coordinate if another line will be printed.
5. Place steps 2, 3, and 4 inside a loop if there are multiple lines to print.

Printing the Contents of a List Box

You can combine the techniques for printing, looping, and the list box properties to send the contents of a list box to the printer. You know how many iterations to make, using the Items.Count property. The Items collection allows you to print out the actual values from the list.

```
// Print out all items in the coffeeComboBox list.

for (int indexInteger = 0; indexInteger < coffeeComboBox.Items.Count; indexInteger++)
{
    // Set up a line.
    printLineString = coffeeComboBox.Items[indexInteger];
    // Send the line to the graphics page object.
    e.Graphics.DrawString(printLineString, printFont, Brushes.Black,
        horizontalPrintLocationFloat, verticalPrintLocationFloat);

    // Increment the Y position for the next line.
    verticalPrintLocationFloat += lineHeightFloat;
}
```

Printing the Selected Item from a List

When an item is selected in a list box or a combo box, the Text property holds the selected item. You can use the Text property to print the selected item.

```
// Set up the line.
printLineString = "Coffee: " + coffeeComboBox.Text
    + " Syrup: " + syrupListBox.Text;
// Send the line to the graphics page object.
e.Graphics.DrawString(printLineString, printFont, Brushes.Black,
    horizontalPrintLocationFloat, verticalPrintLocationFloat);
```

Aligning Decimal Columns

When the output to the printer includes numeric data, the alignment of the decimal points is important. Alignment can be tricky with proportional fonts, where the width of each character varies. The best approach is to format each number as you want it to print and then measure the length of the formatted string. This technique requires a couple more elements: You need an object declared as a SizeF structure, which has a Width property, and you need to use the MeasureString method of the Graphics class. Both the SizeF structure and the MeasureString method work with pixels, which is what you want. It's the same unit of measure as used for the X and Y coordinates of the DrawString method.

The following example prints a left-aligned literal at the left margin and right-aligns a formatted number at position 500.

```
private void columnsPrintDocument_PrintPage(object sender,
  System.Drawing.Printing.PrintPageEventArgs e)
{
    // Print aligned columns.
    Font printFont = new Font("Arial", 12);
    float lineHeightFloat = printFont.GetHeight();
    float yFloat = e.MarginBounds.Top;

    for (decimal indexDecimal = 0m; indexDecimal < 2000m; indexDecimal+=500m)
    {
        e.Graphics.DrawString("Text", printFont, Brushes.Black,
            e.MarginBounds.Left, yFloat);

        string formattedOutputString = indexDecimal.ToString("N");
```

```
    // Measure the string using the font.
    SizeF fontSize = e.Graphics.MeasureString(formattedOutputString,
        printFont);

    // Determine start for number to end at column end.
    float column2Float = 500f - fontSize.Width;

    e.Graphics.DrawString(indexDecimal.ToString("N"), printFont,
        Brushes.Black, column2Float, yFloat);
    yFloat += lineHeightFloat;
    }
}
```

Displaying a Print Preview

A really great feature of the printing model is **print preview**. You can view the printer's output on the screen and then choose to print or cancel. This is especially helpful for testing and debugging a program so that you don't have to keep sending pages to the printer and wasting paper.

The **PrintPreviewDialog component** is the key to print preview. You add the control to your form's component tray; the default name is printPreviewDialog1 (Figure 7.11). Since you can use the same dialog for all print previews, you do not need to rename the component.

You write two lines of code in the event handler for the button or menu item where the user selects the print preview option. The PrintPreviewDialog component uses the same PrintDocument component that you declared for printer output. You assign the PrintDocument to the Document property of the PrintPreviewDialog and execute the ShowDialog method. The same PrintPage event handler executes as for the PrintDocument.

Figure 7.11

Add a PrintPreviewDialog component to your form's component tray.

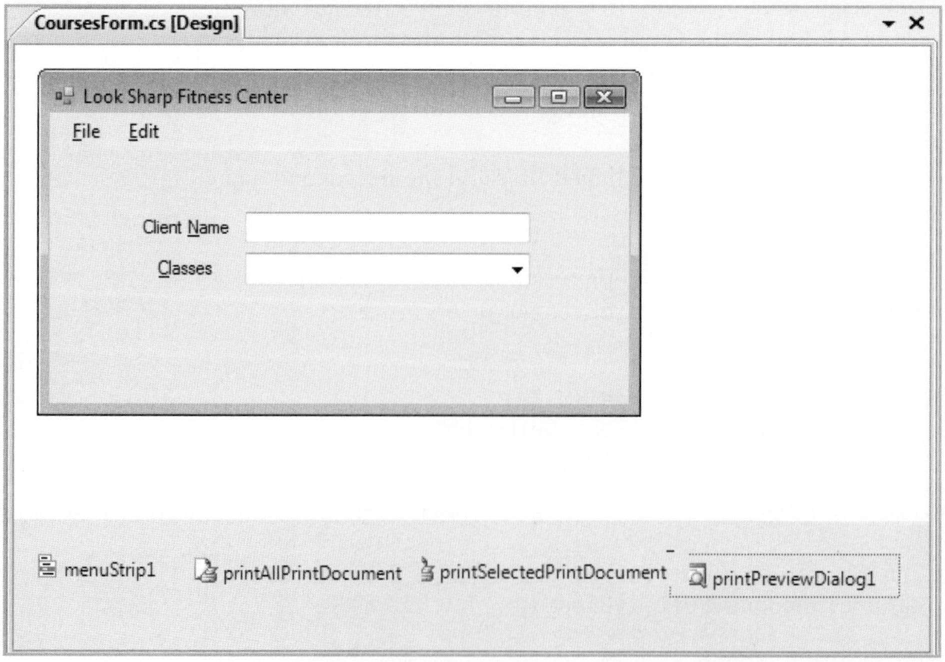

```
private void filePrintPreviewMenu_Click(object sender, System.EventArgs e)
{
    // Begin the process for print preview.

    printPreviewDialog1.Document = printAllPrintDocument;
    printPreviewDialog1.ShowDialog();
}
```

Adding a PrintPreview Dialog to the Print Project—Step-by-Step

Open the Project

STEP 1: Open Ch07Printing.
STEP 2: Add a PrintPreviewDialog component to the form.
STEP 3: Add a printPreview button.

Write the Code

STEP 1: Write the code for the printPreview button.

```
private void printPreviewButton_Click(object sender, EventArgs e)
{
    // Assign the printDialog1 document to the preview.

    printPreviewDialog1.Document = printDocument1;
    // Show the dialog.
    printPreviewDialog1.ShowDialog();
}
```

Printing Multiple Pages

You can easily print multiple pages, both to the printer and to the *Print Preview* dialog box. Recall that the PrintDocument's PrintPage event fires once for each page. You indicate that you have more pages to print by setting the HasMore-Pages property of the PrintPageEventArgs argument to *true*.

The following example prints three pages full of the same line, just to illustrate multiple-page output. Normally you will have a certain amount of data to print and stop when you run out.

```
// Class level variable.
int pageCountInteger = 1;

private void multipagePrintDocument_PrintPage(object sender,
    System.Drawing.Printing.PrintPageEventArgs e)
{
    // Generate a multiple-page report.

    Font printFont = new Font("Arial", 12);
    float printYFloat = e.MarginBounds.Top;
    float lineHeightFloat = printFont.GetHeight();

    // Print a full page.
    do
    {
        e.Graphics.DrawString("Another line", printFont, Brushes.Black,
            e.MarginBounds.Left, printYFloat);
        printYFloat += lineHeightFloat;
```

```
                // Stop at bottom margin.
        } while (printYFloat <= e.MarginBounds.Bottom);
        pageCountInteger++;

        if (pageCountInteger <= 3)
        {
            e.HasMorePages = true;
        }
        else
        {
            e.HasMorePages = false;
            pageCountInteger = 1;    //Reset the page counter.
        }
    }
```

Feedback 7.4

What is the purpose of each of these elements? Where and how is each used?

1. The PrintDocument component.
2. The `Print` method.
3. The PrintPage event.
4. The `DrawString` method.
5. `System.Drawing.Printing.PrintPageEventArgs`.
6. `MarginBounds.Left`.
7. The PrintPreviewDialog component.

Your Hands-On Programming Example

Create a project for Look Sharp Fitness Center that contains a drop-down combo box of the current class offerings. Initially the items collection should contain Pilates, Step, Kickboxing, Body Sculpting, and Spinning. Include a text box for the client name. Print the name when printing the selected course.

An *Edit* menu will contain options for adding or removing a course, clearing the list, or displaying a count of courses. Use a loop to check for duplicates when adding a new course. Verify that the user wants to clear the list before removing all items. When removing an item, check that a course is selected.

The *File* menu should contain menu items for *Print All Courses* and for *Print Selected Course*. Use a separator bar between the *Print*s and the *Exit*.

Send all printer output to the Print Preview window.

Planning the Project

Sketch a form (Figure 7.12), which your users sign off as meeting their needs.

A sketch of the form for the hands-on project.

Plan the Objects and Properties

Object	Property	Setting
CoursesForm	Name	CoursesForm
	Text	Look Sharp Fitness Center
label1	Text	Client &Name
nameTextBox	Name	nameTextBox
	Text	(blank)
label2	Text	&Classes
classesComboBox	Name	classesComboBox
	Items	Spinning
		Step
		Pilates
		Kickboxing
		Body Sculpting
	Sorted	True
fileToolStripMenuItem	Text	&File
printSelectedCourseToolStripMenuItem	Text	Print &Selected Course
printAllCoursesToolStripMenuItem	Text	Print &All Courses
exitToolStripMenuItem	Text	E&xit
editToolStripMenuItem	Text	&Edit
addACourseToolStripMenuItem	Text	&Add a Course
removeACourseToolStripMenuItem	Text	&Remove a Course
clearTheCourseListToolStripMenuItem	Text	C&lear the Course List

(Continued)

Object	Property	Setting
displayCourseCountToolStripMenuItem	Text	Display Course &Count
printAllPrintDocument	Name	printAllPrintDocument
printSelectedPrintDocument	Name	printSelectedPrintDocument
printPreviewDialog1	Name	printPreviewDialog1

Plan the Event Handlers

Method	Actions

printSelectedCourseToolStripMenuItem_Click	If course selected
	    Set the print preview document.
	    Show the print preview dialog.
	Else
	    Display an error message.

printAllCoursesToolStripMenuItem_Click	Set the print preview document. Show the print preview dialog.
exitToolStripMenuItem_Click	Terminate the project.

addACourseToolStripMenuItem_Click	If text is not blank
	    If duplicate item
	        Display "Duplicate" message.
	    Else
	        Add item to the list.
	        Clear the Text property.

removeACourseToolStripMenuItem_Click	If course selected
	    Remove selected item.
	Else
	    Display error message.

clearTheCourseListToolStripMenuItem_Click	Display a message box to confirm the clear. If user clicks Yes Clear the list.
displayCourseCountToolStripMenuItem_Click	Display list count in message box.
printAllPrintDocument_PrintPage	Use a loop to send all courses to the printer.
printSelectedPrintDocument_PrintPage	Send selected item to the printer.

Write the Project Follow the sketch in Figure 7.12 to create the form. Figure 7.13 shows the completed form.

- Set the properties of each object as you have planned.

- Write the code. Working from the pseudocode, write each event-handling method.

- When you complete the code, use a variety of data to thoroughly test the project.

Figure 7.13

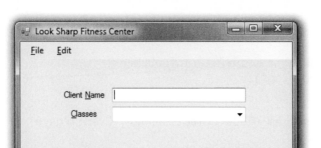

*The form for the hands-on
project.*

The Project Coding Solution

```
/*
 * Project:          Ch07HandsOn
 * Programmer:       Bradley/Millspaugh
 * Date:             June 2009
 * Description:      Maintain a list of courses, print the selected
 *                   course, or print a list of all courses.
 *
 */

using System;
using System.Collections.Generic;
using System.ComponentModel;
using System.Data;
using System.Drawing;
using System.Text;
using System.Windows.Forms;

namespace Ch07HandsOn
{
    public partial class CoursesForm : Form
    {
        public CoursesForm()
        {
            InitializeComponent();
        }

        private void printSelectedCourseToolStripMenuItem_Click(object sender,
            EventArgs e)
        {
            // Print preview for selected course.

            if (classesComboBox.SelectedIndex == -1)
            {
                MessageBox.Show("Select a course to print.", "No Selection");
            }
            else
            {
                printPreviewDialog1.Document = printSelectedPrintDocument;
                printPreviewDialog1.ShowDialog();
            }
        }
    }
```

```csharp
private void printAllCoursesToolStripMenuItem_Click(object sender,
    EventArgs e)
{
    // Print preview for all courses.

    printPreviewDialog1.Document = printAllPrintDocument;
    printPreviewDialog1.ShowDialog();
}

private void exitToolStripMenuItem_Click(object sender, EventArgs e)
{
    // Close the application.

    this.Close();
}

private void addACourseToolStripMenuItem_Click(object sender,
    EventArgs e)
{
    // Add a new course.
    int indexInteger = 0;
    bool itemFoundBoolean = false;

    // Use a loop to test for duplicates.
    if (classesComboBox.Text != string.Empty)
    {
        while (indexInteger < classesComboBox.Items.Count &&
            !itemFoundBoolean)
        {
            if (classesComboBox.Items[indexInteger++].ToString().ToUpper()
                == classesComboBox.Text.ToUpper())
            {
                MessageBox.Show("Duplicate class name.", "Class Not Added",
                    MessageBoxButtons.OK, MessageBoxIcon.Information);
                itemFoundBoolean = true;
            }
        }
        if (!itemFoundBoolean)
        {
            // Add to the list.
            classesComboBox.Items.Add(classesComboBox.Text);
            classesComboBox.Text = string.Empty;
        }
    }
    else
    {
        MessageBox.Show("Enter the new course name.",
            "No Course Name Entered", MessageBoxButtons.OK,
            MessageBoxIcon.Exclamation);
    }
}

private void removeACourseToolStripMenuItem_Click(object sender,
    EventArgs e)
{
    // Remove the selected course.
```

```csharp
        if (classesComboBox.SelectedIndex != -1)
        {
            classesComboBox.Items.RemoveAt(classesComboBox.SelectedIndex);
        }
        else
        {
            MessageBox.Show("Select a course to remove.", "No Selection",
                MessageBoxButtons.OK, MessageBoxIcon.Exclamation);
        }
    }

    private void clearTheCourseListToolStripMenuItem_Click(object sender,
        EventArgs e)
    {
        // Verify and then remove the course.
        DialogResult confirmDialogResult = MessageBox.Show("Remove all items?",
            "Clear Courses List", MessageBoxButtons.YesNo,
            MessageBoxIcon.Question);
        if (confirmDialogResult == DialogResult.Yes)
        {
            classesComboBox.Items.Clear();
        }
    }

    private void displayCourseCountToolStripMenuItem_Click(object sender,
        EventArgs e)
    {
        // Display the number of courses.

        MessageBox.Show("Course Count: " +
            classesComboBox.Items.Count.ToString(),
            "Look Sharp Fitness Center Courses", MessageBoxButtons.OK,
            MessageBoxIcon.Information);
    }

    private void printAllPrintDocument_PrintPage(object sender,
        System.Drawing.Printing.PrintPageEventArgs e)
    {
        // Print a list of all current courses.
        Font printFont = new Font("Arial", 10);
        Font headingFont = new Font("Arial", 14, FontStyle.Bold);
        float verticalPrintPositionFloat = e.MarginBounds.Top;
        float horizontalPrintPositionFloat = e.MarginBounds.Left;
        float lineHeightFloat = printFont.GetHeight();

        // Print heading.
        e.Graphics.DrawString("Current Course List As of "
            + DateTime.Now.ToShortDateString(), headingFont,
            Brushes.Black, horizontalPrintPositionFloat,
            verticalPrintPositionFloat);
        verticalPrintPositionFloat += 2 * lineHeightFloat;

        // Loop through the list to print all courses.
        for (int indexInteger = 0; indexInteger < classesComboBox.Items.Count;
            indexInteger++)
        {
            e.Graphics.DrawString(classesComboBox.Items[indexInteger].ToString(),
                printFont, Brushes.Black, horizontalPrintPositionFloat,
                verticalPrintPositionFloat);
```

```csharp
                verticalPrintPositionFloat += lineHeightFloat;
            }
        }

        private void printSelectedPrintDocument_PrintPage(object sender,
            System.Drawing.Printing.PrintPageEventArgs e)
        {
            // Set up output for selected item.
            Font printFont = new Font("Arial", 12);

            // Print heading.
            e.Graphics.DrawString("Selected Course:", printFont, Brushes.Black,
                100, 100);
            e.Graphics.DrawString(nameTextBox.Text + " \t" +
                classesComboBox.SelectedItem.ToString(), printFont, Brushes.Black,
                100, 140);
        }
    }
}
```

Summary

1. List boxes and combo boxes hold lists of values. The three styles of combo boxes are simple combo boxes, drop-down combo boxes, and drop-down lists.
2. The size of a list box or combo box is determined at design time. If all of the items will not fit into the box, C# automatically adds scroll bars.
3. The values for the items in a list are stored in the Items property, which is a collection. The items can be entered in the Items property in the String Collection Editor. At run time, items are added to lists using the `Items.Add` or `Items.Insert` method.
4. The SelectedIndex property can be used to select an item in the list or to determine which item is selected.
5. The Items.Count property holds the number of elements in the list.
6. The Items collection holds all elements of the list. The individual elements can be referenced by using an index.
7. The `Items.Remove` and `Items.RemoveAt` methods remove one element from a list.
8. The `Items.Clear` method may be used to clear all of the contents of a list box's Items collection at once.
9. Code can be written for several events of list boxes and combo boxes. Combo boxes have a TextChanged event; both combo boxes and list boxes have Enter and Leave events.
10. A loop allows a statement or series of statements to be repeated. `while` and `do/while` loops continue to execute the statements in the loop until a condition is met. Each pass through a loop is called an iteration.
11. `do` loops can have the condition test at the bottom of the loop and `while` loops test the condition at the top of the loop.
12. A `do` loop can be used to locate a selected item in a combo box.
13. A loop index controls `for` loops; the index is initialized to an initial value. After each iteration, the loop index is incremented. The loop is terminated when the condition is met.

14. The PrintDocument and PrintPreviewDialog components can be used to send program output to the printer or the screen.

15. The `Print` method of the PrintDialog control begins a print operation. The control's PrintPage event fires once for each page to print. All printing logic belongs in the PrintPage event handler. The PrintPage event continues to fire as long as the HasMorePages property of the PrintDocument component has a value of *true*.

16. The page to print or display is a graphics object. Use the `DrawString` method to send a string of text to the page, specifying X and Y coordinates for the string.

17. Aligning columns of numbers is difficult using proportional fonts. Numbers can be right-aligned by formatting the number, measuring the length of the formatted string in pixels, and subtracting the length from the right end of the column for the X coordinate.

Key Terms

Review Questions

1. What is a list box? a combo box?
2. Name and describe the three styles of combo boxes.
3. How can you make scroll bars appear on a list box or combo box?
4. Explain the purpose of the SelectedIndex property and the Items.Count property.
5. When and how is information placed inside a list box or a combo box?
6. In what situation would a loop be used in a method?
7. Explain the difference between a pretest and a posttest in a loop.
8. Explain the differences between a `do` and a `while` loop.
9. What are the steps in processing a `for` loop?

10. Discuss how and when the values of the loop index change throughout the processing of the loop.
11. What is the purpose of the PrintDocument component? the PrintPreview-Dialog component?
12. In what method do you write the logic for sending output to the printer?
13. What is the purpose of the X and Y coordinates on a print page?

Programming Exercises

7.1 Create a project that obtains student information, prints the data entered on the form, and prints a list of the schools in the list.

The Form:

- Text boxes for entering the name and units completed.

- Radio buttons for Freshman, Sophomore, Junior, and Senior.

- Check box for Dean's List.

- A list box for the following majors: Accounting, Business, Computer Information Systems, and Marketing.

- A simple combo box for the name of the high school—initially loaded with Franklin, Highland, Midtown, and West Highland. If the user types in a new school name, it should be added to the list. The list should be sorted.

- Print button that prints the data from the form. Include a title and identifying labels for the data. Use the *Print Preview* dialog box.

- An *OK* button that clears the entries from the form and resets the focus. The button should be the Accept button for the form.

Menus: The *File* menu should have an item for *Print Schools* and *Exit*. The *Edit* menu should have an item for *Add High School*; the *Help* menu should have an item for *About* that displays the About box. Include appropriate access keys on your menu items.

   Note: Print your name at the top of the printer output for the schools and include a report title. Display the printer output in the *Print Preview* dialog box.

7.2 R 'n R—for Reading 'n Refreshment needs a project that contains a form for entering book information, prints the information on the screen, and prints out the subjects from the list box.

The Form:

- Text boxes for author and title.

- Radio buttons for type: fiction or nonfiction.

- Drop-down list for subject that will include Best-Seller, Fantasy, Religion, Romance, Humor, Science Fiction, Business, Philosophy, Education, Self-Help, and Mystery. Make the list sorted.

- List box for shelf number containing RC-1111, RC-1112, RC-1113, and RC-1114.

- Print button that prints the data from the form. Include a title on the report and identifying labels for the data. Use the *Print Preview* dialog box.

- An *OK* button that clears the entries from the form and resets the focus. Make this the Accept button.

Menus: The *File* menu will have items for *Print Subjects* and *Exit*. The *Help* menu will have an item for *About* that displays the About box. Include appropriate access keys on your menu items.

   Note: Print your name at the top of the printer output for the subjects, with an appropriate column heading. Display the printer output in the *Print Preview* dialog box.

7.3 Create a project to input chartering information about yachts and print a summary report showing the total revenue, number of charters, and average hours per charter.

Menus: The *File* menu will contain items for *Print Summary*, *Print Yacht Types*, and *Exit*. Place a separator bar before *Exit*. The *Edit* menu should have items for *Clear for Next Charter*, *Add Yacht Type*, *Remove Yacht Type*, and *Display Count of Yacht Types*. Include a separator bar after the *Clear* item. The *Help* menu will contain an *About* item that displays an About form. Include appropriate access keys on your menu items.

The Form:

- The form should contain text boxes for responsible party and hours chartered. The calculated price of the charter should display in a read-only text box or a label.

- A drop-down combo box will contain the type of yacht: Ranger, Wavelength, Catalina, Coronado, Hobie, C & C, Hans Christian, and Excalibur.

- A drop-down list will contain the sizes: 22, 24, 30, 32, 36, 38, and 45. (No new sizes can be entered at run time.)

- An *OK* button will calculate and display the price and add to the totals. The calculations will require price per hour. Use the following chart:

Size	Hourly rate
22	95.00
24	137.00
30	160.00
32	192.00
36	250.00
38	400.00
45	550.00

- A *Clear* button will clear the contents of the screen controls. The functions of the *Clear* button are the same as for the *Clear for Next Charter* menu item.

- Make the *OK* button the Accept button and the *Clear* button the form's Cancel button.

Summary Report: The summary report will print the summary information and send the report to a *Print Preview* dialog box. The summary information will include Number of Charters, Total Revenue, and Average Hours Chartered. Include your name on the output, a report title, and identifying labels for the summary information.

Yacht Types Report: Display the yacht types in the combo box in the *Print Preview* dialog box. Include your name and a title at the top of the report.

7.4 Maintain a list of bagel types for Bradley's Bagels. Use a drop-down combo box to hold the bagel types and use buttons or menu choices to *Add Bagel Type*, *Remove Bagel Type*, *Clear Bagel List*, *Print Bagel List*, *Display Bagel Type Count*, and *Exit*. Keep the list sorted in alphabetic order. Include appropriate access keys on your menu items.

Do not allow a blank type to be added to the list. Display an error message if the user selects *Remove* without first selecting a bagel type.

Before clearing the list, display a message box to confirm the operation. Here are some suggested bagel types. You can make up your own list.

Plain	Poppy seed
Egg	Sesame seed
Rye	Banana nut
Salt	Blueberry

7.5 Modify Programming Exercise 7.4 to not allow duplicate bagel types to be added to the list.

Case Studies

Custom Supplies Mail Order

Create a project for Custom Supplies Mail Order to maintain a list of catalogs. Use a drop-down combo box for the catalog names and allow the user to enter new catalog names, delete catalog names, display a count of the number of catalogs, clear the catalog list, or print the catalog list.

Do not allow a blank catalog name to be added to the list. Display an error message if the user selects *Remove* without first selecting a catalog name. Before

clearing the list, display a message box to confirm the operation.

To begin, the catalog list should hold these catalog names: Odds and Ends, Solutions, Camping Needs, ToolTime, Spiegel, The Outlet, and The Large Size.

Display the printed output in the *Print Preview* dialog box. Include your name and a heading at the top of the report.

Christopher's Car Center

Create an application for the car wash located at Christopher's Car Center.

The form will contain four list box or combo box controls that do not permit the user to type in items at run time. The first list will contain the names of the packages available for detailing a vehicle: Standard, Deluxe, Executive, or Luxury.

Use a drop-down list to allow the user to select the fragrance. The choices are Hawaiian Mist, Baby Powder, Pine, Country Floral, Pina Colada, and Vanilla.

The contents of the other two lists will vary depending upon the package selected. Display one list for the interior work and one list for the exterior work. Store the descriptions of the items in string constants. You must clear the lists for the interior

and exterior for each order and add new items to the lists each time the user makes a selection from the package list.

Include menu items for *Print Order*, *Clear*, and *Exit* with appropriate access keys. The print option should send its output to the *Print Preview* window. Include your name and a heading at the top of the report.

The Order printout will contain the package name (Standard, Deluxe, Executive, or Luxury), the interior and exterior items included, and the fragrance selected. Use a *for* loop when printing the interior and exterior lists.

Hint: Write code in the SelectedIndexChanged method of the list box that contains the various "Packages" for detail.

	Item description	S	D	E	L
Exterior	Hand Wash	✓	✓	✓	✓
	Hand Wax		✓	✓	✓
	Check Engine Fluids			✓	✓
	Detail Engine Compartment				✓
	Detail Under Carriage				✓
Interior	Fragrance	✓	✓	✓	✓
	Shampoo Carpets		✓	✓	✓
	Shampoo Upholstery				✓
	Interior Protection Coat (dashboard and console)			✓	
	Scotchgard™				✓

Note: S—Standard; D—Deluxe; E—Executive; L—Luxury

Xtreme Cinema

Maintain a list of movie categories. Use a drop-down combo box to hold the movie types, keeping the list in alphabetic order. Use buttons or menu choices to *Add a Category*, *Remove a Category*, *Clear All Categories*, *Print the Category List*, *Display the Movie Category Count*,

and *Exit*. Include appropriate access keys on your form and/or menu items.

Do not allow a blank type to be added to the list. Display an error message if the user selects *Remove* without first selecting a movie category. Before clearing the list, display a message box to confirm the operation.

The starting categories are Comedy, Drama, Action, Sci-Fi, and Horror.

Display the printed output in the *Print Preview* dialog box. Include your name and a heading at the top of the report.

Cool Boards

Write a project to maintain a list of shirt styles. Keep the styles in a drop-down combo box, with styles such as crew, turtleneck, or crop top.

Add a *Style* menu with options to *Add Style*, *Remove Style*, *Clear Style List*, and *Count Styles*. Add a *Print Style List* to the *File* menu and include access keys and keyboard shortcuts for the menu items.

Display the printed output in the *Print Preview* dialog box. Include your name and a heading at the top of the report.

CHAPTER

8

Arrays

at the completion of this chapter, you will be able to . . .

1. Establish an array and refer to individual elements in the array with subscripts.

2. Use a `foreach` loop to traverse the elements of an array.

3. Create a structure for multiple fields of related data.

4. Accumulate totals using arrays.

5. Distinguish between direct access and indirect access of a table.

6. Write a table lookup for matching an array element.

7. Combine the advantages of list box controls with arrays.

8. Store and look up data in multidimensional arrays.

Single-Dimension Arrays

An **array** is a list or series of values, similar to a list box or a combo box. You can think of an array as a list box without the box—without the visual representation. Any time you need to keep a series of variables for later processing, such as reordering, calculating, or printing, you need to set up an array.

Consider an example that has a form for entering product information one product at a time. After the user has entered many products, you will need to calculate some statistics, perhaps use the information in different ways, or print it. Of course, each time the user enters the data for the next product, the previous contents of the text boxes are replaced. You could assign the previous values to variables, but they also would be replaced for each new product. Another approach might be to create multiple variables, such as product1String, product2String, product3String, and so on. This approach might be reasonable for a few entries, but what happens when you need to store 50 or 500 products?

When you need to store multiple values of the same datatype, use an array. An array is a series of individual variables, all referenced by the same name. Sometimes arrays are referred to as **tables** or **subscripted variables**. For an array for storing names, you may have nameString[0], nameString[1], nameString[2], and so on.

Each individual variable is called an ***element*** of the array. The individual elements are treated the same as any other variable and may be used in any statement, such as an assignment statement. The **subscript** (which also may be called an ***index***) inside the square brackets is the position of the element within the array. Figure 8.1 illustrates an array of 10 elements with subscripts from 0 to 9.

nameString array

[0]	Janet Baker
[1]	George Lee
[2]	Sue Li
[3]	Samuel Hoosier
[4]	Sandra Weeks
[5]	William Macy
[6]	Andy Harrison
[7]	Ken Ford
[8]	Denny Franks
[9]	Shawn James

Figure 8.1

An array of string variables with 10 elements. Subscripts are 0 through 9.

Subscripts

The real advantage of using an array is not realized until you use variables for subscripts in place of the constants.

```
nameString[indexInteger] = "";

Console.WriteLine(nameString[indexInteger]);
```

Subscripts may be constants, variables, or numeric expressions. Although the subscripts must be integers, C# rounds any noninteger subscript.

A question has probably occurred to you by now—how many elements are there in the nameString array? The answer is that you must declare the array name and the number of elements, but there is no limit to the number of elements you can declare, except for the amount of memory available.

The Declaration Statement for Arrays—General Forms

You can declare arrays using the `public` or `private` keyword or allow them to default to private. And just as with any other variable, the location of the declaration determines the scope and lifetime of the array variables.

When you declare an array, you place opening and closing square brackets after the data type. You can declare the number of elements and/or the initial values of the array elements.

General Forms

```
Datatype[] arrayName = new DataType[NumberOfElements];
Datatype[] arrayName = new DataType[] {InitialValueList};
Datatype[] arrayName = {InitialValueList};
[public|private] Datatype[] arrayName = new DataType[NumberOfElements];
```

The first form of the declaration statement allocates storage for the specified number of elements and initializes each numeric variable to 0. In the case of string arrays, each element is set to an empty string (no characters).

In the second form of the statement, you specify initial values for the array elements, which determine the number of elements. The third form is a shortcut for the second form, and the fourth form shows using the `public` or `private` keyword.

The Declaration Statement for Arrays—Examples

Examples

```
string[] nameString = new string[25];
decimal[] balanceDecimal = new decimal[10];
int[] numbersInteger = new int[] {1, 5, 12, 18, 20};
string[] departmentsString = new string[] {"Accounting", "Marketing",
    "Human Relations"};
private string[] categoryString = new string[10];
public string[] IDNumbersString = new string[5];
string[] nameString = {"Sean", "Sam", "Sally", "Sara"};
```

Array subscripts are zero based, so the first element is always element zero. The upper subscript is the highest subscript—1 less than the number of elements. For example, the statement

```
string[] categoryString = new string[10];
```

creates an array of 10 elements with subscripts 0 through 9.

Notice that you declare a data type for the array. All of the array elements must be the same data type.

Valid Subscripts

A subscript must reference a valid element of the array. If a list contains 10 names, it wouldn't make sense to ask: What is the 15th name on the list? *or* What is the 2½th name on the list? C# rounds fractional subscripts and throws an exception for a subscript that is out of range.

Note: Arrays are based on System.Array, which is a collection.

► Feedback 8.1

```
string[] nameString = new string[20];
const int INDEX_Integer = 10;
```

After execution of the preceding statements, which of the following are valid subscripts?

1. nameString[20]
2. nameString[INDEX_Integer]
3. nameString[INDEX_Integer * 2]
4. nameString[INDEX_Integer * 3]
5. nameString[0]
6. nameString[INDEX_Integer – 20]
7. nameString[INDEX_Integer / 3]
8. nameString[INDEX_Integer / 5 – 2]

foreach Loops

When you use an array, you need a way to reference each element in the array. In Chapter 7 you learned to use `for` loops, which work well to traverse the elements in an array. Another handy loop construct is the `foreach`. The significant advantage of using a **foreach loop** is that you don't have to manipulate the subscripts of the array or know how many elements there are in the array.

Note: Array elements are read-only in the body of a `foreach` loop. You cannot modify the contents of an array element inside the body of a `foreach` loop.

The foreach Statement—General Form

General Form

```
foreach (DataType ElementName in ArrayName)
{
    // Statement(s) in the loop.
}
```

C# automatically references each element of the array, assigns its value to ElementName, and makes one pass through the loop. If the array has 12 elements, for example, the loop will execute 12 times. The variable used for

ElementName must be the same data type as the array elements or an Object data type. It's best to declare the variable for ElementName as part of the `foreach` statement, which creates a block-level variable.

In the following examples, assume that the array nameString has already been declared and holds data, and the variable oneNameString will hold the individual values of nameString, one element at a time.

The foreach Statement—Examples

```
foreach (string oneNameString in nameString)
{
    Console.WriteLine(oneNameString); // Write one element of the array.
}

foreach(decimal oneItemDecimal in allItemsDecimal)//Display all elements in the array.
{
    totalsRichTextBox.Text += indexInteger++ + "\t" + totalDecimal.ToString() + "\n";
}
```

The `foreach` loop will execute if the array has at least one element. All the statements within the loop are executed for the first element. If the array has more elements, the loop continues to execute until all the elements are processed. When the loop finishes, execution of code continues with the line following the closing braces for the loop.

Note: You can use a `break` statement in a loop to exit early.

Structures

You have been using the C# data types, such as int, string, and decimal, since Chapter 3. Now you will learn to combine multiple fields of related data to create a new **structure**. In many ways, a structure is similar to defining a new data type. For example, an Employee structure may contain last name, first name, social security number, street, city, state, ZIP code, date of hire, and pay code. A Product structure might contain a description, product number, quantity, and price. You can combine the fields into a structure using the **struct** statement.

The struct Statement—General Form

```
[public | private] struct NameOfStruct
{
    public Datatype FirstField;
    public Datatype SecondField;
. . .
}
```

The `struct` declaration cannot go inside a method. You generally place the `struct` block at the top of the file with the class-level declarations. You also can place a `struct` outside of the class.

The struct Statement—Examples

```
struct Employee
{
    public string lastNameString;
    public string firstNameString;
    public string SSNString;
    public string streetString;
    public string cityString;
    public string stateString;
    public string ZIPString;
    public DateTime hireDateTime;
    public int payCodeInteger;
}

public struct Product
{
    public string descriptionString;
    public string IDString;
    public int quantityInteger;
    public decimal priceDecimal;
}

struct SalesDetail
{
    public decimal[] saleDecimal;
}
```

By default, a structure is public. You can declare the structure to be public or private, if you wish.

If you include an array inside a structure, you cannot specify the number of elements.

Declaring Variables Based on a Structure

Once you have created a structure, you can declare variables of the structure, just as if it were another data type. You can choose the location to declare variables to have the desired scope.

```
Employee officeEmployee;
Employee warehouseEmployee;
Product widgetProduct;
Product[] inventoryProduct = new Product[100];
SalesDetail housewaresSalesDetail;
SalesDetail homeFurnishingsSalesDetail;
```

Accessing the Elements in a Structure Variable

Each field of data in a variable declared as a structure is referred to as an *element* of the structure. To access elements, use the dot notation similar to that used for objects: Specify *Variable.Element*.

```
officeEmployee.lastNameString
officeEmployee.hireDateTime
warehouseEmployee.lastNameString
```

```
widgetProduct.descriptionString
widgetProduct.quantityInteger
widgetProduct.priceDecimal
inventoryProduct[indexInteger].descriptionString
inventoryProduct[indexInteger].quantityInteger
inventoryProduct[indexInteger].priceDecimal
```

Notice the use of indexes in the preceding examples. Each example was taken from the preceding struct and declaration statements. A variable that is not an array, such as widgetProduct, does not need an index. However, for inventoryProduct, which was declared as an array of 100 elements (0 through 99), you must specify not only the inventoryProduct item but also the element within the array of structures.

Including an Array in a Structure

The SalesDetail structure is a little more complicated than the other structures described above. In this structure, we want to include an array of seven variables, one for each day of the week. However, C# does not allow you to declare the number of elements in the struct declaration.

```
// Class-level declarations.
public struct SalesDetail
{
    public decimal[] saleDecimal;
}

// Class level or inside a method;
SalesDetail housewaresSalesDetail;

// Inside a method:
// Establish the number of elements in the array.
housewaresSalesDetail.saleDecimal = new decimal[7];

// In processing.
housewaresSalesDetail.saleDecimal[dayIndexInteger] = todaysSalesDecimal;
```

Because the saleDecimal element of the SalesDetail structure is declared as an array, you must use a subscript to refer to each individual element within the structure.

Feedback 8.2

1. Write a struct statement to hold student data, which contains last name, first name, student number, number of units completed, and GPA. The new structure should be called "Student".
2. Declare an array of 100 students that will use the structure for student information.
3. Write the struct statement for a structure called "Project" that contains a project name, form name, and folder name.
4. Declare a variable called "myProject" based on the Project structure.
5. Declare an array of 100 elements called "ourProjects" based on the Project structure.

Using Array Elements for Accumulators

Array elements are regular variables and perform in the same ways as all variables used so far. You may use the subscripted variables in any way you choose, such as for counters or total accumulators.

To demonstrate the use of array elements as total accumulators, eight totals will be accumulated. For this example, eight scout troops are selling raffle tickets. A separate total must be accumulated for each of the eight groups. Each time a sale is made, the amount of the sale must be added to the correct total. The statement

```
decimal[] totalDecimal = new decimal[8];
```

declares the eight decimal accumulators with subscripts 0 to 7.

Adding to the Correct Total

Assume that your user inputs a group number into groupTextBox.Text and the sale amount for the tickets sold into saleTextBox.Text. The sales may be input in any order with multiple sales for each group. Your problem is to add each ticket sale to the correct totalDecimal, with subscripts 0 to 7, for groups numbered 1 to 8.

To add to the correct group's total, you can determine the subscript by subtracting one from the group number. For example, if the first sale of 35.00 is for group 4, the 35.00 must be added to totalDecimal[3]. (Figure 8.2 shows the form and the variables used for this example.)

```
// Convert input group number to subscript.
groupNumberInteger = int.Parse(groupTextBox.Text) - 1;
// Add sale to the correct total.
saleDecimal = decimal.Parse(saleTextBox.Text);
totalDecimal[groupNumberInteger] += saleDecimal;
```

Figure 8.2

The group number entered in groupTextBox is used as a subscript to determine the correct totalDecimal array element to which to add.

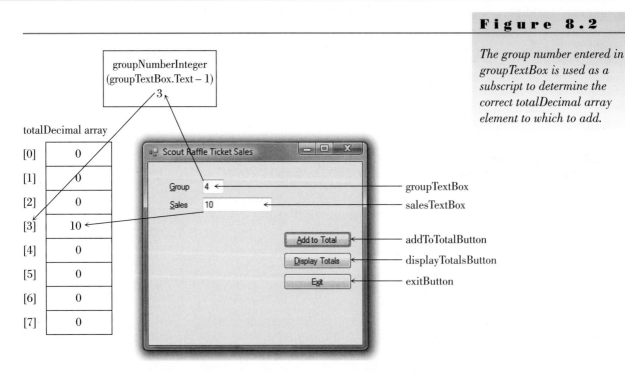

Of course, the user might enter an incorrect group number. Because you don't want the program to cancel with an exception, you must validate the group number.

```
try
{
    // Convert input group number to a subscript.
    groupNumberInteger = int.Parse(groupTextBox.Text) - 1;
    if (groupNumberInteger >= 0 && groupNumberInteger <= 7)
    {
        // Add sale to correct total.
        saleDecimal = decimal.Parse(saleTextBox.Text);
        totalDecimal[groupNumberInteger] += saleDecimal;
    }
    else
    {
        MessageBox.Show("Enter a valid group number (1-8)",
            "Data Entry Error", MessageBoxButtons.OK,
            MessageBoxIcon.Exclamation);
    }
}
catch (FormatException)
{
    MessageBox.Show("Numeric entries required for both group number and sales",
        "Data Entry Error", MessageBoxButtons.OK, MessageBoxIcon.Exclamation);
}
```

Using the group number as an index to the array is a technique called *direct reference*. The groups are assigned numbers from one to eight. You can subtract 1 from the group number to create the subscripts, which are 0 to 7.

Debugging Array Programs

You can view the contents of array elements when your program is in debugging time. Set a breakpoint and view the Autos window (Figure 8.3) or the Locals window (Figure 8.4). You will need to click on the plus sign to the left of the array name to view the individual array elements.

Figure 8.3

View the contents of an array in the Autos window at debugging time.

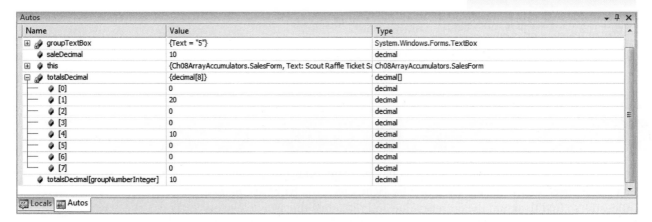

The Locals window contains an entry for each control on the form as well as all variables that are within scope. Click on the plus sign for "this" to see the form elements; click on the plus sign for the array to see the array elements.

Expand the "this" entry

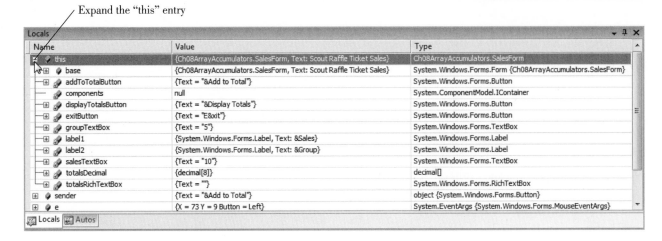

If you are using the Express Edition of Visual C#, the Autos window is not available, but you can use the Locals window. To view the contents of controls on the form, click the plus sign to expand the "this" entry. You also can expand the entry for the array, to see the contents of all elements.

Visual Studio 2008 introduces visualizers, which allow you to pop up the value of an array in the Code Editor window (Figure 8.5). Pause the mouse pointer over the variable or array that you want to display; when the array name pops up, point to the plus sign to display the current contents of each of the elements.

```
if (groupNumberInteger >= 0 && groupNumberInteger <= 7)
{
    // Add sale to correct total.
    decimal saleDecimal = decimal.Parse(salesTextBox.Text);
    totalsDecimal[groupNumberInteger] += saleDecimal;
    // Clear       totalsDecimal  {decimal[8]}
    groupTextB       [0]  0     );
    salesTextB       [1]  20    );
                     [2]  0
    groupTextB       [3]  0     );
}                    [4]  10
else                 [5]  0
{                    [6]  0
                     [7]  0
    MessageBox.Show("Enter a valid group number (1-8)", "Data Entry Error",
        MessageBoxButtons.OK, MessageBoxIcon.Exclamation);
}
```

Use the Visual Studio visualizer to view the current contents of array elements. Point to the array name and then to the plus sign to pop up the array elements.

Table Lookup

Things don't always work out so neatly as having sequential group numbers that can be used to access the table directly. Sometimes you will have to do a little work to find (look up) the correct value and reference the array elements indirectly. Reconsider the eight scout troops and their ticket sales. Now the groups are not numbered 1 to 8, but 101, 103, 110, 115, 121, 123, 130, and 145. The group number and the sales are still input, and the sale must be added to the correct total. But now you must do one more step—determine to which array element to add the ticket sales, using a **table lookup**.

The first step in the project is to establish a structure with the group numbers and totals and then declare an array of the structure. Before any processing is done, you must load the group numbers into the table; the best place to do this is in the Form_Load event handler, which is executed once as the form is loaded into memory.

Place the following statements at the top of the form class:

```
public struct GroupInfo
{
    public string groupNumberString;
    public decimal totalDecimal;
}
public GroupInfo[] arrayGroup = new GroupInfo[8];
```

Then initialize the values of the array elements by placing these statements into the Form_Load event handler:

```
private void Form1_Load(object sender, EventArgs e)
{
    // Load the group numbers.
    arrayGroup[0].groupNumberString = "101";
    arrayGroup[1].groupNumberString = "103";
    arrayGroup[2].groupNumberString = "110";
    arrayGroup[3].groupNumberString = "115";
    arrayGroup[4].groupNumberString = "121";
    arrayGroup[5].groupNumberString = "123";
    arrayGroup[6].groupNumberString = "130";
    arrayGroup[7].groupNumberString = "145";
}
```

During program execution, the user still enters the group number and the sale amount into text boxes.

The technique used to find the subscript is called a *table lookup*. In this example, the object is to find the element number (0 to 7) of the group number and add to the corresponding group total. If the user enters the third group number ("110"), the subscript is 2 and the sale is added to the total for subscript 2. If the seventh group number ("130") is entered, the sale is added to the total with the subscript 6, and so on. Hence, you need a way, given the group number in groupTextBox.Text, to find the corresponding subscript of the arrayGroup array.

When C# executes the statement

```
arrayGroup[groupNumberInteger].totalDecimal += saleDecimal;
```

the value of groupNumberInteger must be a number in the range 0 to 7. The task for the lookup operation is to find the number to place in groupNumberInteger, based on the value of groupTextBox.Text. Figure 8.6 (p. 342) shows the variables used for the lookup. Figure 8.7 (p. 342) shows a UML action diagram of the lookup logic.

Figure 8.6

A lookup operation: The group number is looked up in the arrayGroup array; the correct subscript is found and used to add the sale to the correct totalDecimal.

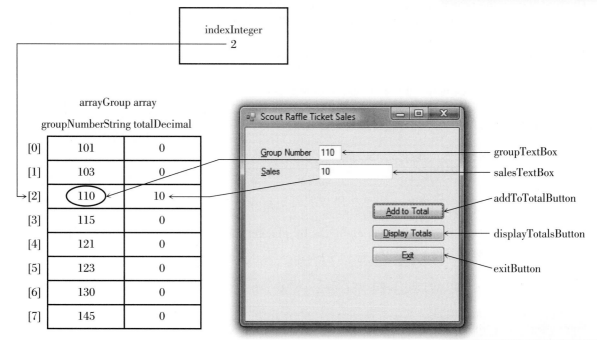

Figure 8.7

A UML action diagram of the logic of a lookup operation.

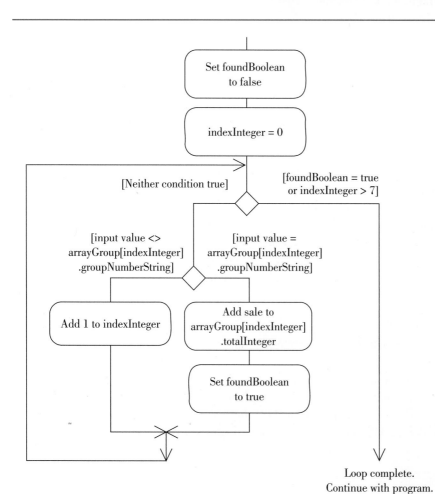

Coding a Table Lookup

For a table lookup, you will find that a `do` loop works better than a `foreach` loop. As you compare to each element in the array and eventually find a match, you need to know the subscript of the matching element. Here is the logic of the lookup operation. The declarations and error trapping have been omitted to better show the lookup logic.

```
// Convert input group number to a subscript.
do
{
    if (groupTextBox.Text == arrayGroup[groupNumberInteger].groupNumberString)
    {
        // A match is found.
        decimal saleDecimal = decimal.Parse(salesTextBox.Text);
        arrayGroup[groupNumberInteger].totalDecimal += saleDecimal;
        foundBoolean = true;
        // Clear the controls.
        groupTextBox.Clear();
        salesTextBox.Clear();
        groupTextBox.Focus();
    }
    groupNumberInteger++;
} while (groupNumberInteger < 8 && !foundBoolean);
```

Once again, you should do some form of validation. If the user enters an invalid group number, you should display a message box. You can check the value of the Boolean variable foundBoolean after completion of the loop to determine whether the loop terminated because of a match or without a match.

```
if (!foundBoolean)
{
    MessageBox.Show("Enter a valid group number.",
        "Data Entry Error", MessageBoxButtons.OK,
        MessageBoxIcon.Exclamation);
}
```

The table-lookup technique will work for any table, numeric or string. It isn't necessary to arrange the fields being searched in any particular sequence. The comparison is made to one item in the list, then the next, and the next—until a match is found. In fact, you can save processing time in a large table by arranging the elements with the most-often-used entries at the top so that fewer comparisons must be made.

Using List Boxes with Arrays

In the previous example of a lookup, the user had to type some information into a text box, which was used to look up the information in an array. A more efficient and friendly solution might be to substitute a list box or combo box for the text box. You can store the eight group numbers in a list box and allow the user to select from the list (Figure 8.8).

Figure 8.8

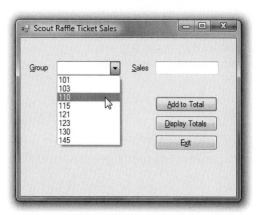

The initial Items collection can contain the values 101, 103, 110, 115, 121, 123, 130, and 145.

You have probably already realized that you can use the SelectedIndex property to determine the array subscript. Remember that the SelectedIndex property holds the position or index of the selected item from the list.

In place of the lookup operation, we can use this code:

```csharp
//Declare class-level variable.
decimal[] totalsDecimal = new decimal[8];

private void addToTotalsButton_Click(object sender, EventArgs e)
{
    // Add to the appropriate total.
    int groupNumberInteger;

    try
    {
        if (groupComboBox.SelectedIndex != -1)
        {
            // Convert input group number to a subscript.
            groupNumberInteger = groupComboBox.SelectedIndex;
            // Add sale to correct total.
            decimal saleDecimal = decimal.Parse(salesTextBox.Text);
            totalsDecimal[groupNumberInteger] += saleDecimal;
            // Clear the entries.
            groupComboBox.SelectedIndex = -1;
            salesTextBox.Clear();
        }
        else
        {
            MessageBox.Show("Select a group.", "Data Entry Error",
                MessageBoxButtons.OK, MessageBoxIcon.Exclamation);
        }
    }
    catch (FormatException)
    {
        MessageBox.Show("Numeric entries required for sales",
            "Data Entry Error", MessageBoxButtons.OK, MessageBoxIcon.Exclamation);
    }
}
```

Multidimensional Arrays

You generally need to use two subscripts to identify tabular data, where data are arranged in **rows** and **columns**.

Many applications of two-dimensional tables quickly come to mind—insurance rate tables, tax tables, addition and multiplication tables, postage rates, foods and their nutritive value, population by region, rainfall by state.

To define a two-dimensional array or table, the declaration statement specifies the number of rows and columns in the array. The row is horizontal and the column is vertical. The following table has three rows and four columns:

The Declaration Statement for Two-Dimensional Arrays—General Form

```
DataType[,] ArrayName = new Datatype[NumberOfRows, NumberOfColumns];
DataType[,] ArrayName = new DataType[,] = {ListOfValues};
```

The Declaration Statement for Two-Dimensional Arrays—Examples

```
string[,] nameString = new string[3, 4];
string[,] nameString = new string[,] = { {"James", "Mary", "Sammie", "Sean"},
    {"Tom", "Lee", "Leon", "Larry"}, {"Maria", "Margaret", "Jill", "John"} };
```

The two example statements both establish an array of 12 elements, with three rows and four columns. Just as with single-dimension arrays, you can specify the number of elements within parentheses and/or specify initial values.

Notice the comma inside the square brackets in the second example: You must use a comma to specify that there are two dimensions to the array. Specify the initial values with the first dimension (the row) first and the second dimension (the column) second. The compiler determines the number of elements from the initial values that you supply. The second example above fills the table in this sequence:

[0, 0] James	[0, 1] Mary	[0, 2] Sammie	[0, 3] Sean
[1, 0] Tom	[1, 1] Lee	[1, 2] Leon	[1, 3] Larry
[2, 0] Maria	[2, 1] Margaret	[2, 2] Jill	[2, 3] John

You must always use two subscripts when referring to individual elements of the table. Specify the row with the first subscript and the column with the second subscript.

The elements of the array may be used in the same ways as any other variable—in accumulators, counts, and reference fields for lookup; in statements like assignment and printing; and as conditions. Some valid references to the table elements include

```csharp
nameString[1, 2] = "New Name";
nameString[rowInteger, columnInteger] = "New Name";
displayLabel.Text = nameString[1, 2];
e.Graphics.DrawString(nameString[rowInteger, columnInteger], printFont,
    Brushes.Black, 100.0, 100.0);
```

Invalid references for the nameString table would include any value greater than 2 for the first subscript or greater than 3 for the second subscript, or less than 0 for either subscript.

Initializing Two-Dimensional Arrays

Numeric array elements are initially set to 0, and string elements are set to empty strings. And, of course, you can assign initial values when you declare the array. But many situations require that you reinitialize arrays to 0 or some other value. You can use nested `for` loops to set each array element to an initial value.

Nested for Loop Example

The assignment statement in the inner loop will be executed 12 times, once for each element of nameString.

```csharp
for (int rowInteger = 0; rowInteger < 3; rowInteger++)
{
    for (int columnInteger = 0; columnInteger < 4; columnInteger++)
    {
        nameString[rowInteger, columnInteger] = ""; //Initialize each element.
    }
}
```

Note: You cannot use a `foreach` loop to initialize an array.

Printing a Two-Dimensional Table

When you want to print the contents of a two-dimensional table, you can use a `foreach` loop. This code prints one array element per line.

```csharp
// Print one name per line.
foreach (string elementString in nameString)
{
    // Set up a line.
    e.Graphics.DrawString(elementString, printFont,
        Brushes.Black, printXFloat, printYFloat);

    // Increment the Y position for the next line.
    printYFloat += lineHeightFloat;
}
```

If you wish to print an entire row in one line, use a `for` loop and set up the X and Y coordinates to print multiple elements per line.

```
// Print one row per line.
for (int rowIndexInteger = 0; rowIndexInteger < 3; rowIndexInteger++)
{
    for (int colIndexInteger = 0; colIndexInteger < 4; colIndexInteger++)
    {
        e.Graphics.DrawString(nameString[rowIndexInteger, colIndexInteger],
            printFont, Brushes.Black, printXFloat, printYFloat);
        printXFloat += 200f;                     // Move across the line.
    }

    // Start the next line.
    printXFloat = e.MarginBounds.Left; // Reset to the left margin.
    printYFloat += lineHeightFloat; // Move down to the next line.
}
```

Summing a Two-Dimensional Table

You can find the sum of a table in various ways. You may sum either the columns or the rows of the table; or, as in a cross-foot, you can sum the figures in both directions and double-check the totals.

To sum the array in both directions, each column needs one total variable and each row needs one total variable. Two one-dimensional arrays will work well for the totals. Figure 8.9 illustrates the variables used in this example.

Figure 8.9

Two one-dimensional arrays hold totals for the two-dimensional array.

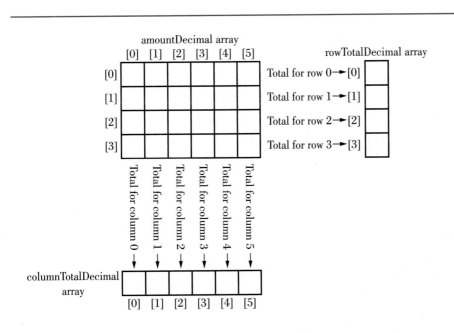

```
// Crossfoot total a 2D table.

// Give the 6 x 4 array values for testing.
//   (Normally you would total values that are accumulated in a program.)
decimal[,] amountDecimal = {{2.5M, 3M, 1.2M, 2.2M, 4.5M, 3.5M},
    {2M, 2M, 2M, 2M, 2M, 2M},
    {3M, 3.1M, 3.2M, 3.3M, 3.4M, 3.5M},
    {4.4M, 4.5M, 4.6M, 4.7M, 4.8M, 4.9M}};
// decimal amountDecimal = new decimal[4, 6];
decimal rowTotalDecimal[4];
decimal columnTotalDecimal[6];
for (int rowInteger = 0; rowInteger < 4; rowInteger++)
{
    for (int columnInteger = 0; columnInteger < 6; columnInteger++)
    {
        rowTotalDecimal[rowInteger] += amountDecimal[rowInteger, columnInteger];
        columnTotalDecimal[columnInteger] += amountDecimal[rowInteger, columnInteger];
    }
}
```

▶ Feedback 8.3

Write the C# statements to do the following:

1. Declare a table called temperatureDecimal with five columns and three rows.
2. Set each element in the first row to 0.
3. Set each element in the second row to 75.
4. For each column of the table, add together the elements in the first and second rows, placing the sum in the third row.
5. Print the entire table. (Write only the logic for printing inside the PrintDocument_PrintPage event handler.)

Lookup Operation for Two-Dimensional Tables

When you look up items in a two-dimensional table, you can use the same techniques discussed with single-dimensional arrays—direct reference and table lookup. The limitations are the same.

1. To use a direct reference, row and column subscripts must be readily available. For example, you can tally the hours used for each of five machines (identified by machine numbers 1 to 5) and each of four departments (identified by department numbers 1 to 4).

```
rowInteger = int.Parse(machineTextBox.Text) - 1;
columnInteger = int.Parse(departmentTextBox.Text) - 1;
hoursDecimal = decimal.Parse(hoursTextBox.Text);
machineTotalDecimal[rowInteger, columnInteger] += hoursDecimal;
```

2. A table lookup is the most common lookup technique.

Many two-dimensional tables used for lookup require additional one-dimensional arrays or lists to aid in the lookup process. For an example, use a shipping rate table (Figure 8.10) to look up the rate to ship a package. The shipping rate depends on the weight of the package and the zone to which it is

Figure 8.10

This shipping rate table in a two-dimensional array can be used to look up the correct shipping charge.

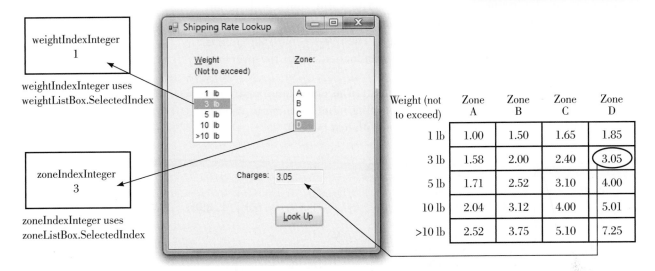

Weight (not to exceed)	Zone A	Zone B	Zone C	Zone D
1 lb	1.00	1.50	1.65	1.85
3 lb	1.58	2.00	2.40	3.05
5 lb	1.71	2.52	3.10	4.00
10 lb	2.04	3.12	4.00	5.01
>10 lb	2.52	3.75	5.10	7.25

being shipped. You could design the project with the weight and zones in list boxes, or you could use a text box and let the user input the data. Using list boxes is preferred because the user is much less likely to make input errors.

Using List Boxes

In the example illustrated in Figure 8.10, a list box holds the weight limits, and another list holds the zones. The values for the two lists are set in the Items properties at design time. The five-by-four rate table is two-dimensional, and the values are set when the table is declared.

```
// Look up values from list boxes.

// Declare class-level variables.
decimal[,] rateDecimal = new decimal[,] {{1M, 1.5M, 1.65M, 1.85M},
                                         {1.58M, 2M, 2.4M, 3.05M},
                                         {1.71M, 2.52M, 3.1M, 4M},
                                         {2.04M, 3.12M, 4M, 5.01M},
                                         {2.52M, 3.75M, 5.1M, 7.25M}};

private void lookupButton_Click(object sender, System.EventArgs e)
{
    // Look up the shipping rate.
    int weightSubInteger = weightListBox.SelectedIndex;
    int zoneSubInteger = zoneListBox.SelectedIndex;
    if (weightSubInteger != -1 && zoneSubInteger != -1)
    {
        chargesLabel.Text = rateDecimal[weightSubInteger,
            zoneSubInteger].ToString("N");
    }
    else
    {
        MessageBox.Show("Select the weight and zone.",
            "Information Missing", MessageBoxButtons.OK,
            MessageBoxIcon.Exclamation);
    }
}
```

Using Text Boxes

If you are using text boxes rather than list boxes for data entry, the input requires more validation. You must look up both the weight and zone entries before you can determine the correct rate. The valid zones and weight ranges will be stored in two separate one-dimensional arrays. The first step in the project is to establish and fill the arrays. The five-by-four rate table is two-dimensional, and the values should be preloaded, as in the previous example.

Note that the try/catch blocks were omitted to clarify the logic. You should always use error trapping when converting input to numeric values. Also note how much more complex the logic is with text boxes.

```csharp
// Look up values from text boxes.

// Declare module-level variables.
decimal[,] rateDecimal = new decimal[,] {{1M, 1.5M, 1.65M, 1.85M},
                          {1.58M, 2M, 2.4M, 3.05M},
                          {1.71M, 2.52M, 3.1M, 4M},
                          {2.04M, 3.12M, 4M, 5.01M},
                          {2.52M, 3.75M, 5.1M, 7.25M}};
int[] weightInteger = new int[] { 1, 3, 5, 10 };
string[] zoneString = new string[] { "A", "B", "C", "D" };

private void lookupButton_Click(object sender, System.EventArgs e)
{
    // Look up the shipping rate.

    int weightSubInteger = 0;
    int zoneSubInteger = 0;
    int indexInteger = 0;
    int weightInputInteger;
    bool weightFoundBoolean = false;
    bool zoneFoundBoolean = false;

    // Look up the weight to find the weightSubInteger.
    weightInputInteger = int.Parse(weightTextBox.Text);

    while (!weightFoundBoolean && indexInteger < 4)
    {
        if (weightInputInteger <= weightInteger[indexInteger])
        {
            weightSubInteger = indexInteger;
            weightFoundBoolean = true;
        }

        indexInteger++;
    }
    if (!weightFoundBoolean)
    {
        weightSubInteger = 4;
        weightFoundBoolean = true;
    }
```

```
// Look up the zone to find the zoneSubInteger.
indexInteger = 0;
while (!zoneFoundBoolean && indexInteger < 4)
{
    if (zoneTextBox.Text.ToUpper() == zoneString[indexInteger])
    {
        zoneSubInteger = indexInteger;
        zoneFoundBoolean = true;
    }

    indexInteger++;
}

// Display the appropriate rate.
if (weightFoundBoolean && zoneFoundBoolean)
{
    chargesLabel.Text = rateDecimal[weightSubInteger,
        zoneSubInteger].ToString("N");
}
else
{
    MessageBox.Show("Enter a valid weight and zone.", "No Match Found",
        MessageBoxButtons.OK, MessageBoxIcon.Exclamation);
}
}
```

Your Hands-On Programming Example

Modify Ch06HandsOn to store all items purchased in each order. When an order is complete, display a receipt for the order that details the drinks ordered, their price, an extended price, and a total for the order. The receipt should display in a *Print Preview* dialog box, so the user has the option of printing it.

Modify the form layout from Chapter 6 to store the drink names in a drop-down combo box instead of radio buttons. You can use the combo box's SelectedItem to retrieve the name of the selected drink.

Create a structure that contains the size, drink, quantity, and price for each item ordered. You will need an array of the structure to store all of the items for an order. When the order is complete and the receipt displayed, clear out the array.

Set up an index to store the number of items in an order. Set the index back to 0 when an order is complete.

Since this project is based on Ch06HandsOn, it has a splash form, an About box, and a summary form. These items are not shown in the planning for this project but should appear in the solution.

Planning the Project

Sketch a form (Figure 8.11), which your users sign off as meeting their needs.

Figure 8.11

A planning sketch of the form for the hands-on programming example.

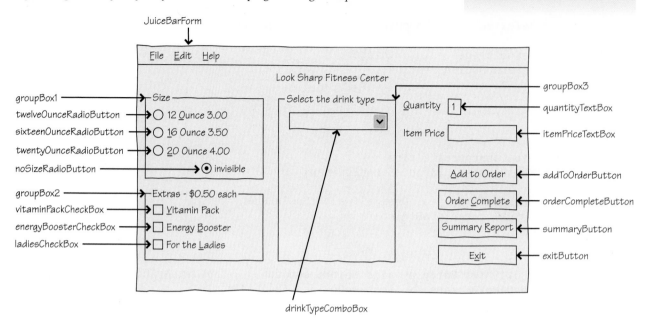

drinkTypeComboBox

Plan the Objects and Properties

Object	Property	Setting
JuiceBarForm	Name	JuiceBarForm
	Text	Juice Bar Orders
	AcceptButton	addToOrderButton
	CancelButton	exitButton
groupBox1	Text	Size
twelveOunceRadioButton	Name	twelveOunceRadioButton
	Text	12 &Ounce 3.00
sixteenOunceRadioButton	Name	sixteenOunceRadioButton
	Text	&16 Ounce 3.50
twentyOunceRadioButton	Name	twentyOunceRadioButton
	Text	&20 Ounce 4.00
noSizeRadioButton	Name	noSizeRadioButton
	Text	invisible
	Checked	true
	Visible	false
groupBox2	Text	Extras - $0.50 each
vitaminPackCheckBox	Name	vitaminPackCheckBox
	Text	&Vitamin Pack
energyBoosterCheckBox	Name	energyBoosterCheckBox
	Text	Energy &Booster

Object	Property	Setting
ladiesCheckBox	Name	ladiesCheckBox
	Text	For the &Ladies
groupBox3	Text	Select the drink type
drinkTypeComboBox	Items	Fruit juice
		Veggie juice
		Pomegranate smoothie
		Strawberry banana smoothie
		Wheatberry smoothie
label3	Text	&Quantity
quantityTextBox	Name	quantityTextBox
	Text	(blank)
label4	Text	Item Price
itemPriceTextBox	Name	itemPriceTextBox
	Text	(blank)
	ReadOnly	true
	TabStop	false
addToOrderButton	Name	addToOrderButton
	Text	&Add to Order
orderCompleteButton	Name	orderCompleteButton
	Text	Order &Complete
	Enabled	false
summaryButton	Name	summaryButton
	Text	Summary &Report
	Enabled	false
exitButton	Name	exitButton
	Text	E&xit
fileToolStripMenuItem	Name	fileToolStripMenuItem
	Text	&File
summaryToolStripMenuItem	Name	summaryToolStripMenuItem
	Text	&Summary
exitToolStripMenuItem	Name	exitToolStripMenuItem
	Text	E&xit
editToolStripMenuItem	Name	editToolStripMenuItem
	Text	&Edit
addToOrderToolStripMenuItem	Name	addToOrderToolStripMenuItem
	Text	&Add to Order
orderCompleteToolStrip-MenuItem	Name	orderCompleteToolStripMenuItem
	Text	&Order Complete
fontToolStripMenuItem	Name	fontToolStripMenuItem
	Text	&Font

Object	Property	Setting
colorToolStripMenuItem	Name Text	colorToolStripMenuItem &Color
helpToolStripMenuItem	Name Text	helpToolStripMenuItem &Help
aboutToolStripMenuItem	Name Text	aboutToolStripMenuItem &About
ColorDialog1	Name	ColorDialog1
FontDialog1	Name	FontDialog1

Plan the Methods You need to plan the actions for the event handlers and general methods. Set up a `struct` and declare an array of the `struct` to hold the sales items.

Object	Method	Action
addToOrderButton	Click	Check if size and drink type are selected. Validate for blank or nonnumeric amount. Save drink type and price in the drinkOrder array. Multiply price by quantity. Store the price in the drinkOrder array. Add to number of drinks. Call clearForNextItem. Enable the Order Complete button. Add 1 to the item count.

orderCompleteButton	Click	If last item not cleared from screen
		   Ask user whether to add it.
		   If yes
		      Call addToOrderButton_Click.
		Display the receipt in a print preview.
		Add to the number of orders and totalSales.
		Reset the controls for the next order.
		Clear the order amount.
		Clear the drinkOrder array.

summaryButton	Click	Display the summary totals in the summary form.
exitButton	Click	Terminate the project.
Size radio buttons	Checked-Changed	Find the price of the selected size. Store in the array.
clearForNextItem	General method	Clear option buttons, check boxes, combo box, text boxes. Set quantity to default to 1.
findExtrasPrice	General method returns a decimal	Clear the extras variable. Find the price of extras.
Check boxes	Checked-Changed	Find the price of extras. Calculate and display the current drink price.

Object	Method	Action
summaryToolStrip MenuItem	Click	Share summaryButton_Click handler.
exitToolStripMenuItem	Click	Share exitButton_Click handler.
aboutToolStripMenuItem	Click	Display the About box form.
fontToolStripMenuItem	Click	Display the Font dialog box. Change the font of the title.
colorToolStrip MenuItem	Click	Display the Color dialog box. Change the ForeColor of the form.
printDocument1	PrintPage	Send heading lines to the print page. Loop through the drinkOrder array. Print one line for each item in the order. Calculate the extended price = price * quantity. Print the order total.

Write the Project Follow the sketch in Figure 8.11 to create the form. Figure 8.12 shows the completed form and Figure 8.13 shows sample report output.

- Set the properties of each object, according to your plan.

- Write the code. Working from the pseudo code, write each event handler and the class-level `struct` and variables needed.

- When you complete the code, use a variety of data to thoroughly test the project. Make sure that the receipt has accurate amounts for each item and for the order total.

Figure 8.12

The form for the hands-on programming example.

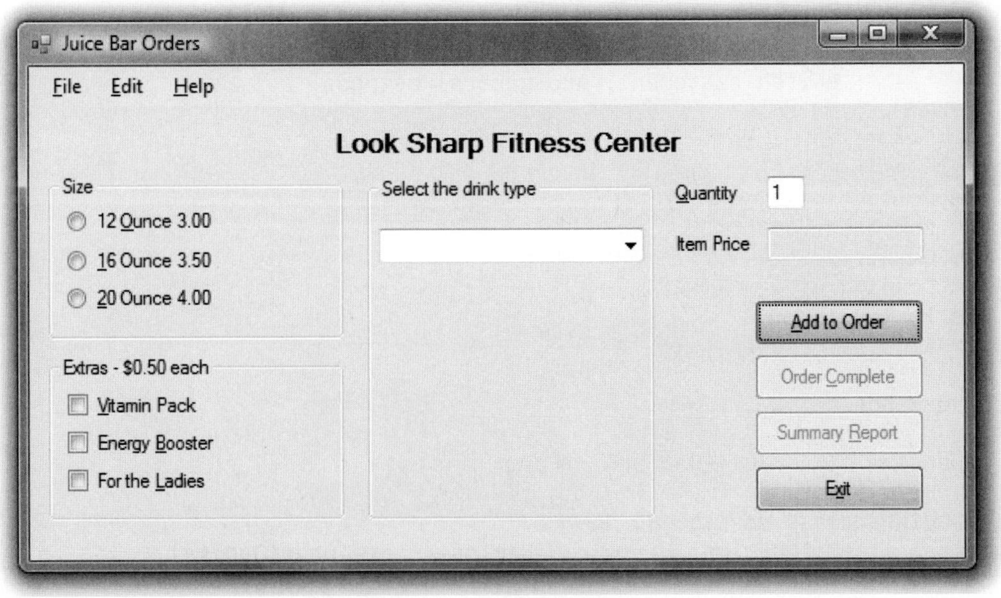

A sample report created by the program.

Look Sharp Fitness Center

Drink Sales Receipt 6/1/2009

Quantity	Size	Drink Type	Unit Price	Extended Price
2	12 oz	Fruit juice	$3.00	$6.00
1	16 oz	Veggie juice	$3.50	$3.50
2	20 oz	Strawberry banana smoothie	$4.00	$8.00
Total:				$17.50

The Project Coding Solution

The splash form, summary form, and About box are unchanged from Ch06HandsOn.

JuiceBarForm

```
/*
 * Program Name:    Ch08HandsOn
 * Programmer:      Bradley/Millspaugh
 * Date:            June 2009
 *
 * Description:     This project calculates the amount due
 *                  based on the customer selection,
 *                  prints a receipt for an order, and
 *                  accumulates summary data for the day.
 *                  Includes menus, common dialog boxes, a
 *                  switch statement, and general methods.
 */

using System;
using System.Collections.Generic;
using System.ComponentModel;
using System.Data;
using System.Drawing;
using System.Text;
using System.Windows.Forms;

namespace Ch08HandsOn
{
    public partial class JuiceBarForm : Form
    {
        // Declare class variables.
        decimal itemSizeDecimal, itemPriceDecimal, totalOrderDecimal,
            totalSalesDecimal;
```

```csharp
    int drinkTotalInteger, orderTotalInteger, itemCountInteger;
    public struct OrderItem
    {
        public string sizeString;
        public string drinkString;
        public int quantityInteger;
        public decimal priceDecimal;
    }
    // Create an array for the items in the order.
    OrderItem[] drinkOrder = new OrderItem[20];

    public JuiceBarForm()
    {
        InitializeComponent();
    }

    private void addToOrderButton_Click(object sender, EventArgs e)
    {
        // Add the current item price and quantity to the order.

        if (noSizeRadioButton.Checked
            || drinkTypeComboBox.SelectedIndex == -1)
        {
            MessageBox.Show("You must select a drink and size.",
                "Missing required entry");
        }
        else
        {
            try
            {
                drinkOrder[itemCountInteger].quantityInteger
                    = int.Parse(quantityTextBox.Text);
                if (drinkOrder[itemCountInteger].quantityInteger != 0)
                {
                    drinkOrder[itemCountInteger].drinkString
                        = drinkTypeComboBox.SelectedItem.ToString();
                    drinkOrder[itemCountInteger].priceDecimal
                        = itemPriceDecimal;
                    totalOrderDecimal += itemPriceDecimal
                        * drinkOrder[itemCountInteger].quantityInteger;
                    drinkTotalInteger += drinkOrder[itemCountInteger]
                        .quantityInteger;
                    clearForNextItem();
                    orderCompleteButton.Enabled = true;
                    itemCountInteger++;
                }
                else
                {
                    MessageBox.Show("Please enter a quantity.",
                        "Missing Required Entry");
                }
            }
            catch (FormatException)
            {
                MessageBox.Show("Invalid Quantity.", "Data Entry Error");
                quantityTextBox.Focus();
                quantityTextBox.SelectAll();
            }
        }
    }
```

```csharp
    private void orderCompleteButton_Click(object sender, EventArgs e)
    {
        // Order is complete, add to summary and clear order.

        // Verify that the last item was added to the total.
        if (!noSizeRadioButton.Checked
            && drinkTypeComboBox.SelectedIndex != -1)
        {
            DialogResult responseDialogResult;
            string messageString = "Current item not recorded. Add to order?";
            responseDialogResult = MessageBox.Show(messageString,
                "Verify Last Drink Purchase", MessageBoxButtons.YesNo,
                MessageBoxIcon.Question);
            if (responseDialogResult == DialogResult.Yes)
            {
                addToOrderButton_Click(sender, e);
            }
        }
        // Display receipt for items purchased in this order.
        printPreviewDialog1.Document = printDocument1;
        printPreviewDialog1.ShowDialog();

        // Add to summary totals.
        orderTotalInteger++;
        totalSalesDecimal += totalOrderDecimal;

        // Reset all for new order.
        summaryButton.Enabled = true;
        summaryToolStripMenuItem.Enabled = true;
        orderCompleteButton.Enabled = false;
        orderCompleteToolStripMenuItem.Enabled = false;
        totalOrderDecimal = 0m;
        itemCountInteger = 0;
        // Clear order array.
        for (int orderInteger = 0; orderInteger < 20; orderInteger++)
        {
            drinkOrder[orderInteger].quantityInteger = 0;
            drinkOrder[orderInteger].priceDecimal = 0;
            drinkOrder[orderInteger].drinkString = "";
        }
    }

    private void summaryButton_Click(object sender, EventArgs e)
    {
        // Display the summary information in a summary form.

        // Display the summary form.
        SummaryForm aSummaryForm = new SummaryForm();

        aSummaryForm.DrinksSold = drinkTotalInteger;
        aSummaryForm.NumberOrders = orderTotalInteger;
        aSummaryForm.TotalSales = totalSalesDecimal;
        aSummaryForm.Show();
    }
```

```csharp
    private void exitButton_Click(object sender, EventArgs e)
    {
        // End the application.

        this.Close();
    }

    private void clearForNextItem()
    {
        // Clear option buttons, combo box, check boxes, text boxes.

        noSizeRadioButton.Checked = true;
        drinkTypeComboBox.SelectedIndex = -1;
        vitaminPackCheckBox.Checked = false;
        energyBoosterCheckBox.Checked = false;
        ladiesCheckBox.Checked = false;
        itemPriceTextBox.Clear();
        quantityTextBox.Text = "1";
    }

    private void twelveOunceRadioButton_CheckedChanged(object sender,
        EventArgs e)
    {
        // Calculate and display the price for the selected item.
        // Handles all size radio buttons.

        // Cast the sender to a RadioButton type.
        RadioButton selectedSizeRadioButton = (RadioButton)sender;

        switch (selectedSizeRadioButton.Name)
        {
            case "twelveOunceRadioButton":
                itemSizeDecimal = 3m;
                drinkOrder[itemCountInteger].sizeString = "12 oz";
                break;
            case "sixteenOunceRadioButton":
                itemSizeDecimal = 3.5m;
                drinkOrder[itemCountInteger].sizeString = "16 oz";
                break;
            case "twentyOunceRadioButton":
                itemSizeDecimal = 4m;
                drinkOrder[itemCountInteger].sizeString = "20 oz";
                break;
        }
        itemPriceDecimal = itemSizeDecimal + findExtrasPrice();
        itemPriceTextBox.Text = itemPriceDecimal.ToString("C");
    }

    private decimal findExtrasPrice()
    {
        // Find price for additives.
        decimal extrasDecimal = 0m;

        if (vitaminPackCheckBox.Checked)
            extrasDecimal += .5m;
        if (energyBoosterCheckBox.Checked)
            extrasDecimal += .5m;
```

```csharp
        if (ladiesCheckBox.Checked)
            extrasDecimal += .5m;

    return extrasDecimal;
}

 private void vitaminPackCheckBox_CheckedChanged(object sender,
    EventArgs e)
{
    // Check price of additives and display current price.

    drinkOrder[itemCountInteger].priceDecimal
        = itemSizeDecimal + findExtrasPrice();
    itemPriceTextBox.Text = drinkOrder[itemCountInteger]
        .priceDecimal.ToString("C");
}

 private void aboutToolStripMenuItem_Click(object sender, EventArgs e)
{
    // Display about form.
    AboutBox1 aboutForm = new AboutBox1();

    aboutForm.ShowDialog();
}

 private void fontToolStripMenuItem_Click(object sender, EventArgs e)
{
    // Change the label's font.

    // Initialize the dialog box.
    fontDialog1.Font = titleLabel.Font;
    // Display the dialog box.
    fontDialog1.ShowDialog();
    // Assign the new font.
    titleLabel.Font = fontDialog1.Font;
}

private void colorToolStripMenuItem_Click(object sender, EventArgs e)
{
    // Change the form's ForeColor.
    // Applies to all controls on the form that haven't had their
    // ForeColor explicitly modified.

    // Initialize the dialog box.
    colorDialog1.Color = this.ForeColor;
    // Display the dialog box.
    colorDialog1.ShowDialog();
    // Assign the new color.
    this.ForeColor = colorDialog1.Color;
}

private void printDocument1_PrintPage(object sender,
  System.Drawing.Printing.PrintPageEventArgs e)
{
    // Display the invoice in a Print Preview dialog box.

    Font printFont = new Font("Arial", 12);
    Font headingFont = new Font("Arial", 14, FontStyle.Bold);
```

```
float lineHeightFloat = (float)printFont.GetHeight() + 2f;
float column1Float = e.MarginBounds.Left;
float yFloat = e.MarginBounds.Top;
float column2Float = 200f;
float column3Float = 250f;
float column4Float = 500f;
float column5Float = 600f;
string lineString;

// Set up heading lines.
lineString = "Look Sharp Fitness Center";
e.Graphics.DrawString(lineString, headingFont, Brushes.Black,
    column3Float, yFloat);
yFloat += (lineHeightFloat * 2);
lineString = "Drink Sales Receipt " + DateTime.Today.ToString("d");
e.Graphics.DrawString(lineString, printFont, Brushes.Black,
    column3Float, yFloat);
yFloat += (lineHeightFloat * 2);
e.Graphics.DrawString("Quantity", headingFont, Brushes.Black,
    column1Float, yFloat);
e.Graphics.DrawString("Size", headingFont, Brushes.Black,
    column2Float, yFloat);
e.Graphics.DrawString("Drink Type", headingFont, Brushes.Black,
    column3Float, yFloat);
e.Graphics.DrawString("Unit Price", headingFont, Brushes.Black,
    column4Float, yFloat);
e.Graphics.DrawString("Extended Price", headingFont, Brushes.Black,
    column5Float, yFloat);
column5Float += 30;
yFloat += (lineHeightFloat * 2);

// Loop through the transactions.
foreach (OrderItem oneOrder in drinkOrder)
{
    // Only print valid orders.
    if (oneOrder.quantityInteger != 0)
    {
        // Set up a line.
        // Quantity.
        e.Graphics.DrawString(oneOrder.quantityInteger.ToString(),
            printFont, Brushes.Black, column1Float, yFloat);

        // Size.
        e.Graphics.DrawString(oneOrder.sizeString,
            printFont, Brushes.Black, column2Float, yFloat);

        // Drink type.
        e.Graphics.DrawString(oneOrder.drinkString, printFont,
            Brushes.Black, column3Float, yFloat);

        // Unit Price.
        e.Graphics.DrawString(oneOrder.priceDecimal.ToString("c"),
            printFont, Brushes.Black, column4Float, yFloat);

        // Extended Price.
        decimal extendedPriceDecimal = oneOrder.priceDecimal
            * oneOrder.quantityInteger;
```

```
            e.Graphics.DrawString(extendedPriceDecimal.ToString("c"),
                printFont, Brushes.Black, column5Float, yFloat);

            // Increment the Y position for the next line.
            yFloat += (lineHeightFloat * 2);
        }
    }

    // Print total.
    e.Graphics.DrawString("Total: ", headingFont, Brushes.Black,
        column1Float, yFloat);
    e.Graphics.DrawString(totalOrderDecimal.ToString("c"), printFont,
        Brushes.Black, column5Float, yFloat);
    }
  }
}
```

Summary

1. A series of variables with the same name and data type is called an *array*. The individual values are referred to as elements, and each element is accessed by its subscript, which is a position number.
2. Array subscripts or indexes are zero based; they must be integers in the range of the array elements. Noninteger values are rounded.
3. You can assign initial values in the array declaration *or* specify the number of elements.
4. A special form of the `for` loop called `foreach` is available for working with arrays. The `foreach` eliminates the need for the programmer to manipulate the subscripts of the array.
5. You can declare a structure to combine related fields and then declare variables and arrays of the structure. The `struct` statement must appear at the class level.
6. Array elements can be used like any other variables; they can be used to accumulate a series of totals or to store values for a lookup operation.
7. The information in arrays may be accessed directly by subscript, or a table lookup may be used to determine the correct table position.
8. You can use the SelectedIndex property of a list box as a subscript of an array.
9. Arrays may be multidimensional. A two-dimensional table contains rows and columns and is processed similarly to a one-dimensional array. Accessing a multidimensional array frequently requires the use of nested loops.

Key Terms

array *332*
column *345*
direct reference *339*
element *332*
`foreach` loop *334*
index *332*
row *345*

struct *335*
structure *335*
subscript *332*
subscripted variable *332*
table *332*
table lookup *341*

Review Questions

1. Define the following terms:
   a. Array
   b. Element
   c. Subscript
   d. Index
   e. Subscripted variable
2. What is a structure? When might a structure be useful?
3. Describe the logic of a table lookup.
4. Name some situations in which it is important to perform validation when working with subscripted variables.
5. Compare a two-dimensional table to an array of a structure.
6. How can you initialize values in a two-dimensional table?

Programming Exercises

8.1 *Array of a structure.* Create a project to analyze an income survey. The statistics for each home include an identification code, the number of members in the household, and the yearly income.

   The menus will include *File*, *Reports*, and *Help*. The *File* menu will contain *Enter Data* and *Exit*. As the data are entered, they should be assigned from the text boxes to the elements of a structure.

   The reports for the project will be sent to the Print Preview window. Each report should include a title, the programmer name, and labels identifying the data.

   Report 1: A report that displays the input data.
   Report 2: A two-column report listing of the identification number and income for each household that exceeds the average income. The calculated average income should display at the top of the report.
   Report 3: The percentage of households that have incomes below the poverty level.

Poverty Guidelines for 2008

Family size	Income
1	10210
2	13690
3	17170
4	20650
5	24130
6	27610
7	31090
8	34570
For each additional person add	3480

Test Data		
ID number	**Number of persons**	**Annual income**
2497	2	32500
3323	5	23000
4521	4	38210
6789	2	38000
5476	1	26000
4423	3	16400
6587	4	25000
3221	4	20500
5555	2	18000
0085	3	19700
3097	8	30000
4480	5	23400
0265	2	19700
8901	3	13000

8.2 *Two-dimensional table.* Modify Programming Exercise 8.1 to assign the data to a multidimensional array rather than use an array of a structure.

8.3 Create a project to keep track of concert ticket sales by your club. Ticket prices are based on the section of the auditorium in which the seats are located. Your program should calculate the price for each sale, accumulate the total number of tickets sold in each section, display the ticket price schedule, and print a summary of all sales.

The form should contain a list box of the sections for seating.

Section	Price
Orchestra	40.00
Mezzanine	27.50
General	15.00
Balcony	10.00

8.4 *Array of a structure.* Create a project that will allow a user to look up state and territory names and their two-letter abbreviations. The user will have the options to *Look up the Abbreviation* or to *Look up the State Name.* In the event that a match cannot be found for the input, display an appropriate error message.

Use radio buttons with a shared method and a `switch` statement to determine which text box (state name or abbreviation) should have the focus and which should be set to ReadOnly.

Data

AL	Alabama	MT	Montana
AK	Alaska	NE	Nebraska
AS	American Samoa	NV	Nevada
AZ	Arizona	NH	New Hampshire
AR	Arkansas	NJ	New Jersey
CA	California	NM	New Mexico
CO	Colorado	NY	New York
CT	Connecticut	NC	North Carolina
DE	Delaware	ND	North Dakota
DC	District of Columbia	OH	Ohio
FL	Florida	OK	Oklahoma
GA	Georgia	OR	Oregon
GU	Guam	PA	Pennsylvania
HI	Hawaii	PR	Puerto Rico
ID	Idaho	RI	Rhode Island
IL	Illinois	SC	South Carolina
IN	Indiana	SD	South Dakota
IA	Iowa	TN	Tennessee
KS	Kansas	TX	Texas
KY	Kentucky	TT	Trust Territories
LA	Louisiana	UT	Utah
ME	Maine	VT	Vermont
MD	Maryland	VA	Virginia
MA	Massachusetts	VI	Virgin Islands
MI	Michigan	WA	Washington
MN	Minnesota	WV	West Virginia
MS	Mississippi	WI	Wisconsin
MO	Missouri	WY	Wyoming

8.5 *Two-dimensional table.* Create a project that looks up the driving distance between two cities. Use two drop-down lists that contain the names of the cities. Label one list *Departure* and the other *Destination*. Use a *Look Up* button to calculate the distance.

Store the distances in a two-dimensional table.

	Boston	Chicago	Dallas	Las Vegas	Los Angeles	Miami	New Orleans	Toronto	Vancouver	Washington, DC
Boston	0	1004	1753	2752	3017	1520	1507	609	3155	448
Chicago	1004	0	921	1780	2048	1397	919	515	2176	709
Dallas	1753	921	0	1230	1399	1343	517	1435	2234	1307
Las Vegas	2752	1780	1230	0	272	2570	1732	2251	1322	2420
Los Angeles	3017	2048	1399	272	0	2716	1858	2523	1278	2646
Miami	1520	1397	1343	2570	2716	0	860	1494	3447	1057
New Orleans	1507	919	517	1732	1858	860	0	1307	2734	1099
Toronto	609	515	1435	2251	2523	1494	1307	0	2820	571
Vancouver	3155	2176	2234	1322	1278	3447	2734	2820	0	2887
Washington, DC	448	709	1307	2420	2646	1057	1099	571	2887	0

8.6 *Two-dimensional table.* Create a project in which the user will complete a 10-question survey. Create a form that contains labels with each of the questions and a group of radio buttons for each question with the following responses: Always, Usually, Sometimes, Seldom, and Never.

Use a two-dimensional array to accumulate the number of each response for each question.

Have a menu or button option that will print an item analysis in the Print Preview window that shows the question number and the count for each response.

Sample of Partial Output

Question	Always	Usually	Sometimes	Seldom	Never
1	5	2	10	4	6
2	2	2	10	2	11
3	17	0	10	0	0

Case Studies

Custom Supplies Mail Order

Create a project that will calculate shipping charges from a two-dimensional table of rates. The rate depends on the weight of the package and the zone to which it will be shipped. The weight column specifies the maximum weight for that rate. All weights over 10 pounds use the last row.

Optional Extra: Add a report that displays all items shipped; include the total charges.

Weight	Zone A	B	C	D
1	1.00	1.50	1.65	1.85
3	1.58	2.00	2.40	3.05
5	1.71	2.52	3.10	4.00
10	2.04	3.12	4.00	5.01
>10	2.52	3.75	5.10	7.25

Christopher's Car Center

Christopher's Car Center (CCC) sells its own brand of spark plugs. To cross-reference to major brands, it keeps a table of equivalent part numbers. Christopher's wants to computerize the process of looking up part numbers in order to improve its customer service.

The user should be able to enter the part number and brand and look up the corresponding CCC part number. You may allow the user to select the brand (Brand A, Brand C, or Brand X) from a list or from radio buttons.

You can choose from two approaches for the lookup table: Store the part numbers either in a two-dimensional table or in an array of a structure. In either case, using the part number and brand entered by the user, look up and display the CCC part number.

CCC	Brand A	Brand C	Brand X
PR214	MR43T	RBL8	14K22
PR223	R43	RJ6	14K24
PR224	R43N	RN4	14K30
PR246	R46N	RN8	14K32
PR247	R46TS	RBL17Y	14K33
PR248	R46TX	RBL12-6	14K35
PR324	S46	J11	14K38
PR326	SR46E	XEJ8	14K40
PR444	47L	H12	14K44

Xtreme Cinema

Create a project that displays the aisle number of a movie category. The movie categories will be in a list box. Store the aisle numbers and categories in an array.

A *Search* button should find the correct location from the array and display it. Make sure that the user has selected a category from the list and use the list box SelectedItem property to find the appropriate aisle number.

Test Data

Aisle 1	Comedy
Aisle 2	Drama
Aisle 3	Action
Aisle 4	Sci-Fi
Aisle 5	Horror
Back Wall	New Releases

Cool Boards

Modify your project from Chapter 6 to keep track of an order in an array. You can then print out the entire order with detail lines for each type of shirt. Convert the event handling for the radio buttons to share an event-handling method. Use a `switch` for selection.

Create an array of a structure, which holds the quantity, size, monogram (Boolean), pocket (Boolean), price, and extended price for each type of shirt ordered. As each shirt type is added to an order, store the information in the array. Add a menu option to print out the order, which will have the customer name and order number at the top, and one line for each shirt type ordered. Use the following layout as a rough guide for your list. Make sure to align the numeric columns correctly. For the two Boolean fields (monogram and pocket), print Yes or No. Do not allow the user to print an invoice until the order is complete.

**Cool Boards Shirt Orders
By Your Name**

Customer name: xxxxxxxxxxxxxxxxxxxxx

Order Number: xxxxx

Quantity	Size	Monogram	Pocket	Price Each	Extended Price
=======	======	======	======	=====	======
xxx	xxx	xxx	xxx	xx	x,xxx

Order Total: xx,xxx

9

Web Applications

1. Explain the functions of the server and the client in Web programming.

2. Create a Web Form and run it in a browser.

3. Describe the differences among the various types of Web controls and the relationship of Web controls to controls used on Windows Forms.

4. Understand the event structure required for Web programs.

5. Design a Web Form using tables.

6. Control the styles used on Web pages using cascading style sheets (CSS).

7. Create multiple pages in a Web application.

8. Navigate using the HyperLink control and the Server object.

9. Validate Web input using the validator controls.

10. Use state management to preserve values in variables.

11. Use AJAX to update a portion of a Web page.

12. Define ASP.NET, XML, WSDL, and SOAP.

C# and Web Programming

So far, all of your projects have been based on Windows Forms and run stand-alone in the Windows environment. In this chapter, you learn to program for the Internet. In C# you use **Web Forms** to create the user interface for Web applications. A Web Form displays as a document in a **browser** such as Mozilla Firefox, Opera, Safari, or Internet Explorer (IE). If you are using the C# Standard Edition, Professional Edition, or above (not Visual Web Developer), you can create documents that display on mobile devices such as cell phones and personal digital assistants (PDAs).

Important software note: Microsoft has a separate product for developing Web applications: Visual Web Developer 2008 Express Edition (VWD), which is a streamlined subset of Visual Studio. The steps and screen captures in this chapter are based on the Professional Edition of Visual Studio and may differ slightly if you are using the Express Edition of Visual Web Developer. If you are using the Express Edition of Visual C# for your Windows applications, you will need to download and install Visual Web Developer for the Web applications.

Client/Server Web Applications

Most Windows applications are stand-alone applications; Web applications require a **server** and a **client**. The server sends Web pages to the client, where the pages display inside a browser application (Figure 9.1).

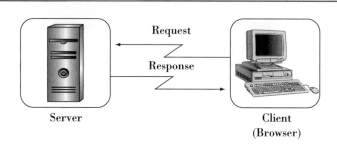

Server — Request / Response — Client (Browser)

Figure 9.1

A server delivers Web pages to a client, where the pages display in a browser window. The server can be on a remote machine or on the same machine as the client.

Web Servers

To develop Web applications, you can either use a remote Web server or make your local machine a Web server. Microsoft provides two pieces of software that can make the development machine function as a server: the new Visual Studio Web server and Internet Information Services (IIS). The server software handles the Web server functions, and the browser acts as the client.

The Visual Studio Web server simplifies development, testing, and debugging. After you have debugged your Web application, you can use the tools in the IDE to transfer the application to an IIS Web server to share with others. The VS Web server is installed automatically when you install Visual Web Developer or Visual Studio.

Web Clients

Browsers display pages written in a markup language. Although the most common format is still hypertext markup language (HTML), many programmers are using the more dynamic features found in extensible hypertext markup language (XHTML). See the World Wide Web Consortuium (W3C) at www.w3.org

for more details. Web pages also may contain programming logic in the form of script such as JavaScript, VBScript, or Jscript, or as Java applets. The browser renders the page and displays it on the local system.

You have likely seen Web pages that look different when displayed in different browsers, or even in different versions of the same browser. Although many browser applications are available, the most common are Internet Explorer, Mozilla FireFox, and Opera.

You may know which browser your users are using, such as when you are programming for a network within a company, called an *intranet*. Or you may develop applications that run on the Internet and might display in any browser. If your projects will run on different browsers, you should test and check the output on multiple browsers.

Web Pages

One characteristic of HTML **Web pages** is that they are **stateless**. That is, a page does not store any information about its contents from one invocation to the next. Several techniques have been developed to get around this limitation, including storing cookies on the local machine and sending state information to the server as part of the page's address, called the uniform resource locator (URL). The server can then send the state information back with the next version of the page, if necessary.

When a user requests a Web page, the browser (client) sends a request to the server. The server may send a preformatted HTML file, or a program on the server may dynamically generate the necessary HTML to render the page. One Microsoft technology for dynamically generating HTML pages is active server pages (ASP).

ASP.NET

The latest Web programming technology from Microsoft is **ASP.NET** 3.5, which represents major advances over the earlier ASP.NET and ASP. The ASP.NET product provides libraries, controls, and programming support that allow you to write programs that interact with the user, maintain state, render controls, display data, and generate appropriate HTML. When you use Web Forms in Visual Studio or Visual Web Developer Express, you are using ASP.NET.

Using C# and ASP.NET, you can create object-oriented, event-driven Web applications.

C# and ASP.NET

Each Web Form that you design has two distinct pieces: (1) the HTML and instructions needed to render the page and (2) the C# code. This separation is a big improvement over older methods that mix the HTML and programming logic (script or applets). A Web Form generates a file with an .aspx extension for the HTML and another file with an .aspx.cs extension for the C# code.

Don't panic if you don't know HTML; the HTML is generated automatically by the Visual Studio IDE. This is similar to the automatically generated code in Windows Forms. You visually create the document using the IDE's designer; you can then view and modify the HTML tags in the Visual Studio editor.

The C# code contains the program logic to respond to events. This code file is called the "code behind" file. The code looks just like the code you have been writing for Windows applications, but many of the events for the controls on Web Forms are different from those of Windows Forms. Another difference is that the C# code is not compiled into an executable (.exe) file as it is for Windows applications. Instead, it is compiled into a dynamic link library (dll) file.

Types of Web Sites

Web applications are referred to as *Web sites* in Visual Studio 2008. VS provides four types of Web sites, which you can see in the *Open Web Site* dialog box (Figure 9.2). Notice the options down the left side of the dialog box: File System, Local IIS, FTP Site, and Remote Site. The icons can vary depending on the version of Visual Studio or Visual Web Developer Express that you are using.

Note: Visual Studio Professional Edition and above also offer a second type of Web site, called a Web project, which more closely resembles the projects that you use for Windows applications. In this text we have elected to use the Web Site template, which is available in VWD and Visual Studio.

F i g u r e 9 . 2

The four types of Web sites supported by Visual Studio and Visual Web Developer appear on the left edge of the **Open Web Site** *dialog box.*

File System Web Sites

A File System Web site stores the Web pages and associated files in any folder on the local computer or other computer on the network. The Web pages are then tested using the Visual Studio Web server. The examples in this chapter all use File System sites.

The features of File System sites and the Visual Studio Web server provide several advantages for Web developers over using IIS. The VS Web server does not expose the computer to security vulnerabilities and does not require administrative rights to create and debug a Web project. Also, the VS Web server can run on the Home Edition of Windows Vista or Windows XP, which most home users are running.

☑**TIP**

Use a File System Web site for development. You can use the *Copy Web Site* feature to convert to IIS or a remote server after you debug the application. ∎

IIS Web Sites

Internet Information Services (IIS) is Microsoft's production Web server and is part of the operating system in Windows 2000, Windows XP Professional, Windows Vista, and Windows Server, but not in Windows XP Home Edition.

IIS includes a Web server, FTP server, e-mail server, and other services. When you run IIS on your local computer, you are hosting a Web server that you must take extra steps to secure.

You must have administrative rights on the computer to create IIS Web projects. If the security on your campus or corporate network does not allow the proper permissions, you cannot create IIS Web applications.

When you create a Web site using local IIS (instead of the new VS Web server), by default the files are stored in the C:\inetpub\wwwroot folder. However, you can create a virtual IIS directory elsewhere on your computer and store your Web site there.

Remote Sites and FTP Sites

It is possible that your campus network will be set up for you to do development on a remote Web server. However, you must be granted administrative rights on the host computer. You cannot use an FTP site to create a new Web site; you only can open a previously created FTP Web site in Visual Studio.

Follow your instructor's directions for the type of site to use.

Creating a Web Site

You can create a new Web application in one of two ways, depending on the edition of the software you are using. For Visual Web Developer 2008 Express Edition, select *File / New Web Site*. If you are using Visual Studio 2008 Professional Edition, you can begin the same way, or you can choose to select *File / New Project* and then select *Web* for the *Project Type*. The following discussion focuses on the *New Web Site* technique since it can be used for either VWD or the Professional Edition.

In the *New Web Site* dialog box (Figure 9.3), you select *ASP.NET Web Site* for the template and *Visual C#* for *Language*. Notice in Figure 9.3 that the *Location* field is set to a suggested folder and project name.

Figure 9.3

Begin a new Web project by entering the location and project name in the New Web Site dialog box.

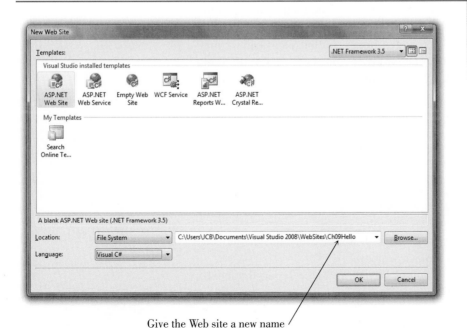

Give the Web site a new name

The default for a File System Web site project location and name is `C:\ Users\UserName\Documents\Visual Studio 2008\WebSites\WebSite1`. You can browse to select a different folder, if you wish. Give your project a name by changing the name on the end (WebSite1) in the *Location* box.

Note: The default for a local IIS project location and name is `http://localhost/ProjectName` (localhost is translated by IIS to your local virtual directory, usually `C:\Inetpub\wwwroot`).

Web Page Files

A new Web site automatically contains one Web page, called Default.aspx, which contains the visual representation of the page. A second file, Default.aspx.cs holds the C# code for the page. This model is very similar to a Windows Form, which also keeps the visual elements separate from the code. But in the case of Web pages, the visual elements are created with HTML tags rather than C# code.

ASP.NET provides two models for managing controls and code. In addition to the **code separation model** described in the preceding paragraph, you also can use a **single-file model**, which combines the visible elements and the C# code in a single file. In early versions of ASP (before .NET), the single-file model was the only format available, so you may see old applications created in this style. We will use the code separation model for all programs in this text.

Caution: Visual Studio also creates a folder for the project's .sln and .suo files. This additional folder appears in the location specified as the Visual Studio projects location, which you can check and modify in *Tools / Options / Projects and Solutions / General.*

Web Forms in the Visual Studio IDE

As soon as you open a new C# Web application, you notice many differences from Windows Forms. Instead of a Windows Form, you see a new Web Form (Figure 9.4), also called a *Web page* or *Web document*. The toolbar is different as is the list of files in the Solution Explorer. The toolbox has different controls, and even those that look the same, such as TextBoxes, Buttons, and Labels, are actually different from their Windows counterparts and have some different properties and events. For example, Web controls have an ID property rather than a Name property.

The IDE allows you to view the Design, the Source (HTML and ASP.NET), or a Split window. Click on the *Design* tab at the bottom of the window (Figure 9.4) to display the page. The Properties window may not appear automatically; press the *Properties* button or select *View / Properties Window* to display it.

Creating Your First Web Form—Step-by-Step

This simple step-by-step exercise creates a Web application that displays a Hello message on a document in a browser window.

If you are using the Express version of Visual Web Developer, the menu choices will be slightly different.

Figure 9.4

The Visual Studio Web Development IDE with a new Web site opened. If the page's Source *tab is selected, click the* Design *tab.*

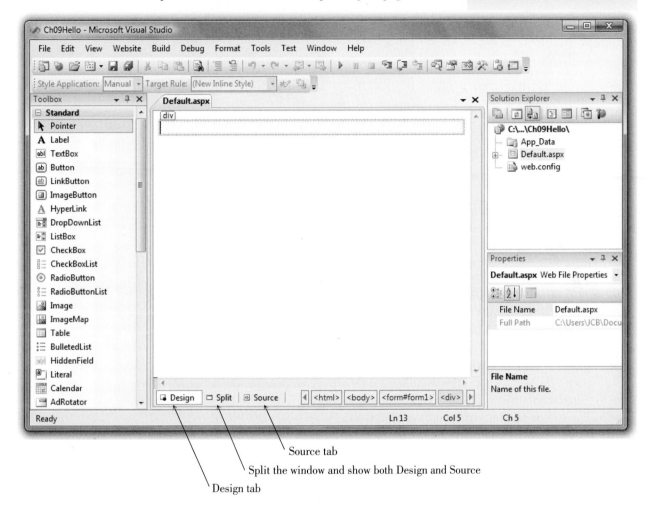

Source tab

Split the window and show both Design and Source

Design tab

Begin the Project

STEP 1: Open Visual Studio 2008 or Visual Web Developer 2008 Express Edition.

STEP 2: From the *File* menu, select *New Web Site* and set the Web site name to "Ch09Hello" by changing the location to "C:\Users\UserName\Documents\Visual Studio 2008\WebSites\Ch09Hello".

    Note: You can use the folder of your choice in place of WebSites. If you are using a shared computer, select a folder in your Documents folder or on your own disk or flash drive. If you are using Windows XP, use a folder in your My Documents folder.

STEP 3: Drop down the *Language* list and select *Visual C#*. The template should be ASP.NET Web Site and the *Location* drop-down list should have *File System* selected. Click *OK*.

STEP 4: If you don't see a blank page in the Document window, click on the *Design* tab at the bottom of the window or on the *View Designer* button in the Solution Explorer (Shortcut: Shift + F7).

Create the User Interface

You add elements to a Web page in a manner similar to writing text in a word processor. You must press Enter to move to a new line and press the spacebar to move across a line.

STEP 1: Click underneath the box at the top of the page, press Enter a few times, and type "Enter Name: ". (Do not include the quotes, but do include the space after the colon to provide separation between the elements.)

STEP 2: Add a TextBox control from the Standard section of the toolbox. You can drag the text box onto the form or double-click the tool in the toolbox; the text box will appear at the insertion point in either case.

Note: The text box is a server control, and the text "Enter Name: " is static HTML. You will learn more about these elements later in this chapter.

STEP 3: Set the ID property of the text box to nameTextBox. You may want to click the *Alphabetical* button in the Properties window to sort the properties. The ID property appears at the top of the list due to the parentheses, just as the Name property appears at the top of the list in Windows Forms.

STEP 4: Click after the text box, press Enter twice, and add a Label control.

STEP 5: Set the Label's ID property to messageLabel and delete the Text property. The label will display its ID property at design time but not at run time.

STEP 6: Click after the label, press Enter a couple of times, and add a Button control. Set the ID property to submitButton and the Text property to "Submit".

STEP 7: In the Properties window, drop down the list of objects and select DOCUMENT, which is the Web Form. Set the BgColor property (background color) to a color of your choice.

STEP 8: Set the document's Title property to "Hello Application". The Title property displays in the title bar of the browser when you run the application. Make sure to press Enter after entering the title.

Note: The Title property sometimes is lost and reverts to "Untitled Page". Make sure to press Enter and save the file after entering the Title property.

STEP 9: Click the *Save All* button to save the application.

Add Code

STEP 1: Double-click on the *Submit* button to go to the Code Editor. Add the following code at the top of the code window.

```
/*
 * Web site:    Ch09Hello
 * Web page:    Default.aspx
 * Programmer:  Bradley/Millspaugh
 * Date:        June 2009
 * Description: Display a Hello message on a Web page.
 *              Concatenate the name and display in a label.
 */
```

STEP 2: Add the following in the submitButton_Click event handler.

```
// Display the name and a message.

messageLabel.Text = "Hello " + nameTextBox.Text;
```

Run the Web Application

STEP 1: Run the project without debugging using Ctrl + F5 or by selecting *Start without Debugging* from the *Debug* menu.

　　　　Note: You also can display a page preview, without actually running the program: Right-click on the aspx file or on the page in the Document window and select *View in Browser.*

STEP 2: The default browser should launch and open the page with your page showing.

　　　　Trouble? If you are running the Windows XP firewall, you may receive a message that the firewall has blocked the Web Server and asking what you would like to do; choose *Unblock* to permit the server to render your page and then refresh the page in the browser window.

STEP 3: Enter a name and press the *Submit* button. A "Hello" message should appear in the label.

STEP 4: Close the browser window to end execution.

Viewing the HTML Code

When you are viewing your Web Form in the designer, you can see three tabs at the bottom of the form: *Design*, *Split*, and *Source*. You can click on the *Source* tab to see the static HTML code. The HTML creates the visual elements on the page and is automatically generated, like the Windows-generated code in a Windows Form. The *Split* tab splits the Document window horizontally and shows you both the design and the source.

Controls

Several types of controls are available for Web Forms. You can mix the control types on a single form. For most of your work, you will use the controls in the Standard section of the toolbox. Refer to Figure 9.5 to view the toolbox.

- *Standard (ASP.NET server controls)*. These are the richest, most powerful controls provided by ASP.NET and the .NET framework. Web server controls do not directly correspond to HTML controls, but are rendered differently for different browsers in order to achieve the desired look and feel. Some of the special-purpose Web server controls are Calendar, CheckBox-List, AdRotator, and RadioButtonList.

- *Data*. This list of controls includes the GridView and DataList for displaying database data.

- *Validation*. These controls are used to validate user input before it is sent to the server.

- *Navigation*. This list includes a Menu control.

- *Login*. Visual Studio includes login controls and wizards.

- *WebParts*. The WebParts set of components enables users to change the appearance and behavior of the interface from the browser.

- *AJAX Extensions*. These are a set of AJAX (Asynchronous JavaScript and XML) controls that provide for faster Web page loading and richer interfaces.

- *HTML.* These are the standard HTML elements that operate only on the client. You cannot write any server-side programming logic for HTML controls. As you submit forms to the server, any HTML controls pass to the server and back as static text. You might want to use HTML controls if you have existing HTML pages that are working and you want to convert to ASP.NET for additional capabilities.

- *Others.* Depending on your version of VS, you may have other sections, such as Reporting.

You can see the available controls in the toolbox when a Web Form is in Design view. Generally, the Standard section is showing (refer to Figure 9.4). Try selecting other toolbox tabs such as *Data*, *Validation*, *Navigation*, *Login*, *WebParts*, and *HTML* (these tools may be in a different order, depending on how you sorted the Toolbox).

In Design view, you can tell the difference between client-side HTML controls and server-side controls. Click on a control and a popup DataTip tells you the type of control and its ID (Name). Figure 9.6 shows two button controls, one an ASP.NET server control and the other an HTML control.

F i g u r e   9 . 5

The Standard section of the toolbox holds the ASP.NET server controls, which you will use primarily. Click on each of the tabs to view the controls in each section of the toolbox.

F i g u r e   9 . 6

The popup Data Tip for each control identifies the type of control and its ID.

ASP server control ———→ asp:button#Button1 | Button

Client-side HTML control ———→ input#Button2 | button

Event Handling

You write C# code for events of Web controls in the same way that you write for Windows controls. The events may actually occur on either the client or the server. The process of capturing an event, sending it to the server, and executing the required methods is all done for you automatically.

The events of Web Forms and controls are somewhat different from those of Windows Forms. For example, a Web Form has a Page.Load event rather than a Form.Load event. You can see the events of the controls in the Properties window if you select the control and click on the *Events* button. If you select a button control, you can see that you still have a Click event, but the list of events is much shorter than it is for Windows controls.

Files

The files that you find in a Web application differ greatly from those in a Windows application (Figure 9.7). Two files make up the form: the aspx file and the aspx.cs file. The aspx file holds the specifications for the user interface that are used by the server to render the page. The aspx.cs file holds the code that you write to respond to events. The aspx.cs file is the code-behind file for the aspx file. When you are designing the user interface, you select the *FormName.aspx* tab and select the *Design* tab at the bottom of the window; when you are working on the code methods, you select the *FormName.aspx.cs* tab.

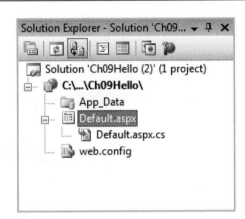

Figure 9.7

The Solution Explorer for a Web application. The Web page called "Default" consists of two files: Default.aspx (the visual elements) and Default.aspx.cs (the C# code-behind file).

Debugging

Running a Web application in the Visual Studio IDE is different from running a Windows application. The IDE does not automatically generate the code necessary for debugging a Web application. If you want to use the debugging tools, such as breakpoints and single-stepping, you must take steps to add the debugging functions to your project.

Run without Debugging

If you choose to run without debugging, you can press Ctrl + F5 or select *Debug / Start without debugging.*

Run with Debugging

To add the necessary support for debugging, your project must have the following line in the Web.config file:

```
<compilation debug="true" />
```

If you try to run with debugging (F5), you receive an error telling you that it can't start with debug mode because debugging is not enabled in the Web.config file (Figure 9.8). It gives you two options: Modify the Web.config file to enable debugging or run without debugging (equivalent to Ctrl + F5).

After you allow modification of the Web.config file, you can set breakpoints, single-step execution, and display the contents of variables and properties. Try

Figure 9.8

This dialog box appears if you attempt to run with debugging. Select Modify the Web.config file *if you want to use the debugging tools; otherwise, select* Run without debugging.

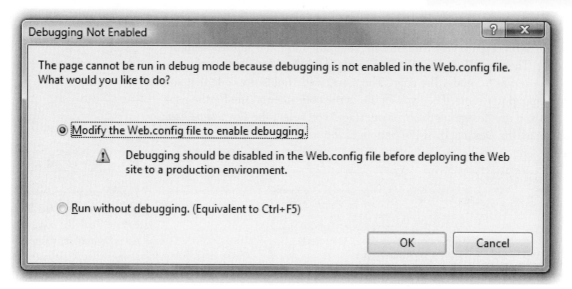

setting a breakpoint in the submitButton event handler and rerun the program. The project compiles and displays in the browser. After you click on the button, the breakpoint halts execution and you can view the code and the values of properties, just as you can in Windows applications. Single-step execution using the F11 and/or F10 keys, as appropriate, and view your objects and properties in the Locals window, or the Autos window if you are using the Professional Edition.

TIP

Always remove debugging support before deploying an application. Debugging code slows the application considerably. ∎

Testing in Other Browsers

You can test your project in another browser such as Mozilla Firefox. From the Solution Explorer window, right-click on the project name and select *Browse With*. You can select from browsers that are installed on your computer.

Feedback 9.1

1. What two files make up a Web Form? What is the purpose of each file?
2. How can you display a preview of how your Web Form will display in a browser without actually running the program?
3. What is the difference between an ASP.NET server control and an HTML control? When might you want to use each type?

Laying Out Web Forms

Using Web Forms, you have considerable control over the layout of a page. However, you must always be aware that users may have different browsers, different screen sizes, and different screen resolutions. ASP.NET generates appropriate HTML to render the page in various browsers but cannot be aware of the screen size, resolution, or window size on the target machine.

Using Tables for Layout

If you want to have more control over placement of elements on your Web page, you can add an HTML **table**. You can add controls and text to the table cells to align the columns as you want them.

The table is an HTML control, which doesn't need any server-side programming. Although there is a Web server Table control, that is generally used when you want to write code to add rows, columns, or controls at run time.

You can either add a table to a Web page by selecting the Table tool from the HTML section of the toolbox or allow the IDE to give you more help. Select *Insert Table* from the *Table* menu. In the *Insert Table* dialog box (Figure 9.9), you can choose the number of rows and columns, as well as set many attributes of the entire table.

F i g u r e   9 . 9

In the Insert Table dialog box, you can create a new table and set many properties of the table.

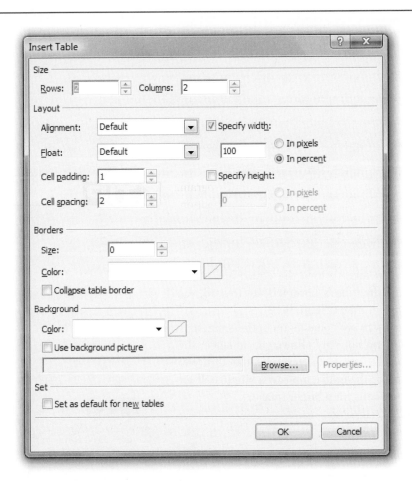

After you create a table, you can set many more properties such as borders, alignment, and background color for the entire table, for individual rows, or for individual cells (Figure 9.10). Note that the HTML colors differ from the ones you can select for the document. You can adjust the column widths by dragging the bar between columns. If you want to move the table, you must click outside the table and insert or delete lines on the page.

To add or delete a table row, first select a row. Then right-click and use the context menu. You can use the same technique to add or delete a column.

Placing Controls or Text in a Table

You can add controls to any table cell or type text in a cell during design time. If you want to be able to refer to the text in a cell at run time, add a label and

Figure 9.10

Move the mouse pointer around to make the various arrows and handles appear. You can click on the arrows to select the entire table, a row, or a column. You also can resize the table by dragging the resizing handles.

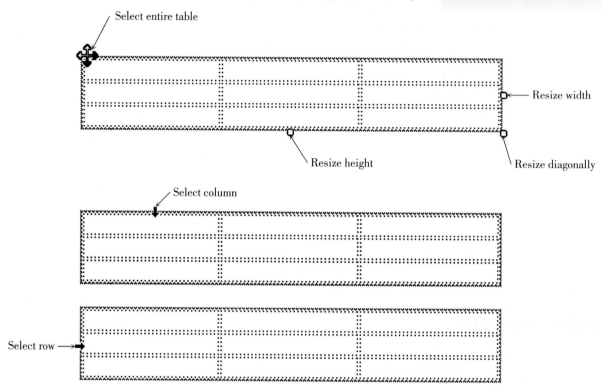

give it an ID; otherwise you can type text directly into the cell. Figure 9.11 shows a table in Design view. Although the table's border is set to zero, the borders appear at design time but not at run time (Figure 9.12).

When you are working with a table, there are some menu options that may help you adjust your table. The *Table* menu not only allows you to select the table, and to insert columns, rows, or cells, but it also provides the ability to merge cells. This means that you can make the entire top row a single cell for your title or you may combine a couple of cells for a larger image.

Figure 9.11

Add text and controls to the table cells. Although the Border property is set to zero, the borders still show at design time.

```
Default.aspx*                                        ▾ ✕

        Name:  ┌─────────────────────────────┐
               └─────────────────────────────┘
     Address:  ┌─────────────────────────────┐
               └─────────────────────────────┘
       Phone:  ┌─────────────────────────────┐
               └─────────────────────────────┘

               ┌──────────┐
               │  Submit  │
               └──────────┘


 ▣ Design   ☐ Split   ▣ Source  │  ◀ <tr> <td> <asp:TextBox#TextBox3>  ▶
```

Figure 9.12

The table at run time. With the Border property set to zero, the borders do not appear.

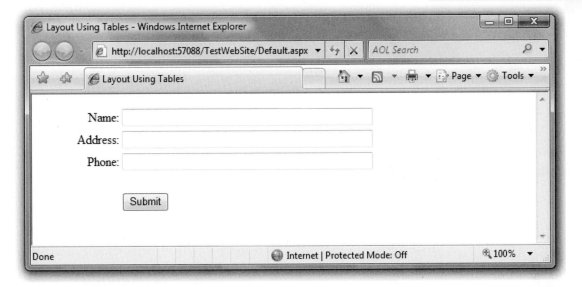

Absolute Positioning

You can choose to place controls on a Web page using **absolute positioning**. This option places controls in a specific X and Y position. If you choose absolute positioning, be aware that controls may not show up if the user has set the browser window to a small size, or they may overlap each other if the user has selected a large font size for the browser window.

To turn on absolute positioning, select *Tools / Options* and check the box to show all settings (Figure 9.13). Go to the tab for *HTML Designer, CSS Styling* and check the box for *Change positioning to absolute for controls added using Toolbox, paste or drag and drop.*

When you are using absolute positioning, you can drag a control using the white tab at the top of a selected control (Figure 9.14).

Absolute positioning keeps controls in the same position relative to the container—the Web page in our case. You also can set individual controls to an absolute position using cascading style sheets, which are discussed later in this chapter.

Including Images on Web Pages

You can add graphics to a Web page using the Image control. The concept is similar to the PictureBox control on Windows Forms, but the graphic file is connected differently due to the nature of Web applications. Each Image control has an ImageUrl property that specifies the location of the graphic file.

To place an image on a Web page, you should first copy the graphic into the Web site folder. Although you can use graphics that are stored elsewhere, your project will be more self-contained and portable if you include graphics in the project folder.

Turn on absolute positioning in the Options dialog box.

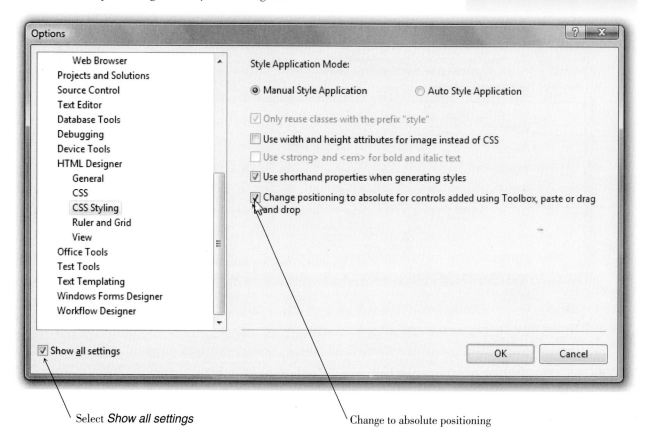

Select *Show all settings*

Change to absolute positioning

Drag a control to a new position using the tab at the top of the selected control.

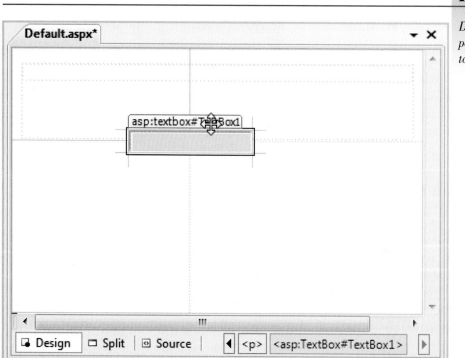

Note: If the project is open in the IDE when you add graphic files, click the *Refresh* button at the top of the Solution Explorer to make the files show up.

You can add an Image control to a cell in a table or directly on a Web page. In the ImageUrl property, click on the Property button (…) to open the *Select Image* dialog box (Figure 9.15). If you have added the graphic to the project folder, and either clicked the Solution Explorer *Refresh* button or reopened the project, the graphic file will appear in the *Contents* pane.

The page in Figure 9.16 is made up of a table of three rows and three columns. The image and company title are in the first row and the text box is in

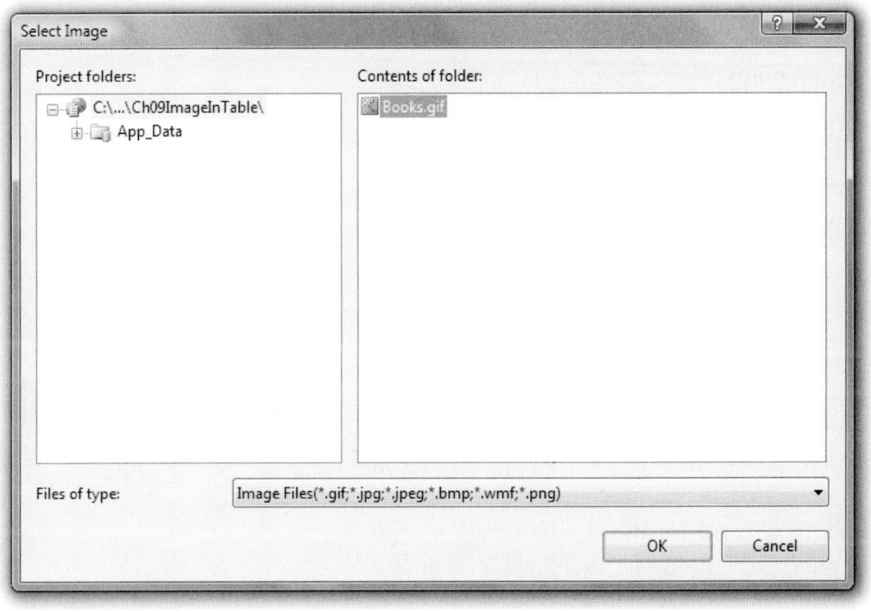

Figure 9.15

Select the graphic for the ImageUrl property of the Image control in the Select Image dialog box.

Figure 9.16

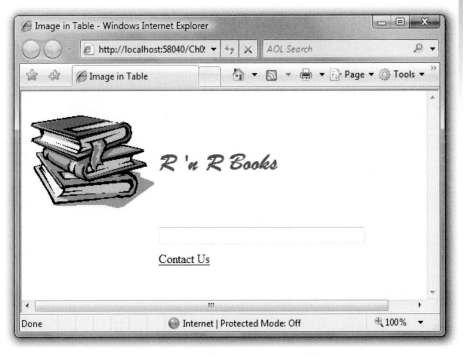

Place images, text, and controls where you want them by using a table. The elements on this page are inserted into table cells. The graphic appears in an Image control.

the second row. The hyperlink shown in the last row is discussed in the section "Navigating Web Pages" later in this chapter.

Feedback 9.2

1. Name two ways to place a button at the bottom of a Web page.
2. What is the difference between an HTML Table control and a Web Table control?
3. Where should you store images for a Web application?

Cascading Style Sheets

One huge improvement in Visual Studio 2008 is the new tools for using styles in Web applications. These new tools, called *Expression Web*, expand, enhance, and simplify using **cascading style sheets (CSS)**. You can use cascading style sheets to create, modify, and apply styles to single elements on a page, one entire page, all pages of an application, or all applications of an organization.

Using Styles

Styles are rules that can specify page layout, position, font, color, alignment, margins, borders, background, and bullet and numbering formats. You can create and apply new styles within a page, attach an external .css file and apply the styles, and even save the styles in a page to an external .css file for use on other pages or Web sites.

You can choose to define styles in several locations, including on the Web page for individual elements, called an *inline style*; in a *style* section of a Web page, called a *page style*; or in an external style sheet (.css file) that is linked or imported into the Web page. Generally programmers use inline styles for elements that appear only once on a page, page styles for elements that may be used in more than one location on the page, and external style sheets for elements that may appear on more than one page of a Web site or in multiple Web sites.

The term "cascading" in cascading style sheets refers to the order of precedence of style rules. More locally created styles override the rules of the more globally created styles. For example, you might apply an h1 style from the style sheet (global) that sets the font, color, size, and alignment. And if you also apply a style defined in the page for the color and size, the local (page-defined) color and size take precedence, but the font and alignment of the style-sheet style are still in effect. And if you also apply an inline style for the size, the inline (more local) style will override the size but keep the color of the page-defined style and the font and alignment of the style-sheet style.

Types of Styles

In Visual Studio, you will use several new tools to define, apply, modify, and change the location of styles. The Apply Styles window and the Manage Styles window, both of which you will learn about in the next section, use the icons in Table 9.1 to identify the various types of styles.

Cascading Style Sheet (CSS) Style Types

Table 9.1

Icon	Style type	How referenced
• (Red dot)	ID-based style; defined in a .css file. Applies to a specific element by ID.	Style name preceded by a pound sign. Example: `#footer`
• (Green dot)	Class-based style; defined in a .css file or the current page. Defines style properties that you want to apply to some, but not all, elements of a particular type, such as some <p> (paragraph) elements.	Style name preceded by a period. Example: `.intro`
• (Blue dot)	Element-based style; defined in the style block of a page. Applies to all elements that use a particular tag, such as <p> (for paragraph) or <td> (for table cell).	Style name only. Example: `p {margin-left: 25px; margin-right: 25px}`
• (Yellow dot)	Inline style. Applies only to the specified item; will not be reused by another element.	In Design view, apply formatting such as font, size, and bold, from the *Format* menu or the formatting toolbar. In Source view, formatting appears using the style element of the opening tag. Example: `<p style="font-weight: bold; font-style: italic>`
◉ (Circled dot)	Indicates that the style is used on the current page.	A dot without a circle indicates that the style is defined but not used.
@ (At sign)	Indicates an imported external cascading style sheet.	

New Style Tools

The Visual Studio 2008 IDE and Visual Web Developer have new windows that make it easy to define, apply, and manage styles. The new windows—CSS Properties, Manage Styles, and Apply Styles—appear by default in the same area as the toolbox and are available from the *View* menu. Also, a new Style Application toolbar appears in the default layout of the IDE. Figure 9.17 shows the new tools.

The Style Application Toolbar

You can use the first drop-down list on the Style Application toolbar to select either *Manual* or *Auto* style application. The *Auto* selection disables the remaining items in the toolbar and allows the software to determine where to place the CSS code. Select *Manual* to choose the location of the styles using the *Target Rule* drop-down list.

As an example, set the Style Application mode to *Manual* and drop down the *Target Rule* list. One option is *New Inline Style*, which places the style code directly into the HTML source code. You also can choose to create an external .css file that can be reused on multiple pages or projects. In this example, we will select the *Apply New Style* option, which will allow us to create a new style in a new or existing .css file.

Figure 9.17

The new style windows and the Style Application toolbar.

Style Application toolbar

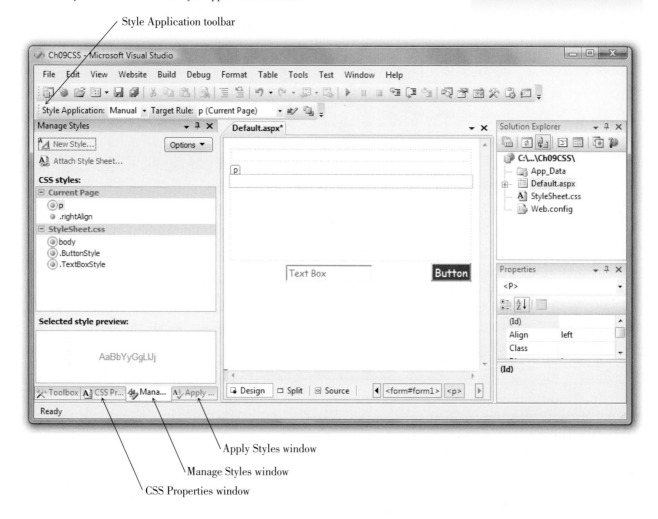

Apply Styles window

Manage Styles window

CSS Properties window

Defining Styles

You define a new style in the *New Style* dialog box (Figure 9.18), which you can display from several locations. Choose *New Style* from the *Format* menu, or select *New Style* in either the Manage Styles window or the Apply Styles window. You also can right-click in the CSS Properties window and choose *New Style* from the context menu.

In the *New Style* dialog box, choose the category and then make settings. For example, click on *Font* in the *Category* list and set the font attributes; click on *Block* and set such attributes as text-align, text-indent, and vertical-align; click on *List* to set bullet and numbering attributes; and *Table* has settings for such attributes as borders and spacing.

Managing Styles

In the Manage Styles window (refer to Figure 9.17), you can see a preview of each style. Hover the mouse pointer over a style name to display the code in the style. You also can see the settings for a given style in the CSS Properties window.

Define a new style in the **New Style** *dialog box. Enter the name for the new style or choose the tag for an element type in the* **Selector** *box. The* **Define in** *box allows you to choose the location for the new style.*

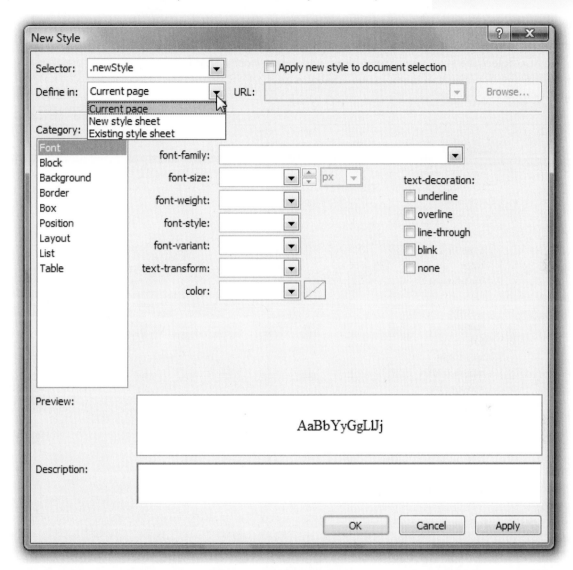

In the Manage Styles window, you can drag styles from one category to another to change the location of the style definition. For example, if you created a style in the current page and want to move it to the .css file so that you can use it in other pages, drag the style name from the Current Page pane to the StyleSheet.css (or other name of a .css file) pane. If you have more than one .css file attached to the page, you can choose the file to which to add a style.

Applying Styles

You can apply styles from several locations, including the Apply Styles window, the Manage Styles window, and the *New Style* dialog box. When you create a new style on the *New Style* dialog box, check the box for *Apply new style to document selection* (refer to Figure 9.18). Using the Apply Styles window, select the element on the page and click the desired style. To use the Manage Styles window, select the element on the page, then right-click the desired style name and select *Apply Style* from the context menu.

Modifying Styles

You can change the attributes of a style from either the Apply Styles or Manage Styles window. Select the style name, right-click, and select *Modify Style* from the context menu. You also can modify style attributes in the CSS Properties window (Figure 9.19).

Figure 9.19

View and modify style elements in the CSS Properties window.

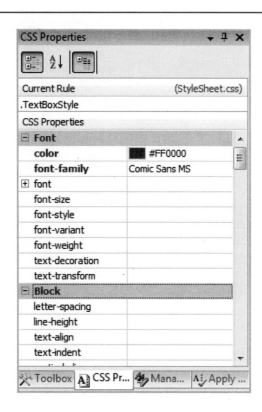

Navigating Web Pages

ASP.NET provides several techniques for navigating from one Web page to another. The easiest form of navigation is to use a HyperLink control.

Using Hyperlinks

You may need to allow your user to navigate to another site or to another page in your application. You can add a hyperlink to a Web page. The **HyperLink control** allows you to enter a Text property for the text to display for the user and a NavigateUrl property that specifies the URL to which to navigate.

When you select the NavigateUrl property for a HyperLink control, the *Select URL* dialog box appears (Figure 9.20). You can select the page from the list. If you want to navigate to another Web site, simply type the Web address as the NavigateUrl property value.

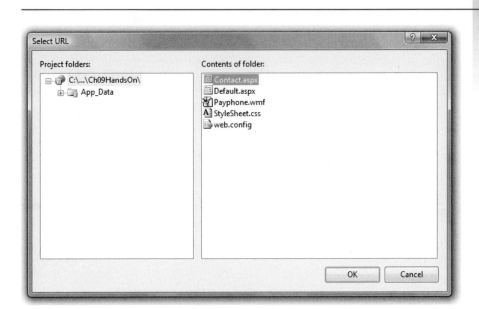

Adding a Second Web Page

Often you need to include multiple Web pages in your application. For example, you can have a separate page to display contact information for your company. You can create a Web Form that contains labels about the company and a HyperLink control to return to the company's home page. The following step-by-step exercise adds a page to the Hello project that you created earlier and adds hyperlinks to each page to navigate back and forth.

Add a New Form to the Hello Project

STEP 1: Open the Ch09Hello Web site in the IDE if necessary.

STEP 2: Select *Add New Item* from the *Website* menu.

      Note: If the templates are not listed, make sure that the project is displaying in the Solution Explorer.

STEP 3: In the *Add New Item* dialog box (Figure 9.21), make sure that the Web Form is selected in the *Templates* list, then set the *Name* box to ContactInfo.aspx. The language should be set to C#.

STEP 4: Make sure that the check box for *Place code in separate file* is selected. This option should be selected for all pages in a project.

STEP 5: Click *Add*. The ContactInfo.aspx file appears in the Document window.

STEP 6: If the source code for HTML is displaying, display Design view by selecting the tab at the bottom of the Document window or by clicking on the *View Designer* button in the Solution Explorer window.

Add Controls to the New Page

STEP 1: Set the document's Title property to "Hello Contact Information".

STEP 2: Add a HyperLink control to the top of the page.

STEP 3: Set the HyperLink's Text property to "Return to Home Page".

Figure 9.21

To add a new Web Form to a Web site, select Web Form in the Add New Item dialog box. Make sure to choose C# for the language and select Place code in separate file.

STEP 4: Click on the Property button for the HyperLink's NavigateUrl property to open the *Select URL* dialog box.

STEP 5: Select Default.aspx (Figure 9.22), the main page of this Web site, and click *OK*.

STEP 6: Click following the control, press Enter three or four times, and enter the contact information. (Make up any information.)

Figure 9.22

Select Default.aspx, the main page of the Web site, as the page to which to navigate.

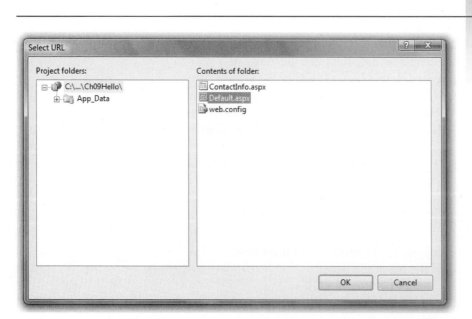

Add a HyperLink to the Main Page

STEP 1: Display Default.aspx in the designer and add a HyperLink control to the bottom of the page.

STEP 2: Set the Text property of the control to "Contact Information". Set the NavigateUrl property to ContactInfo.aspx.

Set the Start Page

For a Web site with multiple pages, you need to set the start page.

STEP 1: In the Solution Explorer, right-click on Default.aspx and choose *Set as Start Page*.

Run the application. Test the links on both pages, which should navigate back and forth between the two pages.

Transferring Pages in Code

Sometimes you cannot use the hyperlink to navigate because you need to perform some other action in code prior to the transfer. To transfer to another page in code, use the `Server.Transfer` method.

```
Server.Transfer("Offer.aspx");
```

Feedback 9.3

1. What property of a HyperLink control indicates to which Web page the control is linked?
2. Describe how to set up the HyperLinks to navigate from a main page to a second page and back again to the main page.
3. Write the line of code for the submitButton that transfers to ThankYou.aspx.

Using the Validator Controls

ASP.NET provides several controls that can automatically validate input data. You add a **validator control**, attach it to an input control such as a text box, and set the error message. At run time, when the user inputs data, the error message displays if the validation rule is violated. These validation controls run on the client-side, so the page does not have to be submitted to the server to view and clear the message. Table 9.2 lists the ASP.NET validator controls.

Note that a blank entry passes the validation for each of the controls except the RequiredFieldValidator. If you want to ensure that the field is not blank *and* that it passes a range check, for example, attach both a RangeValidator and a RequiredFieldValidator control to a field.

For the ErrorMessage property of the validator controls, you can either enter a complete message or set the property to an asterisk. When the user leaves the field blank or enters invalid data, the asterisk will appear.

The ASP.NET Validator Controls   T a b l e   9 . 2

Control	Purpose	Properties to set
RequiredFieldValidator	Requires that the user enter something into the field.	ControlToValidate ErrorMessage
CompareValidator	Compares the value in the field to the value in another control or to a constant value. You also can set the Type property to a numeric type and the CompareValidator will verify that the input value can be converted to the correct type.	ControlToValidate ControlToCompare *or* ValueToCompare Type (to force type checking) ErrorMessage
RangeValidator	Makes sure that the input value falls in the specified range	ControlToValidate MinimumValue MaximumValue Type (to force type checking) ErrorMessage
RegularExpressionValidator	Validates against a regular expression, such as a required number of digits, or a formatted value, such as a telephone number or social security number. Use the Regular Expression Editor to select or edit expressions; open by selecting the Property button on the ValidationExpression property.	ControlToValidate ValidationExpression ErrorMessage
ValidationSummary	Displays a summary of all of the messages from the other validation controls.	DisplayMode (Can be set to a list, bulleted list, or a single paragraph.)

Feedback 9.4

Describe how to validate a text box called numberTextBox using validator controls. A numeric entry is required, in the range 0 to 1000. The field must not be blank.

Maintaining State

As you learned earlier, a Web page holds static data. Each time a page is displayed, or redisplayed, it is a new "fresh" copy of the page. In fact, each time the page is posted back to the server, a new fresh copy of the *program* is loaded. The server responds to the postback, handles any events that have occurred, sends the page back to the client (the browser), and releases the memory used by the program. Unless steps are taken to maintain the values of variables and the controls on the page, called the *state* of the page, all values will be lost in every postback.

Retaining the Contents of Controls

Although regular HTML does not retain the contents of controls during a post-back, ASP.NET *can* retain and redisplay control contents. Web controls have an EnableViewState property, which indicates that you want the server to send the control's contents back with the page. EnableViewState is set to *true* by default, so control contents reappear for each postback.

Retaining the Values of Variables

Local variables in a Web application work just like local variables in a Windows application: The variables are re-created each time the method begins. But class-level variables in Web applications do not work like the ones you are used to in Windows. Because the program is reloaded for each postback, the values of class-level variables are lost unless you take steps to save them. You can store the value of a class-level variable in a control on the Web page; the control's EnableViewState property takes care of holding the value during postback.

You can either set up a label with its Visible property set to *false* or use the HiddenField control in the toolbox. Then assign the class-level variable to the invisible control. For an invisible label, use the Text property; for the hidden field, you must use the Value property, which is a string. In the following example, discountHiddenField is a control on the page and discountTotalDecimal is a class-level variable.

```
//Declare a class-level variable.
private decimal discountTotalDecimal;

protected void submitButton_Click(object sender, EventArgs e)
{
    // . . . Calculations omitted.
    discountHiddenField.Value = discountTotalDecimal.ToString();
}
```

Checking for Postback

When an ASP.NET Web application loads, the Page_Load event occurs. But unlike Windows applications, the page is reloaded for each "round trip" to the server (each **postback**). Therefore, the Page_Load event occurs many times in a Web application. The page's IsPostBack property is set to *false* for the initial page load and to *true* for all page loads following the first. If you want to perform an initialization task once, you can test for `IsPostBack == false` (or `!IsPostBack`) in the Page_Load event handler. And if you want to make sure that you perform an action only on postback (not the initial page load), you can check for `IsPostBack == true`, or just `IsPostBack`.

```
protected void Page_Load(object sender, EventArgs e)
{
    // See if the discount has already been entered.

    if (IsPostBack && discountHiddenField.Value != "")
    {
        discountTotalDecimal = decimal.Parse(discountHiddenField.Value);
    }
}
```

Notice that the class-level variable discountTotalDecimal is assigned a value only on postback *and* discountHiddenField already has been assigned a value.

Passing Values to a Second Page

The HiddenField control maintains the value of a class-level variable only for a single page. In many cases, you want to send information such as the user's name to a second page. There are several ways to pass data between pages; we will use the Session variable technique.

Using a Session Variable

One instance of the **Session object** exists for each user of an application, so you can use this object to store information about the user. The Session object is stored on the server.

Each time the user accesses a site, the Session object is created and assigned a unique SessionID. The value is sent to the user through a dynamic cookie and is sent back to the server in the HTTP header when the user navigates to another page.

Session values are maintained as long as the session exists. A Session object usually ceases to exist when the session times out, which is 20 minutes by default (but can be modified). Some sites have a logout option in which the code can call the `Session.Abandon` method. Also, if the service terminates, the Session objects are lost.

Session objects are easy to use, but you must be aware of some drawbacks. Because the information is stored on the server, storing large amounts of data for multiple users could bog down the server. Also, many Web sites split the server load among several systems, referred to as a *Web farm*. It is not uncommon for the user to be routed to a different server in the Web farm for each postback. In this case, the state information might not be on the correct server. This problem is handled in .NET by specifying the name of the machine that stores the session values in the Web.config file.

You use the Contents collection of the Session object to store values in code. Each item in the collection is called a key/value pair. You make up a name (the key) and assign a value to it. For example, this code assigns the value in nameTextBox to a session variable called "UserName".

```
Session["UserName"] = nameTextBox.Text;
```

The session variable is available in all forms of the application. You can retrieve the data using the same session variable name or an index number for the position of the variable within the collection.

If you want the name to appear automatically when a page displays (or redisplays), place the code in your Page_Load event handler.

```
string nameString = Session["UserName"].ToString();

if (nameString != string.Empty)
{
    greetingLabel.Text = "Hello " + nameString;
```

TIP

If you know that you will not be using a Session object, set the document's enableSession property to *false* for improved efficiency. ■

```
}
else
{
    greetingLabel.Text = "Welcome stranger";
}
```

You can clear all session variables by using the `Session.Clear` method.

Feedback 9.5

Why is it necessary to check for a postback when writing Web applications?

AJAX

One of the newest improvements for Web applications is **Asynchronous JavaScript and XML (AJAX)** for creating interactive applications. AJAX allows you to reload only a portion of the Web page, rather than the entire page, on each postback.

Often large portions of a Web page are unchanged for a postback. Using standard protocols, the entire page is redrawn every time. Using AJAX, the loading speed can increase dramatically by downloading and rendering only the portion that *does* change.

AJAX is an open and cross-platform technology that works on many operating systems. Many AJAX objects are available in the tool library, and any developer can contribute more objects due to the open nature of the standards. You can find more information at www.asp.net/community/.

AJAX is included in Visual Studio 2008, so you can use it on your Web pages. Any page that uses AJAX features must include a ScriptManager component, which is available in the toolbox under AJAX Extensions. After you place the ScriptManager component on the page, you can add other controls, such as the UpdatePanel, which is a container for other controls.

Placing controls inside of an UpdatePanel determines what portion of the page updates on a postback. One fun way to test this is to place a label containing the time inside the update panel and another outside the panel. When a *Submit* button posts back to the server, only the time inside the update panel changes.

In the following small program (Figure 9.23), the user enters a name in a text box and clicks the *Submit* button. The page then welcomes the user by name. The large image is outside the UpdatePanel so it does not redraw when the page posts back the response.

```
Private void submitButton_Click(object sender, EventArgs e)
{
    // Concatenate Welcome to the name.

    welcomeLabel.Text = "Welcome " + nameTextBox.Text;
}
```

A Web page that uses AJAX must have a ScriptManager component. The UpdatePanel holds the controls that should be posted back to the server. The area outside the UpdatePanel remains unchanged.

Managing Web Projects

Moving and renaming Web projects is extremely easy when you are using File System Web sites, as opposed to IIS sites. Always make sure that the project is closed, and then you can rename the project folder, move it to another location on the computer, or copy it to another computer. To open the moved or renamed project, open the IDE first, select *File / Open Web Site*, and navigate to the project's folder.

Using the Copy Web Site Tool

You can use the Copy Web Site tool to copy an entire Web site from one location to another on the same computer, or to another computer on a network, or to a remote site. The tool can copy the Web site to a remote server where it can be accessed by multiple users. See the MSDN Help page: "Walkthrough: Copying a Web Site Using the Copy Web Site Tool". You can select *Website / Copy Web Site* to begin the operation.

Some Web Acronyms

You have seen many acronyms in this chapter, such as HTML, ASP, IIS, and URL. But we have only scratched the surface. As you read the Help files for Visual Studio and begin developing Web applications, you will want to know the meaning of many more. These include the following:

XML	Extensible Markup Language. This popular tag-based notation is used to define data and their format and transmit the data over the Web. XML is entirely text-based, does not follow any one manufacturer's specifications, and can pass through firewalls. See the pages "XML" and "XML Tools in Visual Studio" in Help for further information.
SOAP	Simple Object Access Protocol. An XML-based protocol for exchanging component information among distributed systems of many different types. Since it is based on XML, its messages can pass through network firewalls. See www.w3.org/TR/soap12-part1/
HTTP	Hypertext Transfer Protocol. The protocol used to send and receive Web pages over the Internet using standardized request and response messages.
Web Service	Code in classes used to provide middle-tier services over the Internet.
WSDL	Web Services Description Language. An XML document using specific syntax that defines how a Web service behaves and how clients interact with the service.

Your Hands-On Programming Example

Look Sharp Fitness Center needs a Web site to display promotional offers and contact information. The site should contain three pages: the Default page, a Contact Information page, and an Offer page.

On the Default page, the user should enter his or her name, e-mail address, and the promotion code. The name and e-mail address are required fields. Use a regular expression validator to make sure that the e-mail address is properly formed.

The current promotion codes are

A1876	A Free Step Class
E7770	Equipment Training
D5420	30% discount on clothing

Create a style sheet with a style that defines the background color and font color. Apply the style to all three pages.

Planning the Project

Sketch the Web Forms (Figure 9.24), which your users sign off as meeting their needs.

Figure 9.24

Sketch the forms for the hands-on programming example; a. the main (default) page, b. the Offer page, and c. the ContactInformation page.

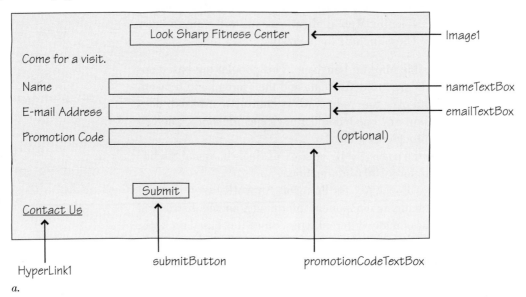

a.

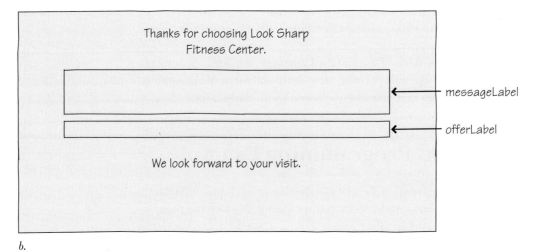

b.

Look Sharp Fitness Center ◄──── Image1

Contact Information:

Phone: 1-800-555-0000

E-mail: looksharpfitnesscenter@fitness.com

Return to Home Page

HyperLink1

c.

Plan the Objects and Properties

The Default Page

Object	Property	Setting
Document	Title	Look Sharp Promotions
HTML Table (9 rows by 3 columns)		
Image	ImageUrl	~/LookSharp.gif
HTML Label	Text	Come for a visit.
HTML Label	Text	Name
HTML Label	Text	E-mail Address
HTML Label	Text	Promotion Code
nameTextBox	ID	nameTextBox
emailTextBox	ID	emailTextBox
promotionCodeTextBox	ID	promotionCodeTextBox
submitButton	ID	submitButton
	Text	Submit
nameRequiredFieldValidator	ID	nameRequiredFieldValidator
	ControlToValidate	nameTextBox
	ErrorMessage	*
emailRegularExpressionValidator	ID	emailRegularExpressionValidator
	ControlToValidate	emailTextBox
	ErrorMessage	Invalid email address.
	Validator Expression	Internet email address
emailRequiredFieldValidator	ID	emailRequiredFieldValidator
	ControlToValidate	emailTextBox
	ErrorMessage	*
HyperLink1	Text	Contact Us
	NavigateUrl	ContactInformation.aspx

The Offer Page

Object	Property	Setting
Document	Title	Look Sharp Promotions
HTML Table (6 rows by 2 columns)		
Static text	Text	Thanks for choosing Look Sharp Fitness Center.
messageLabel	Text	(blank)
offerLabel	Text	(blank)
Static text	Text	We look forward to your visit.

The ContactInformation Page

Object	Property	Setting
Document	Title	Look Sharp Contact Information
Image	ImageUrl	~/LookSharp.gif
Static text	Text	Contact Information:
Static text	Text	1-800-555-0000
Static text	Text	E-mail: looksharpfitnesscenter@fitness.com
HyperLink1	Text	Return to Home Page
	NavigateUrl	Default.aspx

Plan the Methods

The Default Page

Method	Actions
submitButton_Click	Check for promotion code.
	Assign Session variable for promotion type.
	Transfer to the offer page.

The Offer Page

Method	Actions
Page_Load	Check if a promotion code was entered.
	If not, use message to watch for promotions.
	Otherwise, assign the Session variable to the offerLabel.

The ContactInformation Page The contact page has no controls that require event handlers.

Write the Project Follow the sketches in Figure 9.24 to create the Web pages. Figure 9.25 shows the completed pages and Figure 9.26 shows the pages in Design view.

- Set the properties of each of the objects according to your plan.

- Write the code. Working from the pseudocode, write each handler.

- When you complete the code, thoroughly test the project. Make sure to test with empty fields and bad data.

Figure 9.25

The finished Web application; a. the main (default) page, b. the Offer page, and c. the ContactInformation page.

Look Sharp Fitness Center

Come for a visit.

Name

E-mail Address

Promotion Code   (optional)

Submit

Contact Us

a.

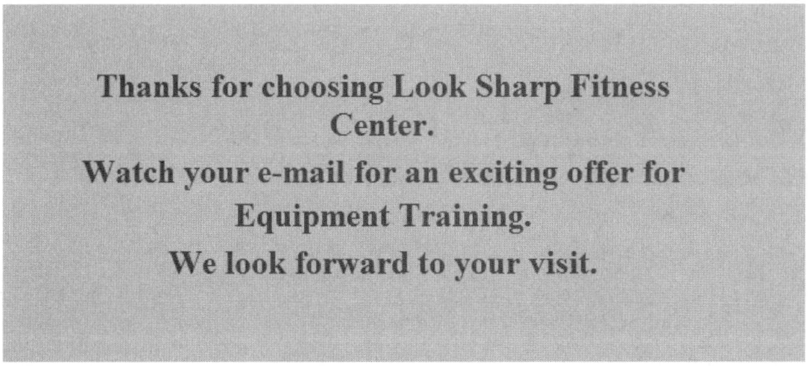

Thanks for choosing Look Sharp Fitness Center.
Watch your e-mail for an exciting offer for Equipment Training.
We look forward to your visit.

b.

Look Sharp Fitness Center

Contact Information:

Phone:1-800-555-0000

E-mail: LookSharpFitnessCenter@fitness.com

Return to Home Page

c.

Lay out the controls in Design view; a. the main (default) page, b. the Offer page, and c. the ContactInformation page.

Look Sharp Fitness Center

Come for a visit.

Name   *

E-mail Address   *Invalid e-mail address

Promotion Code   (optional)

               [Submit]

Contact Us

a.

Thanks for choosing Look Sharp Fitness Center.

[messageLabel]

[offerLabel]

We look forward to your visit.

b.

Look Sharp Fitness Center

Contact Information:

Phone:1-800-555-0000

E-mail: LookSharpFitnessCenter@fitness.com

Return to Home Page

c.

The Project Coding Solution

Default.aspx

```
/*
 * Program:        Ch09HandsOn
 * Programmer:     Bradley/Millspaugh
 * Date:           June 2009
 * Page:           Default.aspx
 * Description:    Web site for Look Sharp Fitness Center Promotions.
 */

using System;
using System.Data;
using System.Configuration;
using System.Web;
using System.Web.Security;
using System.Web.UI;
using System.Web.UI.WebControls;
using System.Web.UI.WebControls.WebParts;
using System.Web.UI.HtmlControls;

public partial class _Default : System.Web.UI.Page
{
    protected void submitButton_Click(object sender, EventArgs e)
    {
        // Test for promotion code.
        switch (promotionCodeTextBox.Text)
        {
            case "A1876":
                Session["PromoType"] = "a free Step class";
                break;
            case "E7770":
                Session["PromoType"] = "Equipment Training";
                break;
            case "D5420":
                Session["PromoType"] = "30% discount on clothing";
                break;
            default:
                Session["PromoType"] = "";
                break;
        }
        Server.Transfer("Offer.aspx");
    }
}
```

Offer.aspx

```
/*
 * Program:        Ch09HandsOn
 * Programmer:     Bradley/Millspaugh
 * Date:           June 2009
 * Page:           Offer.aspx
 * Description:    Web site to display promotional offers for Look Sharp
 *                 Fitness Center.
 */
```

```csharp
using System;
using System.Data;
using System.Configuration;
using System.Collections;
using System.Web;
using System.Web.Security;
using System.Web.UI;
using System.Web.UI.WebControls;
using System.Web.UI.WebControls.WebParts;
using System.Web.UI.HtmlControls;

public partial class FreeClass : System.Web.UI.Page
{
    protected void Page_Load(object sender, EventArgs e)
    {
        // Display the offer from the Session Variable.
        string offerString = Session["PromoType"].ToString();

        if (offerString == String.Empty)
        {
            messageLabel.Text = "Watch your local paper for our promotions.";
        }
        else
        {
            messageLabel.Text = "Watch your e-mail for an exciting offer for";
            offerLabel.Text = offerString;
        }
    }
}
```

Summary

1. A Web application runs in a browser whereas most Windows applications run stand-alone.
2. A Web application has a client, which is the local computer running the Web page in a browser, and a server, which is a local or remote computer that stores the Web page files and renders the page for the client.
3. Different browsers may display Web pages differently. Web developers must test their applications on multiple browsers unless they know that all users will use the same browser, such as in a company intranet.
4. Web pages are static and stateless. They require processing to change the appearance of the page and they cannot store variables on their own.
5. ASP.NET is the Web technology included in Visual Studio. Web Forms in C# use ASP.NET.
6. A different set of files is generated for Web projects than for Windows projects.

7. A Web Form consists of two files: the .aspx file that holds the code to render the user interface and the .aspx.cs file that holds the C# code.

8. The controls for Web pages are different from those used on Windows Forms.

9. In Design view, the *Source* tab displays the HTML that is automatically generated.

10. You can display a page preview as it will appear in a browser.

11. Controls on Web pages may be HTML (client-side) controls or Web server controls, which are the controls provided by ASP.NET. Web server controls are rendered specifically for the browser being used.

12. Although the events of Web controls are somewhat different from those for Windows controls, coding for the events is the same.

13. In a Web page, controls are placed one after another, from top to bottom, similar to a word processing document.

14. You can use an HTML table to lay out controls and text in rows and columns.

15. The positioning of a page or a control may be set to absolute, which allows you to set the location by dragging the control to the desired position.

16. Add graphics to a page using an Image control. The control's ImageUrl property holds the location of the file.

17. Cascading style sheets can be used to set font properties, position, border, and the background for Web pages and controls. The location of the style definition determines the type of style—inline, page, or .css file.

18. A HyperLink control is used for navigation. Set the NavigateUrl property to the page to which to navigate, which can be in the current project or another Web site.

19. You can add multiple pages to a Web application and set up navigation between the pages.

20. Validator controls allow testing for a required field, proper type of data, or a range of values.

21. The EnableViewState property of a Web control determines whether the control maintains its value during postback. To maintain the value of a program class-level variable, assign the variable's value to a hidden or invisible control.

22. A postback occurs for every round trip to the server. The form is reloaded for every postback, so you often must check in the Form_Load event handler to determine whether it is the first time the page is loaded (for initialization steps) or a postback (to handle a second request).

23. Use a Session variable to pass a data value to a second page. Session variables are key/value pairs that exist for each user of the application.

24. To move a Web project from one computer to another, make sure the project is not open in the IDE and copy the project's folder. You also can use the Copy Web Site tool in Visual Studio to copy a Web project.

25. AJAX (Asynchronous JavaScript and XML) improves the speed of Web applications. By using the Update Panel, only a portion of a Web page is submitted and reloaded on a postback.

26. XML is used to store and transfer data on the Internet. XML is tag-based and text-only and can be transmitted through network firewalls. SOAP and WSDL are based on XML.

Key Terms

absolute position *383*

Asynchronous JavaScript and
   XML (AJAX) *397*

ASP.NET *371*

browser *370*

cascading style sheet (CSS) *386*

client *370*

code separation model *374*

HyperLink control *390*

intranet *371*

postback *395*

server *370*

Session object *396*

single-file model *374*

stateless *371*

table *381*

validator control *393*

Web Form *370*

Web page *371*

Review Questions

1. Explain the differences between the execution of a Windows application and a Web application.
2. Differentiate between the client and the server for a Web application.
3. What is meant by the statement that Web pages are stateless?
4. What options are available for locations of Web site files?
5. What are the differences between HTML controls and standard controls?
6. How does event handling differ from that for Windows applications?
7. Describe at least two methods for controlling the layout of controls on a Web page.
8. What functions are done by validator controls? How can you set up a validator control?
9. Describe the purpose and functionality of AJAX. What is meant by open standards?
10. What is a Session object and how would it be used?
11. What is the purpose of XML? of SOAP?

Programming Exercises

9.1 Rewrite your project from Chapter 3 to be a Web project; include validation.

9.2 Rough Riders Rodeo wants to sell tickets online. Allow the user to enter the number of tickets needed. The data entry screen also should include the shipping address for the tickets, a credit card number, expiration date, and a drop-down box allowing the user to select the type of credit card. Also include a check box for attending the Awards Event. Include a hyperlink for confirming the order. Make the link invisible to begin but display it after the *Submit* button has been clicked.

The confirmation page should say "Thank you for your order." and display the amount due.

The tickets are $15 for just the rodeo, $25 if they want to attend the Awards Event. Note that all members of the party must select the same type of tickets.

When the user selects the *Submit* button, display the amount due and display a link to confirm the order (make the existing link visible).

9.3　Create a Web page for entering new customer information. The fields include name, e-mail, username, and password. Include a second text box to confirm the password. Set the TextMode property of the two password fields to "Password". Use a table to lay out your controls.

Validate that all fields contain information. Display appropriate messages for any empty fields. Include a *Submit* button.

When all information is entered and the *Submit* button is pressed, compare the two password fields to see if they are equal. If not, clear both text boxes and display a message to reenter the password information. When the passwords match, display a message that says "Welcome" and the name of the customer.

9.4　Create a Web page for a company of your choosing. Include multiple pages, a HyperLink control, and validator controls.

Case Studies

Custom Supplies Mail Order

Write the Custom Supplies Mail Order project from Chapter 4 as a Web application. Use validator controls for the validation. Place an image or logo on the page located outside an AJAX Update Panel. Include a second page with contact information for the company.

Christopher's Car Center

Write the Christopher's Car Center project from Chapter 3 as a Web application. Use validator controls for the validation. Include a second page with contact information for the company.

Suggestion: Use a RadioButtonList control.

Xtreme Cinema

Write the Xtreme Cinema project from Chapter 3 or Chapter 4 as a Web application. Use validator controls for the validation. Include a second page with contact information for the company.

Suggestion: Use a RadioButtonList control.

Cool Boards

Write the Cool Boards project from Chapter 4 as a Web application. Use validator controls for the validation, including a range validator for the quantity. Include a second page with contact information for the company.

Suggestion: Use a RadioButtonList control.

10

Database Applications

1. Use database terminology correctly.

2. Create Windows and Web projects that display database data.

3. Display data in a DataGridView control.

4. Bind data to text boxes and labels.

5. Allow the user to select from a combo box or list box and display the corresponding record in data-bound controls.

6. Query an object using LINQ.

Databases

Most data handling today is done with relational databases. Many manufacturers produce database management systems (DBMS), each with its own proprietary format. One challenge for software developers has been accessing data from multiple sources that are stored in different formats. Most of the new tools available to developers, including Microsoft's Visual Studio, attempt to handle data from multiple locations (servers) and data stored in different formats.

C# and Databases

You can use C# to write applications that display and update the data from databases. C# uses ADO.NET, which is the next generation of database technology, based on Microsoft's previous version called *ActiveX Data Objects (ADO)*. One big advantage of ADO.NET is that information is stored and transferred in Extensible Markup Language (XML). You will find more information about XML in the section "XML Data" later in this chapter.

ADO.NET allows you to access database data in many formats. The basic types of providers are OleDb, SQLClient for SQL Server (Microsoft's proprietary DBMS), Odbc, and Oracle. Using OleDb you can obtain data from sources such as Access, Oracle, Sybase, or DB2. The examples in this text use Microsoft's SQL Server Express (SSE), which installs automatically with Visual Studio.

Database Terminology

To use databases, you must understand the standard terminology of relational databases. Although there are various definitions of standard database terms, we will stick with the most common terms, those used in SQL Server and Access.

A database file (with an .mdf or .mdb extension) can hold multiple tables. Each **table** can be viewed like a spreadsheet, with rows and columns. Each **row** in a table represents the data for one item, person, or transaction and is called a **record**. Each **column** in a table is used to store a different element of data, such as an account number, a name, an address, or a numeric amount. The elements represented in columns are called **fields**. You can think of the table in Figure 10.1 as consisting of rows and columns or of records and fields.

Most tables use a **primary key field** (or combination of fields) to identify each record. The primary key field is often a number such as an employee number, account number, identification number, or social security number; or it may be a text field such as a last name or a combination such as a last name and first name.

A relational database generally contains multiple tables and relationships between the tables. For example, an Employee table may have an Employee ID field, and the Payroll table also will have an Employee ID field. The two tables are related by Employee ID. You can find the employee information for one payroll record by retrieving the record for the corresponding Employee ID in the Employee table. One reason to create relationships between tables is to keep the data compact and easy to maintain. By having multiple payroll records related to one employee record through the Employee ID, an employee's

Figure 10.1

A database table consists of rows (records) and columns (fields).

ISBN	Title	Author	Publisher
0-111-11111-1	89 Years in a Sand Trap	Beck, Fred	Hill and Wang
0-15-500139-6	Business Programming in C	Millspaugh, A. C.	The Dryden Press
0-394-75843-9	Cultural Literacy	Hirsch, E. D. Jr.	Vintage
0-440-22284-2	Five Days in Paris	Steel, Danielle	Dell Publishing
0-446-51251-6	Megatrends	Naisbitt, John	Warner Books
0-446-51652-X	Bridges of Madison County	Waller, Robert James	Warner Books
0-446-60274-4	The Rules	Fein/Schneider	Warner Books
0-451-16095-9	The Stand	King, Stephen	Signet
0-452-26011-6	Song of Solomon	Morrison, Toni	Plume/Penguin
0-517-59905-8	How to Talk to Anyone, Anytime, Anywhere	King, Larry	Crown
0-534-26076-4	A Quick Guide to the Internet	Bradley, Julia Case	Integrated Media Group

Record or row

Field or column

address, for example, can be changed in one spot without having to go to each payroll record to update it.

Any time a database table is open, one record is considered the current record. As you move from one record to the next, the current record changes.

XML Data

XML is an industry-standard format for storing and transferring data. You can find the specifications for XML at www.w3.org/XML, which is the site for the World Wide Web Consortium (W3C).

You don't need to know any XML to write database applications in C#. The necessary XML is generated for you automatically, like the automatically generated C# code and HTML. However, a few facts about XML can help you understand what is happening in your programs.

Most proprietary database formats store data in binary, which cannot be accessed by other systems or pass through Internet firewalls. Data stored in XML is all text, identified by tags similar to HTML tags. An XML file can be edited by any text editor program, such as Notepad.

If you have seen or written any HTML, you know that opening and closing tags define elements and attributes. For example, any text between <b> and </b> is rendered in bold by the browser.

```
<b>This text is bold.</b> <i>This is italic.</i>
```

The tags in XML are not predefined as they are in HTML. The tags can identify fields by name. For example, following are three records of a database exported to XML.

```
<?xml version="1.0" encoding="UTF-8"?>
<dataroot xmlns:od="urn:schemas-microsoft-com:officedata">
    <Books>
        <ISBN>0-15-500139-6</ISBN>
        <Title>Business Programming in C</Title>
        <Author>Millspaugh, A. C.</Author>
        <Publisher>The Dryden Press</Publisher>
    </Books>
    <Books>
        <ISBN>0-446-51652-X</ISBN>
        <Title>Bridges of Madison County</Title>
        <Author>Waller, Robert James</Author>
        <Publisher>Warner Books</Publisher>
    </Books>
    <Books>
        <ISBN>0-451-16095-9</ISBN>
        <Title>The Stand</Title>
        <Author>King, Stephen</Author>
        <Publisher>Signet</Publisher>
    </Books>
</dataroot>
```

In addition to an XML data file, you usually also have an XML schema file. The schema describes the fields, data types, and any constraints, such as required fields. ADO.NET validates the data against the schema and checks for constraint violations. The schema also is defined with XML tags and can be viewed or edited in a text editor.

The format of XML data offers several advantages for programming. Because an XML schema provides for strong data typing, the various data types can be handled properly. And ADO.NET can treat the XML data as objects, allowing the IntelliSense feature of the Visual Studio environment to provide information for the programmer. In addition, data handling in XML and ADO.NET executes faster than in earlier forms of ADO.

Feedback 10.1

1. Assume you have a database containing the names and phone numbers of your friends. Describe how the terms *file, table, row, column, record, field,* and *key field* apply to your database.
2. What is an advantage of transferring data as XML, rather than a proprietary format such as Access or SQLServer?

Using ADO.NET and C#

In C#, you can display data from a database on a Windows Form or a Web Form. You add controls to the form and bind data to the controls. The controls may be labels or text boxes or one of the special controls designed just for data, such as the DataGridView or DataList. However, just as you found in

Chapter 9, the controls for a Windows application are different from the controls for a Web application and have different properties and events. In this chapter, you will write database applications using both Windows Forms and Web Forms. Figure 10.2 shows a data table displaying in a DataGridView on a Windows Form.

You must use several classes and objects to set up data access in C#.

Figure   10.2

The DataGridView control is bound to a table in a dataset. The data fields display automatically in the cells of the grid.

First Name	Last Name	Home Phone	E-mail	Cell Phone	Membership Date
Alison	Paugh	9495556222	apgirl@sprite.net	9495551111	8/5/2006
Breana	Holmes	9495558766	bree@hotmail.com		7/8/2004
Derek	Ball	9495558888			8/5/2006
Dillan	Young	9515551222	dyoung@crox.net		12/7/2007
Drew	Shelton	9495551010	speedrew@msn....	9495559999	7/12/2007
Elena	Holmes	9495556666	elena456@hotm...		7/8/2004
Kathleen	Mills	9515551234	kmills@yahoo.com		1/10/2004
Kevin	Spade	9515553456		9515553456	5/5/2004
Rich	Alcanter	9495553455	richA@crox.net	9495550000	8/5/2005
Zach	Smyth	9495558766	soccerboy@msn....		3/12/2005

Look Sharp Fitness Center

Data Access in Visual Studio

The Visual Studio Data Sources window provides an easy way to create data-bound controls on a form. As you will see later in this chapter, you can drag tables and fields from the window onto a form to automatically create controls that are bound to the data. You can display the data in grids or in individual fields, which are referred to as *Details*. You also can drag a field from the Data Sources window and drop it on an existing control, which causes **data binding** to be set up automatically.

When you add data-bound controls to a form, two things occur: An .xsd file is added to the Server Explorer window, and BindingSource, TableAdapter, and DataSet objects are added to the form's component tray, along with a Binding-Navigator.

The following list is an overview of database objects; each of the classes is further described in the sections that follow.

- *Binding source.* A binding source establishes a link to the actual data, which is a specific file and/or server.

- *Table adapter.* A table adapter handles retrieving and updating the data. A table adapter automatically generates SQL statements that you can use to access or update data. SQL, or Structured Query Language, is an industry-standard language that is used to select and update data in a relational database.

- *Dataset.* A dataset contains the actual data. The data in a single dataset may come from multiple binding sources and/or multiple table adapters.

- *Binding navigator.* A binding navigator is a toolbar that provides for database navigation and updating.

  Figure 10.3 shows a visual representation of the required steps.

F i g u r e 1 0 . 3

To display database data in bound controls on a form, you need a binding source, a table adapter, and a dataset.

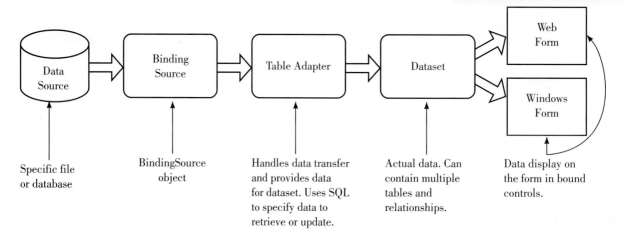

Binding Sources

A **BindingSource** object establishes a link from a specific file or database to your program. In this chapter, you will use a wizard to automatically create BindingSource objects. You also can add new BindingSource objects using the Data Sources window or the *Data* menu.

Note: Earlier versions of C# used Connection objects rather than BindingSources.

Table Adapters

A **table adapter** does all of the work of passing data back and forth between a data source (the binding source) and a program (the dataset). The binding source for a table adapter does not have to be a database; it also can be a text file, an object, or even an array. No matter where the actual data (the source) for the binding source are, the table adapter transfers data from the source to the dataset (fills) or transfers data from the dataset back to the source (updates), all via XML.

Datasets

A **dataset** is a temporary set of data stored in the memory of the computer. In ADO.NET, datasets are disconnected, which means that the copy of data in memory does not keep an active connection to the data source. This technique is a big improvement over the recordsets in previous versions of ADO, which maintain open connections to the data source. A dataset may contain multiple tables; however, the examples in this chapter use only one table per dataset.

Any controls that you have bound to the dataset will automatically fill with data.

Feedback 10.2

Explain the purpose of and the differences between *binding sources*, *table adapters*, and *datasets*.

Creating a Database Application

In the following step-by-step exercise, you will create a Windows application that displays data from the Customers table of the LookSharp.mdf SQLServer database. You will display the fields from the table in a **DataGridView control** on a Windows Form. Refer to Figure 10.2 for the finished application.

A Windows Database Application—Step-by-Step

This step-by-step exercise uses the LookSharp.mdf SQLServer database file, which is available from the text Web site (www.mhhe.com/C#2008). Make sure that the file is available before starting this project.

Start a New Project

STEP 1: Start a new Windows Application project called "Ch10DataGridView".

STEP 2: Name the form "CustomerForm" and set the Text property to "Look Sharp Fitness Center". Widen the form to about three times the original size.

STEP 3: Select *Save All* from the *File* menu or the toolbar button.

Add a Grid to Display the Data

STEP 1: Add a DataGridView control to the from. You can find the control in the toolbox in both the *All Windows Forms* tab and the *Data* tab. Click the *Smart Tag* arrow to pop up the smart tag (Figure 10.4).

Figure   10.4

Add a DataGridView control to a form and pop up its smart tag.

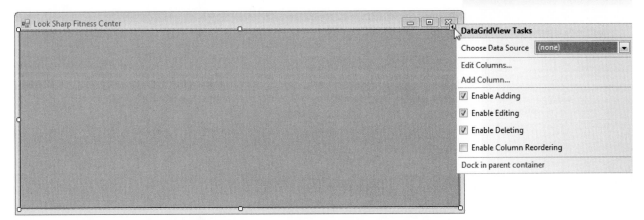

STEP 2: On the smart tag, drop down the list for *Choose Data Source* . Select *Add Project Data Source* from the drop-down (Figure 10.5), which activates the Data Source Configuration Wizard. Click *Next*.

Figure 10.5

*Add a new data source to a
project from the smart tag of
the DataGridView.*

STEP 3: Select *Database* (Figure 10.6) and click *Next*.

Note that it isn't necessary to copy the database .mdf file into the project folder; the wizard will ask you later if you want to add the data file to the project, which automatically copies the file to your project folder. You can select the file from anywhere it is available, such as a folder on the local computer, a network share, or a CD. When the project runs, it uses the copy in your project folder. If you want to use a database file stored somewhere else, for example to share with other applications, you will not add the file to your project.

STEP 4: Select *New Connection* to set up the connection for the binding source object. The next dialog asks what type of database you want to use. Select *Microsoft SQL Server Database File (SqlClient)*, which will use SQL Express, unless you are using the full version of SQL Server.

Figure 10.6

*Select Database in the first
page of the Data Source
Configuration Wizard.*

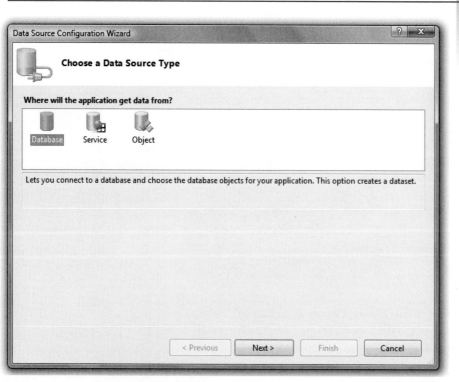

STEP 5: In the *Add Connection* dialog box (Figure 10.7), the Data source should
be set to "Microsoft SQL Server Database File (SqlClient)." Browse to
select the LookSharp.mdf file. You can find it anywhere it is available, including on a CD; later the file will be added to your project.
Click *Open* and then *Test Connection*; you should see a message that
the test connection succeeded. Click *OK*.

Figure 10.7

*Select New Connection to
display the Add Connection
dialog box and set up the
connection to the database file.*

STEP 6: Back on the wizard page, your new connection should now appear
selected; click *Next*.
     A dialog pops up asking if you want to add the file to your project
(Figure 10.8). Click *Yes*, which will make your project portable, so
that you can run it on different computers without worrying about the
file location.

Figure 10.8

*This dialog gives you the
option of making a copy of the
database file in the current
folder. Select Yes.*

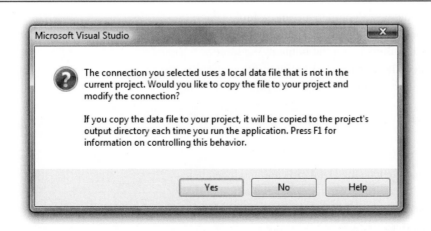

STEP 7: Click *Next*. The database objects in the LookSharp database will appear.

STEP 8: Expand the *Tables* node and place a check mark in front of Customer (Figure 10.9). Click *Finish*.

Figure 10.9

Click on the plus sign for **Tables** *to expand the node and select the Customer table.*

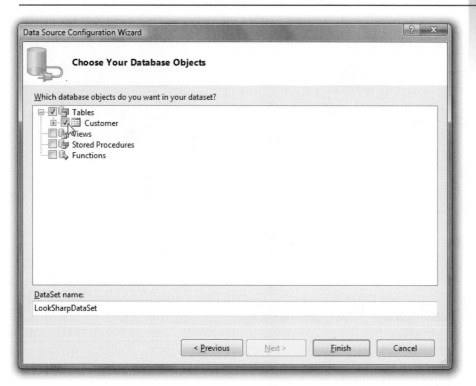

STEP 9: Notice that the grid column headings now have the names of the fields. Later you will learn to resize the widths of the columns.

Run the Data Application

STEP 1: Run your program. The grid should fill with data. At this point, the user can resize the columns by dragging the dividers between column headings.

STEP 2: Close the form or click the *Stop Debugging* button (Shift + F5) in the IDE to stop program execution.

Examine the Components

STEP 1: Take a look in the components tray (Figure 10.10). Your form now contains a DataSet component, a BindingSource component, and a TableAdapter component. The wizard automatically names the dataset with the name of the database source and the others using the name of the table.

STEP 2: Now look at the form's code. The Form_Load method automatically contains the code to fill the dataset from the table adapter.

```
this.customerTableAdapter.Fill(this.lookSharpDataSet.Customer);
```

Format the DataGridView

STEP 1: Switch back to the designer and click on the DataGridView and then click on the *Smart Tag* arrow—the small arrow on the upper-right side of the grid. In the smart tag that pops up, select *Edit Columns* (Figure 10.11).

Figure 10.10

The data components that were generated by the Data Source Configuration wizard appear in the component tray of the form.

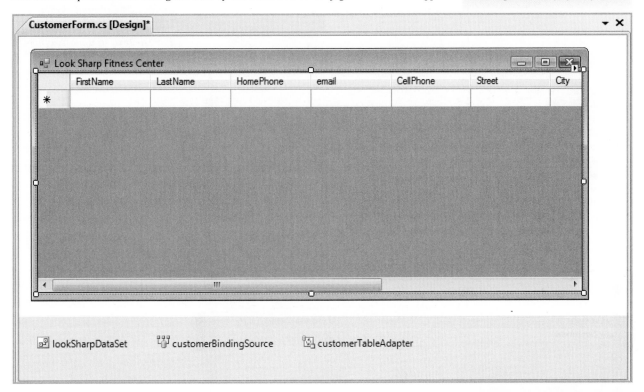

Figure 10.11

Pop up the smart tag and select Edit Columns to format the grid.

STEP 2: In the *Edit Columns* dialog box (Figure 10.12), you can add, remove, and reorder the columns. You also can select any of the columns on the left side of the dialog box and view or modify its properties on the right side. For example, you can set the width of a column and change its heading text (HeaderText property).

STEP 3: Remove the address field, so that the grid displays only the FirstName, LastName, HomePhone, email, CellPhone, and MembershipDate fields.

STEP 4: Select the FirstName field and locate the HeaderText property, which is in the *Appearance* group. Type a space between the two words and press Enter to make the HeaderText "First Name".

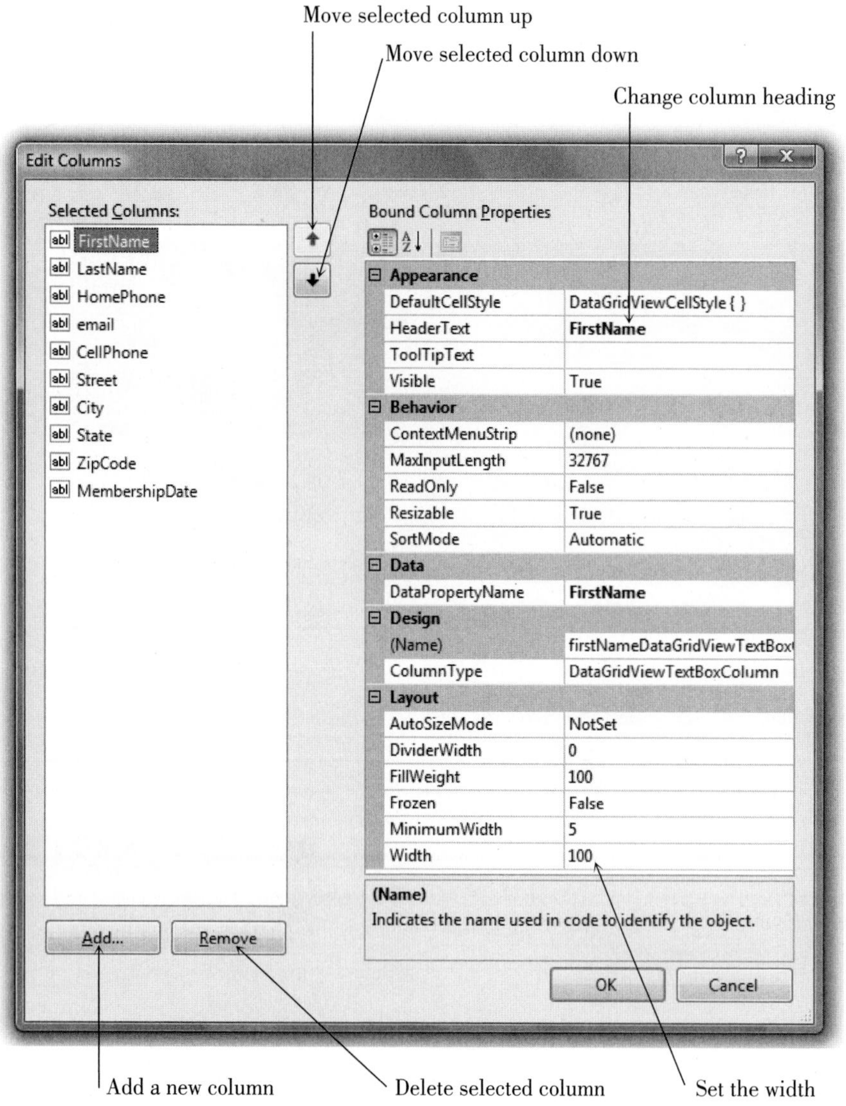

Figure   10.12

Format the columns of the grid in the **Edit Columns** *dialog box. You can set HeaderText, ToolTip Text, and many other properties of a column.*

Move selected column up

Move selected column down

Change column heading

Add a new column   Delete selected column   Set the width

STEP 5: Make each of the other two-word fields have a space in their name: LastName, HomePhone, CellPhone, and MembershipDate. Select the email field and change the HeaderText to "E-mail". Click *OK*.

STEP 6: You may want to resize the grid and/or form to fit the columns in the grid. Or, you could choose to dock the grid in the form.

Run the Application

STEP 1: Run the application and make note of any changes that would improve the layout.

STEP 2: Return to design time, make any further modifications, and run the application again.

The Grid's Smart Tag

Earlier you used the smart tag to edit the properties of grid columns. You also can use the smart tag to add and edit columns and to dock the grid in its parent container (the form). Docking the grid makes it fill the form, even when the form is resized.

The Database Schema File

When you add a new data source to a project, a file with the extension .xsd is added to the Solution Explorer. This file contains the XML schema definition, which has the description and properties of the data. You can double-click on the .xsd file to open the **Data Designer** (Figure 10.13). The schema shows the names of the table(s) and fields, the primary keys for each table, and the relationships among the tables if more than one table is represented. You can click on the table name or a field name to display the properties in the Properties window.

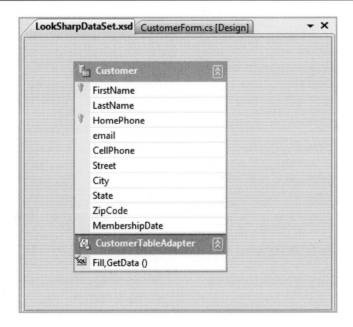

Right-click on the .xsd file in the Solution Explorer, select *Open With*, and select *XML Editor* to view the actual XML in the Visual Studio XML editor. ■

Notice in Figure 10.13 that at the bottom of the schema appears the TableAdapter for the table. The TableAdapter handles the `Fill` and `GetData` methods for the table. You can click on the *TableAdapter* row to display its properties in the Properties window or click on the *Fill,GetData()* row to view the properties of the Fill Query.

Binding Individual Data Fields

You can bind table fields from your dataset to many types of controls, such as labels, text boxes, combo boxes, and check boxes. Controls that are connected to fields in the database are referred to as **bound controls** or **data-bound controls**. The easiest way to create bound controls is to use the automatic binding features of the Data Sources window. You can set the data to display as details and then drag the table to the form. This technique creates individual text box controls for each field of data and a navigation control, which allows the user to move from one record to another. Figure 10.14 shows a form with data-bound text boxes; you will create this form in the next section.

Figure 10.14

Each text box is bound to one field from the table. As the user clicks the navigation buttons, all controls change to display the data for the next record.

The Data Sources Window

You can display the Data Sources window by selecting *Show Data Sources* from the *Data* menu. In a new project, you can use the Data Sources window to add a new data source (Figure 10.15).

Figure 10.15

Add a new data source in the Data Sources window.

When you select the option to add a new data source, the Data Source Configuration Wizard opens and steps you through selecting the file and table, just as you did in the earlier step-by-step exercise. The new data source appears in the Data Sources window. You can click on the table name to make a drop-down list available, from which you can select *Details* (Figure 10.16). Note that the default view is DataGridView, which is the view that you used in the previous step-by-step exercise. After you select Details view, the table's icon changes to match the view (Figure 10.17).

Note: The form's designer must be open for the table's check mark to appear.

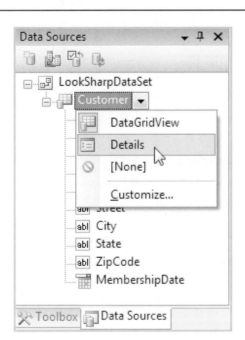

Figure 10.16

Drop down the list for the table name and select Details to bind each field to its own TextBox control.

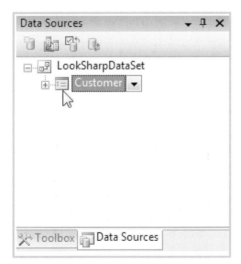

Figure 10.17

The table's icon changes to indicate Details view.

Database Details Program—Step-by-Step

This step-by-step exercise creates the data-bound Details view shown in Figure 10.14.

Begin a New Project

STEP 1: Create a new Windows project called Ch10IndividualFields.

STEP 2: Change the form's filename to "CustomerForm" and set the form's Text property to "Look Sharp Fitness Center".

STEP 3: Save all.

Set Up the Data Source

STEP 1:　Open the Data Sources window by selecting *Show Data Sources* from the *Data* menu.

STEP 2:　Click on *Add New Data Source* in the Data Sources window.

STEP 3:　In the Data Source Configuration wizard, make sure that *Database* is selected and click *Next*. Then click on the *New Connection* button.

STEP 4:　Browse to locate a copy of the LookSharp.mdf database file and click *Open*. Click *OK* and *Next*.

STEP 5:　Respond *Yes* to the question about copying the file to your project folder and click *Next* again.

STEP 6:　Open the *Tables* node and click in the box for the Customer table. Click *Finish*.

Create the Bound Controls

STEP 1:　In the Data Sources window, click on *Customer*, which makes a down arrow appear to the right of the name (Figure 10.18). *Warning*: The Form Designer must be open for the down arrow to appear.

F i g u r e   1 0 . 1 8

Click on the table name to make the drop-down list available.

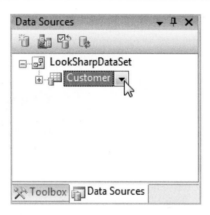

STEP 2:　Click on the down arrow and select *Details* (refer to Figure 10.16).

STEP 3:　Point to the Customer table name and drag the table to a position about an inch down from the top of the form.

STEP 4:　Change the text on the labels, the widths of the text boxes, and the form as desired. Notice in Figure 10.19 that the component tray holds five new components: a DataSet, BindingSource, TableAdapter, TableAdapterManager, and BindingNavigator, which provides the navigation buttons at the top of the form.

　　　Also notice the text of the labels on the form. The designer is smart enough to figure out multiple-word field names. For example, if your table names contain underscores or multiple capital letters, the smart labels will have the words separated by spaces. The Customer table has fields called "FirstName" and "LastName", but the labels say "First Name" and "Last Name".

STEP 5:　Run the project. Try the navigation buttons to step through the records.

Note: Remember that the ADO.NET dataset is loaded into memory and is disconnected from the database, so you can make changes to the records and use the navigation bar buttons for *Add New* (the record is added to the end of

Figure 10.19

Resize the form and controls of the automatically generated controls. The component tray holds the five automatically generated database components.

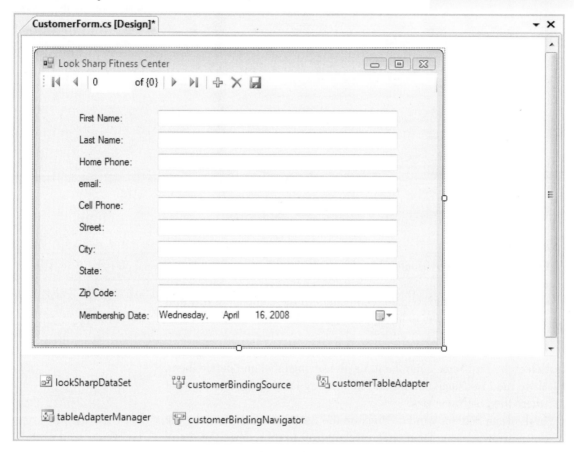

the dataset), *Delete*, and *Save* without making any changes to the original data file. To see any updates from one run to the next, set the database file's "Copy to Output Directory" property to "Copy if newer".

Selecting Records from a List

Many applications allow the user to select an item to display from a list. You can fill a list box or combo box with values from a database. Consider the previous program. A better approach might be to display the list of names in a drop-down list and allow the user to make a selection. Then, after the name is selected, the corresponding data elements fill the remaining fields (Figure 10.20).

You can easily select the control type for a bound control in the Data Sources window. The choices are TextBox, ComboBox, Label, LinkLabel, and ListBox.

Converting to Combo Box Selection—Step-by-Step

This step-by-step exercise converts the previous exercise to a selection application. Figure 10.20 shows the completed form.

Figure 10.20

The user can select a last name from the combo box. The labels automatically fill with the field values that correspond to that name.

Begin the Project

STEP 1: Open your Ch10IndividualFields project. It should contain text boxes for the data.

STEP 2: Click on the BindingNavigator component in the component tray and press the Delete key to delete the navigation bar from the form.

Change the Controls and Properties

STEP 1: Select the LastName control and its identifying label and delete them.

STEP 2: Move the FirstName control and identifying label down into the spot where the LastName was.

STEP 3: In the Data Sources window, click on the LastName field to make the down-arrow appear. Then click on the arrow to drop down the list of possible control types (Figure 10.21). Select *ComboBox* and notice that the icon for the LastName field changes to indicate a combo box.

Figure 10.21

Select ComboBox for the LastName field.

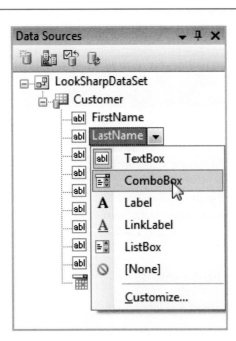

STEP 4: Drag the LastName field from the Data Sources window to the form, which will automatically create a ComboBox control and identifying label. Move and resize the combo box to match the text boxes (refer to Figure 10.20).

STEP 5: Click on the *Smart Tag* arrow for the combo box and select *Use data bound items*, which pops up some new fields for *Data Binding Mode* (Figure 10.22). Drop down the list for *Data Source* and select *customerBindingSource*. Select *LastName* for *Display Member*.

Figure 10.22

Set up the data binding for the LastName combo box using the smart tag.

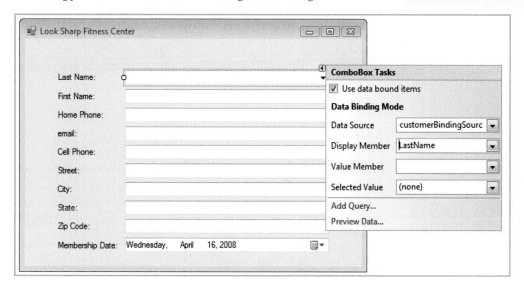

STEP 6: With the combo box still selected, scroll to the top of the properties in the Properties window and expand the entry for *(DataBindings)*. Click in the entry for *(Advanced)* and click its Properties button to open the *Formatting and Advanced Binding* dialog box. Drop down the entry for *Data Source Update Mode* and select *Never*. Click *OK*.

Note: Without this setting, each time the user makes a selection from the combo box, the database updating routines will attempt to add the selection as a new person to the table and generate a "duplicate" error message.

STEP 7: Reset the tab order for the controls on the form. You want the combo box to appear selected when the application begins, so it must be at the top of the tab sequence.

Run the Application

STEP 1: Run the program.

STEP 2: Drop down the combo box and select another last name. The other controls automatically fill with the data for the selected customer.

Selecting Fields from the Table

Often you only need to display some of the fields from a database table. You can select individual fields when you create the new data source, or select the fields later after you have created the data source.

Selecting Fields When You Create the Data Source

To set up a new dataset with selected fields, choose the *Add New Data Source* option from the *Data* menu or the Data Sources window. The Data Source Configuration wizard appears as described earlier. When you get to the *Choose Your Database Objects*, expand the *Tables* node and place a check mark on just the fields that you want (Figure 10.23).

Figure 10.23

Select only the fields that you want to include in the Data Source Configuration wizard.

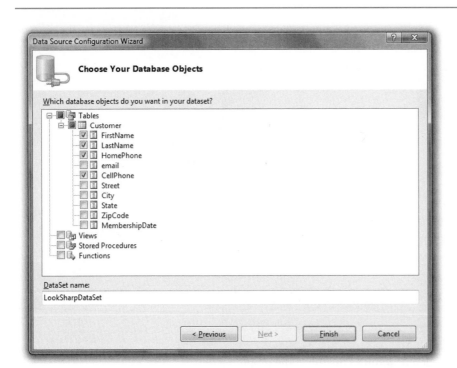

Selecting Fields after the Data Source Is Created

To modify the fields in a dataset after it has been created, select the dataset name in the Data Sources window. You can either click the *Configure DataSet with Wizard* button at the top of the window or right-click and choose the same option. You can make the field selection from the wizard as described in Figure 10.23, which will change the schema for your dataset.

Sorting the List Data

You cannot sort bound data in a combo box or list box using the Sorted property of the control. However, you can sort the records in the query that selects the data for the dataset. Although the SQL SELECT statement is generated automatically by the designer, you can find and modify it. In the Solution Explorer, double-click on the dataset's schema file, with the .xsd extension. In the displayed schema (Figure 10.24), click on the *Fill,GetData()* entry at the bottom, which displays the properties of the Fill command in the Properties window. Click on the Property button (. . .) for the CommandText property; the *Query Builder* dialog box will open. If you have any experience creating queries in Access, this dialog will look very familiar to you.

Figure 10.24

Click on the Fill,GetData() entry in the dataset schema to display the properties of the Fill *command in the Properties window.*

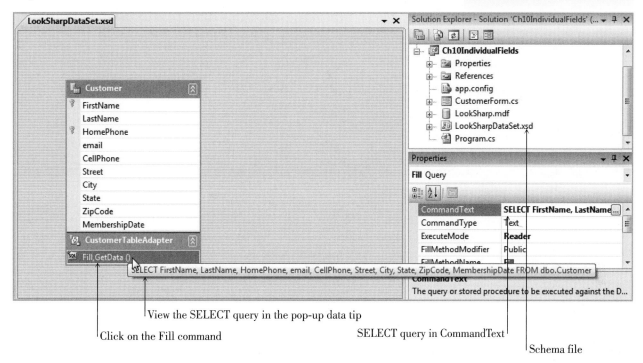

View the SELECT query in the pop-up data tip

Click on the Fill command

SELECT query in CommandText

Schema file

In the Query Builder, you can modify the SQL SELECT command that selects the data for the dataset. To sort by a field, drop down the *Sort Type* list for the desired field and choose *Ascending* or *Descending*. After you make the selection and press Enter, the SQL statement changes to include an ORDER BY clause (Figure 10.25), which sorts the data records as they are retrieved and makes the list items appear in sorted order. You also can type directly into the SELECT statement to make modifications, if you wish. Notice at the bottom of the Query Builder window that you can execute the query to preview its output in the lower part of the window. When you click *OK* on the *Query Builder* dialog box, you may receive a prompt asking if you want to regenerate update commands; say *Yes*.

Choosing the Control Type for Fields

When you drag a Details view to a form, by default text fields are represented by text boxes. You saw earlier that you can select a different type of control in the Data Sources window before dragging a control to the form. In the Data Sources window, click on a field name; a small down arrow appears to the right of the field name. Drop down the list and choose the control type (Figure 10.26). You can choose the control type for all controls and then drag the table to the form to create the Details view.

Note: You must have the form displayed in the Form Designer to select the control type for the field.

Select Ascending *for the* Sort Type *to sort the data by the LastName field. The SQL statement changes to include an* ORDER BY *clause.*

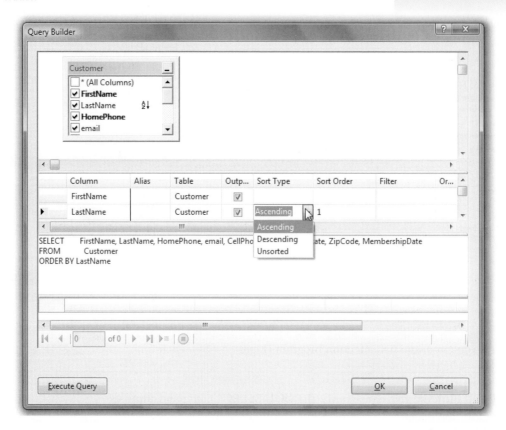

Select the control type for each control before creating the Details view.

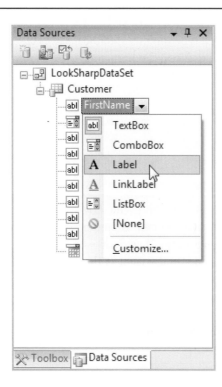

1. You drag a table name from the Data Sources window onto a form. What determines whether the action produces a bound grid or a set of individual fields?
2. How can you create data-bound text boxes? data-bound labels?
3. What properties of a ComboBox control must you set to bind the control to a data field?
4. How can you make the list items in a data-bound combo box appear in sorted order?

Selecting Records Using Web Forms

When you write database programs for the Web instead of Windows, you have a few more considerations. You still set up data sources and bind to controls, but the Web controls are considerably different from their Windows counterparts. You also have additional security issues for Web-based database applications.

A Web database application operates somewhat differently than a Windows application due to the nature of Web pages in a client/server environment. Remember that a Web page is stateless. Each time a page displays, it is a "new fresh page."

In the Web version of the list selection program (Figure 10.27), each time the user makes a selection from the list, a **postback** occurs, which is a round-trip to the server. After a postback, the Web page redisplays with only the selected data.

Figure 10.27

Allow the user to select a last name from the drop-down list; then the rest of the fields display for the selected name.

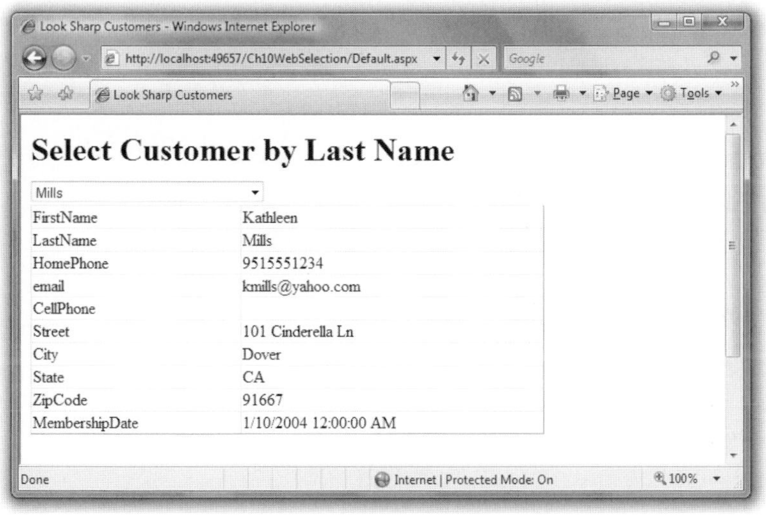

Security in Web Database Applications

Security is much tighter for Web database applications than for Windows applications. You wouldn't want an unauthorized user to be able to access data from the Web. If you set up a Web application that displays or allows modifications to data, you must require user authentication and set permission levels. Visual Studio integrates security features, which are generally strict by default, so that data will be secure unless you take steps to unprotect your files.

For the programs in this text, which introduce the basic features of Web programming, the challenge is to avoid security restrictions, rather than to secure your database. You will use a SQL Server database file, stored in the App_Data folder beneath the project folder. This folder has the necessary permissions for the default user of development projects.

Note: If you wish to use a database file stored in a folder other than the ProjectName\App_Data folder, the folder must have read and write permissions for the ComputerName\ASPNET user.

Creating the Web Selection Application—Step-by-Step

This step-by-step exercise develops the Web version of the selection program that you created earlier in Windows. The Web version must use two data sources rather than one. The drop-down list must have a separate data source from the one used for the individual fields of data. The finished application appears in Figure 10.27.

Begin a New Web Site

STEP 1: Select *File / New Web Site* and set the *Location* to the folder of your choice and "Ch10WebSelection" for the name. *Example*: C:\WebSites\ Ch10WebSelection.

STEP 2: Switch to Windows Explorer and copy LookSharp.mdf into the project's App_Data folder. *Example*: C:\WebSites\Ch10WebSelection\App_ Data\LookSharp.mdf. Or you can copy the file from another location and then click on the App_Data folder in the Solution Explorer window and paste the file (Ctrl + V). The database appears in the App_ Data folder after you click the Solution Explorer's *Refresh* button (Figure 10.28).

Figure 10.28

Click the Refresh button after you have copied the file into the App_Data folder to see the changes in the Solution Explorer.

Refresh button

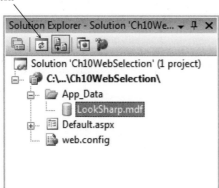

STEP 3: Click on the *Design* tab for Default.aspx.

STEP 4: Select *DOCUMENT* in the Properties window *Object* drop-down list and set the Web page's Title property to "Look Sharp Customers". Press Enter and save the file to make sure that the title is correctly saved.

STEP 5: Click at the top of the Web Form and type "Select Customer by Last Name". Select the text and enlarge the font and make it bold. You also can change the font, if you wish.

STEP 6: Click after the text and press Enter two or three times to move the insertion point down the page.

Set Up the Drop-Down List

STEP 1: Add a DropDownList control from the toolbox. In the smart tag select *Choose Data Source*.

STEP 2: In the Data Source Configuration wizard, drop down the list for *Select a data source*, select *New data source. . . .*

STEP 3: In the next page of the wizard, select *Database* (Figure 10.29). You can leave the ID of the data source set to SqlDataSource1. Click *OK*.

Figure 10.29

Set the data source to a SQL database.

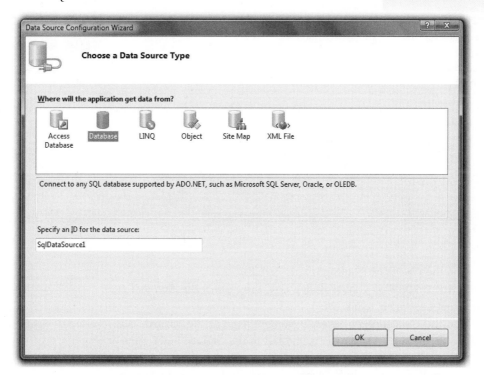

STEP 4: Next you set up the connection: Click on the *New Connection* button. If the data source does not say "Microsoft SQL Server Database File (SqlClient)", click on the *Change* button and make that selection.

STEP 5: In the *Add Connection* dialog box, browse to select the LookSharp. mdf file in the App_Data folder beneath the project folder. Click *Open*, *OK*, and *Next*. Click *Next* again.

STEP 6: On the *Configure the Select Statement* page, you will select the data fields for the dataset for the drop-down list. Click on (check) *LastName*.

*Select the **LastName** field and click on the **ORDER BY** button to set the sort order for the data.*

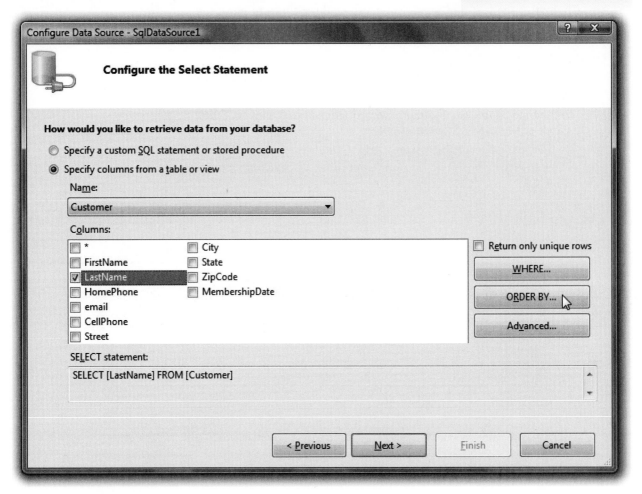

STEP 7: Click on the *ORDER BY* button (Figure 10.30).

STEP 8: In the *Add ORDER BY Clause* dialog box, drop down the *Sort by* list and select *LastName*. Click *OK*.

STEP 9: Back on the *Configure the Select Statement* page of the wizard, you can see the new ORDER BY clause added to the SQL SELECT statement (Figure 10.31).

STEP 10: Click *Next*. Before you click *Finish*, you can click on the *Test Query* button if you would like to see the records returned from the query you just created. Click *Finish*. The Data Source Configuration Wizard reappears.

STEP 11: In the *Choose a Data Source page*, LastName should be selected for both the data to display and the value of the field. Click *OK*.

STEP 12: Display the smart tag for the drop-down list again and select *Enable AutoPostBack* (Figure 10.32). This important step specifies that each time the user makes a new selection from the list, the page should be sent back to the server. This step is necessary to select and display the data for the selected customer.

Figure 10.31

An ORDER BY *clause is added to the* SQL SELECT *statement.*

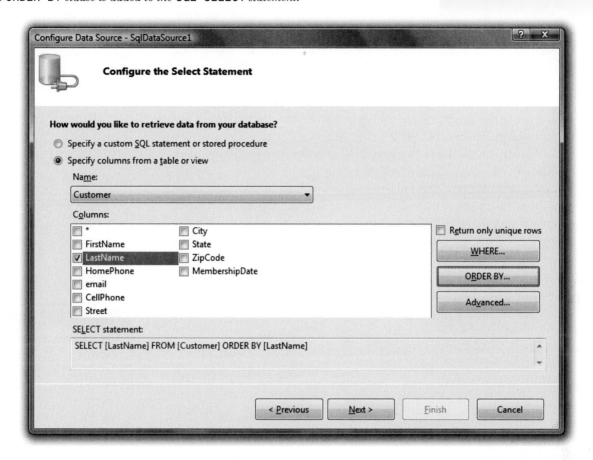

Figure 10.32

Select Enable AutoPost-Back *from the smart tag so that the user's selection will be sent to the server.*

STEP 13: Widen the DropDownList control so that it is wide enough to hold a customer's last name.

STEP 14: Press Enter two or three times following the list control.

Set Up the Additional Fields

STEP 1: In the toolbox, open the *Data* tab and click to view the available controls and components.

You can see tools for data sources, which is another way to add a new data source. The controls near the top of the list are those that can be bound to data.

STEP 2: Add a DetailsView control to the Web page. In the smart tag, drop down the *Choose a Data Source* list and select *New data source....* Do not choose *SqlDataSource1*, which you already created. The data for the DetailsView must be different from the data for the list.

STEP 3: Select *Database* and click *OK.* Then drop down the list and select the connection for LookSharp.mdf that you already created. The two data sources will share the same connection since they both refer to the same database file. Click *Next.*

STEP 4: For *Configure the Select Statement*, click on the box for all columns (the asterisk) and click the *WHERE* button.

STEP 5: In the *Add WHERE Clause* dialog box, you will set up the parameter used to select the correct data for the individual fields. Drop down the *Column* list and select *LastName*; then drop down the list for *Source* and select *Control.* The *Parameter properties* pop up on the right side of the dialog box. For *Control ID* select *DropDownList1* and notice the *SQL Expression* (Figure 10.33). This type of query is called a *parameterized query.*

Set up the selection parameter in the Add WHERE Clause dialog box.

STEP 6: Click on *Add* and view the WHERE clause at the bottom of the dialog box. It should say "[LastName] = @LastName" and the Value shows "DropDownList1.SelectedValue". If it isn't correct, you can click *Remove* and repeat step 5. Click *OK.*

Back on the *Configure Data Source* page, the SELECT statement should read:

```
SELECT * FROM [Customer] WHERE ([LastName] = @LastName)
```

STEP 7: Click *Next* and *Finish*.

STEP 8: Select the DetailsView control and click in the Width property in the Properties window. Although by default VS gives the control an absolute size based on pixels, you can base the size on a percentage. For the width, type "75%". Your form should resemble Figure 10.34; if it doesn't, select *Refresh Schema* from the SqlDataSource's *Smart Tag.*

If the font is too large, select the DetailsView control, select *Format / Font,* and choose a smaller font size.

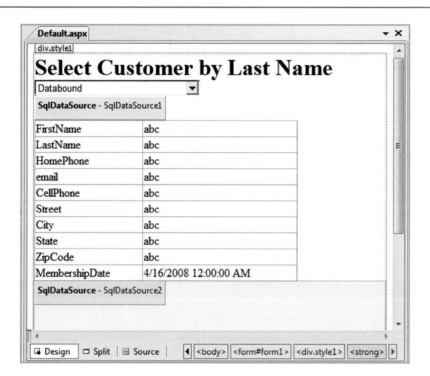

Figure 10.34

Set the Width property of the DetailsView control to 75%.

STEP 9: Save all.

Run the Application

STEP 1: Press Ctrl + F5 to test the application.

STEP 2: Make new selections from the list; the data fields below should change to match the selection.

Make the Project Portable

This optional step will make your Web application portable. The Web.config file has a hard-coded path for the connection to the database file. If you move or rename the Web site folder, the connection fails due to the path. You can modify the connection entry to make the project portable.

STEP 1: Open the Web.config file from the Solution Explorer and scroll to find the entry for the connection string. The path for AttachDbFilename will show the current folder where you created the Web site.

```
<appSettings/>
    <connectionStrings>
        <add name="LookSharpConnectionString" connectionString="Data
Source=.\SQLEXPRESS;AttachDbFilename=&quot;C:\Users\UserName\Documents\Visual
Studio2008\WebSites\Ch10WebSelection\App_Data\LookSharp.mdf&quot;;Integrated
Security=True;Connect Timeout=30;User Instance=True"
            providerName="System.Data.SqlClient" />
    </connectionStrings>
```

STEP 2: Very carefully select the text that shows the path (but not the file-name). Replace the highlighted text with "|DataDirectory|". (That is, "DataDirectory" with a vertical bar before and after, with no spaces.)

The completed entry should look like this:

```
AttachDbFilename=&quot;|DataDirectory|LookSharp.mdf&quot;;
```

STEP 3: Save and close the project.

After you have changed the Web.config file, you can rename your project folder and move it to another location. The portable connection string will always point to the database file in the Web site's App_Data folder. Make sure that the project is not open in the IDE and copy the complete folder from one computer or location to another. When you move a Web project, you must first open the IDE, select *Open Web Site*, and browse to the folder.

LINQ

This section introduces and demonstrates **Language-Integrated Query (LINQ)**, a recent addition to Visual C#. LINQ is a general-purpose query language that can ask a question of any data that are defined as an object, a database, or XML. The source of the data may be a database but could also be any collection such as an array or the collection for a list box. C# includes a LINQ to SQL component to convert database items to objects and a LINQ to XML component for converting XML document collections to objects.

Setting up a Query

You write a LINQ query using operators that are standard, regardless of the source of the data. The primary operators in a query (Table 10.1) are `from`, `in`, `where`, and `select`. You can see a complete list of LINQ operators, which includes operators for ordering and grouping, in the MSDN Help page "Query Keywords (C# Reference)".

The LINQ Query—General Form

```
variableName = from itemName in objectName select fieldName|listOfFields|items
```

Primary LINQ Operators

Operator	Purpose	Example
from	Name of a single element.	from anItem
in	Specifies the source of the data (all of the elements to query).	in amountDecimal
where	A Boolean expression that specifies the condition for the query.	where anItem < 100m
select	Execute the query. The identifier determines the type of data element(s) that will be returned from the query.	select anItem

The variableName in the format does not need a data type assigned. In Visual Studio 2008, if the data type is not specified, the compiler can assign a type in a process called *type inference*. To see an example of type inference, type var anAmount = 5; and use anAmount in another statement, such as anAmount++;. Hover the mouse over anAmount in the second statement and the editor pops up the data type, which is inferred to be int. Change the original assignment to 5.5 and hover over anAmount again; this time the type is double. Although it is not wise to use type inference when you know the type of the data, the feature was introduced into C# to allow some of the operators in LINQ (order by, where) to be used on unspecified data types.

The result of the query is retrieved from the object represented by variableName.

The LINQ Query—Example

```
var belowMinimumQuery=
    from anItem in amountDecimal
    where anItem < 100m
    select anItem;
```

In this example, amountDecimal is an array and anItem is a single element, which is not declared elsewhere. The query is similar to a foreach—it steps through the array, assigns each element to anItem, and performs the comparison. Use belowMinimumQuery to retrieve the result of the query.

Creating a LINQ Project—Step-by-Step

The following step-by-step example queries an array of decimal numbers. The query selects each element from the array and determines whether it is less than 100. The select statement executes the query. The results of the query are displayed in a ListBox control, by assigning the ToList method of the query to the DataSource property of the ListBox control.

In this example, you will use the ToList method of a collection, which works much like the ToString method but returns a list of items.

Set up the LINQ Project

STEP 1: Open a new Windows application project, calling it Ch10LINQ.

STEP 2: Name the form LinqForm and set its Text property to "Execute a LINQ query".

STEP 3: Add a ListBox control; name it belowMinimumListBox.

STEP 4: Add a Button control. Name it executeButton and set the Text to "Display Results of LINQ Query".

Write the Code

STEP 1: Double-click on the button to access the executeButton_Click event handler.

STEP 2: Type in the following code:

```
// Display the amounts below the minimum of 100.
decimal[] amountDecimal = { 100m, 50m, 35.75m, 123.1m, 12.4m };
var belowMinimumQuery =
    from anItem in amountDecimal
    where anItem < 100m
    select anItem;
belowMinimumListBox.DataSource = belowMinimumQuery.ToList();
```

Run the Program

STEP 1: Run the program. It should retrieve the numbers less than 100, convert them to a list, and assign the list as the data source of the list box (Figure 10.35).

Figure 10.35

Using a LINQ query to fill a ListBox control.

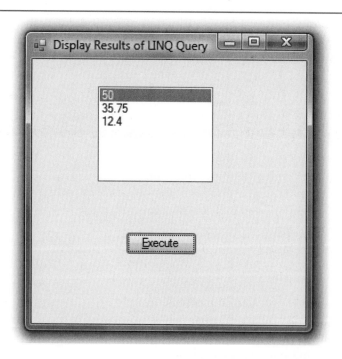

LINQ to SQL

You can apply a LINQ query to a relational database, even though the database's language is not based on objects. To use LINQ with a database, you need to add a new item to a database project called the "LINQ to SQL Classes" template. In a project that already has a data source defined, select *Project / Add New Item* and select *LINQ TO SQL Classes* from the *Templates* list (Figure 10.36).

Add the LINQ to SQL Classes template to a database project to query a database.

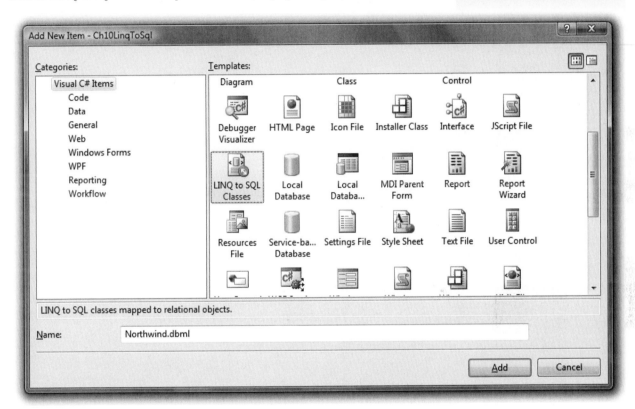

When you add the LINQ to SQL template to a project, you create a strongly typed DataContext class. You set up the object database model using a new design surface with two panes, which appears in the main Document window (Figure 10.37). Using the visual designer, you can simply drag database tables from the Server Explorer (or the Database Explorer in the Express Edition) to the design surface. The tables that you add to the left pane are referred to as *entities*; the right pane holds optional stored procedures or methods. Figure 10.38 shows the design surface with the Employee class. You may notice that Visual Studio changes the plural table name to singular when it creates a class; the Employees table became the Employee class.

When writing the code, you refer to the DataContext. The Employees table is a member of the Northwind database. The corresponding DataContext is automatically called the NorthWindDataContext. Once you have created the DataContext class, you can create a DataContext object in code. You can then

Figure 10.37

Adding the LINQ to SQL Classes template to a database project creates a new design surface for visualizing your data.

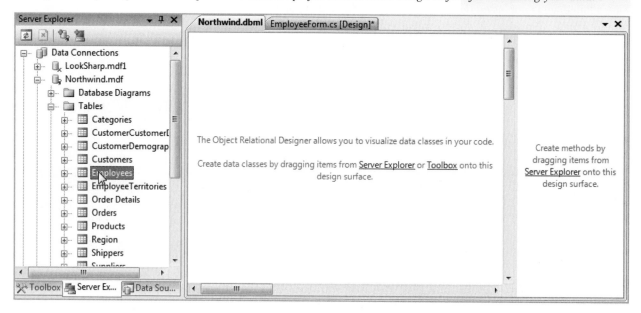

query the database using the same LINQ operators that you saw in the previous section.

```
// Class-level declaration.
NorthwindDataContext northWindDataBase = new NorthwindDataContext();

private void EmployeeForm_Load(object sender, EventArgs e)
{
    // Query the Employees table using LINQ and the Employee class.
    var employeeQuery =
        from anEmployee in northWindDataBase.Employees
        select anEmployee;

    employeeDataGridView.DataSource = employeeQuery.ToList();
}
```

Next, let's add a `where` clause to list only the ladies. Figure 10.39 shows the completed output.

```
// Class-level declaration.
NorthwindDataContext northWindDataBase = new NorthwindDataContext();

private void EmployeeForm_Load(object sender, EventArgs e)
{
    // Query the Employees table using LINQ and the Employee class.
    var employeeQuery =
        from anEmployee in northWindDataBase.Employees
        where anEmployee.TitleOfCourtesy.ToString() == "Ms."
        select anEmployee;

    employeeDataGridView.DataSource = employeeQuery.ToList();
}
```

Figure 10.38

The new Employee class, based on the Employees table of the Northwind database.

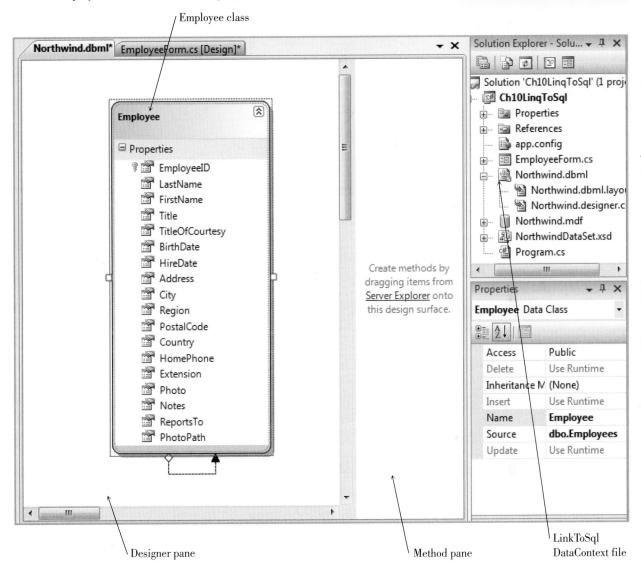

Employee class

Designer pane

Method pane

Create methods by dragging items from Server Explorer onto this design surface.

LinkToSql DataContext file

Figure 10.39

Using a LINQ query to retrieve and display employee data in a DataGridView control.

> ## Feedback 10.4

1. What is LINQ?
2. What can be queried with LINQ?
3. Explain what is meant by type inference.

Your Hands-On Programming Example

Create a Windows application that contains a drop-down list of last names from the LookSharp.mdf database file. When the user selects a last name, display the corresponding first name, phone numbers, and e-mail address in text boxes. Sort the last names in ascending order.

Planning the Project

Sketch the form (Figure 10.40), which your users sign off as meeting their needs. Figure 10.41 shows the form in Design mode.

Select the control types for the controls in the Data Sources window before dragging the Details view to the form.

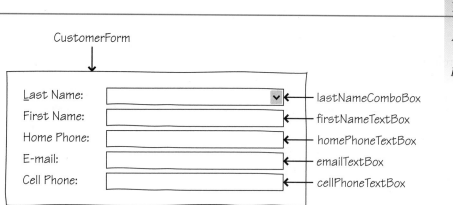

Figure 10.40

A planning sketch of the Windows form for the hands-on programming example.

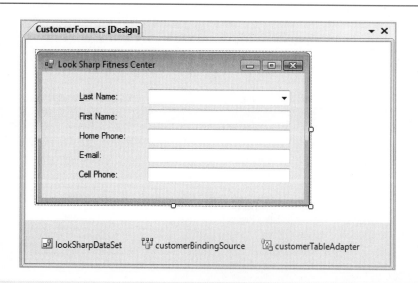

Figure 10.41

The form for the hands-on programming example in Design mode, showing the component tray.

Plan the Objects and Properties

Object	Property	Setting
CustomerForm	Text	Look Sharp Fitness Center
customerBindingSource	Name	CustomerBindingSource
lookSharpDataset	Name	LookSharpDataset
customerTableAdapter	Name	CustomerTableAdapter
lastNameLabel	Name Text	lastNameLabel &LastName
lastNameComboBox	Name DataSource DisplayMember DataSourceUpdateMode	lastNameComboBox customerBindingSource LastName Never
Text boxes	Name	Keep the default names

Plan the Procedures No code is required if all properties are correctly set.

Write the Project

- Create a new Windows project.

- Create the new SQL Server data source based on the LookSharp.mdf data file. Include only those fields that appear on the finished form.

- Set the control types to a combo box and text boxes for the fields.

- Drag a Details view of the data to the form and rearrange the controls to match the sketch in Figure 10.40. Figures 10.41 and 10.42 show the completed form.

- Set the properties of the combo box according to your plan.

- Thoroughly test the project.

F i g u r e   1 0 . 4 2

The form for the hands-on programming example.

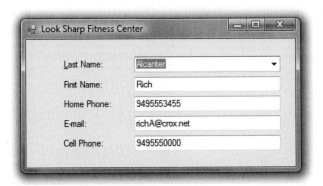

The Project Code

Isn't it amazing that so powerful a program doesn't require any code at all?

Summary

1. Visual Studio uses Microsoft's ADO.NET technology to access databases in many different formats.

2. ADO.NET provides several types of connections for databases: OleDb, SQL Server, Odbc, and Oracle.

3. Databases are composed of tables of related information. Each table is organized into rows representing records and columns containing fields of data.

4. The primary key field uniquely identifies a row or record in a table.

5. ADO.NET stores and transfers data using a format called XML (Extensible Markup Language), which can be used by many different platforms.

6. Many controls can be bound to a database including labels, text boxes, list boxes, or a DataGridView.

7. A binding source establishes a link to a data source, which is a specific data file or server.

8. A table adapter handles the transfer of data between a data source and a dataset.

9. A dataset stores information from the database in the memory of the computer. A dataset can contain multiple tables and their relationships.

10. You can create datasets by using the configuration wizard that displays when *Add New Data Source* is selected from the *Data* menu or the Data Sources window.

11. A table adapter uses a SQL SELECT statement to specify the data to retrieve.

12. You can add a DataGridView to a form and automatically bind the grid to a data source.

13. The dataset's schema is defined in the .xsd file that appears in the project folder.

14. To bind individual controls to data fields, select *Details* for the table in the Data Sources window and drag the table to the form.

15. You can select a different type of control to display bound data in the Data Sources window.

16. It is common to allow the user to select a value from a list and then display the data values for the selected item in bound labels.

17. To use a bound combo box for selection, you must set its DataSource and DisplayMember properties. You also should set the DataSourceUpdate-Mode to *Never*.

18. You can select a subset of the fields in a table for a dataset.

19. In a Web database application, you must be very aware of the security requirements.

20. Each selection from a list requires a postback to the server to fill the bound controls. You must set the AutoPostBack property of the drop-down list to *true* to make the postback occur.

21. A Web selection program requires a parameterized query to retrieve the data matching the list selection. The Windows program does not have the same requirement.

22. LINQ is a query language that works on object data types.

Key Terms

BindingSource *416*
bound controls *423*
column *412*
data binding *415*
Data Designer *423*
data-bound controls *423*
DataGridView control *417*
dataset *416*
field *412*

Language-Integrated
  Query (LINQ) *440*
postback *433*
primary key field *412*
record *412*
row *412*
table *412*
table adapter *416*
XML *413*

Review Questions

1. Explain the purpose of a binding source.
2. Explain the purpose of the table adapter component.
3. What is a dataset?
4. How is a DataGridView control used?
5. Explain the steps to change a data source from DataGridView to Details.
6. What options are available for styles of a bound control?
7. What is the purpose of the Data Sources window?
8. How do a Windows and a Web version of a list selection program vary? Why?
9. What is a parameterized query? When would it be used?
10. What is a postback? When does it occur?
11. What is the purpose of LINQ? Name three operators.

Programming Exercises

Each of the database files can be found in the StudentData folder on the text Web site (www.mhhe.com/C#2008).

Note: Each of these exercises can be written as a Windows application or as a Web application.

10.1: Write an application to display book information from the RnrBooks.mdf database. Display the Books table in a grid. *Hint*: For a Web application, use a DataList or GridView control for the grid.

    Optional: Use a LINQ query.

10.2: Write an application to display book information from the RnrBooks.mdf database. Display an alphabetized list of titles in a drop-down list for selection. When the user selects the Title, display the corresponding ISBN, Author, and Publisher in labels.

10.3: Write a project to display the Publishers table from the Contacts.mdf database. The Publishers table has the following fields: PubID (the key field), Name, Company Name, Address, City, State, Zip, Telephone, and Fax.

    Allow the user to select the publisher name from a sorted drop-down list; display the rest of the fields in labels or text boxes.

Case Studies

Custom Supplies Mail Order

1. Create a Windows application to display the Custom Supplies Mail Order Customer table from the CsMail.mdf database in labels. Use the navigation bar to move from record to record.
2. Create a Web application to display the Customer table in a grid on a Web Form. *Hint*: Use a DataList or GridView control for the grid.

The Customer table holds these fields:
CustomerID
LastName
FirstName
Address
City
State
ZipCode

Christopher's Car Center

Create a Windows application or a Web application to display the Christopher's Car Center Vehicle table from the CCCar.mdf database. Display the InventoryID sorted in a combo box. Display the remaining fields in individual controls.

The table holds these fields:
InventoryID
Manufacturer
ModelName
Year
VehicleID
CostValue

Xtreme Cinema

1. Create a Windows application to display the information from the Studio table in the XtremeCinema.mdf database. Allow the user to select the studio name from a sorted drop-down list and display the rest of the fields in labels.
2. Create a Windows or Web application to display the Studio table in a grid. *Hint*: Use a DataList or GridView control for the grid.

The Studio table contains these fields:
StudioID
StudioName
ContactPerson
Phone

Cool Boards

1. Create a Windows application to display the Product table from the CoolBoards.mdf database file. Allow the user to select the product ID from a sorted drop-down list and display the rest of the fields in labels.
2. Create a Windows or a Web application to display the Product table in a grid. *Hint*: For a Web application, use a GridView control for the grid.

The Product table contains these fields:
ProductID
Description
MfgID
Unit
Cost
LastOrderDate
LastOrderQuantity

11

Data Files

1. Store and retrieve data in files using streams.

2. Save the values from a list box and reload for the next program run.

3. Check for the end of file.

4. Test whether a file exists.

5. Display the standard *Open File* and *Save File As* dialog boxes to allow the user to choose the file.

Data Files

Many computer applications require that data be saved from one run to the next. Although the most common technique is to use a database, many times a database is overkill. Perhaps you just need to store a small amount of data, such as the date of the last program run, the highest ID number assigned, a user preference, or the property values of an object to transfer to another application. This chapter deals with techniques to store and retrieve **data files** on disk.

   Note that default security policy for the Internet and for intranets does not allow access to disk files. This chapter presents only basic file input and output (I/O) for Windows applications.

File I/O

You can read and write data in a disk file. You may have the user enter data into text boxes that you want to store in a file; that is called *writing* or *output*. At a later time, when you want to retrieve the data from the file, that is *reading* or *input* (Figure 11.1).

Figure 11.1

Write output from a program to a file; read input from the file into a program.

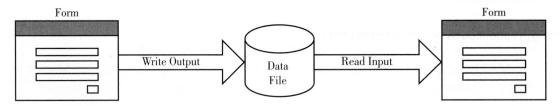

Simple File I/O

The .NET Framework includes classes to support simplified data file input and output (IO). You can use the methods of these classes to quickly and easily write and read data files.

Writing and Reading Text Files

The quickest and easiest way to write text files in C# is to use the **WriteAllText, WriteAllLines,** or **AppendAllText methods** of the **File class**. These methods specify the filename and the text string or array to write to the file. Using WriteAllText or WriteAllLines replaces any existing file. The AppendAllText method adds (appends) the data to the end of the file. The File class is in the System.IO namespace, so you must add using System.IO to the top of your code or use the full name System.IO.File for each reference.

The WriteAllText Method—General Form

General Form

```
File.WriteAllText(FileName, StringToWrite);
```

The WriteAllLines Method—General Form

```
File.WriteAllLines(FileName, ArrayToWrite);
```

The AppendAllText Method—General Form

```
File.AppendAllText(FileName, StringToWrite);
```

When you use these methods, there is no need to open or close a file. Each of the methods opens a file, creates a file if one does not already exist, writes the data, and closes the file. For WriteAllText and WriteAllLines, if the file already exists, it is overwritten; for AppendAllText, the new data are written at the end of an existing file. For the filename, you also can specify a complete path; if the path does not exist, an exception occurs.

The File Write Methods—Examples

```
File.WriteAllText("C:\FinalCount.txt", CountInteger.ToString());

string[] phoneData = new string[10];
File.WriteAllLines("TextFile.txt", phoneData);

File.AppendAllText("Names.txt", nameString);
```

You may want to write just one field, such as a date or a reference number, to a file. The best choice for that situation is the WriteAllText method. When you want to add data to an existing file, use the AppendAllText method.

A Simple File Write Example

The following example allows the user to enter names and phone numbers (Figure 11.2). It concatenates a name and phone number together with New-Line characters and appends each string to the end of the file.

```
private void saveButton_Click(object sender, EventArgs e)
{
    // Save the record to the end of the file.

    string fileString = "TextFile.txt";
    string recordString = nameTextBox.Text + "\n" + phoneTextBox.Text + "\n";

    // This line opens the file, appends text to the end of the file, and closes it.
    System.IO.File.AppendAllText(fileString, recordString);

    // Clear the screen fields for the next record.
    phoneTextBox.Clear();
    nameTextBox.Clear();
    nameTextBox.Focus();
}
```

Figure 11.2

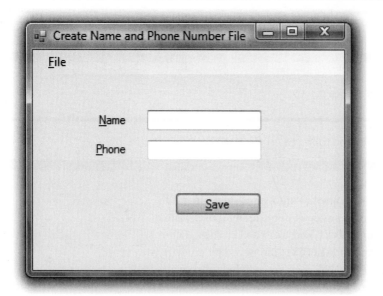

The user enters data into the text boxes and clicks the Save button, which writes this record in the file.

Another alternative for the name and phone number file is to save the data into an array and then perform a single file operation with the WriteAllLines method. Note that this version of the program replaces any previous data with a new file.

```
//Program:        Ch11SimpleFileWriteAllLines
//Programmer:     Bradley/Millspaugh
//Date:           June 2009
//Description:    Allows the user to enter names and phone numbers and
//                saves them in a file, overwriting any previous data.
//                Uses the simplified file access methods.
//Folder:         Ch11SimpleFileWriteAllLines

using System;
using System.Collections.Generic;
using System.ComponentModel;
using System.Data;
using System.Drawing;
using System.Linq;
using System.Text;
using System.Windows.Forms;
using System.IO;

namespace Ch11SimpleFileWriteAllLines
{
    public partial class PhoneForm : Form
    {

        // Class-level variables.
        string[] phoneData = new string[10];
        int indexInteger;

        public PhoneForm()
        {
            InitializeComponent();
        }
```

```
        private void ExitToolStripMenuItem_Click(object sender, EventArgs e)
        {
            // Close the form.

            this.Close();
        }

        private void saveButton_Click(object sender, EventArgs e)
        {
            // Write to the file.
            File.WriteAllLines("TextFile.txt", phoneData);
        }

        private void addButton_Click(object sender, EventArgs e)
        {
            // Add data to the array.
            phoneData[indexInteger++] = nameTextBox.Text;
            phoneData[indexInteger++] = phoneTextBox.Text;

            // Clear the fields for the next record.
            phoneTextBox.Clear();
            nameTextBox.Clear();
            nameTextBox.Focus();
        }
    }
}
```

To read the data back into an array, you can use either the **ReadAllText** or **ReadAllLines method**. The ReadAllText method reads the entire file into a single string; the ReadAllLines method reads the file into a string array.

The ReadAllText and ReadAllLines Methods—General Forms

```
aString = File.ReadAllText(FilePath);
anArrayString = File.ReadAllLines(FilePath);
```

Both the ReadAllText and ReadAllLines methods fail if the file or path does not exist, so you should place the methods in a try/catch block.

The ReadAllLines Method—Example

```
try
{
    // Read the entire file into an array.
    string[] fileString = File.ReadAllLines("TextFile.txt");
    // Display the array in a list box.
    phoneListBox.DataSource = fileString.ToList();
}
catch
{
    MessageBox.Show("File or path not found or invalid.");
}
```

This example reads an entire file into an array and displays the data in a list box.

The ReadAllText Method—Example

```
try
{
    // Read entire file into a single string.
    string fileString = File.ReadAllText("TextFile.txt");
    // Split the string into individual fields of a string array.
    string[] aFieldString = fileString.Split('\n');
    // Display the array in a list box.
    phoneListBox.Items.AddRange(aFieldString);
}
catch
{
    MessageBox.Show("File or path not found or invalid.");
}
```

As you can see, it takes one extra step to split the long string into individual strings when you use the `ReadAllText` method.

Note: You can easily display an array in a list box by using either of the two methods shown in the two example boxes: setting the list's DataSource property to an array, as shown in the `ReadAllLines` example, or using the `Items.AddRange` method, as shown in the `ReadAllText` example. You can use either technique for either method.

The `ReadAllText, ReadAllLines, WriteAllText, WriteAllLines`, and `AppendAllText` methods are handy when you need to read or write a small amount of data.

Viewing the Contents of a File

After you run your project, you can view the new file using a text editor such as Notepad. You also can view the file in the Visual Studio IDE. Unless you specified a path to a folder in a different location, by default your new file is created in the bin\Debug folder in your project folder.

To view the file, select the project name in the Solution Explorer. If you don't see the bin and obj folders listed, click on the *Show All Files* button at the top of the window. Then you can expand the bin folder and the Debug folder, find the data file's name (Figure 11.3), and open it. The contents of the file should appear in the Editor window. If the filename does not appear when you open the bin\Debug folder, click on the *Refresh* button at the top of the Solution Explorer.

.NET File Handling

The simple file handling that you saw in the previous section can work well for small amounts of data in a program. But for more robust and universal file handling, which is the same for all .NET languages, you will want to use streams.

Figure 11.3

View the contents of your new file in the Visual Studio IDE.

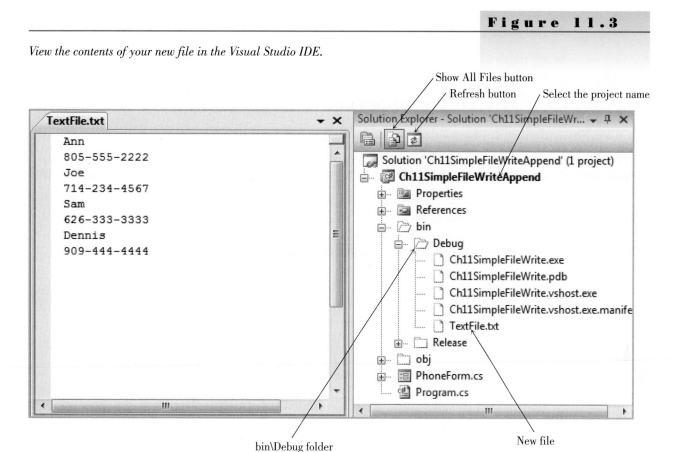

Show All Files button

Refresh button

Select the project name

bin\Debug folder

New file

File Handling Using Streams

.NET uses streams for file input and output. A **stream** is designed to transfer a series of bytes from one location to another. Streams are classes that have methods and properties, just like any other class. The stream classes are found in the **System.IO namespace**. You can save the trouble of fully qualifying references by adding a `using` statement to the top of the file, before the `namespace` statement.

```
using System.IO;

namespace Ch11WriteFile
```

In C#, the most straightforward way to read and write small amounts of data is to use the **StreamReader** and **StreamWriter** classes. Generally, you write the StreamWriter code first, to create the data file. Then you can write the StreamReader code to read the file that you just created.

Writing Data in a File Using a StreamWriter

To write data to a file, you first have the user input the data into text boxes and then write the data to the disk. The steps for writing data are

- Declare a new StreamWriter object, which also declares the name of the data file.

- Use the StreamWriter's `WriteLine` method to copy the data to a buffer in memory. (A buffer is just a temporary storage location.)

- Call the StreamWriter's `Close` method, which transfers the data from the buffer to the file and releases the system resources used by the stream.

Instantiating a StreamWriter Object—General Form

```
StreamWriter ObjectName = new StreamWriter("FileName");
StreamWriter ObjectName = new StreamWriter("FileName", BooleanAppend);
```

You declare a new StreamWriter object for writing data to a file. The first argument in the constructor specifies the name of the file. The default location for the file is where the program executable (.exe) is placed, which is the bin\Debug folder beneath the folder for the current project. You also can specify the complete path of the file.

In the second version of the StreamWriter constructor, you can specify that you want to append data to an existing file. Specify *true* to append. By default, the option is set to *false*, and the old data file is deleted and a new data file is created, in effect overwriting any existing data.

Instantiating a new StreamWriter object opens the file. The file must be open before you can write in the file. If the file does not already exist, a new one is created. If you don't use a full qualifying path, then the file is opened or created in the project's bin\Debug folder where the program executable is located. Because no exception occurs whether or not the file exists, you can declare the StreamWriter object at the top of the class or inside a method. If you do use a full path in the filename, then you should instantiate the StreamWriter object in a `try`/`catch` block in case the path does not exist.

Use .txt as your extension to follow conventions and allow for easy viewing of the file in Notepad. ∎

Instantiating a StreamWriter Object—Examples

```
StreamWriter phoneStreamWriter = new StreamWriter("Phone.txt");
StreamWriter namesStreamWriter = new StreamWriter("C:\\MyFiles\\Names.txt");
StreamWriter logStreamWriter = new StreamWriter("C:\\MyFiles\\LogFile.txt", true);
StreamWriter namesStreamWriter = new StreamWriter(@"C:\MyFiles\Names.txt");
```

Note: To include a literal backslash in a string, you can either use the escape sequence (\\) or place an at-sign (@) before the literal, which specifies that a backslash not be treated as an escape sequence. You also can replace the backslash in a path with a forward slash, which is easier to do and works perfectly well.

The StreamWriter object has both a **Write** and a **WriteLine method**. The difference between the two is a carriage-return character. The `Write` method places items consecutively in the file with no delimiter (separator). The `WriteLine` method places an Enter (carriage return) between items. We will use the `WriteLine` in this chapter because we want to easily retrieve the individual data elements later.

The WriteLine Method—General Form

```
ObjectName.WriteLine(DataToWrite);
```

The DataToWrite argument may be string or numeric. The `WriteLine` method converts any numeric data to string and actually writes string data in the file.

The WriteLine Method—Examples

Examples

```
phoneStreamWriter.WriteLine(nameTextBox.Text);
phoneStreamWriter.WriteLine(phoneTextBox.Text);
namesStreamWriter.WriteLine("Sammy");
bankBalanceStreamWriter.WriteLine(balanceDecimal.ToString());
```

If you are inputting data from the user and writing in a file, you generally place the `WriteLine` in a button click event handler. The following phone list example is similar to the earlier file-writing program but uses a StreamWriter object, rather than the `AppendAllText` method. You can refer to Figure 11.2 to see the data entry form.

```
private void saveButton_Click(object sender, System.EventArgs e)
{
    // Save the record to the file.

    phoneStreamWriter.WriteLine(nameTextBox.Text);
    phoneStreamWriter.WriteLine(phoneTextBox.Text);
    nameTextBox.Clear();
    phoneTextBox.Clear();
    nameTextBox.Focus();
}
```

The *Save* button writes the data from the screen to the StreamWriter object and then clears the screen.

Closing a File

After you finish writing data in a file, you must close the file. Closing a file is good housekeeping; it finishes writing all data from the stream's buffer to the disk and releases the system resources. Use the StreamWriter's **Close method**, which is similar to closing a form. A common location for the `Close` method is in your program's `Exit` command or the form's FormClosing event handler (see page 470).

```
private void exitButton_Click(object sender, System.EventArgs e)
{
    // End the project.

    phoneStreamWriter.Close();
    this.Close();
}
```

If you fail to close a file when you are finished with it, the file may remain open for an indefinite time and sometimes may become unusable. See "The Form_FormClosing Event Handler" section later in this chapter.

TIP

It's best to open a file only when it is needed and close it as soon as you are done with it so that you don't tie up system resources unnecessarily. ∎

Reading Data from a File Using a StreamReader

You use the StreamReader class to read the data from a file that you created with a StreamWriter.

The steps for reading the data from a file are the following:

• Declare an object of the StreamReader class. The constructor declares the filename and optional path. This statement opens the file so that you can read from it.

• Use the `ReadLine` method to read the data. You may need to use a loop to retrieve multiple records.

• When finished, close the stream using the StreamReader's `Close` method.

Declaring and Instantiating a StreamReader Object—General Form

```
// Declare a class-level variable.
private StreamReader ObjectName;

// Inside a method.
ObjectName = new StreamReader("FileName");
```

The StreamReader class works in much the same way as the StreamWriter. However, the file must exist in the location where the application expects it. If no such file exists, an exception occurs. For this reason, you must instantiate the StreamReader object in a method so that you can enclose it in a `try`/`catch` block.

Declaring and Instantiating a StreamReader Object—Examples

```
try
{
    StreamReader namesStreamReader = new StreamReader("C:\\MyFiles\\Names.txt");
}
catch
{
    MessageBox.Show("File does not exist.");
}

// Declare a class-level variable.
StreamReader phoneStreamReader;
...
// In a method, to catch an exception for a missing file.
try
{
    phoneStreamReader = new StreamReader("Phone.txt");
}
catch
{
    MessageBox.Show("File does not exist.");
}
```

Using the ReadLine Method

Use the StreamReader's **ReadLine method** to read the previously saved data. Each time you execute the method, it reads the next line from the file. Assign the value from the read to the desired location, such as a label, a text box, or a string variable. The ReadLine method has no arguments.

```
nameTextBox.Text = phoneStreamReader.ReadLine();
```

Checking for the End of the File

Use the StreamReader's **Peek method** to check for the end of file. The Peek method looks at the next element without really reading it. The value returned when you peek beyond the last element is negative 1 (−1).

```
if (phoneStreamReader.Peek() != -1)
{
    nameLabel.Text = phoneStreamReader.ReadLine();
    phoneLabel.Text = phoneStreamReader.ReadLine();
}
```

Note that the ReadLine method does not throw an exception when you attempt to read past the end of the file.

You must always make sure to read the data elements in the same order in which they were written. Otherwise, your output will display the wrong values. For example, if you reversed the two lines in the program segment above, the phone number would display for the name and vice versa. The ReadLine method just reads the next line and assigns it to the variable or property that you specify.

The File Read Program

Here is the completed program that reads the name and phone numbers from a file and displays them on the form (Figure 11.4). Each time the user clicks

Figure 11.4

Each time the user clicks Read Next, the next record is read from the file and displayed in the labels.

Read Next, the program reads and displays the next record. Note that for this example program, we copied the Phone.txt file from the bin\Debug folder of the Ch11WriteFile project to the bin\Debug folder of this project. You also could specify the exact path of the file.

```csharp
/*
Program:       Ch11ReadFile
Programmer:    Bradley/Millspaugh
Date:          June 2009
Description:   Retrieve the information stored in a data file
               and display it on the screen.
               Uses a StreamReader.*/

using System;
using System.Drawing;
using System.Collections;
using System.ComponentModel;
using System.Windows.Forms;
using System.Data;
using System.IO;

namespace Ch11ReadFile
{
    public class DisplayFileForm : Form
    {

        private StreamReader phoneStreamReader;

        public DisplayFileForm()
        {
            InitializeComponent();
        }

        private void exitButton_Click(object sender, System.EventArgs e)
        {
            // End the project.

            phoneStreamReader.Close();
            this.Close();
        }

        private void DisplayRecord()
        {
            // Read and display the next record.

            if (phoneStreamReader.Peek() != -1)
            {
                nameLabel.Text = phoneStreamReader.ReadLine();
                phoneLabel.Text = phoneStreamReader.ReadLine();
            }
        }

        private void nextButton_Click(object sender, System.EventArgs e)
        {
            // Read the next record.

            DisplayRecord();
        }
```

```
        private void DisplayFileForm_Load(object sender, System.EventArgs e)
        {
            // Open the file and display the first record.

            try
            {
                phoneStreamReader = new StreamReader("Phone.txt");
                DisplayRecord();
            }
            catch
            {
                // File is not found.
                MessageBox.Show("File does not exist.");
            }
        }
    }
}
```

▶ Feedback 11.1

1. Write the statement to create an inventory StreamWriter object that will write data to a file called "Inventory.txt".
2. Code the statement to write the contents of descriptionTextBox into the inventory stream.
3. Why should the declaration statement for a StreamReader object be in a try/catch block? Does the declaration statement for a StreamWriter object need to be in a try/catch block? Why or why not?
4. Write the statement(s) to read a description and a product number from inventoryStreamReader, assuming that it has been opened as a Stream-Reader object. Make sure to test for the end of the file.

Using the File Common Dialog Box

In the preceding file read and write programs, the filenames are hard-coded into the programs. You may prefer to allow the user to browse and enter the filename at run time. You can display the standard Windows *Open File* dialog box, in which the user can browse for a folder and filename and/or enter a new filename. Use the **OpenFileDialog** common dialog component to display the dialog box, and then use the object's FileName property to open the selected file.

OpenFileDialog Component Properties

You will find the following properties of the OpenFileDialog component very useful:

Property	Description
Name	Name of the component. You can use the default openFileDialog1.
CheckFileExists	Display an error message if the file does not exist. Set to *false* for saving a file since you want to create a new file if the file does not exist. Leave at the default *true* to read an existing file.
CheckPathExists	Display an error message if the path does not exist. Set to *false* for saving a file since you want it to create the new folder if necessary.
FileName	The name of the file selected or entered by the user, which includes the file path. Use this property after displaying the dialog box to determine which file to open. You also can give this property an initial value, which places a default filename in the dialog box when it appears.
Filter	Filter file extensions to display. Example: `Text Files (*.txt)|*.txt|All files (*.*)|*.*`
InitialDirectory	Directory to display when the dialog box opens. Set this in code to System.IO.Directory.GetCurrentDirectory() to begin in the current directory.
Title	Title bar of the dialog box.

Displaying the Open File Dialog Box

To display an *Open File* dialog box (Figure 11.5), you must first add an Open-FileDialog component to your form. The component appears in the component tray. At design time, set initial properties for Name, CheckFileExists, Check-PathExists, Filter, and Title (see the preceding table for the values). In code, set the InitialDirectory property to **Directory.GetCurrentDirectory**, display the dialog box using the ShowDialog method, and retrieve the FileName property.

Note: Directory.GetCurrentDirectory is in the System.IO namespace. If your program does not include a using statement for System.IO, you must fully qualify the name: System.IO.Directory.GetCurrentDirectory().

Display the Windows **Open File** *dialog box using the OpenFileDialog component. The Filter property determines the entries that display in the drop-down box.*

```
private void OpenFileToolStripMenuItem_Click(object sender, System.EventArgs e)
{
    // Open the file.
    DialogResult responseDialogResult;

    // Begin in the project folder.
    openFileDialog1.InitialDirectory = Directory.GetCurrentDirectory();
    // Display the File Open dialog box.
    responseDialogResult = openFileDialog1.ShowDialog();

    if (responseDialogResult != DialogResult.Cancel)
    { // User didn't click the Cancel button.
        // Open the output file.

        phoneStreamWriter = new StreamWriter(openFileDialog1.FileName);
    }
    nameTextBox.Focus();
}
```

Notice that the user may click on the *Cancel* button of the *Open File* dialog box. Check the DialogResult for *Cancel*. And if the user *does* click *Cancel*, that presents one more task for the program: You cannot close a StreamWriter object that isn't open.

Checking for Successful File Open

In the preceding file-open procedure, the statement

```
phoneStreamWriter = new StreamWriter(openFileDialog1.FileName);
```

may not execute. In that case, the StreamWriter is not instantiated. You can verify the object's instantiation using the C# keyword **null**. An object variable that has not been instantiated has a value of null.

```
if (phoneStreamWriter != null) // Is the file open?
{
    phoneStreamWriter.Close();
}
```

Place this code in the form's FormClosing event handler.

Checking for Already Open File

It's possible that the user may select the *File / Open* menu item twice, which can cause a problem. A second open instantiates another file stream, and the Close method will never execute for the first file. It's best to check for an active instance of the file stream before instantiating a new one.

```
private void fileOpenMenuItem_Click(object sender, System.EventArgs e)
{
    // Open the file.
    DialogResult responseDialogResult;

    if (phoneStreamWriter != null) // Is the file already open?
    {
        phoneStreamWriter.Close();
    }
```

```
        // Begin in the project folder.
        openFileDialog1.InitialDirectory = Directory.GetCurrentDirectory();
        // Display the File Open dialog box.
        responseDialogResult = openFileDialog1.ShowDialog();
        if (responseDialogResult != DialogResult.Cancel)
        { // User didn't click the Cancel button.
            // Open the output file.
            phoneStreamWriter = new StreamWriter(openFileDialog1.FileName);
        }
        nameTextBox.Focus();
}
```

Using the SaveFileDialog Component

In addition to the OpenFileDialog, you also can choose to display a SaveFile-
Dialog component, which displays the standard system *Save File As* dialog box.
The SaveFileDialog allows the user to browse and enter a filename to save; it
has most of the same properties as the OpenFileDialog component. By default,
the SaveFileDialog component checks for an already-existing file and displays
a dialog box asking the user whether to replace the existing file.

The Open and Write File Program

Here is the complete listing of an Open and Write File program, which allows
the user to select the filename. The user can select the *Open* command from the
File menu. But if the *Save* button is clicked and the file is not yet open, the
Open File dialog box displays automatically.

```
/*
Program:       Ch11OpenAndWriteFile
Programmer:    Bradley/Millspaugh
Date:          June 2009
Description:    Create a file using a StreamWriter.
               Displays the File Open dialog box for the user to
               enter the file and path.
*/

using System;
using System.Collections.Generic;
using System.ComponentModel;
using System.Data;
using System.Drawing;
using System.Text;
using System.Windows.Forms;
using System.IO;

namespace Ch11OpenFileDialog
{
    public partial class PhoneForm : Form
    {
        StreamWriter phoneStreamWriter;

        public PhoneForm()
        {
            InitializeComponent();
        }
```

```
        private void saveButton_Click(object sender, System.EventArgs e)
        {
            // Save the record to the file.

            if (phoneStreamWriter != null)      // Is the file open?
            {
                // Save the record.
                phoneStreamWriter.WriteLine(nameTextBox.Text);
                phoneStreamWriter.WriteLine(phoneTextBox.Text);
                nameTextBox.Clear();
                nameTextBox.Focus();
                phoneTextBox.Clear();
            }
            else     // File is not open.
            {
                MessageBox.Show(
                    "You must open the file before you can save a record",
                    "File Not Open", MessageBoxButtons.OK,
                    MessageBoxIcon.Information);
                // Display the File Open dialog box.
                openFileToolStripMenuItem_Click(sender, e);
            }
        }

        private void openFileToolStripMenuItem_Click(object sender, EventArgs e)
        {
            // Open the file.
            DialogResult responseDialogResult;

            // Is the file already open?
            if (phoneStreamWriter != null)
            {
                phoneStreamWriter.Close();
            }

            // Begin in the project folder.
            openFileDialog1.InitialDirectory = Directory.GetCurrentDirectory();
            // Display the File Open dialog box.
            responseDialogResult = openFileDialog1.ShowDialog();

            if (responseDialogResult != DialogResult.Cancel)
            { // User didn't click the Cancel button.
                // Open the output file.

                phoneStreamWriter = new StreamWriter(openFileDialog1.FileName);
            }
            nameTextBox.Focus();
        }

        private void exitToolStripMenuItem_Click(object sender, EventArgs e)
        {
            // Close the file and the form.

            if (phoneStreamWriter != null)      // Is the file open?
            {
                phoneStreamWriter.Close();
            }
            this.Close();
        }
    }
}
```

> ## Feedback 11.2
>
> 1. What is the Filter property setting to display only .txt files?
> 2. Write the statement to set openFileDialog1 to begin in the current directory.
> 3. Write the statement to close phoneStreamWriter; make sure to allow for the possibility that the file is not open.

Saving the Contents of a List Box

In Chapter 7 you wrote a program to maintain a list. The user was allowed to add items and remove items, but the next time the program ran, the list changes were gone. The changes were not saved from one execution to the next.

Now that you know how to save data in a file, you can save the contents of a list when the program exits and reload the list when the program reopens. The techniques that you need to use for this project are

- Do not give any values to the list's Items collection at design time. Instead, when the program begins, open the data file and read the list elements into the Items collection.

- If the file holding the list elements does not exist when the program begins, give the user the option of creating a new list by adding the items.

- If the user makes any changes to the list, ask whether to save the list when the program ends.

- Include a menu option to save the list.

The examples in this section use the hands-on example from Chapter 7, which allows the user to make changes to the Courses list (Figure 11.6). We will load the list from a file in the Form_Load method and query the user to save the list if any changes are made.

Figure 11.6

The form for the list save program, taken from Chapter 7.

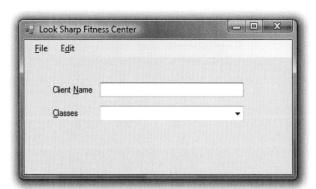

Loading the List Box

Assuming that the list items are stored in a data file, you can read the file into the list in the Form_Load method. Loop through the file until all elements are read, placing each item in the list with the `Items.Add` method.

```
while (classesStreamReader.Peek() != -1)
{
    classesComboBox.Items.Add(classesStreamReader.ReadLine());
}
```

Checking for Existence of the File

When you create a StreamReader object, the constructor checks to make sure the file exists. If the file does not exist, what do you want to do? Maybe the user wants to exit the program, locate the file, and try again. Or maybe the user prefers to begin with an empty list, add the list items, and create a new file. This technique is a good way to create the file in the first place.

You can catch the exception for a missing file and display a message box asking if the user wants to create a new file.

```
responseDialogResult = MessageBox.Show("Create a new file?", "File not Found",
    MessageBoxButtons.YesNo, MessageBoxIcon.Question);
```

If the user says Yes, allow the program to begin running with an empty list; the file will be created when the program exits or the user saves the list. If the user says No, exit the program immediately.

```
private void CoursesForm_Load(object sender, EventArgs e)
{
    // Load the combo box.
    DialogResult responseDialogResult;

    try
    {
        StreamReader classesStreamReader = new StreamReader("Classes.txt");
        while (classesStreamReader.Peek() != -1)
        {
            classesComboBox.Items.Add(classesStreamReader.ReadLine());
        }
        classesStreamReader.Close();
    }
    catch
    {
        responseDialogResult = MessageBox.Show("Create a new file?",
            "File not Found", MessageBoxButtons.YesNo,
            MessageBoxIcon.Question);
        if (responseDialogResult == DialogResult.No)
        {
            // Exit the project.
            exitToolStripMenuItem_Click(e, new System.EventArgs());
        }
    }
}
```

Saving the File

In this program, the user can choose a menu option to save the file. Open a StreamWriter object and loop through the Items collection of the list box, saving each element with a WriteLine method.

```
private void saveCoursesToolStripMenuItem_Click(object sender, EventArgs e)
{
    // Save the list box contents to a file.
    StreamWriter classesStreamWriter = new StreamWriter("Classes.txt");
    int indexInteger, maximumInteger;

    maximumInteger = classesComboBox.Items.Count;
    for (indexInteger = O; indexInteger < maximumInteger; indexInteger++)
    {
        classesStreamWriter.WriteLine(classesComboBox.Items[indexInteger]);
    }
    classesStreamWriter.Close();
    isDirtyBoolean = false;
}
```

The last line in this procedure needs some explanation. The next section explains the reason for `isDirtyBoolean = false;`.

Querying the User to Save

If your program allows users to make changes to data during program execution, it's a good idea to ask them if they want to save the changes before the program ends. This is similar to working in a word processing program or the C# editor. If you close the file after making changes, you receive a message asking if you want to save the file. But if you haven't made any changes since the last save, no message appears.

To keep track of data changes during execution, you need a class-level Boolean variable. Because the standard practice in programming is to refer to the data as "dirty" if changes have been made, we will call the variable isDirtyBoolean. In each method that allows changes (Add, Remove, Clear), you must set isDirtyBoolean to *true*. After saving the file, set the variable to *false*.

Just before the project ends, you must check the value of isDirtyBoolean; if *true*, ask the user if he or she wants to save; if *false*, you can just exit without a message.

The Form_FormClosing Event Handler

If you want to do something before the project ends, such as ask the user to save the file, the best location is the form's **FormClosing event** handler. This is a much better place for such a question than your exit method because the user can quit the program in more than one way. The Form_FormClosing event handler executes before the form closes when the user clicks on your *Exit* button or menu command, clicks on the window's Close button, or even exits Windows.

```
private void CoursesForm_FormClosing(object sender, FormClosingEventArgs e)
{
    // Ask user to save the file.
    DialogResult responseDialogResult;

    if (isDirtyBoolean)
    {
```

```
    responseDialogResult = MessageBox.Show(
        "Class list has changed. Save the list?", "Class List Changed",
        MessageBoxButtons.YesNo, MessageBoxIcon.Question);
    if (responseDialogResult == DialogResult.Yes)
    {
        saveCoursesToolStripMenuItem_Click(sender, new System.EventArgs());
    }
    }
}
```

Feedback 11.3

1. Write the loop to save all of the elements from namesListBox using namesStreamWriter, which is a StreamWriter already opened and connected to Names.txt.
2. In what method should the code from Question 1 be placed?
3. Write the statements in the Form_Load event handler to load the list of names into namesListBox.

XML Files

An increasingly important topic, XML files, is covered in Chapter 14. See "XML Data Files" for terminology and examples, including XDocument and XElement objects, and LINQ to XML.

Your Hands-On Programming Example

Modify the hands-on programming example from Chapter 7 to save the changes to the Classes list from one run of the program to the next. The user can add items to the list, remove items, and clear the list. If there are any changes to the list, allow the user to save the list. When the program begins, load the list from the disk file so that it displays the list as it appeared during the last run.

Do not give the Classes list initial values; if the user has not entered any classes, the list should be blank. If the file holding classes is not found, allow the user to enter the new classes at run time.

Add a *Save Courses List* menu item on the *File* menu. Also query the user to save the file when the program closes if the list has changed.

Note: We have removed the printing routines from the Ch07HandsOn program to better focus on the file-handling routines.

Planning the Project

Sketch the form (Figure 11.7), which your users sign off as meeting their needs.

Figure 11.7

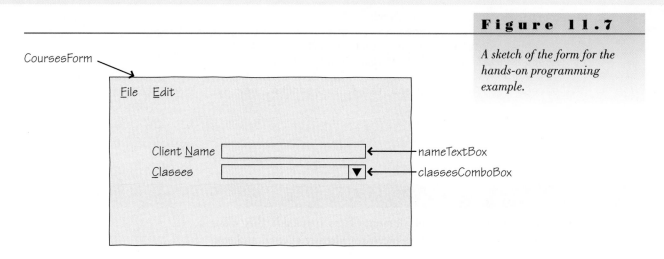

Plan the Objects and Properties See the planning for the Chapter 7 hands-on programming example and make the following addition:

Object	Property	Setting
saveCoursesToolStripMenuItem	Name	saveCoursesToolStripMenuItem
	Text	&Save Courses

Plan the Methods Refer to the planning for the Chapter 7 hands-on programming example and make the following changes. You can remove the controls and procedures for printing.

Method	Actions
saveCoursesToolStripMenuItem_Click	Open the file. Save the list items in the file. Close the file. Set isDirtyBoolean to *false*.
Form_Load	try Open the file. Read the file contents into the Classes list. Close the file. catch (file is missing) Query the user to create the new file. If answer is No Exit the program.
CoursesForm_FormClosing	If the list has changed (is dirty) Query the user to save the list data. If Yes Call saveCoursesToolStripMenuItem_Click.
Each method that changes the list	Set isDirtyBoolean to *true*

Write the Project Begin with the Chapter 7 hands-on programming example. See "Basing a New Project on an Existing Project" in Chapter 5 for help. Figure 11.7 shows the sketch and Figure 11.8 shows the completed form.

Figure 11.8

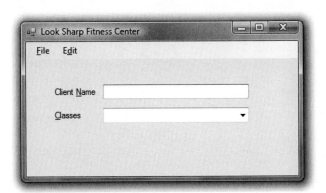

- Add the menu item and set the properties according to your plan.

- Make sure to add the new using statement:

  `using System.IO;`

- Add the class-level variable isDirtyBoolean.

- Write the code for the new menu item based on the pseudocode.

- Write the new code for the Form_Load and Form_FormClosing event handlers, based on the pseudocode.

- When you complete the code, thoroughly test the project. Fill the list, save the list, and rerun the program multiple times. Make sure that you can modify the list and have the changes appear in the next program run. Also, test the option to not save changes and make sure that it works correctly.

The Project Coding Solution

CoursesForm

```
/*
 * Project:        Ch11HandsOn
 * Programmer:     Bradley/Millspaugh
 * Date:           June 2009
 * Description:    Maintain a list of courses and allow user to save
 *                 the list for the next program run.
 *
 */

using System;
using System.Collections.Generic;
using System.ComponentModel;
using System.Data;
using System.Drawing;
using System.Text;
using System.Windows.Forms;
using System.IO;
```

```csharp
namespace Ch11HandsOn
{
    public partial class CoursesForm : Form
    {
        private bool isDirtyBoolean = false;

        public CoursesForm()
        {
            InitializeComponent();
        }

        private void CoursesForm_Load(object sender, EventArgs e)
        {
            // Load the combo box.
            DialogResult responseDialogResult;

            try
            {
                StreamReader classesStreamReader = new StreamReader("Classes.txt");
                while (classesStreamReader.Peek() != -1)
                {
                    classesComboBox.Items.Add(classesStreamReader.ReadLine());
                }
                classesStreamReader.Close();
            }
            catch
            {
                responseDialogResult = MessageBox.Show("Create a new file?",
                    "File not Found", MessageBoxButtons.YesNo,
                    MessageBoxIcon.Question);
                if (responseDialogResult == DialogResult.No)
                {
                    // Exit the project.
                    exitToolStripMenuItem_Click(e, new System.EventArgs());
                }
            }
        }

        private void addACourseToolStripMenuItem_Click(object sender,
            EventArgs e)
        {
            // Add a course, use a loop to test for duplicate.
            int indexInteger = 0;
            bool itemFoundBoolean = false;

            if (classesComboBox.Text != String.Empty)
            {
                while (indexInteger < classesComboBox.Items.Count &&
                        !itemFoundBoolean)
                {
                    if (classesComboBox.Items[indexInteger++].ToString()
                        .ToUpper() == classesComboBox.Text.ToUpper())
                    {
                        MessageBox.Show("Duplicate class name.", "Class Not Added",
                            MessageBoxButtons.OK, MessageBoxIcon.Information);
                        itemFoundBoolean = true;
                    }
                }
            }
```

```csharp
        if (!itemFoundBoolean)
        {
            // Add to the list.
            classesComboBox.Items.Add(classesComboBox.Text);
            isDirtyBoolean = true;
            classesComboBox.Text = String.Empty;
        }
    }

    private void removeACourseToolStripMenuItem_Click(object sender,
        EventArgs e)
    {
        // Remove the selected course.

        if (classesComboBox.SelectedIndex != -1)
        {
            classesComboBox.Items.RemoveAt(classesComboBox.SelectedIndex);
            isDirtyBoolean = true;
        }
        else
        {
            MessageBox.Show("Select a course to remove.", "No Selection",
                MessageBoxButtons.OK, MessageBoxIcon.Exclamation);
        }
    }

    private void displayCourseCountToolStripMenuItem_Click(object sender,
        EventArgs e)
    {
        // Display the number of courses.

        MessageBox.Show("Course Count: " + classesComboBox.Items.Count
            .ToString(), "Look Sharp Fitness Center Courses");
    }

    private void clearTheCourseListToolStripMenuItem_Click(object sender,
        EventArgs e)
    {
        // Verify and then remove the course.
        DialogResult confirmDialogResult = MessageBox.Show(
            "Remove all items", "Clear Courses List", MessageBoxButtons.YesNo,
            MessageBoxIcon.Question);

        if (confirmDialogResult == DialogResult.Yes)
        {
            classesComboBox.Items.Clear();
            isDirtyBoolean = true;
        }
    }

    private void saveCoursesToolStripMenuItem_Click(object sender, EventArgs e)
    {
        // Save the list box contents to a file.
        StreamWriter classesStreamWriter = new StreamWriter("Classes.txt");
        int indexInteger, maximumInteger;
```

```csharp
            maximumInteger = classesComboBox.Items.Count;
            for (indexInteger = 0; indexInteger < maximumInteger; indexInteger++)
            {
                classesStreamWriter.WriteLine(classesComboBox.Items[indexInteger]);
            }
            classesStreamWriter.Close();
            isDirtyBoolean = false;
        }

        private void CoursesForm_FormClosing(object sender, FormClosingEventArgs e)
        {
            // Ask user to save the file.
            DialogResult responseDialogResult;

            if (isDirtyBoolean)
            {
                responseDialogResult = MessageBox.Show(
                    "Class list has changed. Save the list?", "Class List Changed",
                    MessageBoxButtons.YesNo, MessageBoxIcon.Question);
                if (responseDialogResult == DialogResult.Yes)
                {
                    saveCoursesToolStripMenuItem_Click(sender,
                        new System.EventArgs());
                }
            }
        }

        private void exitToolStripMenuItem_Click(object sender, EventArgs e)
        {
            // End the program.

            this.Close();
        }
    }
}
```

Summary

1. You can add a `using System.IO` statement to the top of a file so that you do not have to fully qualify references to classes in the namespace.
2. For simple text file handling, you can use `WriteAllText`, `WriteAllLines`, `AppendAllText`, `ReadAllText`, and `ReadAllLines`. These methods automatically open and close the data files.
3. A stream object is used to transfer data to and from a data file. The StreamWriter outputs (writes) the data and the StreamReader inputs (reads) data.
4. The constructors for a StreamWriter and StreamReader take the name of the file, with an optional path, as a parameter.
5. The `WriteLine` method writes a data line to disk.
6. A `Close` method should be used as soon as you are done with the stream. Make sure the stream is closed prior to the termination of a program that uses streams.

7. The `Peek` method looks at the next element, which allows testing for the end of the file. The `Peek` method returns −1 at the end of file.

8. List box data may be saved to a stream. The Items collection should be filled in the Form_Load method if the file exists. Any changes should be saved back to the file when the program terminates.

9. A Boolean variable is used to track whether changes have been made to the data.

10. The form's FormClosing event handler is a good location for the code to prompt the users whether to save any changes.

11. The OpenFileDialog and SaveFileDialog components can be used to display the *Open File* and *Save As* dialog boxes and allow the user to select the filename.

Key Terms

`AppendAllText` method *452*

`Close` method *459*

data file *452*

Directory.GetCurrentDirectory *464*

File class *452*

FormClosing event *470*

`null` *465*

OpenFileDialog *463*

`Peek` method *461*

`ReadAllLines` method *455*

`ReadAllText` method *455*

`ReadLine` method *461*

stream *457*

StreamReader *457*

StreamWriter *457*

System.IO namespace *457*

`Write` method *458*

`WriteAllLines` method *452*

`WriteAllText` method *452*

`WriteLine` method *458*

Review Questions

1. Explain what occurs when a stream object is instantiated.
2. Name two types of stream classes. What is the difference between the two?
3. What is the difference between a `Write` method and a `WriteLine` method?
4. What steps are necessary for storing the list items from a list box into a disk file?
5. What is the format for the statements to read and write streams?
6. What method can be used to determine the end of file?
7. When is exception handling necessary for stream handling?
8. Explain when a form's FormClosing event occurs and what code might be included in the FormClosing event handler.

Programming Exercises

11.1 Rewrite Programming Exercise 8.4 using a file to store the state names and abbreviations. You need two projects: The first will allow the typist to enter the state name and the abbreviation in text boxes and store them in a file. The second project will perform the functions specified in Programming Exercise 8.4.

Optional extra: Allow the user to select the file to open using the *Open File* dialog box.

Note: For help in basing a new project on an existing project, see "Basing a New Project on an Existing Project" in Chapter 5.

11.2 Write one project that creates a file for employee information; call the file Employee.txt. Each record will contain fields for first name, last name, employee number, and hourly pay rate.

Write a second project to process payroll. The application will load the employee data into an array of structures from the file with an extra field for the pay. The form will contain controls for the information from the array (display one record at a time) and a text box for the hours worked.

A button called *FindPay* will use a `for` loop to process the array. You will calculate the pay and add the pay to the totals. Then display the information for the next employee. (Place the pay into the extra field in the array.)

The *Exit* button will print a report in a print preview dialog and terminate the project. (Print the array.)

Processing: Hours over 40 receive time-and-a-half pay. Accumulate the total number of hours worked, the total number of hours of overtime, and the total amount of pay.

Sample Report

Ace Industries

Employee name	Hours worked	Hours overtime	Pay rate	Amount earned
Janice Jones	40	0	5.25	210.00
Chris O'Connel	35	0	5.35	187.25
Karen Fisk	45	5	6.00	285.00
Tom Winn	42	2	5.75	247.25
Totals	162	7		929.50

Optional extra: Allow the user to select the file to open using the *Open File* dialog box.

11.3 Modify Programming Exercise 7.4 or 7.5 to store the list box for Bradley's Bagels in a data file. Load the list during the Form_Load event handler and then close the file. Be sure to use error checking in case the file does not exist.

In the FormClosing method, prompt the user to save the bagel list back to the disk.

Optional extra: Allow the user to select the file to open using the *Open File* dialog box.

Note: For help in basing a new project on an existing project, see "Basing a New Project on an Existing Project" in Chapter 5.

11.4 Create a simple text editor that has one large rich text box (with its Multiline property set to *true*). Set the text control to fill the form and set its Anchor property to all four edges so that the control fills the form even when it is resized.

Allow the user to save the contents of the text box in a data file and load a data file into the text box using the *Open File* dialog box.

Use a StreamWriter and StreamReader or `File.WriteAllText` and `File.ReadAllText`.

11.5 Create a project that stores personal information for a little electronic "black book." The fields in the file should include name, phone number, pager number, cell phone number, voice mail number, and e-mail address. Use text boxes to enter the data.

Create a second project to load the names into a list box and use a structure to hold the fields of data. Perform a "look up" and display the appropriate information for the selected name.

Optional extra: Allow the user to select the file to open using the *Open File* dialog box.

Case Studies

Note: For help in basing a new project on an existing project, see "Basing a New Project on an Existing Project" in Chapter 5.

Custom Supplies Mail Order

Modify your project from Chapter 7 to save the changes to the catalog name combo box from one run to the next. When the program begins, load the list from the data file. If the file does not exist, display a message asking if the user wants to create it.

Allow the user to save changes from a *Save* menu item. When the program terminates, check to see if there are any unsaved changes. If so, prompt the user to save the changes.

Optional extra: Allow the user to select the file to open using the *Open File* dialog box.

Christopher's Car Center

Write a project to store vehicle information including model, manufacturer, year, and VIN number.

Create a second project that loads the data from the file into memory and loads a drop-down combo box with the VIN numbers. When a number is selected from the combo box, display the appropriate information regarding the vehicle.

Optional extra: Allow the user to select the file to open using the *Open File* dialog box.

Xtreme Cinema

Modify your project from Chapter 7 to save the changes to the movie combo box from one run to the next. When the program begins, load the list from the data file. If the file does not exist, display a message asking if the user wants to create it.

Allow the user to save changes from a *Save* menu item. When the program terminates, check to see if there are any unsaved changes. If so, prompt the user to save the changes.

Optional extra: Allow the user to select the file to open using the *Open File* dialog box.

Cool Boards

Modify your project from Chapter 7 to save the changes to the shirt style combo box from one run to the next. When the program begins, load the list from the data file. If the file does not exist, display a message asking if the user wants to create it.

Allow the user to save changes from a *Save* menu item. When the program terminates, check to see if there are any unsaved changes. If so, prompt the user to save the changes.

Optional extra: Allow the user to select the file to open using the *Open File* dialog box.

12

OOP: Creating Object-Oriented Programs

1. Use object-oriented terminology correctly.

2. Create a two-tier application that separates the user interface from the business logic.

3. Differentiate between a class and an object.

4. Create a class that has properties and methods.

5. Declare object variables and assign values to the properties with a constructor or property methods.

6. Instantiate an object in a project using your class.

7. Differentiate between static members and instance members.

8. Understand the purpose of the constructor and destructor methods.

9. Inherit a new class from your own class.

10. Use visual inheritance by basing a form on another form.

Object-Oriented Programming

You have been using objects since Chapter 1. As you know quite well by now, **objects** have properties and methods and generate events that you can respond to (or ignore) if you choose. Up until now, the classes for all objects in your projects have been predefined; that is, you could choose to create a new object of the form class, a button class, a text box class, or any other class of control in the toolbox. In this chapter, you will learn to define your own new class and create objects based on that class.

Object-oriented programming (OOP) is currently the most accepted style of programming. Some computer languages, such as Java, C#, and SmallTalk, were designed to be object oriented (OO) from their inception. Other languages, such as Visual Basic and C++, have been modified in recent years to accommodate OOP.

Writing object-oriented programs is a mind-set—a different way of looking at a problem. You must think in terms of using objects. As your projects become more complex, using objects becomes increasingly important.

Objects

Beyond the many built-in choices you have for objects to include in your projects, C# allows you to create your own new object type by creating a **class**. Just like other object types, your class may have properties, methods, and events. Remember: Properties are characteristics and methods are actions that can be performed by a class of objects.

An object is a *thing* such as a button. You create a button object from the button tool in the toolbox. In other words, *button* is a class but *exitButton* is an actual occurrence or **instance** of the class; the instance is the object. Just as you may have multiple buttons in a project, you may have many objects of a new class type.

Defining your own class is like creating a new tool for the toolbox; the process does not create the object, only a definition of what that type of object looks like and how it behaves. You may then create as many instances of the class as you need using the new keyword. Your class may be a student, an employee, a product, or any other type of object that would be useful in a project.

Many people use a cookie analogy to describe the relationship of a class and an object. The cookie cutter is the class. You can't eat a cookie cutter, but you can use it to make cookies; the cookie is the object. When you make a cookie using a cookie cutter, you **instantiate** the cookie class, creating an object of the class. You can use the same cookie cutter to make various kinds of cookies. Although all the cookies made will have the same shape, some may be chocolate; others are lemon, or vanilla; some may be frosted or have colored sprinkles on top. The characteristics of the cookie, such as flavor and topping, are the properties of the object. You could refer to the properties of your cookie object as

```
Cookie1.Flavor = "Lemon";
Cookie1.Topping = "Cream Frosting";
```

What about methods? Recall that a method is an action or behavior—something the object can do or have done to it, such as Hide, Clear, or Show.

Possible methods for our cookie object might be Eat, Bake, or Crumble. Using object terminology, you can refer to Object.method:

```
Cookie1.Crumble();
```

Sometimes the distinction between a method and an event is somewhat fuzzy. Generally, anything you tell the object to do is a method; if the object does an action and needs to inform you, that's an event. So if you tell the cookie to crumble, that is a method; if the cookie crumbles on its own and needs to inform you of the fact, that's an event.

Object-Oriented Terminology

Key features of an object-oriented language are encapsulation, inheritance, and polymorphism.

Encapsulation

Encapsulation refers to the combination of characteristics of an object along with its behaviors. You have one "package" that holds the definition of all properties, methods, and events. For example, when you create a button, you can set or retrieve its properties, such as Text, Name, or BackColor. You can execute its methods, such as Focus, Hide, or Show, and you can write code for its events, such as Click or Double-click. But you cannot make up new properties or tell it to do anything that it doesn't already know how to do. It is a complete package; you can think of all of the parts of the package as being in a capsule.

You can witness encapsulation by looking at any program. The form is actually a class. All of the methods and events that you code are enclosed within the braces. The variables that you place in your code are actually properties of the specific form class that you are generating.

When you understand and use encapsulation successfully, you can implement *data hiding*. Each object can keep its data (properties) and methods hidden. Through use of the public and private keywords, an object can "expose" only those data elements and methods that it wishes to allow the outside world to see.

Inheritance

Inheritance is the ability to create a new class from an existing class. You can add enhancements to an existing class without modifying the original. By creating a new class that inherits from an existing class, you can add or modify class variables and methods. For example, each of the forms that you create is inherited from, or derived from, the existing Form class. The original class is known as the **base class**, the **superclass**, or the **parent class**. The inherited class is called a **subclass**, a **derived class**, or a **child class**. Of course, a new class can inherit from a subclass—that subclass becomes a superclass as well as a subclass.

Look closely at the first lines of the class file for a form:

```
public partial class Form1 : Form
```

The base class is Form and Form1 is the derived class. Inherited classes have an "is a" relationship with the base class. In the form example, the new Form1 "is a" Form.

The real purpose of inheritance is **reusability**. You may need to reuse or obtain the functionality from one class or object when you have another similar situation. The new Form1 class that you create has all of the characteristics and actions of the base class, System.Windows.Forms.Form. From there you can add the functionality for your own new form. Other classes that you have reused multiple times are the Button class and the TextBox class.

You can create your own hierarchy of classes. You place the code you want to be common in a base class. You then create other classes from it, which inherit the base class methods. This concept is very helpful if you have features that are similar in two classes. Rather than writing two classes that are almost identical, you can create a base class that contains the similar methods.

An example of reusing classes could be a Person class, where you might have properties for name, address, and phone number. The Person class can be a base class, from which you derive an Employee class, a Customer class, or a Student class (Figure 12.1). The derived classes could call methods from the base class and contain any methods that are unique to the derived class. In inheritance, typically the classes go from general to the more specific.

The derived classes inherit from the base class.

Polymorphism

The term *polymorphism* actually means the ability to take on many shapes or forms. As applied to OOP, polymorphism refers to methods that have identical names but have different implementations, depending on the situation. For example, radio buttons, check boxes, and list boxes all have a `Select` method. In each case, the `Select` method operates appropriately for its class.

Polymorphism also allows a single class to have more than one method with the same name. When the method is called, the argument type determines which version of the method to use. Each of the identically named methods should perform the same task in a slightly different manner, depending on the arguments.

Later in this chapter, you will use both **overloading** a method and **overriding** a method to implement polymorphism. You have already seen examples of *overloading*, such as the `MessageBox.Show` method that gives you several argument lists for calling the method. *Overriding* refers to a method that has the same signature (name and parameter list) as a method in its base class. The method in the subclass, or derived class, takes precedence over, or overrides, the identically named method in the base class.

Reusable Classes

A big advantage of object-oriented programming over traditional programming is the ability to reuse classes. When you create a new class, you can then use that class in multiple projects. Each object that you create from the class has its own set of properties. This process works just like the built-in C# controls you have been using all along. For example, you can create two PictureBox objects: pictureBox1 and pictureBox2. Each has its own Visible property and Image property, which will probably be set differently from each other.

As you begin creating classes in your projects, you will find many situations in which classes are useful. You might want to create your own class to provide database access. You could include methods for adding and deleting data members. If you work frequently with sales, you might create a Product class. The Product class would likely have properties such as description, quantity, and cost. The methods would probably include finding the current value of the product.

Multitier Applications

A common practice for writing professional applications is to write independent components that work in multiple "tiers" or layers. Each of the functions of a **multitier application** can be coded in a separate component, and the components may be stored and run on different machines.

One of the most popular approaches is a three-tier application. The tiers in this model are the Presentation tier, Business tier, and Data tier (Figure 12.2). You also hear the term "n-tier" application, which is an expansion of the three-tier model. The middle tier, which contains all of the business logic, may be written in multiple classes that can be stored and run from multiple locations.

Figure 12.2

The three-tier model for application design.

Presentation Tier	Business Tier	Data Tier
User Interface Forms, controls, menus	**Business Objects** Validation Calculations Business logic Business rules	**Data Retrieval** Data storage

In a multitier application, the goal is to create components that can be combined and replaced. If one part of an application needs to change, such as a redesign of the user interface or a new database format, the other components do not need to be replaced. A developer can simply "plug in" a new user interface and continue using the rest of the components of the application.

The Presentation tier refers to the user interface, which in C# is the form. Consider that, in the future, the user interface could be redesigned or even converted to a Web page.

The Business tier is a class or classes that handle the data. This layer can include validation to enforce business rules as well as the calculations.

The Data tier includes retrieving and storing the data in a database. Occasionally an organization will decide to change database vendors or will need to retrieve data from several different sources. The Data tier retrieves the data and passes the results to the Business tier, or takes data from the Business tier and writes them in the appropriate location.

Classes

The classes that you have worked with up until now have generated visual objects such as text boxes and labels. These were easily created from the toolbox at design time. You also can create objects at run time. In Chapter 6 you instantiated objects of the Forms class, and in Chapter 7 you instantiated objects of the Font class in your printing routines. In both cases, you used the new keyword to instantiate the objects.

Designing Your Own Class

To design your own class, you need to analyze the characteristics and behaviors that your object needs. The characteristics or properties are defined as variables, and the behaviors are methods. For a simple example, assume that you have a user interface (form) that gathers the unit price and the quantity of a product. You can design a class to perform the calculations. For the class to calculate the extended price, it must know the unit price and the quantity. The form needs to retrieve the extended price. The price, quantity, and extended price are stored in private variables in the class; those variables are accessed through property methods.

The form will instantiate the class, pass the price and quantity to it through property procedures, call a method to calculate the extended price, and then display the extended price on the form by retrieving it from a property method (Figure 12.3).

Figure   1 2 . 3

A presentation tier class and a business tier. The data are entered and displayed in the presentation tier; calculations are performed in the business tier. Pass in the Product ID, Quantity, and Unit Price and then you can retrieve the Extended Price.

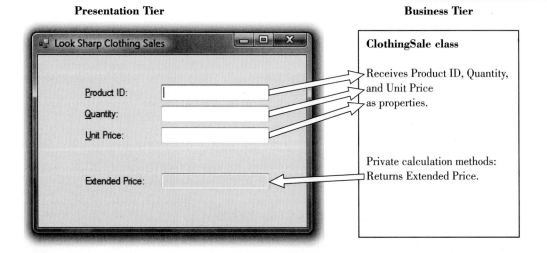

Presentation Tier   **Business Tier**

Creating Properties in a Class

In Chapter 6 you created properties of the form to pass the summary data. The same concept applies for the classes that you create.

Inside your class you define private member variables, which store the values for the properties of the class. Theoretically, you could declare all variables as `public` so that all other project code could set and retrieve their values. However, this approach violates the rules of encapsulation that require each object to be in charge of its own data. Remember that encapsulation can be used for *data hiding*. To accomplish data hiding, you will declare all variables in a class as `private` or `protected`. Protected variables behave as private, but are available in any class that inherits from this class. As a private or protected variable, the value is available only to methods within the class, the same way that private class-level variables are available only to methods within a form's class code.

Use property `set` and `get` methods to pass the values between your class and the class where objects of your class are instantiated.

Class Methods

You create methods of the new class by coding public methods within the class. Any methods that you declare with the `private` keyword are available only within the class. Any methods that you declare with the `public` keyword are available to external objects created from this class or other classes. And a method that you declare with the `protected` keyword behaves like private in the current class and any classes that inherit from it.

```
// Private method used for internal calculations.

private void calculateExtendedPrice()
{
    // Calculate the extended price.

    extendedPriceDecimal = quantityInteger * priceDecimal;
}
```

Constructors and Destructors

A **constructor** is a method that executes automatically when an object is instantiated. A **destructor** is a method that executes automatically when an object is destroyed. A constructor method has the same name as the class.

Constructors

The constructor executes automatically when you create an instance (an object) of the class. Because the constructor method executes before any other code in the class, the constructor is an ideal location for any initialization tasks that you need to do, such as setting the initial values of variables and properties.

The constructor must be public because the objects that you create must execute this method.

Note: If you do not write a constructor for a class, the compiler creates an implicit default constructor, which has an empty parameter list. If you do write a constructor, the compiler-supplied default constructor is no longer available.

Overloading the Constructor

Recall from Chapter 3 that *overloading* means that two methods have the same name but a different list of arguments (the signature). You can create over-loaded methods in your class by giving the same name to multiple methods, each with a different argument list. The following example shows an empty constructor (one without arguments) and a constructor that passes arguments to the class.

```
public ClothingSale()
{
    // Empty constructor.
}

public ClothingSale(string productNumberString, int quantityInteger,
    decimal discountRateDecimal)
{
    // Code statements to assign property values.
}
```

Parameterized Constructor

The term **parameterized constructor** refers to a constructor that requires arguments. This popular technique allows you to pass arguments as you create the new object.

```
ClothingSale aClothingSale = new ClothingSale(productString,
    int.Parse(quantityTextBox.Text),
    decimal.Parse(discountRateTextBox.Text));
```

You must assign the incoming values to the properties of the class. One way would be to just assign each incoming argument to its class-level property vari-able. But the better way is to assign an argument to the property name, which then uses the set method. Often validation is performed in the set methods.

```
public ClothingSale(string productNumberString, int quantityInteger,
    decimal discountRateDecimal)
{
    ProductNumber = productNumberString;
    Quantity = quantityInteger;
    DiscountRate = discountRateDecimal;
    calculateExtendedPrice();
}
```

Creating a New Class—Step-by-Step

In this step-by-step exercise, you will create a new class to hold clothing sale information for Look Sharp Fitness Center.

The user interface for this project has already been created so that you can focus on writing the class for the middle-tier component. The partially com-pleted project is available in the StudentData folder, which you can download from the text Web site (www.mhhe.com/C#2008). You will open the Windows project and add a new class to perform the calculations.

Open the Project

STEP 1: Locate and open the Ch12SBS project. ("SBS" stands for *step-by-step*). You can find Ch12SBS in the Student Data folder on the text Web site (www.mhhe.com/C#2008).

Begin a New Class

STEP 1: Select *Add Class* from the *Project* menu. The *Add New Item* dialog box will appear (Figure 12.4) with the Class template already selected.

Figure 12.4

*Add a new class to a project in the **Add New Item** dialog box.*

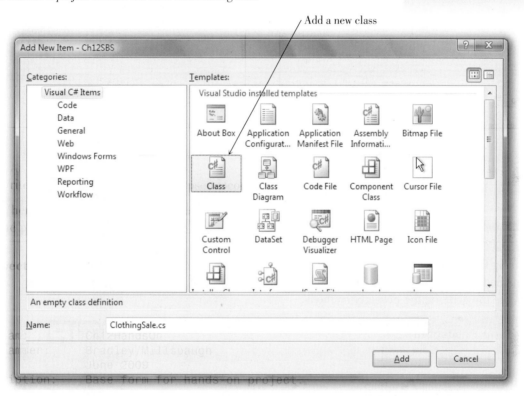

Add a new class

STEP 2: In the *Add New Item* dialog, with the *Class* template selected, type "ClothingSale.cs" for the class name and click on *Add*. You will see a new tab in the Document window for the new class. Note that a new class does not have a user interface; you will have only the Code window.

Define the Class Properties

STEP 1: In the Code Editor window, add a new line between the opening and closing braces following the `Class` statement. Declare the class-level `private` variables, which will hold the values for the properties of your new class:

```
private string productIdString;
private int quantityInteger;
private decimal unitPriceDecimal, discountRateDecimal,
    extendedPriceDecimal;
```

This class has private class-level variables: productIdString, quantity-Integer, unitPriceDecimal, discountRateDecimal, and extendedPriceDecimal

(Figure 12.5). Because the variables are declared as private, they can be accessed only by methods within the class. To allow access from outside the class, you must add property methods.

Figure 12.5

Declare the class-level variables to hold the class properties.

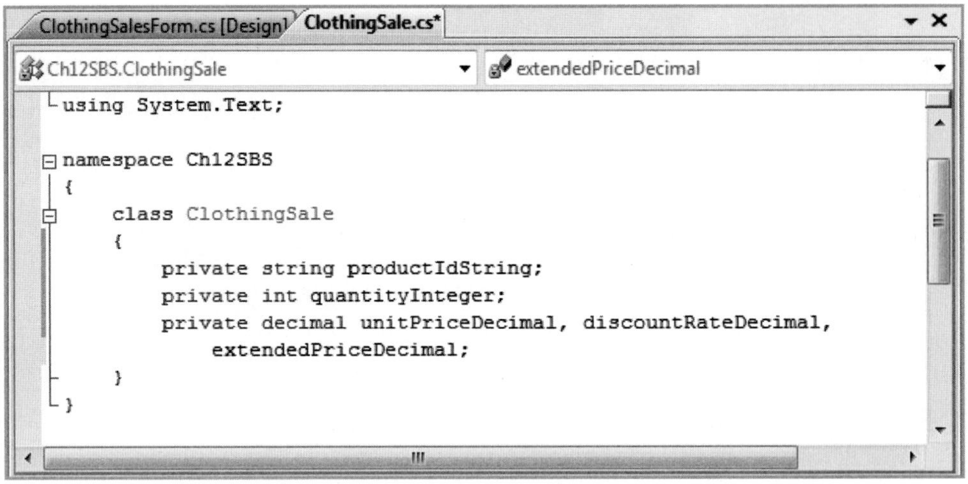

```
ClothingSalesForm.cs [Design]   ClothingSale.cs*                              ▾ ✕

 Ch12SBS.ClothingSale                     ▾      extendedPriceDecimal              ▾
      using System.Text;

    namespace Ch12SBS
      {
          class ClothingSale
          {
              private string productIdString;
              private int quantityInteger;
              private decimal unitPriceDecimal, discountRateDecimal,
                  extendedPriceDecimal;
          }
      }
```

Add the Property Methods

STEP 1: In the Code Editor window, after the property declarations, type "public string ProductId". Press Enter and type the brace. Inside the property method you will create a public get method and a private set method.

STEP 2: Write the code for the property methods.

```
public string ProductId
{
    get
    {
        return productIdString;
    }
    set
    {
        productIdString = value;
    }
}

public int Quantity
{
    set
    {
        quantityInteger = value;
    }
}

public decimal UnitPrice
{
    set
    {
        unitPriceDecimal = value;
    }
}
```

✔**TIP**

Follow variable naming conventions for the class-level variable to hold the property value; use a friendly name for the property name in the property method. ■

✔**TIP**

Use snippets to automatically create the code for a property. In the Editor, type "prop" and press the Tab key twice. You can enter the data type and property name, or press Tab again to accept the defaults. Press Enter when finished and then fill in the *get* and *set* clauses. ■

```
public decimal DiscountRate
{
    set
    {
        discountRateDecimal = value;
    }
}

public decimal ExtendedPrice
{
    get
    {
        return extendedPriceDecimal;
    }
}
```

Write the Constructor

STEP 1: Type the code for the constructor.

```
public ClothingSale(string productIdString, int quantityInteger,
    decimal unitPriceDecimal, decimal discountDecimal)
{
    ProductId = productIdString;
    Quantity = quantityInteger;
    UnitPrice = unitPriceDecimal;
    DiscountRate = discountDecimal;
    calculateExtendedPrice();
}
```

The call to calculateExtendedPrice is flagged as an error. You will code that method next.

Code a Method

For this class, you will add a method to calculate the extended price, which is the price per item multiplied by the quantity.

STEP 1: Type the code for the method:

```
private void calculateExtendedPrice()
{
    // Calculate the extended price.

    extendedPriceDecimal = unitPriceDecimal * (1 - discountRateDecimal)
        * quantityInteger;
}
```

Add General Comments

STEP 1: Type the comments at the top of the file, before the using statements.

```
/* Class Name:   Ch12SBS
 * Programmer:   Your Name
 * Date:         Today's Date
 * Description:  Handle clothing sale information.
 */
```

STEP 2: Save all.

The Complete Class Code

```
/* Class Name:      Ch12SBS
 * Programmer:      Your Name
 * Date:            Today's Date
 * Description:     Handle clothing sale information.
 */

using System;
using System.Collections.Generic;
using System.Text;

namespace Ch12SBS
{
    class ClothingSale
    {
        private string productIdString;
        private int quantityInteger;
        private decimal unitPriceDecimal, discountRateDecimal,
            extendedPriceDecimal;

        public string ProductId
        {
            get
            {
                return productIdString;
            }
            set
            {
                productIdString = value;
            }
        }

        public int Quantity
        {
            set
            {
                quantityInteger = value;
            }
        }

        public decimal UnitPrice
        {
            set
            {
                unitPriceDecimal = value;
            }
        }

        public decimal DiscountRate
        {
            set
            {
                discountRateDecimal = value;
            }
        }
```

```
                    public decimal ExtendedPrice
                    {
                        get
                        {
                            return extendedPriceDecimal;
                        }
                    }

                    public ClothingSale(string productIDString, int quantityInteger,
                        decimal unitPriceDecimal, decimal discountDecimal)
                    {
                        // Assign incoming values to the class properties.

                        ProductId = productIdString;
                        Quantity = quantityInteger;
                        UnitPrice = unitPriceDecimal;
                        DiscountRate = discountDecimal;
                        calculateExtendedPrice();
                    }

                    private void calculateExtendedPrice()
                    {
                        // Calculate the extended price.

                        extendedPriceDecimal = unitPriceDecimal * (1 - discountRateDecimal)
                            * quantityInteger;
                    }
            }
}
```

Property Methods with Mixed Access Levels

It is possible to set the property statement as public and then to assign either
the get or the set method to a more restrictive level such as private.

```
public string EmployeeID
{
    get
    {
        return employeeIDString;
    }
    private set
    {
        employeeIDString = value;
    }
}
```

This code allows public access to the get method but the set method is
private.

Creating a New Object Using a Class

Creating a new class defines a new type; it does not create any objects. This is similar to creating a new tool for the toolbox but not yet creating an instance of the class.

Generally, you will create new objects of your class in a two-step operation: first declare a variable for the new object and then instantiate the object using the new keyword. You can declare the variable as public; generally, you will allow variables to default to private.

```
ClothingSale aClothingSale;
```

This line merely states that the name aClothingSale is associated with the ClothingSale class, but it does not create an instance of the object. You must use the new keyword to actually create the object.

```
aClothingSale = new ClothingSale();
```

In C# it is legal to declare and instantiate an object in the same statement:

```
ClothingSale aClothingSale = new ClothingSale();
```

If you will need to use the object variable in multiple methods, you should declare the object at the class level. But when you instantiate an object, you may need to include the new statement in a try/catch block to allow error checking, and a try/catch block *must* be inside a method. Make sure to enclose the instantiation in a try/catch block if you are converting and passing values that a user enters in a text box so that you catch any bad input data.

The preferred technique is to include the new statement inside of a method at the time the object is needed. And if the object is never needed, it won't be created needlessly.

If you are using a parameterized constructor, you must pass the values for the arguments when you instantiate the object.

```
// Instantiate the ClothingSale object and set the properties.
ClothingSale aClothingSale = new ClothingSale(productIdTextBox.Text,
    int.Parse(quantityTextBox.Text), decimal.Parse(unitPriceTextBox.Text),
    decimal.Parse(discountRateTextBox.Text));
```

Defining and Using a New Object—Step-by-Step

To continue the step-by-step exercise for the ClothingSale class, the next step is to write the code for the user interface. Figure 12.6 shows the completed user interface, which has text boxes for the user to enter the product ID, quantity, and unit price and a check box for discount. The Discount Rate text box is not visible unless the user selects the Discount check box. When the user selects the menu option to calculate the sale, the program creates an instance of the ClothingSale class and assigns the input values for product ID, quantity, unit price, and the discount rate to the properties of the ClothingSale object.

The ExtendedPrice property in the ClothingSale class returns the amount of the sale, which you will display on the form.

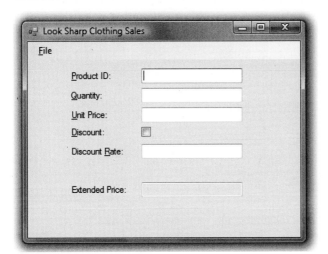

Placing all calculations in a separate class is a good thing. You are seeing your first example of dividing a program into a presentation tier and a business tier.

Examine the Form

This is a continuation of the step-by-step exercise for this chapter. If the project is not still open, open it now.

STEP 1: Open ClothingSalesForm in the Form Designer.

STEP 2: Open the menus in the menu designer to see the available options.

STEP 3: Examine the properties of the form controls. Notice that the Discount Rate text box is set to `Visible = false` and that the controls have ToolTips assigned to aid the user.

STEP 4: Open the code in the Code Editor window and modify the program comments at the top of the file.

STEP 5: Examine the methods that are already written. Notice that the calculateSaleToolStripMenuItem_Click method performs validation on the input values but does not perform any calculations or display the output (the extended price).

Write the Code

STEP 1: In the calculateSaleToolStripMenuItem event handler, write the code to instantiate the ClothingSale object, assign the values to the properties, calculate the extended price, and assign the result to extendedPriceTextBox. Notice that IntelliSense pops up with the properties and method of your new ClothingSale class.

```
// All passed validation; perform the calculation and display
// the output here.
// Instantiate a ClothingSale object.

ClothingSale aClothingSale = new
    ClothingSale(productIdTextBox.Text, quantityInteger,
    unitPriceDecimal, discountRateDecimal);
```

```
// Display the output.
   extendedPriceTextBox.Text =
        aClothingSale.ExtendedPrice.ToString("N");
```

Save Your Work

STEP 1: Click the *Save All* toolbar button to save the project, class, and form.

Run the Project

The next step is to watch the project run—hopefully without errors.

STEP 1: Run the program; your form should appear.

STEP 2: Fill in test values. Select the *File / Calculate Sale* menu item. What did you get for the extended price? Is it correct? Try entering something other than a number for Quantity. What happens when you calculate the sale?

STEP 3: Stop program execution using the *File / Exit* menu item.

Single-Step the Execution

If you get an error message or an incorrect answer in the output, you will need to debug the project. The quickest and easiest way to debug is to single-step program execution. Single-stepping is an interesting exercise, even if you *did* get the right answer.

To single-step, you need to be in debugging mode. Place a breakpoint on the first line in the calculateSaleToolStripMenuItem_Click method (the `try` statement). Run the program, enter test values, and select *File / Calculate Sale*. When the program stops at the breakpoint, press the F11 key repeatedly and watch each step; you will see execution transfer to the code for the Clothing-Sale class for each property and for the `calculateExtendedPrice` method. If an error message halts program execution, point to the variable names and property names on the screen to see their current values.

When the Click event method finishes, if the form does not reappear, you can click on your project's taskbar button.

Instance Variables versus Static Variables

The class properties that you have created up to this point belong to each instance of the class. Therefore, if you create two ClothingSale objects, each object has its own set of properties. This is exactly what you want for properties such as quantity and price, but what if you need to find a total or count for all of the ClothingSale objects? You don't want each new object to have its own count property; there would be nothing to increment.

The variables and properties that we have declared thus far are called **instance members**. A separate memory location exists for each instance of the object. Now we will create **static members**. A static member is a single variable, property, or method that exists, or is available, for all objects of a class.

Terminology varies from one OOP language to another. In some languages, static members are called *class variables* or *shared variables*. Microsoft documentation refers to *instance members* and *static members*, which include both properties and methods. In general, a static member has one copy for *all* objects of the class and an instance member has one copy for *each* instance or object of the class. You can declare both variables and methods as `static`; both are considered static members.

Another important point is that you can access static members without instantiating an object of the class. When you display class documentation in MSDN Help, static members display with a yellow *S* next to the name (Figure 12.7). You must reference these static members with `ClassName.Property` or `ClassName.method()`, whether or not you have instantiated an object from the class.

Creating Static Members

Use the **static keyword** to create a static member.

```
[public|private] static Datatype variableName;
[public|private] static Datatype methodName(ArgumentList);
```

Note: The `static` keyword can appear before or after the `public` or `private` keyword.

If we want to accumulate a total of all sales and a count of the number of sales for our ClothingSale class, we need **static properties**:

```
private static decimal salesTotalDecimal;
private static int salesCountInteger;
```

You will want to make the properties for the static members read-only so that their values can be retrieved but not set directly. The values of the properties are accumulated inside the class; each time a new sale is calculated, the extended price is added to the total sales and the sales count is incremented by one.

Figure 12.7

Static members display in MSDN Help with a yellow S.

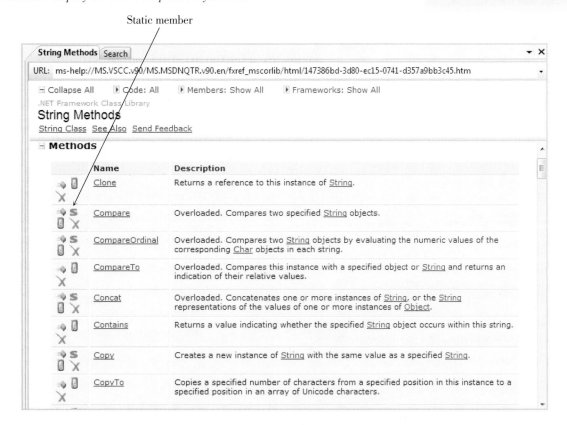

```
public static int SalesCount
{
    get
    {
        return salesCountInteger;
    }
}

public static decimal SalesTotal
{
    get
    {
        return salesTotalDecimal;
    }
}
```

Note that the `static` keyword on the `private` class-level variable makes it a static member; the `static` keyword on the property method is optional. You need to use it if you plan to retrieve the property without first creating an instance of the class.

Adding Static Properties to the Step-by-Step Exercise

You will now make the ClothingSale class calculate the total of all sales and a count of the number of sales. You will need static properties for the sales total and sales count in the class. Then, on the form, you will add a menu option for *Summary* that displays the totals in a message box.

Add Static Properties to the Class

If the chapter step-by-step exercise is not still open, open it now.

STEP 1: In the ClothingSale class, add the private class-level declarations for salesTotalDecimal and salesCountInteger.

```
private static decimal salesTotalDecimal;
private static int salesCountInteger;
```

STEP 2: Add the property methods for these two static read-only properties.

```
public static decimal SalesTotal
{
    get
    {
        return salesTotalDecimal;
    }
}

public static int SalesCount
{
    get
    {
        return salesCountInteger;
    }
}
```

Modify the Class Code to Calculate the Totals

STEP 1: In the ClothingSale class, add a private method for calculating the totals. This method will be called inside the class but cannot be called from an object outside the class.

```csharp
private void addToTotals()
{
    // Add to summary information.

    salesCountInteger++;
    salesTotalDecimal += extendedPriceDecimal;
}
```

STEP 2: Modify the constructor method to call the addToTotals method.

```csharp
public ClothingSale(string productIDString, int quantityInteger,
    decimal unitPriceDecimal, decimal discountDecimal)
{
    // Assign incoming values to the class properties.

    ProductId = productIdString;
    Quantity = quantityInteger;
    UnitPrice = unitPriceDecimal;
    DiscountRate = discountDecimal;
    calculateExtendedPrice();
    addToTotals();
}
```

Modify the Form

STEP 1: Add a menu item for *File / Summary* to the form. The easiest way to do this is to add the *Summary* item to the bottom of the *File* menu and drag it up to the correct position; the new item will be correctly named. If you insert a menu item, it is given a default name and you will have to rename it manually.

STEP 2: Write the event-handling method for summaryToolStripMenuItem to display the sales total and sales count from the properties of the class. Use a message box and format the sales total to display dollars and cents. Note that you retrieve the static members of the ClothingSale class using the name of the class, not using an instance of the class: ClothingSale.SalesTotal.

```csharp
private void summaryToolStripMenuItem_Click(object sender, System.EventArgs e)
{
    // Display the sales summary information.
    string messageString;

    messageString = "Sales Total: " + ClothingSale.SalesTotal.ToString("N") +
        "\nSales Count: " + ClothingSale.SalesCount.ToString();
    MessageBox.Show(messageString, "Look Sharp Clothing Sales Summary",
        MessageBoxButtons.OK, MessageBoxIcon.Information);
}
```

STEP 3: Test the program. Try entering several sales and checking the totals. Also try selecting *Summary* without first calculating a sale.

Destructors

If there is special processing that you need to do when an object goes out of scope, you can write a *destructor*. The destructor is a method with the same name as the class preceded by a tilde (~) such as

```
~ClothingSale()
{
    // Any cleanup code goes here.
}
```

The destructor method automatically calls the `Object.Finalize` method from the base class of the object. The programmer has no control over when the destructor is called because it is handled by the CLR as part of the garbage collection. Microsoft advises against writing destructors in classes since they have an adverse effect on the performance of the .NET garbage collector.

Garbage Collection

The **garbage collection** feature of the .NET Common Language Runtime cleans up unused components. Periodically the garbage collector checks for unreferenced objects and releases all memory and system resources used by the objects. If you have written a destructor method, it executes during garbage collection. Microsoft recommends that you rely on garbage collection to release resources and not try to finalize objects yourself. Using this technique, you don't know exactly when your objects will be finalized since the CLR performs garbage collection on its own schedule, when it needs to recover the resources or has spare time.

Feedback 12.1

1. What is the difference between an object and a class?
2. Given the statement

   ```
   private Product aProduct;
   ```

   is aProduct an object or class? What about Product?
3. What actions are performed by the following statement?

   ```
   aProduct.Quantity = int.Parse(quantityTextBox.Text);
   ```

4. Write the property declarations for a Student class that will contain the properties LastName, FirstName, StudentIDNumber, and GPA. Where will these statements appear?
5. Code the property method to set and retrieve the value of the LastName property.
6. Code the property method to retrieve the value of the read-only GPA property.

Inheritance

When you create a class, the new class can be based on another class. You can make the new class inherit from one of the .NET existing classes or from one of your own classes. Recall that a form uses inheritance using the statement

```
public partial class ClothingSaleForm : Form
```

The inheritance clause must follow the class header prior to any comments.

```
public class NewClass : BaseClass
```

Inheriting Properties and Methods

When writing code for a derived class, you can reference all public and protected data members and methods of the base class. If you want the derived class to have a different implementation for a base-class method, you must write the method in the derived class that overrides the base-class method.

In the past you have used the `public` and `private` keywords. You also can declare elements with the **protected** keyword, which specifies that the element is accessible only within its own class or any class derived from that class.

Overriding Methods

You can create a method with the same name and the same argument list as a method in the base class. The new method is said to *override* the base-class method. The derived class will use the new method rather than the method in the base class.

To override a method in C#, you must declare the original method (in the base class) with the **virtual** or **abstract** keyword and declare the new method (in the subclass) with the `override` keyword. The access modifier for the override method must be the same as the base-class method.

Base Class

```
protected virtual decimal calculateExtendedPrice()
```

Inherited Class

```
protected override decimal calculateExtendedPrice()
```

In a base class, you can use the `virtual`, `abstract`, or `override` keyword on a method that can be overridden. Use `virtual` when you are writing a new method that has code; use `abstract` for a method header for an empty method. **Abstract methods** are designed to be overridden by subclasses and have no implementation of their own. The only time that you declare a base-class method with the `override` keyword is when the method is overriding a method in *its* base class.

When you use the word `virtual` for a base-class method, in the derived class you have the option of using the base-class implementation for the method or overriding the method by supplying new code. However, if you use the `abstract` keyword on a base-class method, the method does not have any code; the derived class *must* provide its own code for the method. A class that has any method declared as `abstract` is considered an **abstract class**, which can be used only for inheritance. You cannot instantiate objects from a class that contains abstract methods.

Accessing Properties

Your derived class can set and retrieve the properties of the base class by using the property **accessor methods**. Usually your derived class needs to make use of properties and methods of the base class. You can call the base-class constructor from the subclass constructor, which allows you to use the property values from the base class. In the following example, the derived Member-ClothingSale class inherits from ClothingSale. Notice the constructor, which uses the `base` statement to call the constructor of the base class. If the constructor requires arguments, you can pass the argument values when you call the constructor:

```
class MemberClothingSale : ClothingSale
{
    public MemberClothingSale(string productIdString, int quantityInteger,
        decimal unitPriceDecimal, decimal discountDecimal)
        :
        base(productIdString, quantityInteger, unitPriceDecimal, discountDecimal)
    {
        // Calls the base-class constructor and passes arguments.
    }
}
```

After you have assigned values to the properties of the base class, you can refer to the properties in methods in the derived class. In the following example, the calculateExtendedPrice method in the derived class uses properties of the base class by property name.

```
// Method in the derived class that overrides the method in the base class.
protected override void calculateExtendedPrice()
{
    // Find the ExtendedPrice.
    decimal discountDecimal;

    discountDecimal = DiscountRate + MEMBER_DISCOUNT_Decimal;
    ExtendedPrice = unitPriceDecimal * (1 - discountDecimal) * Quantity;
}
```

Note that to use base-class properties in the derived class as in this example, the properties must have both a `get` and a `set` accessor method. Read-only or write-only properties cannot be accessed by name from a derived class.

Creating a Derived Class Based on ClothingSale

The ClothingSale class could be considered a generic class, which is appropriate for most sales. But now we want another similar class, but with some differences. The new class should have all of the same properties and methods of the ClothingSale class but will calculate sales with a member discount of 10 percent. We also want a new static property in the new class to hold the total of the member discounts.

Our new derived class will be called MemberClothingSale; the base class is ClothingSale. Figure 12.8 shows the UML diagram to indicate the inherited

Figure 12.8

The diagram for a base class and an inherited subclass.

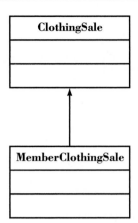

class. The inherited class automatically has all public and protected properties and methods of the base class; in this case, MemberClothingSale automatically has seven properties and any methods listed as protected.

Adding Inheritance to the Step-by-Step Exercise

This continuation of the chapter step-by-step exercise includes adding a new subclass class, overriding a method, and adding a new property.

Change the Private Members to Protected

STEP 1: Open your project, if necessary, and open the ClothingSale.cs file. Change all of the private class-level variable declarations to protected. For example, change

```
private string productIdString;
```

>   *to*

```
protected string productIdString;
```

Add the New Class

STEP 1: Select *Add Class* from the *Project* menu.

STEP 2: In the *Add New Item* dialog, choose *Class*, type "MemberClothingSale.cs" for the class name, and click on *Add*. You will see a new tab in the Document window for the new class.

STEP 3: Modify the class header.

```
class MemberClothingSale : ClothingSale
```

You can ignore the warning error message; it tells you that this subclass must have a constructor, which you will do in the next step.

All of the public and protected properties and methods of the base class will be inherited by the subclass.

Add the Constructor

STEP 1: The subclass must have its own constructor since constructors are not inherited. Write the following code inside the new class:

```
public MemberClothingSale(string productIdString, int quantityInteger,
    decimal unitPriceDecimal, decimal discountDecimal)
    :
    base(productIdString, quantityInteger, unitPriceDecimal, discountDecimal)
{
    // Calls the base-class constructor and passes arguments.
}
```

Add a Constant

STEP 1: Add a constant at the class level to hold the discount rate of 10 percent.

```
const decimal MEMBER_DISCOUNT_Decimal = .1M;
```

Override a Method

When you override a method from the base class in an inherited class, the method name and the argument list must exactly match.

STEP 1: Open the ClothingSale base class in the editor and modify the method header for `calculateExtendedPrice`.

```
protected virtual void calculateExtendedPrice()
```

STEP 2: In the MemberClothingSale inherited class, write the new `calculateExtendedPrice` method, using the `override` keyword.

```
// Method in the derived class that overrides the method in the base class.
protected override void calculateExtendedPrice()
{
    // Find the ExtendedPrice.
    decimal discountDecimal;

    discountDecimal = DiscountRate + MEMBER_DISCOUNT_Decimal;
    ExtendedPrice = UnitPrice * (1 - discountDecimal) * Quantity;
}
```

Add Required Accessors for DiscountRate, Quantity, and ExtendedPrice

STEP 1: In the ClothingSale (base) class, modify the properties to contain both `get` and `set` accessors.

```
public int Quantity
{
    get
    {
        return quantityInteger;
    }
```

```
    set
    {
        quantityInteger = value;
    }
}
public decimal UnitPrice
{
    get
    {
        return unitPriceDecimal;
    }
    set
    {
        unitPriceDecimal = value;
    }
}
public decimal DiscountRate
{
    get
    {
        return discountRateDecimal;
    }
    set
    {
        discountRateDecimal = value;
    }
}
public decimal ExtendedPrice
{
    get
    {
        return extendedPriceDecimal;
    }
    set
    {
        extendedPriceDecimal = value;
    }
}
```

Allow a Method to Be Inherited

The addToTotals method in the base class was declared with the private keyword, which does not allow it to be inherited. If you want to be able to inherit a method, it must be declared as protected or public.

STEP 1: Open the ClothingSale base class, if necessary, and modify the addToTotals method header.

```
protected void addToTotals()
```

Modify the Form to Use the Inherited Class

STEP 1: Add a check box to the form (Figure 12.9). Name the control memberCheckBox and delete the Text property. Add a label with the Text set to "&Member" and reset the tab sequence.

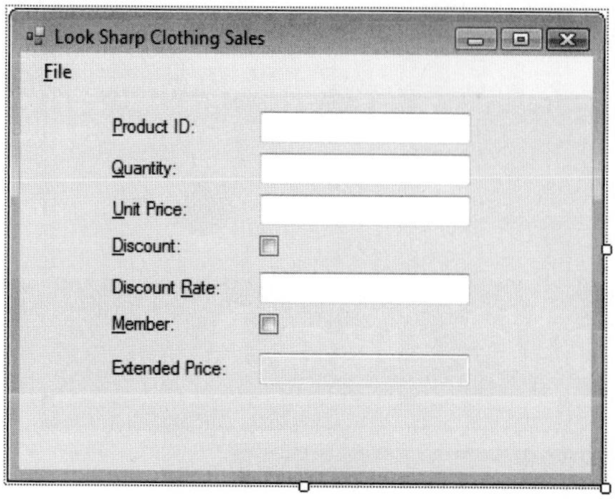

Figure 12.9

Add a Member check box to the form.

STEP 2: Modify the calculateSaleToolStripMenuItem event method to create the correct object, depending on the state of memberCheckBox.

```
if (memberCheckBox.Checked)
{
    MemberClothingSale aMemberClothingSale = new
        MemberClothingSale(productIdTextBox.Text, quantityInteger,
        unitPriceDecimal, discountRateDecimal);
    // Display the output.
    extendedPriceTextBox.Text =
        aMemberClothingSale.ExtendedPrice.ToString("N");
}
else
{
    ClothingSale aClothingSale = new
        ClothingSale(productIdTextBox.Text, quantityInteger,
        unitPriceDecimal, discountRateDecimal);
    // Display the output.
    extendedPriceTextBox.Text =
        aClothingSale.ExtendedPrice.ToString("N");
}
```

Notice that the code uses the ExtendedPrice property in either case. But when memberCheckBox is checked, `ExtendedPrice` is calculated in the subclass; when the check box is not checked, the `ExtendedPrice` is calculated in the base class. Both classes add to the static SalesTotal and SalesCount properties of the base class, which will hold the totals for both classes.

STEP 3: Run the program. Try both member and nonmember sales; check the totals.

STEP 4: Close the project.

Creating a Base Class Strictly for Inheritance

Sometimes you may want to create a class solely for the purpose of inheritance by two or more similar classes. For example, you might create a Person class that you don't intend to instantiate. Instead, you will create subclasses of the Person class, such as Employee, Customer, and Student.

For a base class that you intend to inherit, include the `abstract` modifier on the class declaration. In each of the methods in the base class that must be overridden, include the `abstract` modifier. The method that must be overridden does not contain any code in the base class.

Base Class

```
public abstract class BaseClass
{
    public abstract void someMethod()
    {
        // No code allowed here.
    }
}
```

Inherited Class

```
public class DerivedClass : BaseClass
{
    public override void someMethod()
    {
        // Code goes here.
    }
}
```

Note: You must build (compile) the base class before using it for an inherited class.

Inheriting Form Classes

Some projects require that you have several forms. You may want to use a similar design from one form to the next. You can use **visual inheritance** by designing one form and then inheriting any other forms from the first (Figure 12.10).

Once you have designed the form that you want to use for a pattern, you can add more forms that inherit from your design master, called your *base class*. Your base class inherits from Form, and your new forms inherit from your base class.

When you design the base class, you can include design elements and other controls such as labels, text boxes, and buttons. You also can write methods and declare variables in the base class. Just as you saw earlier, all public and protected methods and variables are inherited from the base class to the subclass. You can write methods in the base class and specify `virtual` or `abstract`, and then in the subclass write the identically named method with the `override` keyword.

To create an inherited form in your project, first create the base class, save, and build the project. You cannot inherit from a form that has not been compiled. Then you can define the inherited form class in two ways:

1. Select *Project/Add Windows Form* and type the name of the new Windows form. In the code window, modify the class header.

```
public partial class NewForm : BaseForm
```

Figure 12.10

Create a base form and inherit the visual interface to new forms. a. The base form; b., c., and d., inherited forms.

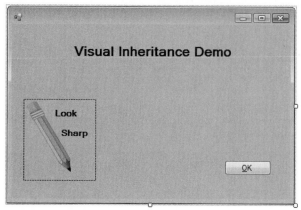

a.

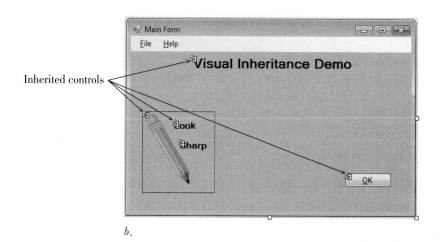

Inherited controls

b.

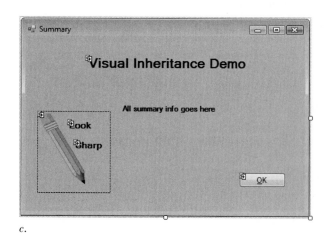

c.

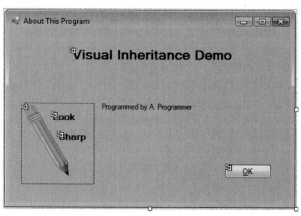

d.

Open the new form in the designer and you should see the inherited visual elements.

2. In the Professional Edition, you also can use this technique: Select *Project / Add Windows Form* and type the name of the new form. Select the *InheritedForm* icon. After clicking on the *Add* button, you are shown a dialog displaying the compiled forms in the project from which to select. The *InheritedForm* template is not available in the Express Edition.

Form Inheritance Example

This example has three forms that inherit from a base class. The base class has an *OK* button, a picture box, and labels. All forms that inherit from the base class will have all of these controls. You cannot delete any of the controls on the inherited forms, but you can make a control invisible. For example, in MainForm, the *OK* button's Visible property is set to *false*.

The base class has an okButton_Click event method, which can be overridden in the subclasses. Note that the okButton_Click event method must be declared as `public` or `protected` to be inherited and overridden in derived classes. In order to set the properties of the okButton (such as Visible) in a derived form, the button must have its Modifiers property set to public or protected (in the designer) and the click event handler must be declared as public or protected. The method access modifier must match in the base class and subclass; for example, if you set the okButton_Click event method to protected, the overriding method in the subclass also must be protected.

TIP

If you receive errors when opening the inherited form in Design View, close the form, rebuild the project, and reopen the form. ■

BaseForm

```
public partial class BaseForm : Form
{
    public BaseForm()
    {
        InitializeComponent();
    }

    protected virtual void okButton_Click(object sender, EventArgs e)
    {
        // Close the form.

        this.Close();
    }
}
```

AboutForm No code required.

MainForm

```
public partial class MainForm : BaseForm
{
    public MainForm()
    {
        InitializeComponent();
    }
```

```csharp
private void MainForm_Load(object sender, EventArgs e)
{
    // Hide the OK button for this form.

    this.okButton.Visible = false;
}

private void exitToolStripMenuItem_Click(object sender, EventArgs e)
{
    // Close the application.

    this.Close();
}

private void summaryToolStripMenuItem_Click(object sender, EventArgs e)
{
    // Display the Summary form.
    SummaryForm aSummaryForm = new SummaryForm();

    aSummaryForm.Show();
}

private void aboutToolStripMenuItem_Click(object sender, EventArgs e)
{
    // Display the About form.
    AboutForm anAboutForm = new AboutForm();

    anAboutForm.ShowDialog();
}
}
```

SummaryForm

```csharp
public partial class SummaryForm : BaseForm
{
    public SummaryForm()
    {
        InitializeComponent();
    }

    protected override void okButton_Click(object sender, EventArgs e)
    {
        base.okButton_Click(sender, e);
        // Could write code to alter the behavior here.
    }
}
```

Coding for Events of an Inherited Class

When you derive a new form class from an existing form, you often want to write code for events of inherited controls. Unfortunately, you can't double-click on an inherited control and have the event method open, like you can for most controls. In the inherited class's code window, type in "public override ok" and then select the okButton_Click event from IntelliSense. Remember that the code must already have been changed to "protected virtual" in the base class and that you must have recompiled the project.

Setting the Startup Form

In Visual Studio, the default behavior of C# applications is to begin execution with a file called Program.cs. You can open and modify this file, which contains a `Main` method that always runs first. Recall that in Chapter 6 you modified the `Main` method to display your splash form before the main form.

The first form added to a project is considered the startup form. If you create a base form first, that's not the form that you want to display. Modify the `Application.Run` method in Program.cs to begin with your main form:

```
Application.Run(new MainForm());
```

Managing Multiclass Projects

This chapter has examples of projects with multiple forms and multiple classes. In each case, every class is stored in a separate file. Although you must keep form classes in separate files, other classes do not have that requirement. You can code multiple classes in one file.

Adding an Existing Class File to a Project

If you have an existing form or other class file that you want to include in a project, you can choose to reference the file in its original location or move or copy it into your project folder. Unless you need to share a class among several projects, it's best to place the class file into the project folder. After you move or copy the desired file into the project folder, add the file to the project by selecting *Project / Add Existing Item* (or right-click the project name in the Solution Explorer and select from the context menu).

Using the Object Browser

The Object Browser is an important tool for working with objects. The Object Browser can show you the names of objects, properties, methods, events, and constants for C# objects, your own objects, and objects available from other applications.

Select *View / Object Browser* or the Object Browser toolbar button (Figure 12.11) to open the Object Browser window (Figure 12.12). You can choose the libraries/namespaces in the *Browse* list. You also can search for specific items using the *Search* box.

The Object Browser uses several icons to represent items. Notice in Figure 12.12 the icons that represent properties, methods, events, constants, classes,

Figure   12.11

Open the Object Browser from the toolbar button.

Object Browser (Ctrl+W, J)

The Object Browser window; notice the icons to indicate the member type.

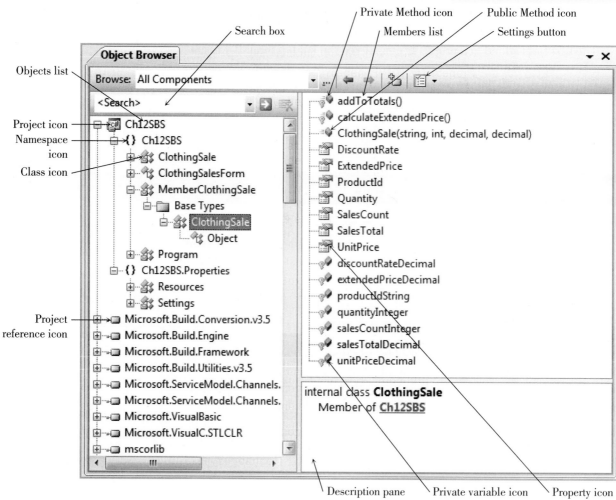

and namespaces. In the lower-right corner of the window, you can see a description of any item you select. Click the *Settings* button to show or hide public, protected, and private members, along with base-class and derived-class information.

Examining C# Classes

You can look up the available properties, methods, events, or constants of a C# class. You can see which elements are defined in the class; what is the base class; and which properties, methods, and events are inherited. In Figure 12.13, notice the entries for System.Windows.Forms.MessageBox; the overloaded constructors appear in the *Members* list. And in Figure 12.14, you can see the constants for MessageBoxButtons.

Examining Your Own Classes

You can see your own classes listed in the Object Browser. With the chapter step-by-step project open, select your project name in the Object Browser. Try

Figure 12.13

Display the members of the System.Windows.Forms.MessageBox class.

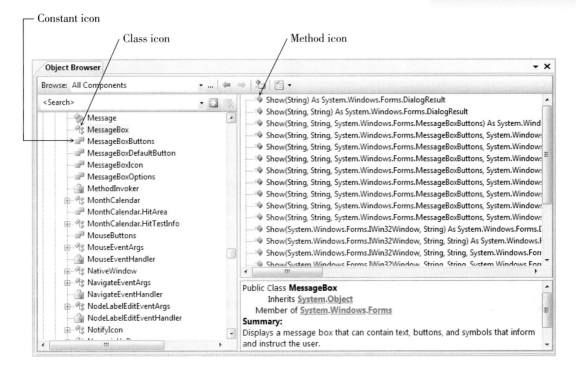

Figure 12.14

Display the MessageBoxButtons constants.

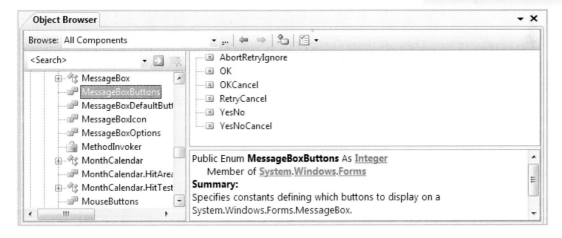

clicking on each class name and viewing the list of properties and methods (Figure 12.15).

You can use the Object Browser to jump to the definition of any property or method by double-clicking on its name in the *Members* list. This technique is also a great way to jump to any of the methods in your forms. Select your form name in the *Objects* list and double-click on the name of the method you want to view.

Figure 12.15

View the properties and methods for your own classes. Double-click on an item in the Members list to jump to its definition in code.

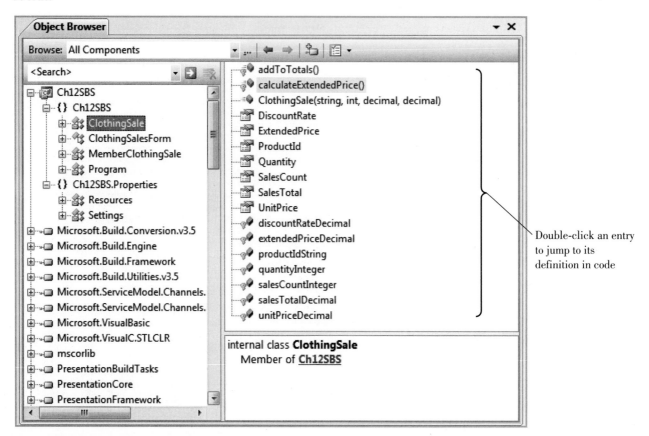

Double-click an entry to jump to its definition in code

Your Hands-On Programming Example

This program must calculate clothing sales for Look Sharp Fitness Center, with an input field for any discount rate and a discount of 10 percent for members. The project will be similar to the ClothingSale and MemberClothingSale classes developed in the chapter step-by-step, but with some modifications.

The user will be able to select the product ID from a drop-down list on the form; each product ID has a predetermined price, so the user will not be required to enter the price. The list of product IDs and their prices could be stored in a database or a small text file and read as a stream. For this program, use the file Products.txt in the StudentData folder to both load the drop-down list and calculate the price. In the ClothingSale class, make the ProductId property an integer and pass the index of the selected item, rather than the string.

The project should have multiple forms that have a static design element (visual inheritance). Include a main form, an About form, and a Summary form that displays the sales summary information.

Design a base form to use for inheritance and make the other three forms inherit from the base form. The About form and Summary form must have an *OK* button, which closes or hides the form. The main form will have menus and no *OK* button.

Main form menu

<pre>
<u>F</u>ile   <u>H</u>elp
   <u>C</u>alculate Sale   <u>A</u>bout
   C<u>l</u>ear
   <u>S</u>ummary
   ────────
   E<u>x</u>it
</pre>

Planning the Project

Sketch a base form for inheritance, a main form, an About form, and a Summary form (Figure 12.16) for your users. The users approve and sign off the forms as meeting their needs.

Figure 12.16

The planning sketches of the forms for the hands-on programming example. a. the base form; b. the main form.

BaseForm

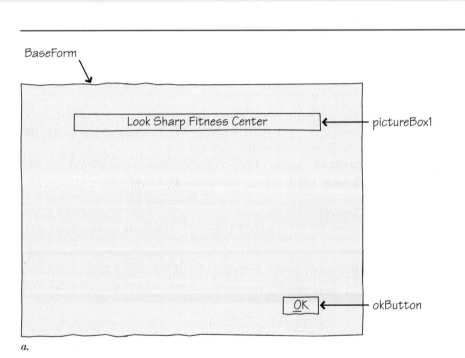

a.

ClothingSaleForm

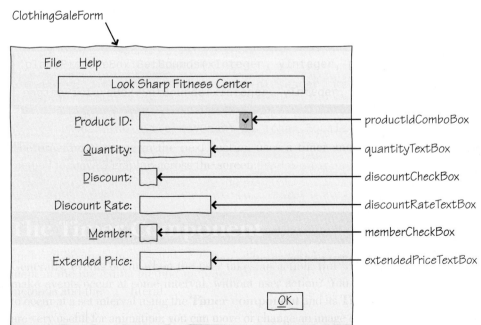

b.

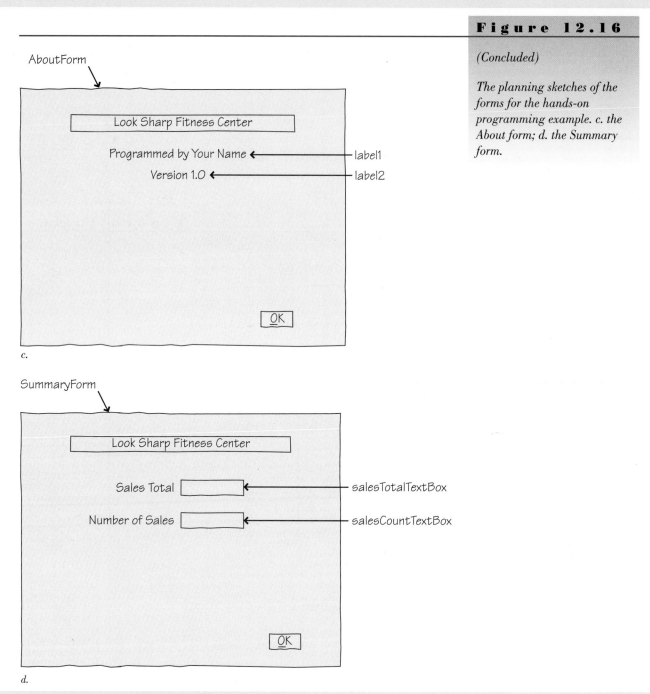

Figure 12.16

(Concluded)

The planning sketches of the forms for the hands-on programming example. c. the About form; d. the Summary form.

AboutForm

Look Sharp Fitness Center

Programmed by Your Name ← ———— label1

Version 1.0 ← ———— label2

OK

c.

SummaryForm

Look Sharp Fitness Center

Sales Total [   ] ← ———— salesTotalTextBox

Number of Sales [   ] ← ———— salesCountTextBox

OK

d.

Plan the Objects and Properties for the Base Form

Object	Property	Setting
BaseForm	Name	BaseForm
	Text	Clothing Sales
	BackColor	light blue
pictureBox1	Name	pictureBox1
	Image	LookSharp.gif
okButton	Name	okButton
	Modifiers	Public
	Text	&OK

Plan the Event Handlers for the Base Form

Event Handler	Actions
okButton_Click	Close the form.

Plan the Objects and Properties for the Main Form

Object	Property	Setting
ClothingSaleForm	Name	ClothingSaleForm
	Text	Clothing Sales
label1	Text	&Product ID:
productIdComboBox	Name	productIdComboBox
	ToolTip	Product ID from the catalog.
label2	Text	&Quantity:
quantityTextBox	Name	quantityTextBox
discountCheckBox	Name	discountCheckBox
	Text	&Discount
	RightToLeft	Yes
discountRateLabel	Name	discountRateLabel
	Text	Discount &Rate:
	Visible	false
discountRateTextBox	Name	discountRateTextBox
	Visible	false
	ToolTip	Enter as a decimal, such as .20 for 20%.
memberCheckBox	Name	memberCheckBox
	Text	&Member:
	RightToLeft	Yes
label4	Name	label4
	Text	Extended Price:
extendedPriceTextBox	Name	extendedPriceTextBox
	ReadOnly	true
	TabStop	false
fileToolStripMenuItem	Name	FileToolStripMenuItem
	Text	&File
calculateSaleToolStripMenuItem	Name	calculateSaleToolStripMenuItem
	Text	&Calculate Sale
clearToolStripMenuItem	Name	clearToolStripMenuItem
	Text	C&lear
summaryToolStripMenuItem	Name	summaryToolStripMenuItem
	Text	&Summary
exitToolStripMenuItem	Name	exitToolStripMenuItem
	Text	E&xit

(Continued)

Object	Property	Setting
helpToolStripMenuItem	Name Text	helpToolStripMenuItem &Help
aboutToolStripMenuItem	Name Text	aboutToolStripMenuItem &About

Plan the Event Handlers for the Main Form

Event Handler	Actions

Form_Load	Hide the inherited OK button.
	Load the combo box with Product IDs.
	If the file is not found
	    Query user to continue.
	      If No
	        Call exitToolStripMenuItem_Click.

calculateSaleToolStripMenuItem_Click	If no Product ID selected
	    Display a message.
	Else
	    If Discounted
	      Parse discount rate.
	      If discount rate >= 1
	        Throw exception.
	    Parse quantity.
	    If member sale
	      Create a MemberClothingSale object.
	      Calculate and format the extended price.
	    Else
	      Create a ClothingSale object.
	      Calculate and format the extended price.
	Catch all parsing errors.
	    Display a message box for input errors.

clearToolStripMenuItem_Click	Clear the combo box selection. Clear the text boxes. Uncheck the discount check box. Hide the discount controls. Set the focus on the combo box.
summaryToolStripMenuItem_Click	Instantiate a Summary form. Set the properties of the form with the summary values. Show the Summary form.
exitToolStripMenuItem_Click	End the project
aboutToolStripMenuItem_Click	Instantiate and show the About form.

discountCheckBox_CheckedChanged	If the check box is checked
	    Set Visibility = true for the discount controls.
	    Set the focus to the discount rate text box.
	Else
	    Set Visibility = false for the discount controls.

Plan the Objects and Properties for the About Form

Object	Property	Setting
AboutForm	Name	AboutForm
	Text	About Clothing Sales
label1	Text	Programmed by A. Programmer (Use your own name.)
label2	Text	Version 1.0

Plan the Event Handlers for the About Form **None required.**

Plan the Objects and Properties for the Summary Form

Object	Property	Setting
SummaryForm	Name	SummaryForm
	Text	Clothing Sales Summary
label1	Text	Sales Total:
salesTotalTextBox	Name	salesTotalTextBox
	ReadOnly	True
	TabStop	False
label2	Text	Number of Sales:
salesCountTextBox	Name	salesCountTextBox
	ReadOnly	True
	TabStop	False

Plan the Properties for the Summary Form

Properties	DataType	Accessor

Declare private class-level variables and write property methods
for all public properties:

SalesTotal	decimal	set
SalesCount	int	set

Plan the ClothingSale Class

Properties

Declare private class-level variables and write property methods for all public properties:
Instance:
    ProductNumber
    Quantity
    UnitPrice
    DiscountRate
    ExtendedPrice
Static:
    SalesTotal
    SalesCount

Methods	Actions
ClothingSale (Constructor)	If first run 　　Call loadPriceList. Set properties for input values. Retrieve unit price from array. Call calculateExtendedPrice. Call addToTotals.
calculateExtendedPrice	Calculate extended price = unitPrice * (1 − discountRate) * quantity.
addToTotals	Add 1 to SalesCount. Add extended price to SalesTotal.
loadPriceList	Declare and instantiate a stream reader. Read the file stream and load the priceDecimal array.

Plan the MemberClothingSale Object Class Inherit from ClothingSale.

Method	Actions
MemberClothingSale (Constructor)	Call the base class, passing the arguments.
calculateExtendedPrice	Calculate discount = member discount plus other discounts. Calculate extended price.

Write the Project Follow the sketches in Figure 12.16 to create the forms. Create the base form and inherit the other three forms from the base form. Figure 12.17 shows the completed forms.

- Set the properties of each of the objects according to your plan.

- Create the ClothingSale and MemberClothingSale classes. You may want to copy the classes from the step-by-step exercise and modify them.

Figure 12.17

The completed forms for the hands-on programming example. a. the base form; b. the main form; c. the About form; and d. the Summary form.

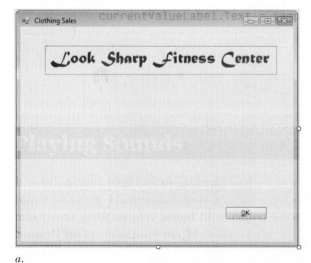

a.

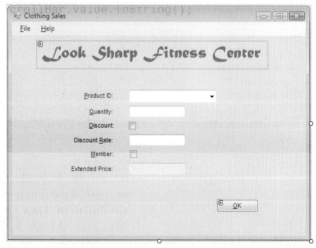

b.

Figure 12.17

(Concluded)

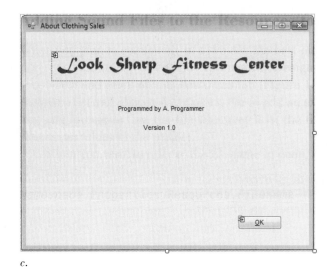

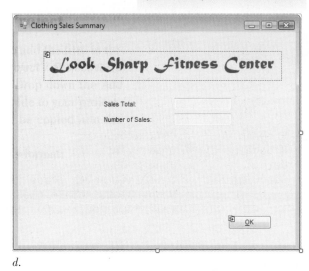

c.   *d.*

- Write the code. Working from the pseudocode, write each method.

- When you complete the code, use a variety of data to thoroughly test the project.

The Project Coding Solution

BaseForm

```
/* Program:        Ch12HandsOn
 * Programmer:     Bradley/Millspaugh
 * Date:           June 2009
 * Description:    Base form for hands-on project.
 */

using System;
using System.Collections.Generic;
using System.ComponentModel;
using System.Data;
using System.Drawing;
using System.Text;
using System.Windows.Forms;

namespace Ch12HandsOn
{
    public partial class BaseForm : Form
    {
        public BaseForm()
        {
            InitializeComponent();
        }
```

```csharp
        public virtual void okButton_Click(object sender, EventArgs e)
        {
            // Close the form.

            this.Close();
        }
    }
}
```

ClothingSaleForm

```csharp
/* Program:         Ch12HandsOn
 * Programmer:      Bradley/Millspaugh
 * Date:            June 2009
 * Description:     Calculate sales price using the ClothingSale and
 *                  MemberClothingSale classes.
 *                  Main form for the Chapter 12 hands-on project.
 */

using System;
using System.Collections.Generic;
using System.ComponentModel;
using System.Data;
using System.Drawing;
using System.Text;
using System.Windows.Forms;
using System.IO;

namespace Ch12HandsOn
{
    public partial class ClothingSaleForm : BaseForm
    {
        public ClothingSaleForm()
        {
            InitializeComponent();
        }

        private void ClothingSaleForm_Load(object sender, EventArgs e)
        {
            // Initialize the form.

            // Hide the ok button.
            this.okButton.Visible = false;

            // Load the drop-down list.
            DialogResult responseDialogResult;
            try
            {
                StreamReader productsStreamReader =
                    new StreamReader("Products.txt");
                string productString, priceString;
                while (productsStreamReader.Peek() != -1)
                {
                    productString = productsStreamReader.ReadLine();
                    priceString = productsStreamReader.ReadLine();
                    productIdComboBox.Items.Add(productString);
                }
```

```
                productsStreamReader.Close();
            }
            catch
            {
                responseDialogResult = MessageBox.Show(
                    "Product File not found. Run anyway?",
                    "File not Found", MessageBoxButtons.YesNo,
                    MessageBoxIcon.Question);
                if (responseDialogResult == DialogResult.No)
                {
                    // Exit the project.
                    exitToolStripMenuItem_Click(e, new System.EventArgs());
                }
            }
        }

        private void calculateSaleToolStripMenuItem_Click(object sender,
            EventArgs e)
        {
            // Calculate the extended price and any discount.
            decimal discountRateDecimal = 0m;

            if (productIdComboBox.SelectedIndex == -1)
            {
                MessageBox.Show("Select a product number.", "Error");
            }
            else
            {
                // A product has been selected.
                // Is there a discount?
                try // Discount rate.
                {
                    if (discountCheckBox.Checked)
                    {
                        discountRateDecimal =
                            decimal.Parse(discountRateTextBox.Text);
                        // Check for decimal fraction.
                        if (discountRateDecimal >= 1M)
                        {
                            throw new ApplicationException();
                        }
                    }
                }
                try // Quantity.
                {
                    int quantityInteger = int.Parse(quantityTextBox.Text);
                    if (membercheckBox.Checked)
                    {
                        // Instantiate a MemberClothingSale object and
                        // set the properties.
                        MemberClothingSale aMemberClothingSale = new
                            MemberClothingSale(productIdComboBox.SelectedIndex,
                            quantityInteger, discountRateDecimal);
                        extendedPriceTextBox.Text =
                            aMemberClothingSale.ExtendedPrice.ToString("N");
```

```
                    }
                    else
                    {

                        ClothingSale aClothingSale =
                            new ClothingSale(productIdComboBox.SelectedIndex,
                            quantityInteger, discountRateDecimal);
                        extendedPriceTextBox.Text =
                            aClothingSale.ExtendedPrice.ToString("N");
                    }
                }
                catch // Quantity.
                {
                    MessageBox.Show("Invalid quantity", "Error");
                }
            }
            catch // Discount rate.
            {
                MessageBox.Show("Invalid discount rate.", "Error");
            }
        }
    }

    private void clearToolStripMenuItem_Click(object sender, EventArgs e)
    {
        // Clear the controls for next entry.

        productIdComboBox.SelectedIndex = -1;
        quantityTextBox.Clear();
        discountRateTextBox.Clear();
        discountCheckBox.Checked = false;
        extendedPriceTextBox.Clear();
        productIdComboBox.Focus();
    }

    private void summaryToolStripMenuItem_Click(object sender,
        System.EventArgs e)
    {
        // Display the sales summary form.
        SummaryForm aSummaryForm = new SummaryForm();

        // Fill the properties.
        aSummaryForm.SalesTotal = ClothingSale.SalesTotal;
        aSummaryForm.SalesCount = ClothingSale.SalesCount;
        aSummaryForm.Show();
    }

    private void exitToolStripMenuItem_Click(object sender, EventArgs e)
    {
        // Close the project.

        this.Close();
    }
```

```csharp
        private void aboutToolStripMenuItem_Click(object sender, EventArgs e)
        {
            // Display the about form.
            AboutForm anAboutForm = new AboutForm();

            anAboutForm.ShowDialog();
        }

        private void discountCheckBox_CheckedChanged(object sender, EventArgs e)
        {
            // Display input field for discount rate if checked.

            if (discountCheckBox.Checked)
            {
                discountRateTextBox.Visible = true;
                discountRateLabel.Visible = true;
                discountRateTextBox.Focus();
            }
            else
            {
                discountRateTextBox.Visible = false;
                discountRateLabel.Visible = false;
            }
        }
    }
}
```

AboutForm

```csharp
/* Program:        Ch12HandsOn
 * Programmer:     Bradley/Millspaugh
 * Date:           June 2009
 * Description:    Calculate sales price using the ClothingSale class.
 *                 About form for hands-on project.
 */

using System;
using System.Collections.Generic;
using System.ComponentModel;
using System.Data;
using System.Drawing;
using System.Text;
using System.Windows.Forms;

namespace Ch12HandsOn
{
    public partial class AboutForm : Ch12HandsOn.BaseForm
    {
        public AboutForm()
        {
            InitializeComponent();
        }
    }
}
```

SummaryForm

```
/* Program:        Ch12HandsOn
 * Programmer:     Bradley/Millspaugh
 * Date:           June 2009
 * Description:    Calculate sales price using the ClothingSale class.
 *                 Summary form for hands-on project.
 */

using System;
using System.Collections.Generic;
using System.ComponentModel;
using System.Data;
using System.Drawing;
using System.Text;
using System.Windows.Forms;

namespace Ch12HandsOn
{
    public partial class SummaryForm : Ch12HandsOn.BaseForm
    {
        public SummaryForm()
        {
            InitializeComponent();
        }
        private decimal salesTotalDecimal;
        private int salesCountInteger;

        public decimal SalesTotal
        {
            set
            {
                salesTotalDecimal = value;
            }
        }

        public int SalesCount
        {
            set
            {
                salesCountInteger = value;
            }
        }

        private void SummaryForm_Load(object sender, EventArgs e)
        {
            // Fill the text boxes.

            salesCountTextBox.Text = salesCountInteger.ToString();
            salesTotalTextBox.Text = salesTotalDecimal.ToString("C");
        }
    }
}
```

ClothingSale Class

```
/* Class Name:      ClothingSale
 * Programmer:      Bradley/Millspaugh
 * Date:            June 2009
 * Description:     Handle clothing sale information.
 */

using System;
using System.Collections.Generic;
using System.Text;
using System.IO;

namespace Ch12HandsOn
{
    class ClothingSale
    {
        protected int quantityInteger, productIdInteger;
        protected decimal discountRateDecimal, unitPriceDecimal,
            extendedPriceDecimal;
        protected static decimal salesTotalDecimal;
        protected static int salesCountInteger;
        protected static decimal[] priceDecimal = new decimal[100];
        private bool runOnceBoolean = false;
        public int ProductNumber
        {
            get
            {
                return productIdInteger;
            }
            private set
            {
                productIdInteger = value;
            }
        }

        public int Quantity
        {
            get
            {
                return quantityInteger;
            }
            set
            {
                quantityInteger = value;
            }
        }

        public decimal UnitPrice
        {
            get
            {
                return unitPriceDecimal;
            }
            set
            {
                unitPriceDecimal = value;
            }
        }
```

```csharp
public decimal DiscountRate
{
    get
    {
        return discountRateDecimal;
    }
    set
    {
        discountRateDecimal = value;
    }
}

public decimal ExtendedPrice
{
    get
    {
        return extendedPriceDecimal;
    }
    set
    {
        extendedPriceDecimal = value;
    }
}

public static decimal SalesTotal
{
    get
    {
        return salesTotalDecimal;
    }
}

public static int SalesCount
{
    get
    {
        return salesCountInteger;
    }
}

public ClothingSale(int productIdInteger, int quantityInteger,
    decimal discountDecimal)
{
    // Constructor.

    if (!runOnceBoolean)
    {
        loadPriceList();
    }
    ProductNumber = productIdInteger;
    UnitPrice = priceDecimal[ProductNumber];
    Quantity = quantityInteger;
    DiscountRate = discountDecimal;
    calculateExtendedPrice();
    addToTotals();
}
```

```
        protected virtual void calculateExtendedPrice()
        {
            // Find the ExtendedPrice.

            extendedPriceDecimal = unitPriceDecimal * (1 - discountRateDecimal)
                * quantityInteger;
        }

        protected void addToTotals()
        {
            // Add to summary information.

            salesCountInteger++;
            salesTotalDecimal += extendedPriceDecimal;
        }

        private void loadPriceList()
        {
            try
            {
                StreamReader productsStreamReader = new
                    StreamReader("Products.txt");
                string productString;
                int indexInteger = 0;
                while (productsStreamReader.Peek() != -1)
                {
                    productString = productsStreamReader.ReadLine();
                    priceDecimal[indexInteger] =
                        decimal.Parse(productsStreamReader.ReadLine());
                    indexInteger++;
                }

                productsStreamReader.Close();
            }
            catch
            {
                // Allow list to default to zeros.
            }
        }
    }
}
```

MemberClothingSale Class

```
/*
 * Class Name:    MemberClothingSale
 * Programmer:    Bradley/Millspaugh
 * Date:          June 2009
 * Description:   Handle clothing sale information for member sales,
                  which receive a 10% discount.
 */

using System;
using System.Collections.Generic;
using System.Text;
```

```csharp
namespace Ch12HandsOn
{
    class MemberClothingSale : ClothingSale
    {
        const decimal MEMBER_DISCOUNT_Decimal = .1M;

        public MemberClothingSale(int productIdInteger,
            int quantityInteger, decimal discountDecimal)
            :
            base(productIdInteger, quantityInteger, discountDecimal)
        {
            // Call the base-class constructor and pass arguments.
        }

        // Method in the derived class that overrides the method in the base class
        protected override void calculateExtendedPrice()
        {
            // Find the ExtendedPrice.
            decimal discountDecimal;

            discountDecimal = DiscountRate + MEMBER_DISCOUNT_Decimal;
            ExtendedPrice = unitPriceDecimal * (1 - discountDecimal) * Quantity;
        }
    }
}
```

Summary

1. Objects have properties and methods, and can trigger events.
2. You can create a new class that can then be used to create new objects.
3. Creating a new object is called *instantiating* the class; the object is called an *instance* of the class.
4. In object-oriented terminology, *encapsulation* refers to the combination of the characteristics and behaviors of an item into a single class definition.
5. Inheritance provides a means to derive a new class based on an existing class. The existing class is called a *base class*, *superclass*, or *parent class*. The inherited class is called a *subclass*, *derived class*, or *child class*.
6. Polymorphism allows different classes of objects in an inheritance hierarchy to have similarly named methods that behave differently for that particular object.
7. One of the biggest advantages of object-oriented programming is that classes that you create for one application may be reused in another application.
8. Multitier applications separate program functions into a Presentation tier (the user interface), Business tier (the logic of calculations and validation), and Data tier (accessing stored data).
9. To plan a new class, you need to model the required characteristics (properties) and behaviors (methods).
10. The variables inside a class used to store the properties should be private, so that data values are accessible only by methods within the class.

11. The way to make the properties of a class available to code outside the class is to use property methods. The `get` portion returns the value of the property, and the `set` portion assigns a value to the property. Validation is often performed in the `set` portion.

12. Read-only properties have only a `get` accessor method. Write-only properties have only a `set` accessor method.

13. A constructor is a method that automatically executes when an object is created; a destructor method is triggered when an object is destroyed.

14. A constructor method must have the same name as the class and may be overloaded.

15. A parameterized constructor requires arguments to create a new object.

16. Property methods may have mixed access levels; that is, the `get` or `set` may have a more restrictive access level than the other.

17. To instantiate an object of a class, you must use the `new` keyword on either the declaration statement or an assignment statement. The location of the `new` keyword determines when the object is created.

18. Static members (properties and methods) have one copy that can be used by all objects of the class, generally used for totals and counts. Instance members have one copy for each instance of the object. Declare static members with the `static` keyword.

19. The garbage collection feature periodically checks for unreferenced objects, destroys the object references, and releases resources.

20. A subclass inherits all public and protected properties and methods of its base class, except for the constructor.

21. To override a method from a base class, the original method must be declared as `virtual` or `abstract`, and the new method must use the `override` keyword.

22. A base class used strictly for inheritance is called an abstract class and cannot be instantiated. The class should be declared as `abstract` and the methods that must be overridden should be declared as `abstract`.

23. You can use visual inheritance to derive new forms from existing forms.

24. You can use the Object Browser to view classes, properties, methods, events, and constants in system classes as well as your own classes.

Key Terms

abstract   *501*

abstract class   *501*

abstract method   *501*

accessor methods   *502*

base class   *483*

child class   *483*

class   *482*

constructor   *487*

derived class   *483*

destructor   *487*

encapsulation   *483*

garbage collection   *500*

inheritance   *483*

instance   *482*

instance member   *496*

instantiate   *482*

multitier application   *485*

object   *482*

overloading   *484*

overriding   *484*

parameterized constructor   *488*

parent class   *483*

polymorphism   *484*

protected   *501*

Review Questions

1. What is an object? a property? a method?
2. What is the purpose of a class?
3. Why should property variables of a class be declared as private?
4. Explain how to create a new object.
5. What steps are needed to assign property values to an object?
6. What actions trigger the constructor and destructor methods of an object?
7. How can you write methods for a new class?
8. What is a static member? How is it created?
9. Explain the steps necessary to inherit a class from another class.
10. Differentiate between overriding and overloading.
11. What is a parameterized constructor?
12. When might you use the protected keyword on a method?
13. What is visual inheritance?

Programming Exercises

Note: For help in basing a new project on an existing project, see "Copy and Move Projects" in Appendix C.

12.1 Modify the program for Programming Exercise 5.1 (the piecework pay) to separate the business logic into a separate class. The class should have properties for Name and Pieces, as well as static read-only properties to maintain the summary information.

12.2 Modify Programming Exercise 12.1 to include multiple forms. Create a base form that you can use for visual inheritance. Display the summary information and the About box on separate forms, rather than in message boxes.

12.3 *Extra challenge*: Modify Programming Exercise 12.2 to have an inherited class. Create a derived class for senior workers, who receive 10 percent higher pay for 600 or more pieces. Add a check box to the main form to indicate a senior worker.

12.4 Modify Programming Exercise 5.3 (the salesperson commissions) to separate the business logic into a separate class. The class should have properties for Name and Sales, as well as static read-only properties to maintain the summary information.

12.5 Modify Programming Exercise 12.4 to include multiple forms. Create a base form that you can use for visual inheritance. Display the summary information and the About box on separate forms, rather than in message boxes.

12.6 *Extra challenge*: Modify Programming Exercise 12.5 to have an inherited class. Create a derived class for supervisors, who have a different pay scale. The supervisor quota is $2,000, the commission rate is 20 percent, and the base pay is $500. Include a check box on the main form to indicate a supervisor and calculate separate totals for supervisors.

12.7 Modify Programming Exercise 5.2 (the check transactions) to separate the business logic from the user interface. Create a Transaction class and derived classes for Deposit, Check, and Service Charges. Display the summary information on a separate form rather than a message box.

> *Optional extra*: Use visual inheritance for the forms.

12.8 Modify Programming Exercise 5.4 (the library reading program) to separate the business logic from the user interface. Create a class with properties for Name and Number of Books. Display the summary information and About box in separate forms rather than message boxes.

> *Optional extra*: Use visual inheritance for the forms.

12.9 *Extra challenge*: Modify Programming Exercise 12.8 to have inherited classes. Have separate classes and separate totals for elementary, intermediate, and high school. Include radio buttons on the form to select the level; display totals for all three groups on the summary.

12.10 Create a project that contains a class for sandwich objects. Each sandwich object should have properties for Name, Bread, Meat, Cheese, and Condiments. Use a form for user input. Assign the input values to the properties of the object, and display the properties on a separate form.

12.11 Create a project that contains a Pet class. Each object will contain pet name, animal type, breed, and color. The form should contain text boxes to enter the information for the pets. A button or menu item should display the pet information on a separate form.

12.12 Modify the project that you created in Chapter 3 to separate the user interface from the business logic (calculations) and return the results through a property.

Case Studies

Custom Supplies Mail Order

Modify your Custom Supplies Mail Order project from Chapter 5 to separate the user interface from the business logic. Create two new classes: one for customer information and one for order items. The order item class should perform the calculations and maintain the summary information.

Add a menu option to display the customer information. Display the properties of the Customer object on a separate form.

Display the About box and the summary information on forms, rather than in message boxes.

Optional extra: Use visual inheritance for the forms.

Need a bigger challenge? Create an inherited class for preferred customers. Preferred customers receive an automatic 5 percent discount on all purchases. Use a check box to determine if the customer is a preferred customer and instantiate the appropriate class. Maintain and display separate totals for preferred customers.

Note: For help in basing a new project on an existing project, see "Copy and Move Projects" in Appendix C.

Christopher's Car Center

Modify your Christopher's Car Center project from Chapter 5 to separate the business logic from the user interface. Create a class for purchases, with properties for each of the options. The class method will calculate the subtotal, tax, total, and amount due.

Make the About box display on a separate form, rather than in a message box.

Need a bigger challenge? Add summary totals for the number of sales, the total sales, and the total trade-ins. Maintain the totals as static read-only properties of the class and display the summary information on a separate form.

Note: For help in basing a new project on an existing project, see "Copy and Move Projects" in Appendix C.

Xtreme Cinema

Modify the Xtreme Cinema project from Chapter 5 to separate the user interface from the business logic. Create a class for each rental. Include a property for title, Boolean properties for video format and members, and static read-only properties for the summary information.

Display the summary information and the About box on forms, rather than in message boxes.

Note: For help in basing a new project on an existing project, see "Copy and Move Projects" in Appendix C.

Cool Boards

Modify the Cool Boards project from Chapter 5 to separate the user interface from the business logic. Create a class for each shirt sale with properties for Order Number, Quantity, and Size. Use Boolean properties for Monogram and Pocket and a method to calculate the price. Maintain static read-only properties for the summary information.

Display the summary information and the About box on forms, rather than in message boxes.

Optional extra: Use visual inheritance for the forms.

Note: For help in basing a new project on an existing project, see "Copy and Move Projects" in Appendix C.

13

Graphics, Animation, Sound, and Drag-and-Drop

at the completion of this chapter, you will be able to . . .

1. Use Graphics methods to draw shapes, lines, and filled shapes.

2. Draw on a drawing surface of a Graphics object using Pen and Brush objects.

3. Create animation by changing pictures at run time.

4. Create simple animation by moving images.

5. Automate animation using a Timer component.

6. Move an image using scroll bars.

7. Play sounds in an application using a SoundPlayer object.

8. Play videos on a form.

9. Incorporate drag-and-drop events into your program.

10. Draw a pie chart using the methods of the Graphics object.

You had your first introduction to graphics when you learned to print documents in Chapter 7. In this chapter, you will learn to draw shapes such as lines, rectangles, and ellipses using the methods of the Graphics object. You can use the Graphics methods to draw pictures and charts in a business application.

You will do simple animation by replacing and moving graphics. You also will use a Timer component to cause events to fire, so that you can create your own animation.

Graphics in Windows and the Web

The term *graphics* refers to any text, drawing, image, or icon that you display on the screen. You have placed a graphic image in a PictureBox control to display pictures on your forms. A picture box also can display animated .gif files, so you can easily produce animation on the screen.

You can display a graphics file on either a Web Form or a Windows Form. Recall that the Web control is an Image control and the Windows control is a PictureBox. Both display graphics files, but the Windows control accepts a few more file formats.

Using Windows Forms, you can draw graphics shapes such as circles, lines, and rectangles on a form or control. The Graphics methods work only on Windows Forms, not Web Forms. Therefore, the programs in the next section use Windows Forms only.

The Graphics Environment

The .NET Framework uses a technology called *GDI+* for drawing graphics. GDI+ is more advanced and an improvement over the previous Graphics Device Interface (GDI) used in previous versions of .NET. GDI+ is designed to be device-independent, so that the programmer doesn't have to be concerned about the physical characteristics of the output device. For example, the code to draw a circle is the same whether the output goes to a large-screen monitor, a low-resolution monitor, or the printer.

Steps for Drawing Graphics

When you draw a picture, you follow these general steps. The sections that follow describe the steps in more detail.

- Create a Graphics object to use as a drawing surface.

- Instantiate a Pen or Brush object to draw with.

- Call the drawing methods of the Graphics object.

Looking over the steps, you realize that this is what you did for creating printer output in Chapter 7. In that chapter, you used the `DrawString` method to place text on the Graphics object; in this chapter, you will use methods that draw shapes.

The Paint Event Handler

You draw lines and shapes on a form by drawing on a Graphics object. And where do you place the code for the drawing methods? In the Paint event handler for the form or the control on which you are drawing.

Each time a window is displayed, resized, moved, maximized, restored, or uncovered, the form's Paint event fires. In the Paint event handler, the form and its controls are redrawn. If you draw some graphics on the form, in say the Form_Load event handler or the click event of a button, the graphics are not automatically redrawn when the form is repainted. The only way to make sure that the graphics appear is to create them in the Paint event handler. Then they are redrawn every time the form is rendered.

So far we have ignored the Paint event and allowed the repainting to proceed automatically. Now we will place code in that event handler. You can write code in the form's Paint event handler to draw on the form or in a control's Paint event handler to draw graphics on the control.

In the Paint event handler, you can use the e.Graphics object or declare a Graphics object. You assign the Graphics property of the handler's PaintEventArgs argument to the new Graphics object.

TIP

To write code for the form's Paint event, select the form in the Designer, select the *Events* button in the Properties window, and select the Paint event. ■

```
private void GraphicsForm_Paint(object sender, PaintEventArgs e)
{
    // Create a graphics object.
    Graphics gr = e.Graphics;
}
```

You also can create a graphic object by calling the `CreateGraphics` method of a form or control. You would use this method when you want to display a graphic from a method other than the Paint event.

```
Graphics gr = this.CreateGraphics();     // Draw on the form.

Graphics gr = drawGroupBox.CreateGraphics();     // Draw on a group box control.
```

Pen and Brush Objects

Using a **Pen object**, you can draw lines or outlined shapes such as rectangles or circles. A **Brush object** creates filled shapes. You can set the width of a Pen and the color for both a Pen and a Brush. Figure 13.1 shows some lines and shapes created with Pen and Brush objects.

When you create a new Pen object, you set the color using the Color constants, such as Color.Red, Color.Blue, and Color.Aquamarine. You also can set the pen's width, which is measured in pixels. The term **pixel** is an abbreviation of *picture element*—a dot that makes up a picture. You are probably most familiar with pixels in the determination of the resolution of a monitor. A display of 1,280 by 1,024 is a reference to the number of pixels horizontally and vertically.

TIP

You can use the form's `Refresh` method to force a Paint event to occur. ■

Figure 13.1

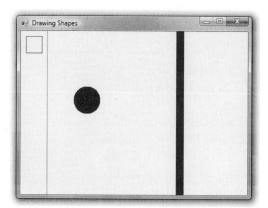

The Pen Class—Constructors

General Form

```
Pen(Color)
Pen(Color, Width)
```

If you don't set the width of the pen, it defaults to one pixel.

The Pen Class—Examples

Examples

```
Pen redPen = new Pen(Color.Red);
Pen widePen = new Pen(Color.Black, 10);
```

You may find that you want several different pens. For each different color or line width, you can create another Pen object or redefine an existing Pen variable if you are finished with it.

If you want to create filled figures, declare Brush objects—one for each different color that you want to use.

The SolidBrush Class—Constructor

General Form

```
SolidBrush(Color)
```

Use the Color constants to assign a color to your Brush objects.

The SolidBrush Class—Example

Example

```
SolidBrush blueBrush = new SolidBrush(Color.Blue);
```

You may have deduced from the name of the SolidBrush class that other types of brushes exist. See Help if you are interested in using a TextureBrush, Hatch-Brush, LinearGradientBrush, or PathGradientBrush.

The Coordinate System

Graphics are measured from a starting point of 0,0 for the X and Y coordinates beginning in the upper-left corner. The *X* is the horizontal position, and the *Y* is the vertical measurement. The starting point depends on where the graphic is being placed. If the graphic is going directly on a form, the 0,0 coordinates are the upper-left corner of the form, below the title bar. You also can draw graphics in a container such as a PictureBox, GroupBox, or Button. In this case, the container has its own 0,0 coordinates to be used as the starting point for measuring the location of items inside the container (Figure 13.2).

F i g u r e   1 3 . 2

The coordinates for graphics begin with 0,0 in the upper-left corner of a form or container.

Each of the drawing methods allows you to specify the starting position using X and Y coordinates. Most of the methods also allow you to specify the position using a Point structure. In some methods, it is useful to use a Rectangle structure, and in others a Size structure comes in handy.

The Point Structure

A **Point structure** is designed to hold the X and Y coordinates as a single unit. You can create a Point object, giving it values for the X and Y. Then you can use the object anywhere that accepts a Point as an argument.

```
Point myStartingPoint = new Point(20, 10);
```

You can see an example of a Point in the design of any of your forms. Examine the Location property of any control; the Location is assigned a Point object, with X and Y properties.

The Size Structure

A **Size structure** has two components: the width and height. Both integers specify the size in pixels. Some Graphics methods accept a Size structure as an argument.

```
Size myPictureSize = new Size(100, 20); // Width is 100, height is 20.
```

You also can see an example of a Size structure by examining the design of any of your forms. Each of the controls has a Size property, which has width and height properties.

For an interesting exercise, examine the automatically generated code for a Button control in the *FormName*.Designer.cs file. The button's Location is set to a new Point object, and the size is set to a new Size object.

The Rectangle Structure

A **Rectangle structure** defines a rectangular region, specified by its upper-left corner and its size.

```
Rectangle myRectangle = new Rectangle(myStartingPoint, myPictureSize);
```

The overloaded constructor also allows you to declare a new Rectangle by specifying its location in X and Y coordinates and its width and height.

```
Rectangle myOtherRectangle = new Rectangle(xInteger, yInteger, widthInteger, heightInteger);
```

Note that you also can create Point, Size, and Rectangle structures for float values. Specify the PointF, SizeF, and RectangleF structures.

Graphics Methods

The drawing methods fall into two basic categories: draw and fill. The draw methods create an outline shape and the fill methods are solid shapes. The first argument in a draw method is a Pen object; the fill methods use Brush objects. Each of the methods also requires the location for the upper-left corner, which you can specify as X and Y coordinates or as a Point object. Some of the methods require the size, which you may supply as width and height, or as a Rectangle object.

> ☑ **TIP**
>
> **R**ather than declaring a pen or brush, you can type `Pens.color` or `Brushes.color` directly in your graphics method. You must declare the Pen or Brush object if you want to change the width. ∎

Graphics Methods—General Form

General Form

```
Object.DrawLine(Pen, x1Integer, y1Integer, x2Integer, y2Integer);
Object.DrawLine(Pen, Point1, Point2);

Object.DrawRectangle(Pen, xInteger, yInteger, widthInteger, heightInteger);
Object.DrawRectangle(Pen, Rectangle);

Object.FillRectangle(Brush, xInteger, yInteger, widthInteger, heightInteger);
Object.FillRectangle(Brush, Rectangle);

Object.FillEllipse(Brush, xInteger, yInteger, widthInteger, heightInteger);
Object.FillEllipse(Brush, Rectangle);
```

The following code draws the outline of a rectangle in red using the **DrawRectangle method** and draws a line with the **DrawLine method**. The **FillEllipse method** is used to draw a filled circle.

```
Private void GraphicsForm_Paint(object sender, PaintEventArgs e)
{
    // Draw a red rectangle.
    // e.Graphics.DrawRectangle(Pens.Red, 10, 10, 30, 30);
    // or
    Rectangle smallRectangle = new Rectangle(10, 10, 30, 30);
    e.Graphics.DrawRectangle(Pens.Red, smallRectangle);

    // Draw a green line.
    e.Graphics.DrawLine(Pens.Green, 50, 0, 50, 300);
```

```
    // Draw a blue filled circle.
    e.Graphics.FillEllipse(Brushes.Blue, 100, 100, 50, 50);

    // Draw a fat blue line.
    Pen widePen = new Pen(Brushes.Blue, 15);
    e.Graphics.DrawLine(widePen, 300, 0, 300, 300);
}
```

Table 13.1 shows some of the methods in the Graphics class.

Selected Methods from the Graphics Class   **T a b l e   1 3 . 1**

Method	Purpose
`Object.Clear();`	Clear the drawing surface by setting it to the container's background color.
`Object.Dispose();`	Release the memory used by a Graphics object.

`Object.DrawArc(Pen, x1Integer, y1Integer, x2Integer, y2Integer, widthInteger, heightInteger);`
 	
`Object.DrawArc(Pen, Rectangle, startAngleFloat, angleLengthFloat);`
	Draw an arc (segment of an ellipse).

`Object.DrawLine(Pen, x1Integer, y1Integer, x2Integer, y2Integer);`
 	
`Object.DrawLine(Pen, Point1, Point2);`
	Draw a line from one point to another.

`Object.DrawEllipse(Pen, xInteger, yInteger, widthInteger, heightInteger);`
 	
`Object.DrawEllipse(Pen, Rectangle);`
	Draw an oval shape. A circle has equal width and height.

`Object.DrawRectangle(Pen, xInteger, yInteger, widthInteger, heightInteger);`
 	
`Object.DrawRectangle(Pen, Rectangle);`
	Draw a rectangle.

`Object.DrawPie(Pen, xInteger, yInteger, widthInteger, heightInteger, angleStartInteger, angleLengthInteger);`
 	
`Object.DrawPie(Pen, Rectangle, angleStartFloat, angleLengthFloat);`
	Draw a partial oval (segment of a pie).

`Object.DrawString(textString, Font, Brush, xFloat, yFloat);`
 	
`Object.DrawString(textString, Font, Brush, PointF);`
	Draw a string of text. Note that coordinates are float.

`Object.FillEllipse(Brush, xInteger, yInteger, widthInteger, heightInteger);`
 	
`Object.FillEllipse(Brush, Rectangle);`
	Draw a filled oval; a circle has equal width and height.

`Object.FillPie(Brush, xInteger, yInteger, widthInteger, heightInteger, angleStartInteger, angleLengthInteger);`
 	
`Object.FillPie(Brush, Rectangle, angleStartFloat, angleLengthFloat);`
	Draw a partial filled oval (segment of a pie).

`Object.FillRectangle(Brush, xInteger, yInteger, widthInteger, heightInteger);`
 	
`Object.FillRectangle(Brush, Rectangle);`
	Draw a filled rectangle.

Random Numbers

Often it is useful to be able to generate random numbers. The **Random class** contains various methods for returning random numbers of different data types. Random numbers are popular for use in games, as well as problems in probability and queuing theory.

```
Random generateRandom = new Random();
```

To generate a different series of numbers for each run, the constructor uses a value from the system clock. This is called *seeding* the random number generator. This feature causes the list of random numbers to begin at a different point each time. On high-performance systems, the system clock value may not work properly. You may find that you need to seed the Random object yourself by passing an integer value. Using the clock is a good way to make sure that a different value is passed each time an object instantiates.

```
// Seed the random number generator.
DateTime currentDateTime = DateTime.Now;
Random generateRandom = new Random(currentDateTime.Millisecond);
```

You seed the Random object once when you instantiate it and generate the random numbers using the Random object's **Next method**, which returns a positive integer number. You can use one of three overloaded argument lists to choose the range for the random numbers. The numbers generated by the Next method do not include the maximum value, but do include the minimum value, if present.

The Random.Next Method—General Form

```
// Any positive integer number.
Object.Next();

// A positive integer up to the value specified.
Object.Next(MaximumValueInteger);

// A positive integer in the range specified.
Object.Next(minimumValueInteger, maximumValueInteger);
```

The Random.Next Method—Examples

```
// Return an integer in the range 0–10.
int generateRandomInteger = generateRandom.Next(10);

// Return an integer in the range 1 to the width of the form.
int randomNumberInteger = generateRandom.Next(1, this.Width);
```

A Random Number Example

This example program draws graphics using the Graphics methods and generates snowflakes using the Random.Next method. Figure 13.3 shows the screen generated by this code.

Figure 13.3

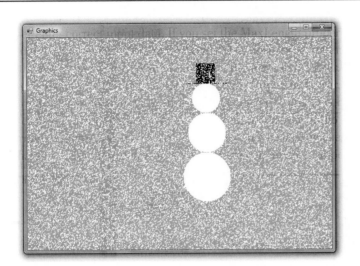

*This program draws the figure
and generates random
snowflakes in the form's Paint
event handler.*

```
/* Program:        Ch13RandomNumbers
 * Programmer:     Bradley/Millspaugh
 * Date:           June 2009
 * Description:    Draw a snowman using filled ellipses and then snow using
 *                 random locations.
 */

using System;
using System.Collections.Generic;
using System.ComponentModel;
using System.Data;
using System.Drawing;
using System.Text;
using System.Windows.Forms;

namespace Ch13RandomNumbers
{
    public partial class GraphicsForm : Form
    {
        Random generateRandom = new Random();

        public GraphicsForm()
        {
            InitializeComponent();
        }

        private void GraphicsForm_Paint(object sender, PaintEventArgs e)
        {
            // Generate dots (snowflakes) in random locations.
            // Draw a snowman at the bottom center of the screen.
            int xInteger = Convert.ToInt32(this.Width / 2),
                yInteger = Convert.ToInt32(this.Height / 2);
            Pen whitePen = new Pen(Color.White, 2);

            // Draw the snowman.
            e.Graphics.FillEllipse(Brushes.White, xInteger, yInteger, 100, 100);
            // Top of last circle.
            yInteger -= 80;
```

```
// Offset for smaller circle.
xInteger += 10;
e.Graphics.FillEllipse(Brushes.White, xInteger, yInteger, 80, 80);
yInteger -= 60;
xInteger += 8;
e.Graphics.FillEllipse(Brushes.White, xInteger, yInteger, 60, 60);

// Add a top hat.
e.Graphics.DrawLine(Pens.Black, xInteger - 10, yInteger,
    xInteger + 80, yInteger);
e.Graphics.FillRectangle(Brushes.Black, xInteger + 10, yInteger - 40,
    40, 40);

// Make it snow in random locations.
for (int indexInteger = 1; indexInteger < 40000; indexInteger++)
{
    xInteger = generateRandom.Next(1, this.Width);
    yInteger = generateRandom.Next(1, this.Height);
    e.Graphics.DrawLine(whitePen, xInteger, yInteger,
        xInteger + 1, yInteger + 1);
}
        }
    }
}
```

▶ **Feedback 13.1**

1. Write the statements necessary to draw a green vertical line down the center of a form.
2. Write the statements to draw one circle inside another one.
3. Write the statements to define three points and draw lines connecting the points.

Simple Animation

There are several ways to create animation on a form. The simplest way is to display an animated .gif file in a PictureBox control. The animation is already built into the graphic. Other simple ways to create animation are to replace one graphic with another, move a picture, or rotate through a series of pictures. You also can create graphics with the various graphics methods.

If you want to create animation on a Web page, displaying an animated .gif file is the best way. Another way is to write script using a scripting language such as VBScript or JavaScript or to embed a Java applet, which creates the animation on the client side. It doesn't make any sense to create animation using server-side controls since each movement would require a round-trip to the server.

Displaying an Animated Graphic

You can achieve animation on either a Windows Form or a Web Form by displaying an animated .gif file (Figure 13.4). Use a PictureBox control on a Windows Form and an Image control on a Web Form.

Figure 13.4

Create animation by display-ing an animated .gif file on either a Windows Form or a Web Form.

Note: You can find the graphics for the programs in this chapter on the text Web site (www.mhhe.com/C#2008).

Controlling Pictures at Run Time

You can add or change a picture at run time using one of several techniques. To speed execution, it is a good idea to have the pictures loaded into controls that you can make invisible until you are ready to display them. Displaying images from the project Resources folder is also very quick. But you can also use the **FromFile method** of the Image object to load a picture at run time.

If you store a picture in an invisible control, you can change the Visible property to *true* at run time; or you may decide to copy the picture to another control.

```
logoPictureBox.Visible = true;
logoPictureBox.Image = holdPicture.Image;
```

To display images from the project Resources folder, as described in Chapter 2, refer to *ProjectName*.Properties.Resources.*ResourceName*. This is the technique used for the example program that follows.

To remove a picture from the display, either hide it or use the null constant.

```
logoPictureBox.Visible = false;
logoPictureBox.Image = null;
```

Switching Images

An easy way to show some animation is to replace one picture with another. Many of the icons in the Visual Studio image library have similar sizes but opposite states, such as a closed file cabinet and an open file cabinet; a mailbox with the flag up and with the flag down; a closed envelope and an open envelope; or a traffic light in red, yellow, or green. This sample program demonstrates switching between a next page and a previous page image (Figure 13.5). The bitmap files are found in the VS2008ImageLibrary\Actions\16Color bitmaps folder. Note that the bitmap images from Microsoft have magenta backgrounds. This program demonstrates how to make the magenta background transparent.

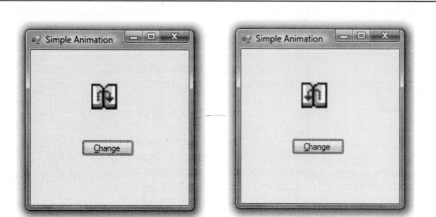

Figure 13.5

Create animation by switching from one image to another. Each of these graphics is placed into the upper picture box when the user clicks the Change button.

```
/*Program:        Ch13SimpleAnimation
 *Programmer:     Bradley/Millspaugh
 *Date:           June 2009
 *Description:    Change one picture to another.
 *                This project uses the graphics in the VS2008ImageLibrary and
 *                makes the magenta background transparent.
 */

using System;
using System.Collections.Generic;
using System.ComponentModel;
using System.Data;
using System.Drawing;
using System.Text;
using System.Windows.Forms;

namespace Ch13SimpleAnimation
{
    public partial class AnimationForm : Form
    {
        public AnimationForm()
        {
            InitializeComponent();
        }

        bool switchBoolean = true;
        Bitmap nextPageBitmap;
        Bitmap previousPageBitmap;

        private void changePictureButton_Click(object sender, EventArgs e)
        {
            // Switch the picture.

            if (switchBoolean)
            {
                displayPictureBox.Image = previousPageBitmap;
                switchBoolean = false;
            }
```

```
        else
        {
            displayPictureBox.Image = nextPageBitmap;
            switchBoolean = true;
        }
    }

    private void AnimationForm_Load(object sender, EventArgs e)
    {
        // Set up the transparent images.

        nextPageBitmap = Ch13SimpleAnimation.Properties.Resources.NextPage;
        nextPageBitmap.MakeTransparent(Color.Magenta);
        previousPageBitmap = Ch13SimpleAnimation.Properties.Resources.PreviousPage;
        previousPageBitmap.MakeTransparent(Color.Magenta);
        displayPictureBox.Image = nextPageBitmap;
    }
}
}
```

Moving a Picture

The best way to move a control is to use the control's **SetBounds method**. The SetBounds method produces a smoother-appearing move than changing the Left and Top properties of controls.

The SetBounds Method—General Form

```
Object.SetBounds(xInteger, yInteger, widthInteger, heightInteger);
```

You can use a control's SetBounds method to move it to a new location and/or to change its size.

The SetBounds Method—Examples

```
planePictureBox.SetBounds(xInteger, yInteger, planeWidth, planeHeight);

enginePictureBox.SetBounds(xInteger, yInteger, widthInteger, heightInteger);
```

The program example in the next section uses a timer and the SetBounds method to move a graphic across the screen.

The Timer Component

Generally, events occur when the user takes an action. But what if you want to make events occur at some interval, without user action? You can cause events to occur at a set interval using the **Timer component** and its **Tick event**. Timers are very useful for animation; you can move or change an image each time the Tick event occurs. You have used the Timer component to display a splash screen.

When you have a Timer component on a form, it "fires" each time an interval elapses. You can place any desired code in the Tick event handler; the code executes each time the event occurs. You choose the interval for the timer by setting its **Interval property**, which can have a value of 0 to 65,535. This value specifies the number of milliseconds between the calls to the Tick event. One second is equivalent to 1,000 milliseconds. Therefore, for a three-second delay, set the timer's Interval property to 3,000. You can set the value at run time or at design time.

You can keep the Tick event from occurring by setting the Timer's Enabled property to *false*. The default value is *false*, so you must set it to *true* when you want to enable the Timer. You can set the Enabled property at design time or run time.

When you add a timer to your form, it goes into the component tray. The tool for the timer is represented by the little stopwatch in the toolbox (Figure 13.6).

This timer example program achieves animation in two ways: it moves an animated .gif file for a steam engine across the screen. When the steam engine moves off the left edge of the form, it reappears at the right edge, so it comes around again. Figure 13.7 shows the form. You'll have to use your imagination for the animation.

Figure 13.6

The tool for the Timer component in the toolbox.

Figure 13.7

Each time the Timer fires, the train moves 10 pixels to the left.

```
/* Program:        Ch13TimerAnimation
 * Programmer:     Bradley/Millspaugh
 * Date:           June 2009
 * Description:    Move a steam engine across the screen.
 */

using System;
using System.Collections.Generic;
using System.ComponentModel;
using System.Data;
```

```csharp
using System.Drawing;
using System.Text;
using System.Windows.Forms;

namespace Ch13TimerAnimation
{
    public partial class TimerForm : Form
    {

        private int xInteger = 200;

        public TimerForm()
        {
            InitializeComponent();
        }

        private void trainTimer_Tick(object sender, EventArgs e)
        {
            // Move the graphic across the form.
            xInteger -= 10;
            if (xInteger <= -enginePictureBox.Width)
            {
                xInteger = this.Width;
            }
            enginePictureBox.Left = xInteger;
        }

        private void TimerForm_Load(object sender, EventArgs e)
        {
            trainTimer.Enabled = true;
        }
    }
}
```

Feedback 13.2

1. Write the statement(s) to move commandButton 10 pixels to the left using the SetBounds method.
2. How long is an interval of 450?
3. What fires a Timer's Tick event?

The Scroll Bar Controls

You can add **horizontal scroll bars** and **vertical scroll bars** to your form (Figure 13.8). These scroll bar controls are similar to the scroll bars in Windows that can be used to scroll through a document or window. Often scroll bars are used to control sound level, color, size, and other values that can be changed in small amounts or large increments. The HScrollBar control and VScrollBar control operate independently of other controls and have their own methods, events, and properties. You can find the HScrollBar and VScrollBar controls on the *All Windows Forms* tab of the toolbox.

Figure 13.8

Horizontal scroll bars and ver-
tical scroll bars can be used to
select a value over a given
range.

Scroll Bar Properties

Properties for scroll bars are somewhat different from the controls we have
worked with previously. Because the scroll bars represent a range of values,
they have the following properties: **Minimum** for the minimum value,
Maximum for the maximum value, **SmallChange** for the distance to move
when the user clicks on the scroll arrows, and **LargeChange** for the distance
to move when the user clicks on the light gray area of the scroll bar or presses
the Page-Up or Page-Down key (Figure 13.9). Each of these properties has a
default value (Table 13.2).

Figure 13.9

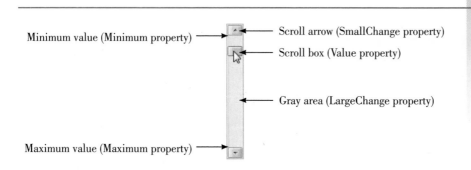

Minimum value (Minimum property) ⟶ ┄ Scroll arrow (SmallChange property)

Scroll box (Value property)

Gray area (LargeChange property)

Maximum value (Maximum property) ⟶ ┄

Clicking on the scroll arrow
changes the Value property by
SmallChange amount; clicking
the gray area of the scroll bar
changes the Value property by
LargeChange amount.

Default Values for Scroll Bar Properties

Table 13.2

Property	Default value
Minimum	0
Maximum	100
SmallChange	1
LargeChange	10
Value	0

The **Value property** indicates the current position of the scroll box (also called the *thumb*) and its corresponding value within the scroll bar. When the user clicks the up arrow of a vertical scroll bar, the Value property decreases by the amount of SmallChange (if the Minimum value has not been reached) and moves the scroll box up. Clicking the down arrow causes the Value property to increase by the amount of SmallChange and moves the thumb down until it reaches the bottom or Maximum value.

Figure 13.10 shows the horizontal scroll bar tool and vertical scroll bar tool from the toolbox.

◄► HScrollBar

▲▼ VScrollBar

Figure 13.10

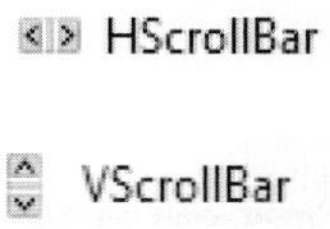

The toolbox tools for horizontal scroll bars and vertical scroll bars, which are found on the All Windows Forms tab of the toolbox.

Scroll Bar Events

The events that occur for scroll bars differ from the ones used for other controls. Although a user might click on the scroll bar, there is no Click event; rather, there are two events: a **ValueChanged event** and a **Scroll event**. The ValueChanged event occurs any time that the Value property changes, whether it is changed by the user or by the code.

If the user drags the scroll box, a Scroll event occurs. In fact, multiple scroll events occur, as long as the user continues to drag the scroll box. As soon as the user releases the mouse button, the Scroll events cease and a ValueChanged event occurs. When you write code for a scroll bar, usually you will want to code both a ValueChanged event handler and a Scroll event handler.

A Programming Example

This little program displays the value of a horizontal scroll bar in a label (Figure 13.11).

Figure 13.11

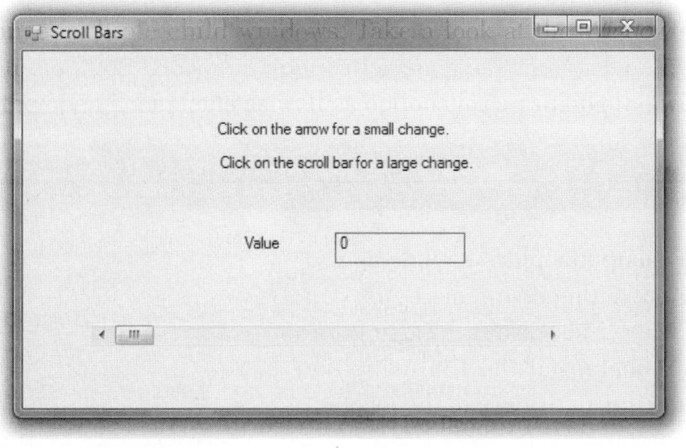

A programming example to demonstrate a horizontal scroll bar. Click on the scroll bar or drag the scroll box to change the value.

```
/*
 * Program:        Ch13ScrollBars
 * Programmer:     Bradley/A. Millspaugh
 * Date:           June 2009
 * Description:    Display the current value of a scroll bar in a label.
 */

using System;
using System.Collections.Generic;
using System.ComponentModel;
using System.Data;
using System.Drawing;
using System.Text;
using System.Windows.Forms;

namespace Ch13ScrollBars
{
    public partial class ScrollForm : Form
    {
        public ScrollForm()
        {
            InitializeComponent();
        }

        private void sampleHScrollBar_Scroll(object sender, ScrollEventArgs e)
        {
            // Assign the scroll bar value to the label.

            currentValueLabel.Text = sampleHScrollBar.Value.ToString();
        }

        private void sampleHScrollBar_ValueChanged(object sender, EventArgs e)
        {
            // Assign the scroll bar value to the label.

            currentValueLabel.Text = sampleHScrollBar.Value.ToString();
        }

        private void ScrollForm_Load(object sender, EventArgs e)
        {
            // Assign the scroll bar value to the label.

            currentValueLabel.Text = sampleHScrollBar.Value.ToString();
        }
    }
}
```

Playing Sounds

It is fun to add sound to an application. Your computer plays sounds as you turn it on or off. There's also likely a sound when you receive e-mail. You can make your program play sound files, called wave files (.wav), by using the **SoundPlayer component**. You can set the location of the file using the SoundPlayer's constructor or set its **SoundLocation property** to the location of the file. The SoundPlayer component comes from the System.Media library, so you should add a using System.Media statement to the program.

Adding Sound Files to the Resources for a Project

When you plan to use sounds in a project, the best plan is to add the files to the project's resources. Open the Application Designer (*Project / ProjectName Properties*) and click on the *Resources* tab (Figure 13.12). Drop down the *Add Resource* list and choose *Add Existing File* to add an existing file to your project. You can browse to find the file wherever it is; the file will be copied into the Resources folder in the project.

When you want to refer to the filename in code, use this format:

```
Namespace.Properties.Resources.Filename
```

Example

```
SoundPlayer myPlayer = new SoundPlayer(Ch13Sounds.Properties.Resources.Chimes);
```

Figure 13.12

*Add sound files to the project resources in the **Resources** tab of the Application Designer.*

A Sound-Playing Program

The following program (Figure 13.13) plays three different sounds from the Resources folder or allows the user to select a file using the OpenFileDialog component. The filter property for the OpenFileDialog is set to wave files (WAV Files (*.wav)|*.wav).

Figure 13.13

The form for the sound-playing
example program.

```
/* Program:        Ch13Sounds
 * Programmer:     Bradley/Millspaugh
 * Date:           June 2009
 * Description:    Play .wav sounds using the SoundPlayer class.
 */

using System;
using System.Collections.Generic;
using System.ComponentModel;
using System.Data;
using System.Drawing;
using System.Text;
using System.Windows.Forms;
using System.Media;

namespace Ch13Sounds
{
    public partial class SoundForm : Form
    {
        public SoundForm()
        {
            InitializeComponent();
        }

        private void chimesButton_Click(object sender, EventArgs e)
        {
            // Play the Chimes.wav file.

            SoundPlayer myPlayer = new
                SoundPlayer(Ch13Sounds.Properties.Resources.Chimes);
            myPlayer.Play();
        }

        private void dingButton_Click(object sender, EventArgs e)
        {
            // Play the Ding.wav file.

            SoundPlayer myPlayer = new
                SoundPlayer(Ch13Sounds.Properties.Resources.Ding);
            myPlayer.Play();
        }
```

```csharp
private void tadaButton_Click(object sender, EventArgs e)
{
    // Play the Tada.wav file.

    SoundPlayer myPlayer = new
        SoundPlayer(Ch13Sounds.Properties.Resources.Tada);
    myPlayer.Play();
}

private void selectButton_Click(object sender, EventArgs e)
{
    // Allow the user to browse for and select the wav file to play.

    openFileDialog1.InitialDirectory = Application.StartupPath;
    openFileDialog1.Filter = "WAV files (*.wav)|*.wav";
    openFileDialog1.ShowDialog();

    // Play the selected file.
    SoundPlayer myPlayer = new SoundPlayer(openFileDialog1.FileName);
    myPlayer.Play();
}
}
}
```

Playing Videos

You have seen how to play sounds using a SoundPlayer control. If you would like to include a video in your Windows application, use the Windows Media Player control (Figure 13.14), which can play audio and video files in many formats, including .avi, .wmv, and .wav.

Figure 13.14

Place a Windows Media Player control on a form to play an audio or video file.

Using the Windows Media Player Control

The Windows Media Player control does not appear in the Visual Studio toolbox by default, so you must add it. Right-click on the toolbox and select *Choose Items*. You will find the control on the *COM components* tab. Place a check mark in the box and press *OK* to add the control. Then you can place a Windows Media Player control on your form.

The URL property of the control determines the file that plays. If you set the property at design time, you must include a hard-coded path, and the file begins playing when the program loads. You also can control the URL property at run time. If you want to copy the files into the project folder for greater portability, place the files in the bin\Debug folder. Although you can use *Resources* for audio files, at this point *Resources* cannot handle video files.

You can set several properties of the Windows Media Player control. If you wish to just play sound, you may choose to set the visibility to *false*. Set CtlenabIed to *true* to allow the user access to the *Play*, *Pause*, and *Stop* buttons. Set the URL property to the path and filename to play, and choose whether the loaded file will begin playing automatically with the settings.autoStart property. For example, set WindowsMediaPlayer1.settings.autoStart = false so that the video won't begin playing until the user clicks the *Play* button. By default autoStart is set to *true* so the video starts playing as soon as it is loaded.

The following program allows the user to select and play a sample file by choosing the file type from a list box. It then assigns the URL property in a switch statement in the list box Selection Committed event procedure.

```
//Program:        Ch13Video
//Programmer:     Bradley/Millspaugh
//Date:           June 2009
//Description:    Uses a Windows media player for wmv, avi, and wav files.
//                Video files are stored in bin\Debug to make the project
//                portable.

using System;
using System.Collections.Generic;
using System.ComponentModel;
using System.Data;
using System.Drawing;
using System.Linq;
using System.Text;
using System.Windows.Forms;

namespace Ch13Video
{
    public partial class MediaForm : Form
    {
        public MediaForm()
        {
            InitializeComponent();
        }

        private void
            mediaComboBox_SelectionChangeCommitted(object sender, EventArgs e)
        {
            // Select the type of file.
            string selectString =
                    System.IO.Directory.GetCurrentDirectory().ToString();
```

```
        switch (mediaComboBox.SelectedIndex)
        {
            case 0:
                axWindowsMediaPlayer1.URL = selectString + "\\bear.wmv";
                break;
            case 1:
                axWindowsMediaPlayer1.URL = selectString + "\\music.avi";
                break;
            case 2:
                axWindowsMediaPlayer1.URL = selectString + "\\applause.wav";
                break;
            default:
                MessageBox.Show("Please select media type.");
                break;
        }
    }
}
}
```

Drag-and-Drop Programming

Often Windows users like to use drag-and-drop to make a selection rather than selecting a menu item or pressing a button. For example, you can copy or move files in My Computer by dragging the file and dropping it on the new location icon.

Drag-and-drop programming requires you to begin the drag-and-drop with a **MouseDown event** and determine the effect of the drop with a **DragEnter event**. The event that holds the code for the drop is the **DragDrop event**. Figure 13.15 shows the objects and events for a drag-and-drop operation.

Figure 13.15

The Source object is dragged to the Target object in a drag-and-drop operation.

Source	→	Target
In the MouseDown or MouseMove event: DoDragDrop method.		The AllowDrop property must be set to true.

In the MouseEnter event (Optional):
    Set cursor to give feedback
    that a drag will occur.
		In the DragEnter event:
		    Set the DragDrop effect (Move or Copy).

		In the DragDrop event: Code to add dragged object to the target.

The Source Object

The item that you wish to drag is commonly referred to as the source object. With .NET programming, you begin a drag-and-drop operation by setting the source object using a control's **DoDragDrop method**.

The DoDragDrop Method—General Form

```
Object.DoDragDrop(DataToDrag, DesiredDragDropEffect);
```

The DragDrop effect specifies the requested action for the operation. Choices include

- `DragDropEffects.Copy`

- `DragDropEffects.Move`

- `DragDropEffects.None`

The DoDragDrop Method—Example

```
nameTextBox.DoDragDrop(nameTextBox.SelectedText, DragDropEffects.Move);
```

Look at the following MouseDown event handler. First, an `if` statement checks to see if the user pressed the left mouse button. If so, the contents of the text box are selected and the effect of the drag is set to a move operation.

```
private void nameTextBox_MouseDown(object sender, MouseEventArgs e)
{
    // Select contents of the text box and invoke the drag/drop.

    if (e.Button == MouseButtons.Left)
    {
        nameTextBox.SelectAll();
        nameTextBox.DoDragDrop(nameTextBox.SelectedText, DragDropEffects.Move);
        nameTextBox.Clear();
    }
}
```

The Target Object

The location where a user releases the mouse, a drop, is the target. A form may have multiple targets. To set a control to be a target, set its **AllowDrop property** to *true*. The target control needs a DragEnter event handler that sets the effect and a DragDrop event handler that executes the action to take when the drop takes place.

In the following example program (Figure 13.16) the value in a text box can be transferred to one of two list boxes. Each list box would be a potential target and must have its AllowDrop property set to *true*. And each target object needs a DragEnter event handler and a DragDrop event handler.

The DragEnter Event

When the user drags a source object over the target, the target control's DragEnter event fires. Notice in the DragEnter's handler header that the `e` argument is defined as `DragEventArgs`, which has some special properties for the drag operation. You assign the desired effect to the `e` argument.

Figure   13.16

The user types a name in the top text box and then drags the name to one of two list boxes.

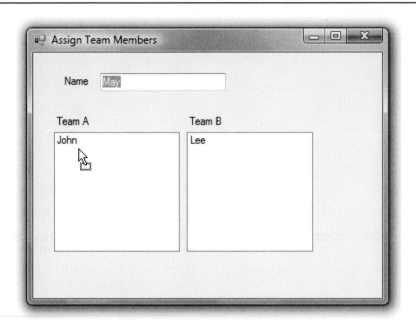

```
private void teamBListBox_DragEnter(object sender, DragEventArgs e)
{
    // Set the desired DragDrop effect.

    e.Effect = DragDropEffects.Move;
}
```

The DragDrop Event

Assume that when the user drops the text value on a list box that we want to add the value to the items collection for the list and clear the original text box. The statements to perform these actions are entered in the list box's DragDrop event handler.

The information that is being dragged is contained in the Data property of the e argument of the DragDrop event handler. You can retrieve the dragged data using the GetData method of the Data object. You also can format the data yourself or use a predefined clipboard data format. The predefined format for text is DataFormats.Text.

```
private void teamBListBox_DragDrop(object sender, DragEventArgs e)
{
    // Add the name to the list box.

    teamBListBox.Items.Add(e.Data.GetData(DataFormats.Text).ToString());
}
```

Note: .NET actually allows the target of the drop to be outside the current application, but that topic is beyond the scope of this text.

The Drag-and-Drop Program

Following is the completed program that is illustrated in Figure 13.16.

```csharp
/* Program:        Ch13DragDropListBoxes
 * Programmer:     Bradley/Millspaugh
 * Date:           June 2009
 * Description:    Drag a name from the text box and drop on a list.
 */

using System;
using System.Collections.Generic;
using System.ComponentModel;
using System.Data;
using System.Drawing;
using System.Text;
using System.Windows.Forms;

namespace Ch13DragDropListBoxes
{
    public partial class DragDropForm : Form
    {
        public DragDropForm()
        {
            InitializeComponent();
        }

        private void nameTextBox_MouseDown(object sender, MouseEventArgs e)
        {
            // Select contents of the text box and invoke the drag/drop.

            if (e.Button == MouseButtons.Left)
            {
                nameTextBox.SelectAll();
                nameTextBox.DoDragDrop(nameTextBox.SelectedText,DragDropEffects.Move);
                nameTextBox.Clear();
            }
        }

        private void teamAListBox_DragDrop(object sender, DragEventArgs e)
        {
            // Add the name to the list box.

            teamAListBox.Items.Add(e.Data.GetData(DataFormats.Text).ToString());
        }

        private void teamBListBox_DragDrop(object sender, DragEventArgs e)
        {
            // Add the name to the list box.

            teamBListBox.Items.Add(e.Data.GetData(DataFormats.Text).ToString());
        }

        private void teamBListBox_DragEnter(object sender, DragEventArgs e)
        {
            // Set the desired DragDrop effect.

            e.Effect = DragDropEffects.Move;
        }

        private void teamAListBox_DragEnter(object sender, DragEventArgs e)
        {
            // Set the desired DragDrop effect.

            e.Effect = DragDropEffects.Move;
        }
    }
}
```

Dragging and Dropping an Image

You also can drag and drop images (Figure 13.17), but with one small difference. The AllowDrop property of a PictureBox is not available at design time, but you can set it in the Form_Load event handler.

```
targetPictureBox.AllowDrop = true;
```

To make the drop appear like a move, set the original picture box to null. To make it a copy, you could leave the original alone.

```
private void TargetPictureBox_DragDrop(object sender, DragEventArgs e)
{
    // Assign the image to the target; original is erased.

    TargetPictureBox.Image = SourcePictureBox.Image;
    SourcePictureBox.Image = null;
}
```

Figure 13.17

The user can drag the source image and drop it on the target control.

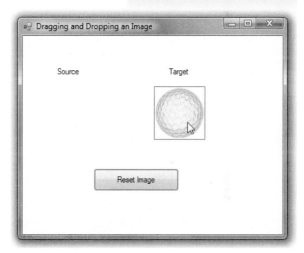

The DragDropImage Program

```
//Program:       Ch13DragDropImage
//Programmer:    Bradley/Millspaugh
//Date:          June 2009
//Description:   Use a picture box for the source and target in a drag-and-
//               drop operation.

using System;
using System.Collections.Generic;
using System.ComponentModel;
using System.Data;
using System.Drawing;
using System.Linq;
using System.Text;
using System.Windows.Forms;

namespace Ch13DragDropImages
{
    public partial class DragDropForm : Form
    {
```

```csharp
public DragDropForm()
{
    InitializeComponent();
}

private void DragDropForm_Load(object sender, EventArgs e)
{
    // Set the AllowDrop for the target.

    TargetPictureBox.AllowDrop = true;
}

private void SourcePictureBox_MouseMove(object sender, MouseEventArgs e)
{
    // Drag the picture.

    SourcePictureBox.DoDragDrop(SourcePictureBox.Image,
        DragDropEffects.Move);
}

private void TargetPictureBox_DragDrop(object sender, DragEventArgs e)
{
    // Assign the image to the target; original is erased.

    TargetPictureBox.Image = SourcePictureBox.Image;
    SourcePictureBox.Image = null;
}

private void TargetPictureBox_DragEnter(object sender, DragEventArgs e)
{
    // Set the effect to a move.

    e.Effect = DragDropEffects.Move;
}

private void resetButton_Click(object sender, EventArgs e)
{
    // Clear the target image and reset the orginal.

    SourcePictureBox.Image = TargetPictureBox.Image;
    TargetPictureBox.Image = null;
}
    }
}
```

Feedback 13.3

1. Code the DragEnter event for taskListBox that will copy the value received in a drag operation.
2. Write the statement for the DragDrop method to add the value to the list box.

Your Hands-On Programming Example

Create a project that will draw a pie chart showing the relative amount of profit for each department for Look Sharp Fitness Center.

Include text boxes for the user to enter the sales amount for Membership, Clothing, Personal Training, and Juice Bar. Include buttons for *Display Chart*, *Clear*, and *Exit*.

Calculate the values for the pie chart in the *Display Chart* button's Click event handler and use a `Refresh` method to force a repaint to occur. In the form's Paint event handler, use the `CreateGraphics.FillPie` method to draw each of the pie segments.

```
CreateGraphics.FillPie(Brush, xInteger, yInteger, widthInteger, heightInteger,
    beginAngleInteger, lengthInteger);
```

Planning the Project

Sketch a form (Figure 13.18) that your users sign off as meeting their needs.

A planning sketch of the hands-on programming example.

Plan the Objects and Properties Plan the property settings for the form and each control.

Object	Property	Setting
PieChartForm	Name	PieChartForm
	Text	Look Sharp Profit Pie Chart
	AcceptButton	displayButton
	CancelButton	clearButton
label1	Text	Enter Profit Amount for Each Department
label2	Text	&Membership
membershipTextBox	Name	membershipTextBox
label3	Text	C&lothing
clothingTextBox	Name	clothingTextBox

Object	Property	Setting
label4	Text	&Personal Training
personalTrainingTextBox	Name	personalTrainingTextBox
label5	Text	&Juice Bar
juiceBarTextBox	Name	juiceBarTextBox
legendLabel	Name	legendLabel
	Text	Membership: Blue, Clothing: Yellow, Personal Training: Red, Juice Bar: Green
	Visible	False
displayButton	Name	displayButton
	Text	&Display Chart
clearButton	Name	clearButton
	Text	&Clear
exitButton	Name	exitButton
	Text	E&xit

Plan the Event Handlers

Event handler	Actions—Pseudocode
Form_Load	Create a graphics object.
displayButton_Click	If text fields are numeric Find total profits. Force form to repaint (Refresh).
Form_Paint	If total profits is not equal to 0 Make legend visible. Calculate ratio of each activity to total profits. Draw portions of the pie for each department.
clearButton_Click	Set each text box and label to blanks. Clear the graphic. Force the form to repaint (Refresh). Set the focus in the first text box.
exitButton_Click	Exit the project.

F i g u r e   1 3 . 1 9

The form for the hands-on programming example.

Write the Project Following the sketch in Figure 13.18, create the form. Figure 13.19 shows the completed form.

- Set the properties of each of the objects, as you have planned.

- Write the code. Working from the pseudocode, write each event handler.

- When you complete the code, use a variety of test data to thoroughly test the project.

The Project Coding Solution

```
/* Program:        Ch13HandsOn
 * Programmer:     Bradley/Millspaugh
 * Date:           June 2009
 * Description:    Draw a chart for relative profit amounts.
 */

using System;
using System.Collections.Generic;
using System.ComponentModel;
using System.Data;
using System.Drawing;
using System.Text;
using System.Windows.Forms;

namespace Ch13HandsOn
{
    public partial class PieChartForm : Form
    {
        public PieChartForm()
        {
            InitializeComponent();
        }

        // Class-level variables.
        bool drawChartBoolean;
        Graphics gr;
        private decimal membershipDecimal, clothingDecimal,
            personalTrainingDecimal, juiceBarDecimal, totalProfitDecimal;

        private void PieChartForm_Load(object sender, EventArgs e)
        {
            // Create a graphics object.

            gr = this.CreateGraphics();
        }

        private void displayButton_Click(object sender, EventArgs e)
        {
            // Draw a pie chart with relative profit amounts.
```

```csharp
            // Find the total profit.
            try
            {
                membershipDecimal = decimal.Parse(membershipTextBox.Text);
                try
                {
                    clothingDecimal = decimal.Parse(clothingTextBox.Text);
                    try
                    {
                        personalTrainingDecimal =
                            decimal.Parse(personalTrainingTextBox.Text);
                        try
                        {
                            juiceBarDecimal = decimal.Parse(juiceBarTextBox.Text);
                            totalProfitDecimal = membershipDecimal +
                                clothingDecimal + personalTrainingDecimal +
                                juiceBarDecimal;
                            // Force a paint of the form.
                            drawChartBoolean = true;
                            Refresh();
                        }
                        catch (FormatException)
                        {
                            MessageBox.Show("Invalid juice bar profit", "Error");
                            juiceBarTextBox.Focus();
                        }
                    }
                    catch (FormatException)
                    {
                        MessageBox.Show("Invalid profit for personal training",
                            "Error");
                        personalTrainingTextBox.Focus();
                    }
                }
                catch (FormatException)
                {
                    MessageBox.Show("Invalid clothing profit", "Error");
                }
            }
            catch (FormatException)
            {
                MessageBox.Show("Invalid membership profit", "Error");
                membershipTextBox.Focus();
            }
        }

        private void PieChartForm_Paint(object sender, PaintEventArgs e)
        {
            // Create the pie chart.
            // Amounts are a portion of the total circle of 360 degrees.
            int xCenterInteger = 380, yCenterInteger = 60;
            int startAngleInteger = 0;

            if (drawChartBoolean)
            {
                if (totalProfitDecimal != 0)
                {
                    legendLabel.Visible = true;
                    int endMembershipInteger = Convert.ToInt32(
                        membershipDecimal/totalProfitDecimal * 360);
```

```
            gr.FillPie(Brushes.Blue, xCenterInteger, yCenterInteger,
                100, 100, startAngleInteger, endMembershipInteger);

            startAngleInteger += endMembershipInteger;
            int endClothingInteger = Convert.ToInt32(
                clothingDecimal/totalProfitDecimal * 360);
            gr.FillPie(Brushes.Yellow, xCenterInteger, yCenterInteger,
                100, 100, startAngleInteger, endClothingInteger);

            startAngleInteger += endClothingInteger;
            int endPersonalTrainingInteger = Convert.ToInt32(
                personalTrainingDecimal/totalProfitDecimal * 360);
            gr.FillPie(Brushes.Red, xCenterInteger, yCenterInteger,
                100, 100, startAngleInteger, endPersonalTrainingInteger);

            startAngleInteger += endPersonalTrainingInteger;
            int juiceBarInteger = Convert.ToInt32(
                juiceBarDecimal/totalProfitDecimal * 360);
            gr.FillPie(Brushes.Green, xCenterInteger, yCenterInteger,
                100, 100, startAngleInteger, juiceBarInteger);
        }
    }
}

private void clearButton_Click(object sender, EventArgs e)
{
    // Clear the text boxes and graphic.
    SolidBrush clearBrush = new SolidBrush(PieChartForm.DefaultBackColor);

    membershipTextBox.Clear();
    clothingTextBox.Clear();
    personalTrainingTextBox.Clear();
    juiceBarTextBox.Clear();
    legendLabel.Visible = false;
    gr.FillEllipse(clearBrush, 380, 60, 100, 100);
    drawChartBoolean = false;
    Refresh();
    membershipTextBox.Focus();
}

private void exitButton_Click(object sender, EventArgs e)
{
    // End the project.

    this.Close();
}
    }
}
```

Summary

1. A drawing surface is created with a Graphics object.
2. The graphics methods should appear in the form's Paint event handler so
   that the graphics are redrawn every time the form is repainted.

3. Pen objects are used for lines and the outline of shapes; brushes are used for filled shapes.

4. Measurements in drawings are in pixels.

5. The coordinate system begins with 0,0 at the upper-left corner of the container object.

6. You can declare a Point structure, a Size structure, or a Rectangle structure to use as arguments in the graphics methods.

7. You can generate random numbers using the Random class. Seed the random number generator when instantiating a variable of the class; use the Next method to generate a series of numbers.

8. An animated .gif file can be displayed in a PictureBox control to display animation on a Windows Form or in an Image control on a Web Form.

9. Animation effects can be created by using similar pictures and by controlling the location and visibility of controls.

10. Pictures can be loaded, moved, and resized at run time; the best way is to use the SetBounds method.

11. The Timer component can fire a Tick event that occurs at specified intervals, represented in milliseconds.

12. Scroll bar controls are available for both horizontal and vertical directions. Properties include Minimum, Maximum, SmallChange, LargeChange, and Value. Scroll and ValueChanged events are used to respond to the action.

13. You can play .wav files using the SoundPlayer class. Other types of multimedia can be played using the Windows Media Player.

14. Drag-and-drop programming allows a source object to be dropped on a target object. The target control has its AllowDrop property set to *true*. The source control calls the DoDragDrop method in its MouseDown event handler. The target control sets the effect of the drag in the DragEnter event handler and the results in the DragDrop event handler.

Key Terms

R e v i e w   Q u e s t i o n s

1. What is a pixel?
2. What class contains the graphics methods?
3. Describe two ways to add a graphics object to a form.
4. Name three methods available for drawing graphics.
5. How is a pie-shaped wedge created?
6. Differentiate between using a Brush and a Pen object.
7. Which function loads a picture at run time?
8. How can you remove a picture at run time?
9. What steps are necessary to change an image that contains a turned-off light bulb to a turned-on light bulb?
10. What is the purpose of the Timer component?
11. Explain the purpose of these scroll bar properties: Minimum, Maximum, SmallChange, LargeChange, Value.
12. What determines the file to be played by a SoundPlayer?
13. Explain the purpose of the following events for a drag-and-drop operation:
    a. MouseDown
    b. DragEnter
    c. DragDrop
14. Explain the parameters of the `DoDragDrop` method.

P r o g r a m m i n g   E x e r c i s e s

13.1 Create a project that contains two buttons labeled "Smile" and "Frown". The *Smile* button will display a happy face; *Frown* will display a sad face. Use graphics methods to draw the two faces.

   Optional: Add sound effects when the faces appear.

13.2 Use graphics methods to create the background of a form. Draw a picture of a house, including a front door, a window, and a chimney.

13.3 Use a PictureBox control with a .bmp file from Windows. Set the Size-Mode property to StretchImage. Use scroll bars to change the size of the image.

13.4 Use graphics from any clip art collection to create a project that has a button for each month of the year. Have an appropriate image display in a PictureBox for each month.

13.5 Use a bicycle image and a Timer component to move the bicycle around the screen. Add a *Start* button and a *Stop* button. The *Stop* button will return the bicycle to its original position.

13.6 Modify the snowman project ("Random Numbers") from earlier in the chapter by adding eyes, a mouth, and buttons. Play an appropriate sound file; you can play it in the Form_Load, in the Form_Activated, or at the end of the Form_Paint method. Do not place the sound in the middle of the graphics code in the Form_Paint method.

13.7 Modify the chapter hands-on example to add two more categories: Drinks and Gifts. Allow the user to enter the additional values and make the pie chart reflect all six categories. Make sure to set the legend label at the bottom of the form to include the new categories.

13.8 Write a project that has list boxes for a potluck party: appetizers, salad, entrée, and dessert. Have a text box for entering attendees' names and then drag them to the appropriate list box.

Optional extra: Code a save feature to save the contents of each of the list boxes to a separate file. Then add a feature to load the list boxes when the program begins.

Case Studies

Custom Supplies Mail Order

Create a logo for Custom Supplies Mail Order using graphics methods. Place the logo in the startup form for the project from Chapter 12. Add appropriate images and graphics to enhance each form. The graphics may come from .bmp files, .gif files, clip art, or your own creation from Paintbrush.

Christopher's Car Center

Have the startup screen initially fill with random dots in your choice of colors. Use graphics methods to draw a Car Center advertisement that will appear on the screen. Have various appropriate images appear in different locations, remain momentarily, and then disappear.

Xtreme Cinema

Use the Timer component and the random number generator to create a promotional game for Xtreme Cinema customers. Create three image controls that will display an image selected from five possible choices. When the user clicks on the *Start* button, a randomly selected image will display in each of the image controls and continue to change for a few seconds (like a "slot machine") until the user presses the *Stop* button. If all three images are the same, the customer receives a free video rental.

Display a message that says "Congratulations" or "Better Luck Next Visit".

Cool Boards

Modify your Cool Boards project from Chapter 8 or 12 to add a moving graphic to the About form. Use the graphic Skateboard.wmf or other graphic of your choice. Include a Timer component to move the graphic across the form. When the graphic reaches the edge of the form, reset it so that the graphic appears at the opposite edge of the form and begins the trip again.

Note: For help in basing a new project on an existing project, see "Copy and Move a Windows Project" in Appendix C.

CHAPTER

14

Additional Topics in C#

// Convert input values to numeric and assign
extendedPriceDecimal = quantityInteger *
discountDecimal=Decimal.Round(
(extendedPriceDecimal * DISCOUNT_RATE
amountDueDecimal = extendedPriceDecimal
totalAmountDecimal += amountDueDecimal;
numberTransactionsInteger++;
// Format and display answers.
extendedPriceTextBox.Text = extendedPrice

at the completion of this chapter, you will be able to . . .

1. Validate user input in the Validating event handler and display messages using an ErrorProvider component.

2. Capture and check an individual keystroke from the user.

3. Use code snippets in the editor.

4. Create a multiple-document project with parent and child forms.

5. Arrange child forms vertically, horizontally, or cascaded.

6. Add toolbars and status bars to your forms using tool strip and status strip controls.

7. Use calendar controls and date methods.

8. Display a Web page on a Windows Form using a WebBrowser control.

9. Use WPF Interoperablility to add Windows Presentation Framework controls to a Windows Form.

10. Create a WPF application.

This chapter introduces some topics that can make your programs a bit more professional. You can use an ErrorProvider component to display error messages to the user and perform field-level validation, rather than validate an entire form. You can display multiple documents from a single instance of an application by using a multiple document interface (MDI), which allows you to set up parent and child forms. Most professional applications have toolbars and status bars, which you learn to create in this chapter.

This chapter also introduces the WebBrowser control, which you can add to a Windows application, and creating of special effects using Windows Presentation Foundation (WPF).

Advanced Validation Techniques

You already know how to validate user input using `try/catch`, `if` statements, and message boxes. In addition to these techniques, you can use ErrorProvider components, which share some characteristics with the Web validation controls. Other useful techniques are to set the MaxLength and/or CharacterCasing properties of text boxes and to perform field-level validation using the Validating event of input controls.

Using ErrorProvider Components

In Chapters 3 and 4, you learned to validate user input and display message boxes for invalid data. Now you will learn to display error messages directly on the form using an **ErrorProvider component**, rather than popup messages in message boxes. Using an ErrorProvider component, you can make an error indication appear next to the field in error, in a manner similar to the validator controls in Web applications.

Although you can add multiple ErrorProvider components to a form, generally you use a single ErrorProvider for all controls on a form. Once you add the ErrorProvider into the component tray, you can validate a control. If the input value is invalid, the ErrorProvider component can display a blinking icon next to the field in error and display a message in a popup, similar to a ToolTip (Figure 14.1).

The logic of your program can be unchanged from a MessageBox solution. When you identify an error, you use the ErrorProvider **SetError method**, which pops up the icon.

ErrorProvider SetError Method—General Form

```
ErrorProviderObject.SetError(ControlName, MessageString);
```

ErrorProvider SetError Method—Examples

```
errorProvider1.SetError(quantityTextBox, "Quantity must be numeric.");
errorProvider1.SetError(creditCardTextBox, "Required field.");
```

Figure 14.1

The ErrorProvider displays a blinking icon next to the field in error. When the user points to the icon, the error message appears in a popup.

The following example is taken from Chapter 3. The message boxes have been removed and replaced with ErrorProvider icons and messages. Notice that all messages are cleared at the top of the calculateButton_Click method so that no icons appear for fields that have passed validation. Figure 14.2 shows the form in Design view.

```
private void calculateButton_Click(object sender, EventArgs e)
{
    // Declare the variables.
    int quantityInteger;
    decimal priceDecimal, extendedPriceDecimal, discountDecimal,
        amountDueDecimal;

    // Clear any error messages.
    errorProvider1.SetError(quantityTextBox, "");
    errorProvider1.SetError(priceTextBox, String.Empty);

    try
    {
        // Convert input values to numeric and assign to variables.
        quantityInteger = int.Parse(quantityTextBox.Text);
        try
        {
            priceDecimal = decimal.Parse(priceTextBox.Text);

            // Calculate values.
            extendedPriceDecimal = quantityInteger * priceDecimal;
            discountDecimal = Decimal.Round(
                (extendedPriceDecimal * DISCOUNT_RATE_Decimal), 2);
            amountDueDecimal = extendedPriceDecimal - discountDecimal;
            totalAmountDecimal += amountDueDecimal;
            numberTransactionsInteger++;
```

Figure 14.2

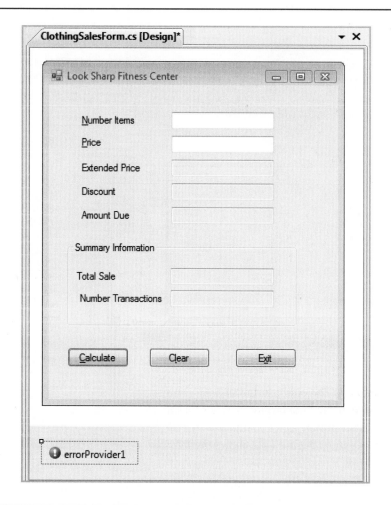

The calculation form from Chapter 3 with an ErrorProvider added.

```
        // Format and display answers.
        extendedPriceTextBox.Text = extendedPriceDecimal.ToString("C");
        discountTextBox.Text = discountDecimal.ToString("N");
        amountDueTextBox.Text = amountDueDecimal.ToString("C");

        //Format and display summary information.
        totalAmountTextBox.Text = totalAmountDecimal.ToString("C");
        numberTransactionsTextBox.Text = numberTransactionsInteger.ToString();
    }
    catch (FormatException)
    {
        // Invalid price.
        errorProvider1.SetError(priceTextBox, "Price must be numeric.");
        priceTextBox.Focus();
        priceTextBox.SelectAll();
    }
}
catch (FormatException)
{
    // Invalid quantity.
    errorProvider1.SetError(quantityTextBox, "Quantity must be numeric.");
    quantityTextBox.Focus();
    quantityTextBox.SelectAll();
}
}
```

The MaxLength and CharacterCasing Properties

You can use the **MaxLength** and **CharacterCasing properties** of text boxes to help the user enter correct input data. If you set the MaxLength property, the user is unable to enter more characters than the maximum. The user interface beeps and holds the insertion point in place to indicate the error to the user. The CharacterCasing property has possible values of Normal, Upper, or Lower, with a default of Normal. If you change the setting to Upper, for example, each character that the user types is automatically converted to uppercase, with no error message or warning. Figure 14.3 shows a State text box on a form. The user can enter only two characters, and any characters entered are converted to uppercase.

F i g u r e   1 4 . 3

To help the user enter only good data, the stateTextBox. MaxLength property is set to 2 and the CharacterCasing property is set to Upper.

Note: Although the MaxLength property limits user input, the program can assign a longer value to the text box in code, if necessary.

Field-Level Validation

So far all of the validation you have coded is for the entire form, after the user clicks a button such as *OK, Calculate,* or *Save.* If the form has many input fields, the validation code can be quite long and complex. Also, the user can become confused or annoyed if multiple message boxes appear, one after another. You can take advantage of the Validating event, the CausesValidation property, and the ErrorProvider components to perform **field-level validation**, in which any error message appears as soon as the user attempts to leave a field with invalid data.

Using the Validating Event and CausesValidation Property

As the user enters data into input fields and tabs from one control to another, multiple events occur in the following order:

Enter
GotFocus
Leave
Validating
Validated
LostFocus

Although you could write event handlers for any or all of these events, the Validating event is the best location for validation code. The Validating event handler's header includes a CancelEventArgs argument, which you can use to cancel the event and return the focus to the control that is being validated.

Each control on the form has a **CausesValidation property** that is set to *true* by default. When the user finishes an entry and presses Tab or clicks on another control, the Validating event occurs for the control just left. That is, the event occurs if the CausesValidation property of the *new* control (receiving the input focus) is set to *true*. You can leave the CausesValidation property of most controls set to *true* so that validation occurs. Set CausesValidation to *false* on a control such as Cancel or Exit to give the user a way to bypass the validation if he or she doesn't want to complete the transaction.

In the Validating event handler, you can perform any error checking and display a message for the user. If the data value does not pass the error checking, set the Cancel property for the **e** argument of the event to *true*. This cancels the Validating event and returns the focus to the text box, making the text box "sticky." The user is not allowed to leave the control until the input passes validation.

```csharp
private void nameTextBox_Validating(object sender, CancelEventArgs e)
{
    // Validate for a required entry.

    // Clear any previous error.
    errorProvider1.SetError(nameTextBox, "");

    // Check for an empty string.
    if (nameTextBox.Text == String.Empty)
    {
        // Cancel the event.
        e.Cancel = true;
        errorProvider1.SetError(nameTextBox, "Required Field");
    }
}
```

One note of caution: If you use the validating event on the field that receives focus when the form is first displayed and require an entry, the user will be unable to close the form without filling in the text box. You can work around this problem by setting e.Cancel = *false* in the form's FormClosing event handler.

```csharp
private void ValidationForm_FormClosing(object sender, FormClosingEventArgs e)
{
    // Do not allow validation to cancel the form's closing.

    e.Cancel = false;
}
```

A Validation Example Program

The following program combines many of the techniques presented in this section. The form (Figure 14.4) has an ErrorProvider component, and all controls have their CausesValidation property set to *true*. The stateTextBox has its MaxLength property set to 2 and its CharacterCasing property set to Upper. The amountTextBox shows an example of numeric range validation.

```csharp
/*
 * Program:       Ch14FieldLevelValidation
 * Programmer:    Bradley/Millspaugh
 * Date:          June 2009
 * Description:   Demonstrate validation using the Validating event
 *                and an Error Provider component.
 */

using System;
using System.Collections.Generic;
using System.ComponentModel;
```

Figure 14.4

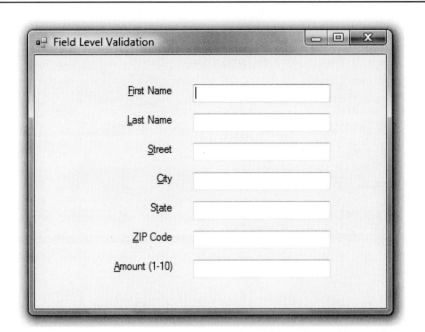

The Validation example form, which provides field-level validation.

```csharp
using System.Data;
using System.Drawing;
using System.Text;
using System.Windows.Forms;

namespace Ch14FieldLevelValidation
{
    public partial class ValidationForm : Form
    {
        public ValidationForm()
        {
            InitializeComponent();
        }

        private void nameTextBox_Validating(object sender, CancelEventArgs e)
        {
            // Validate for a required entry.

            // Clear any previous error.
            errorProvider1.SetError(nameTextBox, "");

            // Check for an empty string.
            if (nameTextBox.Text == String.Empty)
            {
                // Cancel the event.
                e.Cancel = true;
                // Display the error message.
                errorProvider1.SetError(nameTextBox, "Required Field");
            }
        }

        private void ValidationForm_FormClosing(object sender,
            FormClosingEventArgs e)
        {
            // Do not allow validation to cancel the form's closing.
```

```
        e.Cancel = false;
    }

    private void accountNumberTextBox_Validating(object sender,
        CancelEventArgs e)
    {
        // Validate for a required entry.

        // Clear any previous error.
        errorProvider1.SetError(accountNumberTextBox, String.Empty);

        if (accountNumberTextBox.Text.Length == 0)
        {
            // Cancel the event.
            e.Cancel = true;
            // Display the error message.
            errorProvider1.SetError(accountNumberTextBox,
                "Required Field.");
        }
    }

    private void stateTextBox_Validating(object sender, CancelEventArgs e)
    {
        // Make sure the state is two characters.
        // The control's CharacterCasing propety forces uppercase.
        // The MaxLength property limits input to 2 characters.

        // Clear any previous error.
        errorProvider1.SetError(stateTextBox, "");

        if(stateTextBox.Text.Length != 2)
        {
            // Cancel the event and select the text.
            e.Cancel = true;
            stateTextBox.SelectAll();
            // Display the error message.
            errorProvider1.SetError(stateTextBox, "Must be 2 characters.");
        }
    }

    private void quantityTextBox_Validating(object sender,
        CancelEventArgs e)
    {
        // Validate a numeric field for a range of values.
        int amountInteger;

        // Clear any previous error.
        errorProvider1.SetError(quantityTextBox, "");

        try
        {
            amountInteger = int.Parse(quantityTextBox.Text);
            if (amountInteger < 1 || amountInteger > 10)
            {
                // Cancel the event and select the text.
                e.Cancel = true;
                quantityTextBox.SelectAll();
                // Display the error message.
```

```
                    errorProvider1.SetError(quantityTextBox,
                        "Must be between 1 and 10, inclusive.");
                }
            }
            catch (FormatException)
            {
                // Cancel the event.
                e.Cancel = true;
                // Display the error message.
                errorProvider1.SetError(quantityTextBox,
                    "Enter a number from 1 to 10.");
            }
        }
    }
}
```

Capturing Keystrokes from the User

At times you may want to determine individual keystrokes entered by
the user. You can check for the key that the user entered in a control's
KeyDown, KeyPress, or KeyUp event handler. These events occur in the
order listed for most keyboard keys. But keystrokes that ordinarily cause an
action to occur, such as the Tab key and the Enter key, generate only a
KeyUp event.

The e argument of the KeyPress event handler is KeyPressEventArgs,
which has a KeyChar property that holds the character pressed. Another
property of the KeyPressEventArgs is the Handled property, which you can set
to *true* to say, "I have already taken care of this keystroke; it doesn't need any
further processing." This action effectively "throws away" the keystroke just
entered.

In the following code example, the KeyChar property is checked in the
KeyPress event handler. If the character is not a digit or a period, then
e.Handled is set to *true*, which does not pass the keypress on to the text box.
This means that *only* digits or a period are allowed through. You can use this
technique in a text box for which you want to allow only numeric data to be
entered, such as a Quantity or Price text box.

```
private void textBox1_KeyPress(object sender, KeyPressEventArgs e)
{
    // Accept only a digit or a period.
    if (!char.IsDigit(e.KeyChar) && !char.Equals(e.KeyChar, '.'))
    {
        e.Handled = true;
    }
}
```

Note that the e.KeyChar argument is a char data type. To make comparisons, you must use methods of the char class, and single characters must be
enclosed in single quotes, rather than double quotes. Notice that the if statement in the preceding method includes the char.IsDigit and char.Equals
methods and the '.' literal.

Using the Masked Text Box for Validation

Although you learned about the masked text box in Chapter 2, you may not have thought about using it to aid data validation. You can set the Mask property of a masked text box to any of the predefined masks or write your own. The easiest way to write your own is to modify one of the existing masks, or you can follow the syntax rules of a regular expression (see "Regular Expression Syntax" in MSDN Help).

The predefined masks include date, time, phone number, social security number, and Zip code formats. If the user enters invalid data for the mask, such as a letter for a numeric month in the date mask, the character is not accepted.

▶ Feedback 14.1

1. What is the purpose of the following code:

```
errorProvider1.SetError(quantityTextBox, "Quantity must be numeric.");
```

2. Name two properties of a TextBox control that help the user enter correct input data. Describe the function of each.
3. What is meant by field-level validation?

Code Snippets and Samples

A great time-saving feature in Visual C# is the ability to add segments of code for a variety of topics directly in the editor. You may wonder why this topic wasn't covered earlier, but it was really necessary for you to understand the code that you add to your program. Now that you understand the basic concepts, you will find that many of your new tools and techniques come from looking at sample projects. Visual Studio includes many sample projects as well as code snippets.

Code Snippets

Code snippets are small samples of code that can show you how to accomplish many programming tasks. The *Insert Snippet* menu option is available on the context menu (right-click) of the Code Editor window (Figure 14.5). The Snippet categories include the various structures including loops, decisions, exception handling, and arrays. When you select a snippet keyword, the editor places the code right in your program, where you can study it and/or modify and use it. Snippets also appear in IntelliSence when you are typing in the editor.

Sample Projects

Visual Studio includes many sample projects (all editions except the Express Edition) that you can use to learn new techniques. From the *Help* menu, select *Contents*. Expand the nodes for *Development Tools and Languages / Visual Studio / Visual C#* to find the *Visual C# Samples* node. Make sure to have the filter set to *Visual C#*.

Figure 14.5

a. Right-click in the Code Editor window and select Insert Snippet; *select* Visual C# *to see the list of available snippets; b. the code appears in the Code Editor window, where you can modify it for your own use.*

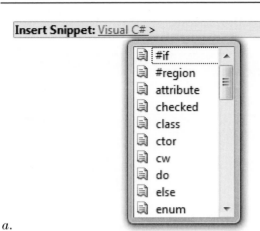

Insert Snippet: Visual C# >

- #if
- #region
- attribute
- checked
- class
- ctor
- cw
- do
- else
- enum

a.

```
// foreach snippet.
foreach (var item in collection)
{

}

// try snippet.
try
{

}
catch (Exception)
{

    throw;
}
```

b.

The walkthroughs in Help are another way to learn to program in C#. These tutorials give a step-by-step introduction to many techniques and controls.

Multiple Document Interface

All of the projects so far have been **single document interface (SDI)**. Using SDI, each form in the project acts independently from the other forms. However, C# also allows you to create a **multiple document interface (MDI)**. For an example of MDI, consider an application such as Microsoft Word 2003. Word has a **parent form** (the main window) and **child forms** (each document window). You can open multiple child windows and maximize, minimize, restore, or close each child window, which always stays within the boundaries of the parent window. And when you close the parent window, all child windows close automatically. Figure 14.6 shows an MDI parent window with two open child windows.

Figure 14.6

The main form is the parent and the smaller forms are the child forms in an MDI application.

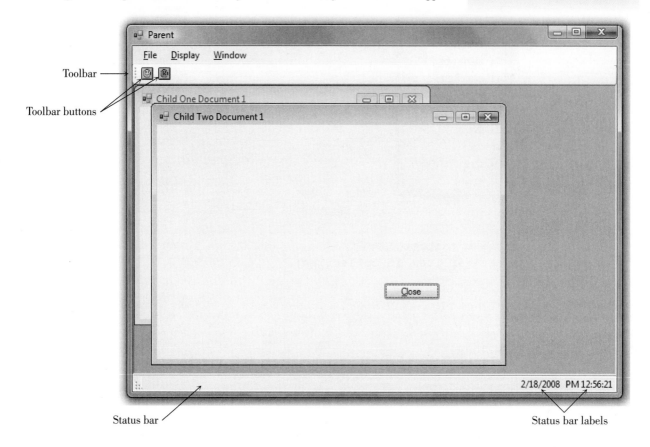

Toolbar

Toolbar buttons

Status bar

Status bar labels

With MDI, a parent and child relationship exists between the main form and the child forms. One of the rules for MDI is that if a parent form closes, all of its children leave with it. Pretty good rule. Another rule is that children cannot wander out of the parent's area; the child form always appears inside the parent's area.

C# allows you to have forms that act independently of each other. You may have a parent form and several child forms *and* some forms that operate independently. For example, a splash form likely should remain SDI.

One feature of MDI is that you can have several documents open at the same time. The menu strip generally contains a *Window* menu that allows you to display a list of open windows and move from one active document to another.

Creating an MDI Project

You can make any form a parent. In fact, a form can be both a parent and a child form (just as a person can be both a parent and a child). To make a form into a parent, simply change its **IsMdiContainer property** to *true* in the Properties window of the designer. One project can have multiple child forms and multiple parents.

Creating a child is almost as easy. Of course, your project must contain more than one form. You make a form into a child window in code at run time. You must declare a new variable for the form, instantiate it, set the child's MdiParent property to the current (parent) form, and then show it. This example instantiates a new form object of the ChildForm class, which has already been created in the project.

```
private void childOneToolStripMenuItem_Click(object sender, EventArgs e)
{
    // Display child one form.

    ChildForm childOneForm = new ChildForm();
    childOneForm.MdiParent = this;
    childOneForm.Show();
}
```

Our example application allows the user to display multiple child windows. Therefore, the title bar of each child window should be unique. We can accomplish this by appending a number to the title bar before displaying the form. This is very much like Microsoft Word, with its Document1, Document2, and so forth.

```
// Class-level declarations.
int childOneCountInteger;

private void childOneToolStripMenuItem_Click(object sender, EventArgs e)
{
    // Display child one form.

    ChildForm childOneForm = new ChildForm();
    childOneForm.MdiParent = this;
    childOneCountInteger++;
    childOneForm.Text = "Child One Document " +
        childOneCountInteger.ToString();
    childOneForm.Show();
}
```

Adding a Window Menu

A parent form should have a *Window* menu (Figure 14.7). The *Window* menu lists the open child windows and allows the user to switch between windows and arrange multiple child windows. Take a look at the *Window* menu in the Visual Studio 2008 IDE or an application such as Word or Excel; you will see a list of the open documents as well as options for arranging the windows.

Figure 14.7

The Window *menu in an MDI application lists the open child windows and allows the user to select the arrangement of the windows.*

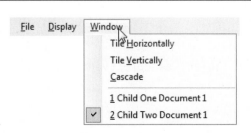

After you create the menus for a MenuStrip control, you can make one of the menus display the list of open child windows. Display the properties of the MenuStrip (not a menu item) in the Properties window. Drop down the list for the **MdiWindowListItem property**, which shows all of the menu items that belong to the MenuStrip, and select windowToolStripMenuItem (Figure 14.8). Include a separator bar at the bottom of the *Window* menu, which will separate the open window list from the other menu choices.

Figure 14.8

Set the MdiWindowListItem property to make the Window menu display the list of open MDI child windows.

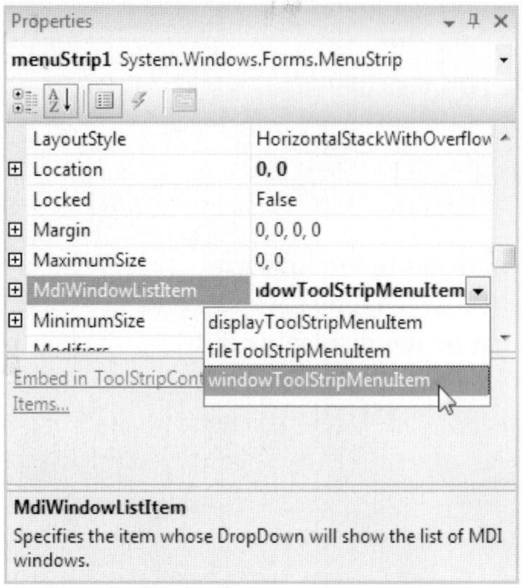

Layout Options

When several child windows are open, the windows may be arranged in several different layouts: tiled vertically, tiled horizontally, or cascaded. You set the type of layout in code with an argument of the **LayoutMdi method**.

```
LayoutMdi(MdiLayout.TileHorizontal);
```

You can use one of the three constants: TileHorizontal, TileVertical, and Cascade.

```
private void tileVerticallyToolStripMenuItem_Click(object sender, EventArgs e)
{
    // Arrange the child forms vertically.

    LayoutMdi(MdiLayout.TileVertical);
}

private void tileHorizontallyToolStripMenuItem_Click(object sender, EventArgs e)
{
    // Arrange the child forms horizontally.

    LayoutMdi(MdiLayout.TileHorizontal);
}

private void cascadeToolStripMenuItem_Click(object sender, EventArgs e)
{
    // Cascade the child forms.

    LayoutMdi(MdiLayout.Cascade);
}
```

Toolbars and Status Bars

You can enhance the usability of your programs by adding features such as a toolbar and/or status bar. You probably find that you use the toolbars in applications as an easy shortcut for menu items. Status bars normally appear at the bottom of the screen to display information for the user.

To create a **toolbar**, you need a **ToolStrip control** and the images in *Resources* to appear on the ToolStrip buttons.

Toolbars

You use the ToolStrip control (Figure 14.9) in the *Menus & Toolbars* tab of the toolbox to create a ToolStrip object for your project. The new ToolStrip is a container that does not yet contain any objects. After you add the ToolStrip, you can add several types of objects. The strip may contain ToolStripButtons, ToolStripLabels, and several other types of objects.

Figure 14.9

The ToolStrip and StatusStrip controls in the toolbox.

Figure 14.9

The ToolStrip and StatusStrip controls in the toolbox.

Setting Up the Buttons

The easiest way to add buttons to a ToolStrip is to drop down the arrow on the tool strip icon and select the type of object that you want to add (Figure 14.10).

Figure 14.10

Add buttons to a tool strip using the drop-down list of objects.

The list allows you to add many types of objects; for now you will use only the button. Click on *Button*, which adds a new ToolStripButton object to the ToolStrip. Then you can set the properties of the new button, such as its Name and ToolTipText properties. Make sure to give the button a meaningful name. For example, a button that displays the Summary window might be called summaryToolStripButton and one that displays the About box might be called aboutToolStripButton.

You also can assign an image to the button's Image property in the Properties window. Additionally, set the button's AutoSize property to *false* to make the image display properly. By default, the DisplayStyle is set to Image, but you can change it to Text and then modify the Text property to have words appear on the button.

Note that with the ToolStrip selected, you can click *Insert Standard Items* from the ToolStrip's smart tag or from the Properties window. You will get *New*, *Open*, *Save*, *Print*, *Cut*, *Copy*, *Paste*, and *Help* buttons with pictures added automatically. However, you must write the code for each button yourself.

Coding for the ToolStrip Buttons

To code the actions for a ToolStrip button, you can create a new event handler for the button click. However, since most buttons are actually shortcuts for menu items, you normally only need to set your ToolStripButton's Click event to the menu item's event-handling method.

Recall that the events display in the Properties window when you select the *Events* button. Find the Click event for the tool strip button, drop down the list of existing event handlers, and select the appropriate handler. For example, if you have a menu item for *Find Product*, you will most likely have an event handler for findProductToolStripMenuItem_Click. For the new *Find Product* ToolStrip button, select the Click event in the Properties window, drop down the list, and select findProductToolStripMenuItem_Click, which makes the one method handle both the menu item and the button.

Status Bars

A **status bar** is usually located at the bottom of a form (refer to Figure 14.6). A status bar displays information such as date, time, status of the Caps Lock or Num Lock keys, or error or informational messages. If you want a status bar on your form, you need to take two steps: add a **StatusStrip control** (refer to Figure 14.9) to your form and add **ToolStripStatusLabel objects** to the StatusStrip.

Just as with ToolStrips, the easiest way to add objects to the StatusStrip object is to drop down the arrow on the status strip and select the type of object. We are going to use the label to display date and time. Set the properties of the toolStripStatusStripLabel, including the object's Name and ToolTipText properties.

You can make the labels appear at the right end of the status bar, as in Figure 14.6, by setting the StatusStrip's RightToLeft property to *true*. The default is *false*. When you set RightToLeft to *true*, the labels will appear in the opposite order that you define them.

Assigning Values to ToolStripStatusLabels

A ToolStripStatusLabel can hold text such as the current date, the time, or error messages. You assign values to the Text property of labels at design time or run time:

```
dateToolStripStatusLabel.Text = DateTime.Now.ToShortDateString();
timeToolStripStatusLabel.Text = DateTime.Now.ToLongTimeString();
informationToolStripStatusLabel.Text = "It's very late.";
```

Displaying the Date and Time

You use the properties and methods of the **DateTime structure** to retrieve and format the current date and time. The **Now property** holds the system date and time in a numeric format that can be used for calculations. You can format the date and/or time for display using one of the following methods: ToShortDateString, ToLongDateString, ToShortTimeString, or ToLongTimeString. The actual display format of each method depends on the local system settings.

You can set the display value of status strip labels in any method; however, the display does not update automatically. Generally, you will set initial values in the Form_Load event handler and use a Timer component to update the time. Or you can skip the Form_Load event, figuring that, in just one second, the timer will fire and the clock will update.

```
private void MainForm_Load(object sender, EventArgs e)
{
    // Set the date and time on the status strip.

    dateToolStripStatusLabel.Text = DateTime.Now.ToShortDateString();
    timeToolStripStatusLabel.Text = DateTime.Now.ToLongTimeString();
}

private void timer1_Tick(object sender, EventArgs e)
{
    // Update the time on the status strip.
    // Interval = 1000 milliseconds (one second).

    timeToolStripStatusLabel.Text = DateTime.Now.ToLongTimeString();
}
```

Don't forget to set the Enabled and Interval properties of your timer.

Controlling the Layout

You can set the Width property of each label or control on your status strip; however, you may want one label to adjust in width as the form changes size. Add a blank label at the beginning of the status strip to move the date and time to the right side of the status strip. Set the Spring property of the blank label to *true*, which causes the blank label to adjust in size when the form is resized. Note that only one control on the strip can have its Spring property set to *true*.

Feedback 14.2

1. Write the statements to display aSummaryForm as a child form.
2. Assume that you have a ToolStrip called toolStrip1 that has buttons for *Exit* and *About*. How are the buttons coded?
3. What steps are necessary to display the current time in a status strip label called currentTimeToolStripStatusLabel?

Some Helpful Date Controls

Have you examined the toolbox? It holds many other controls; you may want to experiment with some of them to see how they work. This section demonstrates two more controls: the DateTimePicker and MonthCalendar controls.

The Calendar Controls

The DateTimePicker and the MonthCalendar controls (Figure 14.11) provide the ability to display calendars on your form. One advantage of the Date-TimePicker is that it takes less screen space; it displays only the day and date unless the user drops down the calendar. You can use either control to allow the user to select a date, display the current date, or set a date in code and display the calendar with that date showing.

Figure 14.11

The calendar controls: The DateTimePicker drops down a calendar when selected and shows the selected day and date when not dropped down; the MonthCalendar control displays the calendar.

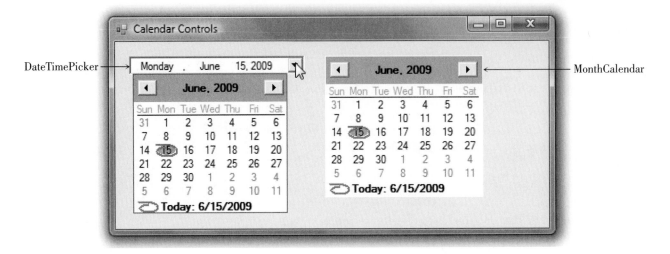

The DateTimePicker control contains a Value property for the date. When the control initially displays, the Value is set to the current date. You can let the user select a date and then retrieve the Value property or you can assign a Date value to the property.

The following example allows the user to enter a birthdate in a text box. It converts the text box entry in a `try`/`catch` in order to trap for illegal date formats.

```
birthdateDateTimePicker.Value = Convert.ToDateTime(birthdateTextBox.Text);
```

This example program demonstrates the use of the calendar, date methods, and some interesting features of C#. Figure 14.12 shows the form for the project.

Figure 14.12

The birthday form with the calendar for the DateTimePicker dropped down.

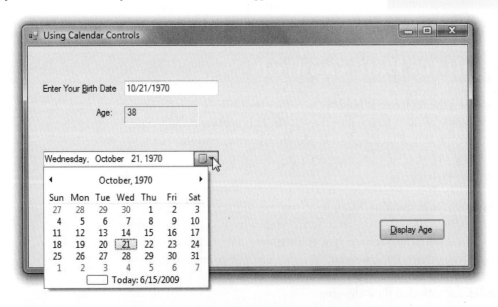

```csharp
/* Program:        Ch14Calendar
 * Programmer:     Bradley/Millspaugh
 * Date:           June 2009
 * Description:    Allow the user to enter a birthdate; calculates his or her age.
 *                 Uses a DateTimePicker and Calendar controls and Date methods.
 */

using System;
using System.Collections.Generic;
using System.ComponentModel;
using System.Data;
using System.Drawing;
using System.Text;
using System.Windows.Forms;

namespace Ch14Calendar
{
    public partial class CalendarForm : Form
    {
        public CalendarForm()
        {
            InitializeComponent();
        }

        private void displayButton_Click(object sender, EventArgs e)
        {
            // If the date is valid, set the calendar and display.

            try
            {
                birthdateDateTimePicker.Value =
                    Convert.ToDateTime(birthDateTextBox.Text);
            }
            catch (FormatException)
            {
                MessageBox.Show("Invalid Date.");
                birthDateTextBox.Focus();
            }
        }

        private void birthdateDateTimePicker_ValueChanged(object sender,
            EventArgs e)
        {
            // Calculate the age when the calendar changes.
            int yearsInteger;

            // Check if birthday has passed this year.
            if (birthdateDateTimePicker.Value.DayOfYear <=
                DateTime.Now.DayOfYear)
            {
                yearsInteger = DateTime.Now.Year -
                    birthdateDateTimePicker.Value.Year;
            }
            else
            {
                yearsInteger = DateTime.Now.Year -
                    birthdateDateTimePicker.Value.Year - 1;
            }
            ageLabel.Text = yearsInteger.ToString();
        }
    }
}
```

Notice the statements in the ValueChanged event handler for the DateTimePicker. You can use all of the properties of the system time on the Value property of the control.

```
yearsInteger = DateTime.Now.Year - birthdateDateTimePicker.Value.Year;
```

You can see all of the methods and properties using Visual Studio's IntelliSense feature. Type "Now." to see the list of methods and properties.

> **Feedback 14.3**
>
> 1. Write the code to assign the date from appointmentDateTimePicker to the variable appointmentDateTime.
> 2. Use the IntelliSense feature or Help to list five of the properties of the Value property for a DateTimePicker control.
> 3. Which of the five properties listed in Question 2 are also available for the Now property?

Displaying Web Pages on a Windows Form

You can add a **WebBrowser control** to a Windows Form and display Web pages on the form. The toolbox includes a WebBrowser control (Figure 14.13). The WebBrowser control can make your form resemble a browser window in Internet Explorer, or you can use the control to display any HTML page, online or offline. Note that you must have a live Internet connection to display Web pages in the WebBrowser control.

Figure 14.13

The Windows WebBrowser control in the toolbox.

The WebBrowser Control

When you add a WebBrowser control to an empty Windows Form, by default the control is set to fill the entire form (`Dock = Fill`). You can add a ToolStrip control to provide navigation. Some useful properties, methods, and events of the WebBrowser control follow:

Url property	Set this property to a URL at design time or run time to navigate to the entered page.
	`webBrowser1.Url = New`
	`    Uri(@"http://www.microsoft.com/");`

`Navigate` method	Execute this method at run time to navigate to the desired page.
	`webBrowser1.Navigate(New`
	`    Uri(@"http://www.microsoft.com/"));`

DocumentCompleted event	A page has finished loading. You can use this event to add the page to the Items property of the combo box.
	`toolStripComboBox1.Items.Add`
	`    (webBrowser1.Url);`

DocumentTitle property	Retrieves the title of the current Web page.

Notice the use of "Uri" in the preceding table. A Uniform Resource Identifier (URI) is a Web address that is more generic than "URL". The WebBrowser control requires that all URLs be instances of the Uri class.

A WebBrowser Program

The following Windows program displays a Web page in a WebBrowser control. The form has a ToolStrip control with a ToolStripComboBox and a ToolStripButton to aid navigation. When the user enters a new URL in the text portion of the combo box, he or she can either press Enter or click the *Go* button on the toolbar. The ToolStripComboBox_KeyUp event handler checks for the Enter key and the ToolStripButton_Click event handler checks for a click on the button. Figure 14.14 shows the completed form with a Web page displayed.

Figure 14.14

This Windows Form displays a Web page in a WebBrowser control. A ToolStrip control contains a ToolStripComboBox item and a ToolStripButton item.

The Program Code

```
/* Program:     Ch14WebBrowser
 * Programmer:  Bradley/Millspaugh
 * Date:        June 2009
 * Description: Display a Web form on a Windows Form using a WebBrowser
 *              control.
 */
```

```csharp
using System;
using System.Collections.Generic;
using System.ComponentModel;
using System.Data;
using System.Drawing;
using System.Text;
using System.Windows.Forms;

namespace Ch14WebBrowser
{
    public partial class BrowserForm : Form
    {

        public BrowserForm()
        {
            InitializeComponent();
        }

        private void webBrowser1_DocumentCompleted(object sender,
            WebBrowserDocumentCompletedEventArgs e)
        {
            // New document loaded. Add the Url to the combo box.

            toolStripComboBox1.Text = webBrowser1.Url.ToString();
            toolStripComboBox1.Items.Add(toolStripComboBox1.Text);
            this.Text = webBrowser1.DocumentTitle;
        }

        private void toolStripButton1_Click(object sender, EventArgs e)
        {
            // Go button clicked; navigate to requested page.

            try
            {
                string testString =
                    toolStripComboBox1.Text.Substring(0,7).ToUpper();
                if (testString != "HTTP://")
                {
                    toolStripComboBox1.Text = "http://" +
                        toolStripComboBox1.Text;
                }
                webBrowser1.Url = new Uri(toolStripComboBox1.Text);
            }
            catch
            {
                MessageBox.Show("Unable to locate the requested page.");
            }
        }

        private void toolStripComboBox1_KeyUp(object sender, KeyEventArgs e)
        {
            // Check for Enter key and navigate to the requested URL.

            if (e.KeyCode == Keys.Enter)
            {
                toolStripButton1_Click(sender, e);
            }
        }
```

```
    private void BrowserForm_Load(object sender, EventArgs e)
    {
        this.webBrowser1.Url = new Uri(@"http://www.microsoft.com/");
    }
}
}
```

Checking for the Enter Key

You may have noticed a strange statement in the previous section:

```
if (e.KeyCode == Keys.Enter)
```

This statement checks to see if the key pressed is the Enter key.

As you learned earlier in this chapter, you can check for the key that the user entered in a control's KeyDown, KeyPress, or KeyUp event handler. But keystrokes that ordinarily cause an action to occur, such as the Tab key and the Enter key, generate only a KeyUp event.

The e argument of the KeyUp event handler is KeyEventArgs, which has KeyCode and KeyData properties. These properties hold a numeric representation of the key pressed, but you can use the constants in the Keys enumeration to call the keys by name. For example, the Enter key has a KeyCode of 13. You can check for the Enter key with either of these statements:

```
if (e.KeyCode == 13)
```

or

```
if (e.KeyCode == Keys.Enter)
```

In the program in the previous section, the user is expected to type a URL into the combo box and press Enter or click a button. To check for the Enter key, you need to code the combo box's KeyUp event handler. Notice that the line of code compares the event argument e with the desired Keys constant.

```
private void toolStripComboBox1_KeyUp(object sender, KeyEventArgs e)
{
    // Check for Enter key and navigate to the requested URL.

    if (e.KeyCode == Keys.Enter)
    {
        toolStripButton1_Click(sender, e);
    }
}
```

XML Data Files

More and more documents are being stored as XML files. In Chapter 10 we discussed XML as a part of database files. The same format is also used for word processing and other types of office files.

There are many advantages to using XML rather than other file formats. XML is a platform-independent format that is not tied to a specific language or vendor. Because it is text-based, you can view and edit the file contents with text-edit tools. It is easy to make changes, such as adding fields. XML is Unicode compliant and can be used internationally.

Nodes, Elements, and Attributes

The following section describes the terminology and structure of XML files using books.xml, a sample file from Microsoft that also is included in your StudentData folder. Here is a listing of books.xml for reference. The terminology follows the file listing.

```xml
<?xml version='1.0'?>
<!-- This file represents a fragment of a book store inventory database -->
<bookstore>
  <book genre="autobiography" publicationdate="1981" ISBN="1-861003-11-0">
    <title>The Autobiography of Benjamin Franklin</title>
    <author>
      <first-name>Benjamin</first-name>
      <last-name>Franklin</last-name>
    </author>
    <price>8.99</price>
  </book>
  <book genre="novel" publicationdate="1967" ISBN="0-201-63361-2">
    <title>The Confidence Man</title>
    <author>
      <first-name>Herman</first-name>
      <last-name>Melville</last-name>
    </author>
    <price>11.99</price>
  </book>
  <book genre="philosophy" publicationdate="1991" ISBN="1-861001-57-6">
    <title>The Gorgias</title>
    <author>
      <name>Plato</name>
    </author>
    <price>9.99</price>
  </book>
</bookstore>
```

The first things you notice when looking at an XML file are the tags. The tags delineate **elements** of the file. The basic structure is a tree, starting with the root **node** (a file can have only one) and branching out in child nodes. A child also can contain child nodes. Nodes that are at the same level are referred to as *siblings*.

Within a node there may be several different values assigned to **attributes**. The value may be placed in either single quotes or double quotes. In the following line, genre, publicationdate, and ISBN are attributes.

```xml
<book genre="autobiography" publicationdate="1981" ISBN="1-861003-11-0">
```

Table 14.1 describes the elements in the books.xml file and Figure 14.15 illustrates the locations of the elements in the file.

XML File Terminology   **T a b l e   1 4 . 1**

Term	Meaning	Example from books.xml
`< > </>`	Start-tag and end-tag. Each element has a start tag and an end tag. If an element is empty, the start and end tags can be combined. For example, `<price/>` is the same as `<price></price>`.	`<price></price>`

Element	Contents within a set of tags.	`<title>The Gorgias</title>`
		`<author>`
		`    <name>Plato</name>`
		`</author>`

Node	A branch on the tree; the root node is the most outside with the child nodes inside.	Root node `<bookstore>` Child (descendant) nodes `<book>` `<title>` and `<author>` are child nodes of `<book>`
Sibling	Nodes at the same level.	`<title>` and `<author>`
Attribute	Named values embedded within an element; the name of the attribute is assigned a value enclosed in either single or double quotes.	`<book genre="autobiography"` `publicationdate="1981" ISBN="1-861003-11-0">`
Text	Value placed within tags.	`<first-name>Benjamin</first-name>`
Comment	Used for remarks only.	`<!-- This file represents a fragment of a book store inventory database -->`

F i g u r e   1 4 . 1 5

The elements in an XML document.

```
                     Element; root node                      Attribute

<book genre="autobiography" publicationdate="1981" ISBN="1-861003-11-0">

    <title>The Autobiography of Benjamin Franklin</title>
                                                      Elements; descendants of
    <author>                                          book

        <first-name>Benjamin</first-name>
                                                      Elements; descendants of
        <last-name>Franklin</last-name>               author

    </author>                                         Element; descendant of
                                                      book
    <price>8.99</price>

</book>
```

For more information about XML and terminology, refer to the W3C recommendations. You can find recommendations at www.w3.org/TR/REC-xml/#sec-terminology.

Writing and Reading an XML File

You can write an XML file from a program using an XmlWriter object. The XmlWriter has many methods that can write properly formed XML files, with the elements and attributes identified by tags.

The following example replaces the text file from Ch11HandsOn with an XML file. The program reads the XML file, loads the classesComboBox when the form loads, and gives the user the option of saving the list when the list has changed.

Only two procedures from Ch11HandsOn have changed: the Form_Load and the saveCoursesToolStripMenuItem_Click. Also, a `using System.Xml` statement replaces the `using System.IO` statement.

Warning: The XmlWriter class is part of the .NET 3.5 platform. If you used the Upgrade Wizard to upgrade an older version of the program, it targets an older version of the platform. Begin a new project in Visual Studio 2008 to target .NET 3.5 when you want to use the XmlWriter.

The XML Version of the ComboBox Save and Read Program

Add a `using` statement to the top of the file:

```
using System.Xml;
```

Load the ComboBox in the Form_Load event handler:

```
private void CoursesForm_Load(object sender, EventArgs e)
{
    // Load the combo box.
    DialogResult responseDialogResult;

    try
    {
        XmlTextReader aReader = new XmlTextReader("Classes.xml");

        while (aReader.Read())
        {
            if (aReader.NodeType == XmlNodeType.Text)
            {
                classesComboBox.Items.Add(aReader.Value);
            }
        }
        aReader.Close();
    }
    catch
    {
        responseDialogResult = MessageBox.Show("Create a new file?",
            "File not Found", MessageBoxButtons.YesNo,
            MessageBoxIcon.Question);
        if (responseDialogResult == DialogResult.No)
        {
            // Exit the project.
            exitToolStripMenuItem_Click(sender, new System.EventArgs());
        }
    }
}
```

Save the XML file in the *Save* menu item's routine:

```
private void saveCoursesToolStripMenuItem_Click(object sender, EventArgs e)
{
    // Save the list box contents to a file.
    try
    {
```

```
        XmlWriter aWriter = XmlWriter.Create("Classes.xml");

        aWriter.WriteStartElement("Classes");

        int indexInteger, maximumInteger;

        maximumInteger = classesComboBox.Items.Count;
        for (indexInteger = 0; indexInteger < maximumInteger; indexInteger++)
        {
            aWriter.WriteElementString("Class",
                classesComboBox.Items[indexInteger].ToString());
        }
        aWriter.WriteEndElement();
        aWriter.Flush();
        isDirtyBoolean = false;
    }
    catch
    {
        MessageBox.Show("Unable to create the file.");
    }
}
```

The XML File The Classes.xml file is created by the program. To see the file properly formatted, double-click on the filename in the bin\Debug folder. If the file is not formatted properly, select *Edit / Advanced / Format Document*.

```
<?xml version="1.0" encoding="utf-8"?>
<Classes>
    <Class>Body Sculpting</Class>
    <Class>Kickboxing</Class>
    <Class>Pilates</Class>
    <Class>Spinning</Class>
    <Class>Step</Class>
</Classes>
```

C# Tools for Reading XML Files

Visual C# 2008 includes some new tools that make working with XML files easier than in the past. In this section you will see XDocument objects, XElement objects, and how to use LINQ to XML queries.

Loading an XML File into an XDocument Object

You can use the Load method of an XDocument to read an XML file.

The XDocument.Load Method—General Forms

General Forms

```
var identifier = XDocument.Load("Filename");
XDocument identifier = XDocument.Load("Filename");
```

For the Filename entry, you can specify a complete path or a URI; otherwise the Load method looks in the current directory, which is bin\Debug in your C# project.

Notice in the first format that the data type is not specified. The Visual Studio editor's new type inference takes care of determining and assigning a strong data type.

The XDocument.Load Method—Examples

Examples

```
var bookXDocument = XDocument.Load("books.xml");
private XDocument customerXDocument = XDocument.Load
    (@"C:\Data\customers.xml");
XDocument inventoryDocument = XDocument.Load(System.IO.Directory.GetCurrentDirectory() +
    "\\inventory.xml");
```

The third example uses `System.IO.Directory.GetCurrentDirectory()` to refer to the current directory.

The following method displays the books.xml file in the Output window, which you can view with *View / Other Windows / Output* :

```
private void readFileButton_Click(object sender, EventArgs e)
{
    // Read the XML file into an XDocument and display the file
    // in the Output window.

    XDocument bookXDocument = XDocument.Load(System.IO.Directory.GetCurrentDirectory()
        + "\\books.xml");
    Console.WriteLine(bookXDocument);
}
```

Output

```
<!-- This file represents a fragment of a book store inventory database -->
<bookstore>
  <book genre="autobiography" publicationdate="1981" ISBN="1-861003-11-0">
    <title>The Autobiography of Benjamin Franklin</title>
    <author>
      <first-name>Benjamin</first-name>
      <last-name>Franklin</last-name>
    </author>
    <price>8.99</price>
  </book>
  <book genre="novel" publicationdate="1967" ISBN="0-201-63361-2">
    <title>The Confidence Man</title>
    <author>
      <first-name>Herman</first-name>
      <last-name>Melville</last-name>
    </author>
    <price>11.99</price>
  </book>
  <book genre="philosophy" publicationdate="1991" ISBN="1-861001-57-6">
    <title>The Gorgias</title>
    <author>
      <name>Plato</name>
    </author>
    <price>9.99</price>
  </book>
</bookstore>
```

Loading an XML File into an XElement Object

In addition to using an XDocument, you also can load an XML file into an XElement object. The difference between the two is that the XDocument contains the information about the document from the top of the file, while the root node is the first item in an XElement object.

```
XElement bookData = XElement.Load("books.xml");
```

Using LINQ to XML to Query an XElement Object

You can use LINQ to XML to retrieve data elements from an XElement or XDocument object. The following examples select data from the bookData XDocument and display the data in a list box. The bookData object was loaded with books.xml in the previous section.

You can refer to the elements in the XElement object on the `In` clause of LINQ as well as in the `Select` clause. Use `bookData.Elements("")` to refer to all child elements of the "book" root node. Use *queryName*.`Element("`*ElementName*`")` to refer to an element that is a descendant of one child.

```
// Read the XML file into an XElement and use LINQ to query the data.
XElement bookData = XElement.Load("books.xml");

// Retrieve the titles.
var bookQuery = from aBook in bookData.Elements()
                select aBook.Element("title").Value; // Get the titles.
titlesListBox.DataSource = bookQuery.ToList();
```

You also can combine the `XElement.Load` and the query:

```
// Retrieve the titles. Combined load and query.
var bookQuery = from aBook in XElement.Load("books.xml").Elements()
                select aBook.Element("title").Value;
titlesListBox.DataSource = bookQuery.ToList();
```

LINQ offers many operators beyond what we have covered up to this point. The next two examples demonstrate `orderby`, which is used for sorting, and `where`, which is used for conditions.

```
// LINQ query that sorts by book title.
var bookQuery = from aBook in bookData.Elements()
                orderby aBook.Element("title").Value ascending
                select aBook.Element("title").Value; // Get the titles.
titlesListBox.DataSource = bookQuery.ToList();

// LINQ query that selects a particular book by using a where clause.
var bookQuery = from aBook in bookData.Elements()
                where aBook.Element("title").Value == "The Confidence Man"
                select aBook.Element("price").Value
                   + " " + aBook.Element("title").Value;
titlesListBox.DataSource = bookQuery.ToList();
```

Stepping through Query Output

If you want to refer to individual attributes in the results of a query, or manipulate the output in some way, you can use a `foreach` statement.

```
// Retrieve ISBN and publicationdate attributes.
var isbnQuery = from aBook in bookData.Elements()
                select aBook;
foreach (XElement anElement in isbnQuery)
{
    titlesListBox.Items.Add((string) anElement.Attribute("ISBN")
        + " " + (string) anElement.Attribute("publicationdate"));
}
```

LINQ to XML Program Examples

The following program reads the books.xml file, uses a LINQ to XML query, and loads the resulting list of titles into a list box (Figure 14.16). Extra queries are included but commented out to illustrate other queries.

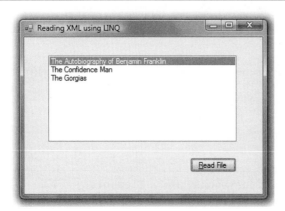

Figure 14.16

The book titles from books.xml are loaded into a list box using LINQ to XML.

```
/* Project:      Ch14LinqToXml
 * Programmer:   Bradley/Millspaugh
 * Date:         June 2009
 * Description:  Read an XML file into an XDocument and use
 *               LINQ to XML to extract the titles and display
 *               in a list box.
 */

using System;
using System.Collections.Generic;
using System.ComponentModel;
using System.Data;
using System.Drawing;
using System.Linq;
using System.Text;
using System.Windows.Forms;
using System.Xml;
using System.Xml.Linq;

namespace Ch14LinqToXml
{
```

```csharp
public partial class XmlListForm : Form
{
    public XmlListForm()
    {
        InitializeComponent();
    }

    private void readFileButton_Click(object sender, EventArgs e)
    {
        // Read the XML file into an XElement and use LINQ to query the data.
        XElement bookData = XElement.Load("books.xml");

        // Retrieve the titles.
        var bookQuery = from aBook in bookData.Elements()
                        select aBook.Element("title").Value;
        titlesListBox.DataSource = bookQuery.ToList();

        // Order by title.
        //var bookQuery = from aBook in bookData.Elements()
        //                orderby aBook.Element("title").Value ascending
        //                select aBook.Element("title").Value;
        //titlesListBox.DataSource = bookQuery.ToList();

        // Retrieve the titles. Combined load and query.
        //var bookQuery = from aBook in XElement.Load("books.xml").Elements()
        //                select aBook.Element("title").Value;
        //titlesListBox.DataSource = bookQuery.ToList();

        // LINQ query that selects a particular book by using a where clause.
        //var bookQuery = from aBook in bookData.Elements()
        //                where aBook.Element("title").Value ==
        //                  "The Confidence Man"
        //                select aBook.Element("price").Value
        //                    + "   " + aBook.Element("title").Value;
        //titlesListBox.DataSource = bookQuery.ToList();

        // Retrieve the title and price.
        //var bookQuery = from aBook in bookData.Elements()
        //                select aBook.Element("price").Value
        //                    + aBook.Element("title").Value;
        //titlesListBox.DataSource = bookQuery.ToList();

        // Retrieve the title and price in a foreach loop.
        //var bookQuery = from aBook in bookData.Descendants("book")
        //                select aBook;
        //foreach (XElement anElement in bookQuery)
        //{
        //    titlesListBox.Items.Add((double)anElement.Element("price")
        //        + "   " + (string) anElement.Element("title"));
        //}
    }
}
```

Windows Presentation Foundation (WPF)

One of the coolest new features in Visual Studio 2008 is **Windows Presentation Foundation**. WPF provides the ability to create richer user interfaces for multiple platform development. Windows Vista uses WPF technology to bring a better multimedia experience to the operating system. The designing capability of WPF is available in Visual Studio as well as in the Microsoft Expression Studio, which consists of Expression Web, Expression Blend, Expression Design, and Expression Media. Microsoft Silverlight (http://silverlight.net/) is a scaled-down version of WPF technology for a rich Web-based interface and works with all leading browsers and on multiple platforms, such as Macintosh. These products offer the ability to integrate vector-based graphics, media, text, animation, and overlays into the Web interface.

When you create a Web page, there are essentially two different tasks: the interface and the code that runs the application. Often the person or artist who creates the interface is referred to as the designer. Making the page useful by creating the logic for database connection and programming is done by a developer (programmer).

Expression Blend allows a Web page designer to create an interface that can be turned over to a developer for adding the code. In Visual Studio, you may have noticed that when you create a new project, there are templates for a WPF application and for WPF Browser Applications (Figure 14.17).

Figure 14.17

You can use the WPF Application and WPF Browser Application templates to create applications in Visual Studio.

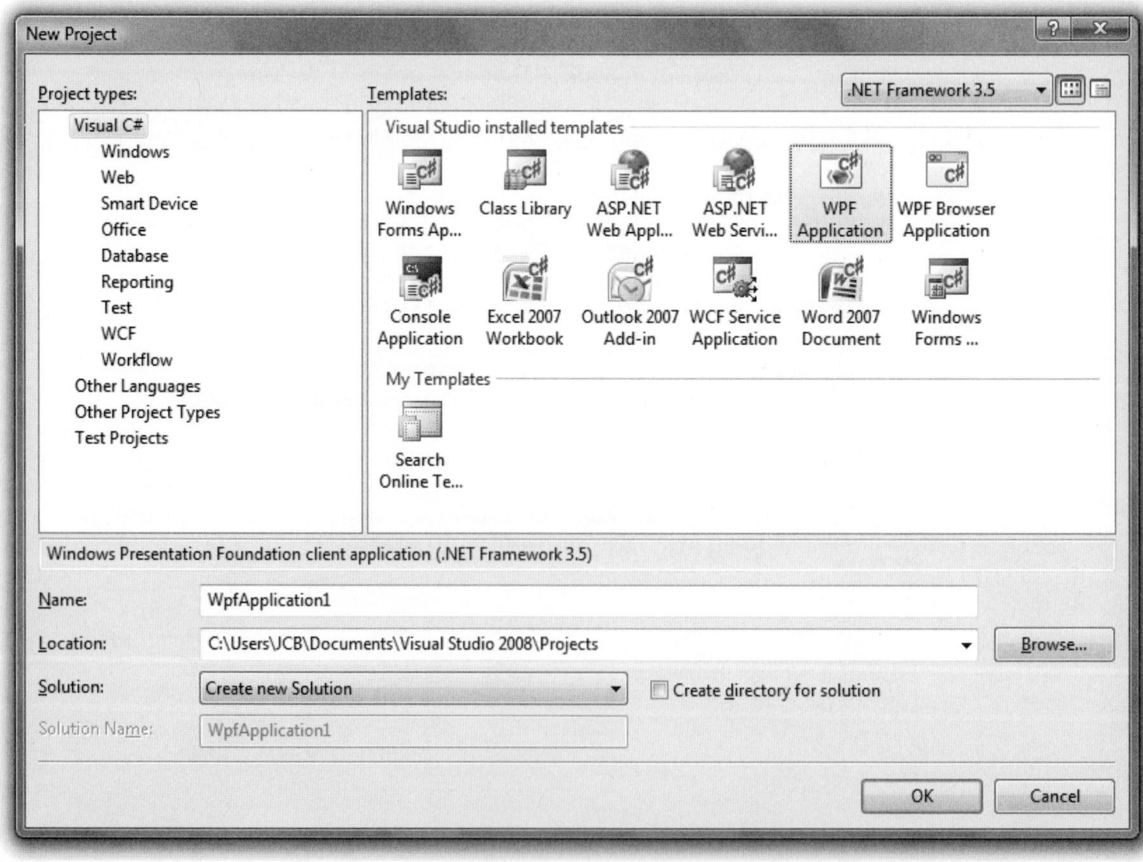

The user interface in WPF applications uses XAML (pronounced "zammel") code rather than HTML. **XAML (Extensible Application Markup Language)** is an XML-based language that is much more interactive than the traditional HTML. The term ***XBAP*** is used to refer to a **XAML Browser Application** that runs in an Internet browser. You can check out some of the existing business applications at http://blogs.msdn.com/chabrook/archive/2007/02/20/cool-wpf-applications.aspx.

We can still write our programs in C# and Visual Studio or Visual Web Developer to supplement the XAML interface. The new technology also allows us to create hybrid applications. You can add WPF features to your Windows Form applications, and the Windows controls that you have learned about can be added to a WPF page.

We will examine both a Windows Form with WPF features and a WPF application.

WPF Interoperability

Using WPF Interoperability you can use WPF controls in a Windows Forms application. The C# toolbox for a Windows project has a category for WPF Interoperability (Figure 14.18). The only control in the group that appears by default is the ElementHost. This control is a container that allows you to add other WPF controls to the Windows Form. Many WPF controls are available, and the list continues to grow. View the list by right-clicking in the toolbox, selecting *Choose items*, and then clicking on the *WPF* tab (Figure 14.19). You do not need to add the controls to the toolbox, as you add the controls at run time rather than design time.

To use WPF Interoperabiltiy, you add the ElementHost control to a Windows Form and then add the WPF controls in code. Your file must include a `using` statement for `System.Windows.Controls`.

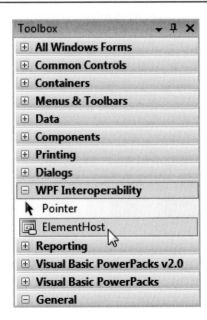

Figure 14.18

The toolbox for a Windows Forms application has an ElementHost control in the WPF Interoperability section, which allows you to add WPF controls to a Windows application.

Figure 14.19

See the list of available WPF controls on the **WPF Components** *tab of the* **Choose Toolbox Items** *dialog box.*

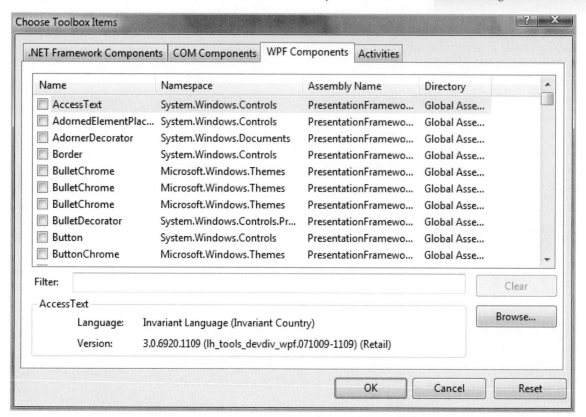

You may have noticed a control that allows a part of the page to show or be hidden. This is a WPF control called an Expander. The Expander's header property indicates the words to display on the form: "More" in Figure 14.20. When the user clicks to expand the control, the value of the Content property displays.

Adding a WPF Control to a Windows Form—Step-by-Step

In the following step-by-step exercise, you will place a WPF Expander control on a Windows Form.

Set Up the Windows Project
STEP 1: Create a new project called Ch14WPFInterop.

STEP 2: Name the form WPFInteropForm, and set the Text property to "Including a WPF Control".

STEP 3: Add an ElementHost control to the form, keeping the default name elementHost1.

Write the C# Code
STEP 1: In the Code Editor window, add a using statement to the top of the file:

```
using System.Windows.Controls;
```

Figure 14.20

An Expander control on a Windows Form, using WPF Interoperability. When the user clicks on "More" or the arrow, the additional information displays.

Click on *More* or the arrow to see the additional information

STEP 2: Add the following code in the Form_Load event handler.

```
private void WPFInteropForm_Load(object sender, EventArgs e)
{
    // Display a WPF Expander control.

    Expander moreExpander = new Expander();

    moreExpander.Header = "More";
    moreExpander.Content = "Now you see additional information.";

    elementHost1.Child = moreExpander;
}
```

Run the Program

STEP 1: Run the program. You can click on either the word "More" or the arrow icon to see the additional information.

Writing a WPF Application

To create a WPF application, you select a different template when you create a new project (refer to Figure 14.17).

After creating a new project, examine the layout of the IDE. You will find that it resembles the layout for an ASP.NET application for creating a Web site.

*The IDE for a WPF application. To design the user interface visually, minimize the **XAML** tab.*

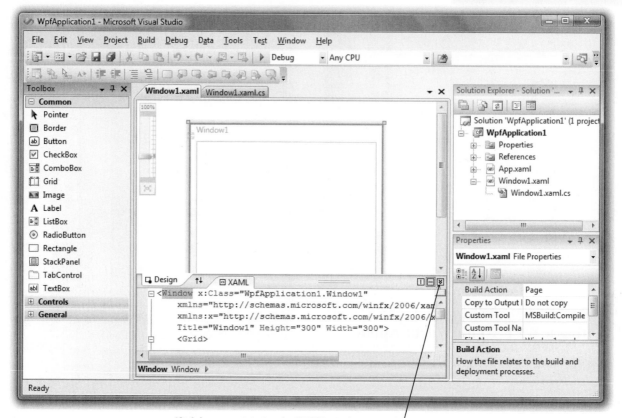

Click here to minimize the XAML window to a tab

The Document window is split, showing the XAML and the design (Figure 14.21). Since you are not going to write in XAML, you can collapse the XAML screen; it doesn't really close; instead, it appears as a tab at the bottom of the Design window. You can control the size of the WPF form using the adjuster bar on the left of the Design window.

Designing the layout of a WPF window is similar to a Web page—both use flow layout, and you must take steps to place controls where you want them. For Web pages, you would probably use a table to lay out the controls on the page. For a WPF window, you do not need to set up a table; if you wish, you can use the grid container that is automatically added to a new window. The grid container displays with a blue border on the left and the top. If you place your cursor inside the blue border, the mouse pointer changes to a crosshair (Figure 14.22), and you can click to set grid lines of whatever height and width that you wish.

Next, look at the toolbox. You will notice many familiar-sounding controls. The controls have the same functionality and feel as the equivalent Windows Forms controls but have many extra properties. Notice the Expander control that we used on the Windows Form ElementHost.

You also will find that some of the terminology is different. WPF creates a window rather than a form. There is no Text property; instead, the window has a Title property and the other controls have a Content property.

Figure 14.22

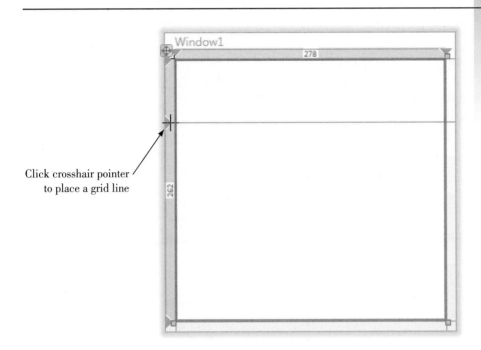

Click crosshair pointer to place a grid line

Creating a WPF Hello World Application—Step-by-Step

We will create a Hello World application to give you a brief overview of some of the features of WPF.

Note: Although you can create this application in Windows XP, the great effects do not appear. You need to be running in Vista to see the special effects.

Set Up the Project

STEP 1: Create a new project using the WPF Application template. Call the project Ch14WpfHelloWorld.

STEP 2: Click the down arrow in the upper-right corner of the XAML window to minimize it into a tab at the bottom of the Document window.

STEP 3: Do not change the name of the window but change the Title to "A Hello World Example".

STEP 4: Save all.

Add Controls

STEP 1: Add a label and set the Name property to messageLabel, which you set in a text box at the top of the Properties window (Figure 14.23).

STEP 2: Set the BorderThickness of the label to 3.

STEP 3: Set the BorderBrush to BurlyWood.

STEP 4: Set the Content property to blank.

STEP 5: Add two buttons, naming them displayButton and exitButton, with the Content property set to Display and Exit.

STEP 6: Select both of the button controls and set the following properties:

Under Appearance, expand *More Properties*, then set the Bitmap-Effect to BevelBitmapEffect.

Select *Hand* from the Cursor property drop-down list. Note that the Cursor drop-down list is not in alphabetic order; you must search the list to find *Hand*.

Figure 14.23

Set the Name property of controls in the text box at the top of the Properties window.

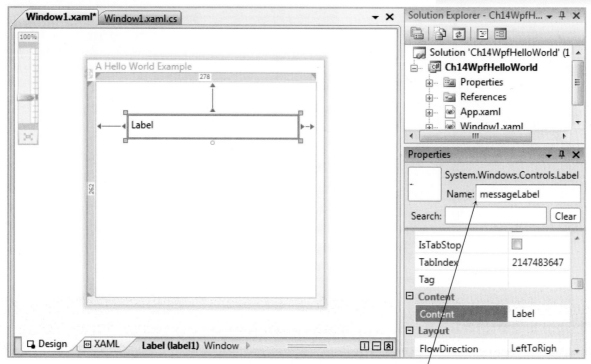

Set the Name property in this text box

Code the Buttons

STEP 1: Write the code for the *Display* button. You can double-click the control to access the xaml.cs Code Editor window, just as you do in a Windows application.

> *Note:* The Text property from a Windows Form is referred to as the Content property in WPF.

```
private void displayButton_Click(object sender, RoutedEventArgs e)
{
    // Display a message.

    messageLabel.Content = "Hello World";
}
```

STEP 2: Write the code for the *Exit* button.

```
private void exitButton_Click(object sender, RoutedEventArgs e)
{
    // Close the program.

    this.Close();
}
```

STEP 3: Write the remarks at the top of the file.

```
//Program:      Ch14WPFHelloWorld
//Programmer:   Your Name
//Date:         Today's date
//Description:  Displays Hello World in a label.
```

Run the Program

As you move your cursor over the buttons, the color changes to blue. Also notice the cursor that we set. You can easily add a ToolTip to the button. There is no need to drag any extra components; the ToolTip property is already on each control.

The Role of Expression Blend

Earlier we mentioned that the XAML code is the same for developers in Visual Studio and for designers in Expression. The project that we just created could be opened in Expression, for a designer to add even more dramatic features. Watch the video at http://channel9.msdn.com/Showpost.aspx?postid=359715 for more information.

Summary

1. An ErrorProvider component can provide an icon and popup error message next to the field that does not pass validation. Specify the text box and the message in the ErrorProvider's `SetError` method.
2. A text box MaxLength property limits the number of characters the user is allowed to enter into the control.
3. The CharacterCasing property of a text box can automatically convert user input to uppercase or lowercase.
4. You can validate individual fields in the Validating event handler for the controls. The Validating event occurs when the user attempts to move the focus to another control that has its CausesValidation property set to *true*.
5. C# code snippets are small samples of code that illustrate coding techniques. You can add code snippets in the editor.
6. Visual Studio includes many sample programs and quick-start tutorials.
7. A multiple document interface (MDI) contains parent and child forms. Closing the parent also closes all child forms. The child forms stay within the bounds of the parent form.
8. To create an MDI parent form, set a form's IsMdiContainer property to *true*. To create a child form, instantiate a new form object and set its MdiParent property to the parent form in code.
9. MDI applications generally have a *Window* menu, which displays a list of open child windows and provides choices for arranging the child windows.
10. To create a toolbar, add a ToolStrip control and add buttons to the control.
11. A toolbar generally provides shortcuts to menu options.
12. A status bar contains information for the user along the bottom of a form. After adding a StatusStrip control to a form, add ToolStripStatusLabels, which you can use to display text.
13. The date can be assigned to the Text property of a ToolStripStatusLabel during the Form_Load event handler, but the time display requires an update routine using a Timer component.

14. The DateTimePicker and MonthCalendar controls have accurate calendars for displaying and inputting dates.

15. The WebBrowser control provides the ability to display Web pages on a Windows Form.

16. You can check the **e** (KeyEventArgs) argument of a control's KeyUp event handler to determine which key was pressed. The e.KeyCode and e.Key-Data properties hold a numeric code for the key, which you can check using the constants in the Keys enumeration.

17. XML files are used to store data as text identified by tags. The files are platform independent and extremely flexible.

18. XML files consist of nodes, elements, and attributes. Each file can have one root node and many child (descendant) nodes. Child nodes at the same level are called siblings.

19. You can save data into an XML file using an XmlWriter object, which inserts the correct tags into the file.

20. Two objects that you can use to read an XML file are XDocument and XElement. You can use a LINQ to XML query to select data elements.

21. Windows Presentation Foundation (WPF) can be used to create rich user interfaces, such as those in Windows Vista.

22. A WPF user interface is coded in XAML; a XAML Browser Application is called *XBAP*.

23. Using WPF Interoperability you can add an ElementHost control and WPF controls to a Windows Form. WPF controls are added to the ElementHost at run time.

24. WPF applications are similar to Web applications in that they are created as two files: one for the user interface and one for the programming logic.

Key Terms

R e v i e w   Q u e s t i o n s

1. Explain how to use an ErrorProvider component when validating the value in a text box.
2. What properties of a text box determine the number of characters a user can enter and the case (upper or lower) of the input?
3. What are code snippets? How might they be used?
4. What is meant by *MDI*?
5. What are the advantages of having parent and child forms?
6. What are the layouts available for arranging child windows?
7. How can a child form be created? a parent form?
8. What steps are necessary to create a toolbar and have its buttons execute menu methods?
9. What must be done to create a status bar? to display a label with the current time? to keep the time display current?
10. Describe two controls that you can use for displaying dates on a form.
11. What property is used to navigate to a Web page at design time using the WebBrowser control? How is this task accomplished at run time?
12. What is the advantage of using XML files over other file types?
13. What is WPF? How does it apply to Windows and Web applications?

P r o g r a m m i n g   E x e r c i s e s

14.1 Convert any of your earlier programs that use message boxes for error messages to use an ErrorProvider component. Remove all error message boxes from the program and display meaningful messages in the popup Error text.

14.2 Write an MDI application that is a simple text editor. Allow the user to open multiple documents, each in a separate child form. For the text editor, use one big TextBox control with its Multiline property set to *true* or a RichTextBox control. Set the control's Anchor property to all four edges so the control fills its form.

The main form should have an *Open* menu item to open previously saved files; the child forms should have a *Save* menu item to save their text to a file. Use the file handling that you learned about in Chapter 11 and display the name of the file in the form's title bar.

14.3 Add a toolbar and a status bar to a previous project to provide shortcuts to the menu items.

14.4 Add a toolbar and a status bar to the calendar program from this chapter. You can first create the calendar program, or your instructor may provide it to you.

14.5 Create an application for displaying movie listings. Add a WebBrowser control that navigates to a page showing the movies.

14.6 Convert your text file project from Chapter 11 to use an XML file.

Case Studies

Note: For help in basing a new project on an existing project, see "Basing a New Project on an Existing Project" in Appendix C.

Custom Supplies Mail Order

Convert any of your earlier Custom Supplies Mail Order programs that use message boxes for error messages to use an ErrorProvider component. Remove all error message boxes from the program and display meaningful messages in the popup Error text.

Add a toolbar and a status bar to the project to provide shortcuts to the menu items.

Christopher's Car Center

Convert any of your earlier Christopher's Car Center programs that use message boxes for error messages to use an ErrorProvider component. Remove all error message boxes from the program and display meaningful messages in the popup Error text.

Add a toolbar and a status bar to the project to provide shortcuts to the menu items.

Xtreme Cinema

Convert any of your earlier Xtreme Cinema programs that use message boxes for error messages to use an ErrorProvider component. Remove all error message boxes from the program and display meaningful messages in the popup Error text.

Add a toolbar and a status bar to the project to provide shortcuts to the menu items.

Cool Boards

Convert any of your earlier Cool Boards programs that use message boxes for error messages to use an ErrorProvider component. Remove all error message boxes from the program and display meaningful messages in the popup Error text.

Add a toolbar and a status bar to the project to provide shortcuts to the menu items.

A

Answers to Feedback Questions

> ## Feedback 1.1

These exercises are designed to help the student become more familiar with the Help system. There are no "correct" answers.

> ## Feedback 2.1

Property	Setting
Name	iconPictureBox
BorderStyle	Fixed3D
SizeMode	StretchImage
Visible	true

> ## Feedback 2.2

1. ```
   companyTextBox.Clear();
   companyTextBox.Focus();
   ```
2. ```
   customerLabel.Text = "";
   orderTextBox.Focus();
   ```
3. (a) Places a check in the checkbox.
   (b) Radio button is selected. All other Radio buttons in the group are deselected.
   (c) Makes the picture invisible.
   (d) Makes the label appear sunken.
   (e) Assigns the value in `cityTextBox.Text` to the text value of `cityLabel.Text`.
   (f) Makes the radio button enabled so the user can select it.

> ## Feedback 3.1

1. Does not have a suffix indicating a data type.
2. Identifiers cannot contain special characters such as #.
3. An identifier cannot contain blank spaces.
4. Periods are used to separate items such as Object.Property.
5. Identifiers cannot contain special characters such as $.
6. *Class* is a reserved word.
7. The name is valid; however, it does not indicate anything about what the variable is used for (unless you work in a sandwich shop).
8. *Text* is a property name and, therefore, it is a reserved word.
9. The name is not valid; the suffix used should clearly indicate the data type.
10. A suffix indicating the data type should be used.
11. Valid.
12. Valid.

▶ Feedback 3.2

Note: Answers may vary; make sure the suffix indicates the data type.

1. (a) `decimal hoursDecimal;`
   (b) `string employeeNameString;`
   (c) `string departmentNumberString;`
2. (a) `int quantityInteger;`
   (b) `string descriptionString;`
   (c) `string partNumberString;`
   (d) `decimal costDecimal;`
   (e) `decimal sellingPriceDecimal;`

▶ Feedback 3.3

Note: Answers may vary; make sure that the suffix indicates the data type.

1. `decimal totalPayrollDecimal;`
   Declared at the class level.
2. `const decimal SALES_TAX_Decimal = .08M;`
   Declared at the class level.
3. `int participantsInteger;`
   Declared at the class level.

▶ Feedback 3.4

1. 4
2. 1
3. 6
4. 5
5. 14
6. 40
7. 14
8. 22

▶ Feedback 3.5

1. (a) `countInteger = countInteger + 1;`
   (b) `countInteger += 1;`
   (c) `countInteger++;`
2. (a) `countInteger = countInteger + 5;`
   (b) `countInteger += 5;`
3. (a) `balanceDecimal = balanceDecimal – withdrawalDecimal;`
   (b) `balanceDecimal -= withdrawalDecimal;`
4. (a) `priceDecimal = priceDecimal * countInteger;`
   (b) `priceDecimal *= countInteger;`

▶ **Feedback 3.6**

1. ```
   averagePayTextBox.Text = averagePayDecimal.ToString("C");
   ```
2. ```
   quantityTextBox.Text = quantityInteger.ToString();
   ```
3. ```
   totalTextBox.Text = totalCollectedDecimal.ToString("N");
   ```

▶ **Feedback 4.1**

1. True
2. True
3. True
4. False
5. False
6. False
7. True
8. False
9. True
10. True
11. True

▶ **Feedback 4.2**

1. frogsRadioButton will be selected.
2. "It's the toads and polliwogs" will be displayed.
3. "It's true" will be displayed.
4. ```
   if (int.Parse(applesTextBox.Text) >
       int.Parse(orangesTextBox.Text))
   {
       mostLabel.Text = "It's the apples!";
   }
   else if (int.Parse(applesTextBox.Text) <
       int.Parse(orangesTextBox.Text))
   {
       mostLabel.Text = "It's the oranges!";
   {
   else
   {
       mostLabel.Text = "It's a tie!";
   }
   ```
5. ```
   if (balanceDecimal > 0)
   {
       fundsCheckBox.Checked = true;
       balanceDecimal = 0;
       countInteger++;
   }
   else
   {
       fundsCheckBox.Checked = false;
   }
   ```
   ```

▶ Feedback 4.3

1.
```
switch (codeString)
{
    case "A":
        outputLabel.Text = "Excellent";
        break;
    case "B":
        outputLabel.Text = "Good";
        break;
    case "C":
    case "D":
        outputLabel.Text = "Satisfactory";
        break;
    default:
        outputLabel.Text = "Not Satisfactory";
        break;
}
```

2.
```
switch (codeString.ToUpper())
{
    case "A":
        outputLabel.Text = "Excellent";
        break;
    case "B":
        outputLabel.Text = "Good";
        break;
    case "C":
    case "D":
        outputLabel.Text = "Satisfactory";
        break;
    default:
        outputLabel.Text = "Not Satisfactory";
        break;
}
```

3.
```
switch (countInteger)
{
    case O:
        MessageBox.Show("Invalid value");
        break;
    default:
        averageDecimal = sumDecimal / countInteger;
        MessageBox.Show("The average is: " +
            averageDecimal.ToString());
        break;
}
```

▶ Feedback 5.1

1.
```
private decimal Average(decimal valueOneDecimal, decimal valueTwoDecimal,
    decimal valueThreeDecimal)
```

2. ```
return (valueOneDecimal + valueTwoDecimal + valueThreeDecimal) / 3;
```
3. The `return` statement is used to send the answer back to the calling method.

---

## ▶ Feedback 6.1

1. Property methods set up the properties of the class. The properties allow controlled external access to data members in an instance of a class.
2. ```
aSummaryForm.DrinksSold = drinksSoldInteger;
```
3. ```
public integer DrinksSold
{
    set
    {
        drinksSoldInteger = value;
    }
}
```

---

## ▶ Feedback 7.1

1. Alphabetizes the items in a list box or combo box.
2. Stores the index number of the currently selected (highlighted) item; has a value of −1 if nothing is selected.
3. Is a collection that holds the text of all list elements in a list box or combo box.
4. Determines whether or not a list box will have a text box for user input. It also determines whether or not the list will be drop down.
5. Stores the number of elements in the Items collection of a list box or combo box.
6. Adds an element to a list at run time.
7. Adds an element to a list and inserts the element in the chosen position (index).
8. Clears all elements from a list box or combo box.
9. Removes an element from the list by referring to its index.
10. Removes an element from a list by looking for a given string.

---

## ▶ Feedback 7.2

```
bool itemFoundBoolean = false;   // Set the initial value of the found
                        // switch to false.
int itemInteger = 0;   // Initialize the counter for the item index.
// Loop through the items until the requested item is found or the
// end of the list is reached
while (! itemFoundBoolean && itemInteger < itemsListBox.Items.Count)
{
```
```

```
    // Check if the text box entry matches the item in the list.
    if (newItemTextBox.Text == itemsListBox.Items[itemInteger].ToString())
    {
        itemFoundBoolean = true;     // Set the found switch to true.
    }
    itemInteger++;                   // Increment the counter for the item index.
}
```

▶ Feedback 7.3

1. (a) Semicolons should be used, not commas.
   (b) indexInteger should be used in the condition as well as the action.
   (c) 4 is not a proper variable name.
   (d) Valid.
   (e) The loop will never execute since indexInteger does not start out less than −10.
2. (a) Will be executed 2 times.
   (b) Will be executed 3 times.
   (c) Will be executed 10 times.
   (d) Will be executed 6 times.

▶ Feedback 7.4

1. A control used to set up output for the printer. Add the control to the form's component tray at design time. Begin the printing process by executing the Print method of the control; the control's PrintPage event occurs.
2. Starts the printing process. Belongs in the Click event handler for the *Print* button.
3. The PrintPage event is a callback that occurs once for each page to print. The PrintPage event handler contains all the logic for printing the page.
4. Sends a line of text to the graphics object. The DrawString method is used in the PrintPage event handler.
5. An argument passed to the PrintPage event handler; holds items of information such as the page margins.
6. MarginBounds.Left is one of the properties of the PrintPageEventArgs argument passed to the PrintPage event handler. The property holds the left margin and can be used to set the X coordinate to the left margin.
7. A control that allows the user to view the document in a Print Preview window. The control is added to the form's component tray at design time. In the event handler where the user selects *Print Preview*, the print document is assigned to this control.

▶ Feedback 8.1

1. Invalid.
2. Valid.
3. Invalid.

4. Invalid.
5. Valid.
6. Invalid.
7. Valid. (It truncates to 3.)
8. Valid.

▶ **Feedback 8.2**

1.
```
struct Student
{
    public string lastNameString;
    public string firstNameString;
    public string studentNumberString;
    public decimal unitsDecimal;
    public decimal GPADecimal;
}
```
2.
```
public Student[] Students = new Student[100];
```
3.
```
struct Project
{
    public string projectNameString;
    public string formNameString;
    public string folderNameString;
}
```
4.
```
Project myProject;
```
5.
```
Project[] ourProjects = new Project[100];
```

▶ **Feedback 8.3**

1.
```
decimal[,] temperatureDecimal = new decimal[3, 5];
```
2.
```
for (columnInteger = 0; columnInteger < 5; columnInteger++)
{
    temperatureDecimal[0, columnInteger] = 0M;
}
```
3.
```
for (columnInteger = 0; columnInteger < 5; columnInteger++)
{
    temperatureDecimal[1, columnInteger] = 75M;
}
```
4.
```
for (columnInteger = 0; columnInteger < 5; columnInteger++)
{
    temperatureDecimal[2, columnInteger] =
      temperatureDecimal[0, columnInteger] +
      temperatureDecimal[1, columnInteger];
}
```
5.
```
for (rowInteger = 0; rowInteger < 3; rowInteger++)
{
    for (columnInteger = 0; columnInteger < 5; columnInteger++)
    {
```

```
        // Set up a line.
        printLineString = temperatureDecimal[rowInteger,
          columnInteger].ToString();
        // Send the line to the graphics page object.
        e.Graphics.DrawString(printLineString, printFont,
          Brushes.Black, printXFloat, printYFloat);
        printXFloat += 200;   // Move across the line.
    }
    printXFloat = e.MarginBounds.Left; // Reset to left margin.
    // Increment the Y position for the next line.
    printYFloat += lineHeightFloat;
}
```

➤ Feedback 9.1

1. .aspx; holds the specifications for the user interface that are used by the server to render the page.
   .aspx.cs; holds the C# code that you write to respond to events.
2. Right-click on the form and select *View in Browser*.
3. The ASP.NET server control is rendered on the server and can include code behind it that you can write. An HTML control is a static control that only runs on the client side. Use these types of controls when you want to convert old pages created elsewhere to work in your project.

➤ Feedback 9.2

1. (a) Press the Enter key until the insertion point is at the bottom of the form and add the button control.
   (b) Add a table to the form and place the button in a cell at the bottom of the table.
2. An HTML Table works on the client side only; the data must be added at design time. A Web Table can be changed dynamically during run time.
3. Store the images files in with the project files. Be sure to copy them in before you reference them.

➤ Feedback 9.3

1. The NavigateUrl property.
2. Add a HyperLink control to both pages. Set the NavigateUrl of each to point to the other page.
3. `Server.Transfer("ThankYou.aspx");`

► Feedback 9.4

Attach a RequiredFieldValidator control so that the field cannot be left blank. Attach a RangeValidator to check if the input falls within the specified range by setting the MinimumValue = 0 and the MaximumValue = 1000 and set the Type to make sure that the entry can be converted to numeric. Change the ErrorMessage property to reflect the error.

► Feedback 9.5

The Page_Load event occurs and the page is redisplayed for every round-trip to the server. If you have initialization code in the Page_Load event handler, you don't want to perform the initialization each time the handler executes.

► Feedback 10.1

1. The *file* is the database.
    The *table* contains the *rows* and *columns*, which hold the information about your friends.
    Each *row/record* contains information about an individual friend.
    A *column* or *field* contains an element of data, such as the name or phone number.
    The *key field* is the field used to organize the file; it contains a unique value that identifies a particular record, for example, the name field.
2. XML is stored as text, which can pass through Internet firewalls and can be edited using any text editor.

► Feedback 10.2

The binding source object creates a link between the original data source and the program. The table adapter passes information back and forth between the data source and the dataset. The dataset holds a copy of the data retrieved from the data source and is used in your program to access the data, either field by field (for labels and text boxes) or by connecting it to a grid.

► Feedback 10.3

1. The drop-down list in the Data Sources window allows you to select Data-GridView or Details view.

2. In the Data Sources window, select *Details* on the drop-down list and drag the table to the form. Change the field type from the default text box to a label, open the drop-down list next to the field name in the Data Sources window and select *Label*, then drag the table to the form.
3. Set the DataSource property of the combo box to the binding source used by the other controls. Set the DisplayMember property to the data field to display in the combo box.
4. To sort the list, modify the SQL SELECT statement used by the table adapter. Add a Sort Type to the required field(s) in the Query Builder.

▶ Feedback 10.4

1. LINQ or Language Integrated Query is a standard language that allows the programmer to write queries in the program code.
2. LINQ can be used to query databases, XML files, or any collection defined as an object.
3. The compiler supplies (infers) the data type for a variable that does not have a type declared.

▶ Feedback 11.1

1.
```
private StreamWriter inventoryStreamWriter
    = new StreamWriter("Inventory.txt");
```
2.
```
inventoryStreamWriter.WriteLine(descriptionTextBox.Text);
```
3. The declaration for the StreamReader object needs to be in a `try`/`catch` block in case the file does not exist. The declaration for the StreamWriter object does not need to be in a `try`/`catch` block because, in this case, the program is generating a file, not trying to locate one unless the full path is specified and does not exist.
4.
```
if (inventoryStreamReader.Peek() != -1)
{
    descriptionLabel.Text =
        inventoryStreamReader.ReadLine();
    productNumberLabel.Text =
        inventoryStreamReader.ReadLine();
}
```

▶ Feedback 11.2

1.
```
Text Files (*.txt)|*.txt
```
2.
```
openFileDialog1.InitialDirectory = Directory.GetCurrentDirectory();
```
3.
```
if (phoneStreamWriter != null)
{
    phoneStreamWriter.Close();
}
```

Feedback 11.3

1.
```
int countInteger = namesList.Items.Count;
for (int indexInteger = O; indexInteger < countInteger; indexInteger++)
{
    namesStreamWriter.WriteLine(nameListBox.Items[indexInteger]);
}
namesStreamWriter.Close();
```

2. The above code should be placed in a `Save` method that should be called from the form's FormClosing event handler.

3.
```
try
{
    StreamReader namesStreamReader =
        new StreamReader("Names.txt");
    while (namesStreamReader.Peek() != -1)
    {
        namesList.Items.Add(namesStreamReader.ReadLine());
    }
    namesStreamReader.Close();
}
catch
{
}
```

Feedback 12.1

1. An object is an instance of a class. A class defines an item type (like the cookie cutter defines the shape), whereas the object is an actual instance of the class (as the cookie made from the cookie cutter).

2. aProduct is an object, an instance of the Product class.

3. The Text property of quantityTextBox is converted to an integer and assigned to the Quantity property of the aProduct object.

4.
```
private string lastNameString;
private string firstNameString;
private string studentIDNumberString;
private decimal gpaDecimal;
```
These statements will appear at the class level.

5.
```
public string LastName
{
    get
    {
        return lastNameString;
    }
    set
    {
        lastNameString = value;
    }
}
```

```csharp
6. public decimal GPA
   {
       get
       {
           return gpaDecimal;
       }
   }
```

▶ Feedback 13.1

```csharp
1. int xInteger = Convert.ToInt32(this.Width / 2);
   int yInteger = Convert.ToInt32(this.Height);
   e.Graphics.DrawLine(Pens.Green, xInteger, 0, xInteger, yInteger);
```
```csharp
2. xInteger = 200; // Or any other value for the center of the circle.
   yInteger = 200; // Or any other value for the center of the circle.
   e.Graphics.DrawEllipse(Pens.Green, xInteger, yInteger, 100, 100);
   e.Graphics.DrawEllipse(Pens.Blue, xInteger + 25, yInteger + 25, 50, 50);
```
```csharp
3. Point firstPoint = new Point(20, 20);
   Point secondPoint = new Point(100, 100);
   Point thirdPoint = new Point(200, 50);
   e.Graphics.DrawLine(Pens.Green, firstPoint, secondPoint);
   e.Graphics.DrawLine(Pens.Green, secondPoint, thirdPoint);
   e.Graphics.DrawLine(Pens.Green, thirdPoint, firstPoint);
```

▶ Feedback 13.2

```csharp
1. int xInteger = commandButton.Left - 10;
   int yInteger = commandButton.Top;
   int widthInteger = commandButton.Width;
   int heightInteger = commandButton.Height;
   commandButton.SetBounds(xInteger, yInteger, widthInteger, heightInteger);
```
2. A little less than half a second.
3. The Tick event fires each time the specified interval has elapsed.

▶ Feedback 13.3

```csharp
1. private void taskListBox_DragEnter(object sender, DragEventArgs e)
   {
       // Set the desired DragDrop effect.

       e.Effect = DragDropEffects.Move;
   }
```
```csharp
2. private void taskListBox_DragDrop(object sender, DragEventArgs e)
   {
       // Add the item to the list box.

       taskListBox.Items.Add(e.Data.GetData(DataFormats.Text).ToString());
   }
```

► Feedback 14.1

1. It will place an icon next to the quantityTextBox control when the user inputs invalid data. The message appears as a ToolTip when the user places the pointer over the icon.
2. The MaxLength and CharacterCasing properties.
   MaxLength: Sets a maximum number of characters that may be entered into a text box. A beep occurs if the user attempts to exceed the maximum.
   CharacterCasing: Automatically converts data entry to uppercase, lowercase, or normal.
3. With field-level validation, the user is notified of an error as the focus leaves a field, rather than waiting until a button's Click event occurs.

► Feedback 14.2

1. ```
SummaryForm aSummaryForm = new SummaryForm();
aSummaryForm.MdiParent = this;
aSummaryForm.Show();
```
2. Select the previously written event handlers for the associated menu items.
3. Add a timer component; set the Interval property to 1000, and include this statement in the timer's Tick event handler and the Form_Load event handler:
   ```
currentTimeToolStripStatusLabel.Text = DateTime.Now.ToLongTimeString();
```

# ► Feedback 14.3

1. ```
appointmentDateTime = appointmentDateTimePicker.Value();
```
2. Hour; Millisecond; Minute; Second; Month; Day; Year; Now
3. All of the above properties are available for the Now property of the DateTime structure.

B

Methods for Working with Dates, Mathematics, and String Operations

The .NET Framework includes many functions and methods that you can use in your C# projects. This appendix introduces functions and methods for handling dates, for mathematical operations, and for performing string operations.

Working with Dates

Chapter 14 has a section introducing dates and the Calendar control. You can use the date functions and the methods of the DateTime structure to retrieve the system date, break down a date into component parts, test whether the contents of a field are compatible with the DateTime data type, and convert other data types to a DateTime.

The DateTime Structure

When you declare a variable of DateTime data type in C#, you can use its extensive list of properties and methods. You can use the static members of the DateTime structure (identified by a yellow "S" in the MSDN Help lists) without declaring an instance of DateTime. For example, to use the Now property:

```
DateTime todayDateTime = DateTime.Now;
```

To use the nonstatic members, you must reference an instance of a DateTime structure, such as a variable of DateTime type.

Example

```
timeLabel.Text = todayDateTime.ToShortTimeString();
```

Following is a partial list of some useful properties and methods of the DateTime structure:

Property or method	Purpose
Add	Add the specified number to an instance of a date/time. Variations include `AddDays`, `AddHours`, `AddMilliseconds`, `AddMinutes`, `AddMonths`, `AddSeconds`, `AddTicks`, `AddYears`. Add positive values to increase a date; add negative values to decrease a date.
Date	Date component.
Day	Integer day of month; 1–31.
DayOfWeek	Enum expression for each day in the form of DayOfWeek.Sunday.
DayOfYear	Integer day; 1–366

(continued)

Property or method	Purpose
Hour	Integer hour; 0–23
Minute	Integer minutes; 0–59
Second	Integer seconds; 0–59
Month	Integer month; 1 = January.
Now (Static)	Retrieve system date and time.
Subtract	Find the difference between date/time values; returns a TimeSpan object.
Today (Static)	Retrieve system date.
Year	Year component.
ToLongDateString()	Date formatted as long date. (U.S. default: Monday, June 08, 2009)
ToLongTimeString()	Date formatted as long time. (U.S. default: 12:00:00 AM)
ToShortDateString()	Date formatted as short date. (U.S. default: 6/8/2009)
ToShortTimeString()	Date formatted as short time. (U.S. default: 12:00 AM)

Retrieving the System Date and Time

You can retrieve the system date and time from your computer's clock using the Now property or the Today property. Now retrieves both the date and time; Today retrieves only the date.

Examples

```
DateTime currentDateTime;
currentDateTime = DateTime.Now;

DateTime currentDate;
currentDate = DateTime.Today;
```

To display the values formatted:

```
dateAndTimeLabel.Text = currentDateTime.ToLongDateString();
dateLabel.Text = currentDate.ToShortDateString();
```

Date Variables

The DateTime data type may hold values of many forms that represent a date. Examples could be June 8, 2009, or 6/8/09 or 6-8-2009.

```
DateTime birthDateTime;
birthDateTime = DateTime.Parse("6-8-09");
timeLabel.Text = birthDateTime.ToString("D");
```

You can format your dates using the methods of the DateTime class or the `ToString` method with an appropriate format specifier. The table below lists some of the format specifiers. See "Date and Time Format Strings" in MSDN for a complete list. The actual format depends on the local format for the system.

Format specifier	Description	Example for U.S. default setting
d	Short date pattern	6/8/2009
D	Long date pattern	Monday, June 8, 2009
t	Short time pattern	12:00 AM
T	Long time pattern	12:00:00 AM
f	Full date/time (short)	Monday, June 08, 2009 12:00 AM
F	Full date/time (long)	Monday, June 08, 2009 12:00:00 AM

Converting Values to a Date Format

If you want to store values in a DateTime data type, you usually need to convert the value to a DateTime type. The `DateTime.Parse` method can convert the value. The `ParseExact` method throws an exception if unable to create a valid date from the argument.

Mathematical Methods

In the .NET Framework, the mathematical functions are included as methods in the System.Math class. To use the methods, you must either include a `using System.Math;` statement or refer to each method with the Math namespace. (This assumes that the `using System;` statement, which is included at the top of each file by default, is still included in the file).

For example, to use the `Abs` (absolute value) method, you can use either of these techniques:

```
answerDouble = Math.Abs(argumentDouble);
```

or

```
// At the top of the file.
using System.Math;

// In a method.
answerDouble = Abs(argumentDouble);
```

A good way to see the list of math methods is to type "Math." in the Editor; IntelliSense will pop up with the complete list. The following is a partial list of the Math methods.

Method	Returns	Argument data type	Return data type
`Abs(x)`	The absolute value of x. $\lvert x\rvert = x$ if $x \geq 0$ $\lvert x\rvert = -x$ if $x < 0$	Overloaded: All numeric types allowed.	Return matches argument type.
`Atan(x)`	The angle in radians whose tangent is x.	Double	Double
`Cos(x)`	The cosine of x where x is in radians.	Double	Double
`Exp(x)`	The value of e raised to the power of x.	Double	Double
`Log(x)`	The natural logarithm of x, where $x \geq 0$.	Double	Double
`Max(x1, x2)`	The larger of the two arguments.	Overloaded: All types allowed. Both arguments must be the same type.	Return matches argument type.
`Min(x1, x2)`	The smaller of the two arguments.	Overloaded: All types allowed. Both arguments must be the same type.	Return matches argument type.
`Pow(x1, x2)`	The value of $x1$ raised to the power of $x2$.	Double	Double
`Round(x)` `Round(x, DecimalPlaces)`	The rounded value of x, rounded to the specified number of decimal positions. *Note*: .5 rounds to the nearest even number.	Overloaded: Double or Decimal; Integer DecimalPlaces	Return matches argument type.
`Sign(x)`	The sign of x. -1 if $x < 0$ 0 if $x = 0$ 1 if $x > 0$	Overloaded: All numeric types allowed.	Return matches argument type.
`Sin(x)`	The sine of x where x is in radians.	Double	Double
`Sqrt(x)`	The square root of x where x must be ≥ 0.	Double	Double
`Tan(x)`	The tangent of x where x is in radians.	Double	Double

Working with Strings

Strings in Visual Studio are **immutable**, which means that once a string is created, it cannot be changed. Although many programs in this text seem to modify a string, actually a new string is created and the old string is discarded.

For string handling, you can use any of the many methods of the String class. You also can use the StringBuilder class, which is more efficient if you are building or extensively modifying strings, since the string *can* be changed in memory. In other words, a StringBuilder is *mutable* (changeable) and a String is *immutable*.

Following is a partial list of the properties and methods in the String class. For static methods, you don't need to specify a string instance; for nonstatic methods, you must attach the method to the string instance. Examples of static methods and nonstatic methods follow:

Static Method

```
if (Compare(aString, bString) > 0)
    // Code to execute if true.
```

Nonstatic Method

```
if (aString.EndsWith("ed"))
    // Code to execute if true.
```

Method or property	Returns
EndsWith(*aString*)	Boolean. True if the string instance ends with the value in aString. Case sensitive.
Equals(*aString*)	Boolean. True if the string instance has the same value as aString. Case sensitive.
Insert(*startIndexInteger*, *aString*)	New string with aString inserted in the string instance, beginning at startIndexInteger.
Length	Returns the length of the string.
Remove()	Removes the specified character.
Replace()	Replaces all occurrences of a character within the string.
ToString()	Converts from another data type to string.

The ANSI Collating Sequence

The comparison of strings is based on the sequence of characters in the collating sequence.

Code	Character	Code	Character	Code	Character
32	Space (blank)	44	, (comma)	56	8
33	!	45	–	57	9
34	"	46	.	58	:
35	#	47	/	59	;
36	$	48	0	60	<
37	%	49	1	61	=
38	&	50	2	62	>
39	' (apostrophe)	51	3	63	?
40	(	52	4	64	@
41	)	53	5	65	A
42	*	54	6	66	B
43	+	55	7	67	C

(continued)

Code	Character	Code	Character	Code	Character
68	D	88	X	108	l
69	E	89	Y	109	m
70	F	90	Z	110	n
71	G	91	[	111	o
72	H	92	\	112	p
73	I	93	]	113	q
74	J	94	^	114	r
75	K	95	_	115	s
76	L	96	`	116	t
77	M	97	a	117	u
78	N	98	b	118	v
79	O	99	c	119	w
80	P	100	d	120	x
81	Q	101	e	121	y
82	R	102	f	122	z
83	S	103	g	123	{
84	T	104	h	124	|
85	U	105	i	125	}
86	V	106	j	126	~
87	W	107	k	127	Del

Comparing Strings

See "Comparing Strings" in Chapter 4, page 163.

Methods for Conversion between Data Types

Each of the following methods converts an expression to the named data type.

Function	Return type
Convert.ToBoolean(*Expression*)	bool
Convert.ToDateTime(*Expression*)	DateTime
Convert.ToDecimal(*Expression*)	decimal
Convert.ToDouble(*Expression*)	double
Convert.ToInt16(*Expression*)	short
Convert.ToInt32(*Expression*)	int
Convert.ToInt64(*Expression*)	long
Convert.ToSingle(*Expression*)	float
Convert.ToString(*Expression*)	string
Convert.ToUInt16(*Expression*)	ushort (unsigned short)
Convert.ToUInt32(*Expression*)	uint (unsigned int)
Convert.ToUInt64(*Expression*)	ulong (unsigned long)

C

Tips and Shortcuts for Mastering the Environment

Set Up the Screen for Your Convenience

As you work in the Visual Studio integrated development environment (IDE), you will find many ways to save time. Here are some tips and shortcuts that you can use to become more proficient in using the IDE to design, code, and run your projects.

Close or Hide Extra Windows

Arrange your screen for best advantage. While you are entering and editing code in the Editor window, you don't need the toolbox, the Solution Explorer window, the Properties window, or any other extra windows. You can hide or close the extra windows and quickly and easily redisplay each window when you need it.

Hiding and Displaying Windows

You can use AutoHide on each of the windows in the IDE. Each window except the Document window in the center of the screen has a push-pin icon that you can use to AutoHide the window or "tack" it into place.

You can AutoHide each window separately, or select *Window / Auto Hide All*. In this screen, all extra windows are hidden.

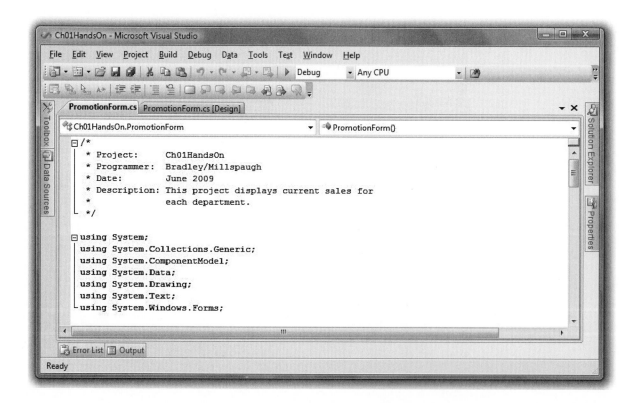

Point to the icon for one of the hidden windows to display it. In the next example, notice the mouse pointer on the Solution Explorer icon, which opens the Solution Explorer window temporarily. When you move the mouse pointer out of the window, it hides again.

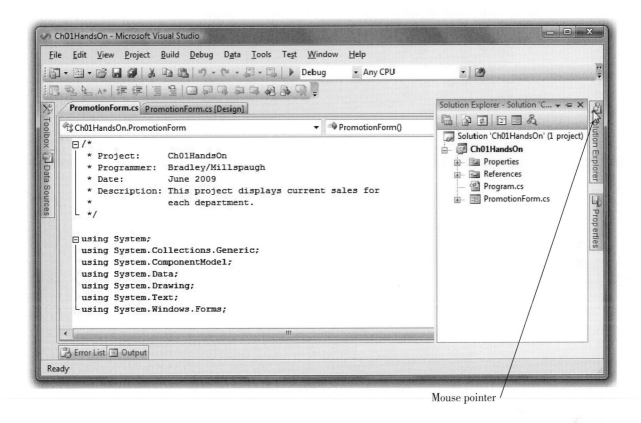

Mouse pointer

To undo the AutoHide feature, display a window and click its push-pin icon.

Each of the IDE windows that has an AutoHide feature also has a drop-down menu from which you can choose to float, dock, AutoHide, hide, or make it into a tabbed window. The tabbed window option is interesting: it makes the window tabbed in the center Document window.

Closing Windows

You can close any window by clicking its Close button. You also can close any extra tabs in the Document window; click on the Close button to the right of the tabs to close the active document.

Displaying Windows

You can quickly and easily open each window when you need it. Each window is listed on the *View* menu, or use the buttons on the Standard toolbar.

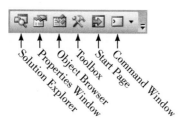

Display Windows Using Keyboard Shortcuts

Solution Explorer window	Ctrl + Alt + L
Properties window	F4
Toolbox	Ctrl + Alt + X

Display the keyboard shortcuts as part of the popup tooltips: select *Tools / Customize / Toolbars tab / Show shortcut keys in ScreenTips.*

Switch between Documents　When you have several tabs open in the Document window, you can switch by clicking on their tabs or using keyboard shortcuts.

Switch from a form's Designer window to the Editor window.	F7
Switch from a form's Editor window to the Designer window.	Shift + F7
Cycle through open document tabs.	Ctrl + F6
Pop up a list of all active windows.	Ctrl + Tab

Visual Studio displays only as many tabs as fit in the current size of the Document window. If you have more documents open than displayed tabs, you can use the drop-down list of active files.

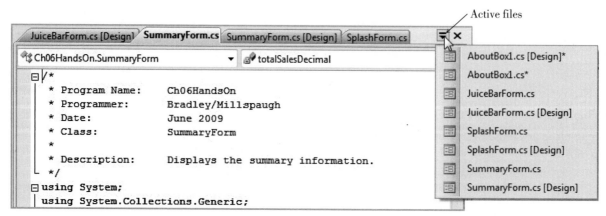

Use the Full Screen

When you are designing a form or editing code, you can work in full-screen mode. This gives you maximum screen space by getting rid of all extra windows. Unfortunately, it also hides all toolbars (the Text Editor toolbar can be a great timesaver while editing code). Select *View / Full Screen* to display in full-screen mode. A small *Full Screen* button appears on the menu, which you can use to switch back to regular display. You also can press Shift + Alt + Enter or select *View / Full Screen* a second time to toggle back. If you want to display the Text Editor toolbar while in full-screen mode, select *View / Toolbars / Text Editor*.

Modify the Screen Layout

For most operations, the Visual Studio tabbed Document window layout works very well. However, if you prefer, you can switch to MDI (multiple document interface). Set this option in the *Tools / Options / Environment / General / Settings*.

Each of the windows in the IDE is considered either a Tool window or a Document window. The Document windows generally display in the center of the screen with tabs. The rest of the windows—Solution Explorer, Properties window, Task List, Output, Server Explorer, and others—are Tool windows and share many characteristics. You can float each of the windows, tab-dock them in groups, and move and resize individual windows or groups of windows.

Dock Windows Using the Guide Diamonds

Guide diamonds are an improvement added to VS 2008. When you start dragging a dockable tool window, the diamonds appear to give you visual cues to help dock to the desired location. As you drag over the arrow, the corresponding area darkens. To tab-dock a window, you need to make the destination location darken. Experiment!

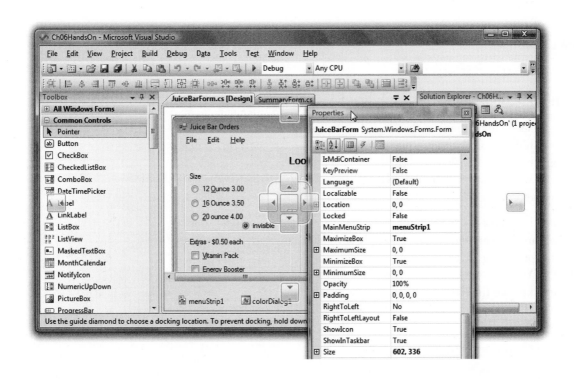

Split the Screen Vertically

You can view the Editor window and the form design at the same time. With at least two tabs open, select *Window / New Vertical Tab Group*. You may want to close the extra windows to allow more room for the two large windows.

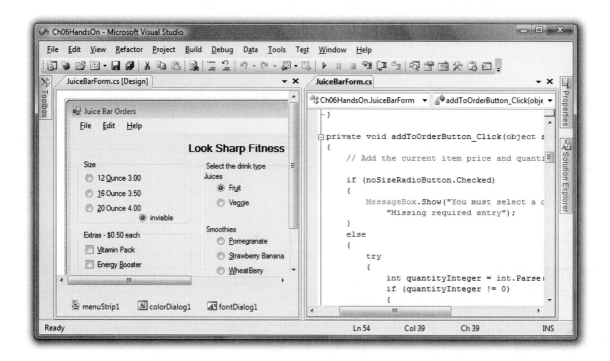

Reset the IDE Layout

To reset the IDE windows to their default locations, select *Window / Reset Window Layout*.

Set Options for Your Work

You can change many options in the VS IDE. Choose *Tools / Options* to display the *Options* dialog box. You may want to click on each of the categories to see the options that you can select.

    Note: If you are working in a shared lab, check with the instructor or lab technician before changing options.

Projects and Solutions: Set the default folder for your projects. It's best to leave the *Build* and *Run* options to automatically save changes, but you may prefer to have a prompt or save them yourself.

Text Editor: You can set options for all languages or for C#. The following presume that you first select C#.

- *General*: Make sure that *Auto list members* is selected and *Hide advanced members* is deselected. You may want to turn on *Word wrap* so that long lines wrap to the next line instead of extending beyond the right edge of the screen.

- *Tabs*: Choose *Smart* indenting; *Tab size* and *Indent size* should both be set to 4.

Use Shortcuts in the Form Designer

You can save time while creating the user interface in the Form Designer by using shortcuts.

Use the Layout Toolbar

The Layout toolbar is great for working with multiple controls. You must have more than one control selected to enable many of the buttons. The same options are available from the *Format* menu.

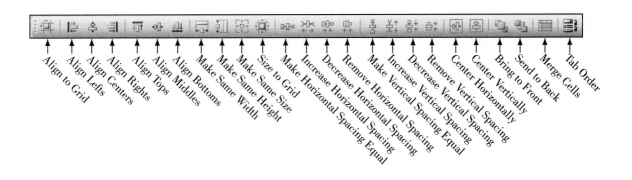

Nudge Controls into Place

Sometimes it is difficult to place controls exactly where you want them. Of course, you can use the alignment options of the *Format* menu or the Layout toolbar. You also can nudge controls in any direction by selecting them and pressing one of the arrow keys. Nudging moves a control one pixel in the direction you specify. For example, the right arrow moves a selected control one pixel to the right. You also can use Ctrl + an arrow key to align a control to the snap line of a nearby control.

Use Snap Lines to Help Align Controls

As you create or move controls on a form, snap lines pop up to help you align the controls, which can be a great help in creating professional-looking forms. Blue snap lines appear to align tops, bottoms, lefts, or rights of controls.

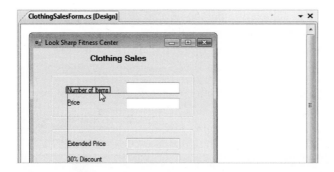

When you see a red line toward the lower edge of a control, that means that the baselines of the text within the controls are aligned.

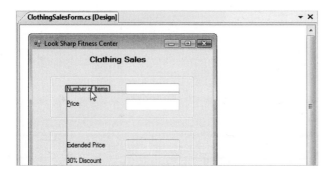

The snap lines also can help you to standardize the vertical spacing between controls. As you drag a control up or down near another control, a small dotted line appears to indicate that the controls are the recommended distance apart.

— Dotted line

Copy Controls Quickly

When you need to create several controls of the same type, you can save time by creating one control, setting any properties that you want for all controls (such as the font or text alignment), and making copies. Although you can use copy-and-paste, there is a quicker way: Hold down the Ctrl key and drag the control, which makes a copy that you can drop in the location that you choose.

Use Shortcuts in the Editor

Several features of the Editor can save you time while editing code. These are summarized in the following sections.

Comment and Uncomment Selected Lines

Comment Selected Lines: Use this command when you want to convert some code to comments, especially while you are testing and debugging projects. You can remove some lines from execution to test the effect without actually removing them. Select the lines and click the *Comment Selected Lines* button (or type Ctrl + E, C); each line will have double forward slashes (//) added at the left end.

Uncomment Selected Lines: This command undoes the *Comment Selected Lines* command (or type Ctrl + E, U). Select some comment lines and click the button; the double slashes (//) at the beginning of the lines are deleted.

Use the Text Editor Toolbar

By default, the Text Editor toolbar displays when the Editor window is open. You also can open the toolbar yourself from the *View / Toolbars* menu item.

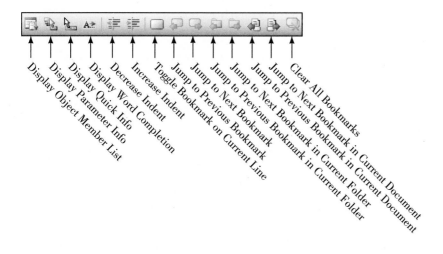

You can save yourself considerable time and trouble if you become familiar with and use some of these shortcuts.

- *Toggle Bookmark*: This button sets and unsets individual bookmarks. Bookmarks are useful when you are jumping around in the Editor window. Set a bookmark on any line by clicking in the line and clicking the *Toggle Bookmark* button (or type Ctrl + B, T); you will see a mark in the gray margin area to the left of the marked line. You may want to set bookmarks in several methods where you are editing and testing code.

- *Jump to Next Bookmark* (Ctrl + B, N) and *Jump to Previous Bookmark* (Ctrl + B, P): Use these buttons to quickly jump to the next or previous bookmark in the code.

- *Clear All Bookmarks*: You can clear individual bookmarks with the *Toggle Bookmark* button or clear all bookmarks using this button (Ctrl + B, C).

Use Keyboard Shortcuts When Editing Code

While you are editing code, save yourself time by using keyboard shortcuts. Note that these shortcuts are based on the default keyboard mapping. Select *Tools / Options* and then *Environment / Keyboard / Keyboard mapping scheme*. Drop down the list and select *Visual C#*, if it isn't already selected.

Task	Shortcut
Cut the current line to the clipboard (insertion point anywhere in the line).	Ctrl + L
Delete the current line without placing it in the clipboard (insertion point anywhere in the line).	Shift + Ctrl + L
Delete from the insertion point left to the beginning of the word.	Ctrl + Backspace
Delete from the insertion point right to the end of the word.	Ctrl + Delete
Create an empty line above the current line. Insertion point can be anywhere in the line.	Ctrl + Enter
Create an empty line below the current line. Insertion point can be anywhere in the line.	Ctrl + Shift + Enter
Swap the two characters on either side of the insertion point (transpose characters).	Ctrl + T
Swap the current word with the word on its right (transpose words). Insertion point can be anywhere in the word.	Ctrl + Shift + T
Complete the word.	Ctrl + Spacebar *or* Alt + right arrow
Jump to a method (insertion point on method name). Use this shortcut while working on the methods that you write. For example, when writing a call to a function, you might want to check the coding in the function. Point to the method name that you are calling and press F12. If you want to return to the original position, set a bookmark before the jump.	F12
Jump to the top of the current code file.	Ctrl + Home
Jump to the bottom of the current file.	Ctrl + End
View the form's Designer window.	Shift + F7
Return to the Editor window. / Return to the form's Designer window.	F7

You can display the keyboard shortcuts as part of the popup tooltips; select *Tools / Customize / Show shortcut keys in ScreenTips*.

Most of the editing and selecting keyboard shortcuts for Microsoft Word also work in the Visual Studio Editor window.

Split the Editor Window

You can view more than one section of code at a time by splitting the Editor window. Point to the Split bar at the top of the vertical scroll bar and drag the bar down to the desired location. To remove the split, you can either drag the split bar back to the top or double-click the split bar.

Split bar

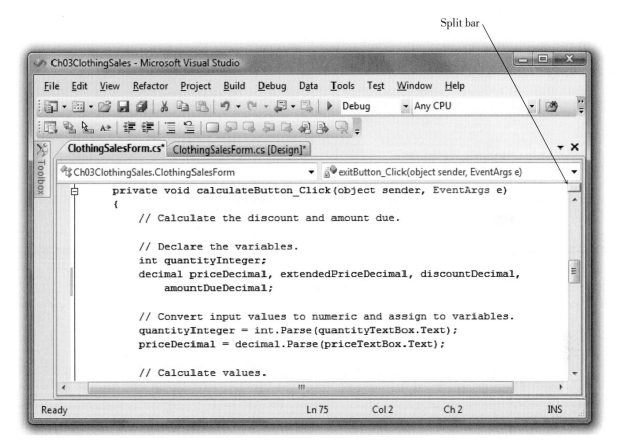

Use Drag-and-Drop Editing

You can use drag-and-drop to move or copy text to another location in the Editor window or to another project. To move code, select the text, point to the selection, and drag it to a new location. You can copy text (rather than move it) by holding down the Ctrl key as you drag.

Use the Task List

The Task List displays error messages after your program is compiled. This makes sense—your tasks are to fix each of the errors. You also can add items to the Task List as a reminder to yourself, so that you don't forget to do something. A very easy way to add items to the Task List is to write a comment in your code with the TODO keyword.

```
// TODO Come back here and write this code.
// TODO Check on this.
```

You also can add tasks to the Task List by clicking on the *Create User Task* button at the top of the list; this creates a new line where you can enter text.

Drag Commonly Used Code to the Toolbox

When you have some lines of code that you use frequently, you can select the text and drag it to the toolbox. Then, when you need to insert the code, drag it from the toolbox to the Editor window. The text appears in the toolbox when the Editor window is open, but not when a form is in design mode.

Caution: This shortcut should not be used on shared computers in a classroom or lab, as the text remains in the toolbox. Use it only on your own computer. You can delete previously stored text from the toolbox by right-clicking and selecting *Delete* from the context menu.

For another way to handle small pieces of code that you reuse often, see "Code Snippets and Samples" in Chapter 14.

Rename Variables and Objects

Use *Refactor / Rename* to automatically rename all occurrences of a variable or object. In the Editor window, right-click on a variable name or an object name and select *Refactor / Rename*. In the *Rename* dialog box, you can enter the new name and the item is renamed everywhere in that form. For a multiform project, the *Rename* dialog box offers the choice of renaming in only the current form or all forms. This feature, called *Symbol Rename*, is part of a more robust feature called **refactoring**, which allows the programmer to modify the name and class of variables and objects.

Reformat the File

Visual Studio offers some advanced formatting options, which can help you to keep the file properly formatted. When you choose to reformat, the Editor formats the file to match the options you have selected in *Tools / Options / Text Editor / C#*. With the Editor window open, select *Edit / Advanced*. Many options appear on the submenu, including *Format Document* and *Format Selection* (which reformats only the selected text). If you have an XML document open in the XML Editor, the format options will properly format and indent the XML tags.

Use Context-Sensitive Help

The quickest way to get Help is to use context-sensitive Help. Click on a control or a line of code and press F1; Help displays the closest-matching item it can locate. You also can get help on the IDE elements: Click in any area of the IDE and press Shift + F1; the Help explanation will be about using the current window or IDE element, rather than about the objects and language.

Use the Debugging Tools

The VS IDE provides many tools to help you debug programs. The most helpful techniques are to examine the values of variables during program execution and to single-step through the program and watch what happens.

The Debug Toolbar and Menu

You can use the *Debug* menu or the tools on the Debug toolbar for debugging. The Debug toolbar appears automatically during run time, or you can display the toolbar by right-clicking any toolbar and selecting *Debug*. The most useful items for debugging your programs are shown in the following table.

Menu command or toolbar button	Purpose	Keyboard shortcut
Start	Begin debug execution.	F5
Continue	Continue execution. (Available at debugging time only.)	F5
Start Without Debugging	Begin execution without invoking the debugger. This option can make a program run sometimes when it won't run with *Start*.	Ctrl + F5
Stop Debugging	Stop execution of a program.	Shift + F5
Step Into	Execute the next statement; steps into any called methods. (Available at debugging time only.)	F11
Step Over	Execute the next statement; rapidly executes any calls to methods without stepping. (Available at debugging time only.)	F10
Step Out	Rapidly finish the current method; reenter break time when the method finishes.	Shift + F11

Set Breakpoints

You can set breakpoints in code, which cause execution to halt on the marked statement. After setting a breakpoint, begin execution as usual. When the breakpoint line becomes current, the program halts, enters debugging time, and displays the code with the current line highlighted (as the *next* statement to execute).

To set a breakpoint, use the *Debug* menu, the Debug toolbar, a keyboard shortcut (F9), or the easiest way: Place the mouse pointer in the gray margin indicator area at the left edge of the Editor window and click; the line will be highlighted in red and a large red dot will display in the margin indicator.

View the Contents of Expressions

At break time, you can view the current values of expressions in several ways. The three most useful techniques are

1. Display the value in a DataTip, which is a ToolTip-like popup in the Editor window. Point to the variable or expression that you want to view and pause; the current value pops up in a DataTip.
2. Use the Locals window, which displays all objects and variables that are within scope at debugging time. You also can expand the `this` entry to see the state of the form's controls.
3. Use the Autos window, which "automatically" displays all variables and control contents that are referenced in the current statement and three statements on either side of the current one.

Single-Step through Code

The best way to debug a project is to thoroughly understand what the project is doing every step of the way. Use the Visual Studio stepping tools to trace program execution line by line and see the progression of the program as it executes through your code.

You step through code at debugging time. Set a breakpoint or choose one of the stepping commands at design time; the program will begin running and immediately transfer to debugging time.

The three stepping commands are *Step Into*, *Step Over*, and *Step Out*. These commands force the project to execute a single line at a time and to display the Editor window with the current statement highlighted. As you execute the project, by pressing a button, for example, the Click event occurs. Execution transfers to the Click event handler, the Editor window for that method appears on the screen, and you can follow line-by-line execution.

Most likely you will use the *Step Into* command more than the other two stepping commands. When you choose *Step Into*, the next line of code executes and the program pauses again in debugging time. If the line of code is a call to another method, the first line of code of the other method displays.

To continue stepping through your program execution, continue choosing the *Step Into* command. When a method is completed, your form will display again, awaiting an event. You can click on one of the form's buttons to continue stepping through code in an event handler. If you want to continue execution without stepping, choose the *Continue* command.

The *Step Over* command also executes one line of code at a time. But when your code calls another method, *Step Over* displays only the lines of code in the current method being analyzed; it does not display lines of code in the called methods as they execute.

You use the *Step Out* command when you are stepping through a called method. It continues rapid execution until the called method completes and then returns to debugging mode at the statement following the method or function call.

When you have seen what you want to see, continue rapid execution by choosing the *Continue* command (F5). If you want to restart execution from the beginning, choose the *Restart* command (Shift + F5).

Write to the Output Window

You can place a `Console.WriteLine` method in your code. In the argument, you can specify a message to write or an object that you want tracked.

```
Console.WriteLine(TextString);
Console.WriteLine(Object);

Console.WriteLine("calculateButton event handler entered.");
Console.WriteLine(quantityTextBox.Text);
```

When the `Console.WriteLine` method executes, its output appears in the Output window. You can clear the Output window: Right-click in the window and choose *Clear All*.

An advantage of using `WriteLine`, rather than the other debugging techniques, is that you do not have to break program execution.

Copy and Move Projects

In a programming class, you often must move projects from one computer to another and must base one project on another one. To create a new project based on a previous one, you should copy the project folder. Then you can move and rename it as necessary.

Copy and Move a Windows Project

You can copy an entire project folder from one location to another using Windows Explorer. Make sure that the project is not open in Visual Studio and copy the entire folder.

To base one project on a previous project, take the following steps:

- Make sure the project is not open. *Note*: This is *extremely* important.

- Copy the folder to a new location using Windows Explorer.

- Rename the new folder for the new project name, still using Windows Explorer.

- Open the new project (the copy) in the Visual Studio IDE.

- In the IDE's Solution Explorer, rename the solution and the project. The best way to do this is to right-click on the name and choose the *Rename* command from the shortcut menu. To rename the solution, you must have the solution name displaying. Select *Tools / Options / Projects and Solutions / General / Always show solution*.

- Rename the forms, if desired. If you rename the startup form, you must open the Program.cs file and change the argument in the `Application.Run` method.

- Open the Project Designer (*Project / Properties*) and change the assembly name and root namespace to match your new project name.

    Warning: Do not try to copy a project that is open using the *Save As* command, attempting to place a copy in a new location.

Copy and Move a Web Project

You can move the folder for a File System Web site from one location to another. You also can rename the folder, which renames the site. To open the moved project, first open Visual Studio, select *File / Open Web Site*, and browse to locate the folder.

Rename and Remove Event Handlers

You can run into problems when you rename or remove an existing event handler unless you understand how C# and the VS IDE set up the event handlers. Once you have set up an event handler for a control, you must be careful when you rename or remove it.

Assume that you have a button called *button1* that you double-click to create the event-handling method, which is automatically named button1_Click. And then assume that you rename the button to *calculateButton*. After renaming the button, the event handler still works properly for the button's Click event, but the method is still named button1_Click. It would be much nicer to have the method name match the control name.

Rename an Event Handler

The best way to rename an event handler is to use *Rename*. Right-click on the event handler and select *Refactor / Rename* from the context menu. The *Rename* dialog box gives you choices to preview the changes and even search in comments, if you wish. By using *Rename*, instead of just changing the name with the Editor, the change is made in all locations, including the designer-generated code. After you change the name of the event-handling method, you can view the change in the Properties window.

Remove an Event Handler

You may want to remove an unwanted event handler. If you accidentally double-click the form or any control, an event handler is automatically added. If you just delete the entire method, you generate an error message because the compiler is still looking for the method. You can avoid the error if you delete the entry for the event in the Properties window; you can do this either before or after deleting the method in the Editor window. Or you can double-click on the error message, which takes you to the FormName.Designer.cs file (discussed in the next section); delete the line that refers to the method that you deleted from the code.

How C# Sets Up Event Handlers

When you set up an event handler in the IDE, code is automatically added to your C# program. However, the code is hidden from view unless you take steps to display it. For each form, the IDE creates both the FormName.cs file and the FormName.Designer.cs file. Under normal circumstances, you should not edit the Designer.cs file directly but allow the IDE to automatically create and modify the code. But in the case of event handlers, you may want to edit the code.

To see the FormName.Designer.cs code, expand the form's node in the Solution Explorer. Then open the file and locate the "Windows Form Designer generated code" section. Expand the region by clicking on the plus sign at the left margin, then search for the section where your control is defined. All controls are declared at the top of the region and then each control has a separate section where the initial properties are set. Following is an example for *button1*:

```
//
// button1
//
this.button1.Font = new System.Drawing.Font("Microsoft Sans Serif", 12F,
    System.Drawing.FontStyle.Regular, System.Drawing.GraphicsUnit.Point,
    ((byte)(0)));
```

```
this.button1.Location = new System.Drawing.Point(51, 67);
this.button1.Name = "button1";
this.button1.Size = new System.Drawing.Size(99, 41);
this.button1.TabIndex = 0;
this.button1.Text = "button1";
this.button1.UseVisualStyleBackColor = true;
this.button1.Click += new System.EventHandler(this.button1_Click);
```

The last line above is the one that assigns the event handler to the Click event of the button. You can (very carefully) change the name of the event handler here, if you wish, but remember to make it exactly match the name of the method. If you have an unwanted event handler, you can delete the entire line.

Deploy Applications

When you are ready to distribute your programs to other computers, you use a process called *deployment*. You can choose to use either Windows Installer or *click-once deployment*.

To use Windows Installer, open the *Build* menu and select *Publish Solution-Name*. Selecting the *Publish* option launches the Publish Wizard, which gives you the option of specifying a file path, a Web site, or an FTP server. Media options for distribution are CD-ROM or DVD, file share (network), or the Web. You also can have the program check for updates online.

If you deploy to a folder on your system, you will find a Setup.exe application inside the folder. Try copying the folder to a CD and then install your program on another machine. For a discussion of the various strategies for deployment, see "Deploying Applications and Components" in Help.

APPENDIX

D

Security

As a programmer, you must be aware of many aspects of security. You must not allow any unauthorized access to programs or data. But you must be able to access all needed resources while you are developing applications. For both sides of the security issue, you need a basic understanding of security topics.

The .NET Framework includes many features for implementing security. And as time passes and hackers and virus writers discover ways to circumvent existing security features, Microsoft is forced to tighten security. Because of this fact, you may sometimes find that programs or procedures that worked previously no longer work after you apply updates to Windows, which include updates to the .NET Framework and CLR.

For programmers, security means **information assurance**. The .NET Framework provides many object-oriented features to assist in the process. The topic of security can fill multiple books and courses; this appendix is intended as an introductory overview for programmers.

Authentication and Authorization

The two topics of authentication and authorization are frequently lumped together because they are so closely related. **Authentication** determines who the user is and **authorization** decides if the user has the proper authority to access information.

Authentication is based on credentials. When you are working with a Windows application, you only need to be concerned with Windows authentication. However, if your application is Web Forms–based (ASP.NET), authentication might be IIS Authentication, Forms–based (not recommended; it is an HTML request for credentials) or it might use Microsoft Passport, which is a centralized profile service for member sites. It is also possible to create a custom authentication method or use none at all. The settings in the Web.config file determine the method of authentication.

The following is an excerpt from the automatically generated Web.config file for an ASP.NET application:

```
<!--
        The <authentication> section enables configuration of the security authentication
        mode used by ASP.NET to identify an incoming user.
    -->
    <authentication mode="Windows"/>
```

For no authentication, you can change the last line in the Web.config file above to

```
<authentication mode ="None"/>
```

Authorization and Impersonation

After the user is authenticated, another step checks for authorization. If ASP.NET does not use impersonation, the ASP.NET user, which is created when the Framework is installed, runs without any privileges. If impersonation is turned on, ASP.NET takes on the identity from IIS. If anonymous access is turned off, ASP.NET takes on the credentials of the authenticated user; otherwise it impersonates the account that IIS uses.

This is where the following code applies:

```
<identity impersonate = "true"/>
```

For a specific user, you can use

```
<identity impersonate = "true" name = "Domain/username" password = "password"/>
```

Writing Secure Code

Programmers need to be aware of how hackers are able to gain access to a database or a network through code. Two primary areas of importance are string injections and error messages that may give away important information about a data source.

SQL Injection

Proper validation of the code is extremely important. A system vulnerability occurs when code is "injected" into a string. A text box or a combo box control allows the user to type in information. It is the responsibility of the programmer to make sure that the input does not contain any scripting code or disruptive characters. When a program is working with a database, there must be no way for the user to inject code into that database.

It is wise to validate the keystrokes to be sure that the input text contains only valid characters.

Error Messages

Another technique that hackers use to find information about a database is to input wrong data, hoping that the error message will give significant information. The default error messages indicate the name of the field containing an error. Plan your error messages so that you don't allow someone to determine valid field names or values. You also can create custom error pages and denote the link in the Web.config file.

Code Access Security

Basically code access security determines what code is allowed to do on a computer; specifically, what resources such as hardware or files the code can access. The settings of the computer ultimately determine if the code can execute or if a resource can be used by the code.

Code access security is based on several Permission classes. The Permission classes are organized into three types: Code Access, Identity, and Role-based. Examples of the code access type include the PrintingPermission class and the RegistryPermission class; SiteIdentityPermission and the UrlIdentity Permission class fall into the Identity permission type. The PrincipalPermission class is the Role-based type for user credentials.

If your program has an OpenFileDialog component, it may be necessary to request permission to access the files from a given system. The following code would appear at the top of the file:

```
using System.Security.Permissions;
```

Then you can apply the attribute to a public/private method in code. Example:

```
[FileDialogPermissionAttribute(SecurityAction.PermitOnly, Unrestricted=true)]
private void OpenFile()
{
    //Place code here to show the Open dialog and read the file.
}
```

Further Reading About Security

You can learn more about security from many locations. Microsoft publishes a free security newsletter; sign up at www.microsoft.com/security/default.mspx. For development information, check out the MSDN Security Developer Center at msdn.microsoft.com/en-us/security/default.aspx. The site provides tutorials, information about community resources, and downloads.

See msdn.microsoft.com/en-us/library/aa302369.aspx for an overview of security in the .NET Framework.

Glossary

A

About box   A window that displays information about the program; usually displayed from the *Help / About* menu item.

absolute positioning   Placing an element on a Web page by X and Y coordinates.

abstract   Modifier on a class definition or a method header. On a class, indicates that the class cannot be instantiated, but instead must be used for inheritance; on a method definition, requires that the method be overridden in an inherited class.

abstract class   A class that cannot be instantiated, but instead must be used for inheritance.

abstract method   A method that must be overridden in an inheriting class.

AcceptButton property   Form property that sets the accept (default) button, which is activated when the user presses the Enter key.

access key   Underlined character that allows the user to select using the keyboard rather than the mouse; also called a *hot key*.

accessor method   `get` and `set` methods written to allow external objects to access the private properties of a class.

AJAX   Asynchonous JavaScript and XML; method of speeding Web page display by updating only the part of the page that has changes.

AllowDrop property   A property of a form or control used for a drag-and-drop operation.

ANSI code   A coding method used to represent characters on a microcomputer (American National Standards Institute).

AppendAllText method   Simplified file handling; opens the file, writes all data at the end of an existing file, and closes the file.

argument   The expression to operate upon in a method; a value being passed to a method.

array   A series of variables; each individual element can be referenced by its index position. Also called a *list*.

ASP.NET   Microsoft's technology for Web applications.

assignment operator   An equal sign (=); assigns a value to the variable or property named on the left side of the sign.

assignment statement   Assigns a value to a variable or property using an assignment operator.

attribute   Application information found in the Assembly Info file.

attribute (XML)   Supplies additional information about an XML element; must appear within single or double quotes.

authentication   Determining who the user is.

authorization   Deciding if the user has the proper authority to access information.

Autos window   Window that opens in IDE during execution; automatically displays all variables and control contents that are referenced in the current statement and three statements on either side of the current one.

B

base class   Class that is inherited from; also called a *superclass* or *parent class*.

BindingSource   Object that establishes a link to a data source.

block variable   A variable declared inside a block of code; only accessible within that block.

Boolean expression   An expression that will evaluate *true* or *false*. May be a comparison of two values (variables, properties, constants) using relational operators.

BorderStyle property   Property of a control that allows the control to appear flat or three-dimensional.

bound control   A control that automatically displays the contents of database fields.

breakpoint   Indicated point in project code where execution should break; used for debugging.

browser   An application used to render and display HTML code; used to display Web pages; in C# used to display the output of Web Forms.

Brush object   Graphical object for drawing filled shapes.

Button   Control used to activate an event-handling method.

C

call (method call)   Execute a method.

callback   An object notifies the program that it needs to do something or that a situation exists that the program needs to handle. The object notifies the program of the situation by firing an event.

camel casing   The naming convention that specifies mixed-case names; the first character must be lowercase and the first character of each word within the name must be uppercase; the rest of the characters must be lowercase.

CancelButton property   Form property that sets the Cancel button, which is activated when the user presses the Esc key.

cascading style sheet (CSS)   A set of styles for formatting elements of Web pages.

case structure   Selection structure; implemented in C# with a switch statement, which can be used in place of an if statement.

casting   Converting from one data type to another.

CausesValidation property   Determines whether the Validating event occurs for a control when the control loses focus; set to *true* by default.

CharacterCasing property   Controls upper- and lowercase data entry in a text box.

check box   A control used to indicate a value that may be *true* or *false*. In any group of check boxes, any number may be selected.

Checked property   Determines if a check box is checked or not. Also used to determine if a radio button is selected or not.

child class   A class that inherits from another class, called the *parent*. Also called a *derived class* or *subclass*.

child form   Multiple Document Interface. A child form belongs to a parent form, is displayed inside the parent, and closes when the parent does.

class   A prototype or blueprint for an object; includes specifications for the properties and methods.

class-level variable   A variable or method that can be used in any method within the current class.

clean compile   Code compiles to Common Language Runtime without errors.

click-once deployment   Simplified method of deploying C# applications to another computer. Provides for installation and automatic updates via the Web.

client   A system that accesses a Web site.

Close method   Closes forms or files; releases resources used by the object.

code   Programming statements in the C# language.

code separation model   A style of Web Form in which the C# code is in a separate file from the HTML code.

code snippets   Small samples of code that illustrate coding techniques; can be added to a program in the editor.

collection   An object that can contain a series of objects; has properties and methods.

color constant   Values assigned in the Color class. Examples: Color.Red and Color.Blue.

column   A vertical section of a grid control. In a database, a field or data element.

ComboBox control   A control that is a combination of a list box and a text box.

comment   A C# statement used for documentation; not interpreted by the compiler.

common dialog   A set of Windows dialog boxes available to C# programmers for *Open*, *Save*, *Fonts*, *Print*, and *Color*.

comparison operator   See *relational operator*.

component tray   Area across the lower edge of a Form Designer window in the IDE; used to store components that are not visible on the form.

compound Boolean expression   Multiple Boolean expressions that are combined by using the logical operators, && or ||.

concatenation   Joining string (text) fields. The plus sign (+) is used to concatenate text.

condition   See *Boolean expressions*.

Console.WriteLine method   A method that writes one line to the Output window.

constant   A value that cannot change during program execution.

constructor A method that runs automatically when an object is instantiated from that class. In C#, the constructor has the same name as the class.

container An object that holds other objects, such as a group box, a form, or a list box.

context menu A popup menu, sometimes referred to as a *shortcut menu* or a *right-mouse menu*.

context-sensitive Help Display of the Help topic that relates to the currently selected object or statement; displayed by pressing the F1 function.

ContextMenuStrip component A container control used to create context menus.

control An object used on a graphical interface, such as a radio button, text box, button, or label.

D

data binding Connecting a control or property to one or more data elements.

data-bound controls Controls that can be set up to display the data from a database.

Data Designer A window of the VS IDE that shows a visual representation of the schema of a database; allows modification of the schema.

data file A file used to store small amounts of information such as the contents of a list box.

data source The original source of database data; may be a file, a server, an array, or other object.

data type Specifies the type of data a variable or constant can hold, such as integer, decimal, or string.

DataGridView control Web control used to display record information in rows and columns.

dataset A temporary set of data stored in the memory of the computer.

DateTime structure Used to retrieve and format the current date and time.

debug time Temporary break in program execution; used for debugging.

debugging Finding and eliminating computer program errors.

declaration Statements to establish a project's variables and constants, give them names, and specify the type of data they will hold.

decrement operator Operator to subtract 1 from the named variable (--).

deployment Distribution of a compiled application to another computer; normally done through a setup.exe file. See *click-once deployment*.

derived class A class that inherits from a base class. Also known as a subclass or child class.

design time The status of the Visual Studio environment while a project is being developed, as opposed to run time or debug time.

destructor A method that is called as an object goes out of scope.

DialogResult object Used to determine which button the user clicked on a message box.

direct reference Accessing an element of an array by a subscript when the value of the subscript is known.

Directory.GetCurrentDirectory The folder from which the application begins execution; in a C# program running from the VS IDE, the project's bin\Debug folder.

disabled Enabled property set to *false*; user can see the control but cannot access it.

do/while loop A series of statements that will be executed as long as a condition is *true*. The condition is written on the while statement and is a posttest loop structure.

Document window IDE window that displays the Form Designer, the Code Editor, the Object Browser, and the Application Designer.

DoDragDrop method Sets an object as a source object for a drag-and-drop operation.

DragDrop event The event that occurs when the user drags an object and drops it on a form or control that has its AllowDrop property set to *true*.

DragEnter event The event that occurs when the user drags an object over a form or control that has its AllowDrop property set to *true*; occurs before the DragDrop event.

DrawLine method Method of the Graphics class.

DrawRectangle method Method of the Graphics class; used to draw squares and rectangles.

DrawString method Method of the Graphics class; sends a line of text to the graphics page.

drop-down combo box A combo box control with a down-pointing arrow that allows the user to drop down the list. Allows efficient use of space on a form.

drop-down list   A list box with a down-pointing arrow that allows the user to drop down the list. Allows efficient use of space on a form.

E

element   Single item within a table, array, list, grid, or structure.

element (XML)   An item in an XML file surrounded by tags.

empty string   A string containing no characters; also called a *null string* or *zero-length string*.

Enabled property   Boolean property that determines whether the control is available to the user.

encapsulation   OOP feature that specifies that all methods and properties of a class be coded within the class. The class can hide or expose the methods and properties, as needed.

entry test   A loop that has its test condition at the top. See *pretest*.

ErrorProvider component A component that can display an error icon and message when a validation rule is violated for the specified text box; used to perform field-level validation.

event   An action that may be caused by the user, such as a click, drag, key press, or scroll. Events also can be triggered by an internal action, such as repainting the form or validating user input. A message sent by an object, to which the application can respond.

event handler   A method written to execute when an event occurs.

event-handling method   See *event handler*.

exception   An error that occurs at run time.

exit test   A loop that has its test condition at the bottom. See *posttest*.

explicit conversion   Writing the code to convert from one data type to another; as opposed to implicit conversion.

Express Edition   A "light" version of Visual C#. Available for download at msdn.microsoft.com/express.

Extensible Application Markup Language (XAML)   Extension of HTML used to create the visual elements of a Windows Presentation Foundation (WPF) window.

F

field   A group of related characters used to represent one characteristic or attribute of an entity in a data file or database.

field-level validation   Checking the validity of input data in each control as they are entered, rather than waiting until the user clicks a button.

file   A collection of related records.

File class   A class in the System. IO namespace used for reading and writing simple text files, using the `WriteAllText`, `WriteAllLines`, `AppendAllText`, `ReadAllText`, and `ReadAllLines` methods.

FillEllipse method   Method of the Graphics object; used to draw filled circles and ovals.

focus   The currently selected control on the user interface. For controls such as buttons, the focus appears as a light dotted line. For text boxes, the insertion point (also called the *cursor*) appears inside the box.

Focus method   Sets the focus to a control, which makes it the active control.

for loop   A pretest loop structure; usually used when the number of iterations is known.

foreach loop   A pretest loop structure that can automatically iterate through a collection or array.

ForeColor property   Property that determines the color of the text.

form   An object that acts as a container for the controls in a graphical interface.

Form.Activated event   Occurs when a form receives focus.

Form Designer   The IDE window for creating the user interface.

Form.Load event   Occurs when a form is loaded into memory.

format   A specification for the way information will be displayed, including dollar signs, percent signs, and number of decimal positions.

format specifier codes Codes used as arguments for the `ToString` method; used to make the output easier to read. Can specify dollar signs, commas, decimal positions, percents, and date formats.

FormClosing event   Occurs before a form unloads. A good location to place the code to prompt the users if they wish to save any changes.

FromFile method   Retrieves an image from a file.

G

garbage collection   Automatic deletion of objects from memory after they are out of scope.

general method   A method not attached to an event.

GetHeight method   A method of the Font class that returns the height of the current font in pixels.

graphical user interface (GUI)   Program application containing icons, buttons, and menu bars.

graphics   Lines, shapes, and images. An image file assigned to a PictureBox control; methods of the Graphics class, such as `DrawString`, `DrawLine`, and `DrawEllipse`.

GroupBox   A control used as a container for other controls, such as a group of radio buttons.

H

handle   A small square on a selected control at design time; used to resize a control. Also called a *resizing handle*.

Help   The collection of reference pages about programming in C# and using the Visual Studio IDE.

Hide method   Method of a form or a control that makes it invisible but does not unload it from memory.

horizontal scroll bar   A Windows control that provides a scroll bar that appears horizontally on the form.

HyperLink control   Used to navigate among Web pages; may link to an external or internal page.

I

IDE   Integrated development environment. See *Visual Studio environment*.

identifier   A name for a variable, method, and named constant; supplied by the programmer.

if statement   Statement for testing a condition and taking alternate actions based on the outcome of the test.

Image property   A graphic file with an extension of .bmp, .gif, .jpg, .png, .ico, .emf, or .wmf.

immutable   The inability of a string to be modified once it is created. A new string must be created for any modifications.

implicit conversion   A conversion from one data type to another that occurs automatically or by default according to specified rules.

increment operator   Shortcut operator for increasing the value of a variable by 1 (++).

index   Position within a list or array.

information assurance   Secure programming measure to provide accurate and timely transfer of information.

inheritance   Ability to create a new class based on an existing class.

instance   An object created from a class.

instance member   Each object created from the class has a separate occurrence of the variable or method.

instantiate   Create an object using the `new` keyword.

integrated development environment (IDE)   Tool for writing projects and solutions; includes an editor, tools, debugger, and other features for faster development.

Interval property   Determines the amount of time until a Timer component fires a Tick event; measured in milliseconds.

intranet   Network within a company.

intrinsic constant   Constants supplied with a language or application such as Color.Blue.

IsMdiContainer property   Used to create a parent form for MDI.

Items property   Collection of elements for a list box or combo box control.

Items.Add method   Adds elements to the Items collection of a list box or combo box.

Items.Clear method   Clears all elements from a list box or combo box.

Items.Count property   Property that holds the number of elements in a list box or combo box.

Items.Insert method   Inserts an element in a list for a list box or combo box.

Items.Remove method   Removes the currently selected item from a list box or combo box.

Items.RemoveAt method   Removes the specified item from a list box or combo box.

iteration   A single pass through the statements in a loop.

L

Label   A control that displays text; cannot be altered by the user.

Language-Integrated Query (LINQ)   New .NET feature that allows SQL-like queries to be written in C# code.

LargeChange property   A property of a scroll bar that determines how far to scroll for a click in the gray area of the scroll bar.

LayoutMdi method   Arranges MDI child windows vertically, horizontally, or cascaded.

lifetime   The period of time that a variable exists.

ListBox control   A control that holds a list of values; the user cannot add new values at run time.

local variable   The scope of a variable or constant that limits its visibility to the current method.

Locals window   Window that opens in IDE during execution; displays all objects and variables that are within scope at break time.

logic error   An error in a project that does not halt execution but causes erroneous results in the output.

logical operator   The operators && (And), || (Or), and ! (Not); used to construct compound Boolean expressions and to reverse the truth of an expression.

loop   A control structure that provides for the repetition of statements.

loop index   A counter variable used in a for loop.

M

MaskedTextBox   A specialized form of text box that includes a Mask property, which can indicate to the user the format of data expected and require the correct data type and format of input.

Maximum property   Scroll bar property for the highest possible value.

MaxLength property   Property of text boxes that limits the number of characters the user can enter as input.

MdiWindowListItem property   Determines whether the menu will display a list of open MDI child windows; used on the *Window* menu.

menu   A list of choices; the available commands displayed in a menu bar.

Menu Designer   Feature of the development environment for creating menus, accessed by adding a MenuStrip component to the component tray.

MenuStrip component   A control used to create menus for forms.

MessageBox   A dialog box that displays a message to the user.

method   Predefined actions provided with objects. A unit of code that performs an action and may or may not return a value.

Minimum property   Scroll bar property for the smallest possible value.

modal   A dialog box that requires a user response before continuing program execution.

modeless   A dialog box that does not require a user response before continuing program execution.

MouseDown event   The event of a form or control that occurs when the user presses the mouse button.

Multiline property   Boolean property of many controls, including labels and text boxes, that allows text to appear on multiple lines. WordWrap must also be set to *true*.

multiple document interface (MDI)   Multiple-form project that has parent and child forms.

multitier application   A program designed in components or services, where each segment performs part of the necessary actions. Each of the functions of a multitier application can be coded in a separate component and the components may be stored and run on different machines.

N

named constant   Constant created and named by the developer.

namespace   Used to organize a group of classes in the language library; the hierarchy used to locate the class. No two classes may have the same name within a namespace.

namespace variable   A variable that can be used in any method within the current namespace; generally the current project.

nested if   An if statement completely contained within another if statement.

nested try/catch block   A try/catch block completely contained within another try/catch block.

new keyword   Used to instantiate an object; creates an object and assigns memory for property values.

NewLine character   Used to set line endings in a string literal. Can use \n in strings; in a text box, use Environment.NewLine.

Next method   Random class method for generating a random number.

node (XML)   A branch of the tree. The file can have only one root node and multiple child nodes.

Now property Current date and time from the Date structure.

null An object variable or string variable that does not have an instance of an object assigned.

O

object An occurrence of a class type that has properties and methods; a specific instance of a control type, form, or other class.

object-oriented programming (OOP) An approach to programming that uses classes to define the properties and methods for objects. Classes may inherit from other classes.

OpenFileDialog Common dialog component used to display the Windows *Open File* dialog box; allows the user to view files and select the file to open.

order of precedence Hierarchy of operations; the order in which operations are performed.

overloading Allows a method to act differently for different arguments. Multiple methods in the same class with the same name but with different argument lists.

overriding A method in a derived (inherited) class with the same name and argument list as a method in the parent (base) class. The method in the derived class overrides (supersedes) the one in the parent class for objects of the derived class.

P

parameterized constructor A constructor that defines a parameter list; as opposed to a default constructor, which has an empty parameter list.

parameterized query A database query that allows a value to be supplied at run time.

parent class A class from which other classes inherit; also called a *superclass* or *base class*.

parent form MDI container for child forms.

pascal casing The naming convention that specifies mixed-case names; the first character must be uppercase and the first character of each word within the name must be uppercase; the rest of the characters must be lowercase.

Peek method Used to look ahead to determine if records remain in a file stream.

Pen object Graphical object for drawing lines and shapes.

PictureBox control A control used to display an image.

pixel Picture element; a single dot on the screen; a unit of measurement for displaying graphics.

Point structure Holds X and Y coordinates as a single unit.

polymorphism OOP feature that allows methods to take different actions depending on the situation. Methods may have the same name but different argument lists. Also refers to the naming convention of naming methods with similar actions the same in each class.

postback A round-trip to the Web server.

postfix operator Increment or decrement operator placed after the variable; calculation is performed after other operations.

posttest A loop that has its test condition after the body of the loop; the statements within the loop will always be executed at least once; also called an *exit test*.

prefix operator Increment or decrement operator placed before the variable; calculation is performed before other operations.

pretest A loop that has its test condition at the top; the statements inside the loop may never be executed; also called an *entry test*.

primary key field The field (or fields) which uniquely identifies a record in a data file.

Print method A method of the PrintDocument class to begin executing code for printing.

print preview View the printer's output on the screen and then choose to print or cancel.

PrintDocument component Contains methods and events to set up output for the printer.

PrintForm A method of a form that prints the form in its current state; can be set to print on the printer or the Print Preview window.

PrintPage event handler Contains the logic for printing.

PrintPreviewDialog component Used to allow printer output to be sent to a Print Preview window.

private Variable or procedure declared with the private keyword; available only inside the current class.

Professional Edition A version of Visual Studio that includes fewer features than the Team System editions. The trial edition included with this text is based on the Professional Edition.

Project Designer   A tabbed window of the IDE used to view and set the project's properties. Displayed from *Project / ProjectName Properties*.

project file   A text file that contains information about the current project. Displays in the Solution Explorer and can be viewed and edited in a text editor.

Properties window   A window in the IDE used to set values for properties at design time.

property   Characteristic or attribute of an object; control properties may be set at design time or run time depending on the specific property.

property accessor   Methods written with `set` and `get` keywords to pass values to and from private variables in a class.

property block   See *property accessor*.

protected   Access modifier for a variable or method; behaves as private but allows inheritance.

pseudocode   Planning tool for code using an English expression or comment that describes the action.

public   The access-level specifier that allows access from all classes.

R

radio button   A control used to indicate a value that may be *true* or *false* (selected or not selected). In any group of radio buttons, only one button may be selected.

Random class   Used to create random numbers.

ReadAllLines method   Simplified file handling; opens a text file, reads all elements of

the file into an array, and closes the file.

ReadAllText method   Simplified file handling; opens a text file, reads all elements of the file into a string variable, and closes the file.

ReadLine method   Reads one record from a file; reads to the end of the line.

record   A group of related fields; relates to data files and database tables.

Rectangle structure   Defines a rectangular region, specified by its upper-left corner and its size.

refactoring   A feature of the IDE that allows the programmer to change the name and/or class of objects.

relational operator   Used to compare two values and return a Boolean (*true*/*false*) result.

resizing handle   Handle on a control or window that may be used to resize the object.

return statement   Returns a value from a method.

return value   Value returned from a function or method.

reusability   Code classes that can be used in multiple projects.

RichTextBox   A specialized form of a TextBox control that allows the text to be formatted in a variety of ways, including character and paragraph formatting.

row   A horizontal section of a grid control; one record of a table.

run time   During the time a project is executing.

run-time error   An error that occurs as a program executes; causes execution to break.

S

scope   The extent of visibility of a variable or constant. The scope may be namespace, class, local, or block level.

Scroll event   Scroll bar event that occurs as the user moves the scroll box.

Select Resource dialog box   A dialog box in which the image and other resource files of a project can be added and selected.

SelectedIndex property   Index of the item currently selected in a list box or combo box.

separator bar   A horizontal line used to separate groups of menu commands.

server   Machine on which a Web application resides.

Session object   An object that exists for one round-trip to the server in a Web application; can be used to store information about the user or program variables.

SetBounds method   Set the location of a control; used to move a control.

SetError method   ErrorProvider method to set up and display a message for the specified control; used for validating input data.

short circuit   Skipping the evaluation of parts of a compound condition that are not required.

shortcut menu   The menu that pops up when the right mouse button is clicked. Also called a *popup menu*, *context menu*, or *right mouse menu*.

Show method   Displays a form or message box. A form displayed with the `Show` method is modeless.

ShowDialog method   Displays a common dialog box or a form; the form is displayed modally.

siblings (XML)   Elements at the same level as each other.

signature   The name and parameter list of a method.

simple binding   Connecting a single data field to a single control, such as a label or text box.

simple combo box   Fixed-size combo box.

simple list box   Fixed-size list box.

single document interface (SDI)   Forms act independently in a multiple-form project.

single-file mode   A style of Web Form in which the C# code and HTML are contained in the same file.

Size structure   A size specified by width and height; measured in pixels.

SizeMode property   Allows the size of an image in a picture box to stretch.

SmallChange property   A property of a scroll bar that determines how far to scroll for a click on the scroll arrow.

snap lines   Guide lines that pop up on a form during design time to help align the controls.

snippet   See *code snippet*.

solution   A C# application; can consist of one or more projects.

Solution Explorer window   An IDE window that holds the filenames for the files included in your project and a list of the classes it references.

solution file   A text file that holds information about the solution and the projects it contains.

Sorted property   Property of a list box and combo box that specifies that the list items should be sorted.

SoundLocation property   A property of a SoundPlayer component that is set to the location of the sound file to play.

SoundPlayer component   A component that can play the sound in a .wav file from a Windows form.

splash screen   A window that appears before the main application window; generally displays program information and gives the appearance of quicker application loading.

Standard Edition   A version of Visual Studio with fewer features than the Professional and Team System editions.

StartPosition property   Determines the screen location of a form when it first appears.

startup form   The main form; the first form to display after the splash screen.

stateless   Does not store any information about its contents from one invocation to the next.

static keyword   Keyword used to designate that a property or method can be shared.

static member   A method that may be accessed without instantiating an object of the class.

static property   Property that can be used by all objects of the class; often used for totals and counts. Only one copy exists for all objects of the class.

status bar   An area along the lower edge of a window used to display information for the user.

StatusStrip control   A container control that creates a status bar across the lower edge of a form.

Step Into   Debugging command; executes each statement, including those in called methods.

Step Out   Debugging command; continues rapid execution until the called method completes, and then returns to break mode at the statement following the call.

Step Over   Debugging command; executes each statement in the current method but does not show statements in called methods.

stream   An object used to transfer a series of bytes from one location to another.

StreamReader   Object used to input small amounts of information stored in a disk file.

StreamWriter   Object used to write small amounts of information to disk.

StretchImage   Setting for the value of the SizeMode property of a PictureBox control.

string literal   A constant enclosed in quotation marks.

struct   Keyword used to create a structure.

structure   A grouping that combines multiple fields of related data.

style   Formatting for a Web form.

subclass   A that inherits from another class; also called a *child class* or a *derived class*.

submenu   A menu within a menu.

subscript The position of an element within an array; also called an *index*.

subscripted variable An element of an array.

superclass A class from which other classes inherit; also called a *parent class* or *base class*.

switch statement C# statement to implement a case structure.

syntax error An error caused by failure to follow the syntax rules of the language; often caused by typographical errors. The Editor informs you of syntax errors.

System.IO namespace Holds the stream objects for reading and writing data files.

T

TabIndex property Determines the order the focus moves as the Tab key is pressed.

table A two-dimensional array.

table (Web) Used for easier page formatting.

table adapter An object that handles retrieving and updating of the data in a dataset.

table lookup Logic to find an element within an array.

TabStop property Determines if a control can receive focus.

Team System Full version of Visual Studio, which contains project management tools in addition to the items found in the Professional Edition.

text box A control for data entry; its value can be entered and changed by the user.

Text property The value that displays on a control such as the words in a text box or label.

TextAlign property Used to change the alignment of text within the control.

this A reference to the current object. In a form's code, reference to the current form.

Tick event One firing of a Timer component; each time the interval passes, another Tick event occurs.

Timer component Fires Tick events at a specified time interval.

ToLower method Converts text to lowercase letters.

toolbar The bar beneath the menu bar that holds buttons; used as shortcuts for menu commands.

toolbox A window that holds icons for tools; used to create controls and components on a form.

ToolStrip control A container control used to create a toolbar on a Windows form.

ToolStripMenuItem Individual controls added to a ToolStrip; each menu name and menu item is a separate control

ToolStripStatusLabel object Area of a ToolStrip control for displaying information.

ToolTip Small label that pops up when the mouse pointer pauses over a toolbar button or control.

ToolTip component Placed on a form to allow the individual controls to display ToolTips. A ToolTip property is added to each control.

ToolTip on ToolTip1 property The new property added to each control when a ToolTip component is added to the form.

ToUpper method Converts text to all uppercase.

try/catch block Traps user errors or program errors.

U

user interface The display and commands seen by a user; how the user interacts with an application. In Windows, the graphical display of an application containing controls and menus.

V

validation Checking to verify that appropriate values have been entered.

validator controls Controls that can automatically validate input data; used on Web Forms.

value keyword Incoming value for a set clause in a property method.

Value property Holds the current setting of a scroll bar control.

ValueChanged event Event that occurs when a scroll bar control is scrolled.

variable Memory location that holds data that can be changed during project execution.

vertical scroll bar A Windows control that provides a scroll bar that appears vertically on the form.

virtual Modifier keyword on a member (property or method) that specifies that, at run time, the member may be replaced by an identically named member of a derived class.

Visible property Determines if a control can be seen or not.

visual inheritance Inheritance of the visual elements of a form.

Visual Studio environment The development environment including tools for designing the interface, editing program code, running, and debugging applications; also called the *IDE*.

void   Keyword that indicates that a method does not return a value.

W

Web Form   Form in Visual Studio for creating pages that display in a browser.

Web page   A static page that displays in a browser application.

WebBrowser control   Allows Internet access from a Windows application.

while loop   A series of statements that will be executed as long as a condition is *true*. The condition is written on the `while` statement and is a pretest loop structure.

Windows Presentation Foundation (WPF)   Technology for creating rich user interfaces, such as those used in Windows Vista. Can use WPF Interoperability to include WPF controls on a Windows Form, use a WPF Application template to write a WPF application, or use a WPF Browser Application template to create a browser application.

WordWrap property   A Boolean property of a TextBox and RichTextBox control that determines whether a long line will be continued to another line. In order to display text on a second line, both WordWrap and MultiLine must be set to *true*.

Write method   Writes one record to a stream object; does not include a carriage return.

WriteAllLines method   Simplified file handling; opens the file, writes all data from an array, and closes the file.

WriteAllText method   Simplified file handling; opens the file, writes all data from a string, and closes the file.

WriteLine method   Writes one record to a stream object; includes a carriage return character at the end.

X

XAML Browser Application (XBAP)   A WPF application that runs in a browser. The user interface is created using XAML. See *Extensible Application Markup Language*.

XML   Extensible markup language. A format for data; popular for data storage and transfer on the Internet.

XMLTextReader   Class used to access information from an XML file.

Index